W9-BNZ-596

Kyle K. Pierce

FUNDAMENTALS OF

GENERAL PSYCHOLOGY

FUNDAMENTALS OF

John Frederick Dashiell

KENAN PROFESSOR OF PSYCHOLOGY

THE UNIVERSITY OF NORTH CAROLINA

HOUGHTON MIFFLIN COMPANY

BF181
D32
1949

GENERAL PSYCHOLOGY

THIRD EDITION

BOSTON · NEW YORK · CHICAGO · DALLAS · ATLANTA · SAN FRANCISCO
The Riverside Press Cambridge

1962

OCT

75913

COPYRIGHT, 1949, by JOHN FREDERICK DASHIELL
COPYRIGHT, 1937, by JOHN FREDERICK DASHIELL
ALL RIGHTS RESERVED INCLUDING THE RIGHT TO REPRODUCE THIS
BOOK OR PARTS THEREOF IN ANY FORM ·

The Riverside Press CAMBRIDGE, MASSACHUSETTS
PRINTED IN THE U.S.A.

150
D26t
1949

TO THE MEMORY OF

JOHN WILLIAM AND FANNIE SOPHIA MYERS DASHIELL

AND OF

CLARA SYLVIA KNOWLES DASHIELL

CONTENTS

vii

IN THE FAST-GROWING field of psychology, a great many new developments have occurred during the twelve years since the publication of the 1937 edition of the present work, developments which warrant a resurvey for the student beginning a study of the subject. True, no new school of thought has arisen in that span to set up one more system to end all systems. No revolution in basic theory, in viewpoint, or in systematic terminology has affected the subject as a whole. But there has been such intensive cultivation in well-established areas, and such noteworthy extensions of the boundaries of some of them, that the story is almost a new one.

As for the first point, increasingly detailed material, both factual and interpretive, has been brought to the surface in the fields of sensory processes and perception, learning, and neurological processes, and in factorial and other statistical techniques. Such advances of knowledge in themselves demand recognition in any fair overview, and so a new survey. In the second place, the experiences of psychologists during World War II have greatly widened our horizons and have brought to the attention of teachers certain fields that were formerly somewhat neglected in general textbooks. Social phenomena are receiving examination as never before. Personnel problems in government as well as in industry and business have attracted the attention of highly competent psychologists who have now given "applied psychology" a scientific recognition it has long awaited. Quantitatively considered, at least, the most notable extension of the boundaries of psychology has been in the direction of the clinical study of individual deviates, a war-emphasized interest that has been considerably accelerated by government-subsidized programs. This new edition, then, seeks to bring into the student's survey of the psychology of today an appreciation of those widened horizons. Some teachers may regret certain omissions, such as the Hullian or Lewinian restatements of certain areas, but the author feared that exposition of such systems might confuse the beginning student.

Frequently in the present edition the attempt is made to combine the classical and the contemporary. For it has seemed desirable to let the student know a little about the great trail-blazers — and the teacher, too, might well read them again instead of relying upon retellings of retellings. Then, in order to complete the perspective, it has seemed well to take the student to the van of present research, so that he may know "what is going on" and may become familiar with at least the names of persons and places important in current psychological studies.

To order the topics of general psychology into one single sequence of chapters requires some temerity. No claim is made that the order in which they are here presented represents the order in which they must be read. Let the individual teacher use them in whatever sequence he prefers; he will in any event find teachers who agree with him and others who do not.

A word as to style. The author hopes that the undergraduate may find this new edition readable and closely related to the phenomena of everyday life but without compromise of scientific soundness. The manner of presentation varies considerably from chapter to chapter, adjusting itself to the varying nature of the contents. For example, sensory or learning phenomena can be much more concisely presented than can personality or social topics, and experimental and statistical yieldings far more concisely than clinical.

The author has not attempted to usurp all of the teacher's functions. He has not drawn all the conclusions, hinted at all the everyday applications, or pointed all the morals. The teacher and his students should not be deprived of these prime privileges of the thoughtful reader, these sure sources of intellectual pleasure and stimulation.

To recent and present colleagues who have read drafts of various chapters and have given most helpful counsel, the author feels deeply in debt. The following especially he must mention: James C. Dixon, Sam B. Lyerly, Ailene Morris, William J. Daniel, Harry W. Crane, James W. Layman, and Emma McCloy Layman. To President Leonard Carmichael of Tufts College, he is grateful for a number of crucial suggestions of technical nature. To Pamela Hotard Shultz he is indebted for careful preparation of typescript and of many figures.

JOHN FREDERICK DASHIELL

FUNDAMENTALS OF

GENERAL PSYCHOLOGY

1

INTRODUCTION TO PSYCHOLOGY

WHAT KNOWLEDGE OF HUMAN NATURE IS SOUND?

SURELY we shall all agree that we find ourselves and our fellow men the most engrossing and fascinating things on earth. Listen in on conversations, scan the columns of your morning paper, analyze motion pictures and radio and television programs, and you will find that in nearly all instances the focal concern is people, their foibles and frailties, their virtues and valors. There is a universal interest in persons, and "the proper study of mankind is man."

Three Sources of Knowledge

Knowledge and understanding of human nature may be acquired in various ways. One is the direct way of everyday practical experience. The preschool child embarks upon this road as he comes into contact with playmates and must respond appropriately to their presence. And throughout life the day-to-day contact with one's fellows furnishes the opportunity — even necessity — to learn better how to get on with them: when to approach and when to avoid. Where is the adult who does not rate himself a good judge of people about him, with plenty of ability to "see them through and through"?

Much of the popular wisdom and shrewdness about human nature thus acquired is generalized and frequently given allegorical form in the proverbs of the people. These rules of prudence, however, are not always based on sound observations. The reader is invited to inspect the proverbs furnished in Table I, and to judge the truth or falsity of each, not as to the literal objective truth of what is stated but as to the human characteristic or human trait that is implied. (After making his

1

own judgments he may compare them with those of the present author in a footnote on page 16.)

TABLE

 Some Proverbs About Human Nature

1. A rose by any other name would smell as sweet.
2. As the twig is bent so the tree's inclined.
3. Forbidden fruit is sweetest.
4. Misfortunes make us wise.
5. Necessity is the mother of invention.
6. Once a knave, always a knave.
7. Once bitten, twice shy.
8. Practice makes perfect.
9. Scalded cats don't fear cold water.
10. Still waters run deep.
11. The fairer the paper, the fouler the blot.
12. The fairest apple hangs on the highest bough.
13. The master's eye makes the horse fat.
14. The watched pot is slow to boil.
15. Unto the pure all things are pure.
16. What soberness conceals, drunkenness reveals.
17. What the heart thinks, the pulse betrays.
18. When children stand quiet, they have done no harm.
19. When the fox preaches, beware of your geese.
20. Zeal is fit only for wise men, but found mostly in fools.

Another avenue of approach to human nature is the indirect route through literature and other fine arts, and through history and biography. By these means human beings are observed at second- or third-hand, and though they lack the concreteness of those encountered in the flesh, a correct understanding of them is presumably furthered by the interpretations of the artist or writer. The interpretations may be offered in astonishing variety of forms, from the detailed analysis of particular people by a Dostoievski or a Henry James to the revelations of one's own inner springs by a Proust or a Poe. This indirect avenue to knowledge of man is celebrated to excess in Pope's lines:

> When first young Maro in his boundless mind
> A work t'outlast immortal Rome designed . . .
> Perhaps he seemed above the critic's law,
> And but from nature's fountains scorned to draw.
> But . . . Nature and Homer were, he found, the same . . .
> Learn hence for ancient rules a just esteem;
> To copy nature is to copy them.

The most direct and definite route to a knowledge of man is that furnished by the methods of natural science, namely, observation and experimentation with statistical refinements. Historically, in the development of Western culture, scientific methods came to be recognized as a kit of intellectual tools invaluable for getting at the facts; and man came to realize the distinct advantage of addressing nature in a detached and impersonal manner. And so with regard to man himself. Putting aside our prides and prejudices, what facts can we discover about him? From this emphasis upon the application of scientific methods to the actions of man, modern psychology was born.

The reader should not become confused. Not just any opinion or information about man and his behavior is "psychology," even though it may claim to be such in newspaper advertisements and wood-pulp magazines; and not everyone who knows his fellow man usefully and adequately is a "psychologist." To call an effective salesman "a good psychologist," or a rabble-rousing political speech "good psychology," is as loose language as to call a successful farmer a good botanist or a trainer for a dog-and-pony show a good zoologist. Properly speaking, then, *the term "psychology" is limited to those interests in human behavior that take the form of true scientific inquiry.*

Scientific Psychology Serves Human Values

Let the idealistic reader not be disturbed. Let him not fear that scientific study is inimical to the values of life — to whatsoever things are true, pure, lovely, and of good repute. Quite the contrary! The study of humankind as an objective thing does not challenge any of the goods of life: it helps us to secure them. And we can properly invert the problem raised by a recent thinker, "The place of values in a world of facts," and inquire rather as to "The place of facts in a world of values." Natural scientific values are instrumental: by knowing more we can provide and maintain those objects and situations in which we have enjoyment of beauty or perpetuation of friendship or addition of comfort. Modern psychology looks to scientific methods to establish the facts of human behavior, but it recognizes the happiness of men as an ultimate ideal.

Different Attitudes Toward the Same Subject

No scientist is a scientist every minute of his day. When the anatomist sits down to his beefsteak he is addressing himself not to a piece of anatomy, but to an appetizing food. When the chemist spreads butter on his toast he is assuredly not manipulating atoms or electrons, nor "glycerides of oleic, stearic, palmitic, butyric, caproic, caprylic, capric, and myristic acids." The astronomer gazing at a sunset is not regarding a certain refraction of ether vibrations due to a certain spatial relationship of the astronomical sun to the planet called the earth. A physicist attending a symphony concert is most certainly not occupying himself with the length, amplitude, and composition of the waves of sound that are being produced by the scrapings and blowings of instruments on the stage; he listens to the sounds as music, and as music he judges them. This total change of attitude that occurs with the donning or doffing of a laboratory apron is well illustrated in the work of the surgeon. The fact that proper surgical treatment is not an affair between friends, but a scientific matter, is shown by the laws in certain states that prohibit a physician's performing major operations on his own near relatives.

Anything can be looked at from different points of view. Let us consider the entity that we call man. If you are an economist, you will look at man as a producer and consumer, and on the ratio between these two things you will estimate his value to the world. If you are a salesman, you will see man as a prospective buyer; that is the viewpoint that will determine your judgment and treatment of him. If you are a teacher, man is a something that can learn; the way in which he is likely to learn, the question of what stimuli you can apply to make the learning more effective, interests you, and you do not care what he produces in economic goods. If you are a religionist or a moralist, man is a soul to be saved. Suppose you are an artist, and take an artist's attitude toward man — he is then a body to be sculptured or painted. As a chemist you will regard him as an enormously complex combination of oxygen, carbon, and hydrogen, plus nitrogen, sodium, and other elements. If you are a politician, you will see him as a ballot-marker. If you are a zoologist or a physician you will look upon man as a specimen of *Homo sapiens*, or as a vast complex of tissues which get out of order easily; and you will not care whether he is one of society's producers, learns well or ill, beats his wife, is an ensemble of good lines and curves, or votes the straight Republican ticket. In short, a particular human being may stand in a great number of separate and mutually unrelated systems of study. We insist, then, that the description and analysis of our psychological object, a man, in terms of physical processes and material mechanisms, does not imply any lessening of man's dignity as viewed from other angles. Psychology challenges no poetical, ethical, religious, social, romantic, or other humanistic conception of his life and destiny. It is merely another way of looking at man. And, in fact, the humanitarians of any field should look to psychology with confidence for the methods of study and the factual findings that it can yield them.

WHAT ARE THE SCIENTIFIC METHODS USED IN PSYCHOLOGY?

To come to closer grips with our subject: What are the particular methods employed? "Scientific method" is a broad term, for astronomers, geologists, physicists, physiologists, zoologists, anthropologists, and other scientists use different techniques that are appropriate to their several kinds of materials. Yet all these techniques have in common certain earmarks that clearly distinguish a natural science research from a legal research or a biographical research or a bibliographical research. How, then, does the particular scientist called the psychologist seek facts?

(1) Experimentation

Natural science may be said to have come of age when the experimental procedure was adopted. A simple and clear example of experiment is afforded by the chemical laboratory. Into a glass test tube containing an accurately known and accurately measured substance, the experimenter introduces one drop of another accurately known and measured substance. What happens? He introduces more drops. Or he applies a flame to raise the temperature ten degrees. What happens? Whatever does happen is assumed to be dependent upon the change of conditions which he has specifically controlled.

So in other fields that make use of the scientific method, in an ideal experiment a *subject* — bit of clover, perhaps, or a frog, or a child, or an adult — is brought into a laboratory, where the experimenter sets all the conditions and surroundings and has instruments for carefully introducing changes in some one of those conditions. He can observe if and when anything "happens" in the clover, frog, child, or adult, when the change in the condition is introduced. He can change one condition after another; and upon an exhaustive trying of many, he will be in a position to say positively with which condition the happening in the clover, frog, child, or adult is associated. Having controlled all other factors and having observed factor *x* to be the one with which the phenomenon is invariably related, he calls the factor *x* an *independent variable* and the phenomenon a *dependent variable*.[1] He — and anyone who reads his report — now has a purchase on that phenomenon; he knows what (in a popular sense) "causes" it, and can produce it at will. It is predictable. It is under control.

---

[1] These terms are rough equivalents of "cause" and "effect," but are preferable because less misleading.

An Example of Experimental Method. Let us explore a popular psychological problem by the methods of the psychological laboratory.

Problem: How do the blind avoid obstacles without contacting them? *Problem re-stated:* Which of the several theoretically possible sensory guides is the necessary one, that is, which of the variables is the determining independent one — (*a*) residual sight, if any, (*b*) touch, (*c*) hearing, or (*d*) a special additional sense? One clear-cut procedure for putting these possible determining factors to actual test would be to introduce and eliminate each of them, one by one, each time noting whether the behavior in question appears or disappears with it.

This very procedure was carried through at Cornell University by Dr. Dallenbach and associates [8].[1] Blind subjects, including some who had demonstrated their ability to travel about alone by bus and train, were deprived of the use of one sense-avenue after another, and tested for their ability to avoid a wall or screen. They were started from various distances on successive tests and required to walk down a wood floor between thick carpet runners. They were to give a right-hand signal when they judged that the obstacle was directly before them, and a left-hand signal when they judged that they were on the point of actually running into it. (See Figure 1, parts 1, 2, 3.) The order of sense-deprivations and of the resultant performances was as follows, the main problem having been broken down into component sub-problems. (The whole research is here much condensed and simplified.)

Problem A: Is some remaining weak vision necessary? *Procedure:* Vision was completely eliminated by blindfolding the subjects. *Results:* Their ability to avoid obstacles was unimpaired. *Conclusion:* The performance does not depend upon sight.

Problem B: Is touch sensitivity in the face and hands necessary? *Procedure:* Touch was eliminated by covering the arms and hands with sleeves and wool-lined leather gauntlet gloves, and covering the head with a felt veil and a hat. (See Figure 1, parts 6 and 7.) *Results:* Under these conditions the subjects could still perceive and avoid the wall-obstacle. *Conclusion:* Touch is not necessary to the performance.

Problem C: Is aural sensitivity necessary? *Negative Procedure:* Use of the ears was eliminated either by plugging them or by subjecting them to a continuous loud noise through headphones. *Results:* No subjects avoided running into the wall. *Conclusion:* Use of the ears was an invariable concomitant and was at least necessary to the performance. *Positive Procedure:* All stimulation except aural was eliminated by having the experimenter himself walk toward the obstacle, carrying a microphone

[1] Numbers in brackets pertain to the References listed at the end of the chapter.

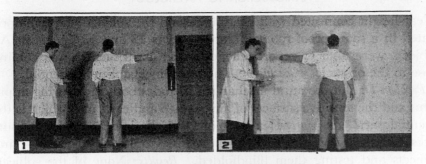

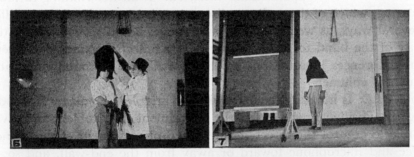

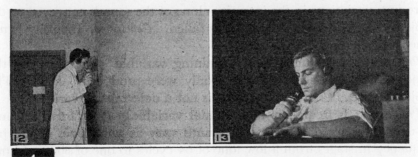

Experiments with the Blind

Explanation in text. (*From K. M. Dallenbach*, et al., AMER. J. PSYCHOL., *1944, 57, 133–183. Pictures by the courtesy of Dr. Dallenbach.*)

at ear-height connected with headphones on the subject who remained seated in a soundproof room (Figure 1, parts 12 and 13). *Results:* All subjects were able to report whenever the experimenter was coming close to the obstacle. *Conclusion:* The aural mechanism is essential.

Problem D: But the aural mechanism includes both the hearing apparatus and the sensitive surfaces of air-passage and eardrum: which is the essential part? *Procedure:* Hearing alone was eliminated, leaving the surfaces of air-passages and eardrum intact, by employing some deaf-blind subjects and testing them blindfolded. *Results:* None of the subjects could perceive the obstacle. *Conclusion:* Hearing alone is a necessary and sufficient condition for the perception of objects by the blind. *Corollary:* To assume a special unknown "obstacle sense" is unnecessary; hence, as it is a cardinal principle of scientific thinking never to multiply explanations beyond necessity, and never to accept a more complicated interpretation when a simpler one is at hand, the idea of an unknown "obstacle sense" somehow possessed by the blind may be set aside as just another superstition.

But the scientist's appetite is now whetted. If the determining variable is hearing, which of the auditory dimensions is involved? Sounds differ in several ways, as we shall learn later (pages 253 ff.). *Problem:* Is the ability of the blind to guide themselves by reflected sounds dependent upon differences in some one of these attributes of sound: intensity, frequency, volume?

Problem E: Is intensity the determining variable? *Procedure:* By modifying the Positive Procedure of the experiment for Problem C, it was possible to control the direction and speed of movement of the sound-source and microphone toward or away from the end-wall, and so to introduce variations in the intensity alone of the sounds conveyed to the subject's ears. *Results:* The subjects failed. *Conclusion:* Intensity is not a necessary variable.

Problem F: Is volume the determining variable? *Procedure:* By the same set-up, variations in volume only were produced. *Results:* The subjects failed. *Conclusion:* Volume is not a determining variable.

Problem G: Is frequency the essential variable? *Procedure:* The same set-up was adapted to make the sounds vary as pure tones of varying frequency in stages from a low tone of 64 cycles to one of 8000 and one of 10,000. *Results:* The subjects were unable to detect the experimenter's approach to the end-wall, except when the reflected sounds were of the highest frequency (pitch), 10,000 cycles. Just as bats, flying about in total darkness, guide themselves by the reflections of very high sounds from wires and other obstacles (in their case the sounds being too high for human ears), so the human blind are guided by reflected sounds of high frequency. (In fundamental physics, this is analogous to the sonar principle used in submarine detection in World War II.)

Thus by introducing and eliminating independent variables, one by one, and noting whether a change occurred in the dependent variable, the single determining one was experimentally isolated.

Multiple Variables. The manipulation of a single variable at a time is an experimental ideal seldom realized. Human nature being what it is, the investigator frequently has to deal with many variables at a time. And even eliminating or altering of one variable alone may produce changes in the effects of other variables — a possibility which the alert investigator keeps before him. He may systematically plan his experiments to let the different variables operate in different combinations, and then make cross-comparisons of his results to throw into relief the relationships of the respective variables to the effects. And he will make his cross-comparisons more precise and effective by applying statistical (mathematical) methods of describing and analyzing the data in quantitative terms: how different variables go together, and the like. We have not room to expand the topic; but most of the references throughout this book will illustrate the general point.

(2) Field Observation

There are some fields of natural science where the phenomena cannot be gotten into a laboratory and put under experimental control. The phenomena of astronomy certainly, much of structural geology, animal and plant ecology, and other disciplines must be sought out and studied where they are; and so, too, must some of the problems of animal and human psychology. Monkeys, chimpanzees, and gibbons have been well studied in their native Africa and Siam, and ants in the wilds of Panama. By going directly to them in their natural habitats it has been possible for human observers to record facts about the social psychology of these animals that simply would not have been available under the artificial conditions of a laboratory. Similar methods have been employed in the analysis of human relations and groupings by studying an American city full of people or by taking up residence in a tribe of tolerant primitive folk. Much work on children has been field-observational rather than experimental, as when observers unobtrusively make precise records of what Jane or Jack or Jim is doing from moment to moment on playground or in kindergarten.

(3) Statistical Procedures and Tools

Even in the conduct of the clean-cut experiment undertaken with blind subjects, attention had to be given to quantitative treatment of the results. What was the average number of contacts with the obstacle made by a number of persons, or by the same person in a number of trials? Does that average represent pretty closely what each individual score was? When, under two different conditions, two different scores were obtained, was that difference an important one or merely a matter of chance? When we start to deal with collections of quantitative data, it becomes clear that we must have some refined methods of getting insight into what they mean. We must employ mathematical techniques of statistical character in order to know exactly what we can and cannot safely conclude. To him who expects to read in the literature of psychology (not watered down and popularized), the need for some understanding of statistical methods cannot be overemphasized. Some of the simpler methods will be presented in later chapters.

(4) Clinical Observation

Data for a science of human beings and how they act often cannot be obtained by direct methods such as are available to him who works on fungi, crayfishes, coal tar derivatives, or quartz crystals. We learn much of human nature from personal peculiarities and things that go wrong. A tenant farmer, when asked whether his new automobile had this or that detail in its engine parts, responded simply, "Ah dunno. It ain't never broke down yit." And so it is with our knowledge of the personal make-up: much of it is derived from studies of deficiencies and impairments. A man, however, cannot be confined indefinitely in a cabinet, fed unknown substances, driven into emotional collapse, for purely experimental purposes. Hence for many a fact about impaired or disordered psychological functioning — as evidenced by memory lapses, color blindness, stuttering, inability to learn, fixed irrational ideas, and the like — the investigator must wait for cases to appear.

But clinical methods are important in psychology for quite another reason than the study of a *pure science of mankind in general*. After all, we are not interested simply in generalizations about the genus *Homo:* we are often and intensely, interested in *this particular man or woman or child*, this particular John Doe or Richard Roe in all his individuality and peculiarities. We may want to study him not as a representative of a type but for his own sake, oftentimes so that we can advise him or help him — to correct a speech difficulty, to get the right kind of job, to overcome a nagging worry that is bothering him as he works, to do a better job of studying. This is a clinical interest.

The "clinical" interest, then, contrasts with the "pure science" interest. The latter leads us to study a person as one of very many persons in terms of some particular trait or problem, in order to arrive at a generalization of a natural law. Clinical interest leads us to study a person as an individual in terms of his own many-sided nature, in order to arrive at a practical judgment concerning him and him alone.

TWO DIRECTIONS OF PSYCHOLOGICAL APPROACH

Objective and Subjective

One feature of psychological investigation that contrasts it sharply with any other natural science is the fact that it can approach its subject-matter, the human being, both by way of the observations made by experimenter or clinician and also in many cases by way of the observations which the subject-matter or "subject" can make on himself. Of the phenomena we are to include in our survey, many are human manifestations which can be noted and reported best by other people — a *public* approach, while others can be noted and reported best by the subject himself — a strictly *private* approach. The emotions of a woman whose car is stalled momentarily on the railroad track before an approaching train can be observed in two ways: by us, as we hear her screams and see her frantic gesticulations and wasted motions; by herself, as she afterward relates how "her heart was in her mouth" and the world seemed to spin around her. In a street car we can observe the behavior of a passenger who is reading the advertisement cards, but only he would be able to tell us what they meant to him. The approach from the public side is known as the *objective* or *behavioristic* approach, that from the strictly private is called the *subjective* or *introspective* approach.

Illustrations. Whether an objective experiment or a subjective experiment is to be performed depends upon the nature of the problem raised and the kind of answer sought. What makes a thing look "lustrous"? Just when is a pain teasingly pleasant? How far back into your early childhood can you recall episodes? Were your emotions more vivid then than now? After gazing at a dark purple object, what after-image do you see? Can you recall the lapping sounds of breakers on the beach? Or the buoying effect of an ocean swell that lifts you off your feet? Have you ever dreamed of going naked down the street? For such questions we employ the subjective approach, for we are asking questions that only the subject can answer; and we treat this approach with proper respect and caution. But we can check up on the subject's verbal descriptions by asking whether or not they correspond to those offered by other subjects concerning their own private experiences.[1]

On the other hand, many phenomena of man are matters which can be best investigated in objective ways. Does X walk in his sleep? Is he awkward in his handling of things? Does negativism (contrariness) usually appear before the age of three years? Is an infant of one year capable of jealousy? Are the child's first notions of causes animistic; that is, does he attribute them to "souls" in things? Is the moron capable of earning a living? Does the depth of one's sleep decrease gradually through the night? Is the schizophrenic patient ever hilarious? Does the psychopath have no respect for the feelings of others? And — since animals really come into psychology's purview — does the dog learn a motor habit more rapidly than the cat? Do apes display a primitive sympathy? Can rats cooperate?

It is apparent, then, that *the nature of the problem and the kind of answer which we are seeking determine the direction of approach*, subjective or objective. Throughout the present book, therefore, we shall present the materials from psychological research, whether obtained by observing others or by observing oneself. As a matter of fact, most current psychological research is objective; but we shall not scruple at including relevant observations made subjectively.

PSYCHOLOGY AND THE STUDENT

Not Prescriptions but Perspectives

The reader is warned not to expect of this book — nor of any other textbook — explicit prescriptions, specific rules to fit whatever concrete personal situation that may confront him. Faced with a particular problem, he need not expect to find the answer ready-made on page such-and-such. Let him but consider any other field of practice, and he will recognize the importance of first developing a sound point of view and equipping himself with established principles and laws in general

---

[1] Sometimes the subjective approach is called *phenomenological;* and the term is useful, because it reminds us that when one consciously experiences something, then that experience is a bona fide natural phenomenon and belongs with other investigable phenomena in the science. Example: When one brings the tips of his right and left middle fingers toward each other, just before the fingers touch physically they are seen to flow or rush together. This rushing-together is *there!* So the mirage on the desert is *there!* So also the sourness of a pickle exists, and the gnaw of a hunger pang. It is a psychological phenomenon, a fact of science. Other examples: the phi-phenomenon (page 465 f.), negative after-images (page 266), Müller-Lyer illusion (page 463); constancy (page 451 ff.); also cf. Figure 78 on page 261.

form. He is the one who must make the applications to specific cases. In medicine, for instance, the student well knows that he must master vast arrays of facts that he probably will never directly use in the form in which he studies them. Again, the student of law or engineering is not expected to memorize judicial or mathematical formulations that he can later apply blindly. He is expected, however, to carry away a training and perspective that will enable him to analyze and bring into sharper focus the concrete problems that he will encounter. The value of a man who has had a long and thorough professional training or many years of intensive business experience lies not so much in his memory for explicit rules or for particular experiences but in the richness and adequacy of his general point of view, in his background, and in the perspective he brings to bear on problems. That is what has always been meant by "wisdom."

The reader, then, is not to suppose that he will find between these covers the answers to all his problems, and that all he needs is an index to direct him to them. First, last, and all the time, an intelligent person will find that in the conduct of his daily affairs he must apply his own judgment. Even if we should depart from the highroad from which we can survey general psychology, and take one of the practical by-paths, such as "how to study effectively" or "how to improve your memory" or "how to develop your personality," the reader would still find that he is forced to pick and choose, to judge for himself how far to apply this fact or that rule to his particular case.

Importance of Both Facts and Methods

There are two requirements for the development of perspectives. One is a substantial knowledge of factual material ranging all the way from concrete particularized findings in a narrowly circumscribed area to broad hypotheses, theories, and laws. Now, in the course of such a survey, a reader will frequently catch himself saying, "But why this fact and that theory? What value have they for me?" It cannot be said too frequently nor too emphatically that it is out of the soil of particular facts and theories that adequate viewpoints grow.

The other requirement for the development of perspectives is an acquaintance with the methods of investigation. Quite possibly the reader may never have occasion to use the apparatus of the psychological laboratory, but there will be times innumerable when in his contacts with people and their opinions he will do well to keep in mind the ideals and general methodology of science as applied to man's behavior.

Above all, he should develop and preserve a keen appreciation of what is and what is not to be used as *evidence*. As the historian must learn to use documentary evidence and as the jurist must learn to sift testamentary evidence, so the scientist must be trained to evaluate factual evidence. For of all fields of fact, none is a richer hunting ground for the quack and the fly-by-night charlatan than is the psychological. If his study of psychology does no more than to make the reader forever critical of the false claims and pet notions current in the popular pseudo-psychological discourse about him — if it does no more than train him to insist upon evidence rather than anecdotes — psychology as a science will have fulfilled one of its missions.

Cultivation of an Impersonal Attitude

When a pet dog with a broken leg snaps at his master who tends him, the master does not cuff him, but recognizes the specific cause for the behavior and seeks to remove or ease it. This is the very attitude a scientist takes toward his subject-matter, and is therefore the attitude encouraged in psychology. A human being is looked upon as an object of inquiry and as a possible object of advice, help, or treatment. It has taken the intelligent civilized world centuries to reach this point of view. Criminal behavior, for one thing, is becoming recognized by a few advanced authorities as a problem for scientific inquiry; for the criminal's activities are recognized as having their causes in the conditions of his home, neighborhood, health, and other factors. From this viewpoint, it becomes obvious that to eliminate criminal behavior we must eliminate the manifold causes.

So, too, those unfortunates called the "insane" are not properly objects of resentment or amusement, for they are results of causal factors. No longer do we send them to "asylums" (which means places of refuge), but to "hospitals." They are ill.

Now, it is a harder thing to maintain, but this same attitude of impersonal, unprejudiced, dispassionate consideration is called for every day. When one of our friends or relatives rages or weeps, is obnoxiously positive in manner or despicably cringing, the most intelligent reaction is not to feel resentment or scorn and to hurl epithets of "wicked" or "silly," but rather to make unemotional inquiry into the causes of this behavior. We should stand outside the sphere of the behavior, and seek to understand the reasons for it.

If our survey of human and sub-human behavior in this book can inculcate a more inquiring and understanding attitude, a major goal will have been attained.

Some Hints on How to Study

We may appropriately close this section on "Psychology and the Student" with some hints on how to study, obtained from a psychology class. At the Ohio State University, Luella Cole selected the best 50 and the poorest 50 students out of a class of 200 in elementary psychology, and compared their methods of studying and of note-taking. She found that their answers to the questions listed in Table II set off the poor students from the good ones rather sharply. The reader is challenged to find out which kind of student he is, by answering the questions sincerely, and then comparing his answers with those obtained in the investigation cited. (The latter are furnished on page 16.) Perhaps this questionnaire will suggest methods of study which will help him to improve his standing as a student.

TABLE

II   "Are You a Good or a Poor Student?"

1. Do you usually study every day in the same place?
2. Do you usually know in the morning just how you are going to spend your day?
3. Does your desk have anything on it that might distract you from work?
4. When studying do you frequently skip the graphs or tables in your textbooks?
5. Do you frequently make simple charts or diagrams to represent points in your reading?
6. When you find a word in your reading that you do not know do you usually look it up in the dictionary?
7. Do you usually skim over a chapter before reading it in detail?
8. Do you usually glance through a chapter looking at the paragraph headings before reading it in detail?
9. Do you usually read the summary at the end of a chapter before reading the chapter?
10. Do you keep your notes for one subject all together?
11. Do you usually take your notes in class just as rapidly as you can write?
12. Do you usually take your notes in lecture in outline form?
13. So you usually take your notes on reading in outline form?
14. Do you usually try to summarize your readings in a sentence or short paragraph?
15. After you have read a chapter and taken notes on it do you usually write a summary of the chapter as a whole?
16. Do you sit up late the night before an exam studying?
17. In preparing for an examination do you try to memorize the text?

From L. C. Pressey, et al., RESEARCH ADVENTURES IN UNIVERSITY TEACHING (*Public School Publishing Co., 1927*). *By permission.*

REFERENCES

1. Andrews, T. G. *Methods of Psychology*. New York: John Wiley and Sons, 1948.
2. Crafts, L. W., *et al.* *Recent Experiments in Psychology*. Revised edition. New York: McGraw-Hill Book Company, 1949.
3. English, H. B. *A Student's Dictionary of Psychological Terms*. New York: Harper and Brothers, 1928.
4. Fisher, R. A. *The Design of Experiments*. Second edition. Edinburgh: Oliver and Boyd, 1937.
5. Garrett, H. E. *Great Experiments in Psychology*. Revised edition. New York: Appleton-Century-Crofts, 1941.
6. Gilliland, A. R. "A study of the superstitions of college students," *J. Abnorm. Soc. Psychol.*, 1930, *24*, 472–479.
7. Pratt, C. C. *The Logic of Modern Psychology*. New York: The Macmillan Company, 1939.
8. Supa, M., M. Cotzin, and K. M. Dallenbach. " 'Facial vision': the perception of obstacles by the blind," *Amer. J. Psychol.*, 1944, *57*, 133–183; P. Worchel and K. M. Dallenbach. " 'Facial vision': perception of obstacles by the deaf-blind," *Amer. J. Psychol.*, 1947, *60*, 502–553.
9. Warren, H. C., ed. *Dictionary of Psychology*. Boston: Houghton Mifflin Company, 1934.

According to the present author's interpretations, the proverbs in Table I that imply *false* notions about human nature are those numbered 1, 6, 8, 9, 10, 15, 18, 20; all others imply true notions. (The author has no proofs for his judgments.)

The good student, in contrast to the poor student, usually answers the questions in Table II as follows: (1) yes, (2) yes, (3) no, (4) no, (5) yes, (6) yes, (7) yes, (8) yes, (9) yes, (10) yes, (11) no, (12) yes, (13) yes, (14) yes, (15) yes, (16) no, (17) no.

2

GENERAL CHARACTERISTICS
OF BEHAVIOR

THE BIOLOGICAL APPROACH

MAN is an animal — a living organism. This is one of the most important things for the reader to keep in mind if he is not to lose his bearings while making a survey of the principles of human behavior. To be sure, man's ways of living and acting are superior in complexity and in refinement to those of any of the humbler forms of life: he can build fifty-story skyscrapers, he can determine the chemical composition of the star Arcturus, and he can produce artistic forms like the symphony. Yet all these capacities are most adequately viewed as only vast complications of animal traits. *Homo sapiens* is moved by essentially the same forces, both without and within, as are the lower animate forms, and he expresses his energies in the same general types of actions and action-tendencies. The differences are only differences of degree, however much the superficial appearances may suggest total differences of kind. Human psychology, in a word, is rooted in living protoplasm, and it is not to be explained in terms totally apart from its antecedent biological history.

We are now ready to inquire: (1) What are some of the most general and fundamental marks or characteristics of human (and other animal) behavior? (2) What is their significance for understanding the human problems that are called "psychological"? The outstanding characteristics of behavior will be best seen and their significance best appreciated if we note some different types of behavior.

SPONTANEOUS EXCESS ACTIVITY

Everyday Examples

Consider a basketful of young kittens or a litter of pups. Their activity seems inexhaustible. At first they are a squirming mass of living bodies. Some days later they roll, romp, and somersault in reckless abandon and *joie de vivre*, expending an enormous amount of energy that apparently has no importance in their lives. And monkeys, with never a need to satisfy, will persist in meddling, chattering, and "monkeying," simply out of a superabundance of animal spirits.

In like manner, the human infant — if healthy, well fed, and comfortable — furnishes a similar picture. Lay him upon his back, and without doing anything to arouse or direct him, watch his activities. He will mildly but continuously wave his arms, work his fingers, kick and hitch his legs, twist his head, work the muscles of his cheeks and eyelids, gurgle and coo. Note that his actions are not provoked by any special outside agencies: he is not reaching or kicking on account of any particular thing, nor are his vocal sounds made in order to attract attention. Note, further, that the movements and vocalizations are not definite and organized, but are random, aimless, and undirected.

Or, consider the adult man. To be sure, much of his daily life is occupied with the manifold demands made upon him by his material and social surroundings; but in odd moments of the busiest day he may be observed drumming on his desk, whistling, clearing his throat, walking about aimlessly, doodling, glancing absently out the window, balancing and rocking back and forth on his chair. Still better, see him after hours, when the external demands relax: he grows more spontaneous and careless, reads some of the comic strips, fills in part of a crossword puzzle, gets out his violin for a while, goes for a walk to nowhere in particular, putters in his garden, or restlessly tramps the house. The central fact is that he does not relapse into mere immobility; and even when his surroundings make fewer demands upon him, his spontaneous activity does not appear to decrease correspondingly.

This spontaneous activity is primarily the expression of the metabolism of the organism. In a limited way the human body may be thought of as an energy exchange. The processes of life are both the up-building (assimilative or anabolic) and the down-wearing (destructive or katabolic). Energy is continually being taken into the body with food and drink and the air that is breathed; and energy is released in various activities, especially in the work done by the muscles in moving the bodily members. Even when a specific sound or sight or contact from

without excites a definite act in a direct way, examination will reveal a
middle term, the release of some internal energy. The external agency,
such as a bright light, an electric current, a taste of sugar, or a painful
burn primarily effects a liberation of energy that is stored up in nerve,
muscle, gland, and other tissues; and this energy liberation takes the
outwardly observable forms of bodily movement.

We may conclude that not all of a man's activity is excited directly
from without. A man is not a football, not the sport of incidental and
accidental forces. His conduct is the expression of his own internal
energies. It is these that impel him. Nor should the word "internal"
here be given any mystical flavor. There is nothing sacrosanct or in-
scrutable about the energies that are generated by processes occurring
in heart, lungs, blood vessels, intestines, striped muscles, or nerve fibers.
They are simply products of physical and physiological operations.

Importance of Activity in Development

From the developmental viewpoint, these spontaneous and excessive
activities are recognized as especially marking the earlier stages of an
individual's life. Living, then, is predominantly activity. As the individual grows older, he becomes more organized and precise, more
directly responsive to the objects about him. Instead of aimlessly working his fingers, he takes more definite grasp of his rattle, of his spoon, of
a pencil, of a surgical instrument. Instead of merely waving his feet
about, he comes to walk and run, to kick a football, to operate a sewing
machine or a pipe organ. Instead of babbling sounds, he voices words
and sentences of ever more subtle and abstract meanings. His energies,
we may say, become increasingly channeled.

Just how these developmental changes come about is one of our primary concerns in psychology. Experience as such plays an important
part, we are ready to say; and many detailed problems of incidental
learning as well as of formal tuition are bound to be raised. But maturation, the natural changing of the child as he grows to manhood, must
be an important factor also, we would suppose. It is natural, therefore,
for us to inquire about the manner and rate of maturing of different
human functions. This we shall do in Chapter 4.

ORGANIZED ROUTINE ACTIVITIES

Examples

In contrast with the sort of human behavior we have just been describing, much of man's activity shows more organization and definiteness.

more coordination of movements in concerted performances that take place smoothly and connectedly. A person's skills and "knowledges," his acts of eating and walking and talking, of posting entries and operating calculating machines, or sweeping and dishwashing, are organized and mechanized performances that make up most of his daily living. These are habits and may be thought of as tools in the individual's possession.

Much of this routine activity goes on without special excitation and guidance from without. Indeed, in extreme cases the activities seem to continue themselves once they get started. Suppose at the sound of a class bell a student gathers his books and papers and starts to walk across the campus: the bell need not continue to ring and the student need not continually remind himself of the bell or its significance in order to keep on walking. The performance is so well established that it maintains itself, subject only to slight cues like the occasional glimpse of the brick walkway, of other people moving this way or that, of doorways, and the like. As he walks, the student may start whistling a popular tune, and once started may continue without being able to tell you later what he was whistling. In the library he may copy an important definition from a reference work, yet even though he concentrates on the substance of the definition, the writing act itself operates as a smooth-running performance, and so far as his fingers are concerned, the student is little more than an automaton. When his cigarette or his pipe is in his mouth, he peacefully draws and puffs and draws in a well-coordinated and timed performance that is more than a random display of energy, yet represents no forced labor, crisis, nor emergency. In all these activities he is merely following his usual routine.

So large a part do these integrated and smooth-running forms of activity play in everybody's daily life, and so large a part of education is given to the forming of such habits and skills and "knowledges," that many questions naturally present themselves to us. What are these integrated forms of behavior? How do they arise? What conditions help and hinder them? These are problems upon which much careful scientific work has been done, work which we shall want to review in later chapters. For the present, however, to get an overview of human-animal behavior, we shall turn to the aspect of behavior which best illuminates the facets of life that are of greatest psychological interest.

The Most Significant Aspect of Behavior

Man's living is not completely described — nor even well described — merely as spontaneous activity or overflow of energy; such an undirected and unharnessed bubbling-up of vitality would get him nowhere. Nor is it well described merely as a set of semi-automatic acts that run themselves off like a job lot of mechanisms; such invariable kinds of behavior would make man only a machine from which the very heart and spark of life were missing. Living things, whether plants or lower animals or man himself, are neither like steam boilers full of raw energy nor like the contrivances of gear-wheels and pulley-belts which that energy drives. If living is anything, it is dramatic. The most significant and interesting things about life are those episodes in which the demand is for some novel mode of activity, some readjustment of behavior to meet the requirements of new or unusual situations. As he grows from infancy to manhood, the human being is faced day by day with new conditions, changes of material surroundings, new groups of human faces; and it is a truism that his mental development is shown in how he meets these ever-changing circumstances by remolding and reshaping his own reactions to them. We must now inquire about the characteristics of this readjustive aspect of so much of human and animal behavior. For our illustrations we shall use scientific material drawn from experimental and clinical studies.

Illustrations of Readjustive Behavior

Examples from Lower Animals. Yerkes, one of America's pioneer students of animal psychology, once in the Harvard laboratory charted the way in which a green frog acts when it is in difficulties [10]. This animal grows restless when high and dry, and moves about until it happens to find water. If repeatedly placed in the same dry spot, it will eventually learn the way to go more and more directly to a wet place it has found. Suppose, then, that route is blocked off: how will the animal act? To put this behavior under experimental observation, Yerkes used the simple maze shown in Figure 2. He let a frog learn in the course of 100 trials the most economical route from the high dry spot A to the tank T: a turn left to avoid the blind alley formed by barrier B, and a turn right to avoid that formed by C. When the frog had learned this well, the experimenter reversed the right-left relations of the barriers and blind alleys. The animal's movements then were thrown into confusion. Instead of reaching the tank in 8 hops, as before, the frog was still unsuccessful after 60 hops. Moreover, the directions of its hopping were exceedingly hit-or-miss; in other words, its movements were undirected.

When a homing bird is released at a faraway point in unknown territory does it promptly fly toward home in a straight line? An answer to this question was obtained by following in an airplane the flight of each of a number of large white gannets. In Figure 3 the path of each is shown up to the point when it was lost to sight from the plane which was going at about 100 miles an hour. Over 60 per cent of all the gannets studied did reach home (after 24 to 75 hours), but from these first segments of their flight-paths we can see that they did a great amount of undirected flying this way and that. Thus when the birds were released

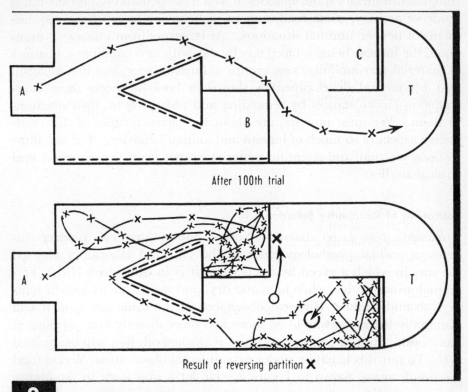

After 100th trial

Result of reversing partition **X**

2   **Readjustive Attempts by a Frog**

Typical records from Yerkes's test of learning in the frog. The solid line marks the general course taken by the animal; and the *X*'s mark its separate hops. (*Redrawn from R. M. Yerkes,* PSYCHOL. MONOGR., *1903, 4, No. 17, by N. Maier and T. C. Schneirla,* PRINCIPLES OF ANIMAL PSYCHOLOGY, *McGraw-Hill, 1935.*)

over strange terrain, their maladjustment prompted them to (1) fly
persistently and (2) fly in varied
and changing directions.

*Examples from Emotional Adjustment
Problems.* Turning now from experimental studies on these simple biological levels, let us draw from
the clinical literature a few examples of readjustment at the more
advanced level of human behavior.

A young man, uncertain as to
whether or not his calling up a
well-to-do girl for a date would
advance his cause with her, spent
an anxious, miserable hour in a
telephone booth, able neither to
put the nickel in the slot and call,
or to pocket it and go home. Each
time his hand approached the coin
box he developed anxiety lest his
calling her might ruin his chances
with her; each time he let his

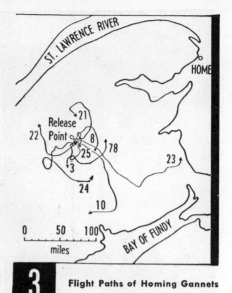

3 **Flight Paths of Homing Gannets**

The arrowhead indicates each
bird's direction of flight when last seen, as
observed from an airplane. (*From D. R.
Griffin and R. J. Hock, "Experiments on bird
navigation,"* SCIENCE, *1948, 107, 347–349.
By permission of the authors.*)

hand fall again he developed anxiety over the possibility of his throwing
away a golden opportunity. He matched every good positive argument
with a good negative one, going into all the intricate ramifications of his contradictory motives, imagining everything the girl and members of her family
might think about his attentions to her and about his neglect of her. He
fantasied in detail, as he sat there, every possible consequence of his decision, to him and to her, on and on into remote contrasted futures. . . .
In the end he had to give up the ambivalent debate and go home, feeling exasperated, chagrined and worn out. He later developed the conviction that, in not making the telephone call, he had missed the chance
of a lifetime for gaining happiness and security.[1]

Frederick was a college sophomore receiving failing grades in all of his
courses. . . . When he came to the college counselor . . . test evidence indicated he had less aptitude for college work than 95 per cent of his classmates. . . . Frederick was on his fraternity basketball team, student manager of the freshman hockey team, chairman of the festival week committee, candidate for the student council, program chairman for the Y.M.C.A.,

[1] Norman Cameron, *The Psychology of Behavior Disorders* (Boston: Houghton Mifflin
Company, 1947), pages 302–303. By permission.

4   **Problem Pictures When Out of Focus**

(*From A. G. Douglas, "A tachistoscopic study of the order of emergence in the process of perception," PSYCHOL. MONOGR., 1947, 61, No. 287. By permission.*)

and one of the organizers of an athletic council. . . . During his first college year he had been continually frustrated in his attempts to do satisfactory class work. Then, giving up the attempt to develop his meager intellectual ability, he concentrated to a pathological extent upon the development of his social skills.[1]

In such clinical cases we can readily see the maladjusted individual struggling this way and that against some obstacle, until he perceives some way out and seizes upon it to establish a more favorable equilibrium.

Examples from an Intellectual Problem. When a person faces the problem of how to recognize correctly something that is indistinct, he casts about in various directions until he hits upon a satisfactory interpretation. An experiment performed in Renshaw's laboratory at Ohio State University has brought this out well.

Some pictures were projected on a screen, each in a series of very brief exposures which ranged progressively from badly out-of-focus to in-focus. (Figure 4 shows two of the pictures used.) After each exposure, each subject stated what he had seemed to see. The reports in two cases will be interesting.

[1] Ralph F. Berdie, "Psychological processes in the interview," *J. Soc. Psychol.*, 1943, *18*, 20. By permission.

Picture [*A*].

    1st exposure: Gray patch of light.

    2nd: Star-shaped. Like what a diamond shines like.

    3rd: Bright and dark patches seem to be radiating from a central point.

    4th: Seems to be squarer now. Definitely rectangular now.

    5th: Seems to be a string with a spider on it. It may be in a cave.

    6th: Well, this picture has depth. Might be just air — the sky, may be deep, clear water. And it's night.

    7th: Your picture is upside down. Lamp posts upside down.

    8th: Well, now we're looking down on a well-lighted courtyard, a row of trees. Very peaceful-looking. Rather moody, too.

    9th: Reflection of a landscape in the water, including some kind of a cause-way, or road.

In-focus: I don't get the upside-downness any more. It's a little square some-where in England. Peaceful. Warm night. Spring, after a rain.

Picture [*B*].

    1st exposure: A piece about a foot wide. Gray streaks running vertically.

    2nd: Same, more diversified.

    3rd: A rough tree on its side.

    4th: A wind-blown landscape.

    5th: Something like an X-ray picture, part of it undeveloped.

    6th: X-ray of a fish.

    7th: Now a feeling of roughness or of blotched. Little ridges.

    8th: It's a ship. Looking over the side of a ship. But more like sand there than water.

    9th: I get the same thing.

In-focus: Wow, brother! What I thought was a man is a bottle. A sailing vessel! What I considered the boat is the side of a wooden house. I got the feeling of some pine cones spread through the picture.[1]

These two cases demonstrate again that (1) faced with a problem the individual goes into action; (2) the solving process itself is one of "try-try-again," on this track or on that, until the adequate procedure is discovered.

Principles Discernible in Readjustive Behavior

The foregoing examples of readjustment, taken from sub-human and human life, should furnish us material for an analysis. What salient principles are to be discerned? A diagram should be helpful (Figure 5).

I. For one thing, some sort of maladjustment of the organism to its particular environment is a basic requirement. The green frog needed water; the gannet was far from home; one young man was paralyzed

[1] From A. G. Douglas, "A tachistoscopic study of the order of emergence in the process of perception," *Psychol. Monogr.*, 1947, *61*, No. 287. By permission.

by his scruples and the other made unhappy by his shortcomings; the picture-observers were challenged by the puzzles. Something was wrong in every case; some of the normal processes of the individual (*1*) were thwarted (*2*). In some instances, the disturbing factors appear to be agents outside the organism (extra-organic), as the too-dry floor of the maze or the strangeness of the country where the birds were released. In other instances they seem to be intra-organic, as in the case of the young men's

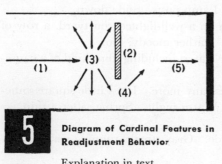

5 Diagram of Cardinal Features in Readjustment Behavior

Explanation in text.

worries. And in still others, both external and internal factors are plainly involved, as in the need to see the pictures correctly. If we take a broader viewpoint, however, it will be clear that the maladjustment is an organism-environment fact, not just the one or the other; and the behavior formula becomes, as the psychologist Lewin preferred to write it, $B = f(PE)$. That is, the behavior is a function of both the person and the environment in dynamic interrelation. In other words, the environment acts upon the person, and he acts upon the environment at the same time. The story of behavior is obviously a story of this interaction.

II. In this condition of being maladjusted, the living organism gets into action (*3*). (*A*) For one thing, as we have repeatedly seen, it displays *persistent activity*, an *increase of vigor* and liveliness. The frog makes hop after hop, the birds keep flying for hours on end; the harassed adult shows worry leading to worry; and the laboratory subjects keep on trying to get the pictures right. (*B*) We have noted also that the behavior becomes more *varied, random, exploratory*. Both frog and bird turn and turn again, in seemingly haphazard directions; the worried young men cast about; the picture-observers report one interpretation following upon the heels of other and very different ones.

III. Eventually, the organism, persisting in its efforts to right the situation, *chances upon a solution* (*4*). In some cases this readjustment takes the form of an escape from the situation; that is, the animal or person avoids the unfavorable and distressing factor. In other cases it takes the form of remaking or remolding the situation. But it is immaterial whether the change be one of the individual to fit his conditions of life more adequately or a change of the conditions to fit the individual. There is a restoration of the optimal relationship; and the individual is said to be *readjusted* (*5*).

Adjustment a Form of Self-Regulation

The readjustive aspect of human and animal behavior will be better interpreted and appreciated if seen against the background of a broader biological concept, that of "self-regulation." All living organisms tend to maintain their normal structures and functions, that is, to maintain a physiological unity and harmony in spite of changes of environmental or even of internal conditions.

The zoologist Jennings has suggested the following somewhat symbolic view:

> The organism is a complex of many processes, of chemical change, of growth, and of movement; these are proceeding with a certain energy. These processes depend for their unimpeded course on their relations to each other and on the relations to the environment which the processes themselves bring about. When any of these processes are blocked or disturbed, through a change in the relations to each other or the environment, the energy overflows in other directions, producing varied changes — in movement, and apparently also in chemical and growth processes. These changes of course vary the relations of the processes to each other and to the environment; some of the conditions thus reached relieve the interference which was the cause of the change. Thereupon the changes cease, since there is no further cause for them; the relieving condition is therefore maintained. After repetition of this course of events, the process which leads to relief is reached more directly.[1]

The physiologist Cannon has pointed out much the same general principles in more particularized ways that emphasize internal body adjustments.[2]

> Here, then, is a striking phenomenon. Organisms, composed of material which is characterized by the utmost inconstancy and unsteadiness, have somehow learned the method of maintaining constancy and keeping steady in the presence of conditions which might reasonably be expected to prove profoundly disturbing. Men may be exposed to dry heat at temperatures from 239 to 257 degrees Fahrenheit without an increase of their body temperature above normal. On the other hand arctic mammals, when exposed to cold as low as 31 degrees below zero do not manifest any noteworthy fall of body temperature. Furthermore, in regions where the air is extremely dry the inhabitants have little difficulty in retaining their body fluids. . . .

[1] From H. S. Jennings, *Behavior of the Lower Organisms* (New York: Columbia University Press, 1906), page 349. By permission.

[2] Whether the temperatures mentioned are accurate is not crucial to the point of the illustration.

Resistance to changes which might be induced by external circumstances is not the only evidence of adaptive stabilizing arrangements. There is also resistance to disturbances from within. For example, the heat produced in maximal muscular effort, continued for twenty minutes, would be so great that, if it were not promptly dissipated, it would cause some of the albuminous substances of the body to become stiff, like a hard-boiled egg. Again, continuous and extreme muscular exertion is accompanied by the production of so much lactic acid in the working muscles that within a short period it would neutralize all the alkali contained in the blood, if other agencies did not appear and prevent that disaster. . . . Somehow the unstable stuff of which we are composed had learned the trick of maintaining stability. . . . The coordinated physiological processes which maintain most of the steady states in the organism are so complex and so peculiar to living beings — involving, as they may, the brain and nerves, the heart, lungs, kidneys and spleen, all working cooperatively — that I have suggested a special designation for these states, *homeostasis*.[1]

On simpler biological levels we have cruder changes that are made to maintain organismic integrity. A starfish that has lost an arm proceeds to regenerate it. A fragment cut out from any part of a polyp will reconstruct itself and grow to a complete individual. So too, the cells appearing after first division of the egg in many animal species will, if separated, develop into two perfect individuals.

Coming closer to phenomena called psychological, we have the organism maintaining its stocks of nutriment and water through the operation of appetites of hunger and thirst, which in turn arouse movements of the whole body toward sources of the needed materials. Striking cases of this biological principle of maintaining equilibrium and integrity through great adversity are displayed as both physiological and psychological in character in the *spes phthisica*, that false feeling of well-being of the tubercular patient, and the refusal of the cancerous patient to accept his fatal diagnosis. Here we are close to the heart of life itself.

Through all animal life, then, an outstanding characteristic runs — from reconstruction by the clipped polyp, to blood-clotting, to hungry foraging, to social evasions — *the tendency of the organism to maintain its normality against internal or external disrupting agencies*. When this takes the form of alterations made by man or animal in his relations to physical and social surroundings, the phenomena are called psychological. Psychological phenomena, it may almost be said, are homeostatic phenomena writ large [4].

---

[1] Reprinted from *The Wisdom of the Body* by Walter B. Cannon, by permission of W. W. Norton and Co., Inc. Copyright 1932 by the author.

Concluding Note

A moment's consideration will make it clear that to describe a person's life activities under three different headings, as we have done in this chapter, is emphatically not to imply a hard-and-fast division of those activities into three distinct and independent kinds. When the individual is reading or writing, he is likely also to be tapping his foot, scratching his head, snuffling or grunting; and it may be hard to decide whether those undirected movements are the expression of superabundant energy or of the excitement and overflow born of an emergency. Certain it is that the behavior of man or beast varies by all degrees between the two poles of unorganized, scattered, overflow activity and the smooth-running performance of well-practiced routine motions. In this continued story of organization, the spotlight of psychological interest plays upon those frequent dramatic episodes we have called readjustments.

THE ANALYSIS OF BEHAVIOR

The Reason for Analysis

In the preceding sections we have noted certain general features of behavior of human beings when considered as whole organisms or persons. It is when regarded from this viewpoint that man is most interesting and most truly human. This is the viewpoint from which we shall take our departure, to which we shall return from time to time throughout our psychological survey, and with which we shall ultimately conclude and summarize. In short, our interest is first and last in persons.

It will be necessary, however, to supplement this consideration of the entire man with more analytic approaches. Our primary interest in alarm clocks or automobiles is in their total performances, and "good" or "poor" clocks or automobiles are those that run well or badly; yet no adequate understanding or control of them can be had without taking them apart to learn how they operate. Our interest in pet dogs or in human friends is likewise centered on total performance; but again no very sound understanding of them can be had without knowing something of their bodily constitution and functioning. We must apply to the field of psychology the same technique of analysis that has played so important a role in all modern scientific study. When the ways in which a person lives and moves and has his being have been resolved into their constituent parts, we shall be better able to appreciate his nature as a whole.

What are the simplest possible divisions of human activity?

One person withdraws his hand quickly from a hot radiator; another drives through dense traffic with admirable ease; another reaches a high note in his operatic aria without perceptible effort or strain; another falls in love and neglects his business or his studies; still another sees ghosts in a haunted house. In all these performances it should be possible for us to disentangle simpler component acts.

Through the discussion of the preceding sections there runs a biological dualism. On the one hand is the *organism*, on the other the *environment*, the two being in complex interaction. If the organism is to make a living, it must be *sensitive* to conditions about it, that is, to stimuli such as food, poison, the opposite sex, an enemy, a friend. On the other hand, it must be able to *react* to the stimulations of such conditions — positively to the food, to the sex (under certain social conditions), to the friend; negatively to the poison, to the sex (under other conditions), to the enemy. And it is obvious that the reaction must be *appropriate* to the stimulation. The differentiation of these two general processes, stimulation and response, and especially a determination of the adequacy of the one to the other, comprises a large part of the investigative work of the psychologist. If we could always say with complete assurance that, given a certain stimulus, such as a friend *A*, a person *B* would be certain to respond in a definitely predictable way, or if we could be absolutely sure that when a person acts in a particular manner this is due to his being stimulated and controlled by such and such stimulus-conditions, then knowledge of human nature would be ideally complete. What further could be asked, for either theoretical or practical purposes? Much psychological inquiry, then, is cast in the form of *stimulation-leading-to-response* ($S \longrightarrow R$).

A First Step in Analysis: The Single Episode

It would be impossible to attempt a complete listing of all the stimulations that have played upon an individual throughout his life, and of all his reactions. But we must find some point from which to begin our simplification of the phenomena we are to study; and the most natural way is to start with a particular episode or event. Hence we shall suppose a person's total behavior-stream to be cut across during some particular moment or short period of time.

Consider a taxi-driver at a street intersection. On the stimulus side, he is being bombarded through the eye with lights and shadows and colors, with other cars, pedestrians, a traffic policeman, and his own dashboard; through the ear, with tones and noises of many degrees of loudness, suddenness, and pitch, emanating from his passengers, from other cars, and from his own. Stimulations reach him through the skin of hands and feet, from manifold pressures of pedals, steering wheel, and gear shift; through the skin of back and legs, from cushions on which he is sitting; through the nose, from odors of gas exhausts and perhaps burning rubber or oil; and internally, from his posturing, his moving legs and arms, his eyes and throat. On the reaction side, the picture is equally complex. Five fingers grasp the gear shift while five others hold the wheel, one foot pushes in the clutch pedal as the other presses the brake, eyes and head move right and left to scan the traffic conditions, vocal organs keep up a conversation with a passenger, and supporting it all is the steadily maintained set of concerted pulls by trunk muscles that keep the body erect. An enormous tangle of incoming and outgoing processes! Yet out of it all emerges total behavior that is integrated and adequate.

A Second Step in Analysis: The Sensori-Motor Arc

In the example just furnished, such an array of processes occurring at the same time cannot be effectively studied until broken up further. The total behavior is too much to handle. It must be formally simplified by the isolation of parts for preliminary treatment, so that, later on, we can better understand the whole. Specifically, our method must be to analyze further by directing attention to some particular detail of the stimulation in which we happen to be interested, and to that particular detail of the response with which, more than anything else, it appears to be connected.

Consider the case of Mr. X who enters the railroad station just as the conductor calls "All aboard!" He catches his breath, his eyelids and his head jerk up, and his heart stops and then palpitates as his legs quicken their movements. Perhaps our belated passenger sees a friend and calls out briefly, "Hello there, Joe!" Perhaps also a cinder gets in his eye, causing his eyelids to close forcibly and tears to flow. Here in this brief moment of Mr. X's life a number of different behavior acts can be differentiated and re-stated as stimuli and responses, $S \longrightarrow R$'s. Cinder in eye $\longrightarrow$ lid closing and tears flowing: almost a complete story within itself, having no significant connection with preceding or simultaneous happenings. Sight of friend $\longrightarrow$ crying a greeting: a fairly complete event, too, though clearly having backward and even forward implications. Hearing "All aboard!" $\longrightarrow$ arrest of breathing, jerking head, palpitation of heart: not at all complete in itself, for it is not the sound as sound but as a learned signal that constitutes the stimulus, and the excited response is certainly related to the whole physical surroundings as well as to the general "set" or intention established in the passenger, namely, to board that train.

Each of these cases might be diagrammed as the operation of a given sensori-motor arc. The arrow, in each of our descriptions, could be expanded and divided into afferent and efferent pathways connecting through nerve centers. However, it would certainly be false to assume that by merely bunching together a number of such processes we get typical total behavior-patterns. With this caution, then, let us proceed a bit further with our analysis.

A Third Step in Analysis: Receptors, Connectors, Effectors

Such accounts as these may be schematized and still further analyzed by use of Figure 6. (Let the reader carefully trace the proper lines on this figure as he reads the following paragraphs.) The cry "All aboard!" falls upon the ear, which is a sensitized part of the body surface called a *receptor* or *sense organ*. Other *stimuli* such as sight of the train and pressure of luggage handle against the palm and fingers, excite receptors in eye and skin. The physical excitations thus set up — called "neural impulses" — are transmitted speedily along *afferent*[1] or *sensory nerves*, in the direction indicated by the arrowhead, to *nerve centers* in the central nervous system. Here the impulses are transferred to *efferent*[1] or *motor nerves*, leading to *effectors* or *motor organs*, such as the striped muscles attached to the bones of arms and legs and moving them, the muscles of the voice when one gives an exclamation of surprise, and the glands of the skin through which a perspiration is secreted.

There are other complications. In the very act of moving, the muscles of arm, leg, and voice excite in sense organs buried therein new afferent impulses which pour back into the central nervous system over their own afferent pathways. These now play the important role of re-exciting the same and other muscles, so that a continuous series of acts is smoothly performed. The belated passenger sets one foot ahead of the other in an alternating order of steps, each exciting the next one. He does not need the further stimulus of repeated calls from the train announcer, for once the running process is started it takes care of itself by this repeated circular sort of self-stimulation.

Still further complications are induced by the suddenness of the call. When the passenger is startled, his heart stops, then palpitates, his stomach is temporarily arrested in its digestive work, and the processes

---

[1] Afferent (from *ad* + *ferre*) = leading inward to the central nervous system; efferent (from *ex* + *ferre*) = leading outward away from the central nervous system.

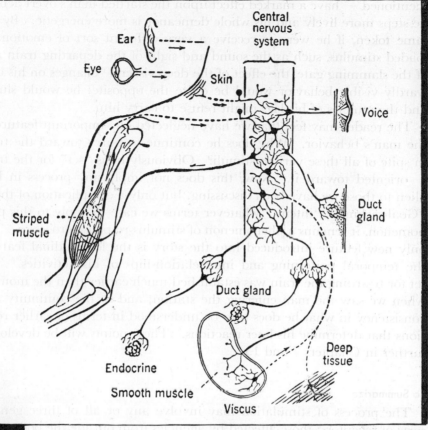

6 **Different Types of End Organs Involved in Different Forms of Stimulation-and-Response**

Afferent or sensory nerves are represented by broken lines, efferent or motor nerves by continuous lines. (The different lines of this figure should be traced out in connection with the analyses of examples in the text.)

of other organs are suddenly altered. This we can trace back to an over-flow of neural impulses from the central nervous system, out over other efferent nerves to (mostly) smooth muscle effectors and to glands in those organs. At the same time some excitation of endocrine or ductless glands occurs, the secretion from these glands changing the blood stream in important ways.

Finally, let us note that this emotional reaction of being startled has important bearings upon our passenger's observed behavior. From the disturbed internal organs and tissues there are returned still other afferent impulses; and these — as well as the change in the blood stream just mentioned — have a marked effect upon the startled man's overt acts — he steps more lively and his whole demeanor is more energetic. By the same token, if he were to receive a very different sort of emotionally loaded stimulus, such as the sound and sight of the departing train and of the slamming gate, the effect of the deep visceral[1] changes on his out-wardly visible behavior would be quite the opposite: he would slump and the muscles of his legs might refuse to carry him.

The reader may feel that we have neglected one important feature of the man's behavior. Why does he continue to hurry toward the train in spite of all these various stimuli? Obviously he is "set" for the train — oriented toward it. Now, this does not imply any process in him alien to those we have been discussing, but only a complication of them. "Goal-seeking," "intent," whatever terms we care to apply to this phe-nomenon, it remains a phenomenon of stimulus-response processes. The only new feature introduced into the story is the longitudinal feature, the temporal patterning and interrelationships of his activities. The set for boarding the train was established much earlier than the moment when we saw the man entering the station; and so the continuity and consistency in what he does is to be understood in terms of earlier reac-tions that determine his later reactions. These points will be developed further in Chapters 7 and 13.

To Summarize

The process of stimulation may involve any or all of three general sorts of receptors: those affected by agencies from outside the body — in the eye, the ear, the nose, the tongue, the skin; those affected by move-ments of muscles; and those affected by changes in the deeper-seated viscera. The process of response may involve any of four kinds of effec-tors: the striped muscles of skeletal movement, that is, overt behavior; the smooth musculature of the internal organs; the duct glands of ali-mentary canal and of the outside of the body; and the endocrine or ductless glands that secrete directly into the blood.

When all of these have been canvassed and listed it still remains true that the most important phases of the whole process of behavior lie in the central nervous system. How does it happen that certain modes of stimulation awaken certain manners of response and not others? The answer is plain: it depends on the central mechanisms; the system of connections and re-connections there is the heart of the story.

---

[1] Visceral = pertaining to the viscera or internal soft organs of the body, as intestines, heart, lungs, etc.

A Warning

By this time the reader should be free from certain common misunderstandings of the phrase "stimulus and response," or $S \longrightarrow R$. Since we shall use these concepts repeatedly throughout our study of human beings and their ways of acting, it will be imperative that he keep in mind certain principles, as follows:

A response may be vocal in nature.

A response may be emotional in nature.

A response may be a maintained posture or set of the body or of a limb.

One response may inhibit another.

Many stimuli are internal stimuli.

Many $S \longrightarrow R$'s are connected in series.

General conditions of the organism modify the $S \longrightarrow R$.

A given $S \longrightarrow R$ is a part of a whole activity-pattern, and gets its final interpretation in terms of that pattern.

(It would make a valuable exercise for the reader to identify illustrations for each of these from examination of the two cases of behavior given above.)

REACTION TIMES

Introduction

How long does it take a person to react to an external stimulation; that is, how much time is required for a complete isolated $S \longrightarrow R$ function to operate? Even for relatively simple functions the investigation of this question has a long and technical history; but even though we merely skim the results, we shall bring into clearer focus the foregoing exposition of "stimulus-arousing-response."

First, however, let us view the problem of reaction times in nontechnical settings. The quickness with which a person can, upon receipt of a stimulus, make the appropriate movement has important consequences in many a practical situation. In some industrial jobs fast-moving saws, punches, and conveyor belts demand quick reactions from the workman, not only that he may operate them in proper tempo with the other machinery but also that he may avoid personal injuries. In many military situations, as in recognizing a newly sighted plane as friend or enemy, prompt apprehension and report may be a matter of life and death; and it is made an objective of months of training. Quick response by an automobile driver has avoided many an accident. On the athletic field, quick reactions are the essence of certain sports. The

7 **Measuring Reaction Times of Football Players**

The players are crouched realistically, with cleated shoes planted in the ground and with heads against vertical triggers. The starter (Dr. Miles) calls "Position — signal — hike!" The men are instructed to charge on hearing the word "hike" and not before. The times elapsing between the pressing of the starter's trigger as he calls "hike" and the forward pushes on the head triggers are each recorded by electric circuit connections to markers on a large rotating drum shown near the ground. The records are then exhibited to the men. (*From W. R. Miles*, THE RESEARCH QUARTERLY [*Stanford University*], *1931, 2, No. 3; facing page 6. Photo by the courtesy of Dr. Miles.*)

sprinter's snappy get-away at the crack of the starting pistol gives him a heavy advantage in the race. Babe Ruth's unusually short reaction time, as measured in the Columbia University laboratory, undoubtedly contributed much to his achievements in meeting ball with bat and in getting started on a "steal." The effectiveness of a charging football line depends in part upon split-second quickness. Dr. Miles measured the charging times of various members of the Stanford University football squad, in the manner shown in Figure 7; and his resulting individual rankings of the players corresponded remarkably to those given by their coaches. Said one coach: "It took me two years to decide on those selections, but apparently you got a line on some of the men in about twenty minutes."

For demonstrations, the experimental apparatus may be fairly simple.

One set-up is shown in Figure 8. For research work, however, which calls for greater precision in marking the exact time interval, as well as more control over the stimuli and the responses, much more elaborate arrangements are entailed. Ordinarily the reaction time is read in thousandths of a second, or milliseconds (ms.) [5, 9].

Simple Reactions

The time required for a person to make a simple response to a simple stimulus, such as closing or opening a key at a click sound, will vary for that same person in ways that depend upon a number of incidental factors. One factor is the sense organ being stimulated. Simple responses to auditory stimuli vary from 120 ms. to 180 ms.; to visual stimuli, from 150 ms. to 225 ms.; to tactual pressure, from 130 ms. to 185 ms. Reactions to warmth and cold, to pain, to tastes, and to smells have not been so thoroughly studied, but they tend to be much slower. Paradoxically enough, from a broad biological viewpoint, the reaction time to pain is notoriously long.

8 | **A Simple Reaction Time Arrangement**

The subject, *S*, is first instructed to hold down (close) his key; then when he hears the experimenter, *E*, snap his key down, he is to release his own key as quickly as possible. During the brief interval between the closing of *E*'s key and the opening of *S*'s key, the circuit is closed, and electricity generated at the battery operates the clock-like chronoscope and its dial hand. The length of the interval can then be read off in terms of the distance the dial hand has traveled.

Reaction time measurements are much used to help determine what condition a person is in. Practice ordinarily shortens the reaction times and also makes them less variable. Fatigue lengthens them and makes them more variable. Concentration of the reactor's energies upon the task in hand tends to shorten the times. In this connection, an interesting difference has been repeatedly exhibited between the times taken when the reactor is concentrating especially upon the reaction he is to make (called the "muscular" reaction) and the times taken when he is concentrating carefully upon the stimulus that is about to appear (the "sensorial" reaction); for the former are so uniformly the shorter that the point can easily be demonstrated in the classroom with untrained subjects.

The effects of drugs on the simple reaction time will be discussed later (pages 662, 664, 666).

Complex Reactions

The situations of daily life as well as of the scientific laboratory usually call for a more complicated kind of quick performance than is represented by the simple reaction time, and hence for more complication of apparatus and setting. The subject may be instructed that he will see either of two lights, a white or a green, and that he is to react with his right hand to the white light, with his left hand to the green. This is the *choice* reaction. Again, he may be told that a certain type of material is to be presented (such as colors or printed words), and that he is to call out the name of the specific stimulus when it appears. This *perceptual* reaction, as it is called, is more complex than a choice reaction because the reactor does not know more than that the stimulus is to be of a certain type or class, and he is required to respond to only one out of five, ten, or even more possibilities. By this technique some curious facts about reading were exhibited long ago by Cattell. He found that perceptual reaction furnished a delicate test of familiarity with a language, in that if the reactor is a Frenchman bred, he requires a few thousandths of a second more to give the German names to pictures or objects than to give the French, even though he has a good reading knowledge of German; whereas the reverse is true of a native German who reads French with ease.

Word-Association Reactions

It is possible to measure the time of word-associations. The reactor is told that he will hear a spoken word and is to respond by speaking aloud the very first word that occurs to him, regardless of what it is. As contrasted with this *free* association, much use is made of *controlled* associations. For example, the subject may be told to be prepared to respond with the opposite of whatever word he hears; or with a subordinate word, as when to "animal" he answers "horse"; or to be prepared for a noun-subject and to give a verb, as when to "dog" he answers "barks." This is probably the form of reaction time measurement most widely useful to psychology; and we shall have more to say about it in later connections.

REFERENCES

1. Berdie, R. F. "Psychological processes in the interview," *J. Soc. Psychol.*, 1943, *18*, 3–31.
2. Cameron, N. *The Psychology of Behavior Disorders.* Boston: Houghton Mifflin Company, 1947.

3. Douglas, A. G. "A tachistoscopic study of the order of emergence in the process of perception," *Psychol. Monogr.*, 1947, *61*, No. 287.
4. Freeman, G. L. *The Energetics of Human Behavior*. Ithaca, N.Y.: Cornell University Press, 1948.
5. Garrett, H. E. *Great Experiments in Psychology*. Revised edition. New York: Appleton-Century-Crofts, 1941. Chapter 14.
6. Griffin, D. R., and R. J. Hock. "Experiments on bird navigation," *Science*, 1948, *107*, 347–349.
7. Maier, N., and T. C. Schneirla. *Principles of Animal Psychology*. New York: McGraw-Hill Book Company, 1935.
8. Miles, W. R. "Studies in physical exertion: II. Individual and group reaction time in football charging," *The Research Quarterly of Amer. Phys. Ed. Assoc.* (Stanford University), 1931, *2*, No. 3.
9. Titchener, E. B. *A Text-Book of Psychology*. New York: The Macmillan Company, 1910. Pp. 428–447.
10. Yerkes, R. M. "The instincts, habits and reactions of the frog," *Psychol. Monogr.*, 1903, *4*, No. 17.

THE HEREDITARY BACKGROUND

3

A QUESTION OF INTEREST AND IMPORTANCE

IN THE YEAR 1799 some huntsmen in the forest of Aveyron pursued and captured a wild boy. He was dirty and naked, mute and fearful; he was as inattentive to loud noises as to gentle tones; his sense of smell was so uncultivated that neither perfumes nor the fetid odors from his filthy bed affected him; he was totally unresponsive to any overtures by gesture or voice; and he was unable to adapt himself to any new conditions. The boy was taken to Paris for examination and training. But the doctors disagreed, one holding the boy an incurable idiot by original nature, another contending that all he needed was education and opportunity. As it turned out, both were in a measure correct: he was deficient in his natural endowment, but he had been handicapped, too, by his wild mode of living. Both nature and nurture had conspired against him.

The problem of nature versus nurture is one that we can apply to many questions that affect ourselves. For example, what is the meaning of the A. B. degree? Is it a badge of proof that the holder has the raw native ability to clear the hurdles of the academic course, or is it more properly to be regarded as evidence that he has been equipped with more or less standard arrays of knowledge and mental habits? Does it represent selection on the basis of innate capabilities or does it serve as a kind of transcript of courses? Nature or nurture? Heredity or environment?

A quotation from the memoirs of the Manchu Emperor K'ang-Hse (1662–1723), translated from *L'Empire Chinois* by E. R. Huc, will illustrate an early recognition of the importance of heredity by application of the pedigree method of establishing a desirable form of life.

> On the first day of the sixth moon I was walking in some fields where rice had been sown to be ready for the harvest in the ninth moon. I observed by chance a stalk of rice already in ear. It was higher than all the rest and was ripe enough to be garnered. I ordered it brought to me. The grain was very fine and well-grown, which gave me the idea to keep it for a trial and see if the following year it would preserve its precocity. It did so. All the stalks which came from it showed ear before the usual time and were ripe in the sixth moon. Each year has multiplied the produce of the preceding, and for thirty years it is the rice which has been served at my table.[1]

No problems are of more vital importance to man than those concerning his immediate biological background and its significance in his affairs. No questions are more persistently interesting, either; for they furnish a perennial source of discussion in almost any informal gathering of thoughtful people, particularly in connection with the behavior of persons — both noted and notorious — who figure in the headlines of the daily newspapers.

"Is the criminal born or made?" This is no merely academic question. If we act on the assumption that he is born with a make-up fatalistically determining him to a criminal career, there can be little choice of public policy other than to segregate him for the duration of his life or perhaps even to relieve him of that life altogether. If, on the contrary, we judge that the crimes he has committed spring not from some original and ineradicable taint but are the consequences of faulty habits and unworthy ideals acquired from family or neighborhood gang or school associates, then our faces are set in quite a different direction, and our duty is a double one, that of trying to re-train and reform him in a very different sort of social setting, and at the same time to break up or change the family-gang-school combination of causes so that no more such products may appear as its fruits. And so the study of criminology, with all its weighty import for the future of society, inevitably revolves in no small measure about the heredity-environment controversy.

Is "insanity" an illness that is inborn or does one acquire it, perhaps as he might acquire any more strictly physical disease? What more agitating question than this! If we answer that insanity is inborn, then the procedure indicated is to isolate and protect the man himself, and for the sake of the future, to prevent his procreation. Suppose, however,

[1] From H. E. Walter, *Genetics* (4th ed.; New York: The Macmillan Company, 1938), page 46. By permission of the publishers.

we answer that this illness has no hereditary basis but is brought on by excessively trying conditions of life; in that case there is indicated treatment for him that is remedial in aim, and an easing of life's stresses for others as well.

Is a genius what he is because genius will out, or because he has had most fortunate and favorable opportunities? And even when we see a man's brilliance reflected in his brilliant relatives and ancestry, is this evidence that he is possessor of shares in a family stock of brilliance, or is it evidence that his cultural tradition and opportunities have stimulated him to talent?

Our Limited Mode of Treatment

Any attack upon this general problem in a book devoted primarily to psychology would have to be limited in scope. What we can best hope to do is, first, to grasp the most fundamental biological concepts of evolution and genetics, without undue attention to details; and second, to make a brief survey of some psychological evidences that have bearing on the issues.

Even when he is thinking along specifically psychological lines, the student will often find himself assuming one or another set of more basic biological notions. It is desirable, then, that he be properly oriented, that his assumptions be critically examined and solidly grounded. The first part of this chapter will therefore present very briefly the outstanding concepts relevant to the general problem. No pretense of completeness of detail, of argument, nor of evidence is to be made. But the student who understands these few matters will be unquestionably set in the right direction.

OUTSTANDING CONCEPTS OF EVOLUTION

The Non-Inheritance of Acquired Traits

Let us start with a popular superstition. It is believed by many persons that the fetus may be profoundly influenced by specific changes in the mother during pregnancy, by her mental states. One hears tales of how deformities of certain infants were so caused: how, for example, a baby was born with an imperfect spine because shortly before his birth his mother was frightened by a squirming snake, or how another baby has a baboon-like face and head that can only be explained by the fact that while he was being carried *in utero* his mother was terrified by a circus monkey. Such cases of *prenatal marking* turn out upon logical analysis to be based on unwarranted reasoning backward (the fallacy of *post hoc, ergo propter hoc*), whereby one is all too likely to find what he is looking for. It is well to bear in mind the well-established fact that the fetus is not truly a part of the mother organism. Its nervous system develops from the first as a totally independent one. Even its blood system is separate from the mother's, for what transfer there is from one to the other of oxygen, nutriment, waste products, and the like, is effected only by diffusion through separating membranes. There is only a chemical interchange, then; and it is inconceivable and impossible that the mother's seeing of a physical object could determine the conformation of the fetal organism.

Less superstitious perhaps, but with little better scientific status today, is the claim made by the naturalist *Lamarck* about 1800 that the evolutionary change of a species is attributable to the transmission from one generation to the next of those variations in the former that resulted from use or disuse. The giraffe, it was asserted, is in modern times a long-necked, long-legged animal because its ancestors for many generations stretched themselves to feed on the foliage of trees, and the contemporary animal inherits the stretched-out condition. In similar vein, one hears it said that the children in a given mill-town do poorly in their school work and are generally low in intelligence because their parents and grandparents had no schooling; that is, that the children are born with poorly exercised or poorly trained brain cells.

Now, it is fair to say that from Lamarck's day to the present no single thoroughly established demonstration has ever been furnished for this view that the characteristics acquired by an individual in its lifetime are transmitted biologically to its offspring and thus produce evolutionary changes. One after another, claims for such proof have turned out to be false; and the reasonable position for the psychologist to take is simply that until some absolute evidence is furnished one cannot assume the operation of any such processes. "The fathers have eaten sour grapes, and the children's teeth are set on edge. . . . Ye shall not have occasion any more to use this proverb." The reader would do well to bear in mind such everyday observations as the following. The children of a war veteran who has lost an arm are not born one-armed; or, as it has been crudely expressed, "Wooden legs do not run in families even though wooden heads may." The child of a literary man must in his turn learn the A B C's; the child of a mathematician has to be taught that 2 and 2 make 4.

The principle of the non-transmission of acquired traits was most clearly brought out a century later by Weismann, who distinguished between those cells that form the *germ* or reproductive plasm in an individual organism and those that form the body or *soma*. As is well known, the fertilized ovum from which the individual develops goes through elaborate stages of cell-division and cell-differentiation, some of the differentiated cells becoming skeletal tissue, some neural, some epithelial, and so on. According to Weismann, one type retains the peculiar characteristics of the reproductive cells and furnishes the material from which the next generation is to spring. The processes of living and learning that the individual organism goes through involve changes in the somatic plasm — his blood and sinew and brain and bone — but it is not from these that the next generation springs, but rather *from the germ plasm (cells) alone*. (See Figure 9.) Playing a piano keyboard, calculating profits and losses, scanning poetry, reading a cookbook, repairing automobile engines, and all the divers and sundry learned activities of the father or mother would be the functioning only of various somatic cells and not of the germ cells at all; and it follows that the latter, being unaffected, will not transmit to offspring any of these acquisitions. The child may be "a chip off the old block," but the "block" is the germ plasm and not the parent's somatic plasm. Indeed the germ plasm is not individually the parent's own, for he is but the carrier or trustee thereof. When both parent and offspring, then, show the traits of eminent musicians or of excellent mathematicians, or when they show similar awkwardness of

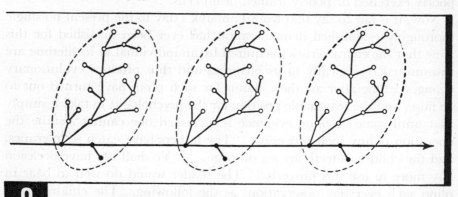

9 **The Continuity of the Germ Plasm**

A diagram to represent the principle of Weismann. Each individual in the line of descent develops from a single ovum. The germ plasm, represented by a succession of dividing germ cells (solid black dots), is continuous from generation to generation. Each individual (in a broken-line oval) develops from one of these germ cells, his body or soma being built up by the differentiation of somatic cells (circles). But these somatic cells are not continuous from generation to generation; and the child is descended not from the parent's soma but only from his germ plasm. (For simplicity's sake the contribution of the other parent to each child is not shown, but it is the same in principle.)

gait or cleverness of fingers, or resemble each other in temperament, the reason lies not in what has happened to the parent's body in the course of his individual experience, but rather in the characteristics of the stock from which both parent and child have sprung.

Natural Selection

A question now presents itself forcibly. If evolutionary changes in a line do not come through somatic modifications of the individuals in that line, how then are the evolutionary changes possible at all? The first clear-cut answer was given by Darwin in 1859 in his *Origin of Species*. Nature, he said in essence, operates as does the stock breeder. Starting with a given population, the breeder selects those individuals that show most of those traits in which he is interested, keeps them for breeding purposes; and by repeating this artificial selection he changes gradually the character of his stock.

Now let the role of selector be played by the natural conditions of life as they favor the survival of some individuals and lead to the early death of others. The process of *natural selection* will follow the same logic, and may be stated in five steps.

(1) *Overproduction.* More individuals are born into a given environment than can possibly survive, on account of limitations of food, ground-space, and other necessary conditions.

(2) *Variation.* No two individuals are ever born exactly alike. The expression "as like as two peas" becomes very much qualified as soon as one examines the peas with a lens or a delicate balance. If the leaves of one and the same tree, or the individuals in one litter of guinea pigs, or the left middle finger of all grown children in a large human family are carefully measured for length, it will be discovered that no two are precisely identical. Most such measurements will cluster about an average, with fewer and fewer to be found toward the extremes. This is shown in Figure 10 in the parent generation, P, and (better) in each of the two strains of the last generation, F_8.

(3) *Competition.* The overproduction of individuals results in some kind of struggle for existence, not simply a tooth-and-nail combat of each against his fellows, but also a peaceful enough rivalry for food and space, or a competition of speed or of protective coloring in escaping enemies, or even a competition in resistance to disease and other decimating agencies.

(4) *Selection.* In consequence of the variations among the competing individuals or groups some of them are better equipped for meeting the peculiar demands of the living conditions than are others; and hence it

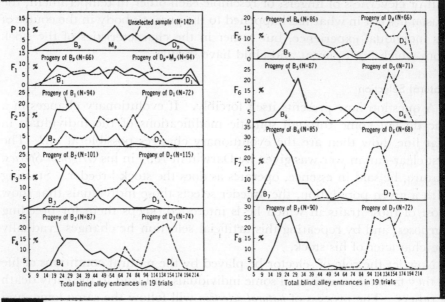

10 **Effects of Selective Breeding for a Psychological Trait**

The 142 individuals of the original parental stock, *P*, were tested for their ability to learn the correct pathway through a maze (such as partly shown in Figure 129, page 412). Their scores were distributed in a long curve showing the percentages of the group that entered 5, 9, 14, 19, 24, etc., blind alleys of the maze in the course of 19 trials. It will be seen that their scores were much scattered among the bright, B_p, the median, M_p, and the dull, D_p, animals. Individuals of the next or filial generation, F_1, were likewise tested for maze learning. The scores of those that were progeny of the original bright rats, and the scores of the progeny of the original median and dull rats, were separated and plotted, forming scattered curves but with a slight divergence. This procedure of separating the progeny of the bright and the dull as a result of maze tests was repeated for eight filial generations, producing — or separating — two distinct strains. This is an example of artificial selection of natural variants. (*From R. C. Tryon,* COMPARATIVE PSYCHOLOGY [*Moss, ed.*], *Prentice-Hall, rev. ed., 1942.*)

is they who show the so-called "survival of the fittest." (It is not necessarily the most pugnacious nor the best armed that survive: it is often the ones best protected against cold or heat, most immune to certain diseases, best cared for by the parent, or most socially organized.)

(5) *Transmission.* Those individuals or groups that survive become the parents of the next generation; and — since they carry germ cells that differ slightly from those of the non-survivors — they establish the new average about which that next generation is to vary. Given a sufficient number of generations appearing under identical life conditions, these small shifts in the average of the stock will become sum-

mated to furnish marked alterations in the breed amounting even to changes of species. Thus, the materials by which evolutionary changes are made possible are the *selected natural variations*.

Artificial Selection

A clear-cut demonstration of this general story appears to be furnished from the University of California in an investigation of a psychological trait (intelligence or learning ability) in a common laboratory animal, as shown in Figure 10. Let the reader study both figure and legend carefully, and let him note that the traits of "brightness" and of "dullness" characterizing the two strains of rats produced by the eighth filial generation (F_8) are not the results of the actual maze training given their ancestors but of the selection, based upon test results, from among the different individuals of each generation.

What was found for brightness and dullness has also been demonstrated for emotionality. As is well known, an animal (and a human being, too) when frightened is likely to defecate and urinate; and hence those individuals that show the more persistent occurrence of such acts when repeatedly placed in a certain situation may be said to betray the greater emotional instability. This was employed as a useful test on white rats at the Western Reserve laboratory. A heterogeneous population of rats was placed one at a time in a standardized enclosure. This was the parental (P) generation. The most emotional males and females were then interbred; as were also the least emotional males and females. The degree of emotionality in their offspring, the various rats of the F_1

TABLE

III   Selective Breeding for Emotional
and Unemotional Behavior

Generation	Persistence of Emotional Behavior, in Days	
	Progeny of Emotional Individuals	Progeny of Unemotional Individuals
P	3.9	
F_1	3.1	0.5
F_2	4.7	1.9
F_3	3.9	1.0
F_4	4.7	1.4
F_5	5.0	.4
F_6	6.9	.5
F_7	7.8	.2
F_8	8.4	1.0

generation, was noted; and the selective breeding of the most emotional males and females of each generation, and also of the least emotional males and females, was continued. The results are exhibited in Table III. Similarly successful results have been obtained in producing active and inactive strains and earlier and later maturing strains.

Mutations

An important amplification of these principles is now generally accepted. The production of apparently new strains, as in the breeding of bright and dull rats, may be only the isolation of different strains that composed the original population; and the emphasis has shifted to the suddenly appearing variations known as *mutations*. According to De Vries (1901), species have arisen not by the very gradual accumulation of very small individual differences but by jumps through sudden transformations, which are due to changes in the germ plasm. And these mutations are then transmitted to descendants. Black sheep, albino rats and guinea pigs, and mule-footed pigs are a few of the more striking sorts of mutations in animals, and six-fingered hands and six-toed feet in man. Though more or less sudden in appearance, the mutations may yet be so small that they are masked by the effect of the somatic modifications and are to be detected only by special experiments, as irradiation with X-rays or radium.

Natural selection, therefore, is to be considered as at least in part a selection of mutations, large or small. Little is known of why or how mutations originate. But in any case, they are germinal variations; and to a brief study of the latter we now turn.

THE MECHANISMS OF HEREDITY

Mendelism

The first clear-cut indications of the part played by the germ plasm in determining inheritable characteristics were set forth by the Austrian monk, Gregor Mendel (1822–1884), in a neglected paper re-discovered in 1900, which gave the results of some epoch-making experiments. Although he worked with the garden pea, Mendel's findings are more quickly grasped from description of another experiment (Figure 11). When a black fowl is crossed with a white one, the *hybrid* offspring, the F_1 generation, turn out to be all blue Andalusians. But if these hybrid blues be interbred with each other, their offspring, the F_2 generation, will consist of different colored fowls in definite ratios: $\frac{1}{4}$ black, $\frac{1}{2}$ blue,

¼ white. Further breeding will show that the blacks alone or the whites alone will breed true (that is, will have only descendants like themselves) throughout later generations, while the blue Andalusians will continue to produce in the above-mentioned ratios. The black and the white individuals will breed true because each carries the germ units for black, or for white, twice present, but the blues will not breed true, since each carries one black and one white unit. Crossing of the blues with the blacks or the whites will give offspring that follow equally definite ratios.

Frequently one of a pair of units is called *dominant* to the other, which in turn is called *recessive*. They are so named because in the hybrid organism developed from both kinds only the former trait will appear in its visible bodily make-up. For example, the offspring of gray and white mice will all be gray, though in the second filial generation the white will appear in its usual ratio of ¼ against ¾ for gray. In the case of the fowls, if the determiner for black had been dominant and that for white recessive, then in Figure 11 the blue Andalusians would appear

F_1

F_2

F_3

11

Mendelian Inheritance in Fowls

When black is crossed with white, all the F_1 birds are *blue*. These, if bred together, produce ¼ black, which breed true; ½ blue, which breed like the F_1 blue; and ¼ white, which breed true. (*From E. W. Sinnott and L. C. Dunn,* PRINCIPLES OF GENETICS, *3rd ed., McGraw-Hill Book Co., Inc., 1939, page 44. By permission of the publishers.*)

black. From such phenomena, Mendel framed his law of *segregation*, that the different determiners for any given trait in the germ-cells of a hybrid *remain separate units*, and in a second filial generation may become separated to produce individuals of distinct characters.

A further aspect of the matter appears when we consider more than one character of a plant or animal organism. For instance, at one stage of his experimentation on the fruit-fly, Morgan crossed white-eyed yellow-winged flies (*WY*) with red-eyed gray-winged ones (*RG*). It was found that in the filial generations a given color of eye did not inevitably go with any given color of wing but that the four mathematically possible combinations of either eye-color with either wing-color were all represented by many individual cases: *WY*, *WG*, *RY*, and *RG*. Findings of this general type had led Mendel to his *law of independent assortment*, namely, that the segregations of the different kinds of units may be independent of each other in greater or less degree.

Multiple Determiners

Many traits of plants, animals, and men are found to vary in a population not in the ways of all-or-nothing nor in such simple ratios as 1:2:1. The trunk thicknesses in a grove of cedars, the longevity of the members of a given family stock, the heights or the weights of the male students on a college campus, the intelligence of a class of third-grade pupils — traits such as these (and they appear to include the vast majority of human mental traits) vary by seemingly continuous degrees, and have formerly been called blending traits. However, even such minute and gradual variations can be brought under Mendelian principles if once we recognize that a given trait may be produced by more than one determiner, each determiner producing it in some degree.

The pioneer case of wheat will serve us an illustration (Nilssen-Ehle). In wheat showing several shades of brown in the chaff of the different plants, there were found to be two independent determiners of this brown color. Suppose one of these determiners be designated by B and the other by B', and the absence of them by b and b', respectively. Then how many combinations of the two determiners (or their absences) in one parental germ and of the two determiners (or their absences) in the other parental germ can be expected? From Figure 12 it can be seen that there will be sixteen possible combinations, and that these will result in five degrees of the brown color determiner from $BBB'B'$ (very brown) to $bbb'b'$ (white). And it is important to note that these five different degrees of brownness can be expected to occur in frequencies that can be plotted in a bell-shaped curve (Figure 13). (Cf. Figures 31

		From one parent		
	BB′	Bb′	bB′	bb′
BB′	BB′ BB′ [4]	Bb′ BB′ [3]	bB′ BB′ [3]	bb′ BB′ [2]
Bb′	BB′ Bb′ [3]	Bb′ Bb′ [2]	bB′ Bb′ [2]	bb′ Bb′ [1]
bB′	BB′ bB′ [3]	Bb′ bB′ [2]	bB′ bB′ [2]	bb′ bB′ [1]
bb′	BB′ bb′ [2]	Bb′ bb′ [1]	bB′ bb′ [1]	bb′ bb′ [0]

(left margin label: From other parent)

12   **A Case of Multiple-Determiner Inheritance**

Diagram of possible combinations of independent similar determiners from brownness in wheat chaff. Each square represents the germs from which an individual of the progeny will develop. B and B' = two independent determiners of the same trait; b and b' = absence of, or effect contrary to, B and B', respectively. By counting the B's and B''s in each square the total effect of that germinal combination in producing brown color in that organism is easily calculated (as shown in brackets).

and 32 on pages 114 and 117, and discussion there.) It is interesting to learn that this very analysis has been used to explain the variations in skin color in the children of mulattoes [1].

Since it can be assumed that some traits depend for their appearance in the organism upon many more than six independent determiners, and since these determiners may have different degrees of potency, it becomes easy for us to realize how the Mendelian laws of heredity may be applicable even to the so-called blending traits. And for psychologists this is significant, since many psychological traits vary from person to person in quantitatively graduated ways. Some hold that intelligence is one of them; and a scheme has been worked out by which the distribution

Number of cases	0	1	2	3	4
6			bb' BB'		
5			Bb' Bb'		
4		bb' Bb'	bB' Bb'	Bb' BB'	
3		bb' bB'	Bb' bB'	bB' BB'	
2		Bb' bb'	bB' bB'	BB' Bb'	
1	bb' bb'	bB' bb'	BB' bb'	BB' bB'	BB' BB'

Number of Brownness-Determiners (B, B')

13 Distribution of a Trait Produced by Two Independent Determiners

The individual cases of Figure 12 are arranged according to their number of determiners (B, B'). Result: a column diagram of normal distribution.

of intelligence scores of 388 English parents and their 812 offspring can be explained by positing one dominant determiner and five modifying determiners [6].

The Cells, Chromosomes, and Genes

Let us now approach the matter from another direction, that of knowledge of the germ cell and its changes. The typical living cell consists of a nucleus, which contains irregular, faint clumps of matter, and the surrounding plasm. In ordinary growth, cells multiply to form large tissues and organisms by dividing. Now, when an egg or *ovum* (female cell) is fertilized by a sperm or *spermatozoon* (male cell) to bring about the beginnings of a totally new organism from this combination of cells of two distinct parents, in that process (called *fertilization*) the clumps of matter in the nuclei of both become rearranged into rods or other-shaped bodies known as *chromosomes*. These have previously been reduced to half their usual number when the germ cells were *maturing* in preparation for this reproductive function. The chromosomes then split; and each half of those from the sperm unites with a half from the ovum, to furnish the chromosomes for a new filial organism. Each of the offspring, then, develops from a cell of which half the chromosomes come from each parent. (See Figures 14 and 15.)

Within the chromosomes reside the *genes*, those special factors to which are referred the heritable characteristics of an individual. The genes are much too small to be seen through the microscope; their existence is inferred, but on grounds as substantial as those from which the physicist infers sub-atomic particles. The genes, then, are the important carriers of heredity.[1]

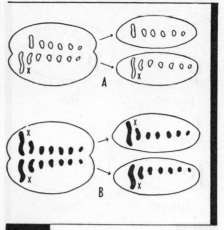

14 **The Chromosomes in Maturation**

The chromosomes of the male are drawn in outline; those of the female in solid black. *Left:* a cell of each parent. In the male, before the reduction, there occur six pairs of chromosomes and one X-chromosome; in the female, six pairs and two X-chromosomes. *Right:* germ cells ready for the process of fertilization. Note that only half the germ cells from the male contain an X-chromosome, while all those from the female contain it. The diagram is highly schematic, as there are actually 24 pairs of chromosomes in man. (*Reprinted from* GENETICS *by H. S. Jennings, by permission of W. W. Norton and Company, Inc. Copyright, 1935, by the publishers.*)

EXPERIMENTAL AND STATISTICAL STUDIES WITH HUMAN BEINGS

In the geneticists' experimental work on simpler animal forms, it was possible absolutely to control either the matings on the one hand, or the life conditions on the other. On the human species, such scientifically ideal procedures are manifestly out of the question. Yet some approximations to them have been at least attempted. In some cases the environmental surroundings have presumably been held constant while the

---

[1] For more detailed presentation of how they are said to operate, the student should consult works on genetics and on heredity. See References, pages 63–64.

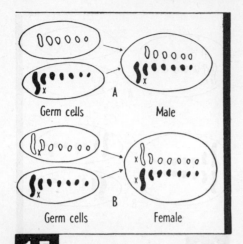

Germ cells   Male

Germ cells   Female

15 **The Chromosomes in Fertilization**

Continuation of Figure 14. A germ cell from one parent unites with a germ cell from the other parent. At the left are shown the two possible combinations, as concerns the number of X-chromosomes. When only one is present, the organism developing from the germ cell is male; when two, female. Note particularly that each organism of the filial generation develops from a germ cell containing chromosomes from both parents. (*Reprinted from* GENETICS *by H. S. Jennings, by permission of W. W. Norton and Company, Inc.   Copyright, 1935, by the publishers.*)

hereditary contributions have been systematically varied; in others, heredity has been held as constant as possible while environment has been varied.

Environment Held Constant; Heredity Varied

Where should we look to find people living under nearly identical conditions, yet varying among themselves as to their genetic constitution? The best answer seems to be: under the same family roof. and especially where children o different degrees of biological relationship to each other live together. Such children include *siblings*, brothers and/or sisters, born at different times; *fraternal twins*, born at the same time but originating from different ova fertilized by different sperm cells; and *identical twins*, originating from the same single ovum fertilized by one and the same sperm. (The distinction between fraternal and identical twins is a matter of inference and is based upon the degree of resemblance in many bodily characteristics: finger and palm prints, pigmentation of irises, hair patterns on the hands, blood agglutination, capillary structures in the skin — all are useful, particularly when combined.) Further, since siblings born in different years doubtless have been subjected to less similar living conditions both inside and outside the home than have twins, the strictest scientific method of holding the environment constant would seem to call for leaving the siblings out of consideration and comparing the inter-twin resemblances between the fraternal pairs with those between identical pairs. And also, since fraternals include many a brother-sister pair while identical are invariably of the same sex, the comparison should be made between the similarities of identical twins and those of like-sexed fraternal twins.

The Method of Comparing Test Scores. The final results from two of the best-conducted studies of this sort, both done at the University of Chicago, we may consider together [5, 10]. They are presented in terms of "coefficients of correlation," [1] in Table IV. In every one of the traits measured, the identicals proved much more alike than did the fraternals (that is, the value of *r* was higher); and as their genetic origins were more alike, too, the differences in the two arrays of values is eloquent testimony to the heavy contribution that original nature makes to achievement.

Nature is about equally effective with nurture in producing twin differences. To the question so often asked — "What percentage of a

TABLE IV Resemblances (Correlations) Between Fraternal Twins Compared with Resemblances Between Identical Twins, in a Variety of Traits

Traits	Fraternal	Identical
Height	.65	.93
Weight	.63	.92
Head length	.58	.91
Pursuit of moving target	.51	.95
Speed of turning drill	.56	.82
Speed of card sorting	.39	.85
Speed, accuracy of spool packing	.44	.71
I.Q. (general intelligence) on Binet test [1]	.63	.88
Word meanings	.56	.86
Educational age: school tests [2]	.70	.89
Personality questionnaire [3]	.37	.56

[1] For this test, see pages 90 ff. below.
[2] The Stanford Achievement Test.
[3] The Woodworth-Mathews Inventory, for a related form of which see pages 630 f. below.

Combined from Q. McNemar, J. GENET. PSYCHOL., *1933, 42, 94, and K. J. Holzinger, J.* EDUC. PSYCHOL., *1929, 20, 247.*

[1] The coefficient of correlation is an index of the degree to which the various measurements in one group resemble those in a related group. Suppose in the above case one of the members of each pair is put into one group, and the other member of each pair is put into a second group. If the various members of the first group make scores that are the same as their partners in the second group, it is said that there is a perfect correspondence, represented by the value, *r* = 1.00. If, however, the members of the second group make scores that show no correspondence at all to the scores of their partners in the first group, then this value is *r* = .00. Finally, the degree of correspondence may vary, of course, from perfect to none at all, and the values of *r*, therefore, may vary from 1.00 to .00. For fuller explanation, see below, Chapter 6.

person's achievement is due to heredity and what percentage to environment?" — the answer suggested by the above results is "fifty-fifty."

The Method of Comparing the Occurrence of Mental Disorders. Another method of using identical and fraternal like-sexed twins for exhibiting a differential role played by hereditary factors in constant environments, is to note the frequency of occurrence of certain personality traits that are fairly recognizable as either present or absent. The argument then runs as follows. If·a given trait occurs more frequently in both members of identical pairs (which developed from the same fertilized ovum) than in both members of fraternal pairs (which developed from separate ova), then that trait may be inferred to be significantly associated with the nature of the germ-plasm. Starting in 1930, Rosanoff and his associates in Los Angeles collected over a thousand cases of twin-pairs, both identicals and fraternals, one or both of whose members exhibited certain mental disorders. Considering one disorder at a time, they noted all twin-pairs in which *one or both* members were affected and the relative frequency with which *both* were affected [14]. A condensed summary appears in Table V. Examination of the table brings to light the fact that all the disorders mentioned, with the probable exception of juvenile delinquency, have far greater occurrence in both members of identical twin-pairs than in both members of fraternal pairs. The greater resemblance, then, seems to be due to the identity of the genetic origin. More generally, each disorder (with the exception noted) appears to have a germinal basis.

One caution! In presenting the foregoing studies we have accepted the assumption that the environment has been held constant, that the fraternal twins are subjected to no more differences in living conditions

TABLE V   Occurrence of Certain Mental and Behavioral Disorders in Identical and in Fraternal Twins (represented in each case as a ratio of occurrence-in-both to occurrences-in-one-or-both members of pairs)

Pairs	Mongolism	Epilepsy	Adult Criminal	Juvenile Delinquency	Problem Child	Schizophrenia	Manic Depressive	Mental Deficiency
Identicals	8/8	14/23	25/37	39/42	41/47	28/41	16/23	115/126
Fraternals	0/13	7/39	5/28	20/25	26/60	10/53	8/35	62/101

From a series of papers by A. J. Rosanoff, L. M. Handy, et al., Amer. J. Dis. Child., *1934, 48, 764–779;* J. Crim. Law Criminol., *1934, 24, 923–934;* Arch. Neurol. Psychiat., *1934, 31, 1165–1193;* Amer. J. Psychiat., *1935, 91, 247–286, 725–762;* Psychol. Monogr., *1937, 48, No. 216.*

than are the identicals. But this assumption may be unwarranted. Indeed, one factual study of the environments has seemed to show that a pair of fraternal twins will encounter somewhat more different situations than will a pair of identicals [18]. They are more likely to be separated by vacations, to be differently approached by friends and teachers, and in turn they are more likely to develop different likes in games and school subjects, in foods and occupations.

Heredity Held Constant; Environment Varied

Studies of Identical Twins Reared Apart. A highly interesting method of holding heredity practically constant, and letting environmental differences do their worst, is to take cases of identical twins that have been reared apart under different social and material living conditions. Some nineteen cases are included in a recent record. An additional case appears in Figure 16. The environments for most of the pairs were strikingly different. Alice, for example, had been adopted into a large family living in a crowded middle-class section in London and had suffered deprivations during the war, while her twin, Olive, was early brought to Canada as an only child in a family of good social standing

16 **Identical Twins Reared Apart**

Case XX, Lois and Louise, who were separated 8 days after birth, not to meet until both entered Baylor University at the same time. (*From I. V. Gardiner and H. H. Newman, J. HERED., 1940, 31, 120. By permission of the editor.*)

in a small town. Eleanore had been kept at home to do housework for an illiterate foster mother, while Georgiana had studied in a convent, academy, and normal school. Ada and Ida had both suffered childhood hardships in their different homes of adoption; but Ada had later lived an unhappy married life in cities, while Ida's married life was placidly spent on a farm. Raymond was adopted by a well-to-do physician in a large city, Richard by a truck farmer. In spite of such disparities of social and cultural opportunity and of nutritional and hygienic surroundings, some rather striking resemblances appeared when the pairs were brought together for observation — the resemblances extending not only to details of physique but also to the measurable emotional-temperamental attitudes and interests, to intellectual capacities, and even to items in their disease histories. And where differences between the two were at all prominent, the more favorable difference was not always to the child that had had the more favorable environment.

These are qualitative statements chosen somewhat at random from the accounts furnished us. But what about quantitative comparisons based if possible upon accurate measures? Some of this kind of evidence was obtained also. In Table VI a few measurements for many identical twins, separated throughout most of their formative years, are presented in comparison with some obtained for identicals reared together and for fraternals reared together. These data can be analyzed in several ways. Previously we have recognized that any clear difference in the amount of inter-twin resemblance of fraternals as compared with that between identicals might be ascribed to the effect of the greater hereditary dissimilarity of fraternals. Extending this argument, we recognize that any considerable decrease in the inter-twin resemblance of identicals reared separately as compared with that between identicals reared together should be credited to the effectiveness of the differential environment in the former cases. Upon inspecting Table VI we find only insignificant differences in the amount of resemblance between the separated identicals and between the unseparated identicals as far as anatomical dimensions are concerned, but more marked differences for the measurements of general intelligence and school work. According to this evidence, the role of environment is something that must be taken into account with respect to a person's intellectual abilities and his achievements, if not his physique. It may be worth noting, too, that such a personality trait as emotional stability would seem to be more a matter of heredity than of environment — a conclusion that is strengthened by the observed contrast between the correlation coefficients for the fraternals and for the unseparated identicals.

TABLE VI   Resemblances (Correlations) Between Identical Twins Reared Apart, Compared with Resemblances Between Identicals Reared Together, and Fraternals Reared Together

Traits	Separated Identical	Unseparated Identical	Unseparated Fraternal
Height	.97	.98	.93
Weight	.89	.97	.90
Head length	.92	.91	.69
I.Q. (Binet)	.67	.91	.64
Educational age	.51	.96	.88
Personality	.58	.56	.37

From H. H. Newman, F. N. Freeman, and K. J. Holzinger,
Twins *(Chicago: University of Chicago Press, 1937), 347.*

A Study of Foster Children.   The importance of nurture may further be checked by comparisons between children who are of equivalent original nature but who have been living under contrasted home conditions; between adopted children, for example, and "own" children. In one such investigation at the University of Minnesota [9] the basis of comparison was the child-parent resemblances; and the logic followed was this. Suppose that Sue Smith, Jane Jones, Beth Brown, Janet Johnson, and Willa Williams are children in whom a certain mental trait is found to be graded in amount and decreasing in the order in which the children are listed. Suppose, too, that the Smith parents taken together, the Jones parents, the Brown parents, the Johnson parents, and the Williams parents, are discovered to have that same mental trait in a decreasing order that parallels their children's order. Such a parallelism would be accepted as due not merely to chance but to some determining factors. It is to be assumed that any chance order of children when compared with any chance order of parents would yield on measurements a correlation coefficient in the neighborhood of .00. Then the child-parent resemblance in physical and mental measurements under the two aforesaid conditions, in foster homes and in own homes, can be represented by the obtained values of *r* under the two conditions.

In the Minnesota research, 194 adopted children were finally matched with the same number of own children of same sex, same age, same paternal occupation, same paternal and maternal amounts of schooling, same "race," and same size of city. Tests were given children and parents. In each of the two groups the distribution of the I.Q.'s of the children was found to parallel the distributions of various traits of their parents and homes in the degrees of correlation shown by values of *r* in

TABLE VII   Correlations Found Between Children's I.Q.'s and Various Traits of Their Parents: For Foster and for Own Children

Child's I.Q. Correlated with	Foster Children	Own Children
Father's intelligence (Otis)	.19	.51
Mother's intelligence (Otis)	.24	.51
Father's vocabulary	.26	.47
Mother's vocabulary	.24	.49
Cultural index of the home	.26	.51
Child training index	.22	.52
Economic index	.15	.37
Sociality index	.13	.42
Father's education	.19	.48
Mother's education	.25	.50
Father's occupational status	.14	.45
Assumed correlation between unselected children .00		

From A. M. Leahy, Genet. Psychol. Monogr., *1935, 17, No. 4, 283.*

Table VII.   If foster children resemble their foster parents more than would a chance assortment of children, the heightened correlation would testify to the importance of the environment in producing the resemblance; while in the case of own children a heightened correlation would represent the effectiveness of both a common environment and a common heredity.

A look at the table shows two rather impressive consistencies of coefficients: for the foster children clustering closely about .20; for the own children about .50 (this latter agreeing well with many studies of parent-child resemblances).   If now we compare the correlations for the foster children with an assumed correlation of .00 for *unselected* children, we conclude that common home environment is certainly important.   But again, from the coefficients of own children, since they run distinctly higher than those of foster children, we must acknowledge that a common heredity has much to add to common environment in shaping individual development.[1]

[1] The investigator, from further statistical considerations, concluded that the hereditary component is the heavier in determining intelligence level, but is the lighter in determining emotional stability.

SOME CONCLUSIONS FOR THE PSYCHOLOGIST

Can We Change Fundamental Human Nature?

Is the human stock improvable? Yes; but only *by selection*. There are very many selective agencies in human society, war being undeniably the poorest as well as the most devastating of all. Meanwhile, *eugenic* investigations go on, and various programs seek to gain ever more accurate knowledge of which human traits are inheritable and what the best means are for their selection and transmission.

By the same principle, much that is "human" is certainly transmissible by "social inheritance," through family life, education, religion, and other institutional channels. This is "culture" in its technical meaning; this type of change is the subject matter of history, for since man became man on the earth, the changes that have come about are far less changes in his nature than changes in his material things and his institutions. Physically and intellectually, says the biologist Osborn, we are probably no whit superior to the men of twenty-five thousand years ago.

Which Is the More Important, Nature or Nurture?

Surely, if we have learned anything from our survey of biological principles and of experimental and statistical studies, it is that such a question is naïve in the extreme. So stated, it belongs with all those easy and vague generalizations that become the bane of intelligent discourse, and a way from which science works toward more definite and particularized fact. It represents a mental vacuum to be avoided. It is weak because too general. More intelligently restated, the question becomes: "In the production of the psychological trait X, does nature or nurture contribute more?" From the evidences furnished by studies cited in this chapter, we would be justified in substituting a few explicit values for X and in rendering a provisional answer. In the cases of genius, feeble-mindedness, the middle levels of intelligence, some forms of insanity, motor abilities, and apparently also certain emotional-temperamental traits, the contributions of heredity are heavy. And it is only fair to assume that the weight of heredity would be equally considerable in cases of many other traits where there is close dependence upon details of bodily structure. Heredity is *most* likely to be an important factor in basic abilities such as a general factor in intelligence, motor skills, sense organ capacities; it is *less* likely to be important for temperamental traits of emotional stability and for general activity; and *least* likely to be important for attitudes, beliefs, and manners of thinking. But observe that these are *general capacities;* they are not specific details of performance.   Particular *skills, knowledges, likes-dislikes* must await the opportunity and practice which are afforded by environment.   Who will attempt to say how much of the expert bookkeeper's efficiency is a matter of general capacity and how much a matter of learning, or what part of a writer's art is ascribable to his experience and what to his native talent?

Two rules may be worth keeping in mind.   (1) To the extent that a trait depends upon anatomical structures, it may be expected to be determined largely by heredity; and, conversely, to the extent that the trait is demonstrably subject to training or conditioning, heredity may be discounted.   (2) In the degree that a trait is a general capacity of the person, it may be determined largely by genetic factors; but in the degree that it involves specific details of performance in skills, knowledges, likes-dislikes, it is more likely a product of opportunities.   But these are generalizations!

Not Heredity versus Environment, but Development

But, lest we oversimplify the problem, we must remember that heredity does not stop its work at the individual's birth, providing him with a blank tablet to be inscribed upon by the stylus of experience which is now in exclusive operation.   In mammals, to be sure, there is an early period in which the conditions surrounding the organism, which lies protected in the mother's body, are almost wholly beyond influence; and we have become accustomed to calling "inherited" those characteristics that are determined before it leaves that isolated state, and "acquired" all those determined later.   No conception could be more erroneous.   As a matter of established biological fact, what is going on from the moment of fertilization to the moment of the individual's death is an astonishingly complex interaction of the protoplasmic material and its surroundings.

When, for example, the ovum is fertilized by the spermatozoon, the genes of each are in interaction not only with each other but with surrounding plasms of each cell and even with the chemical products of activities in the cells nearby.   As the fertilized cell is dividing again and again to lay down the base plan for the organism, an experimental change of the salts in the water actually may change the fundamental architecture of the whole organism; two-headed monsters and other new and unusual individuals may be developed.   Or again, sections of one developing form, when transplanted to another form, may assume quite new structural and functional characteristics.

At every step, then, it is the intricate interplay of the protoplasmic unit (gene, cell, organ, or organism) with its surrounding conditions that determines what the next stage shall be.   It is the intrinsic factors interacting subtly with extrinsic factors, and in so complicated a way that what may be regarded as intrinsic from the point of view of a larger unit (such as an organ) may often be regarded as extrinsic to a smaller contained unit (as a cell).

This is a profoundly significant viewpoint for psychology.   Instead of debating whether walking, for instance, is entirely "instinctive" or entirely "learned," we will do better to observe it as *a succession of stages*. Even such a process as remembering is now coming to be treated as a function not simply of practice but of growth as well.   No longer obsessed with an obligation to sort the phenomena of human psychology into the purely hereditary and the purely environmental, we shall be freer to study the actualities of development in an empirical and factual way.

We now turn to development in the individual.

REFERENCES

1. Davenport, C. G., and F. H. Danielson. "Heredity of skin color in Negro and white crosses," *Publications of the Carnegie Institution of Washington*, No. 188, 1913.
2. Gardner, I. C., and H. H. Newman.   "Mental and physical traits of identical twins reared apart.   Case XX: Twins Lois and Louise," *J. Hered.*, 1940, *31*, 119–126.
3. Gates, R. R. *Human Genetics*. 2 vols. New York: The Macmillan Company, 1946.
4. Hall, C. S. "The inheritance of emotionality," *Sigma Xi Quarterly*, 1938, *26*, 17–27. Cf. also *Psychol. Bull.*, 1941, *38*, 921–922.
5. Holzinger, K. J. "The relative effect of nature and nurture influences on twin differences," *J. Educ. Psychol.*, 1929, *20*, 241–248.
6. Hurst, C. C. "The genetics of intellect," *Eugenics Review*, 1934, *26*, 33–45.
7. Itard, J. M. G. *The Wild Boy of Aveyron*. New York: Appleton-Century-Crofts, 1932.
8. Jennings, H. S. *Genetics*. New York: W. W. Norton and Company, 1935.
9. Leahy, A. M. "Nature-nurture and intelligence," *Genet. Psychol. Monogr.*, 1935, *17*, No. 4.
10. McNemar, Q. "Twin resemblances in motor skills and the effect of practice thereon," *J. Genet. Psychol.*, 1933, *42*, 70–99.
11. Macklin, M. T. "The hereditary factor in human neoplasms," *Quart. Rev. Biol.*, 1932, 7, 255–281.
12. Newman, H. H., F. N. Freeman, and K. J. Holzinger. *Twins: A Study of Heredity and Environment*. Chicago: University of Chicago Press, 1937.
13. Roberts, J. A. F. "Resemblance in intelligence between sibs selected from a complete sample of urban population," *Proc. Int. Genet. Congr.* Cambridge, Eng.: Cambridge University Press, 1939.

14. Rosanoff, A. J., L. M. Handy, *et al.* Articles on etiology of mongolism, criminality, epilepsy, schizophrenia, manic-depressive, and mental deficiency. *Amer. J. Dis. Child.*, 1934, *48*, 764–779; *J. Crim. Law Criminol.*, 1934, *24*, 923–934; *Arch. Neurol. Psychiat.*, 1934, *31*, 1165–1193; *Amer. J. Psychiat.*, 1935, *91*, 247–286, 725–762; *Psychol. Monogr.*, 1937, *48*, No. 216.
15. Shull, A. F. *Heredity.* Third edition. New York: McGraw-Hill Book Company, 1938.
16. Sinnott, E. W., and L. C. Dunn. *Principles of Genetics.* Third edition. New York: McGraw-Hill Book Company, 1939.
17. Walter, H. E. *Genetics.* Fourth edition. New York: The Macmillan Company, 1938.
18. Wilson, P. T. "A study of twins with special reference to heredity as a factor determining differences in environment," *Human Biology*, 1934, *6*, 324–354.

EARLY DEVELOPMENT OF
THE INDIVIDUAL

INTRODUCTION

To THE MODERN WAY of thinking it is almost axiomatic that to understand a given occurrence or phenomenon properly one must take account of its genesis. Social events are rooted in history; and biological facts have their rationale based on their developmental past. This is emphatically true of psychological phenomena. No individual person can be adequately understood without some knowledge of his individual past; and in general, no solid science of human adult behavior can claim anything like competence unless it is based upon the available data and principles of human development. In the present chapter, then, we will try to get a running start for our later tasks of understanding man, in the fullness of his adult stature and the complexity of his ripened capacities, by noting the more outstanding things that characterize him in his earlier stages.

No contrast is more vivid than that presented by the same person as infant and as adult. The family album, with its amusing repository of photographs taken at widely separated ages, merely hints at the remarkable changes that occur in one and the same individual without after all changing his personal identity. And who has not speculated as to the potentialities of a tiny baby, wondered what would be its later actualities, and what the story of the changes to be wrought? Popular thinking seems not, however, to have resolved the matter into specific questions; and our own approach will be guided to a large extent by the outcomes of investigative research.

Reflexes

In America the use of strict scientific methods in the observation of the human infant and child may be said to have begun about 1910. In a psychological laboratory attached to the maternity ward of the Johns Hopkins Hospital, Watson and his colleagues had the opportunity of studying newborn subjects in experimentally controlled ways. Taking one infant at a time, they applied a great number of simple stimuli and noted the subjects' reactions in detail.

Figure 17 shows the application and results in three kinds of stimulation. The following condensed notes will suggest the type of observations that were made [2].

Reactions of respiratory apparatus. Sneezing was the earliest reflex noted, appearing in one case even before the birth cry. *Crying* usually had to be artificially

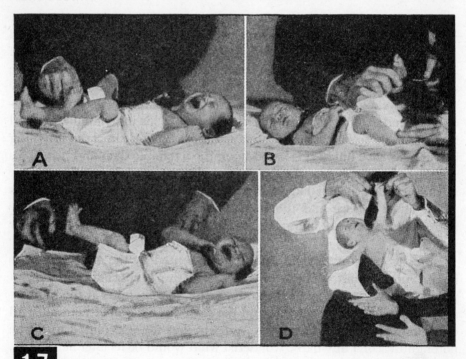

17   **Infant Reflexes**

A. Defensive reflex, with left foot, to slight pinch on inner surface or right knee. *B*. Stimulation. The blunt end of a match is rubbed across the sole of the foot. The result is shown in *C;* the great toe shows contraction, the small toes flexion. (This is a very variable reflex so far as the pattern is concerned.) *D*. Grasping reflex (infant 12 days old). (*From J. B. Watson,* PSYCHOLOGY FROM THE STANDPOINT OF A BEHAVIORIST, *2nd ed., Lippincott, 1924. By permission of author and publishers.*)

stimulated at birth in order to establish breathing — by rubbing, slapping, or immersion. Its nature varied from individual to individual. *Hiccoughing* was noted as early as at six hours of age. *Yawning* was twice noted within five minutes after birth.

Reactions of eyes, face, and head. An inequality of *eye movements* was not uncommon, for the two eyeballs did not always turn together in perfect unison. Fixation upon a bright light was common soon after birth. Following a slowly moving object that reflected light — a hand, a nurse's uniform, a spot of sunlight on a wall past which the baby was being carried — was noted at later dates. *Tears* were not shed by many infants until many days of age; and *smiling* was also delayed. Ability to *hold up the head* when the trunk was supported in a sitting position was observed at varying ages, from 2 to 15 days. Nearly all subjects (4 to 29 days of age) gave some definite response to light rattling *sounds* of paper, some turning the head and eyes directly to the sound (localizing). *Sucking* appeared invariably at the first test. But readiness in *swallowing* was not so certain. The *cheek reflex* (turning the head toward a tap on the cheek) and *lip* and *tongue* adjustments for nursing were elicited soon after birth.

Reactions of arms and hands, legs and feet. The *grasping* reflex (reflex closure of fingers over a rod put in contact with the palm) was highly definite, and but little influenced by other bodily activities and conditions occurring simultaneously. Two infants in whom life was almost extinct clung tenaciously to the rod. *Spreading of fingers* was observed in a few cases. *Kicking* and, to a lesser extent, *moving of arms* were practically continuous during the waking hours of some infants; and much *stretching of fingers, toes, arms, legs, arching of trunk,* and so on, followed removal of clothing. *Pain stimuli* at a toe (needle prick to draw blood) excited kicking movements of the other foot; at a finger (lancing), vigorous arm movements and lusty crying. Very light pin pricks at the wrists elicited minor movements of the hands. To *cold* certain clear responses were obtained: a drop of alcohol on the lower half of the abdomen aroused kicking — if on the left side of the abdomen, by the left leg, if on the right side, by the right leg. No preferential use of either hand was observed.

This list gives a pretty full picture of simple reactions to simple stimulations. And from it one might conclude, as some enthusiasts in the past have concluded, that the infant might fairly be described as a *bundle of reflexes,* his behavior consisting of a great unorganized number of specific local reactions to specific simple stimulations. And as for his further development into, through, and beyond childhood, that would obviously be a story of the hitching-together or integration of these action-units into more complex habits. The cheek reflex, sucking, lip and tongue movements, swallowing, grasping, and other isolated reactions gradually become associated into a well-patterned feeding response. Certainly this *atomistic* conception is a neat and simple one! Does it take account of all the facts of infant behavior?

Mass Activity

In the work of Weiss and his colleagues at Ohio State, we find a radically different set of observations that led to very different interpretations. These investigators, carrying the implications of experimentation still further, introduced a considerable advance in technique by controlling all the stimulating conditions and having the infant's responses automatically recorded.

The baby to be observed was placed in a cabinet measuring about 3 by $4\frac{1}{2}$ by 5 feet. The cabinet itself provided control of light and sound, and it was equipped with heater, thermostat, and humidifier to control the air. (See Figure 18.) The infant was laid upon a "stabilimeter," consisting of a light bed or platform on roller bearings, and so constructed that whenever and whichever way the infant moved, the bed wobbled and its motions were transmitted along cords to two recording pens tracing upon a traveling strip of paper. To these completely automatic records were added the personal observations of two workers watching through special apertures and tapping off their notes in a code that was inscribed upon the same paper.

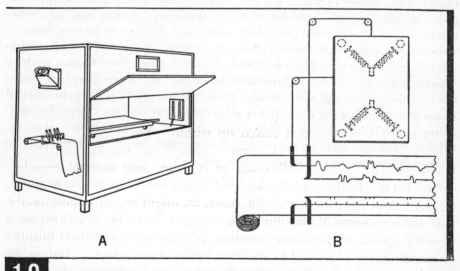

18 Apparatus for Controlled Observations on Infants

A. The cabinet. The stabilimeter and air-controlling devices are seen through the opened door. Two windows in the walls offer opportunity to watch the infant. A motor-driven continuous strip of paper takes the ink records. *B.* The stabilimeter rests on ball bearings and is held in place by four light springs. Any motions imparted to the stabilimeter by movements of the baby are transmitted to two of the recording devices on which pens are mounted. The other pens are operated by an observer and by a time-marker. (*Adapted from Pratt, Nelson, and Sun,* "*The behavior of the newborn infant,*" OHIO STATE UNIV. CONTR. PSYCHOL.. *1930.* 10.)

When the infant was left lying *without any specific or localized stimulations given it from without*, the most striking characteristic it exhibited was the great amount of energy it seemed to expend in indefinite massive activities. The body squirmed, twisted, and rolled, the back arched up, the hips swayed from side to side, the head rolled from side to side, the arms and feet slashed about and kicked, hands and feet and fingers and toes were continually in movement, it made sucking and smacking sounds and loud crying noises — presenting, all in all, a picture of continuous but vague activity that should be familiar to every nurse or mother. The important thing to note is that all these movements occurred as components of a mass activity of the body generally, and not as strictly local acts occurring at specific points and involving the play of single muscles or muscle-groups [9]. This, then, was behavior characteristic of the unstimulated baby. But should we assume that the infant was entirely unstimulated? On the contrary, its activity was greatest during evident hunger, bowel evacuation, intestinal disturbances, regurgitation, and sometimes micturition; and it was concluded that this mass behavior was therefore *initiated by internal (organic) stimulations* and possibly intrinsic rhythmic activity of the central nervous system.

The reader can afford to dwell for a moment on this picture. The newborn is distinctly active. And his activity is not that of a marionette-baby with head and limbs bobbing up and down under the manipulation of outside agencies. Quite the contrary: he is an active energy-transforming organism in which the raw materials of food, oxygen, and the like get most intricately worked over inside him, and furnish the energy which eventually finds its outlet largely in the form of overt muscular activity. Enormous energies stored up within, physiological processes going on without any guidance from without, and on occasion these energies and processes overflowing, as it were, into skeletal muscle activities — this is the truer picture of the baby.

When the infant is under external stimulation, we might expect to find more of the localized kinds of response. To test for this, other experimenters [13] carefully applied particular stimuli to the newborn as it lay in the cabinet. White and colored lights were flashed; sounds were made with snapper or electric bell; taste substances were dropped on the tongue; temperature cylinders were applied to the skin; pressures were applied to the soles of the feet and to the face; and the infant's nostrils were closed or its arms restrained. Now, if the baby be a bundle of reflexes, we would expect under such circumstances definite eyeball and eyelid responses to the lights with very little accompaniment of movements elsewhere; definite head-turnings to the sounds; tongue movements and swallowings to the tastes; sniffings to the odors, and the like. In actual fact, however, the reactions of the baby were for the most part general in nature.

Stimulation of almost any group of receptors by almost any kind of stimulus will lead to a response in almost any part of the organism. The *reaction tends, however, to manifest itself most strongly in that part of the organism which is stimulated,* and from there *spreads out with decreasing frequency and intensity* to the other segments of the body [the phenomenon of "irradiation"]. . . . The newborn infant is equipped with quite a number of reflexes, but the degree of their specificity and their significance seem to have been unduly exaggerated. For the most part these reflexes are vegetative in character, and even the others are in no way peculiar to human beings.

To sum up the results of the Weiss researches, the activity of the newborn is at first *mass activity of the body as a whole:* not a totality of discrete acts but a matrix of action in general and over the whole body, with more involvement now of arm or finger, now of leg or toe, now of face or eyes, and now of the trunk muscles themselves. A corollary is that the specific movements that later make up so much of the child's effective actions result from *differentiation* out of this mass activity and *integration* into complex coordinated activities having definite structure and effectiveness.

Thus, we are presented with two radically different conceptions of the behavior of organisms at their birth and in the process of learning: the reflexological and the mass-action-leading-to-differentiation. Fortunately we are not logically compelled to accept one and reject the other. As a matter of history, the concrete experimental procedures and findings in both the Watson- and the Weiss-inspired researches have been duplicated and verified by other investigators [4].

Patterned Responses

Up to this point, we might be tempted to state, in the words of the jingle, that

> The newborn babe is just a squirming lump,
> Lawless and chaotic, head to rump.

But is this a true picture? The analytic work of still other students has established the fact that mass activity and reflexes do not exhaust the forms of behavior in infancy, but that, on the contrary, one can make out in many series of motion-picture records a number of *patterns* of responses that *remain identifiable* as patterns from frame to frame [5, 7]. They are not chance combinations of reflexes nor inchoate vague movements. A few will illustrate: the "startle response" (described on page 214), the sleeping position, with its regular combination of certain hand, arm, and leg positions; the "springing position," wherein each time the infant is held upright and inclined forward, the arms extend forward and the legs are brought up.

Behavior of the Newborn Is Adjustive in Some Degree

The reader may have gained the impression that in such investigations the psychologist looks upon the baby's behavior in purely descriptive terms and gives no interpretative thought to it, that psychological observation is nothing but an enumeration of actions and reactions. This would be an error. It is psychologically important not only to know something of the repertoire of mechanisms in action on the part of the newborn, but also to appraise their adjustive significance. Psychology is concerned with not a mere inventory of stimuli and movements, but with some appreciation of their value or lack of value to the organism and its biological needs. Or, to translate freely a remark by the Viennese child psychologist, Charlotte Bühler [3]:

> In what are we really interested when we take an inventory of the baby's activities? It is the success or failure of his efforts to reach *objectives*. The relationship of his activity and the outcome, *the effect of his successes or failures upon the situation*, these are the main factors of psychological interest. We should keep a record which would include changes that are brought about in the object or the situation as results of the child's reactions.

A good example is afforded by the defense movements that an infant makes when his head or arms are held in restraint or when pressure is applied to his chin. One study will serve as an illustration [14]. The infant was placed on his back and a nurse gently held his head in midposition. The examiner applied an accurately measured pressure of 750 grams for the constant period of 30 seconds; and the movements

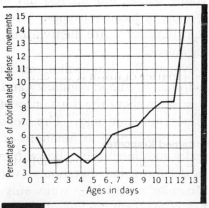

19 Age Changes in Frequency of Coordinated Defense Movements

At each age-period, the percentage of times that each infant reacted to the stimulus with the movement in question is averaged for all the infants of that age. (*From M. Sherman, I. Sherman, and C. D. Flory,* COMP. PSYCHOL. MONOG., *1936,* 12, *No. 59.*)

made by both arms were noted, those that produced some contacts with the pressure apparatus being recorded as truly defensive. Records were secured for infants ranging from just-born to thirteen days of age, and plotted as in Figure 19. By inspection of the figure we can see that very few combined coordinated defense movements appeared before the sixth day, but after that there was rather steady increase of efficiency with age.

A point of cardinal significance is the fact that there was some adequacy from the very first. The newborn is not a totally helpless individual, but reveals some forms of adaptive response to unfavorable and to favorable agents applied to him. However tender the age of the baby, then, he is always and ever an *adjustive living organism* and his overt behavior is as truly *regulative* (cf. Chapter 2) as are the more hidden processes of heartbeat, breathing, digestion, excretion, temperature-maintenance, and the like. To call him only a complicated array of mechanisms, mechanisms that have no particular rhyme or reason in his life-economy, is as libelous to the baby himself as it would be considered insulting by his parents.

Vegetative Processes

In the foregoing summary of the native behavior equipment of very young babies, our interest has been in motor mechanisms or reactions of more or less overt types. Are babies as helpless on the "inside" as on the "outside"? Are their various visceral and organic functions as poorly organized?

Not at all. Respiration, once it is established in the newborn, operates with fair rhythmic regularity and smoothness. The beating of the heart ever since about the third or fourth week of fetal life has been continuing almost automatically. The blood has been circulating through the fetal mass, performing its functions of interrelating the different parts chemically and nutritively. Bowel movements may sometimes occur previous to delivery; and digestion — with all its complexity of glandular and muscular processes — waits only upon the intake of food. For months before his birth the baby has been living; orderly and coordinated processes have been going on within him. (Of course the coordinations of physiological functions are not by any means perfect, and we must recognize that most of the concern of mother, nurse, and pediatrician during the first days and months is related to the establishment of efficiently regular digestion and other complicated visceral processes.) "Our viscera know how to live," it has been said, but "our motor mechanism does not know how to carry to the viscera the things we must have to live on. And we are infants-in-arms until our motor mechanism learns to perform that service for us."

DEVELOPMENT IN INFANCY AND EARLY CHILDHOOD

Emergence in Maturing

The term *inventories* employed in the heading for the preceding section of this chapter will be misleading if it suggests that in our survey of the equipment of the newborn we find the raw materials out of which the child's developing activities and abilities are to arise by combination, recombination, and the like. This would be to overlook one of the most salient characteristics of the maturing process [15]. Consider an analogy. Press a bean into a pot of warm moist earth, and see that it is well watered daily. What happens? A shoot appears — and after a predictable number of days. Then a splitting off of leaves. Then a flower. Then the flower changes to a seed again. And each occurrence is predictable in its timing! Note that each of these appearances is unique. From the sight of the bean, no one unacquainted with the life-cycle could possibly have predicted that flower: it simply was not in the bean in any observable or inferable way. So too with the first shoot, the leaves, the final seed. To him with experience of such things, however, each of these *emergent*, unique phenomena is conforming to earlier observations of the species; and he is able to predict both the sequence of appearings and the timing in the story of serial unfolding.

A Comparison of Species

In the literature of psychology there are several stories, both ancient and modern, of human children of presumably normal parentage who have been lost and eventually cared for and adopted by wolves or other animals. Such tales have never been authenticated, but they can give rise to speculation as to whether the child in such circumstances would grow up as a child or as a wolf. Would the emerging phases of his behavior be the same in order and in timing and in very character? We can speculate, but that is all. On the other hand, we do now have scientific evidence from a reversal of the story.

A female chimpanzee $7\frac{1}{2}$ months of age was taken into a family containing a boy $2\frac{1}{2}$ months older. Chimp and child were reared together as companions and playmates for a period of nine months, their treatment being as nearly alike as it was possible to make it, even to feeding, dressing, toilet training, playthings, endearments, kissing, and vocal commands [10]. (See Figure 20.) Tests, comparative observations, and

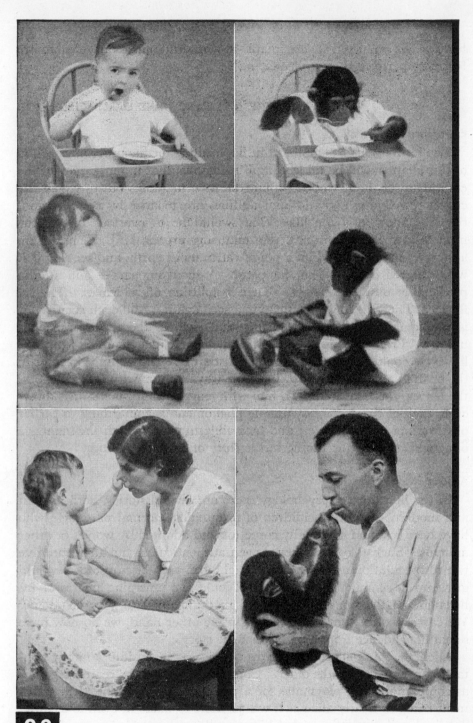

20   Child and Ape in Early Stages of Development

(*From W. N. Kellogg and L. A. Kellogg,* THE APE AND THE CHILD, *McGraw-Hill Book Co., 1933, pages 131, 221. By permission of the publishers. Photos by courtesy of Dr. and Mrs. Kellogg.*)

experiments were made upon both subjects alike throughout that period.
In the earlier weeks the young ape showed equality and even superiority
in some ways. Greater muscular strength and more accurate as well as
quicker movements — for these we might be prepared. But the observers
found her equal to the child, or more advanced, in a variety of activities
— skipping, opening doors, eating and drinking with spoon and glass,
bladder and bowel training. Further, she was observed to be more
cooperative, more quick to obey, more inclined to make use of the kissing
approach for forgiveness. In short, the ape early showed a faster rate
of learning that paralleled her earlier rate of maturing. That, however,
is not the complete story. Toward the end of the nine-month period of
the experiment, the ape seemed to lose some of this momentum as the
child advanced more and more rapidly in the acquiring of manual and
verbal skills.

These comparative observations are, after all, consistent with the well-
accepted view that with different species of animals it may often be said
that the more advanced the species, the greater the helplessness of its
infancy and the longer the period of its infancy. More specifically, we
find that in the developing young of the human and of a sub-human
form, maturation is equally striking, but that there are some differences
in the specific kinds of behavior that appear and significant differences
in their timing.

How do the Basic Behavior-Patterns Appear?

We shall want to know: (1) what are the important stages in the
development of each behavior-pattern in the human baby; and (2)
whether in each case the order of development is the same for different
children. The caterpillar must pass through the pupa stage before
becoming a butterfly; the frog's egg must hatch a tadpole before a frog
appears; and though such changes can be altered in their speed by
thyroxin and other drugs, no stage is skipped. By analogy, shall we
expect the development of activities in the human species to pass through
regular stages?

Developmental Stages in a Gross Motor Activity: Locomotion

Out of the several clear-cut studies of the antecedents and beginnings
of walking we select the one by McGraw [12]. Working with the fraternal twins Johnny and Jimmy, she was able to demonstrate a uniformity of sequence and approximate uniformity of age-timing in the way
the stages in locomotion appeared in both boys. Two of her figures
with their captions tell us the heart of the story of the successive stages

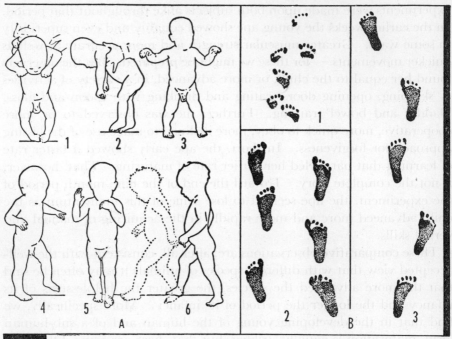

21   **Stages in Development of Walking**

A. Some phases through which a child passes in developing erect carriage in walking: 1. Newborn general flexion of all extremities and neck. Feet make lateral contact with floor. 2. Trunk forward, upper extremities extended, progression of feet by toe contacts only (shown in footprints of *B,* 1). 3 and 4. Balancing self and stepping alone; steps wide spread and flatfooted (shown in *B,* 2). 5. Steps less spread (as in *B,* 3), and stepping is from heel-to-toe. 6. Other movements become associated with the walking, making a well-integrated pattern of activity. (*From M. McGraw,* GROWTH: A STUDY OF JOHNNY AND JIMMY, *Appleton-Century-Crofts, 1935. By permission of the publishers.*)

(Figure 21). All children pass through stages of development such as these, with slight variations in the ages.

We would find the same type of story unfolded in analyses of the development of general body posturing leading up to the appearance of walking [16] or in the development of a finer motor activity such as picking up an object with the fingers [8]. It is, on the one hand, a *differentiating* of finer out of grosser activity; and, on the other, an *integrating* of smaller activities into more organized wholes; and this is a *continuous* growth process in which, however, we can discern certain phases, or stages of development, which are common to all the individuals of a species.

The Method of Co-Twin Control

The reader may question whether training may not have played a greater part than is stated in such studies. It is reassuring, then, to turn to a method adopted at the Yale Clinic of Child Development, to determine whether or not maturation does play the major role, a method in which the factor of training is controlled. A pair of presumably identical twins aged 46 weeks were given differential experience. Twin *T* was given training daily in stacking cubes and in climbing stairs, while Twin *C*, to serve as a control, was given no training of either sort. After *T* had had the practice for 6 weeks, her performance was compared with that of *C*. A day-by-day analysis of *T*'s work had shown the usual stages and advances; yet when tested at the 52d week of age, *C*, with no training at all, was her equal in the cube work and not greatly inferior in the stair-climbing. Moreover, after 2 weeks of practice at this age, *C* was able to surpass *T*'s performance in the latter task. Evidently, to be most effective training must be introduced at the proper stage of maturation. (Such indeed is the conclusion drawn by some half-dozen other investigators who have repeated this kind of work.)

Vocalization. The examples of infant and child behavior which we have been examining in this section have been of the manual-pedal, or better, skeletal, class in which smaller or larger segments of the body are moved through space by the moving of jointed parts of the skeleton. But some of the most significant human functions are not skeletal in that larger sense. For instance, sound production with the voice. We shall give the development of vocal and verbal powers only a brief introduction here, leaving a somewhat fuller treatment to the chapter on language behavior.

The initial repertoire of sounds in the newborn is scanty, consisting of little but crying. With days and weeks of age, however, an increasing number of sounds are at his disposal. These are not put at his disposal by the adults around him, for he seems not to imitate others at all in these early months, but have their genesis in a growing vocal apparatus that becomes gradually more versatile.

A conclusive experiment on this point extended the procedure of co-twin control to language acquisition, employing the same identical twins mentioned above [16]. Twin *T* was given intensive training in naming common objects for a period of 5 weeks, beginning when she was 84 weeks old and continuing through her 88th week. Twin *C* was given the same course of training for 4 weeks, beginning at her 89th. When the achievements of the two were compared for equivalent learning trials — but an age disparity of 5 weeks — the superiority of *C* was quite marked. She learned the same words more quickly. The difference of five weeks' time in which to mature further was a critical point. This is not to deny that language learning is learning, but it does emphasize the fact that learning is by no means the whole story, and that it must be built upon the substructure of organic growth.

Further, we can anticipate that a thorough analysis of the process of language acquisition will illustrate again the double process of differentiating the various sounds and integrating them into new sound-combinations.

Sensory and Perceptual Aspects of Development in Infancy

Along with the refinement of motor response in the developing infant go refinements and elaboration on the receptive side as well. Suppose that an irritant like a light pin prick is applied to the skin of an infant only a few days old. (1) Whether he responds to the pricking or not — and many an infant does not at first — he certainly manifests no noticeable response to the sight of the approaching pin. (2) A few weeks later, he comes to notice the pin, may gaze at it, reach for it, and even play with it as with a toy. But he does not apply it to his skin, nor otherwise show that he has grasped any relation between pin and pain. (3) As the infant continues to develop, upon seeing the pin or the approaching hand of the experimenter, he starts crying or fussing or turning bodily away or ducking his head or (if he is mature enough to talk) whining "no pin." Clearly he has made an association between seeing the stimulus and feeling the cutaneous irritation. (4) As this recognition of the pin and its use becomes more and more complete, the baby comes to defend himself aggressively, or to accept the game stoically by grasping his arm or leg while it is being subjected to the stimulation or even pricking himself in a sporting spirit. Figure 22 graphically shows the ages of appearance of these phases in different children, as well as of phases in the development of motor aspects.

The role of the simpler reflexes to the local sensitivities that was so clear in the picture of the newborn now has become in a sense submerged in the perceptual and understanding behavior made possible by the growing dominance of his cerebral cortex, the highest part of the brain.

Social Behavior Has Maturational Bases

The gradual appearance of behavior that manifests some recognition of *personal* as versus non-personal elements in the environment has received the attention of those who have studied infants, from Tiedemann

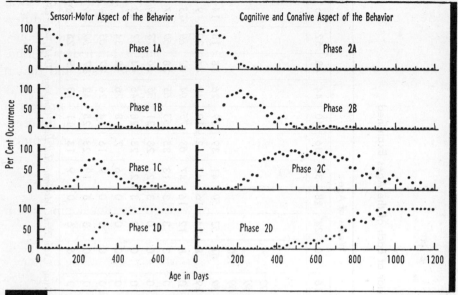

22 **Ages of Occurrence of Different Types of Infant Response**

Sensori-Motor: 1A. Diffuse. Widespread bodily movements, accompanied by crying. Common in first days, reducing to zero before 220 days of age. *1B. Inhibition.* Diminution of the diffuse bodily movements. Probably due to inhibitory influence of maturing cortex upon subcortical centers. Especially observed between 100 and 200 days. *1C. General Localization.* Infant begins to localize place being stimulated. Most frequently observed around 250 days. *1D. Specific Localization.* Carries hand to stimulated spot. Universal after 500 days. *Cognitive-Conative: 2A. Passive.* Makes no detectable response to pin. Condition of newborn. *2B. Objective Perception.* Notices, reaches for pin. No differentiation of pin from other things seen. Commonly observed at 250 days. *2C. Association.* Sight of pin provokes fussing, crying, withdrawal movements. Most frequent from 400 to 800 days. *2D. Integration.* Child not only associates pin and pain, but appraises whole situation. This fuller understanding appears between 800 and 1000 days. (*From M. McGraw,* THE NEUROMUSCULAR MATURATION OF THE HUMAN INFANT, *Columbia University Press, 1943, page 107. By permission of the publishers.*)

in 1787 down to the present. Clear-cut verifications come from Gesell's laboratory, where infants were given thoroughly standardized and systematized examinations at regular intervals on a great variety of behavior items, of which some bore on social patterns and capacities. Some of the observations are collected in Table VIII. For each behavior item, the number of infants in whom it was observed at each of the respective age-periods is indicated in percentage of all infants of that age. Thus, at the age of 4 weeks, only 8 per cent of the subjects responded when the experimenter smiled at them and talked to them;

TABLE VIII

The Percentage of Infants that Showed Each Kind of Behavior at Each of the Ages Examined

Behavior Items	Weeks of Age														
	4	6	8	12	16	20	24	28	32	36	40	44	48	52	56
1. Responds to smiling and talking	8	62	63	...	...										
2. Visually pursues moving person	12	69	74	...	...										
3. Knows mother	3	21	39	87	92										
4. Sobers at strangers	0	3	4	35	56										
5. Turns head on sound of voice	0	3	26	42	50	100									
6. Accepts strangers	100	100	100	100	80	61	52	59	41	39	39	26	18	18	14
7. Withdraws from strangers	0	0	0	0	19	8	24	16	47	42	19	48	44	30	9
8. Adjusts to words					0	8	12	16	47	68	75	94	82	89	73
9. Responds to "bye-bye"					0	3	3	3	13	35	53	65	38	59	27
10. Adjusts to commands					0	0	0	3	22	23	31	55	56	73	50
11. Responds to inhibitory words					0	0	0	3	25	23	28	45	44	52	23
12. Responds to "So big"					0	0	0	0	6	7	8	26	18	34	...
13. Elicits attention					0	0	0	0	9	16	14	26	27	53	50
14. Plays pat-a-cake					0	0	3	6	19	23	25	42	27	50	9
15. Plays peek-a-boo					0	6	6	0	9	13	11	13	9	25	9

From A. Gesell and H. Thompson, INFANT BEHAVIOR (New York: McGraw-Hill Book Company, 1934), page 258.

while at the ages of 6 and 8 weeks, 62 per cent and 63 per cent responded. As we run our eyes down the table we can note some progressive differentiations. Taking the first two items, it appears that the average baby comes to react differently to the personal than to the non-personal features in his surroundings between his 4th and his 6th week of age. His face brightens up at sight of a person and his eyes try to follow him. Later he differentiates his mother, and a bit later distinguishes between strangers and persons with whom he is familiar. When he is 36 weeks old he begins to be responsive to words, not by understanding their symbolic meanings (see Chapter 18), but by reacting to words as cues to simple motor responses, as "Pat-a-cake" or "No! No!" "We do not gain the impression that this social development is radically dependent upon the emergence of a series of differentiated instincts. Pervasive general propensit'es. . . . are present from birth." Yet "Personal and social behavior expresses itself in characteristic patterns and capacities which are subject to laws of growth." "A growth process is molding the patterns of social behavior" [6].

Other child psychologists, working more speculatively, have been able to trace stages during these early months in the attaining of a feeling of self, some *ego-formation*. This stems from the child's experiences in connection with his physical body and with things other than his own body. The resistances he meets in inanimate objects and the oppositions he encounters in other people force him to distinguish himself from external things. Tennyson put the general matter as clearly as anyone has done:

> The baby new to earth and sky,
>   What time his tender palm is prest
> Against the circle of his breast,
>   Has never thought that "this is I";
>
> But as he grows he gathers much,
>   And learns the use of "I" and "Me,"
> And finds "I am not what I see,
>   And other than the things I touch."
>
> So rounds he to a separate mind
>   From whence clear memory may begin,
> As thro' the frame that binds him in
>   His isolation grows defined.[1]

[1] From *In Memoriam, XLV.* See also pages 166 f. below.

REFERENCES

1. Barker, R. G., J. S. Kounin, and H. F. Wright. *Child Behavior and Development*. New York: McGraw-Hill Book Company, 1943.
2. Blanton, M. G. "The behavior of the human infant during the first thirty days of life," *Psychol. Rev.*, 1917, *24*, 456–483.
3. Bühler, C. *The First Year of Life* (trans. by Greenberg and Ripin). New York: John Day Company, 1930.
4. Carmichael, L., ed. *Manual of Child Psychology*. New York: John Wiley and Sons, 1946.
5. Dennis, W. "A description and classification of the responses of the newborn infant," *Psychol. Bull.*, 1934, *31*, 5–22.
6. Gesell, A., and H. Thompson. *Infant Behavior: Its Genesis and Growth*. New York: McGraw-Hill Book Company, 1934.
7. Gilmer, B. v. H. "An analysis of the spontaneous responses of the newborn infant," *J. Genet. Psychol.*, 1933, *42*, 392–405.
8. Halverson, H. M. "An experimental study of prehension in infants by means of systematic cinema records," *Genet. Psychol. Monogr.*, 1931, *10*, Nos. 2–3.
9. Irwin, O. C. "The amount and nature of activities of newborn infants under constant external stimulating conditions during the first ten days of life," *Genet. Psychol. Monogr.*, 1930, *8*, No. 1.
10. Kellogg, W. N., and L. A. Kellogg. *The Ape and the Child*. New York: McGraw-Hill Book Company, 1933.
11. Lewin, K. *Dynamic Theory of Personality* (trans. by D. K. Adams and K. Zener). New York: McGraw-Hill Book Company, 1935.
12. McGraw, M. B. *Growth: A Study of Johnny and Jimmy*. New York: Appleton-Century-Crofts, 1935.
13. Pratt, K. C., A. K. Nelson, and K. H. Sun. "The behavior of the newborn infant," *Ohio State Univ. Contr. Psychol.*, 1930, *10*.
14. Sherman, M., I. Sherman, and C. D. Flory. "Infant behavior," *Comp. Psychol. Monogr.*, 1936, *12*, No. 59.
15. Shirley, M. M. *The First Two Years*. I. Postural and Locomotor Development, 1931; II. Intellectual Development, 1933; III. Personality Manifestations, 1933. Minneapolis: University of Minnesota Press.
16. Strayer, L. C. "Language and growth," etc., *Genet. Psychol. Monogr.*, 1930, *8*, No. 3.

5

INDIVIDUAL DIFFERENCES

AND THEIR TESTING

THE GENERAL AND THE PARTICULAR

IN ANY NATURAL SCIENCE and in many another field of learning called science, the primary interest is in the *typical* phenomena and the *general* laws of the field. When studying frogs, the zoology student ordinarily applies himself to the characteristics that are common to frogs in general, to the whole genus *Rana;* and the fact that the specimen (note the word!) he is dissecting today may be slightly larger or have a slightly different reflex than the one yesterday is set aside as an "accident" of no importance. Today's animal is regarded only as an example or instance of a class; and by dissecting or experimenting with it the zoologist hopes to learn what is true of that class — general principles or laws. As Gordon Allport has written, *Scientia non est individuorum.*

So it is with the science of human nature. We seek out general laws. And so it should be in a first introduction to that field as embodied in a general textbook like the present one.

There is no denying, however, that much of the more practical interest in human nature centers in individual persons and the differences between persons. To the employment manager, mankind in general is of no concern; he hires and fires particular persons, and his problem is always a question of "which ones." Is the new applicant X better fitted for a clerical or a mechanical job; has he the intelligence and the training for an advanced position or does he belong at the bottom rung of the ladder; is he likely to work well with the cranky boss of Department A or had he better be put with the more easy-going boss of B? From the applicant's point of view it is not an essentially different story. Not wanting to be a square peg in a round hole, he seeks advice and counsel as to just for what he — as one individual particular person — is best fitted. In educational psychology, too, the emphasis swings away from man as a type to the specific persons to be educated, as they vary in age, in sex, in intelligence, and the like. The college student does much of his thinking about himself and his fellow students in such terms as, "*J* is better able to work in the natural sciences than in literature," or "*K* is a poor student and would cut a poor figure in campus politics, but he made the college orchestra and the Monogram Club." The instructor grades his students — and the student grades his instructors. And if the reader will but stop to consider, he will be struck with the exceedingly small amount of conversation about people that is about mankind in general, and the enormous amount devoted to the special peculiarities, even idiosyncrasies, of this person and that.

It is also to be admitted that a sound and solid science of the genus *Homo* must not disregard the differences among the men upon whom studies are made. Hasty generalizing is a bane to natural science; and the beginning student does well to protect himself against the evil by first appreciating some of the variations and shadings from man to man, and especially by gaining some acquaintance with the safeguards that have been found necessary in studying them.

SOME AREAS OF REPUTED DIFFERENCES

Differences Supposedly Due to Sex

When asked, "Which is the more intelligent, man or woman?" Dr. Samuel Johnson is said to have retorted, "Which man, which woman?" Though an eighteenth-century celebrity, he could not have anticipated twentieth-century thinking more to the point; for it is well recognized today that any flat assertion about a class or group of people is hazardous to the extent that the individuals within that class or group vary from each other. (As we shall want to put it statistically, the variability or dispersion of the group is as important as the mean.)

Of all the reputed differences that have become a part of the lore of untutored folk, doubtless those supposed to exist between men and women are the richest in variety and give rise to the most opiniated beliefs. This area is a favorite hunting ground for the writers of syndicated columns and for the editors of Sunday newspaper supplements. Certainly the intelligent student of human nature should seek to learn what is scientifically acceptable and what is not.

As we search for psychological differences between the sexes, we recognize certain clear *physical* differences over and beyond those directly associated with the reproductive functions: the adult male physique is more angular, the voice has changed, the distribution of hair is quite different, the body as a whole is heavier and taller, the musculature more powerful. We may then recognize those psychological or behavioral differences that depend quite directly upon physique. As one can confirm readily by consulting the *World Almanac* of any year, men surpass women in nearly every branch of athletic endeavor. Further, it seems certain that among nearly all peoples of all times the physical differences between the sexes have led also to occupational differences: the males doing most of the warring and hunting, the females undertaking most of the care of the young they have borne and the associated household affairs.

There is a more subtle but real physiological difference that is *endocrine* in nature, since the androgen hormones dominate in the male, and the estrogens in the female (see pages 301 ff.); and it is impossible accurately to estimate how much unlikeness in temperament and emotionality may be the consequence of that difference in human beings — though its effects can be ascertained with the experimental animals. In any case, whether the physiological factors contribute 10 per cent, 50 per cent, or 90 per cent to the divisions of labor between man and woman, these divisions tend to become established as customs, and at that point the entrance of social factors confuses the picture of what is and what is not primarily masculine and primarily feminine. It is said that men commonly evince an interest in exploit and adventure, in outdoor and physically strenuous occupations, in machinery and tools, and in business and commerce. They are aggressive and self-assertive (at least in overt manners), rougher in language, less expressive of sentiment. Women, on the other hand, evince more interest in domestic duties and in esthetic objects and exercises, as well as in activities that are of ministrative nature, to the young, the aged, the helpless. They express themselves in ways that are more compassionate and sympathetic, they are more timid, more fastidious, more esthetically sensitive, more emotional. All this reads like the outpourings of the armchair psychologist, yet each descriptive point is deduced from (*a*) anthropological notes on primitive peoples and (*b*) objective tests of the interests of men and women unaware that the tests were getting at the problem of sex differentiation [9]. Many such points seem to be implied in the findings of a questionnaire that was aimed at determining the relative strengths within an individual of the six great classes of time-honored human values: the esthetic, the religious, the social, the economic, the theoretical, and the political. These are graphically and concisely presented in Figure 23.

As an empirical datum it may be noted that in a great number of

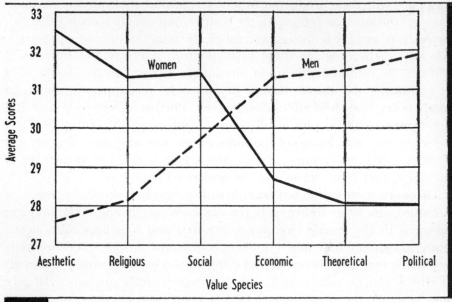

23 Relative Predominance of Different Values in the Lives of Men and of Women

Determined from the answers of 463 men and 313 women to disjunctive questions, such as, "Which do you prefer . . .?" "Which should be the aim of . . .?" (*From P. E. Vernon and G. W.·Allport, J. ABN. SOC. PSYCHOL., 1931, 26, 246, as adapted by E. G. Boring, et al., AN INTRODUCTION TO PSYCHOLOGY, Wiley, 1939, page 129. By permission of the authors.*)

investigations of children of elementary school, high school, and college rank, boys have pretty consistently done better in mathematics and the natural sciences while girls have done better in verbal and literary tests as well as in those that call for memorizing. Is this again a result of social rather than biological differences [6]? With these results may be compared the findings by a number of investigators who have employed the interesting and simple technique of listening in on spontaneous conversations overheard on city streets or during intermissions at concerts. The data, furnished in Table IX, point to clear sex dissimilarities. It is not easy, however, to give a precise summary of their significance; the reader may find it an interesting task to attempt formulation of general principles from the two kinds of research.

Of one human trait something definite can be set down. In native *general intelligence*, no dissimilarities between the sexes are found;[1] and the popular assumption of a superior male rationality to be contrasted

[1] We must except a slight superiority in girls during those childhood years when they are developing in every way slightly in advance of boys.

TABLE

IX Sex Differences in Conversation Topics. Revealed by Percentage Distribution of Conversation Among Various Topics

Topic	Moore (1922, N.Y.C. streets)		M. H. Landis (1924, Columbus streets)		C. Landis (1927, London streets)		Carlson (1936, concerts)		Baker (1937 Boston and N.Y.C. streets)	
	Men to Men	Women to Women	Men to Men	Women to Women	Men to Men	Women to Women	Men to Men	Women to Women	Men to Men	Women to Women
Business and money	48	3	49	12	35	5	19	2	55	17
Men	13	44	12	22	15	14	14	17	4	23
Women	8	16	4	15	5	2	12	30	17	13
Clothes and decoration	2	23	5	19	5	16	1	9	5	23
Sports and amusements	14	4	15	11	16	0	18	12	9	7
Self	..	..	7	13	7	20	..	..	3	10

From S. L. Pressey, J. E. Janney, and R. G. Kuhlen, LIFE: A PSYCHOLOGICAL SURVEY *(New York: Harper and Brothers, 1939). By permission of authors and publisher.*

with the female's so-called intuition is a related superstition that has been laid to rest.

Finally, there is the long-held notion that the male sex is more *variable* than the female, more productive, say, of geniuses and of idiots. This is one more superstition about to be buried. As two critical reviewers [5, 6] have pointed out, in all the extensive literature of psychological tests greater variability of scores is shown by the males in 320 instances, by the females in 322, by neither in 24.

Differences Supposedly Due to Race

There is probably no greater source of emotionalized social and political confusion than the modern assumption of psychological differences between the races of mankind. Since the writings of Gobineau, published in the 1850's, modern peoples of the Western World have been beset by the conviction that there is some kind of hierarchy in which the different races of the earth may be ranged in an order of relative advancement or retardation, with themselves of course at the top.

Some general points deserve consideration at once. *What*, when we come down to it, *is the meaning of "race"*? (1) We find ethnologists using varying differentiae. Some classify races on the basis of skin color —

the white, the red, the yellow, the black.   Some use hair textures as the basis, setting the peoples of straight hair (round in cross section) over against those with hair that is woolly or kinky (oval in cross section). Then there are those who make the "cephalic index," that is, the ratio of head breadth to head length, the distinguishing feature.   (2) On the negative side, we must note that a "race" is not to be confused with a religion, as the Jewish; with a nationality, as the Germans or Japanese; nor with a language, as the Latins or the Aryans.   (3) Some races at least are not fixed.   Boas and others have found clear evidence that the children born in this country of long-headed Sicilian immigrants are themselves less long-headed, while those born of round-headed Southeast European immigrants are less round-headed: both groups change toward an "American type," if we may use such an expression.   (4) If the different so-called races or ethnic groups are to be judged as more and less primitive in terms of their degrees of greater and less resemblance to the anthropoid apes, some interesting anomalies greet us.   Judged by arm-length the Negro would be found most primitive, but judged by thinness of lip he would be most advanced.   Likewise, if we judge by the prominence of the supra-orbital ridges or by the hairiness of the body, the white man is clearly more like the apes and so is somewhat less evolved than the black man and very much less so than the yellow man. (5) It is even debatable whether the rarity of pure ethnic types can be explained as the result of intermixtures and mongrelization of originally distinct races, or is really due to the fact that pure races never have existed and the assumption of types has been made simply for purposes of classification.[1]

Neglecting, however, the confusions that beset the very term *race* even in its proper biological sense, let us inquire into the results of psychological measurements and observations.   Considerable excitement was aroused in 1943 by the publication of a small pamphlet [2] in which the median scores on intelligence tests on Southern White and Northern Negro recruits in World War I (shown in Table X-*A*) were printed on the same page.   There were protests that such a juxtaposition implied an inferiority of Whites to Negroes.   This could have been avoided had the further data of Table X-*B* appeared on the same page.   And the second variable (environmental opportunity) thus brought out for Whites, could have been shown for Negroes from such data as those of Table X-*C*.

The best controlled comparative study of intelligence test scores, however, is that done by Klineberg in Europe [4].

[1] In the treatment of the present topic the author has followed many leads from Klineberg's work [4].

TABLE

X   Median Scores on Intelligence Tests on Southern
White and Northern Negro Recruits

A		B	C	
Southern Whites	Northern Negroes	Northern Whites	Residence in N.Y.	N. I. T. Scores
Miss. 41.25	N.Y. 45.02	N.Y. 64.0	1 and 2 years	72
Ky. 41.50	Ill. 47.35	Ill. 63.0	3 and 4 years	76
Ark. 41.55	Ohio 49.50	Ohio 66.7	5 and 6 years	84
			7 and 8 years	90
			9 and more years	94

Intelligence has been the trait most widely used for comparative purposes because it is most accurately measured. But shrewd observations of *emotional* behavior have led to equally skeptical conclusions as to variations between races. One hears much of the stoical American Indian and of the laughter-loving Negro. Yet there are occasions when Indian tribes give themselves over to unrestrained outbursts of weeping; and there are reports of mid-African folk whose stoicism in face of adversity is so persistent that it actually irritates the white explorer.

There may be some truth in a certain sociologist's phrase: "Nothing is either Jew or Greek but thinking makes it so."

The material presented in this section has been largely negative; and it does not accord with the opinions of all psychologists and ethnologists. But until more evidence is available, it seems that the burden of proof is on him who asserts that there are great genetically-determined differences between so-called races.

Differences Supposedly Due to Nationality

From the preceding paragraphs we are prepared to be skeptical of much that goes as "race psychology." We are ready to recognize the enormous contributions of culture, and to insist that it is not simply who he is, but where and among whom he is, that makes the man. Yet again we may fall into error. We may get into the easy habit of assuming that common environments make common men. We say we can tell an Italian from a Greek every time, or a Pole from a Serb, or a Scotsman from an Irishman. These assured opinions are strengthened as we stroll through a cosmopolitan city from Little Italy through the near-Ghetto to Germanville. Such general impressions based on masses of people may be reliable and sound; but what about this individual boy coming around the corner or that individual girl passing with a basket on her head? Can we apply our judgments to individuals with perfect assurance?

Here we shall not attempt to cite scientific literature. We shall be content with a simple demonstration. In 1930 an International Congress on Mental Hygiene was held in Washington. Portraits of twenty-one eminent foreign members of the Congress were published. From these, twelve have been picked *at random* and reproduced in Figure 24. The reader will find it instructive to try to judge the nationality of the man appearing in each picture, and then to check his successes and failure by reference to the note on page 109. The nations represented by these men were, in alphabetical order:

Austria	Cuba	Holland
Belgium	Finland	Hungary
Brazil	France	Spain
Canada	Germany	Sweden

TESTS OF GENERAL INTELLIGENCE

Any attempt to inquire into the differences between people, if it is to be raised to a level above that of folklore, must have refined tools for the work and refined techniques of using them. The tools are psychological tests. The techniques are statistical methods. The former we shall take up in this chapter; the latter in the following one. It has been estimated that in 1944 alone, 60 million tests were administered to some 20 million people. Testing has indeed become Big Business. Why? How? [39].

The Binet Scale

Quite the best-known and quite the most satisfactorily developed of all the tests are those originally assembled in the first decade of this century by Binet and Simon, of the psychological laboratory at the Sorbonne. They sought a tool that would measure the differences between children, in terms of their ability to profit by schooling, more accurately than did the teachers' marks and judgments. They collected a great variety of tasks, puzzles, and measures from the laboratories, and tried them out on Parisian children. The tests were varied. The child was asked to execute simple commands; to name familiar objects; to copy designs; to give rhymes; to say what he would do in certain everyday situations; to give the meanings of words; and so forth. These little

24 **Nationalities and Individuals**

Officers of national societies for mental hygiene in twelve different nations. These pictures were not "handpicked" but taken by chance. (*From* MENTAL HYGIENE, *1930*, 14, *following page 462.   By permission of the editor.*)

tasks were designed to reveal the degree to which a given child, in his thinking, (1) could maintain a definite goal-direction, (2) could make adaptations in order to attain the goal, and (3) could be critical of his own attempts and adaptations. These were the *marks* of one's general aptitude, or, as it is usually called, his *general intelligence*.

It is important to bear in mind that the method of selecting the tests was *empirical* and not *a priori*. The investigators tried out the many different tests upon some two hundred normal children ranging from three to fifteen years of age in order to find which tests would differentiate children of different levels of intelligent behavior. For example, if a given test was successfully passed by two-thirds to three-fourths of the ten-year-olds, but by a much smaller proportion of the nine-year-olds, it was set up as a suitable test of ten-year-old intelligence. The tests selected were then combined into an age-scale.

Thus, when an individual was examined, the level of his general ability could then be located in terms of age in the general population. If, for example, he could pass tests that had been passed by the great majority of eight-year-olds, but not those that had been passed by the majority of nine-year-olds, he was called eight years old in intelligence or was given the "mental age" (M.A.) of eight. To say that Marie had "eight-year-old intelligence" meant nothing more mysterious or abstruse than that she was as intelligent as the normal eight-year-old.

The scale purported to get at *native capacities*, independent of special training. Of course, it would be idle to seek to measure some tendencies or capacities in a ten-year-old child that had never been affected by any experience. The only way to bring out differences, then, in native capacity is to take children of a common environment (with equal opportunities to learn) and to measure the relative extent to which the respective individuals have profited by such opportunities.

The Stanford Revision

The great value of the Binet-Simon arrangement in a scaled series was promptly grasped in America, where the test was variously revised and adapted for the American child living in an environment different from the French and speaking another language. One of the most successful adaptations is that known as the *Stanford Revision* [34], arranged by Terman with Merrill in 1937. A list of the tests for some of the years included in that scale follows:

Year II (first half year) (6 tests, 1 month credit each)
  1. Fits blocks into holes of a form-board.
  2. Names six small objects shown him: button, cup, etc.

3. Points to parts of the body of a doll: hair, mouth, etc.
4. By imitation builds a tower of four blocks.
5. Names objects in a picture.
6. Obeys simple commands: "Give me the kitty," etc.

Year VI (6 tests, 2 months credit each)
1. Vocabulary: gives meaning of words.
2. By imitation strings beads in a certain order.
3. Tells missing parts of mutilated pictures.
4. Picks up requested number of blocks.
5. Selects unlike picture from several.
6. Traces a maze.

Year XIV (6 tests, 2 months credit each)
1. Vocabulary
2. Discovers the rule followed in a series of paper-foldings.
3. Points out absurdities in a picture.
4. Ingenuity: tells how to measure out 3 pints using a 4-pint and a 9-pint can.
5. Directional orientation: "Suppose you were going west, then turn to your right . . ."; etc.
6. Meanings of abstract words.

Tests were provided for each year from 2 to 15, supplemented at the upper end with three sets of successively more difficult tests, for "superior adults."

The method of scoring the results on such a scale is simple enough: the subject is credited with all tests below a year group in which he passes all, and also with all tests that he happens to pass above this point. By totaling "months" and "years" of test scores the "mental age" (M.A.) is determined.

The M.A., however, is an incomplete measure. As a child matures this may be expected to increase, and so a more constant index is desirable. Stern had proposed the use of a mental quotient. This was called by Terman an "intelligence quotient" (I.Q.), and it expresses the ratio of a child's mental age (M.A.) to his chronological age (C.A.) by a fraction:

$$IQ = \frac{MA}{CA}$$

For example: if the value of the resulting fraction is around 100 per cent the child is rated normal (that is, about as bright as the average of his age); if it is 130 or higher, he is clearly supernormal (brighter than most of his own age) or "gifted"; if it is only 70 or lower, he is subnormal.

One highly gifted child at the age of two years began keeping a written diary. At the age of eight, she composed the following:

Let the Bumble Be

One day I saw a bumble bee bumbling on a rose,
And as I stood admiring him, he stung me on the nose. . . .
And now, dear children, this advice, I hope you'll take from me,
And when you see a bumble bee, just let that bumble be.[1]

At the other extreme we find the imbeciles, whose I.Q.'s range from 50 down to 20, and the idiots, whose lack of development is more profound.

Some Other Tests of General Intelligence

Limitations in the Binet method of examining have led to the development of supplementary methods.

(1) The Binet method has not been so successfully employed with adults as it has with children. An interesting criticism is that many of the Binet items put a premium on the speed at which the testee works, whereas it has been established that in middle maturity the human being slows down somewhat, though without losing in accuracy. For the examination of *adults* one can now turn to scales such as the Wechsler-Bellevue Intelligence Scale. The final score of brightness is not calculated from the mental age values of the tests passed by the examinee but from the total number of points made by him on all tests, this being then re-stated as a distance (in "standard deviations," cf. page 121) above or below the average score made by adults of all ages. Psychologists have found two further advantages in utilizing the Wechsler-Bellevue. For one, its component tests fall into two general sorts, the verbal and the performance; and this makes it possible to compare an examinee's facility in using words and symbols with his ability to manipulate objects and perceive designs — a difference of considerable moment. Furthermore, the patterns of high scores and low scores on the respective component tests of the Bellevue scale differ in characteristic ways with certain different psychiatric groups (such as the "schizophrenic," the "neurotic," the "defective"). This makes the test useful not only for determining the individual's level of general brightness but also for suggesting what clinical type of deviate personality he may be.

(2) The Binet type of test depends much upon the examinee's ability to use language, oral and written; yet it may be desirable to examine

[1] From *Facts in Jingles*, by Winifred Sackville Stoner; copyright 1915, 1943. Used by special permission of the publishers, the Bobbs-Merrill Company.

those who are illiterate or deaf or unfamiliar with the English language. For them, *performance* tests have been devised and standardized. A few are represented in Figure 25. The oldest and best-known is the "form-board" type (*A*) consisting of a baseboard bearing holes of varying shapes into which the examinee is instructed — by wordless hand motions if need be — to fit the blocks that are supplied. There is also the "picture completion" task (*B*) which tests the child's ability to grasp each of a number of life-situations, to be evidenced by his ability to fill each hole with that block bearing the most appropriate picture-detail. The "picture assembly" test (*D*) combines the block-fitting and the picture-completing demands. Paper-and-pencil "mazes" (*C*) furnish the examinee with the problem of tracing his way out from a center through confusing passageways to the outside. Again, there is the "cube imitation" test (Knox). A row of four cubes is set before the examinee, the tester taps a fifth block upon these four in more and more complex irregular order, and the examinee is to repeat the tapping, which seems simple enough, yet is capable of unlimited complication, from an easy

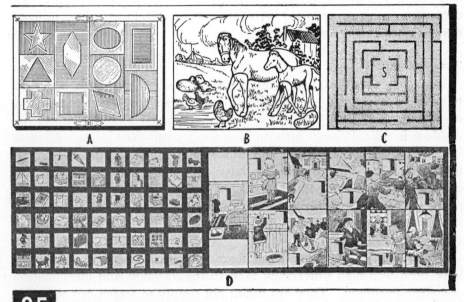

25   **Sample Performance Tests**

A. Form-board, Cornell model. Movable blocks permit spatial arrangements of presentation. *B.* Picture assembly test, Healy-Fernald mare-and-foal model. Heavy lines mark out the insets. *C.* Maze test, Porteus model. *D.* Picture completion test, Louise Wood model. Each of the 11 pictures represents an event in a child's day. (D *from L. Wood*, "*A new picture completion test*," J. GENET. PSYCHOL., *1940, 56, 383–409. By permission of author and editor.*)

1–2–4–3 to a 3–4–2–3–1–4–2–1, etc.   In the "block design" test (as Kohs') the subject is shown a colored pattern printed on a card and is instructed to duplicate the pattern by putting together colored cubes with different-colored faces and half-faces.   These are but a few of the many kinds of performance tests.

(3) The Binet method of intelligence measurement is designed for examining one individual at a time.   But there are occasions when it is desirable to test many at once, if possible; and hence *group* intelligence tests were developed.   When the United States entered World War I there was the practical need of sorting out army recruits of varying levels of intelligence for promotion, discharge, special training, and differential assignments.   The examinees were provided with printed booklets containing a variety of tests, each usually printed on a separate page so that it could not be seen in advance.   Many group intelligence tests have followed, among them the National Intelligence Test and the Otis Group Intelligence Scales, with its various forms.

Just as in individual examining, so in group examining there was seen to be a need for tests of the non-language or performance type.   To meet this demand, printed problems were developed that utilized designs rather than words.

Some Applications

Intelligence tests originated out of practical school demands, and they have been most useful in connection with educational problems.   For one thing, they have been quite widely employed to differentiate the children in school classes into rapid, average, and slow in rate of learning; and over a wide area the differential teaching and treatment methods of the different sections have brought gratifying results.   In dealing with the individual child, of course sensible administrators recognize that many other factors contribute to the pupil's school success: health, home environment, motivation, industry, and a number of other considerations.

Group tests of the general intelligence type, though not so labeled, have been well-nigh universally used in the selection and classification of college freshmen.   They are useful not simply to screen out those for whom college work is inadvisable, but also to furnish data for later reference in cases where individuals need or desire counseling.

Undoubtedly one of the most important uses of tests of intelligence, along with educational and military applications, is in vocational guidance and vocational selection.   Insofar as different occupations and trades are most successfully pursued by people of different ranges of intelligence level, a knowledge of the intelligence test score of a given young person is very material to guiding him successfully. With an I.Q. score of 88 he would not be successful in engineering or medicine or law; with a score of 128 he would with almost equal certainty not be happy nor thoughtfully occupied as a shoe clerk, restaurant busboy, or night watchman. However, success in a given occupation so obviously depends upon many other factors — a person's interests, special aptitudes, social competence, personality, and others — that the tests of general intelligence may be said to have more an eliminative than a positive selective value. From the employer's viewpoint, these same considerations must be kept in mind.

How Are Degrees of Intelligence Distributed?

To evaluate a given person's intelligence score it is helpful to see how it stacks up with the scores of the general population of which he is a member. Of the many intelligence surveys we will note the outcomes of two. Terman and Merrill, when standardizing the Stanford scale, collected results on nearly 3000 children and adolescents in eleven states. These they at one time divided into two groups according to whether the density of the population was over or under 1000 per square mile. The resulting distribution of I.Q. scores appears in Figure 26, A. We have

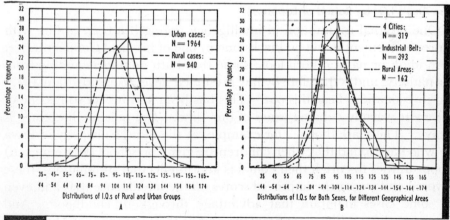

Distributions of I.Q.s of Rural and Urban Groups

A

Distributions of I.Q.s for Both Sexes, for Different Geographical Areas

B

26 **Distributions of I.Q.'s in Nation-Wide Populations**

A. Frequency of cases found at each I.Q. score interval in a study of American children. (*From L. M. Terman and M. A. Merrill,* Measuring Intelligence, *Houghton Mifflin, 1937. Used by permission.*) *B.* Frequencies found in a study of Scottish children. (*From A. H. Macmeeken,* The Intelligence of a Representative Group of Scottish Children, *University of London Press, 1939. Used by permission.*)

also the distributions of I.Q.'s obtained from all children born on the first day of February, May, August, and November, 1926, in three different types of population areas throughout Scotland. See Figure 26, *B*. (The methods of measuring were slightly different in the two studies.)

On inspection of the two graphs we are struck by two points especially. In all five sub-populations the distribution of the scores approaches a *bell-shaped curve* — the Gaussian curve of normal distribution to be discussed in the following chapter — which means that very many individuals achieve middle scores, and a diminishing few achieve very high or very low ones. To make a quantitative approach to the study of individual differences, one must grasp this principle first and foremost, as the one fundamental to the understanding of all others.

In both the American and the Scottish results, children of *rural* areas tended to make slightly lower I.Q. scores than those of *urban* areas. The explanation? A hint is to be found in Terman and Merrill's mention that the I.Q. scores of the rural children drop when they enter the school age, whereas those of urban children in semi-skilled workers' families begin to improve at about that time. The better school opportunities of city life, it is suggested, may be a potent factor in affecting a child's intelligence measurements. And this raises a question of great import.

Can One's I.Q. be Raised or Lowered?

One original assumption in intelligence testing has been in line with a pronouncement made by Blackstone in one of his legal Commentaries: "An idiot, or natural born fool, is one that hath no understanding from his nativity, and is therefore by law presumed never likely to attain any." Do investigations bear this out? This has been and in fact still is one of the most warmly debated issues of our time. The polemic literature is heavy. There are those — for example, at the State University of Iowa — who have found that when children are given preschool (kindergarten) opportunities to enrich their contacts and intellectual stimulations, these favored children make improved scores on the intelligence tests and even in some cases maintain that advantage throughout childhood. And there are those critics — at Stanford and at the University of Minnesota and elsewhere — who claim to see faults in the procedures, controls, and statistical treatments in the studies that have resulted in such findings. We do not have space to go into the merits and demerits of the controversy, but the interested reader can find them set forth elsewhere [22, 27, 35, 38]. In a general way, the part of wisdom is probably to assume that a given child's I.Q. score on a general intelligence test is likely to remain substantially the same year after year, but that it may be raised or lowered slightly (up to 6 or 8 points, say) by increased or decreased opportunity to acquire information and intellectual stimulation and to develop social rapport and feelings of personal security. In any case, it is well to remember that an I.Q. is nothing but a score made on a test given at a certain time and place.

SOME OTHER PSYCHOLOGICAL TESTS

Tests of Achievement

The impression made on educators by the successes of the intelligence test movement led to the widespread adoption of similar methods for measuring what students have accomplished in a course or curriculum. In school-subject examinations, various question forms are used that free their scoring from the influence of subjective impressions on the examiner's part. Examples of types of objective tests are the true-false, the multiple-choice, the matching, and the completion. Examples follow:

True-False

T (F) A dominant trait is that hereditary trait which predisposes to the development of a dominant type of animal or person.

(T) F There is a regular sequence in the stages of unfolding that is to be observed in the social behavior of all normal babies.

T (F) Lack of educational opportunities for generations leads often to feeble-mindedness in offspring.

Multiple Choice

__4__ Pressing one key on seeing a light and another on hearing a sound would be a case of reaction-type called . . . .
(1) perceptual, (2) simple, (3) free, (4) choice.

__2__ Systematic study of the incantation practices of the Dobu people would illustrate the method of . . . .
(1) experimentation, (2) field observation, (3) clinical observation, (4) statistical treatment.

Matching

__4__ behavior of newborn   1. chronoscope
__3__ maturation   2. foster children
__1__ reaction times   3. co-twin control
__5__ self-regulation   4. stabilimeter
                                   5. homeostasis

_3_ ear		1. efferent nerve
_2_ brain		2. nerve center
_5_ optic nerve		3. receptor
_4_ muscle		4. effector
		5. afferent nerve

Completion (filling blank)

If, upon the adding of a co-worker, the activity of worker X is speeded up, the speeding effect would be called the *dependent* variable.

When the human individual studies himself by observing his own experiences he is making an introspective or *subjective* approach.

Tests of Aptitudes

The widening application of objective testing methods has led to the development of tests to measure those characteristics that predict a person's ability to acquire with training some particular skill or knowledge [13]. A celebrated battery of aptitude tests is that for *musical* talents devised by Seashore. He has held that ability in music really involves many components in a complex hierarchy; and for some of these he provided specific testing procedures. Phonograph disks produce the sounds used in testing ability to discriminate differences in pitch, intensity, time interval, consonance, and (later) rhythm, and to evaluate tonal memory. The scores derived from these tests are then represented graphically as distances from a zero-line, and the resulting profile presents a kind of picture of some of the examinee's elementary musical abilities. These individual component measures are not a complete and adequate measure of musical talent as a whole: they are only a battery of measures of some specific abilities in which a certain degree of capacity is essential to success in a musical career. (See Figure 27.) Vocabulary and question tests have also been devised to measure knowledge of music. Tests of musical aptitude have been widely employed to direct attention to pupils who may have unsuspected abilities calling for musical training, and they have been equally valuable for showing that for others such training would be an unwise investment.

Aptitude testing has made great advances in examining candidates' capacity for *mechanical* training. Some tests put a premium on the subject's ability to get the hang of a mechanical device, by asking him to assemble correctly into a working unit the separated parts of a bicycle bell, of a monkey wrench, of an electric light socket, and other articles. Other tests are directed at manual dexterities, as those involved in handling a complicated form-board or in stacking together some "wig-

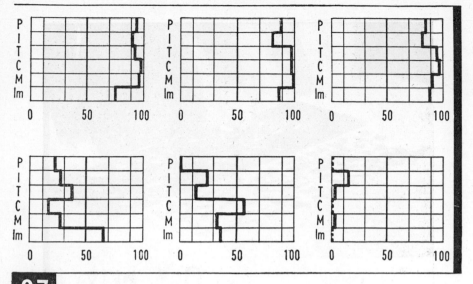

27 **Types of Musical Profiles**

Results obtained with six applicants for admission to the Eastman School of Music. The battery included tests for recognizing Pitch, Intensity, Time intervals, Consonance, tonal Memory, and tonal Imagery. Each square diagram shows the scores made on the six items by one applicant, each score being represented by a vertical bar drawn at the proper distance from the zero point. Candidates whose profiles appear in the top row were rated "safe"; those with profiles in the lower row, "to be discouraged." (*From H. Stanton, reproduced in C. E. Seashore,* PSYCHOLOGY OF MUSIC, *McGraw-Hill, 1938. By permission.*)

gly" blocks. A few mechanical aptitude tests are pictured in Figure 28 (see also Figure 87, page 285) [30]. Then there are paper-and-pencil tasks, such as the kind that asks which pictured tool (screw driver, wrench, etc.) is used with each pictured object (a nut, a bit, etc.), or that demands the quick putting of dots into small circles, or that involves counting how many blocks touch other blocks in a pictured pile of them (see Figure 29) [29].

Increased interest in vocational counseling, as well as the felt need for screening applicants for admission to the professional schools, has supported attempts to apply principles of aptitude measuring to the *learned professions*. The validity of the tests has been measured by comparing the examinees' scores with the grades they later made in professional school studies rather than with the degrees of success they later achieved in professional practice. Hence the predictiveness of these tests is to that extent limited. Nevertheless, they are of value in selecting the persons who will do well in the professional training as such. Schools

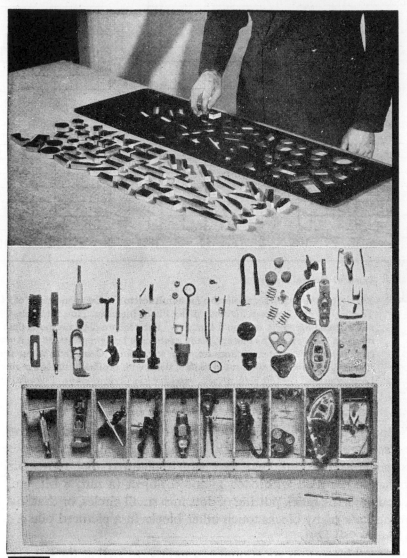

28   **Motor Tests of Mechanical Aptitude**

Above: Minnesota Spatial-Relations Test. One of the four boards constituting the test. *Below:* Minnesota Mechanical Assembly Test. One of three boxes. Somewhat similar tests are shown in Figure 87 on page 285. (*From D. G. Paterson,* et al., MEN, WOMEN, AND JOBS, *University of Minnesota Press, 1936. By permission.*)

of medicine and of engineering have shown interest in this development [24].

The Army General Classification Test

A considerable achievement by the Adjutant General's Office of the United States Army in World War II was the construction and validation of a test of capacity for performing army duties and for profiting by training for a commission. Not unlike group intelligence tests in form, the A.G.C.T. included items especially devised to tap the recruit's ability along verbal, numerical (both computing and reasoning), and spatial lines, with the items arranged in order of increasing difficulty. On the basis of the scores, the candidates were classified into five grades. One finding that served to validate the test was that at several camps those soldiers making higher scores on A.G.C.T. were also more likely to earn commissions. The administering of this test has become regular army routine. (For obvious reasons none of the items is reproduced here.)

These are but a few of the many ways in which psychological differences between individuals are being measured. There are many others: by tests of one's interests, of his value judgments, of his attitudes on public questions, of his emotional-temperamental stability, of his character-organization, of his personality structure, of his motor capacities and of his sensory capacities — they are legion. Mention of them will be made in their appropriate places in our survey.

CONSTRUCTING AND EVALUATING TESTS

A Technical Matter

If testing is big business as has been said, then test construction is a technical business. The giving of sound examinations does not result from a natural gift for testing, but from procedures that involve self-criticism and statistical cautions and precautions. There is a whole literature devoted to the subject; and as some college teachers and all the personnel workers in business and industry and in the armed forces know well, he who would use psychological tests must know something of the main points brought out in this literature [11, 16, 21, 23, 28, 36]. In the case of the industrial personnel expert, it is most imperative, since the fitting of square pegs to square holes in the case of this, that, and the other particular job frequently demands not the routine employment of tests already available and happily standardized but the devising and applying of new tests.

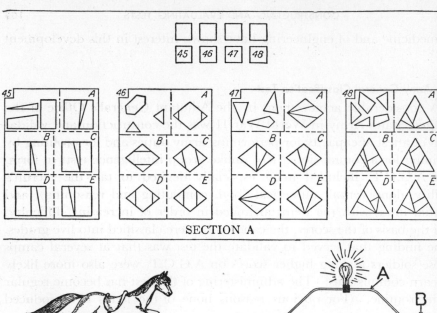

SECTION A

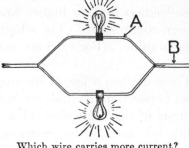

Which end of the toy horse will buck more
when it is pulled along the floor?

Which wire carries more current?

SECTION B

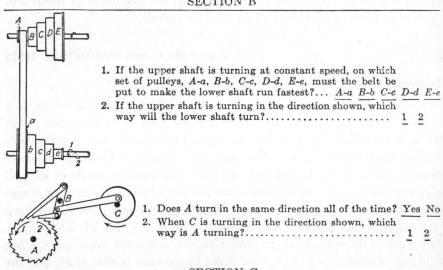

1. If the upper shaft is turning at constant speed, on which
   set of pulleys, *A-a, B-b, C-c, D-d, E-e,* must the belt be
   put to make the lower shaft run fastest?... <u>A-a</u> <u>B-b</u> <u>C-c</u> <u>D-d</u> <u>E-e</u>

2. If the upper shaft is turning in the direction shown, which
   way will the lower shaft turn?...................... <u>1</u> <u>2</u>

1. Does *A* turn in the same direction all of the time? <u>Yes</u> <u>No</u>

2. When *C* is turning in the direction shown, which
   way is *A* turning?........................... <u>1</u> <u>2</u>

SECTION C

29 **Sample Paper-and-Pencil Tests of Mechanical Aptitude**

Section *A* is selected from the Likert revision of the Minnesota Paper Formboard;
Section *B* from the Bennett Test of Mechanical Comprehension, Form AA; Section
C from the Thurstone Mechanical Movements Test. (*As reproduced in H. Moore,*
Psychology for Business and Industry, *2nd ed., McGraw-Hill, 1942.*)

What, then, are the marks of a sound test; and what are the procedures and precautions to be observed in making up original ones?

There are very many types of psychological tests, not only as regards the human traits tested but as regards the forms of the tests. There are *individual* and *group* tests; there are *verbal* and *performance* tests; there are *paper-and-pencil* and *instrumental* tests; there are *achievement* and *aptitude* (potentiality) tests; there are *speed* and *power* tests. In our limited space we shall confine ourselves to the main considerations that arise in constructing group paper-and-pencil power tests, in which every examinee is given opportunity to attempt every item, his score being the number of items he answers correctly. Though not the most common form, this type of test permits the simplest working out of principles.

Reliability

The first consideration is usually the reliability of the test. That is, does it measure in a consistent way? There are variable errors in all measurements, as we have seen in Chapter 1; and the degree to which one has kept out these chance factors when using a given test is indicated by the degree to which the test produces the same scores consistently. Let us suppose that in a case of fifty applicants for a job, their individual scores on a test of finger dexterity range from a low of 68 to a high of 137; and suppose further that Mr. Smith makes scores on successive days of 104, 107, and 102, and that his rank among the applicants is, as a result, 38th, 40th, and 35th from the top, respectively. The consistency with which he makes his scores and maintains his relative position in his group, indicates that his scores were probably not greatly affected by accidental differences in the items of the test, such as catch questions, emotionally loaded ones, subtle ones, peculiarly formulated ones, nor by learning, nor by such transitory factors as boredom, inattention, and the like. If the same is found true for all members of the group, then a single set of the scores can be relied upon.

To determine the degree of reliability (self-consistency) of a test, certain procedures are followed. One is to repeat the same test on a later occasion (the *test-retest* method), as was done with the group of which Mr. Smith was a member, and then see if consistent scores are obtained. Another is not to repeat the test but to separate the scores made by the different examinees on the odd-numbered items from those on the even-numbered items, and determine the degree of consistency or correlation between the two sets of scores (the *split-half* method). A third is to administer an alternative comparable form of the test, and compute the correlation between the scores made on it with those made on the original test. In all these methods it will be noted that reliability is measured by the amount of self-consistency within a test, which is determined by the statistical method of measuring *correlation* (see page 55 n. and pages 122 ff.).

A few practical rules may be mentioned. The longer the test and the more items it contains, the more reliable it is, up to a certain limit. The greater the range of ability of the examinees, the higher the reliability of their scores. The narrower the range of difficulty of the test items, the greater the reliability is likely to be. And it is often found that the more independent the items are of each other, the greater the relia-bility.

Validity

Obviously, a test's value depends upon the extent to which it predicts what it is supposed to predict. Suppose, for instance, that the three tests from which the items are selected in Figure 29 yielded high scores for men who actually did well in operating a milling machine and low scores for those who did poorly on that job; its validity as a test for pre-dicting aptitude for milling machine operation would be high. But if, when administered to candidates for a job in engraving or in armature winding, it yielded scores that failed to correspond with the individual differences of competence in actual jobs of engraving or of winding arma-tures, its validity for these particular purposes would be quite low. To estimate the validity of a test, then, one determines the degree to which the individual scores obtained on it agree with the distribution of scores on some *criterion*. The validity, then, is expressed most exactly as a coefficient of correlation (see pages 122 ff.). The criterion, then, is all-important; if it is slighted, the labor spent on constructing the tests is wasted. Here the need of analyzing the job itself becomes a primary one.

The general method of establishing the validity of a program of testing may be illustrated from a report of the Army Air Forces. Throughout World War II a major effort of the Aviation Psychology Program was the repeated evaluating of the classification tests being used to predict air-crew success. The criterion of success generally used was graduation versus elimination (for flying deficiencies, for fear, or at own requests) from the course of flight training.[1] Figure 30 presents in a bar graph the results for many pilot classes taken collectively. It shows plainly

---

[1] The ultimate criterion or "pay-off" would of course have been the men's degrees of success in combat, but for certain reasons such data were not available in sufficient quantity to do more than furnish material for a general validating.

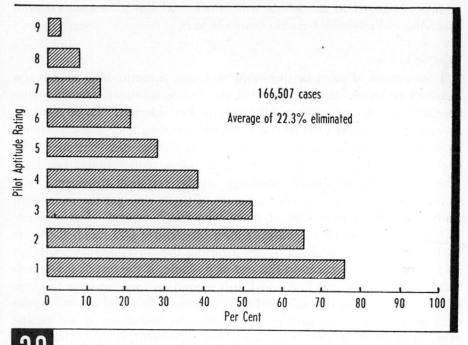

166,507 cases

Average of 22.3% eliminated

30 Validation of Test Results by Criterion of Training Success

The 166,507 candidates for A.A.F. flight training are broken up into nine levels of score on their aptitude tests, from lowest level, *1*, to highest, *9*. The percentage of those at each test-score level who were "washed out" is indicated by length of bar. (*From* A.A.F. AVIATION PSYCHOLOGY PROGRAM, REP. No. 2. *By permission of the Office of the Air Surgeon.*)

that the percentage of elimination from training was the highest for men who had stood lowest on the psychological tests (about 76 per cent), the next highest for those who had scored next lowest, and so on up to the smallest percentage of "washout" (about 4 per cent) found among those who made the best scores on the tests. This graphic presentation is supported by the coefficient of correlation, found to be .51.

The validation of selection tests has, of course, its financial aspects. The taxpayer would be interested in one phase of the A.A.F. research. One thousand young men who wanted to fly were admitted to training without any selection tests; a second thousand, with only average test scores; a third thousand, with superior test scores. The washout in the first group was so great that the average cost of those who survived to become pilots was $62,000 per pilot. Similarly calculated, the average cost in the second group was under $38,000; and in the third group, it was $32,000. Multiply these single-man savings by the number of pilots engaged in the whole war effort, and the monetary value of psychological selection tests becomes obvious.[1]

Selection of Items

Tests consist of parts or questions or items, sometimes as many as a hundred or more; and the value of the test as a whole rests upon the care with which each component item has been selected. To be retained as valid a particular item should certainly show some degree of validity as measured by the outside criterion; that is, the distribution of the various individuals' scores on the item taken alone should correlate with the same individuals' standings on the criterion measures. For example, the average criterion measure of those who get the item right should be higher than that of those who get it wrong. Determining this, however, may be a needlessly long procedure; and much the same result can often be obtained by determining the correlation of scores on each item with the scores on the test as a whole, if the test as a whole is valid. If Johnny ranks first and Edith second on their answers to question 5 of an arithmetic quiz, and they also rank first and second on the quiz as a whole, and, further, if the distribution of the scores of the other individuals on that item closely correlates with the distribution of their scores on the whole quiz, then the examiner is warranted in judging question 5 to be valid and worth retaining.

Out of statistical research a few rules of thumb may be inferred. For instance, a test is improved (as said before) if it includes a goodly number of items, provided that these items do not interlock or depend on each other.

Objectivity

To reduce the inaccuracies that creep from many irrelevant personal factors into the scores assigned to examinees, the objective types of examinations have established themselves almost everywhere. Consider that in the *administering* of a test, two examiners are likely, if not guided by definite rules, to give the test in different ways: with different preliminary instructions to the examinees, with differing amounts of help to them, with differing degrees of personal *rapport*, and the like. Therefore, quite strict rules are set up to govern the precise ways in which a test is to be given. That is, the procedure is *standardized*.

Again, accidental and inconstant factors connected with the person

---

[1] It may be pointed out that a prerequisite of a test's validity is its reliability, for if a test does not correlate with itself, it cannot be expected to correlate with anything else. On the other hand, it may be highly reliable yet not measure what we want it to measure.

who does the *scoring* or grading of the test papers may result in great unfairness to the examinees, unless the grading is made a clerical task so simple and so mechanical as to be unaffected by the grader's likes-dislikes, alterations of attention and of mood, and feelings of tiredness, interest, and so on. Hence most tests are printed with the possible answers so prepared that the scorer need only tally them, and indeed can sometimes have that work done by a machine.

In a word, the fairest test of individual differences eliminates as far as possible any influences arising from the personal make-up of the administrator or the scorer. Putting the principle more positively, a test is considered objective if different examiners get consistent results on applying the test to the same people.

In discussing some considerations that enter into a scientific study of how human individuals differ, and in surveying some principles of test-construction, we have hinted that the psychologist must know how to handle numerical data statistically. Such knowledge is demanded in other psychological areas as well; and it is not too much to say that until a student has learned to think a little in statistical terms his understanding of people can be only superficial. It is none too early, then, for us to seek at least a speaking acquaintance with statistical methods. We do this in our next chapter.

Note on Figure 24, page 91

The men shown are:

A. (C. M. Hincks) Canada	G. (Gustav von Olah) Hungary
B. (Gustavo Reidel) Brazil	H. (K. Herman Bouman) Holland
C. (August Ley) Belgium	I. (Robert Sommer) Germany
D. (Josef Berze) Austria	J. (Genil-Perrin) France
E. (Josef Lundahl) Sweden	K. (Reino Lagus) Finland
F. (S. Ramon y Cajal) Spain	L. (Francisco M. Fernandez) Cuba

REFERENCES

On Individual Differences

1. Anastasi, A. *Differential Psychology*. New York: The Macmillan Company, 1937.
2. Benedict, R., and G. Weltfish. *The Races of Mankind*. New York: Public Affairs Committee, 1943.
3. Garrett, H. E. "A note on the intelligence scores of Negroes and Whites in 1918," *J. Abn. Soc. Psychol.*, 1945, *40*, 344–346.
4. Klineberg, O. *Race Differences*. New York: Harper and Brothers, 1935.
5. McNemar, Q., and L. M. Terman. "Sex differences in variational tendency," *Genet. Psychol. Monogr.*, 1936, *18*, No. 1.
6. Rhinehart, J. B. "Sex differences in dispersion at the high school and college levels," *Psychol. Monogr.*, 1947, *61*, No. 282.

7. Shapiro, H. L. *Migration and Environment.* New York: Oxford University Press, 1939.

8. Taylor, H. C., and J. T. Russell. "The relationship of validity coefficients to the practical effectiveness of tests in selection," *J. Appl. Psychol.*, 1939, *23*, 565–578.

9. Terman, L. M., and C. C. Miles. *Sex and Personality.* New York: McGraw-Hill Book Company, 1936.

10. Tyler, L. E. *The Psychology of Human Differences.* New York: Appleton-Century-Crofts, 1947.

On Testing

11. Adkins, D. C. *Construction and Analysis of Achievement Tests.* Washington, D.C.: U.S. Civil Service Commission, 1947.

12. Arthur, G. *A Point Scale of Performance Tests.* 2 vols. New York: Commonwealth Fund, 1930.

13. Bingham, W. V. *Aptitudes and Aptitude Testing.* New York: Harper and Brothers, 1937.

14. Bronner, A. F., W. Healy, G. M. Lowe, and M. E. Shimberg. *A Manual of Individual Mental Tests and Testing.* Boston: Little, Brown, 1927.

15. Buros, O. K., ed. *The Third Mental Measurements Yearbook.* New Brunswick: Rutgers University Press, 1949.

16. Conrad, H. S. "Investigating and appraising intelligence and other aptitudes." In T. G. Andrews, *Methods of Psychology.* New York: John Wiley and Sons, 1948.

17. Cornell, E. L., and W. W. Coxe. *A Performance Ability Scale.* Yonkers, N.Y.: World Book Company, 1934.

18. Dorcus, R. M. *Handbook of Employee Selection.* New York: McGraw-Hill Book Company, 1949.

19. DuBois, P. H., ed. *A.A.F. Aviation Psychology Program. The Classification Program, Rep. No. 2.* Washington, D.C.: U.S. Govt. Printing Office, 1947.

20. Garrett, H. E., and M. R. Schneck. *Psychological Tests, Methods, and Results.* New York: Harper and Brothers, 1933.

21. Ghiselli, E. E., and C. W. Brown. *Personnel and Industrial Psychology.* New York: McGraw-Hill Book Company, 1948.

22. Goodenough, F. L., L. M. Terman, B. L. Wellman, *et al.* Articles in *Yearb. Nat. Soc. Stud. Educ.*, 1940, *39* (I and II).

23. Greene, E. B. *Measurements of Human Behavior.* New York: Odyssey Press, 1941.

24. Kandel, I. L. *Professional Aptitude Tests in Medicine, Law, and Engineering.* New York: Teachers College, Columbia University, 1940.

25. Lawshe, C. H. *Principles of Personnel Testing.* New York: McGraw-Hill Book Company, 1948.

26. Macmeeken, A. M. *The Intelligence of a Representative Group of Scottish Children.* London: University of London Press, 1939.

27. McNemar, Q. "A critical examination of the University of Iowa Studies," *Psychol. Bull.*, 1940, *37*, 63–92. "More on the Iowa I.Q. Studies," *J. Psychol.*, 1940, *10*, 237–240.

28. Mursell, J. L. *Psychological Testing.* New York: Longmans, Green and Company, 1947.

29. O'Rourke, L. J. *O'Rourke Mechanical Aptitude Test.* Washington, D.C.: Psychological Institute.

30. Paterson, D. G., *et al. Minnesota Mechanical Ability Tests.* Minneapolis: University of Minnesota Press, 1930.

31. Seashore, C. E. *Psychology of Music.* New York: McGraw-Hill Book Company, 1938.

32. Seashore, C. E., *et al. Measures of Musical Talents.* Revised edition. Camden, N. J.: Educ. Dept., R.C.A. Mfg. Co., 1939.

33. Stoddard, G. D. *The Meaning of Intelligence.* New York: The Macmillan Company, 1943.

34. Terman, L. M., and M. A. Merrill. *Measuring Intelligence.* Boston: Houghton Mifflin, 1937.

35. Thorndike, R. L. " 'Constancy' of the I.Q.," *Psychol. Bull.*, 1940, *37*, 167–186.

36. Tiffin, J. *Industrial Psychology.* New York: Prentice-Hall, 1942.

37. Wechsler, D. *The Measurement of Adult Intelligence.* Baltimore: Williams and Wilkins, 1944.

38. Wellman, B. L., *et al.* "Review of McNemar's Critical Examination," *Psychol. Bull.*, 1940, *37*, 93–111.

39. Wolfle, D. "Testing is Big Business," *Amer. Psychologist*, 1947, *2*, 26–28.

6

STATISTICAL METHODS

THE DISTRIBUTION OF INDIVIDUAL DIFFERENCES

INDIVIDUAL DIFFERENCES, we can now realize, are for the most part quantitative rather than qualitative, a matter of degree, not a matter of all-or-none. True, the man in the street speaks as if people flatly have or have not certain characteristics. He will say that Dick has ability in mathematics, Joe in sprinting, Harry in persuasive argumentation, when in truth Dick can sprint a little and can talk fairly well; and by the same token both Joe and Harry have a certain degree of competence in each of these areas. Carrie Co-ed, who shivers at the thought of freshman mathematics, can do a little number work, is able to compare prices, and probably could even do well enough in trigonometry if she would but give herself a fair chance. Comparing people, then, is largely a question of more and less, in this or that way. Accordingly, if we are to advance beyond the most naïve guesswork, we shall need to employ quantitative methods of surveying our human material. We shall need to make our descriptions exact. We shall want accurately to trace out possible relationships in our material.

Statistical procedures have a twofold advantage. First, they enable us to handle large numbers of items economically, to identify certain characteristics of the data which mere inspection alone would not reveal. When a football fan glances down the list of weights given for the forty-odd players of the visiting squad, and again down that for the home squad, he may reach some rough judgment, as "Those Siwash fellows sure are a beefier bunch!". But such a judgment is not only a hazy and rough one; it may actually be untrue. Or again, if a school official were handed a list of the five hundred grades made by the five hundred entering freshmen in 1946, and a similar list for the five hundred who entered in 1947, he would be unable to judge, merely from looking over these lists, which group had done the better. So many data are too difficult to handle: we need methods of grouping them and representing them by single and simple quantitative indices.

A second advantage in the use of statistical methods comes close to the heart of our practical interest in individual differences. For these methods enable us to make predictions — to extend and generalize from a sample group of a few persons to a whole population, or from a few actual events to the probabilities of their recurrence. Historically, one of the earliest interests that led to the discovery of probabilities was gambling. To a player at the green table, it was obviously an advantage to be able from a study of falls of dice to predict the likelihood of certain falls in the future. Again, experiments in agriculture, whereby the plant breeder keeps careful count on the occurrences of variations, are of patent economic value. And since in much of our everyday discourse about human nature we assume that what we have observed in the cases of Smith, Jones, Brown, and Johnson is going to be true of men in general, we can recognize the crucial importance of some guides to greater accuracy in such predictive thinking.

DESCRIBING A DISTRIBUTION

The Normal Curve

At the beginning of the nineteenth century Gauss and other astronomers, physicists, and mathematicians became interested in the fact that it is possible to calculate the variability of a scientific observer, that is, the number of errors (variations in his readings or estimates) he makes, and the sizes of the errors. Indeed this variation follows the same mathematical laws of frequency as do the laws of chance. This "normal law of error" is a way of stating the relative frequency with which errors of different size are likely to be made in the course of a series of observations. When the mathematical formulation is cast into a graphic form it assumes a bell-shaped curve. This curve, then, can be used to represent either (A) the occurrence of impersonal events due to chance (such as the results of flipping coins) or (B) the occurrence of variations in the performance of a human being under the same conditions. (The latter point is obviously of psychological importance, and in the treatment of massed data in a laboratory experiment, such a means of representing them visually is advantageous.) (C) Later it was discovered that the same laws of chance operate in the distribution in a population of many anatomical traits, such as the heights of French soldiers or the chest girths of Scottish soldiers, as well as of more distinctly psychological traits.

In Figure 31 we see how all these different manifestations of chance approximate a common bell-shaped type of curve, often called the

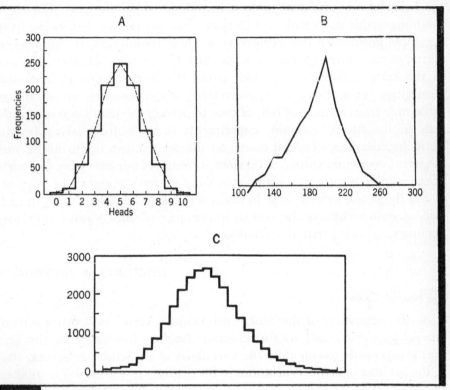

31 **The Normal Distribution Curve**

A. A curve based on data to be derived from a series of *chance physical events*. The vertical distances to the midpoints of each horizontal "step" represent the frequencies with which the various numbers of heads that are indicated on the base line will occur in the course of 1024 tosses of ten coins. (These frequencies are represented mathematically by the coefficients in the expansion of $(a + b)^{10}$.) This figure is drawn both as a *column diagram* (in continuous line) and as a *frequency polygon* (in broken line). *B.* A curve based on data obtained by *repeated measurements on the same individual* under conditions held as constant as possible. Vertical distances represent the frequencies with which the subject made reactions of each of the time-lengths shown in part on the base line in $\frac{1}{1000}$ second. This is drawn as a *frequency polygon*. *C.* A curve based on data obtained from *single measurements on very many individuals*. Vertical distances represent the number of individual cases making each of thirty different scores (not indicated) on the Army Alpha group intelligence test; 25,200 cases in all. This is drawn as a *column diagram*.

Gaussian curve. In general it shows that the middle scores will occur the most frequently, but the extreme scores very rarely, and that the gradation of frequency from the middle scores to the extreme scores is not of the straight-line order but S-shaped like either side of the top of a bell.

What is Meant by "Chance"?

In the tossing of a coin, what determines which face will lie upward when it has fallen to the table? Slight variations in the way the thumb and finger hold it, variations in the amount of flip imparted to it as it leaves the hand, variations in the height to which it is tossed, variations in the direction it is tossed, possible variations in directions of air pressure at the instant — these and other factors we could surmise. Thus we see that the actual fall of the coin is determined by a very great number of small factors, each operating in innumerable degrees, the joint product of their effects being unpredictable for any given throw but predictable in the long run for a large number of throws.

We have already taken note of those hereditary traits of man that appear in all degrees — such as skin color in a family — yet which turn out to be explainable in simple Mendelian terms as the results of the composite operation of a number of independent determiners. And it would be well to note again at this time the shape of the distribution curve in Figure 13 (page 52).

So it is with a person's reaction-times. From one reaction to another he varies in the intensity of his concentration, varies in the direction of his attending, varies in the vigor with which he moves his hand, varies in his interest in the task; he has varying (increasing) practice, he has varying (increasing) fatigue; his signal varies in its loudness, and so forth. His actual time depends, therefore, upon an uncounted number of independent contributory factors that are present in all degrees. This is true even when the experimental conditions are kept as constant as possible.

And again, so it is with the achievement of any single member of a group of people on an intelligence test. What makes one individual brighter than another? We do not know. That is to say, we cannot attribute it to one single factor in his makeup. We know his thyroid is important, and his pituitary, perhaps; we are pretty certain that his schooling has something to do with it, also the treatment he receives at home, and even the physical condition of the home; we know that the functions of his cerebrum are important, but we do not know just what these are, nor how many there are; and so we could go on. What makes one individual differ from another even in a single kind of test is a function of innumerable independent variables that exert each its own effect in all variations of amount.

For mathematical reasons that we cannot go into here,[1] the *composite effect of a large number of factors working independently* to affect an event is, in a large number of such events, expressed by the normal distribution curve of which we have spoken above.

Let us look at some results of measurements of some physical and psychological traits that were found in a psychology class of 77 men recently taught by the writer (Figure 32).[2] It will be seen that they all tend roughly to approximate the normal curve. It is reasonable to assume that had the class included ten times as many members, drawn from the same campus population, the curves would have approximated the normal curve far better, for this reason: the unusual and exceptional individuals that are to be found even in small groups will offset each other in larger samplings of a population, and also will be rendered less striking by the multiplication of the more usual individuals. Here we see the importance of getting large samplings if we are to draw any reliable conclusions concerning a population.

At the same time, it would be an error to suppose that all distribution curves to be met in psychological work are Gaussian, for there are many other types. Figure 33 represents one of them where the distribution is *skewed* to the right. This may be because of the effect on the scores of some special factor that is more important in determining the group scores than any of the countless factors entering by chance. Consider the composition of any large college class, for example. If we measured the students for their general intelligence we would expect the range to be limited at the lower (duller) end, for by no means all persons of an unselected population could pass the school work preliminary to that of college grade; while there would be no special limitation on the upper (brighter) end.

Skewness may also be due to the fact that equal intervals of the test score do not truly correspond throughout the scale to equal amounts in the trait being measured. A difference of 5 points between test-scores 15 and 20 may not be equal to the difference of 5 points between scores 85 and 90. A difficult test in a school subject might well produce results which when plotted resemble Figure 33, while an easy test would be as likely to show skewness to the left. However, the beginning student will find a knowledge of the normal curve and its general properties sufficient for him as a point of departure.

---

[1] These are best understood in terms of the expansion of the binomial in elementary algebra.

[2] The reader should compare also figures to be found on pages 46, 97, 274, and 604.

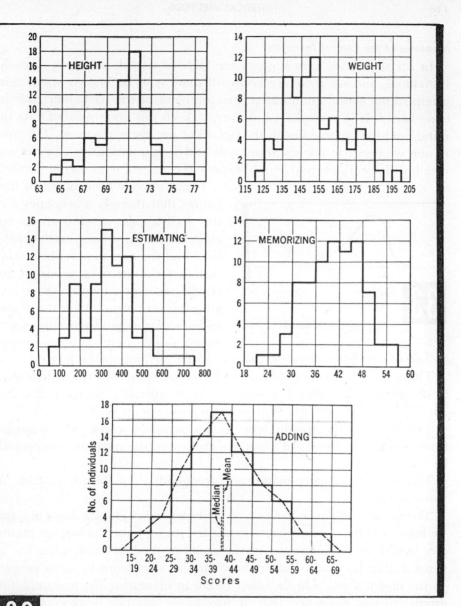

32   Some Sample Distributions

A class of 77 male college students were given two physical and three psychological tests: (1) Height, in inches; (2) Weight, in pounds; (3) Memorizing, in number of ideas reproduced after hearing a prose selection; (4) Estimating, in number of marbles guessed to be in a glass jar seen (actual number 326); (5) Adding, in number of columns added in a given period of time. A column diagram is drawn for the scores of each test. For the Adding test a frequency polygon is also shown, as well as the location of certain measures to be described later.

Measures of the Central Tendency

In all the above distributions we have obtained measures of each individual, and we therefore know all there is to be known about this group so far as the quantitative measurement of the particular trait is concerned. It is impossible, however, to keep this great mass of data in mind, and we become lost in the details of the discrete scores. For this reason we resort to statistical analysis and seek quantitative description which will accurately and simply express the general tenor of our results.

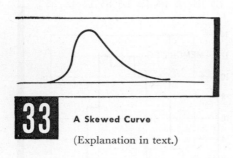

33

A Skewed Curve

(Explanation in text.)

It has already been noted in the figures that there is a tendency for the individuals in the group to cluster around one point on the baseline; and the first step in the statistical description of a group is to obtain an expression which represents this clustering. Thus the *central tendency* of the group is condensed into a simple figure and expressed by one of the three averages, the mean, the median, or the mode.

The *mean* is the total of the scores divided by the number of individuals in the group. It is what is loosely called the average. In the series, 28, 30, 34, 35, 36, 38, 42, 42, 48, the mean score would be 37.

The *median* is the middle score of the series of scores as they range from lowest to highest. In the series just given, the median score would be 36.

The *mode* is the score made most frequently. In the above case, it would be 42.

The use of any particular one of these depends upon the kind of data we have, and upon what we are interested in. A haberdasher, for example, would not be interested in the mean or median-sized shirt that is worn, rather he would like to know the size shirt worn by most people — the modal shirt. On the other hand, in measuring the learning of a group of subjects we find that on any given trial one or more subjects may make unusual scores, on account of a headache, a night of insomnia, or noises outside the laboratory. Since we are not interested in these exceptional cases but in the group as a whole, and since we are not studying the effect of insomnia or noise on learning, we use the median, a measure that will not be distorted by these aberrations. Finally, a different measure would be used if we wished to gauge the batting strength of a baseball team. Since all nine men bat almost equally often we must take into consideration the number of hits the clean-up man as well as the "weak sister" will make; so we use the mean to characterize our ball club, for this average will best tell us how many hits the team as a whole can be expected to make in a certain number of times at bat.

We see, then, that all these measures of central tendency have certain characteristics peculiar to themselves, and in the treatment of our data we pick the measure whose particular characteristics will give us the most pertinent information about what we are interested in.

Grouping the Distribution

Whenever the number of scores that have to be dealt with is very large, much labor is saved by grouping the scores into convenient *class-intervals* of, say, 3 or 5 or 10 points to the interval, depending upon the range of the whole group. For example, on the Adding test given the class of 77 students (as described in an earlier paragraph) the scores ran as follows: 54, 29, 44, 53, 30, 41, 56, 46, and so on. They were grouped for more convenient handling into the intervals of score shown in Table XI, first and third columns. (This is easily done by first making out the intervals, then marking tallies in the appropriate spaces as the scores are read off.)

From grouped scores the determination of the averages is somewhat different. In calculating the mean and the mode, simply treat each score falling within a given interval as having the value of the midpoint of that interval. Thus in the table of Adding scores, two cases are said to have scored 62.5, two cases 57.5, six cases 52.5, and so on. The rest of the computation of mean and mode should be easily made out from the table.

Finding the median of a grouped distribution involves an additional detail of method. When a middle score is one of several in the same interval, precisely what value is it given (how far up the interval)? In the table for the Adding test, the middle case — the 39th — was found in the interval, scores 35–39, along with 16 others. We assigned the bottom score-value of the interval, 35, to the first of these, and dividing the whole interval (5 score-points) into 17 steps (because there are 17 persons whose scores are in that interval), assigned 5/17 score-points to each case. But when we reached the interval we had counted off 30 cases, leaving us 9 more to go. The resulting operation is indicated in the table.

Measures of Variability

It is conceivable that two groups of individuals may make the same score, as a group, yet the scores of individuals of one group may vary

TABLE

Scores on an Adding Test

Class Intervals	Midpoint*	Frequency	F × Midpt.	Deviation of Midpt. from Mean	F × Dev.	F × Dev.²
60–64	62.5	2	125.	24.4	48.8	1190.72
55–59	57.5	2	115.	19.4	38.8	752.72
50–54	52.5	6	315.	14.4	86.4	1244.16
45–49	47.5	8	380.	9.4	75.2	706.88
40–44	42.5	12	510.	4.4	52.8	232.32
35–39	37.5	17	637.5	.6	10.2	6.12
30–34	32.5	14	455.	5.6	78.4	439.04
25–29	27.5	10	275.	10.6	106.0	1123.60
20–24	22.5	4	90.	15.6	62.4	973.44
15–19	17.5	2	35.	20.6	41.2	848.72
		77	2937.5		600.2	7517.72

Σ = "sum of." N = number of cases.

$$\text{Mean} = \frac{\Sigma \, F \times \text{Midpt.}}{N} = \frac{2937.5}{77} = 38.1$$

$$\text{Median} = \left(\frac{N+1}{2} = 39\right) = 35 + \frac{5}{17} \times 9 = 37.6 \qquad\qquad \text{Mode} = 37.5$$

$$\text{Mean deviation (from the mean)} = \frac{\Sigma \, F \times \text{Dev.}}{N} = \frac{600.2}{77} = 7.794$$

$$\text{Standard deviation (from the mean)} = \sqrt{\frac{\Sigma \, F \times \text{Dev.}^2}{N}} = \sqrt{\frac{7512.72}{77}} = 9.877$$

* When scores are interpreted as whole numbers only (example: "60" as "60" only and not as "60 ......60.99") the fraction ".5" should be dropped in this column.

more widely from the central tendency than do the scores of the individuals of the other group. For example, if group *A* makes the scores 1, 2, 3, 4, 5, 6, 7, 8, 8, 9, 10, 11, 12, and 12, and group *B* the scores 5, 5, 5, 6, 6, 7, 7, 7, 8, 8, 8, 8, 9, and 9, they would give the same mean (7) but would vary widely in their extremes. What is needed, then, is an expression of the *variability* of the distribution. One form is the *mean deviation*, which is arrived at by finding the amounts of deviation of the respective scores from the central tendency, and averaging them. With grouped scores this means that for each interval we must find the amount of deviation of its midpoint from the central tendency, and multiply that by the number of cases within that interval. Then these products are summed and divided by the total number of cases. The process is illustrated in the table, using the mean to represent the central tendency — though the median and even the mode are sometimes used.

A more common description of group variability is the *standard deviation* (sigma, σ), a measure which places greater emphasis on the extreme variations.[1] It is similar to the mean deviation, save that the process of squaring is introduced. It is obtained by squaring the individual deviations from the central tendency, averaging them, then extracting the square root. With grouped data of course one deals with the class-intervals instead of individual scores, squaring the deviation of the midpoint of each from the central tendency. This is also demonstrated in Table XI.

The arithmetical labor in the foregoing operations is lightened by short-cut methods in which means or medians are *guessed* and are then corrected to give the true ones. These methods are to be found described in any handbook on statistical methods.

The standard deviation has another special utility. If a distribution is normal, and we mark off the value of the standard deviation as a distance to right and to left of the central tendency (the mean is generally used here), it is found that 68 per cent of the scores will be included between these two points. (See Figure 34.) Further, if we mark off two of these σ distances (two standard deviations, or 2 S.D.'s) we include 96 per cent of the scores, and if we mark off three, we include practically all of them, 99.7 per cent. Now, let us remind ourselves that the normal distribution represents the composite action of innumerable chance factors that determine the scores made by the various individuals. We can now utilize the standard deviation in a new way: since it can be taken as a unit of variation, it makes possible a precise comparison between an individual's relative standing in one group and his relative standing in another, even when the scores used in the two groups are in very different units and seem not to be readily comparable.

In the same general manner, but with a little more mathematics, we can compare two groups to see whether a difference between their two central tendencies is a *reliable difference*. A difference that is reliable is one that indicates that there are different causal factors operating in the two groups, and that the found difference is not to be explained by chance variation. It is expressed as the ratio of the difference,

$$\frac{\text{diff}}{\sigma_{\text{diff}}}.$$

[1] The student should note that in the measurement of dispersion the standard deviation is very helpful; for now we are not interested in the central point about which the measures tend to cluster, but rather in how they tend to vary from this point.

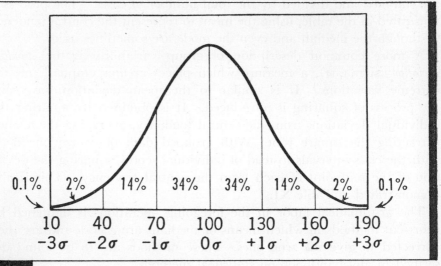

34 **Frequency Curve with Standard Deviation as a Unit of Measure on the Base Line**

The mean score of the distribution is 100 points, the standard deviation is 30 points. Note the area of the curve (i.e., number of individual cases) comprehended by 1, 2, and 3 σ's, respectively, taken above and below the mean.

Generally, a ratio of 3 is taken as the standard or the *critical ratio*, and a ratio between 2 and 3, though not significant, may be taken as suggestive of a true difference. The ratio takes into consideration not only the size of the difference of means, but also the number of cases in each group, and the amount of variability in the scores of each group. For these operations the simple formulae to be employed can be found in books on statistical methods.

As a practical matter, it deserves to be mentioned that with modern calculating machines, punched card equipment, and other mechanical aids, we can nowadays dispense with class intervals, guessed means, and other laborious procedures, for all computations can be made quickly and easily in terms of raw (original) scores or coded (simplified) scores. Labor-saving by such equipment is most gratifying when one is handling very many correlations.

CORRELATIONS

A Graphic Introduction

So much for measuring many individuals in regard to one performance. But it is often desirable to know about the relationship between the distributions of one performance and of another performance in the same group of individuals; as in such questions as: "Do ability in history and ability in arithmetic go together?" "Does weight of children indicate anything regarding their health?" The *coefficient of correlation* is a measure of the degree to which two series of scores go together.

A simple approach to the notion of correlation may be made graphically. Suppose twelve persons be measured in two performances, X and Y. Suppose that when laid out on a scale their respective scores on the two tests are as shown in Figure 35, A. John Doe makes the highest score on each test, Richard Roe makes the second highest, a third person makes third highest on both tests, and so on. It will be seen that from one performance to the other, the individual ranks remain the same; so that, from the knowledge of an individual's position in one series, we could safely predict his position in the other. The correlation between the two series is then said to be a high positive one, and is represented by $+1.00$. But now suppose the individuals' scores in the two performances are as shown in Figure 35, B, John Doe making the highest score on test X but a very low one on test Y, while Richard Roe makes

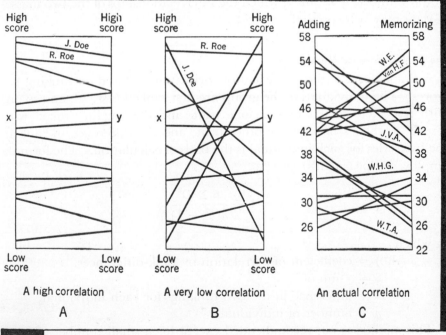

A high correlation	A very low correlation	An actual correlation
A	B	C

35 **Graphic Representation of Correlations**

A and B, hypothetical; C, actual. Each line represents an individual and connects his scores in two different distributions.

high scores on both, and the other individuals change positions considerably. We then could not predict from knowledge of an individual's score on X how he would score on Y. The correlation is then said to be very low, approaching zero or no-correlation, which is represented by 0.00.

When high scores in the one distribution go with low scores in the other, this is not *no* relationship but an *inverse* one, and is given a negative sign. Hence a negative correlation (e.g., $-.68$) is as significant as a positive correlation of the same numerical value ($+.68$).

Let us take, as an actual case, two of the tests applied to the college class mentioned previously (page 116), limiting our treatment for simplicity's sake to the first twenty members. The scores (which are furnished numerically in Table XII) are here represented by points on two scales, for Adding and for Memorizing, as shown in Figure 35, *C*. It will be evident on inspection that we have by no means a perfect correlation; nor do we have an entire absence of correlation for prediction from one series to the other would be somewhat better than chance. But how much? What is needed is a more definite numerical index, a simple number by means of which the interrelationships of the two masses of data may be expressed.

The Rank-Difference Method

A simple form of the coefficient of correlation is based on ranking the scores. The individuals of the group are first ranked (1st, 2d, and so on) with respect to their scores on one trait, and then again ranked with respect to their scores on the other trait; and the difference in rank in the two series for each individual is the basis of calculation. The formula employed (Spearman's) is:

$$\rho = 1 - \frac{6 \, \Sigma \, D^2}{n(n^2 - 1)}$$

in which

ρ (rho) = coefficient of correlation by rank-differences,

Σ = "sum of,"

D = difference in the two rankings for each individual,

n = number of individuals.

This method is not recommended except for a small number of cases (under 30). It is not precise, for it fails to take account of the *amounts* of difference between individual scores in each distribution. To do so let us make another graphic approach.

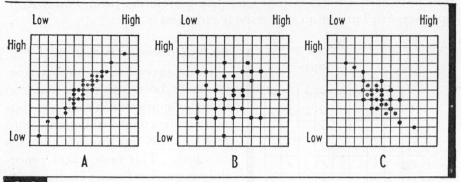

36 **Scatter Diagrams for Two Variables**

A. A high positive correlation.   *B.* A very low correlation.   *C.* A fairly high negative correlation.

The Scatter Diagram

Suppose that we represent low-to-high scores in a trait X by points in space ranging left-to-right, and low-to-high scores in another trait Y by points ranging bottom-to-top. Individuals scoring high in both will be represented in the right-upper area on the plot; those scoring low in both traits, in the left-lower area. Individuals scoring high in X but low in Y, or low in X but high in Y, will be indicated by entries in the lower-right or upper-left portions of the space, respectively. Then, in Figure 36, *A* would represent a very high correlation of X and Y scores; *B*, a very low correlation; and *C*, a fairly high negative correlation.

Now let us utilize this general idea in arranging actual numerical scores for computation. We prepare a diagram in which we can locate each individual by his scores in both distributions. One distribution (the X-scores) is represented horizontally, by the use of class intervals as in Table XI. The other, the Y-distribution, is arranged vertically, also in class intervals. (In this concrete case we shall let X represent the Adding and Y the Memorizing scores.) Tabulating the scores is now a simple tallying. For each pair of scores (as for Adding score 54, and Memorizing score 40) a single tally is entered in the proper square, under the X class interval and opposite the Y class interval. When all tallies have been entered, they are totaled for each square and the numbers written in. The scores shown graphically as individual scores in Figure 35, *C*, and numerically in the correlation sheet in Table XII are graphically shown as grouped scores in relationship in Figure 37. As in the purely graphic method, this charting of the tallies will give us an overview of the two distributions and their relationship. In the present case we can discern a trend toward a positive correlation (from lower-left tc upper-right), but not an impressively close one.

	X — scores							
	20-24	25-29	30-34	35-39	40-44	45-49	50-54	55-59
55-59		/		/				
50-54				//				
45-49					/	/	/	
40-44					/		/	/
35-39				/	/	/		
30-34	//	//						
25-29			///					
20-24	/							

Y — scores

37 A Scatter Diagram Arranged for Tabulating

The data, as tallies, are distributed in general manner as in Figure 35, C, but by class intervals, permitting further numerical operations.

The Product-Moment Method

In the preceding graphic exercise we have been arranging data so that the scores within each distribution can be compared not only as to relative ranks but also as to amounts of scores. This more exact procedure is carried further by the product-moment method in which the correlation between two distributions is determined by taking account of the amount that each individual *deviates from his group mean* in each distribution. The formula (Pearson's) employed is:

$$r = \frac{\Sigma xy}{N \sigma_x \, \sigma_y}$$

in which

r = amount of correlation,

x = the respective individual deviations from the mean in one trait,

y = the respective individual deviations from the mean in the other trait,

N = number of cases,

σ_x = standard deviation of the scores in one trait,

σ_y = standard deviation of the scores in the other trait.

Thus, "the amount of correlation is the sum of the products of each score in one trait by the same individual's score on the other, divided by the whole expression: the number of cases times the standard deviation of the scores in one trait times the standard deviation of the scores in the other trait."

The procedure is illustrated in Table XII where it is applied to the same group of 20 individuals referred to in Figures 35, C, and 37, but using now the actual scores and their deviations from the group means.

The Interpretation of Correlation Coefficients

The correlation coefficient found between the Adding and Memorizing scores referred to above was $+.59$. The degree to which the class-members varied on each test as compared with how they varied on each of the others is shown in the *table of intercorrelations* (Table XIII).

TABLE

XII

A Correlation Sheet

Subject	Score X (Adding)	Score Y (Memorizing)	Dev. x	Dev. y	x^2	y^2	xy
1	54	40	13.8	1.6	190.4	2.6	22.1
2	29	23	− 11.2	− 15.4	125.4	237.2	172.5
3	44	39	3.8	.6	14.4	.4	2.3
4	53	49	12.8	10.6	163.4	112.4	135.7
5	30	34	− 10.2	− 4.4	104.0	19.4	44.9
6	41	50	.8	11.6	.6	134.6	9.3
7	56	42	15.8	3.6	249.6	13.0	56.7
8	46	45	5.8	6.6	33.6	43.6	38.3
9	38	26	− 2.2	− 12.4	4.8	153.8	27.3
10	39	27	− 1.2	− 11.4	1.4	130.0	13.7
11	31	31	− 9.2	− 7.4	84.6	54.8	68.1
12	47	37	6.8	− 1.4	46.2	2.0	− 9.5
13	44	46	3.8	7.6	14.4	57.8	28.9
14	42	56	1.8	17.6	3.2	309.8	31.7
15	26	33	− 14.2	− 5.4	201.6	29.2	76.7
16	37	29	− 3.2	− 9.4	10.2	88.4	30.1
17	44	53	3.8	14.6	14.4	213.2	55.5
18	34	35	− 6.2	− 3.4	38.4	11.6	21.1
19	28	30	− 12.2	− 8.4	148.8	70.6	102.5
20	42	44	1.8	5.6	3.2	31.4	10.1
	$\Sigma X = 805$ $MX = 40.2$	$\Sigma Y = 769$ $MY = 38.4$			$\Sigma x^2 =$ 1452.6	$\Sigma y^2 =$ 1715.8	$\Sigma xy =$ +938.0*

$$\sigma_x = \sqrt{\frac{\Sigma x^2}{N}} = \sqrt{\frac{1452.6}{20}} = \sqrt{72.63} = 8.52$$

$$\sigma_y = \sqrt{\frac{\Sigma y^2}{N}} = \sqrt{\frac{1715.8}{20}} = \sqrt{85.79} = 9.26$$

$$r_{xy} = \frac{\Sigma xy}{N\sigma_x\sigma_y} = \frac{938}{20 \times 8.52 \times 9.26} = \frac{938}{1577.9} = .594$$

* This is an algebraic sum.

Note: In practice the product-moment method is not ordinarily used for less than 30 cases. A smaller number are handled in this table in order to simplify the arithmetic for demonstration.

TABLE

XIII

Intercorrelation Table

	Height	Weight	Adding	Memorizing	Estimating
Height	—	.60	.07	.12	− .06
Weight	.60	—	.18	− .02	.13
Adding	.07	.18	—	.39	.44
Memorizing	.12	− .02	.39	—	.21
Estimating	− .06	.13	.44	.21	—

One must not confuse a correlation coefficient with a simple percentage: he must not suppose that with a correlation of .44 he can predict with one half as much certainty as he can with a correlation of .88. On the contrary, the *prediction value of a coefficient of correlation* drops away with accelerated speed as the coefficient reduces. If between two tests, X and Y, a perfect correlation is obtained ($r = 1.00$), then we can predict with absolute accuracy what John Jones will score on Y from what he scored on X. But if the r is reduced only to .86 the safety of predicting is reduced to 50 per cent — halfway between absolute certainty and the error we would be making if we assigned Jones the mean score of the group on Y. There are practical applications, however, in which even smaller correlation coefficients are found useful [8].

Again, one must guard against confusing a high correlation coefficient between an X series and a Y series with a necessary connection between those two series. The coefficient may still have to be interpreted. Two amusing cases are to the point here. At the Brookings Institution someone found that through a period of eight years the variations in the death rate in the state of Hyderabad, in central India, were correlated highly (.86) with variations in the membership of the International Association of Machinists! Better yet, some statistician once discovered on an odd day that over a period of years the birth rate in Norway was correlated highly with the number of storks counted year by year. Statistical procedures have their reasons — and statistical findings must be interpreted.

Having acquainted ourselves with the fundamentals of statistical methodology, we shall see how these techniques aid us in the solution of many psychological problems. Some were raised in Chapter 3. A few will be given in this chapter. Others will come into our survey incidentally in other places.

INTERRELATIONS WITHIN THE INDIVIDUAL

Do Abilities Tend to Go Together?

For centuries men have speculated about the interrelationships of the different traits or abilities that combine to make up a person.

In what respects are the various analyzable traits of a given individual related to each other, and to what extents? Much research has recently been concerned with determining the degree to which specified human behavior traits are correlated. Does great capacity for remembering names and faces go with great capacity for recalling mathematical formulae? If a child excels in arithmetic, may we expect him to excel also in grammar? If he can acutely distinguish differences in loudness, may we expect him to be acute at discriminating colors? Is a man who is cautious in his investments likely to be equally cautious in his political or religious convictions? Is one who is quickly aroused to anger also quickly aroused to grief, or to fear? The general trend of scientific findings gives but weak support to popular opinions on such questions as these.

The layman's notions about the makeup of human nature are likely to err in two diametrically opposite directions. On the one hand he invests such terms as "memory," "school ability," "caution," and "emotionality" with unwarranted substance. He reasons that a person who can recall names with ease has "a good memory" and hence he must be good at remembering figures and formulae. The fallacy lies in the assumption that when two or more forms of behavior may be described in a way involving the *same conventional name*, then those forms of behavior must be the operations of one and the same fundamental process or capacity. For statistical treatments of the results of psychological tests have exploded any such extreme conception, and have led to a more widespread recognition of some *specific* character in every distinguishable human function.

At the other extreme the layman is apt to assume that a high degree of capacity in one area is likely to be offset by a low degree in another. A high school boy, let us say, does inferior work on literary subjects; accordingly, many of his friends will conclude that he must possess superior ability in mathematics, or, failing that, in manual training or in athletics. Again, it will be assumed that a man with highly trained taste in music or in painting must be inept in things mechanical; that a child who is a genius in intellect is underdeveloped in some other way; that the fast worker is inaccurate. In short, there is a tendency to balance one ability against another — a tendency that perhaps stems from an exaggerated democratic tradition — and to make judgments accordingly. But, again, scientific findings are at variance with popular assumption; for they point to the conclusion that, as Thorndike has put it, *in original nature the rule is correlation, not compensation.* This point is borne out by the fact that the intercorrelations of human abilities, while not running high, are overwhelmingly positive. High ability of one kind is likely to accompany high ability of another kind.

Are Human Abilities of Broad or Narrow Scope?

If we are genuinely curious, we shall not be content to know that abilities do (or do not) tend to go together; we shall want to know how these abilities are constituted. It would seem obvious that different talents are involved in, for instance, the ability to keep books for a business firm, to play a viola acceptably, to punt out-of-bounds near the goal line, and to design and make a dress. Shall we then speak of book-keeping ability, viola-playing ability, punting-out-of-bounds-near-goal-line ability, and dress-designing ability, and assign to each a separate and complete ability which has no relationship to any other? Probably everyone would condemn this as too naïve. (1) Shall we, then, conceive of these achievements as due to *one broad, general human capacity* that makes for success in each and any line, so that the same person who shows high achievement in one way could — if he would — show high achievement in other ways? (2) Or shall we assume that each achievement is due to some one of *several rather general sorts of capacity* but is operating under specific conditions that call for specific abilities also: business ability which, in the bookkeeper's office, involves ability to write and figure; musical talent which, when devoted to the viola, demands also skillful fingering and a good ear; football "know-how" which happens to be devoted at times to punting and so involves nice timing of the foot; a talent for domestic art which, when directed to costume-designing, calls upon specific abilities to visualize, to cut accurately, to sew neatly, and the like? (3) Or again, shall we think of each of these achievements as due to a composite of *very many* simple and *specific* capacities, and say that the form of the achievement depends solely upon the particular pattern of capacities which is called forth?

Psychology has developed certain tools of research that make it possible to investigate these questions in concrete terms, with some hope of solving them. One of these kits of tools is the vast array of psychological tests now available. Another is the development of statistical methods of handling test results.

In a general way, an investigation starts with the results of many tests, combined and compared in a table of intercorrelations. In Table XIII, for example, we note a fairly high correlation between Height and Weight scores, and we would conclude that these two traits must have something in common. Again, we see a suggestive coefficient between Adding and Memorizing: to what can this be due? Does it reveal a broad general human capacity operating in the two cases; or does it indicate an ability somewhat more restricted, such as the ability to work subvocally on symbolic school materials; or does it show simply very many specific abilities such as holding and using a pencil, listening, sitting erect, reading letters and figures, and so on?

Further, we note that Adding scores are also correlated to some extent with Estimating scores. Are we to infer from this that whatever abilities are common to Adding and Memorizing are involved also in Estimating? Or would it be better to assume that whatever ones are common to Adding and Memorizing are different from those common to Adding and Estimating? But then we note that Estimating scores are correlated also with Memorizing scores. Does this justify us in concluding that the same abilities then run through all three types of performance?

It should now be clear that we could hardly hope to get ahead by mere inspection of such tables. We would have to have recourse to more analytic methods. But these techniques lie beyond the scope of our present survey.

The Present Status. The English psychologist Spearman long championed the view that throughout all demonstrations of cognitive ability or intelligence there is evidence of the operation of a *general* ability, or *g*, as well as many specific abilities that vary from one test to another [7]. He would have said that our sample table of intercorrelations, Table XIII, furnishes internal evidence of some general capacity operating along with the various specific ones necessary for such particular performances as naming opposites, completing sentences, immediately recalling a series of digits, and the like. Though there has been much polemic writing on both sides of the Atlantic, the conception of a general ability running through performance on all mental tests is apparently well accepted. And Spearman's claim that Binet assumed this *g* ability in developing his famous scale of tests for general intelligence is a strong point.

Spearman and others have also emphasized the part played by a great many highly *specific* abilities. That is, (*a*) ability to recall immediately a series of digits heard may be independent of (*b*) ability to recall digits heard after a day's lapse, and of (*c*) ability to read digits quickly, and of (*d*) ability to recall letters seen, and of (*e*) ability to recall letters heard; and so on. And, as another example, good ability to guess the sizes of small triangles may be not at all related to good ability to guess the sizes of large triangles. In short, according to this theory each performance is the operating of certain specific abilities in those specific materials only.

Factor Analysis

Meanwhile a shift of interest to methodology has led to the development in the last few years of statistical methods aimed at explaining the many possible intercorrelations by a small number of components or factors. Conceivably we could set up tests for any and every form and manifestation of a person's abilities, but we should soon be swamped with vast tables of intercorrelations derived from them. What we need is to see whether or not the intercorrelations can be compared and cross-compared to bring out a very limited number of human abilities that can be taken as involved in most human achievements. Statistical methods are being devised for treating the data in highly analytic ways, and it seems that there are but a few fundamental abilities involved in the very many performances measured [9, 10]. Their exposition, however, is highly mathematical, and would be out of place here.

Suffice it to say that by these methods of factor analysis some results can already be stated. Among the many workers using factor analysis methods there is some agreement as to certain *group factors* as follows [11]: *verbal* ability, as shown on analogies tests, vocabularies, etc.; *spatial* ability, shown in reading blueprints or detecting differences in geometrical designs; *numerical* ability, as appears in the simple arithmetical operations of adding, etc.; *immediate memory* factor, involved in recalling paired-associates, nonsense syllables, etc.; *speed* factor, shown best on very simple materials that demand few other abilities; *logical* ability, shown in discovering the rule in a number series or in recognizing true and false syllogisms.

Non-Cognitive Factors

The same methods of mathematical analysis of test-result intercorrelations have been applied to human motor and mechanical abilities; but the correlations between different kinds of performance — turning a drill, steadiness, tapping speed, and the like — are so low that no important general abilities in these aspects of human capacity have been isolated.

Is it possible that factorial analyses can bring some order into the broad problems of personality? Certain group factors have been indicated: introversion, depression, emotional immaturity, hypersensitivity. Will further research verify these as truly independent factors in the individual's personality make-up? We shall raise the question in a later and more appropriate place (pages 601 ff.).

REFERENCES

1. Garrett, H. E. *Statistics in Psychology and Education.* Third edition. New York: Longmans, Green and Company, 1947.
2. Guilford, J. P. *Psychometric Methods.* New York: McGraw-Hill Book Company, 1936.
3. Holzinger, K. J., and H. H. Harman. *Factor Analysis.* Chicago: University of Chicago Press, 1941.
4. McNemar, Q. *Psychological Statistics.* New York: John Wiley and Sons, 1949.
5. Morton, R. L. *Laboratory Exercises in Educational Statistics.* New York: Silver Burdett, 1928.
6. Peatman, J. G. *Descriptive and Sampling Statistics.* New York: Harper and Brothers, 1947.
7. Spearman, C. *The Abilities of Man.* New York: The Macmillan Company, 1927.
8. Taylor, H. C., and J. T. Russell. "The relationship of validity coefficients to practical effectiveness of tests," *J. Appl. Psychol.*, 1939, 23, 565–578.
9. Thomson, G. H. *The Factorial Analysis of Human Ability.* Boston: Houghton Mifflin Company, 1939.
10. Thurstone, L. L. *Multiple-Factor Analysis.* Chicago: University of Chicago Press, 1947.
11. Walker, H. M. *Mathematics Essential for Elementary Statistics.* New York: Henry Holt and Company, 1934.
12. Wolfle, D. "Factor analysis to 1940," *Psychometr. Monogr.*, 1940, No. 3.

7

THE BASES OF MOTIVATION

IT IS THE DAY of the big game. Shouted salutations. Noise. Bustle. Automobiles. Crowds. More crowds. The team, collectively and individually, has now been pretty accurately rated as to muscular power and speed and stamina, alertness and athletic prowess and canniness; and its season's record has been known and rated thoroughly from coast to coast. And the opposing team has been as thoroughly analyzed. What, then, is awaited by these crowds and by the thousands that continue to arrive on special trains? When two opposing forces are well known and measured, what remains but to make a mathematical calculation and settle it all on paper? But, you answer truly, no one can know absolutely every detail of ability in every player concerned. Then there are the elements of chance, the "breaks," that may lead to unexpected results But still another factor enters into this opposition of human forces. Why are the underdogs known sometimes to upset all the cold calculations by humbling their greatest rivals? Why the brass band? Why the talks by the coaches in the dressing-room? Why the banner-waving and lusty cheering in the stands? In the language of the mass meeting on the night before, it puts "pep" in the players. What, psychologically, is the source of this "pep"?

Again, why do men work? Those who write on economic matters frequently come up against this question. Is there some unidentifiable "instinct of industry," some "instinct of workmanship"? Is it because recurring pangs of hunger force men to earn money for bread? Or is it because they fear being called "bums"? In his considerations of producing and consuming agents, the economist does well to raise such questions as why men work, and why labor and skill are more easily recruited for one type of industry than for another, why men like to buy this thing and not that, and so create demands and markets. And it is just as legitimate to ask why a given man will not work.

In a word, whether we are considering athletics or economics, we are running up against the problem of motive.

Motive figures largely in the law. A Scotland Yard detective, when asked how he would proceed in the investigation of a certain murder case, remarked: "I would first seek to establish the motive. After that I could know in what direction to look for my man."

Courts of law in modern times make distinctions between motives such as were unknown to primitive justice. The *lex talionis*, "an eye for an eye," has lost its validity — except for lynching parties or for that private form of retaliation known as the "unwritten law." Killing by accident is no longer to be avenged in the same way as killing by deliberate intent. We now speak of murder in the first degree, in the second degree, manslaughter, and accidental homicide, and the progress of legal philosophy may be measured by the progress in recognizing finer and finer distinctions in man's motives.

And in the field of education, the technique of teaching no longer assumes that a pupil is a learner and then concerns itself only with that which is to be presented to him. It recognizes that effective teaching presupposes a will to learn, a disposition on the pupil's part to seek instruction — in a word, motivation. What was once secured largely through a generous use of the rod is now being sought through incentives of a less negative and less crude type. The pupil must somehow be interested, not by urging from behind, but by the exploitation of interests already actively at work in his behavior.

Such concrete incidents and problems bring to light the fundamental need of a scientific knowledge not alone of how a man acts and of what he does but of *why* he gets into action and *why* he acts as he does. Not only the machinery of the organism but also the way it is energized and operated is a pertinent psychological problem. This distinction, however, is not to be taken as a final one, for surely one thing we have learned already is that the human being, or any other living organism, is not a truly inert machine to be set into operation by the application of a power source more or less distinct from itself. Mechanical analogies fit life processes very imperfectly! Nevertheless, even though the distinction between a mechanism and the way it is energized is a difference of emphases more than of entities, it will advance our purposes if we make use of it, and for the present emphasize the dynamic aspect of human life and conduct.

External Stimuli as Releases

One source of differential triggering or setting off of organic activity is, of course, external stimulation. The electromagnetic and air vibrations that initiate processes leading to sight and hearing, the chemical agencies that affect smell and taste receptors, the changes of temperature and the impact of physical masses at the skin surface — these are all readily recognized as moving forces in human behavior. If you would see a man get into action, touch him with a needle point or sound an auto horn behind him, call him by name, slap him on the back, announce a circus parade or a fashion parade, call out the word "fire!" Among the conditions that activate human nature we could list, then, all those classes of stimuli we shall canvass in Chapter 10.

But even in the crude illustrations just offered it does not need much discernment to note that these extra-organic (exteroceptive) stimulations tell by no means the whole story. Human nature is not a football. It is not immediately and solely subject to the actions of external forces alone.[1] Rather, these exteroceptive stimuli serve mainly to release, to touch off, the energies stored and systematized within that extremely complex balanced mass we call a living organism.

To be sure, there are numerous types of reaction that are dependent only in a minor degree upon intra-organic conditions and to a major degree upon the direct, unequivocal result of exteroceptive stimulation. The knee jerk and the pupillary reflex are examples of this order. They are to be described and explained more in terms of their immediate stimuli than in terms of the chemical disequilibrium of the whole organism or of the inadequacy of a specific organ or tissue. However, such relatively unmotivated responses play only the role of extras on life's stage. Eyelid twitchings and finger jerks, necessary as they are to the behavior of man, have no central part in determining in what way or with what energy a person will act.

Let us make sure of our orientation again. In an earlier chapter we saw from concrete examples that it is of the essence of animal and human behavior to seek or to maintain optimal conditions for oneself so that one's intra-organic processes will be adequately furthered. The key to man and to sub-human forms is to be sought more in the enormously

---

[1] This is one reason for a common misunderstanding of a scientific psychology that seeks to know man in terms of cause-and-effect relationships. It is a very superficial view of the science that characterizes it as making man into a robot, a puppet, a marionette, acting out his whole drama of life merely in response to external promptings. But it is equally as impossible and absurd to suppose that the only alternative is to assume mysterious agencies, entities, daemons implanted in man's nature and operating him.

complex energy exchanges going on within him than in the chance play of outside energies working upon him. You can lead a horse to water, but the sight of water will not be an effective stimulus unless he is thirsty; in that case an untethered horse will lead himself to the trough. A mate does not excite the pigeon or the frog to sexual advances except when in a certain physiological state. It is even said that a lion must be hungry to attack a peaceful and unaggressive man. Is the child hungry? Then and only then will he approach the food. Is he tired? The bed now invites him as it did not while he was in the flush of play. It is when he is cold that the warm radiator can attract him, when he is in pain that he runs to his nurse. Some of the primary drives to persistent forms of animal and human conduct are tissue-conditions, local and general, within the organism, giving rise to stimulations exciting the organism to overt activity. A man's interests and desires may become ever so elaborate, refined, socialized, sublimated, idealistic; but the raw basis from which they are developed is found in the phenomena of living matter.

THE ENERGETICS OF ACTIVITY

Organismic Self-Regulation

In 1859 Claude Bernard enunciated the epoch-making notion of the *milieu interne*. Besides the general environment surrounding the organism as a whole, he said, there is the *internal environment* surrounding the body's organs and tissues, the circulating fluids (blood and lymph) that carry nourishment to all the cells and bear away the products of their excretion. The remarkable character of this internal environment is its constancy. A vital part of the work of the bodily organs is to maintain a fixed balance of temperature, of oxygen, of water, of fats, of sugars, of salts.

Subsequent research, especially by endocrinologists (see pages 138 ff. and 294 ff.), has added richer details to the idea of internal environment. The general principle is clear enough: the living organism maintains its integrity, regulates itself to fine degrees, by ever ready compensatory adjustments in all sorts of ways. Nothing in the natural world is more impressive than the

> various mechanisms and processes which serve to control, order and adjust the various activities to varying conditions in such manner as to maintain the physiological unity and harmony of the organism in the changing environment to which it is subjected. Through such mechanisms and processes the activities of organisms are "regulated" within certain limits, and physiologists have very naturally come to call them regula-

tory mechanisms and processes. We know more or less concerning many such mechanisms in organisms; e.g., the mechanism of the regulation of heat production and heat loss in the warm-blooded animals, of respiration, of blood flow and blood volume, of neutrality in the blood and tissues, of blood sugar, of the heart beat, of various digestive functions, of various internal secretions, of the transport of water, salts and carbohydrates in plants, and so on.[1]

To this principle that the organism seeks to maintain a *steady state*, Cannon has applied the name "homeostasis";[2] and some physiological psychologists have adopted it as a key concept for interpreting and clarifying psychological processes [6].

Self-Regulation as Behavior

Enlarging our horizon, we must next recognize that these regulatory functions involve and dominate the total organism's behavior with respect to its external environment also. Richter has directed a series of researches in which the steady state of the white rat organism has been disturbed by the operative removal of one or another endocrine gland [18, 19].

In one case the sodium balance of the organism was upset by removing the adrenal glands (see pages 297 ff.), the loss of which allowed the kidneys to pass salt (sodium chloride) out of the body in excessive amounts. Does the operated animal do anything about this? Some normal animals were placed in cages with two water bottles, one filled with tap water, the other with salt water. After several weeks, their adrenals were removed. Almost immediately the animals drank larger and larger amounts of the salt solution, up to twenty times as much as before. Figure 38 shows the record of one such rat, and, for comparison, the records on another rat that had been offered no salt water. It is clear that when an animal's chemical condition is thrown off balance by the loss of salt, its behavior changes dramatically as it goes after salt to repair the loss. It is under the drive of a salt craving. This finding is supported by the case of a three-year-old boy who ate salt by the handfuls, then when unwittingly restricted to a normal diet died in seven days. Autopsy revealed that he had previously lost adrenal tissue by tumerous growths.

The same experimental procedure has exhibited other examples of homeostatic regulation of the animal's behavior, depending upon the

[1] From C. M. Child, *Physiological Foundations of Behavior* (New York: Henry Holt and Company, 1924).

[2] At this point it is important for the student to re-read pages 27 f., above.

particular direction in which its internal equilibrium has been disturbed. And the resulting behavior has been shown to be highly selective. Normal white rats were offered a number of different kinds of foods, cafeteria-wise, in a number of separate measured containers. Given this opportunity to select their own foods, the animals thrived as well as they ordinarily do on the standardized mixtures [19, 30]. What is more, some rats whose utilization of fats and carbohydrates had been disordered by removal of the pancreas (cf. page 302), when allowed similar self-selection in their diets chose those substances that maintained them on a normal internal metabolism.

The principle of self-regulation can further be verified in experiments with human subjects. Infants of weaning age who had never tasted other foods than mother's milk were presented with thirty-four different varieties of simple foods, including all that are ordinarily included in babies' diets [4]. The items of the entire list were divided and served at three meals a day, each meal including a wide variety. Each article was set out in a separate dish. The baby was allowed to reach for anything and to eat with his fingers or in any way he chose. Some of the infants were in poor physical shape to start with, rickets being promi-

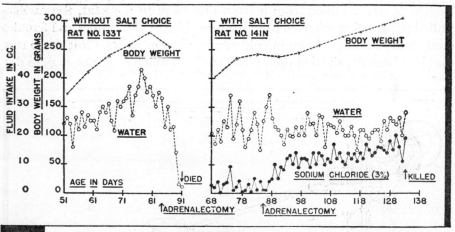

38 Effect of Loss of Adrenals on Behavior and Weight of the Rat

Left: Rat without access to salt. Note that its drinking of water and its body weight increased steadily, from the age of 51 days, until after its adrenal glands had been removed on the 84th day. Thereafter it drank decreasing amounts of the saltless water and lost weight until it died only 7 days later. *Right:* Rat with access to salt. Note that its water drinking and body weight increased much like the other rat's; then, after loss of its adrenals on the 86th day, it drank heavily of the 3 per cent salt water and continued gaining weight as long as used in the experiment. (*From C. P. Richter,* THE HARVEY LECTURES, *series 38, 1942–43.*)

nent; but within a reasonable time the nutritional condition of every one came up to full standard as measured by blood counts, X-rays, urinalyses, and other medical tests. And more than one specialist pronounced them all beautiful specimens in both physique and behavior.

A curious thing about the self-selected diets was their variety. In the long run, they all conformed to scientific nutritional principles and standards; yet the selections varied most remarkably from infant to infant and from meal to meal. Strange meals some of the babies had; yet in the end, they balanced up. The experiment shows well the organismic control of overt selective behavior.

Let us consider one more example of experimentally aroused appetite or tension. It is known that the delicate mechanism which regulates the temperature of the organism depends upon the rate of the metabolic processes of the body, and these in turn depend upon secretions of the pituitary glands (cf. pages 299 ff.), for one thing. Remove this gland and the temperature falls. But the animal will then make efforts to maintain the temperature nearer the optimal level by building himself a nest of much greater than normal size and warmth. Quantitative studies were made by placing rats, operated and unoperated, in individual cages, each equipped with a roll of soft paper and a cyclometer to measure the lengths of paper pulled from it from one noon to the next, the earlier-pulled paper being removed from the nest (Figure 39). Males and females used equal amounts, more in cold rooms than in warm. But those rats that had been deprived of their pituitary built much larger nests than did

39 **Effect of Loss of Pituitary Gland on Nest-Building Activity of the Rat**
Side view of nest-building cage, showing paper roll and cyclometer.

the normals, some actually using up the whole roll of 500 feet. In short, to restore its disturbed body-temperature equilibrium the rat will intensify his nest-building. Here we have a very general body condition corrected by a direct overt performance.

A Generalization

The phenomena described in the preceding sections suggest that in the motivating of the human or animal organism the basic fact is a disequilibrium, a disturbance of the steady state, of the body as a whole, which the organism seeks to correct. The unbalanced state drives the organism into activity, and the activity *continues until the steady state is restored.* And as the particular character of the disequilibrium varies (as we have seen in the different examples) we may speak of different organic needs or *physiological drives.*

The needs of the body in many cases are more or less localized, and specific organs and tissues are the foci of body needs. For instance, although it is the body that demands food (which demand we experience as *appetite*), the digestive apparatus which serves the body's need for food has developed its own special demand (which we experience as the pangs of *hunger*). Since hunger is generally considered the most typical of the specific organ demands, we shall use it for illustration.

The Localized Hunger Drive

The fact that food-lack operates as a drive[1] to increase overt activity has been assumed and used experimentally in nearly all research into animal learning. A genuinely hungry rat or cat will get into activity and keep in activity until its hunger is satisfied, and if obstacles to hunger are interposed it will show exploratory activity until it surmounts them.

A direct study of the connection between hunger drive and general

---

[1] Certain terms in the psychology of motivation are given varying uses by contemporary authorities. For the sake of clarity in our own discussion let us adhere to the following meanings. By a *drive* let us understand a certain organ or tissue condition by which an animal is set into activity. An *incentive* then will refer to the object or situation toward or away from which the drive-originated activity is impelled. Examples: hunger-driven behavior is, or comes to be, directed toward a food-incentive; pain-driven behavior is, or comes to be, directed away from a hot-wire-incentive. The word *motive* we shall employ throughout our treatment in its widest sense, to cover every form of impulsion, from the simplest physiological drive to the most elaborated, sophisticated, and intellectualized ideal. Similarly, "motivated" will be used with breadth of meaning. *Desire* is best applied to those motives and their objectives of which the individual is well aware, as when one says he is thirsty and desires a drink or says he desires to graduate at the next Commencement. The term *interest* is used when the emphasis is upon a motive as predisposing its possessor to pay attention to a certain thing or class of things, as an interest in Chinese porcelains, in politics, or in pig-raising.

bodily activity was made by Miss Wada. From earlier work it was known that hunger, as distinguished from appetite, is traceable to contractions of the smooth musculature of the stomach walls, the contractions appearing and disappearing in rhythmic alternations for periods varying between a half-hour and an hour and a half. Under the bed of a subject a receiving tambour was arranged with the rubber diaphragm connected to the under surface of the bed by a spiral spring and made so sensitive that every overt bodily movement of the subject, even the moving of a finger, affected the tambour. By means of a rubber tubing the movements were communicated to a recording tambour and pointer placed in another room, and were traced on a long paper kymograph, which was also equipped with a time marker. A simultaneous record of stomach contractions (hunger) was made with an inflated balloon communicating with a recording manometer, much like the one shown in Figure 40.[1] By comparing the two lines traced upon the kymograph record, Miss Wada was able to show that both during sleep and during a quiet waking state (that of reading a book) there was a very close correlation between the rhythmic occurrences of hunger and the rhythmic occurrences of gross striped muscular activity.[2] Further, by awakening sleeping subjects at different times she obtained some evidence of a greater tendency to dream during the hunger contraction periods; and by testing waking subjects at various intervals, with a hand dynamometer and with intelligence tests, she found that hunger apparently facilitated both gross reactions and the finer thinking reactions.

Besides this demand of hunger traceable directly to the stomach, we must recognize a more general demand of appetite which is certainly more difficult to localize in the body. The evidence is that this is fundamental to the hunger and is of chemical and probably hormonal nature. Animals in which the afferent nerve fibers leading from the stomach are cut off, or from which the stomach has actually been removed, continue

---

[1] A "tambour" is a metal air-chamber with top covered by a rubber diaphragm. It has a single inlet-outlet for tube connection. In the receiving type, varying external pressures on the diaphragm are transmitted as varying pressures through the connecting tube. Conversely, in the recording type variations in air pressure in the connecting tube raise and lower the diaphragm and the writing-lever resting upon it. A "manometer" is a U-tube partially filled with liquid. One arm of it is connected by air through the tubing with the balloon or other receiving apparatus; the other arm contains a cork float upon which is mounted a rod and writing-point. Changes of air pressure in the connecting tube displace the liquid and so raise and lower the writing-point. "Time markers" are of several types, one being an enclosed clockwork operating a pointer once per second. (See Figure 40.)

[2] Striped muscles are the skeletal muscles usually attached at one end to a fixed part of the body and at the other end to a movable member. See pages 277 ff.

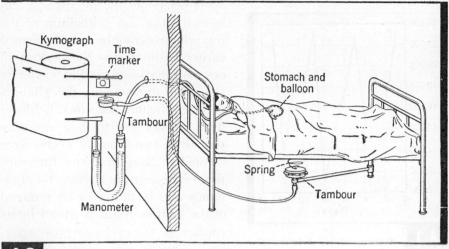

40

Registration of Body Movements and of Stomach Contractions

Any slight movement of the sleeper affects spring and receiving tambour under bed, and, by pneumatic connection, operates a recording tambour with its writing lever bearing on the kymograph drum. Stomach contractions compress rubber balloon swallowed by subject. These compressions are pneumatically transmitted to a manometer with its writing point. A time marker is also mounted (at the top) on the drum. (*Redrawn from T. Wada*, ARCH. PSYCHOL., *1922, No. 57.*)

to seek food in a normal way. A human patient whose stomach had been removed (and esophagus connected directly to intestine) did not lose his experienced desires for food [13].

The Localized Sex Drive

On account of the formidable, impelling character of this bodily urge on the one hand, and of the complicated restrictions that society has placed upon its satisfaction on the other, the sex drive is nowadays recognized as one of the greatest of all sources of maladjustment of human beings to their social environments. Freud, indeed, once held it to be the one and only drive of importance in the genesis of mental disorders. Sometimes he and others have used the word *libido* in this narrow sense; but many psychoanalysts maintain that this is unwarranted, and that the word should have a more general meaning, as "life energy."

The sex drive arises from a condition in the sex apparatus. Wang used a revolving cage and counter and confirmed earlier observations that the adult female albino rat showed rhythmic changes in the amount of general bodily activity in cycles of about four days' length. What drives a female rat, he asked, to show such regular cyclic changes of

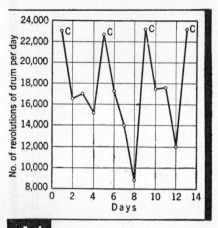

41

Correspondence Between Oestrous Rhythm and Cycles of General Bodily Activity in a Female Rat

Encircled dots indicate examinations made of reproductive tract. At those marked *C* were found cornified epithelial cells, indicative of "heat." The vertical distance of each dot represents the total amount of general bodily activity of the animal on the day the examination was made. (*G. H. Wang*, COMP. PSYCHOL. MONOG., 2, *No. 6.*)

overt behavior? By microscopic examination of the epithelium of the reproductive tract he then confirmed earlier findings that the periods of oestrus (heat) occurred in cycles of the same duration as the changes of the epithelium (Figure 41). Moreover, he was able to show not only that these two kinds of cycles were coincident, but that any interruption of the oestrous rhythm by pregnancy and lactation or by removal of the ovaries resulted in an interruption of the cycles of gross activity. Thus it was proved that the hypertonicity and hyperactivity of the animal was excited by stimulations of intra-organic origin (in the sex apparatus) when it was in certain physiological conditions.

The male rat does not show the same rhythmic phases in his sex life; yet the dependence of his excess overt activity in large measure upon excitation from the sex apparatus was demonstrated clearly. It is a familiar fact that if castrated the male of any domestic animal is less aggressive and less restless; and in Richter's laboratory the point was put on the same level of scientific evidence as was the activation of the female. (See Figure 42.)

The excess activity resulting from the afferent neural currents as well as chemical conditions that arise in the sex apparatus is by no means limited to the striped musculature but is evident also in effectors distributed through the viscera. The tension, in other words, is not merely one of overt posturings and restlessness; it is also strongly emotional. And such emotional conditions are themselves in turn important in energizing the individual.

The part played in sex behavior by external stimuli is originally minor and secondary to the intra-organic; but early in the life of an organism the whole pattern of emotion becomes conditioned to (excitable by) the sight, smell, touch, or other form of stimulation from mates, so that these external kinds of excitation later come to play an increasingly important part in arousing the sex drive.

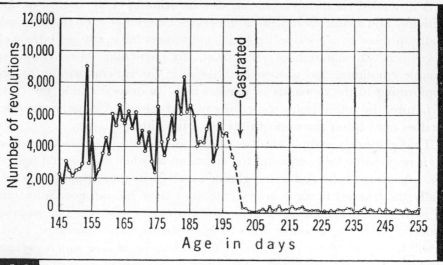

42   **Effect of Castration on General Activity**

(*From C. P. Richter, "Animal behavior and internal drives,"* QUAR. REV. BIOL., *1927, 2, No. 3.*)

Other Organic Sources of Needs

With the operation of these two types of physiological drives before us, we may sketchily refer to other inadequacies in the condition of organic tissues that form the basis of drives to overt behavior.

In frequent association with the hunger drives are the *thirst* drives. These are basically systemic in nature, though the first signal of water shortage takes the form of afferent nerve impulses from the dry throat. The importance of thirst drives in the life and behavior of a human being needs no particular exposition, nor the degree to which they have determined many phases of the individual's relations with his fellows. And because certain group mores forbid certain kinds of drinking, while the desire to drink in those ways is a definite one, frequent conflicts among a person's impulses result, and make for personality problems and perhaps call for clinical guidance.

The *respiratory* and *circulatory* systems are still other organic sources of needs. To a man twenty feet under water, the drive to breathe becomes of greater intensity than all other motives. As a result of old associations, the sight of the boundless prairie may to a city cliff-dweller be as breath-releasing as the congested alleys of the metropolis are breath-constricting to a plainsman — and in either case there may be some anxiety and a basis laid for a phobia (of which more on pages 191 ff.).

A distended condition of *bladder* or *colon* stimulates the organism into activity, and if unrelieved often generates emotional excitement, especially in those in whom polite social inhibitions have not yet been well developed. Evacuation of the bowels, in particular, often comes to assume emotional and anti-social character; for by conforming or not conforming to the demands of parents bent on domesticating the child of nature, the infant holds something of a whiphand. Whether he does or does not exploit the opportunity is an individual matter.

That extremely complicated set of organs called the *reproductive apparatus* is responsible for energizing the organism in other than sexual behavior. As some of the endocrine glands involved in that apparatus (especially the female) become active, the animal or human goes into lines of activity that pertain directly to the caring for young. The *maternal* group of drives is of course one of highest biological importance. And it will be a part of our program later to take note of how much psychological importance it has, too. The effect of deficient or excessive expression of this urge in the behavior of the parent upon the character formation of the individual young is of great moment (Chapter 21). Furthermore, its role in shaping social-cultural organizations is a key concept.

The *skin* is so loaded with receptors that when it is subjected to injury, violent defensive reactions are at once set up. Avoidance of pain stimulation has motivated not a little of the social submissiveness of the slave, of the prisoner of war, of the convict in the turpentine camp, of the suspect in a back room at the police station, of the school child, and of the younger brother. In case the pain condition is persistent or intense, the motor effects include extensive visceral disturbances which may lead to powerful emotional outbursts, as in the pet dog which, when his foot is caught in a trap, snaps at his own master, or the child with a cut finger who alternately cries in terror and berates his nurse. Both the rage and the fear types of excitement are to be observed in man or beast under such circumstances.

Very different conditions at the skin may arouse correspondingly different forms of behavior. Skin that is mildly stroked and patted, and thus probably facilitated in its blood circulation and in other normal metabolic processes, gives rise to afferent impulses that excite inhibitory motor innervations, leading to muscular relaxation. The effect of this on young and old is marked, and such manipulation has been used to quiet the restless baby, to bring sleep to an uneasy adult, and to serve as a form of therapy for a nervous patient. At particular points of the skin there are special *sensitive zones* where gentle stimulations have special effects that are more excitatory but still of a general, positive, accepting type. For a good example, the well-known tickling response will serve us. A light scratching on the soles of the feet or a firm rubbing of the skin over the ribs awakens laughter and wriggling movements of body and limbs. A variety of responses clearly belonging to the same category may be elicited at lips, armpits, nipples, and other sensitive zones, in the form of smiling, gurgling, arching of back, and squirming. All such behavior involves emotional components, but at present we know little about them in detail.

The *striped musculature* in a condition of fatigue provides automatic stimulations taking the form of the inhibitory tendency to cease activity, to rest, to sleep. In the opposite physico-chemical condition (when one is rested), the striped musculature sometimes gives rise to stimulations of excitatory nature, and the individual is urged into some kind of muscular exercise. This is often classed as an activity drive or need. The developed interests in athletics, in hunting or in tramping, in the use of certain stimulant drugs, in physical education, as well as the interests in a restful bed or chair, in an easy living at the seashore, in the use of sedatives, are a few of the many aspects of human behavior motivated fundamentally by conditions of these muscle tissues.

Another characteristic of striped muscle that leads to the development of a drive is the rhythmic character of its contractions. When an external source of stimulation is acting rhythmically, the efforts of the auditor, spectator, or hand worker to adjust himself to that stimulation are modified and influenced by the subject's own rhythms, and a tendency to follow an easily reproduced rhythm becomes strong. It is easy to see how this drive is connected with interest in dancing, music, and poetry. Incidentally, rhythmic activity appears to have emotion-arousing value — at least if it is intense and long maintained — as is shown in the arts just mentioned, and is dramatically exhibited by war dancers, whirling dervishes, and camp-meeting orators, whose excitement mounts to a veritable frenzy.

In the general category of activity drives we must recognize the reactions of *sensory apparatus*. Nearly all the receptors have associated motor tissues. Consider the eye and its three pairs of muscles to rotate the eyeball, its sphincter muscle to regulate the size of the pupil, and its ciliary muscle to adjust the lens for distances. Consider also the receptors of the skin: they may not have muscular tissues so completely identifiable as integral parts of the sense organ, but for them much the same part is played by the skeletal muscles that move exploring fingers over and around objects. The tendency of the eyes to be turned to a light, of the ears to be cocked in the direction of a sound, of the fingers to move about a tactually stimulating object, of the tongue to expose itself to a sapid substance — all such simple receptor-adjusting tendencies furnish some part of the behavior in infancy and throughout life. The organism from birth is equipped "with an overwhelming number of reflexes which go out to meet the stimulus, get more of it, repeat or reproduce the stimulation" [7]. Such reflex adjustments seem to be an expression of the metabolism of the receptors, for they give place to stimulus-avoiding reflexes whenever the light or noise or other external agency becomes intense. Is it possible that in these phenomena we have the core of the very attention-giving that, apart from any other drive to exploratory movement, is at the basis of the type of behavior we call *curiosity*?

One more activity drive (or set of drives) has only recently become recognized. May it not be that *nerve tissue* itself furnishes a certain drive? Analogous to the tendency of rested muscles to become active, or of receptors to orient themselves into receptive positions and even to become self-acting (as when one sees coruscating colors with his eyes closed in the dark), it is possible that neural tissue may be self-active. Some of the electrical changes in the brain suggest spontaneous origin of processes there (cf. pages 336 ff.). Furthermore, research has confirmed that in the central nervous system, particularly the brain, there are closed circuits of nerve cells. An activity once set up may continue itself (cf. page 315; also [10]). This concept would serve as a basis for understanding the continuity of much of our behavior: the recurrent tune that keeps running in the head; the harking back to a talked-out grievance; the search for the elephant hidden in the picture; the not-to-be-distracted attention of the flutist to score and to conductor; or the not-to-be-diverted interest of the research worker. This is far from contending that all maintenance of direction in thinking or other operations is a matter of simple closed-circuit repetitiveness; that would be clearly absurd. We shall have more to say on this point in Chapter 13. Meanwhile, whatever the detailed characteristics of neural tissue and its action, we may pretty safely rely upon our observations of everyday life, in which we see that people "like to use their brains." The student in any field of knowledge quickly becomes aware that the thinkers in that field — be it marine zoology, metaphysics, historical biography, structural engineering, or Latin epigraphy — are not satisfied to *know*, but must be forever ferreting out new problems and forever trying to solve them, only to ferret out some more. The term "brain drive" may strike us at first as ludicrous, but we dare not dismiss the possibility that the nervous system has activity needs of its own.

We have marshaled the foregoing extensive list of tissue demands for a double reason. One can hardly fail to be impressed with the richness of basic needs which present themselves in the human child and out of which rise the possibilities of indefinite variety in men's motives, interests, and values. And while the reader may have been a bit startled at the first prospect of man's highest ideals arising out of what are originally raw anatomical stuffs, it is hoped that by this time he is ready to recognize that we do not debase the ideals by relating them to the stuffs so much as we dignify and ennoble the stuffs by relating them to the ideals.

EMERGENCY RESPONSES: INSTINCTIVE BEHAVIOR

Examples

The living organism is set into action not only by the internal conditions of an upset equilibrium but also by certain extra-organic conditions. Our treatment of human or animal motivation would be oversimplified indeed if we were to neglect the fact that, regardless of where his energies come from, the arousal of those energies is often by environmental agents — by animals and people around him, and occasionally by inanimate forces as well.

(A) At the sounds of the approaching tiger the cobra reared its head. Its neck spread to a widened hood as it faced those gleaming eyes of the terror of the jungle; while the cat on his part, startled by this small but sudden sight, halted the advancing paw while yet midair.

(B) Then when the captive Christian maiden beheld her lover's form bound between the horns of the beast that was being goaded into the arena, she tore herself loose from her jailors to fall prostrate again at the feet of the praetor.

(C) Outside it was raining. Inside all was still, with that stillness that presses on one's eardrums. Then — he heard it. Again. Again. His long hour of tense waiting was not to be fruitless. For though the eye could make out nothing, the ear took in every creak and crackle of those stairs. Nearer! Then, it was too much: with a hoarse cry he stumbled frantically for the door.

(D) When darkness came the aged parents crept their toilsome way up the hill. With infinite pain in their aching arms they raised the scythe together and cut slowly through the gallows rope that had been holding the form aloft. Then, trundling the precious burden down to the village churchyard, they gave it decent burial in God's own sacred half-acre.

(E) "You leave him 'lone!" But again the new little boy pushed Jimmy into the mud. With one full sweep she caught the bully's sleeve and threw him to the ground.

(*F*) To see the new baby nestled and fondled in the arms that had been his was too much for Tim's sensitive soul. He looked askance, he hung aloof; then with no premeditation or design he pulled the baby's toe and pinched its nose and made a spitting sound right in its face.

(*G*) As the ship's deck sunk lower in the washing lashing water the bewildered Tony made one more fighting dash for a place in the lifeboat.

(*H*) With each fresh flash of lightning the ward patients cowered further into their corners.

(*I*) With each fresh crash of china from the kitchen the merry guests grew bolder in their jests.

Life is full of incidents like these, incidents in which the organism is galvanized into action of one or another sort, not by any internal metabolic deficit but by some displacement in the external environment, some turn in outward events. The organism is caught unprepared in some way. And it reacts more or less appropriately — if we employ the word broadly — to an *emergency*.

Some Terms

We can try to classify a few of these externally excited kinds of behavior:

CHARACTER OF SITUATION	BEHAVIOR AROUSED
sudden; strange	startle
dangerous; pain-inflicting	escaping or defending
obstructing; pain-inflicting; retreating	attacking
tension releasing; incongruous	laughter
aloneness	restless going to and fro
novelty and movement	attentive regarding

But to essay a complete list of native responses to emergencies would be unscientific. For to draw sharp demarcation lines would be to ignore the vagueness and imperfection in many of nature's provisions for the adjustment of the organism to the surrounding world. While most of the response patterns are more or less distinguishable, they do overlap in respect either of their excitant stimuli or of the details of the aroused activity. A number of lists have been attempted, some basing their classification on the ends or objectives or purposes of the behaviors [8], some emphasizing the emotional experiences attending the behaviors [11], others less concerned with classifying and more with straightforward concrete reporting of the many ways in which humans and animals are aroused by environmental agents [25, 28].

The term *instincts* had formerly been assigned to these phenomena of animal and human life; but as it came to be used more glibly and less scientifically, it acquired the connotation of little daemons or agents or jack-in-the-boxes called into play by the key-pressing punches of environment. Recently the term in its adjective form, *instinctive*, has returned to scientific favor. There will be no harm, then, in speaking of those modes of behavior which we are considering in this section as *instinctive* types of behavior, so long as we never reify, or objectify, the idea by converting the adjective into a noun, thus making a purely descriptive term do duty as an explanation. For example, if we state that the child is instinctively frightened by a sudden loud noise, that is an acceptable description; but to state that the child *has* an instinct of fear, or jumps *because of* the fear instinct in him, is meaningless.

Many instinctive forms of response — as we may now call them — are complex on the physiological side. The raging person shows a racing heart and widened eyes and upset digestion. Now that, in both popular and scientific phrase, is *emotion*. It would be sound enough for us to call the different types of response to external exciting things by the name of emotions: the emotion of startle, the emotion of fear, the emotion of anger, of amusement, of curiosity, and so on. And in a later chapter we shall do just that, for then we shall want to examine experiential aspects (that is, how they "feel") and also to identify the most prominent types. Here, however, let us content ourselves with one classic illustration.

Cannon [3] pointed out how certain situations, particularly those of potential danger, throw the organism into an *emergency* pattern of total reaction. As the animal or person prepares to spring or flee, a number of physiological changes occur, all in support of the muscles about to do the springing or fleeing. The bulk of the blood supply is diverted from deeper organs to bring to the muscles augmented supplies of the energy-furnishing sugar now also being secreted into the blood by internal glands; and even the nature of the blood itself changes, the better to support the muscle and to repair skin damage. (This interesting story is presented in more detail on pages 299 and 326.) In Cannon's phrase, the animal or person now goes on a war footing. This is total war!

Overlapping Effects of Internal Needs and External Excitants. We must be careful not to force our treatment of human nature into oversimplified molds. Some behavior is motivated by both physiological needs and external seen, heard, smelled, or "felt" stimulus-patterns. Sex behavior is a clear case.

Emotional Participation in Energizing

Perhaps the reader is ready to remonstrate: If we are interested in activity, why not go where we find it at highest pitch — in a person or animal who "rips and tears and screams and rares"? Why not take him when he is excited? We know from common everyday observation that a man's behavior is never so vigorous as when he is "worked up." It is then that he slams doors instead of quietly closing them in his usual manner. It is then that his words are loud-spoken or even replaced by cries and screams. He runs, not like a rabbit but like a frightened rabbit; he charges, not like a bull but like a maddened bull. And much so-called "practical psychology" is devoted to exploiting the motivational efficiency of goad and gadfly, caffeine and heroin, rest and air cures. The ancients recognized well enough these energizing effects: *quamlibet infirmas adjuvat ira manus* (anger assists the hands however weak); *furor arma ministrat* (rage supplies weapons); and *pedibus timor addidit alas* (fear gave wings to his feet).

But there is another well-recognized effect that emotional conditions may have on outward behavior.

> Desponding fear, of feeble fancies full,
> Weak and unmanly, loosens every power.

The paralyzing effect of some fears that flesh is heir to, the enormous weighting down of him that is beset by grief, the slothfulness that peaceful comfort often breeds — such cases can be multiplied a hundredfold. A stomach distended with a heavy dinner, a skin submitted to a warm bath, a severely injured skin or other tissue, a fatigued muscle — each in its own way is likely to set up visceral changes that produce some emotional inhibition or depression of overt behavior.

We must, then, bring into line with our survey of energetics those more diffuse conditions of a person's viscera that lead not only to increased vigor in his overt activity (*emotional reenforcement*) but also to sluggishness and quiescence (*emotional inhibition*). In Figure 43 an attempt is made to suggest the manner in which these emotional segments of a man's total response play an important intermediate role between the original stimulus and the skeletal segments of the response that is made. A stimulus, external or internal ($S_{e \text{ or } i}$), may excite not only the more overt response segments involving skeletal musculature (R_s) but also visceral response segments of smooth musculature and glands (R_v). These visceral changes may in turn set up stimulations (S_v) that strengthen ($+$) or weaken ($-$) the overt response. For example, pain ($S_{e \text{ or } i}$) excites withdrawal movements (R_s) but also at times rage (excitement) (R_v), which in turn reenforces (S_v+) the withdrawing movements.   Receipt of bad news (S_e) evokes not only such actions as talking and writing (R_s) but also grieving (a depressed visceral condition, R_v), which in turn slows down and weakens (S_v-) the overt talking and writing.   The effect of visceral conditions upon overt behavior is not always exercised over neural pathways but is sometimes a more direct chemical effect through the blood stream (*e.g.*, see pages 297 ff.).

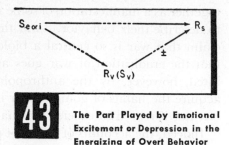

43 **The Part Played by Emotional Excitement or Depression in the Energizing of Overt Behavior**

(Explanation in text.)

As Spinoza wrote in 1665, "by emotion we mean the modifications of the body by which the body's power of acting is increased or diminished, assisted or restrained, and also the consciousness of these modifications."   But further description and analysis at this point is unwise. The emotional phases of human life are so subtle, so complex, so variable, that we shall wish to devote a special chapter to the topic (Chapter 9).

SOME UNIVERSAL HUMAN HABITS: COENOTROPES [1]

So far we have been examining behavior motives that are inborn and unlearned, that are primarily biological.   To clear the ground, we should note that human beings in many ways of living and acting reveal the operation of other motives which are ordinarily supposed to be native but which in reality are learned.   These coenotropes are *forms of learnea behavior that are common to all men because of commonly shared environmental features.*   For example, all men are exposed to weather hazards, and practically all have learned to protect the skin with some sort of clothing and housing; we should, then, speak of clothing and building (universal) habits, rather than of instinctive "clothing" or "home-building drives." Again, all men get hungry, and in the course of trial-and-error they learn to relieve their hunger by catching and eating animals, birds, and fish. It is not necessary to assume that they act on an inborn "hunting impulse" or "fishing impulse."   And in the scramble for sustenance in a country with limited food supply and seasonal famine, men are forced to store up their meat and roots and nuts; but they do not thereby show

[1] From the Greek κοινος meaning "common" and τροπος, "habit."   The term was suggested first by Smith and Guthrie [22].   Its usefulness deserves a wider acceptance than it has received.

that they are urged by some "hoarding instinct." Furthermore, many species of animals and all men survive best if they live and work together, and accordingly they become gregarious; but to speak of their herding together as a manifestation of some native "gregarious instinct" is merely to describe their behavior. And finally one hears even high authorities claim that war is so central a biological fact in the "fighting instinct" that the eradication of war goes against human nature. They are refuted, however, by the anthropologists' observations that individuals acquire the habits of going to war if they are reared in certain societies, but not if reared in others (cf. Chapter 17).

Indeed, the accounts of different peoples of the earth by contemporary anthropologists is a good antidote to the overworked doctrine of inborn instincts. The biological contributions to psychology must not blind us to those aspects which are cultural and acquired. The recognition of coenotropes and of the role of learning prepares us to inquire further into motivation.

THE DEVELOPMENT AND ELABORATION OF MOTIVES

The Problem Stated

We have traced the original sources of the energizing of human behavior back to tissue demands in the organism. Energies generated within take the outward expression of motor activity, activity which is partly guided by the exteroceptive stimulation-patterns received from the world about. But if all human ideals and aspirations, plans, and purposes be sprung originally from such protoplasmic soil, what can have been the processes of their growth? At first blush it would seem a far cry from sensitive zones to filial devotion, from glandular secretion to romantic poetry, from circulatory changes to activity in politics, from sense organ reflexes to a planned tour of Europe.

Juxtaposed in this bald manner, such extremes taken from the whole range of interests of humankind may seem utterly foreign to each other; but between them lie all manner of intermediate degrees. If we read the genetic story of the child's development, we find that the primitive and immediate wants of the child-animal become gradually and progressively modified into the mature and sophisticated interests and aims of the civilized man.

To what extent is the activity of the human being patterned in the first place? This broad, general question is basic to all that follows. Let us present it concretely by taking one kind of behavior as observed in animals of different evolutionary levels.

Of all bodily appetites, it might be presumed that the sexual is the one most likely to point the organism toward its appropriate goal-objects and to awaken the particular behavior-pattern most adequate and suitable. This is, in fact, what has been found for white rats, both male and female. When a white rat reaches the age of puberty, it finds or is receptive to an appropriate member of the opposite sex, and its whole new pattern of activity is well integrated in such a degree that no previous experience is at all necessary for the complete performance, for this will appear complete in males reared in isolation [1]. The pattern of the copulatory performance is highly uniform for rats of the same genus, even though from genus to genus they differ considerably [17].

If now we turn to higher forms, on the road to man, these pictures of direction of an animal's motivated activity by the kind of drive that is operative become much less clear-cut. The rise of sexual activities in young chimpanzees and monkeys, for example, is much less clearly defined than in rats. A variety of elementary acts — acts that are frequently observed as parts of other organized series of responses, by the way — are only gradually organized into the sort of copulatory response usual in adults, and only by degrees become directed to members of the opposite sex and to those that are receptive. Moreover, this organization or integration seems to result from the animals' random play experiences rather than to be predetermined by any particular internal physiological factors or external stimuli; that is, learning rather than maturing is the key here.

In this connection, it will be of interest to note that Freud styled the human child "polymorphous perverse," that is, one in whom sexual interests are likely to assume a very great variety of forms and tendencies, with little or nothing predetermined about them. While not constituting evidence of experimental character, this observation by a deep student of human motivation is worth attention.

It is helpful to bear in mind the principle that the evolution of higher and higher forms of life is marked by increasing plasticity, or modifiability. As motivated behavior becomes more variable and plastic with progressively higher forms of life, so *in human behavior* we may assume *a minimum of biological determination and a maximum of capacity to change and modify the directions* of even one's most basic interests. We can state this concept in general neurological terms: What in the lower animals is a matter of complicated reflexes, in the higher animals and notably in man falls under the control of the cerebral cortex — from lower spinal and sub-cortical centers to the higher centers where readjustment and learning are possible.

Some Principles in the Development of Directions

As implied in the preceding paragraphs, the developing of a person's interests is a matter of his learning. Now, the process of learning is far from simple, as we shall see in Chapter 15. At this point, however, it will help us if we bear in mind two well-recognized characteristics of learning:

(I) When in the course of random activities a child (or other organism) happens to do something that eventuates in a better adjustment (such as removing an irritant from the skin or obtaining a bit of food), on later occasions he will tend to repeat this act more and more directly and effectively. This is known as the "trial-and-error" character of learning.

(II) When a child (or other organism) is making a definite response to a particular stimulus, any frequently accompanying stimulus is likely to be responded to in much the same way. This is known as the "associative" or the "conditioned" character of learning.

Through the discussions that follow, the reader should bear in mind these two aspects of all learning.

Principle I. An external stimulus becomes increasingly potent in arousing an organism's activity. The baby will feed when and only when he is hungry. Offer him breast or bottle or (later) candy or orange after he is sated, and you will get a refusal in no uncertain manner. But offer him the candy or orange a year or two later, and even if he has just told you he feels full from his dinner, he will fall upon the delicacy in a way that bespeaks not an internal need but a learned habit. Similarly in an adult's eating, certain foods (desserts) are reserved for the end of the meal on account of their potency to appeal even after the diner's intra-organic hunger demand is stilled.

When an infant's muscles are well rested we see random kicking and finger-working; when they have exercised much, we see a cessation of the activity and a lapse into sleep. But in the same person four years later activity is not started and stopped by muscular needs in a simple and direct way, for dolls and tin soldiers and the sights and sounds of playmates induce the child to continue his play long beyond the point of initial fatigue. Those things which have served to release his original internal tensions have acquired interest on their own account.

If the mother eases the baby's skin irritation by removing a pricking pin or loosening too-tight clothing, he shows such reflex behavior as smiling, gurgling, freer movements of the limbs, and unquestionable visceral changes of the smooth-running sort. And if the mother is frequently the agent that brings about this release, the mere sight of her face or touch of her ministering hands will come to excite this type of behavior. That is, the mother now has become a stimulus to the pattern of behavior called filial love.

Thus, things which have served to release internal tensions come to acquire interest (or what the psychoanalyst calls *cathexis*) on their own account. Caviar, Benedictine, Lucky Golds, a good mashie, a detective story — it would be an endless task to catalogue all the things that have acquired their interest for man from their original associations — however remote — with the satisfaction of his primary tissue demands.

Principle II a.   A mode of behavior that is excitable by a certain object or situation may become excitable by other associated objects or situations as well.

The baby who has acquired the habit of accepting and eating fruit or candy, whether hungry or not, will develop interest in circumstances associated with the fruit or candy — in the confectionary shop around the corner, in pennies that will buy the delicacies, in uncles who furnish the pennies. The way to a child's heart is through his stomach.

The child who has come to enjoy playing, regardless of fatigue or rest, gradually extends his interest to organized games, to recess periods and spring vacations, and other situations associated with play.

After learning to welcome the very sight or touch of mother or father or nurse, regardless of any physiological urge, the child will come to welcome innumerable accompanying things: their voices in the other room, their spoken names, nurse's beau, Mother's Day, Father's Day, and the like.

The interest in sex furnishes a rich field of associations. The restraining forces of civilization enhance the interest-exciting value of sights, odors, sounds, pictures, articles of clothing, music, and all sorts of things connected with the original sex object. The astonishingly subtle ramifications of these networks of associated interests furnish much of the raw material of psychoanalytic research.

The sucking response at first established to the nipple becomes elicitable by many another object that can be mouthed; and when the child is weaned too forcibly and suddenly, his mouthing response, now so strongly established, turns itself (so to speak) to any easily available substitute, and thumb-sucking is established.

Principle II b.   Words and other symbols come to play much the same stimulus role as the things they represent. For the child the mere sound of the word "candy" soon becomes a potent substitute for that class of objects which it frequently accompanies; and the adult makes more subtle connections between things and their symbols, as the marks on a telegraph blank or

```
                                        fixing radio
                 toys                   fixing auto_____   to be an
          ___ (mechanical) ____ fixing toys _____  "Popular          engineer
         /                              Science"
       ge/
     George
      /                                 athletics
     /                   playing ball   "Baseball         to be profess-
S₁ ─►R ─── toys ───────── with ──────── ─Magazine"─── ional athlete
(urge     Frank (ball)   neighbor boys  "American       coach
  to    \                                 Boy"           sports writer
muscular Pauline
activity) \                             patching up
           \                            playmates_____  to be trained
            \_ dolls _____ patching up _____ talk about       nurse
                             dolls              medicine
```

44 From Biological Urge to Occupational Ideal

A few selected steps in the development of interests out of one arbitrarily chosen tissue demand. The divergence of lines of development is due to differences in environmental opportunities and no doubt also to intrinsic differences in the three personalities. Further explanation is given in the text.

a word that is packed with associations.[1] Using the names for toys and games, learning the rules for counting out and for playing the game, telling riddles and solving puzzles, or being called into action by "Come play ball" or "Let's go swimming" — these are but a few illustrations of the motivating value of words. They grow so important with use that it is not surprising that names gain almost magical potency among some peoples. Primitive tribes have held that names are real and concrete things, often so sacred as to be unmentionable except in certain prescribed situations [21]. At the other extreme, the exploitation of names in modern advertising is familiar to us all; in one American metropolis a proud promoter has set his name in letters twelve feet high atop a tower so that it may be visible for miles around.

Illustrations

Rested musculature, in the absence of other strong internal or external stimuli, will awaken movement-play, which in infancy appears as finger-play. Taking this as one example of primitive drive, let us note some further developments that have appeared with different children in different situations, as noted by the writer. (Consult Figure 44.)

George, who especially enjoyed among his toys building-blocks and

---

[1] A dramatic illustration will be found in Figure 54, page 210, where it is shown that the profound emotional disturbance aroused in a Belgian woman in a London laboratory when she heard the noises of a German air raid occurred also on another day when she heard only the word "bombs" from the experimenter.

mechanical construction sets, developed manual activity interest in constructing miniature bridges and houses, and then in making new building supplies and new toys. This interest, strengthened and fixated, appeared in a later absorption in tearing up and reassembling old alarm clocks and various gadgets about the house. When permitted, he tinkered with the radio and the automobile. His reading turned to the popular science magazines. Eventually this interest determined his choice of the engineering profession.

Frank, playing much with balls and toys that call for romping activity, soon was looking to the day when he could play ball with the neighbor boys, then on to the day when he would participate in high-school athletics. The interest showed itself in its verbalized form: always it was the sporting page and the athletic magazines that he read by preference. And when the time came for choosing a career, he was already oriented in a general way; he planned to be a coach or athlete or sports writer.

Pauline, with dolls as her toys, chanced a few times to glue a broken arm or sew up a sawdust leak. The process of patching up, performed with gratifying results, became an established interest; and soon she was wrapping Susan's finger or dropping iodine on Jane's cut toe. Now she began to prick up her ears when conversations turned to medicine; and by her high-school days she was planning to train as a nurse.

In a study of interest-autobiographies, one appeared that corresponds closely to the last case.

> "As I advanced in the primary grades," reported a young woman, "I took to dolls. I enjoyed treating them for sickness, bandaging their wounds and breaks, and the thought came to me, it would be wonderful to be a nurse to help the sick, relieve them of their pain and suffering, offering them helping hands in their weakness; and after sharing this thought for some time, I was taken to the hospital where I remained for over a month, becoming more acquainted with a nurse's life and their duties. I just longed for their life; all my thoughts centered around the hospital and the sick. When I finished my sophomore year at high, I revealed my thoughts to my parents." [1]

Farfetched, these cases? They seem so only because the years are telescoped, for the processes described are identical in kind with those to be observed every day in pre-school, in school, on the playground. These illustrations, though suggested to the writer by three actual

[1] From D. Fryer, *The Measurement of Interests* (New York: Henry Holt and Company, 1931).

children he has observed, suffer by appearing too sketchy. Instead of five or six periods and crucial incidents there are literally thousands in any child's development. For another thing, the illustrations suffer by appearing too selected; for at any one of the periods named other basic drives play a part. The number of environmental factors in operation is certainly legion, and the chances of interests sprouting in other directions is high indeed. But it is hoped only that the illustrations will give concrete form to the principles enumerated for the development of directions.

Interests Become Complex: Sentiments or Attitudes

To McDougall we owe an insight into the structuring of motivated behavior by means of the concept of *sentiments*. Although this word is employed in many different ways in common parlance, he gave it the technical meaning of *a relatively permanent system of emotional dispositions toward some object, person, or idea.*

It was a favorite device of George M. Cohan to arrange some excuse for unfurling the American flag toward the end of the first act of nearly every play he staged. His canniness is readily understood: any typical American audience is made up of individuals who have established favorable emotional reactions whenever the Stars and Stripes are displayed, and such behavior enkindled in an audience will have an important effect upon their response to the play itself. This producer was capitalizing on a sentiment.

For an honor system to operate effectively on a college campus the individual student must be strongly disposed to react negatively to any infringement of a certain code of rules. He must possess the proper sentiment. Again, a slighting remark about Texas or South Carolina or Kansas may be a fighting word, for it is likely to awaken resentful behavior on the part of a native of the particular state; he has an enduring tendency to defend the state's name. So with the sentiments one develops toward Santa Claus and Christmas and the Glorious Fourth, or toward communism, one's church or lodge or political party, one's rival in business or love. All such concepts or symbols or objects are what they are because of the sentiments of the people concerned with them.

The important thing to note is that one's sentiment toward any of the objects or persons or ideas used for illustration above is in every case a *system* of dispositions. The national emblem will arouse joy or grief, resentment or camaraderie, *depending upon the circumstances* in which it is sighted. If the object of regard is one's rival in business or love, one chuckles at his discomfiture, is irritated by his friendliness, is envious of his achievements to the point of discounting them, and is ready to drink a boisterous toast if the fellow's fortunes go wrong. When a man has acquired the sentiment of love for a person or other object, he is apt to experience tender emotion in its presence, fear or anxiety when it is in danger, anger when it is threatened, sorrow when it is lost, joy when the object prospers or is restored to him, gratitude towards him who does good to it, and so on; and when he hates a person, he experiences fear or anger or both on his approach, joy when that other is injured, anger when he receives favors, gratitude to whoever in any way lowers his power [11].

The significance of sentiments in human life is tremendous. The organization of emotional reactions into habitual and integrated forms of activity furnishes stability in human behavior and human social relations, and molds a man's ways of loving and hating, his likes and dislikes in foods, dress, automobiles, and fiction, his loyalties and his cynicisms, into regular and consistent modes of behavior. His neighbors, family, office force, and club members can deal with him to some purpose because they know how he is likely to respond in almost any given circumstances. Character training, whether broadly or narrowly conceived, is a process of training desirable sentiments so that socially valuable rather than harmful behavior will be aroused by "whatsoever things are true, whatsoever things are honest, whatsoever things are just."

Attitudes. When one's (more or less) emotional disposition toward some object, person, or idea is considered less in terms of its emotional structure and more in terms of the kind of ultimate response to which it will lead, it has become common to apply the name *attitude.* Nowadays the term is being employed in a technical way to *an enduring acquired predisposition to react in a characteristic way, favorably or unfavorably, toward a given type of person, social group, or ideal.* These *pro* and *con* dispositions, as we may fairly call them, are of especial concern to the social scientist. He wants to learn, for example, whether a certain kind of college lecture course has any effect in making students more liberal or more conservative; whether the people of California are more prejudiced against the Japanese than against the Chinese; whether members of a Calvinist faith believe in infant damnation for man's original sin; whether individualists in dress are likely to be individualists in political thought; whether workmen react more loyally to a management that increases pay and decreases hours or to one that gives them voice in management and a slot-box for their complaints. To obtain data on such questions the social scientist employs the attitude-scale methods. Discussion of these as a technique, and of the allied public opinion polling methods, will be postponed to Chapter 17, "Social Behavior."

Like a habit, a person's attitude toward an object is acquired. (*a*) It may be a *residuum of many somewhat similar responses*, a result of cumulative experience operating by both individuation and integration. This is shown, for example, in the attitude toward honesty, which develops only gradually out of many specific cases of acting honestly, and even in later childhood has not yet become well generalized and unified (see pages 603 ff. below). Such was found also to be the case of many atheists who had reached their convictions gradually after months of reflections upon their readings in history and science. (*b*) Or the attitude may have been formed and fixated after *one dramatic experience*. This is true of a celebrated case in which an intense fright at a locomotive engine suffered by a child of two years who had wandered near the forbidden tracks, established in him a lifelong dread of locomotives, which had become for him avenging gods; and this in spite of his insight and better judgment. (*c*) Or again, the attitude may have been *adopted ready-made*, taken over from one's associates. This is illustrated by the white child who himself has no prejudice against or dislike for Negroes until after he has seen and heard people poke fun at the polysyllabic utterances, the shuffling gait, or the superstitions of Sambo.

Attitudes and Hasty Judgments: Stereotypes

Attitudes established in extreme form are called *stereotypes*. People are feeling and thinking in stereotyped ways when they show fixed attitudes of acceptance or aversion toward mere names or labels. In an undiscriminating manner they pre-judge new persons or things merely according to the name or label. Stereotypes play an important role in social psychology.

If a man has heard the mere names "Republican" or "Negro" or "bloated bondholder" or "professor" used often enough in one consistent prejudiced and partisan way, he will be a remarkable man indeed if he does not soon get rooted within him reaction-tendencies toward such labels, and of such strength that thereafter, upon meeting a Republican or Negro or capitalist or professor he will unthinkingly and as a matter of course treat that individual according to his preconceived pattern.

As we shall see upon closer analysis of emotional behavior in a chapter to follow, one can learn to become afraid or unafraid of this object or that if one's associates are afraid or are unafraid; moreover, one will then come to show the same response to the mere name and mention of the thing. What is more, a person learns to become afraid of, or resentful toward, or enthusiastic about, mere symbols, names, tags, applied to things he has never seen nor expects to see, if only the other people he meets daily and the printed matter he reads daily reveal that fear or resentment or enthusiasm, for early in life he has established the habit of doing much as other people do.

This fact is sometimes exploited by certain members of the public press. A comparison was once made between the terms and labels employed in publishing the same news stories in two metropolitan newspapers [20]. Where the *New York Times* used such words as those appearing in the left-hand column of Table XIV, the *Chicago Tribune* for the very same items used the words to be read in the right-hand column. What one paper calls a "senate investigation" the other dubs "government witch hunting," and what the former names "home relief" the latter terms "the dole." As a test with sixty college students proved, the words which the *Tribune* was given to using were such as to touch off emotional attitudes: they were stereotypes. And the accounts appeared on the news pages, not in the editorial columns!

The hamstringing effect of stereotypes is well shown negatively by a Jew's explanation of how he survived two Nazi concentration camps. He kept out of his mind the Gestapo stereotype of "*the* Jew" so that his conduct was not influenced by it; nor did he allow himself to regard any of his guards in terms of the stereotype of "*the* Gestapoman." Consequently he succeeded in creating an interpersonal situation in which one individual, a Gestapoman, dealt with one individual, a Jew; and the Gestapoman, freed of compulsion from stereotypes, could use his own judgment and common sense [2].[1]

Hierarchies of Motives Appear: Value Areas

From the inventory (in the first part of this chapter) of the modes in which the human organism is impelled to action and the analysis of how these activations change, we realize that motivations are many and varied and even incompatible. Any person, any organism, would be distraught and utterly ineffective if there were no organization among his many impulses. Hence one way of telling the psychological story of human life is to highlight the incidents through which one interest gives

[1] The exercise in Chapter 5 on the judging of nationalities from photographs brings out the errors that follow too ready a reliance on stereotypes of what a Cuban or a Swede or a Canadian must look like because of his national classification label.

TABLE XIV	Comparison of Terms Used by the "New York Times" and Those Used in the Same Series by the "Chicago Tribune"

"New York Times"	"Chicago Tribune"
Progressive	Radical
Senate investigation	Government witch hunting
Regulation	Regimentation
Maritime leader	Communist C.I.O. leader
Labor organizer	Labor agitator
Home relief	The dole
Crop control	Farm dictatorship
Nonstrikers	Loyal workers
Investigator	Inquisitor
C.I.O. Chieftain	C.I.O. Dictator
Foreign	Alien
Picketing	Mass picketing

From S. S. Sargent, SOCIOMETRY, 1939, 2, 74.

place to another, so that in the course of months and years priorities are set up, hierarchies established. The two-year-old may quite naturally snatch a toy from another child; but in a ten-year-old such an impulse will be promptly sidetracked by other impulses. As a ten-year-old, John may look upon the life of a big leaguer who bats .300 as the highest of callings; but by the time he is sixteen, that ideal is likely to have been superseded by awesome regard for the industrialist or the professional man. Let us try to set up a few of the principles by which one's values come to assume relations of dominance and subordination.[1]

(1) With increasing knowledge and intelligence, the more remote objectives assume priority over the more immediate. Thus, nearly any college senior who receives the offer of an enticing job is likely to turn it down to stay on and complete his college program, in the hope of a still better job and a better claim to being called an "educated man" after graduation.

(2) The demands of the group tend to supersede the demands of the individual. In the very process of learning to live and let live among others, the individual is subjected to the controls of the group, and he learns to give them precedence. The "mores" come to have a "moral" control over him.

[1] For a different treatment of hierarchies, see A. H. Maslow, "A Theory of Human Motivation," Psychol. Rev., 1943, 50, 370–96.

(3) When an individual sets up an important objective, other interests are likely to be sorted into those that advance and those that hinder the attainment of the objective. Attending weeknight dances at the Country Club is an acceptable pleasure unless it interferes with one's fitness for work on the mornings after.

There are, of course, exceptional occasions when these acquired relations of dominance and subordination break down. Basic biological needs, when seriously threatened, seize the right of way. The drowning man clutches his rescuer with a lethal hold, or the loyal member of the Underground groans out the names of his confederates to halt the agonies of his torture.

A person may be said to possess an integrated personality to the extent that his motives are self-consistent, non-conflicting, and therefore ordered into a system of prepotencies and priorities. But never, short of extreme cases of paranoia, are all of a person's interests subordinated into one hierarchy. To have a number of independent interests and to be able to shift from one to another — from business to music to gardening to love to politics — has always been recognized as contributory to mental health.

In the history of human culture, the primitive acceptance-rejection acts and attitudes toward "good" and "bad" in vague and general ways have come to be differentiated reactions to situations as ethically good or bad, esthetically good or bad (beautiful or ugly), intellectually good or bad (true or false), economically good or bad, and so forth. Different human societies have been marked by the extent to which they have made judgments in one or another of these ways; the esthetic and intellectual predominated in Athenian Greece, the political in Rome, the religious in medieval Europe, the economic and political in modern Europe, the ethical in Scottish and other Northern peoples, and so on. Individual men, too, are marked in history by their major values.

This many-sidedness of the evaluating attitude of man reveals itself in another way. When looking at a wedding ring, for instance, one may regard it as made of fourteen-carat gold (theoretical or factual), as worth probably twenty-five dollars on the market (economic), as a badge of love and loyalty (social), as a symbol of rights and duties (political), as an emblem having sacred significance (religious), or as an example of metalcraft (esthetic).

A test has been devised [27] for determining the relative strength within an individual of these six classes of valuing attitudes.[1] It consists

---

[1] The scale was suggested by the classification by Spranger in his *Types of Men*, but does not follow his theoretical and speculative tenets.

of questions like the following (arbitrary answers are given here to clarify the method):

> The main object of scientific research should be the discovery   (a)   (b)
> of pure truth rather than its practical applications.
> (a) Yes; (b) No.   3   0
>
> [answers numbered according to relative importance on a scale of 3]
> If you should marry do you prefer a wife who
> ..4..can achieve social prestige, commanding admiration from others;
> ..1..likes to stay home and keep house;
> ..2..is fundamentally spiritual in her attitude toward life;
> ..3..is gifted along artistic lines.
>
> [answers numbered in order of preference]

This test has brought to light some interesting differences between sexes, between people of different occupations, between students at different colleges, and between students of differing cultural backgrounds; and it has checked well with tests of newspaper reading, with examinees' statements of qualities attributed to ideal persons, and their statements of qualities attributed to leaders.

THE EGO AS A CENTER OF MOTIVE ORGANIZATION

A Self-Reference Comes to the Surface

"A poor song, my lord, but mine own." Launcelot was simply recognizing and making explicit the self-implication that is found in most of man's motivated activity. As we have seen (page 81), the maturing infant gradually learns to differentiate between self and not-self. Many of the biographical studies of infant development that form the historical background for child psychology[1] include notes that assemble themselves into a coherent account of the process; and it has been confirmed in modern child laboratories.

(1) The movements of the newborn baby, the stirrings of head and wavings about of arms and legs, bring him into contact with physically resistant objects. The touch of cribside, rattle, breast, nurse's hands, tight garments, and the like, provide sensory stimulations, especially when pain receptors are excited. Free movement, then, must be disciplined. And this control aspect of the experience is the basis of the awakening sense of objectivity. Things are real because and if we bump into them.

(2) At the same time the active muscles are returning their own kind

---

[1] By Preyer, Shinn, Moore, Piaget, and others.

of afferent impulses; and the child is gaining those kinesthetic experiences which experimentalists have found to be the necessary matrix out of which voluntary action is to arise. Here then, by contrast with the tactual experiences, is the soil from which a realization of oneself is to grow. *We* are real because and if we experience ourselves to be much in motion.

(3) The ever-active going concern we call a baby now seeks sensory stimulation on his own. His self-perception is enriched by the initiative character of his explorations. We come to appreciate ourselves as agents because and if we *make* motion.

(4) A social factor enters to heighten these effects, as the attentive parents and solicitous sister and brother play up to the baby by applauding each accomplishment and paying him court by the hour.

(5) The perception of self or ego is not a sudden discovery, as is indicated by the way the child of two will speak of himself in the third person: "Give George ball," "Billy hungry." And the differentiation between the centermost ego and the body which appertains to it comes about slowly, as shown by the little girl who after a too-sudden sitting arose with hand on backsides and the remark, "My self hurts."

But of more interest to us here than the development of intellectual apprehension of self is the motivational side of the story. As Freud has so well put it, the infant in its first months is *narcissistic*. Like the mythological youth, Narcissus, who was enamored of his own image mirrored in the pool, the human baby shows only self-love. First his organic needs and later his desires impel him to satisfy only them. Naturally, then, he seeks only his own pleasures. This "ego-involved" character is thenceforth to be traced through most of his later interests and motives [21].

With advance in intelligence and increased opportunities for observing others and oneself in similar situations, some appreciation of others ripens. (*A*) In Billy's first days at the nursery school the cries and other outward aspects of distress in another child Joe may at first cause Billy merely to stare: he may not "see" the distress or the situation which causes it, for only the sounds and sights as such draw his attention. The other child might as well be a mechanical Judy. (*B*) His curiosity aroused, however, Billy comments on the other child's dramatic behavior, asks us about it, or asks the child. Then (*C*) as he comes to realize that other children are sentient like himself, active sympathy appears [14]. He is now in a social world; and there are other interests and wants besides his own. Contrasts and conflicts appear between the urgings of his own nature and play motives and those of others. The lifelong question whether to cater to one's own or others' desires and needs is now opening up.

The Ego Is Not the Physical Body: Identification

The ego or self is an elastic concept. This is well shown by the attitudes that develop when individuals are thrown into closely-bound collective action. The individual person comes to identify himself with the others, not by losing himself in them, really, but by absorbing them into himself. The phenomenon was widely noted during the recent war in small compact ground units as well as in submarine and airplane crews. Psychiatrists observing the latter have written:

> It is an interesting fact that, although the members of combat crews are thrown together only by chance, they rapidly become united to each other by the strongest bonds while in combat. The character of these bonds is of the greatest significance in determining their ability to withstand the stresses of the combat situation. . . .
>
> All members of the crew are dependent upon each other to an unusual degree. Day after day, on mission after mission, this mutual dependence is made to pay dividends in safety and effectiveness of the combat crew. It is no wonder then that the emotional relationships between these fliers assume a special character. The men and their plane become identified with each other with an intensity that in civil life is found only within the family circle. Crew members habitually refer to each other as "my pilot," "my bombardier," "my gunner," and so on, and their feeling for their plane is equally strong, since its strength and reliability are as important as those of any human members of the crew. . . .
>
> In truth, they are brothers-in-arms in more than a figurative sense. They actually feel toward each other as if they were brothers. It is a very common thing to hear a flier say of his buddy, "He reminds me of my brother" or "I felt closer to him than to my own brother." [1]

Levels of Aspiration

The degree of his self-esteem certainly has much to do with a person's interests and endeavors. If it is true that some of his keenest interests get their keenness from being supported by his self-regard, then it becomes a matter of scientific inquiry to attempt to measure that self-regard and to identify factors that affect it. One expression of ego-supported motivation is to be found in the phenomenon that the human being is continuously setting himself higher goals of achievement. No sooner does he succeed in reaching an objective toward which he has

[1] From R. R. Grinker and J. P. Spiegel, *Men under Stress* (Philadelphia: Blakiston, 1945). By permission of the publishers.

striven than he aspires to another on yet higher level. As Robert Browning put it:

> Ah, but a man's reach should exceed his grasp,
> Or what's a heaven for?

A psychological attack on the question has taken the form of experiments upon one's level of aspiration. The general experimental design is simple. The subject is given a series of tasks, such as placing rings on fast-moving hooks, throwing darts at a target, pitching quoits, canceling out certain letters, giving synonyms, adding examples, or substituting digits for symbols. A number of trials is run. After each trial he is informed of the score he made (or this score treated by elaborate statistical procedures), and he is then asked to state what score he expects to make on his next trial.

Example: He is throwing a dart at a target with a bull's-eye score of 10, and on learning that he scores 7, he says that he is going to try to score 8, but makes only a 6. What will he set as the level to which he will aspire in the next trial? Will he lower it, or will he keep it the same, or even raise it? Suppose, however, he was informed that his score was 8, not 6. How high will his next aim be? All investigators recognize that this situation affords a favorable opportunity for spotting traits of individuals that bear upon their self-regard (ego-level) and also upon their purposiveness (goal-behavior).

For one thing, would we suppose that all subjects make careful impersonal judgments of what they are most likely to score the next time based upon their information about their preceding scores; or would some of them be led by their emotional reactions — especially their sensitive concern over their personal status in the group — to make wilder estimates? A few of the variables that have had some experimental attention are worth noticing. (As the findings are sometimes not decisive, and sometimes too complicated for simple statement, we shall do best simply to gain some appreciation of the rich possibilities of application by mentioning the problems only [5].)

Is one's level of achievement on one task likely to affect his level of aspiration on another task?

Are children who are successful in their school work likely to set up different goals in this experiment than do those who are less successful?

Is one's level of aspiration related in any way to his general attitude of security or insecurity?

Is it related to the degree to which he is satisfied-dissatisfied with his ego-status in his group?

Is it raised or lowered when his performances are compared with those of a racial group often superior to his?

Will a partner who does not participate in the task but merely makes judgments as to the probable achievements of his active partner be likely to set them at the same levels?

Can this procedure be turned into a test for use with manic-depressive patients?

A factor not adequately recognized in the earlier studies is the way the formulated instructions he has received will influence the subject's manner of making his estimates.   One subject's estimates will be based upon careful factual appraisal of his previous performances.   These are "realistic" aspirations.   Another subject's will be based upon his hopes, wishes, fears, and such emotional factors.   These are "irrealistic" aspirations.   Either attitude can be established by instructing the subject "to make a cool intellectual appraisal of what he actually will achieve," or on the other hand, "to state what he thinks maybe he could make if he is in particularly good form, or is lucky."   Table XV reveals the outcome of an experiment in which the task set was throwing darts at a target. ·It confirms what was probably the reader's guess.

DIRECTIONS OF INTEREST

Changes of Interest with Age

From our knowledge of the physical maturation of the child, we should infer just what we observe in daily life — that as one grows older his directions of interests and values show changes that are both quantitative and qualitative.   One's interests at any time are legion; but it is possible to group some of them and so to observe their fate in the average man's life history.

TABLE

XV

Mean Levels of Aspiration as Set Up by Subjects on Realistic and Irrealistic Bases

(Two groups were studied independently)

Nature of the Aspiration	Experimenter I	Experimenter II
Expectation (realistic)	82.5	80.0
Hope (irrealistic)	116.9	101.5

From M. G. Preston, A. Spiers, and J. Trasoff, "On Certain Conditions Controlling the Realism and Irrealism of Aspirations," J. Exp. Psychol., 1947, 37, 48–58.

Students from the sixth grade through college were asked to check on a long list of recreations and amusements those in which they had some interest and to double-check those of pronounced interest. A total count of the checks by the one hundred students (combining in this way both the number of students interested and the intensity of their interest) was made within each of several interest-groupings. These are shown for the two sexes at each grade-age in Figure 45. Some understanding of the descending and the ascending curves is helped by reducing the interests to more basic biological age changes. The young child is muscularly active; but as he matures through the years of puberty, sex-based motives come to the fore.

Equally instructive are the changes that interests undergo during later years of life. Data were obtained from 2340 men between the ages of twenty and sixty years by Strong on his Vocational Interest Blank (described below). From the very many items of wide range, a few

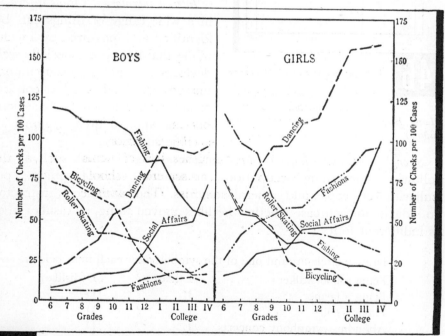

45

Changes in Certain Interests with Age

Shown by number of checks for each interest per 100 students at each grade from the sixth through college. Students were directed to check items in which they were interested, and double-check those in which they were very much interested. Data from 4187 cases. (*From S. L. Pressey, J. E. Janney, and R. G. Kuhlen,* Life: A Psychological Survey, *Harper, 1939. By permission of authors and publishers.*)

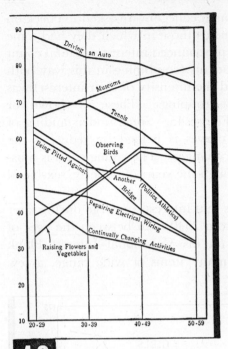

are selected for presentation in Figure 46. Comparison of the trends represented by the different curves suggests that with increasing age men take less to recreations that involve muscular activity, and less also to those involving personal competition; more to those of sedentary, observing, and contemplative character.

SOME WAYS OF MEASURING MOTIVES

Methods of impression are to be described elsewhere, on pages 225 ff. below.

Interest Inventories. One's interests in a wide range of things can be identified and measured by a technique that has been especially well developed to aid in occupational diagnosis and advice. It consists of an elaborate set of questions bearing upon a great number of specific situations.

46 Changes in Interests of Older Men

(From Pressey, Janney, and Kuhlen, Life: A Psychological Survey, *Harper, 1939. By permission of authors and publishers.)*

Strong's Vocational Interest Blank furnishes lists of items such as the following, concerning occupations, amusements, school subjects, peculiarities of people, and general activities. The examinee is instructed to indicate in each case whether he likes a given thing, or dislikes it, or is indifferent to it.

Draw a circle around one of the symbols after each item below:

Being a floorwalker	L(like)	?	D(dislike)
Being a farmer	L	?	D
Playing golf	L	?	D
Attending symphony concerts	L	?	D
Reading *New Republic*	L	?	D
Cowboy movies	L	?	D
Studying geography	L	?	D
Studying algebra	L	?	D
Repairing a clock	L	?	D
Acting as cheer leader	L	?	D

Looking at shop windows	L	?	D
People with gold teeth	L	?	D
Religious people	L	?	D

If the examiner wants to know whether or not his subject has the interests presumably fitting him for the engineering profession, his responses on the blank are compared with the responses previously obtained for many successful engineers, by means of a specially scored reference stencil. If the subject's interest fitness for ministerial or medical or legal or life insurance or many other occupations is in question, his responses are checked against the scores made by successful men in each.

The Kuder Preference Record is somewhat different in choice and arrangement of items. One form appears as follows:

Each question in the booklet consists of a description of two activities. These activities are numbered *1* and *2*, and are followed at the right by two small enclosed spaces which are also numbered *1* and *2*. Indicate which one of the activities you would ordinarily prefer by blackening the space corresponding in number to the activity you have chosen.

In the example below, the person marking the pairs has blackened space *1* for Question A to indicate that he would usually rather go to a movie than attend a symphony concert. In Question B, he has blackened space *2* to show that he would prefer to play a musical instrument at home to going to an amusement park. In Question C, by blackening space *1*, he has shown that he would rather take a photograph of a champion swimmer than take a photograph of a table he would like to make.

EXAMPLE

Put your answers in column *0*

O

A. (1) Go to a movie
    (2) Attend a symphony concert   1   2   A

B. (1) Go to an amusement park
    (2) Play a musical instrument at home   1   2   B

C. (1) Take a photograph of a champion swimmer
    (2) Take a photograph of a table you would like to make   1   2   C

Some of the activities named involve a certain amount of preparation. In such cases, indicate the activity you would prefer if you could first have the necessary training and experience in both activities named.

In some cases you may find that you like both activities very much; in other cases, you may find both unpleasant. In each pair, however, be sure to indicate which activity you would prefer *if you had to choose one or the other*.

(The pencil-blackening of a numbered space is done to make fast machine scoring possible. The graphite furnishes a short circuit between two electrodes pressed against the paper at the two ends of the space for "correct" answers; and the computing part of the machine registers and totals the "corrects" on the whole blank at one time.)

Looking Forward

Resorting to the somewhat forced metaphor of the mechanical engine, we have provisionally drawn a contrast between the mechanisms — its cranks and wheels and piston rods — and the driving energies that make it go — derived from coal or electricity or water power. In the present chapter we first directed our attention particularly to the latter aspect of man and animal. But we found animate things far more than mechanical engines: they are energized not simply by materials stoked into them from without but much more by the much subtler processes expressing the equilibrating, self-regulating functions of the living organism. What has been rather poetically named the "will to live" is seen in homeostatic processes on the inside and adjustmental processes toward the environment on the outside — though that distinction is not a clear-cut one.

Through the chapter we have traced some features of the development of this motivating of the organism, from raw tissue needs to man's highest and holiest values, as the individual matures biologically and as his experiences of living among people multiply. We have not, however, taken much note of what happens when the person finds his motivated behavior blocked and frustrated, or when he is caught in a contest and conflict between some of his different motives. Since so much of human life that is interesting, dramatic, and downright important centers about such interferences, and since so much about an individual's personality is revealed by the ways in which he meets them, we can well afford to devote a special chapter to outlining some personal problems of motivation.

REFERENCES

1. Beach, F. A. "Comparison of copulatory behavior of male rats raised in isolation, cohabitation, and segregation," *J. Genet. Psychol.*, 1942, *60*, 121–136.
2. Bettelheim, B. "The dynamism of anti-Semitism in Gentile and Jew," *J. Abn. Soc. Psychol.*, 1947, *42*, 153–168.
3. Cannon, W. B. *Bodily Changes in Pain, Hunger, Fear, and Rage.* Second edition. New York: Appleton-Century-Crofts, 1929.

4. Davis, C. M. "Results of the self-selection of diets by young children," *Canadian Med. Assn. J.*, 1939, N.S. *41*, 257–261.

5. Frank, J. D. "Recent studies of the level of aspiration," *Psychol. Bull.*, 1941, *38*, 218–226.

6. Freeman, G. L. *The Energetics of Human Behavior.* Ithaca, N.Y.: Cornell University Press, 1948.

7. Holt, E. B. *Animal Drive and the Learning Process.* Holt, 1931.

8. Kirkpatrick, E. A. *Fundamentals of Child Study.* Second edition. New York: The Macmillan Company, 1917.

9. Kuder, G. F. *Preference Record.* Chicago: Science Research Associates.

10. Lashley, K. S. "Experimental analysis of instinctive behavior," *Psychol. Rev.*, 1938, *45*, 445–471.

11. McDougall, W. *An Introduction to Social Psychology.* Second edition. Boston: Luce, 1909.

12. Maslow, A. H. "A theory of human motivation," *Psychol. Rev.*, 1943, *50*, 370–396.

13. Morgan, C. T. *Physiological Psychology.* New York: McGraw-Hill Book Company, 1943.

14. Murphy, L. B. *Social Behavior and Child Personality.* New York: Columbia University Press, 1937.

15. Pressey, S. L., J. E. Janney, and R. G. Kuhlen. *Life: A Psychological Survey.* New York: Harper and Brothers, 1939.

16. Preston, M. G., A. Spiers, and J. Trasoff, "On certain conditions controlling the realism and irrealism of aspirations," *J. Exp. Psychol.*, 1947, *37*, 18–58.

17. Reed, C. A. "The copulatory behavior of small mammals," *J. Comp. Psychol.*, 1946, *39*, 185–206.

18. Richter, C. P. "The internal environment and behavior: V. Internal secretions," *Amer. J. Psychiat.*, 1941, *97*, 878–893.

19. Richter, C. P. "Total self-regulatory functions in animals and human beings," *Harvey Lectures*, 1942–43, *38*, 63–103.

20. Sargent, S. S. "Emotional stereotypes in the *Chicago Tribune*," *Sociometry*, 1939, *2*, 69–75.

21. Sherif, M., and H. Cantril. *The Psychology of Ego-Involvements.* New York: John Wiley and Sons, 1947.

22. Smith, S., and E. R. Guthrie. *General Psychology in Terms of Behavior.* New York: Appleton-Century-Crofts, 1924.

23. Strong, E. K. *Changes of Interests with Age.* Stanford University, Calif.: Stanford University Press, 1931.

24. Strong, E. K. *Vocational Interest Blank.* Stanford University, Calif.: Stanford University Press.

25. Thorndike, E. L. *Educational Psychology: I. The Original Nature of Man.* New York: Teachers College, Columbia University, 1913.

26. Thurstone, L. L., and E. J. Chave. *The Measurement of Attitude.* Chicago: University of Chicago Press, 1929.

27. Vernon, P. E., and G. W. Allport. "A test for personal values," *J. Abn. Soc. Psychol.*, 1931, *26*, 231–248.

28. Watson, J. B. *Behavior: An Introduction to Comparative Psychology.* New York: Henry Holt and Company, 1914.

29. Young, P. T. *Motivation of Behavior.* New York: John Wiley and Sons, 1936.

30. Young, P. T. "Studies of food preference, appetite, and dietary habit. II," *J. Comp. Psychol.*, 1944, *37*, 371–391.

PERSONAL PROBLEMS

OF MOTIVATION

8

INTRODUCTION: SOME CLINICAL CASES

WHAT are some of the personal problems that frequently beset the college student? A typical psychological clinic has been established at the University of Missouri as part of the Student Health Service. All case records are kept strictly confidential. The students are encouraged to use the services of the clinic, and they do so. Below are thumbnail sketches of a few typical cases.

(*A*) The sorority wanted to depledge this girl because her behavior was annoying and her conduct not becoming. She couldn't get along with the other girls, refused to cooperate in fulfilling her responsibilities toward the house, ignored criticism and suggestions, and her conduct on dates was not acceptable. She was regarded as a detriment to the house and was put on probation.

(*B*) Came in voluntarily and discussed his relationships with students of his own age and of the opposite sex. Has always spent too much time in extracurricular activity instead of developing these relationships. Also discussed his vocational choice.

(*C*) Student was referred by the Dean. He had been suspended for cutting classes and reinstated on condition that he not cut again. He cut and was awaiting expulsion. Believed he was not the type to attend classes; said his intellect was too high and the classes were too easy! He blamed the school. His fraternity brothers had told him to mend his ways or get out. He refuses to fit into their routine and displays preposterous plans and characterizations of himself.

(*D*) Student had broken up with his girl friend because she started

177

going with other fellows. He doesn't get along well with other fellows at the dorm and in various organizations. He is very stubborn and dogmatic, but has high standards and is very ambitious.

(*E*) Student was depressed and wanted to leave school. She was worried about her grades. She didn't know what profession to enter. She started out in Physical Education, transferred to Home Economics, and now doesn't like either of them.

(*F*) Girl is engaged to a boy who wants to be a psychiatrist. They want to get married before the boy is able to support them. The mother is opposed to the marriage.

(*G*) Student was worried over a $300 debt. She comes from an Italian Catholic family. Feels she is too inhibited with boys. She has not had much experience with them. She has broken away from her religion and no longer attends church.

(*H*) Student had had rheumatic arthritis, was unable to walk and then, after treatment, was cured. Through occupational therapy, he helped cure himself. Problem now is going down steps. He is afraid to go down one foot over the other, and instead descends one foot at a time. Wanted to know if fear had anything to do with this.

(*I*) Student wanted suggestions about getting along with other fellows. He is too hostile and has a temper. He is sensitive about being a Jew, is not prone to admit his Jewish ancestry and hasn't got along well with Jewish boys. He was unhappy and also a major health problem.

(*J*) Student was referred by members of the faculty because he seems to have ability but was making low grades. Also believed he had acne and was very sensitive about it. His mother had told him this was caused by masturbation and his relationships with the opposite sex. This worried him. He said he felt inferior and lacked confidence; was also concerned about his mother who is emotionally attached to him.

(*K*) Student was referred by clinic doctor. Symptoms which brought her to the hospital: Had nausea, desire to vomit, discomfort on right side, and loss of appetite. There were no physical findings except a temperature of 99°. Developed during interview that she couldn't get along with her employer.[1]

If the reader will examine these cases, he will note that each is a complex one. Rarely does an individual report but a single complaint. And the reader will note also that the problems are of many sorts. Emotional problems appear most frequently, with motivational and social difficulties almost as prevalent. Academic and sexual problems come

[1] From F. McKinney, *J. Consult. Psychol.*, 1945, *9*, 206–207. By permission of author and editor,

next; while those concerned with schedule, discipline, and financing also appear.

Readjustive Behavior Again

Different as the foregoing cases are one from another, when we get away from concrete particulars we are able to recognize that all of them fit into the pattern of adjustment-readjustment by the living organism that finds itself in difficulties (see Chapter 2). Let us reproduce here, as Figure 47, a variation of Figure 5 on page 26. The interested and motivated student (1) encounters one or another blockage in his personal contacts, in his scholastic situation, or in his own peculiarities (2), which puts him into a disturbed condition marked by

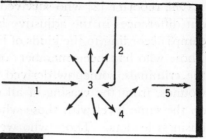

47   A Diagram to Represent a Conflict of Motives

Compare directly with Figure 5 representing readjustive behavior in general. Here instead of the motivated organism running into an obstruction in the more literal sense, one of its powerful motives (1) runs into conflict with another motive (2), and a crisis arises (3), in which here again "persistent activity" that is "varied and exploratory" leads perchance to a "solution" (4), that restores "favorable relationship," a "readjustment" (5). Compare also the two examples on pages 23 f.

some tension (3). It is hoped that the services of the clinic will assist him in discovering a best way out (4), so that he can proceed effectively in his college and vocational life (5).[1]

REACTIONS TO FRUSTRATIONS: IN GENERAL

Some Readjustments to Extreme Frustration

Among the most severe of all frustrations must surely be counted those that beset the prisoners of the concentration and extermination camps of Nazi Germany. All the victim's personal attachments were severed; all his plans catastrophically terminated; physical and mental tortures were his daily portion; and death in some violent form might at any time interrupt the bodily decay from disease and malnutrition. Facing such hideous blockades of nearly every motive, what do such persons do?

[1] The evidence for much that is to be presented on the following pages is of clinical character. Accordingly, the reader will not expect to find the various principles demonstrated by clean-cut laboratory experiments where most extraneous factors are eliminated. The clinician works with people as he finds them living their lives in the midst of things; and he cannot perform experimental tests on all the insights he gains into his patients' motivations. On the other hand, the broadness of his purview is advantageous: he can relate and interpret widely scattered incidents and details so as to bring them under common simplifying principles.

One reporter [2] who survived Dachau and Buchenwald has pointed out differences in the adjustive behavior of the victims of those torture camps according to the kinds of lives they had had before imprisonment. Those who had been members of the lower classes of society, especially the criminals, somehow derived some satisfaction, some balm for their wounds, from the erasing of all class differences, which now put them on the same level with those who had been judges and physicians and business leaders. Those who were imprisoned for political reasons extracted some nourishment for their ego-esteem from the fact that the Gestapo had singled them out as important. Those who had come from the upper classes got what satisfaction they could by assuming some sort of leadership over groups of middle-class followers. Those who were of noble blood felt so much superior to all other human beings in or out of prison that nothing could touch their self-esteem. In one or another way, then, each man resorted to *some* device, however specious, by which he could in a measure discount or offset the threat of annihilation.[1] Truly the resources of human nature in extremity are measureless!

Some Distortion of Behavior May Result

But there must have been many who failed to make adjustments, or as we might better say, who made adjustments that we must call abnormal. Consider a case taken from a very different source where the solution was *hysterical*.

A young man who had been a dancer and acrobat in a circus enlisted in the army long after the [first] World War. Here he found the discipline rigid, his duties irksome, and his experiences monotonous. He longed for the travel, excitement, attention, and opportunity for exhibition enjoyed in his former life. The situation became quite intolerable, but to leave meant that he would be treated as a deserter. A hysterical reaction resulted which was prompted by two conflicting motives, the one to conform to the requirements of military life, the other to secure escape from a hated situation. The hysterical reaction consisted of a dissociation of the conscious sensory and motor functions of his lower extremities, and it provided a solution which permitted him to gain his own end of obtaining immunity from unpleasant experiences and tasks, and at the same time enabled him to maintain his self-respect. On arrival at the mental hospital to which he was transferred he could neither walk nor stand, and his legs were anesthetic to even vigorous prickings by a pin. At the same time he displayed a signifi-

---

[1] That they did not commit suicide in greater numbers is testimony to the "will to live," as it is called, the never-say-die that is the most fundamental and impressive characteristic of all biological organisms.

cant attitude of satisfaction with his disabilities although as far as he was consciously aware they were complete and incurable. His lack of concern is to be explained by the fact that the penalty was less than the gain, although one must not conclude that this weighing of advantages and disadvantages was at all a matter of conscious reflection. A few months later the man was discharged from the army on a surgeon's certificate of disability. Soon the suspended motor and sensory functions began to return. Persistent efforts to walk gradually met with success and in another three months he left the hospital practically well.[1]

And the record files of clinical psychologists and of psychiatrists are full of similar instances. On its face, this case of the acrobat possesses elements of the bizarre; to the man in the street, it is even a bit incredible. However, its unusual character and its exaggeration of the "normal" ought to do us some service by throwing into prominence the salient features of the topic before us.

Note first that the man's paralysis and anesthesia were useful to him, that the incapacities furnished a way around his difficulties, a solution. This is not accident. In this as in other hysterical cases, the very type of disorder and the particular times of its onset and disappearance put it beyond doubt into the class of *an adjustive device*. Or, as commonly stated, it was *wish fulfilling*. The hysterical disabilities furnished a way out, when military routine, and the ignominy and discipline meted out to him who disobeys, combined to make a situation which this man found intolerable. Here the powerful motive to get away from army life ran into the obstacle of another motive not to incur penalties. The distraught man may have displayed excess activity in the form of worried excitement, and it is certain that he cast about, whether deliberately or not, in search of some graceful escape. At length the sensory and motor paralyses enabled him to detour the barrier and attain the objective toward which he had been so strongly impelled.

We are not to suppose that this solution was concocted deliberately and with clear intent. We dare not accuse him of malingering (intentional feigning). So far as he was aware his illness was genuine and real. From knowledge of other cases, however, we may hypothetically reconstruct the antecedents to this illness. We may suppose that in his unhappy quandary he chanced to see or hear or read about or recall a case of a paralytic. It is possible that he deliberately said to himself, "What a lucky fellow; *he's* not in the army!" And with a nervously unstable person that would be suggestion enough: some fine morning he would

[1] From A. P. Noyes, *Modern Clinical Psychiatry*, Saunders, 3d ed., 1948. By permission of the publishers.

simply awaken to find himself lame. Perhaps the reader may object: "But that is impossible on two counts. How could a 'thought' work if he wasn't thinking it? And anyhow, how could a 'thought' lame the body?" That, however, is no more mysterious than are those many mechanisms of self-regulation we have noted in the last chapter, mechanisms which occur on the purely physiological level. The soldier's incapacity is *as if* he had planned it so; but likewise the quick production of sweat which cools the skin when the body temperature is raised a fraction of a degree is *as if* it were intentional and planned. Richter's rats turned to the salt water *as if* they knew they needed the sodium; and the rats and babies that throve on self-selected diets chose foods *as if* they realized what was good for them.

A 28-year-old man was brought into a hospital with the complaint of blindness after having been involved in a minor automobile accident. Hospital examinations failed to show any signs of physical injury, and no organic reason could be found for the blindness. Diagnosis: hysterical blindness.

Now, the patient had had the accident while driving to visit his wife. His spontaneous remark was that since he was now blind his first duty to his wife was to be divorced.

An analysis was undertaken of the patient's life history to understand why that symptom had developed. His father was slight in build, a dependent type of personality, economically unsuccessful. The mother ruled the household with an iron hand. Early in life, as usually happens, he had built up his attitude toward the sexes on the basis of his own parents. He liked the kind father, but pitied his dependence. He respected the mother, but at the same time resented her domineering ways. Fearing a fate similar to that of his father, he had determined never to get married. Eventually he became much attached to one girl; she suggested marriage; and in a weak moment he aquiesced.

About two years after, she became pregnant. All through these weeks he hoped that the pregnancy would not mature, for he had had hopes of some day breaking away from his wife. Then the news came that he was the father of a boy. It was on his way to the hospital after this news that the accident occurred, which resulted in his blindness. As the clinician's interviews and analysis progressed, the patient became aware of the reason for the symptom. His blindness disappeared. His adjustment to his general situation became possible, however, only after further interviews. For with all his natural independence, he was hampered by his early conditioning at home; and unconsciously he had sought a mate who resembled his mother. Consequently, he had developed a dependence upon this wife which she had not wanted but had accepted. Discussions with the two resulted in his gaining the position in the house which he had always feared was impossible; and both were quite contented.[1]

In this case, as in the case of the soldier, it becomes obvious that the physical disorder served as an adjustive device: it was *wish fulfilling*. This time the motives in conflict are a bit more complicated, though they are discernible enough. Some additional points merit our attention.

In the first place, the contemporary events had their roots *in the patient's life history, extending back* into his boyhood. It would be hard to exaggerate the importance of this truth in the practice of modern clinical psychology and psychiatry. We do not need to go the whole way with Freud and some of his followers in frequently tracing all dominant motives back to infancy. But we do need to keep before us the biographical perspective if we hope to untangle the *why's* in human motives.

A second and related point is the extent to which the patient's attitudes toward roles and characters had been determined by his *parent models*. Both the clinical psychologist with his individual patients and the anthropologist with his group cultures are now tracing out the persistence of the father-role and the mother-role in the ideals and attitudes of persons and in the ideologies and religions of peoples.

A third point may be given passing mention. The patient's emotional attitudes toward each parent had been *ambivalent*, that is, had been in contradictory contrast toward one and the same personal object. His father he "liked" but he "pitied." His mother he "respected" but "resented." Such antagonism of emotions toward the same individual is held by some psychoanalysts as characteristic of normal infants but as being continued into adult years only in neurotic personalities. (An ambivalence implies a conflict itself.)

REACTIONS TO FRUSTRATIONS. SOME SPECIAL TYPES: DYNAMISMS

Inspired by the leadership of Freud, psychopathologists and psychiatrists through three decades have been acquiring greater understanding of human nature by finding out more about the *unconscious motivations* that are operating in people, normal as well as abnormal. We cannot here go deeply into this specialized field, but it will be useful to acquaint ourselves with some of the processes that are near the surface. These

[1] Somewhat condensed from W. Malamud, "The Psychoneuroses," in J. McV. Hunt, *Personality and the Behavior Disorders* (2 vols.; New York: Ronald Press, 1944). By permission of author, editor, and publisher.

are collectively given a variety of names: "Methods of readjusting to difficulties," "modes of reacting to frustrations," "devices of substitute satisfaction," "modes of resolving crises," or, briefly, "mechanisms" (but better called "dynamisms"). The processes are grouped together in different ways by different authorities; so that our order of presenting them will have to be somewhat arbitrary [8, 9, 14, 16, 17].

Aggression

The elemental reaction to a frustration is aggression. Interference with what the organism wants to do is one of the most stimulating conditions for rage and attack [5]. Even the infant of a few days will stiffen, kick, fling his arms about, and scream, if his bottle is taken away too soon. Many an adult will show equivalent signs of anger when his sleep is prevented or interrupted. And similar behavior occurs when the more elaborate motives are blocked. When your fountain pen runs dry while you are engrossed in your writing, when a clumsy lout gets in your way as you hurry to catch a train, when the icy sidewalk puts you in danger of falling, when the other fellow wins your sweetheart, when a bit player steals the show from you — when these interferences provoke you, you may react aggressively. Frequently it is not an overtly aggressive reaction, to be sure; it may take shape only in imagination and in dreams, or in the more deliberate planning of revenge.

For much the same reason, aggressive behavior not uncommonly is *displaced* to some innocent object. A white rat deprived of food or stung by an electrically charged floor will fight his nestmates, or in their absence will cuff a doll found in the cage or even the water bottle (Figure 48). After a disastrous defeat of the varsity football team a professor was observed berating a groundkeeper at some length for a trivial thoughtlessness. Social workers report that father-son conflicts increase when both are unemployed. Recent history affords a notorious instance of the displacement of aggressive behavior: the German Fascists made *scapegoats* of the Jews so that the common people would vent their discontent on them instead of on the Nazi bullies. And in all sorts of concrete ways we see that persons who are thwarted from talking back to more dominant persons are apt to release their dammed-up emotions upon those less dominant (Figure 49).

Finally, the frustrated individual sometimes turns against himself. For instance, a boy who showed aggression toward adults received punishment; he turned his aggression then toward other children only to be punished again; whereupon he finally attacked himself. A man curses himself for his absent-minded error or is furious with himself for letting

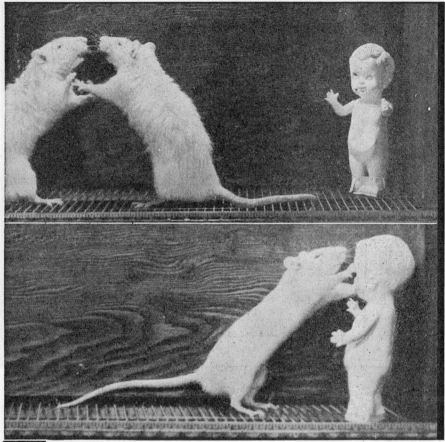

48   **Displaced Aggression**

When two rats were placed in the apparatus along with a doll, they struck at each other as soon as the electric shock was given them in the floor grid. When either was placed in the apparatus alone with doll, it struck at the doll. (*From N. E. Miller*, J. ABN. AND SOC. PSYCHOL., *1948, 43, 157. By permission of author and editor.*)

his bridge opponent take the trick. It may be that this form of aggression is one of the sources of suicidal motives.

(1) Compensation

Just as in the homeostasis of the organism one organic function (as an endocrine) often compensates or makes up for the weakness of another, so may a person compensate for an organic inferiority by *overreacting* in some other way [1]. One student, thwarted by infantile paralysis, had an automobile especially designed for him in which he built up an

THE SATURDAY EVENING POST

49   **Displaced Emotion**

This cartoon amusingly illustrates an everyday instance of release of emotion upon the less dominant rather than the more dominant object. By permission of the artist.

unenviable record for speeding, until it led directly to his death. But vast numbers of others, equally blocked by the after-effects of the same disease, meet the situation with the very different compensation of unfailing gayety and good sportsmanship.

The same dynamism appears in the concealment of an undesirable non-physical trait, so that the individual himself is unaware of it and his self-regard is unthreatened.

Margaret was a somewhat stocky and awkward student of mediocre mental ability. In her junior year in college, she decided that she should take a greater interest in social affairs, and for a time she made a serious effort to improve her appearance and mix with classmates of the opposite sex. Her efforts, however, met with meager success, so she gave up her social interests and concentrated on her studies. Possessing only average intelligence, she was unable to become an outstanding student. This double failure led to arrogant and aggressive behavior. She forced her attention upon others and frequently engaged in heated arguments about trivial matters with the girls in her dormitory. Her favorite trick was to look up some topic in the encyclopedia and then dominate the table conversation with a recital of her superior knowledge.[1]

The basis for much compensatory behavior, as has been hinted, is some *feeling of inferiority*, some true or false recognition of the individual's own weakness in physique or appearance or mental ability or family social level or economic handicap or other circumstance which — it is important to note — he assumes to be a handicap *in the eyes of other people*. This social implication in turn is a threat to his self-esteem: he must resort to some means of avoiding this depreciation of himself.

Let us be reminded, however, that compensatory behavior does not necessarily lead to conduct that is socially maladjustive. We need but to think of Demosthenes and his pebbles, of the Theodore Roosevelt who had been a physical weakling. And college life itself furnishes plentiful illustrations of high achievements in new fields of endeavor that offset or mask poor ability to achieve in other fields.

(2) Projection

Members of some college fraternities were once asked to rate each other and to rate themselves on these traits: *stinginess, obstinacy, disorderliness,* and *bashfulness.* Examination of the rating blanks brought out some interesting facts. Those individuals who were rated by their intimate friends as having a great degree of a trait, but who showed lack of insight into the fact (as revealed by a wide divergence between their self-ratings and the average ratings of them by their friends), tended to attribute more than the average degree of that trait to others. This was true for both the acceptable and the unacceptable traits [15]. The present writer once found that those children in a third-grade group who were rated by their classmates as most likely to cheat were the best judges of cheating in others, and those who were rated as brightest were the best judges of brightness in others (as determined by class-average and teacher ratings).

It is easy to see how Freud found that this tendency — to attribute one's own qualities to others — serves well for the individual who cannot bear to acknowledge to himself his own baser qualities, but instead *projects* them into other people. Or into other things, as so well expressed in such popular sayings as "A bad workman quarrels with his tools," and "The dub at golf wraps his club around a tree."

[1] From J. D. Page, *Abnormal Psychology* (New York: McGraw-Hill Book Company, 1947), page 41. By permission.

The egotistical person finds other persons about him so egotistical that he can scarcely bear with them. The coward likes to assume cowardice in others; hence he is a potential bully. What has been heartlessly called "old maid's insanity" — but is not limited to women — is the delusion that every other person of the opposite sex who happens to look at one is ready to fall in love. And rare indeed is the motorist so fair in judgment that in case of collision he is not readier to blame his brakes or the other driver than himself. So common is this penchant for projecting one's own weakness into other people that there is much truth in the remark that whenever you encounter a surprisingly intense prejudice concerning some human shortcoming you can look first for that shortcoming or a related one in the prejudiced person himself. For, in one of Oscar Wilde's neat epigrams, "All criticism is a form of autobiography."

(3) "Sour Grapes"

Related to the projective manner of — in a fashion — attacking others, is the *sour grapes* dynamism, by which the unattainable objectives are turned into undesirable ones and their motive power thus changed, so that the crisis ends.

> Mary T., who was not invited to the party, explains that it is a low-brow party anyway, that they never have a good time at parties given by Catherine, and that she has other things more interesting and important to do.
>
> Allen, who failed his entrance examinations for the college of his choice, later explains that it is just as well since the standards of work at this college are not very high and hence it would be a waste of time to go there.
>
> The boy who could not marry a rich girl later is heard to say that rich girls in general have bad characters. The truth of the matter is that this boy had particular financial needs which could have been filled had he married a wealthy girl, and had to find some excuse to justify his failure.[1]

He who fails to achieve wealth is convinced that riches are only a source of evil, that it is the poor who are the blessed. The jilted lover sees a hundred failings in his erstwhile sweetheart. Possibly we have here one root of a popular error that is mentioned in several places in this book — the opinion that he who is superior in one regard must be inferior in another: that the student of high scholarship must surely be inept at sports or campus politics; that the infant prodigy is certain to be physically unfit; that the beautiful are dumb. Even the most pro-

---

[1] From P. M. Symonds, *The Dynamics of Human Adjustment* (New York: Appleton-Century-Crofts, 1946). By permission of author and publishers.

found attitudes of humankind may be dictated by this mode of thinking. Instead of meeting the difficulties that life presents, the Buddhist, the Stoic, the Mohammedan dervish, and the ascetic Christian flee the field of contest and take refuge in reviling the flesh and contemplating either the utter nothingness of Nirvana or the unearthly bliss of a future life.

(4) Rationalizing

In each of the foregoing dynamisms the behavior is frequently characterized by some form of *rationalizing*. To rationalize is to attribute one's actions and beliefs to motives that are socially and personally acceptable, instead of to the true and unacceptable motives. It is important to bear in mind that a person is frequently quite unconscious of his true motives. Often a frustrated motive gets release when its possessor happens to find a way of verbally describing it in such manner as to weaken the antagonism between conflicting tendencies, or, to speak less abstractly, when he (often unawares) concocts plausible though false reasons for his attitudes or actions. He is rationalizing, or, in colloquial language, he is "kidding himself with his alibis." Such behavior is certainly very common. If the train conductor overlooks a passenger's ticket and the man does not call the conductor's attention to the oversight, the conflict between this particular expression of his money-saving tendencies and his more highly socialized tendencies to honorable dealing is weakened by such remarks as "This railroad is making too much money, anyhow," or "I don't wish to embarrass the conductor." In the same vein, the business world knows many a Babbitt who talks endlessly of Service. And in international relations the pronunciamentos put forth to justify the action of a state are all too often couched in language tending to weaken opposition between the aims that are behind the actual procedures set up and the aims maintained by intelligent citizens, as, for example, establishing a "protectorate," carrying the "white man's burden," "protecting" three thousand nationals with an intervention army of twenty thousand. A father goes to the circus or buys an electric train "for the boy"; a girl eats all the candy without sharing it with her younger brother because "it isn't good for him"; a boy fails in his arithmetic and grammar because "he has a poor teacher in those subjects"; a man drinks liquor because "one can't refuse a friend under such circumstances." It is too cynical to say, as has been said, that all systems of philosophy "are nothing more than unconscious apologies for our faults — a gigantic scaffolding to hide the philosophers' own sins," but certain it is that the resolution of conflicts between antagonistic desires or ideals all too often takes this form of deceiving one's self by a rephrasing of the true motive-causes at work. Polonius's admonition, "To thine own self be true," is more often honored in the breach than in the observance.

(5) Regressing

A characteristic way of meeting frustrations — and one that overlaps other dynamisms — is to fall back upon childish or infantile ways of reacting. Finding his problem difficult of solution in any mature and adequate way, a person may resort to more rough-and-ready, more spontaneous, more primitive behavior. Instances of regression are not hard to find. We all know adults who frequently indulge in temper tantrums or in sulking spells. A certain scientist when emotionally wrought up is likely to explode in the dialect of the mountain region where he lived as a child. Many of the prisoners in the Nazi concentration camps began to live like adolescents, fighting and swearing deep hatred for each other at one moment, only to become chummy again at the next. They boasted and bragged about how they had tricked and cheated, and then when proved to be lying, they were not at all embarrassed. They were as children [2]. Regression takes many varied forms. When singing for service camps in the Pacific, Bing Crosby found most requests were for Brahms's "Lullaby." And from the earlier World War, there comes a harrowing account of a wounded French poilu caught in a barbed-wire entanglement and piteously sobbing, "Maman! Maman!"

Even children can under stress regress to stages yet younger than those they have attained. In one experiment with nursery children, each was observed by himself through a one-way-vision screen as he played with a number of toys ("free play"). On a later day, he was allowed to play a few minutes with some more attractive toys in another part of the large room; then he was led back to the old part of the room and a wire partition was lowered which allowed him merely to see the more attractive toys ("frustration"). See Figure 50. A measuring rod for regressive behavior was then devised. The ways in which each child played with his toys on each occasion was rated on a scale of "constructiveness," ranging from, e.g., sitting on floor and simply picking up a toy truck (value 2), through such play as hitching and unhitching the truck and other cars (value 5), to, e.g., "We're going fishing in this truck, and we'll go to the gas station first" (value 7), and a still higher value (8). The more mature the child, the more constructive his play. Now, when the scale was used to grade the play shown in the original free-play period and that shown in the frustration period, numerical

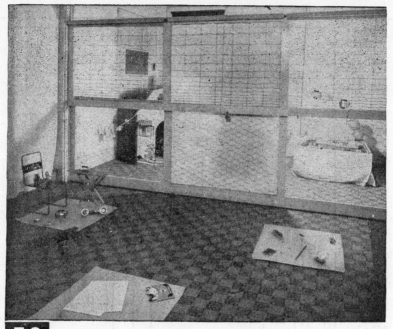

50

A Frustrating Situation with Young Children

A wire partition blocks the child's attempts to play with the more attractive toys visible to him. (*From R. G. Barker, T. Dembo, and K. Lewin,* Univ. Iowa Stud. Child Welf., *1941, 18, No. 1. By permission of authors and publishers. Figure by courtesy of McGraw-Hill Book Co.*)

results were of striking character. As the reader will see in Figure 51, 22 children showed a decrease in the constructiveness of their play when placed in the frustrating situation, and only 5 showed an increase.

(6) Repression

In many of the everyday illustrations given on the preceding pages, as well as in more severe cases like that of the hysteric, the reader will have noticed that the true motive at work in the person is one of which he is not clearly or not at all aware. It has undergone a certain type of forgetting. Yet it has not been rendered wholly ineffective but continues to energize and to direct conduct and thinking, as we have seen. It is repressed. Sometimes this repressing goes to pathological limits, as the following two cases will show.

A man suffered from a phobia [uncontrollable fear] of being grasped from behind, the disturbance appearing early in childhood and persisting to his fifty-fifth year. When walking on the street he was under a compul-

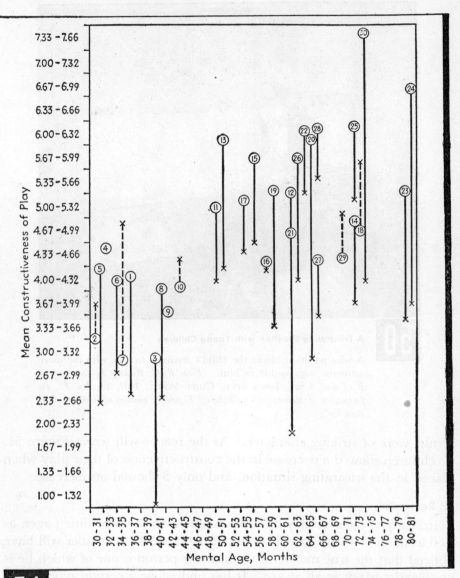

Effect of Frustration on the Constructiveness Shown in Play by Children of Different Mental Ages

Circles represent the constructiveness shown by individual children when in the original free-play situation; crosses, their constructiveness when in the frustrating situation. Degree of constructiveness in each case is shown as a vertical distance, representing the values mentioned in the text. (*From Barker, Dembo, and Lewin, op. cit. By permission.*)

sion to look back over his shoulder at intervals to see if he was closely followed. In social gatherings he arranged to have his chair against the wall. It was impossible for him to enter crowded places or to attend the theater. . . . He could give absolutely no explanation of the origin of his fear. In his fifty-fifth year he returned to the town in which he had spent his childhood. After inspecting his old home, he went to the corner grocery and found that his old boyhood friend was still behind the counter. He introduced himself and they began to reminisce. Finally the grocer said this, "I want to tell you something that occurred when you were a boy. You used to go by this store on errands, and when you passed you often took a handful of peanuts from the stand in front. One day I saw you coming and hid behind a barrel. Just as you put your hand in the pile of peanuts, I jumped out and grabbed you from behind. You screamed and fell fainting on the sidewalk." The episode was remembered and the phobia, after a period of readjustment, disappeared.[1]

In the famous "Bell Tower" case described by Morton Prince, a woman had a phobia for towers and church steeples, especially those in which bells might ring. She was utterly unable to explain it. But while she was in a condition of hypnosis (a condition resembling sleep in which the subject is highly suggestible and sometimes shows unusual recall) some memories of an incident in her childhood were brought out. In her abstracted state she wrote: "G—— M—— church and my father, took my mother to Bi—— where she died, and we went to Br—— and they cut my mother. I prayed and cried all the time that she would live, and the church bells were always ringing and I hated them." She wept during this writing. After becoming fully awake she was able to reconstruct a substantial part of the story, under guiding questions from the examiner. Her mother had once undergone a major surgical operation, the outcome of which was fatal; and the overly conscientious daughter who feared she had not given her every care in the nursing was meanwhile in a protracted agony of mixed grief and remorse —— "and the church bells were always ringing." Now, this later recall of the full story did not at first shake the phobia. It persisted until Prince had finally succeeded in persuading the woman that her childhood attentions to her mother had actually been most devoted and that the fatal outcome was due to a sequence of causes quite out of her control.

In both cases the traumatic (injury-producing) experience was one not only intensely emotional but also involving some sense of guilt, that is, some *dread* of it based upon early socialized behavior.

In the last remark is found the key to the clinician's interpretation of pathological repression. It is "protective forgetting," or, more broadly, it is a form of adjustive response to an object of fear — not now in the physical surroundings but in the self-condemning attitude — which is

[1] From E. Bagby, *The Psychology of Personality* (New York: Henry Holt and Co., 1928).

avoided by being forgotten. The phobias in the two cases just presented simply represent the patients' avoidance of those stimuli that might occasion recall of the original episodes, with their dreaded attitude of self-condemnation. The very operation of the phobias eloquently testifies to the continued functioning in some fashion of the repressed experiences. They were "forgotten" yet remained as motivating factors in behavior.

How is this possible? Two well-established psychological principles are involved.

(1) Much as a person withdraws from a painful physical stimulus, so also he can in some instances "withdraw" from a painful memory, that is, he can actively *forget* it. The process is probably some form of *inhibition*, that is, a sidetracking of one function by another — as when a dog that is scratching himself with his right hind leg, upon receiving a pain stimulus at the left foot stops scratching to use the right foot for standing while the left is sharply retracted, or as when a child about to reach for a piece of forbidden cake is restrained by voice or sight or memory of the forbidding adult.

(2) If a process is inhibited from overt expression or even if it is kept from the subject's awareness, the process is not thereby necessarily rendered inert. Many phases of human psychology present illustrations of this general truth. A person is unaware of just how he performs this and that act of skill and indeed may be quite unable to perform it if he pays attention to the processes involved. Most people are unaware of the motives urging them toward their dominant interests. Most striking of all is the fact that, as we shall see later on, productive thinking processes can go on while a person is attending to something quite different, or while he is actually sleeping. Like these and other phenomena, then, a repressed or actively forgotten motive may continue to be active and responsive to organic or to environmental stimuli.[1] And consequently, the crisis still exists.[2]

(7) Fantasy

The last point leads us to another major way of meeting the frustrations of one dominant urge by another. As we are to see later,[3] the

---

[1] In psychoanalytic usage, this is the meaning of a "complex," that is, an emotional attitude which though repressed still influences thought and action.

[2] Let the reader be warned against a certain manner of misrepresenting these facts of unconscious functioning: they do not point to the working of a Subconscious Mind, nor even of a Subconscious or the Unconscious. Such notions are (a) needless. Moreover they are (b) burdensome, for, far from explaining anything, they themselves need explanation. Often, in fact, they are used as (c) a last refuge of ignorance. Historically they (d) hark back to the pre-scientific mode of thought in which human actions are explained by the operations of daemons residing within.

[3] In Chapter 19.

function of imaginary representation is one of incalculable value to the human being who must anticipate the morrow; and the fertility of his capacity so to imagine is an important determiner of the effectiveness of his thinking. The unimaginative person is the humdrum bore who can contribute nothing to general discourse nor save himself from the tread-mill of routine. But what concerns us here especially is that imagining furnishes an avenue of temporary escape from the day's drab events. In this lies much of the *raison d'être* not only of religion but of fiction, poetry, and the drama. These afford temporary surcease and refreshment from the actualities of life, and so have a function that, even from the narrow-est practical considerations, is wholesome and valuable.

A danger lurks, however.

> If you can dream — and not make dreams your master,
> If you can think — and not make thoughts your aim . . .

If the dreamer would only return from his moments in the clouds re-freshed and strengthened for tackling the problems actually at hand, or if he would bring down with him a new project or an inspiration to be tried, the adjustive value of this function would be immense and indis-putable. But many a daydream has been used only as an escape-mechanism, the air castles as a city of refuge from the responsibilities of everyday life. The evils of *fantasy-forming*, as it is called, are recognized by all clinicians, for whom fantasy has great significance in two types of cases especially. In one type it is a symptom of a fixed habit of with-drawing into oneself before all unpleasantness, all thwartings of one's interests, a habit that grows to such proportions that its possessor comes to spend most of his day in the non-real world, and even to lose appre-ciation of the difference between non-real and real. That way madness lies — madness in which the victim becomes more and more inaccessible to others. The other type of fantasy viewed with particular concern by the clinical expert is that in which "dangers bring fears and fears more dangers bring"; for out of the frustration of this or that primary urge may grow a mounting dread and suspicion of everyone. That way, too, madness lies — a madness in which delusions may steel their possessor to violent deeds against others or himself.

Not only in daydreams but also in nocturnal dreams as well may a person reveal blocked motives and attempts to satisfy them, perhaps by the most unrealistic means. Arctic explorers have repeatedly testified that after weeks of privation and short-rationing their sleeping hours were filled with dream-pictures of bountiful feasts. And a psychologist investigating orphanage children reported that the most common dream was of being taken home — to somebody's home. For this general reason, Freud early recognized that a patient's dreams furnished most valuable lodes from which clever drilling could unearth the patient's basic interests and frustrations. But he pointed out the exceeding complexity of this mining task, for many a human motive only half-reveals itself.

Moreover, we must recognize that the stuff of dreams has other sources. Dreaming is affected by the physically present sensory stimulations, as when he who has been dreaming of Eskimos and a whale-blubber breakfast awakens to find that he has kicked off his blankets in a wintry room. This present sensory control of dream-stuff can be experimentally produced.[1] Dreaming is affected, too, by the return of vivid experiences of the preceding day. Finally, let us bear in mind that there is no clear borderline marking off dreams from waking experiences. This will be recognized by anyone who recalls those absurd creatures and shapes that emerge from the darkness as he drives too long and late, or who in his bed notes the utterly fantastic distortions of events and sequences as he is lapsing from consciousness.

A Word of Caution

These and other ways of finding substitute avenues of satisfaction furnish to the skilled clinician helpful concepts in unraveling the difficulties of his patients and uncovering motivation sources of which the patients themselves are hardly or not at all aware. But these methods of analysis have also caught the imagination of the non-technically trained public; and not only in the recent wave of debunking biographies but also in everyday conversations they have been perverted into what one might term a highbrow form of gossip. This is an indoor sport that is pleasant and easy and at the same time has about it a flavor of subtlety and profundity. But it is dangerous! The chances that untrained persons will make unfair judgments are tremendous. Furthermore, interpreting everybody else's behavior in terms of methods of substitute satisfaction may itself become a mode of substitute satisfaction.

Perhaps, after all, the principal profit from the foregoing survey lies not in our learning the specific devices resorted to by people in resolving crises. The real value is more likely to be gained through developing a wholesome respect for the complexity of motives at work in anyone of higher mental complexity than the moron. Whether introspectively or objectively sought out, the reasons for a man's conduct are difficult to analyze.

[1] M. Maury, *Le Sommeil et les Rêves* (1865).

SOME CONSIDERATIONS OF MENTAL HEALTH

Assimilating the Source of Frustration

In our brief survey of some outstanding methods that people chance upon to secure indirect satisfaction for their thwarted motives, we have

52 Some Frustrating Occasions

What is the very *first* reply that comes to your mind in each of the above instances? Avoid a humorous response. (*Adapted but not copied from S. Rosenzweig's P–F Study, described in* J. PERSONALITY, *1945,* 14, *3–28. By permission.*)

found that in very many cases these methods are used in inadvisable
ways. Hence the satisfactions secured are temporary or illusory or half-
way. Or the readjustments may cause further complications in relationships with other people. Paths of indirection are often insecure and
treacherous. A general formula for the maintenance of a balanced
perspective on self and world, for the preservation of robust mental
health, might be phrased informally as follows:

> Meet and recognize your difficulties as they arise. Face the music; do
> not dodge or run away. Like a fully rational adult human being do not
> regress to childish or "small" ways of acting; do not simply grow emotional,
> but looking the problems fully in the face apply intelligence and rational
> analysis to the whole matter. As in any other of life's emergencies, "don't
> be a big baby, but use your head." This is often not so easy as it sounds;
> and one may need to consult with a psychological adviser. But his or her
> aid would be directed to helping you do just this; the aid would not solve
> the problem for you. You must save your own soul.
>
> Therein the patient
Must minister to himself.

This attitude will help one to *assimilate* the difficulty. The term has
one root in sociology. It is illustrated by the process of Americanization
of an immigrant, a process in which the foreign individual goes through
a certain amount of conflict until he learns how to get along with others
and comes to adopt their attitudes. The same thing happens with the
fraternity or lodge initiate, the religious neophyte, the newly hired member of a construction gang or steamship crew. By analogy, we may
speak of a material or social situation that blocks one's motivated behavior as being a foreign element that needs assimilation into his personal
systems of attitudes and habits. Unless thoroughly thought through and
made consistent with his other dominant motives, it will be like the grain
of sand within the oyster's shell, a source of irritation and disturbance to
the whole organism.

Importance of Controlling Emotional Excitement

When people in crises fall back upon various inadequate devices of
substitute satisfaction (such as we have reviewed), they frequently display enormous emotional tension; and an adequate solution of their
problems means not only an end to frustration but also a lessening of
this tension. Excessive emotion is important enough to deserve a few
words on its own account.

Crile has roughly likened the effect of emotion upon the body mechanism to that produced on an automobile mechanism when its engine

is kept running at high speed while the vehicle stands stationary. It is a matter of common observation that emotional excitement of sthenic (strengthening) types, such as rage, fear, love, joy, tends to re-enforce the activity of striped muscles, but only at the expense of the more delicate integrations; it will lend wings to a person's feet and power to his arm, but it will impair his judgment and thinking. (A convincing laboratory demonstration of this general point is reported on pages 203 f.) Stage fright is an excellent illustration here. The conduct of a man in a lynching mob, or of a woman in a bargain-counter crush, or of a child in a fire panic, serve as further examples. Every boxer knows this principle in his own way; learning not to get angry at any cost is as important as skill in blocking and jabbing and punching, for once the fighter grows enraged, the skillful coordinations trained into him break down, and he fights not wisely but too well and leaves himself unprotected.

> When anger rushes, unrestrain'd, to action,
> Like a hot steed, it stumbles on its way:
> The man of thought strikes deepest, and strikes safest.

For much the same reason, love is proverbially held to be blind; a scientific seeking of fact for fact's sake must be divorced from personal prejudices; a court must tolerate in the spectators no excitement that might be communicated to the jurors. "He that is slow to anger is better than the mighty; and he that ruleth his spirit than he that taketh a city." And the true lady is "mistress of herself, tho' china fall."

To counteract the tendency to emotional tension the recipe is, in formulation at least, simple. Visceral reactions are like other reactions; if they are not to be aroused, either the *stimulus* (situation) must be *removed* or its *character altered*, or *another stimulus* must be provided to *set up a different activity* to divert the individual's energies.[1]

Work has been called a savior of the soul; and certainly many everyday observations prove the aptness of the phrase. Any occupation that provides a series of stimuli that arouse appropriate activity by the worker, particularly if the activity called for is absorbing, will relieve his tensions by setting up a different (antagonistic) activity. Many a grief-stricken person has found that concentrated work serves as a distractor sufficient to keep him on his mettle enough hours of the day to weaken

[1] This contrast between the emotional aspects of behavior and the intellectual aspects which can exert controlling influences over them has received a physiological interpretation that goes far to support the claims and the exhortations of Buddha and Confucius and all the moralists of history. The control of the emotions by the intellect is the control of hypothalamic-centered visceral activities by cerebral inhibitory influence. (See page 324.)

in some degree the intensity of the emotion. The work motive need not be of the highly emotional sort: the oft-repeated duties of a daily job, when they have acquired habit-arousing potency, will serve to direct some of the individual's total activity, and to that degree will save him from emotional excesses. For work to be effective in reducing strain, it would seem that it must either (a) elicit much interested (motivated) attention or (b) provide for vigorous grosser behavior. The former we have illustrated; the latter is shown in many familiar devices. The solicitations of recurring sex drives and the attendant emotions are partly overcome by a strenuous participation in athletics, and a mounting rage is worked off satisfactorily at the woodpile. On the other hand, a fear that is prevented from taking overt form in the use of fists or heels becomes all the more intense as a visceral disturbance. It is because of this that release through working at one's occupation is so valuable.

More Knowledge of Emotions Is Needed

In the preceding chapter and especially in the present one we have referred often to the emotional phases of man's behavior, particularly as they affect the adequacy of his general conduct toward other people and toward the turns in his own individual fortunes. But we must dig deeper. We must obtain a more precise knowledge of what emotional behavior is, and, so far as possible, return to the laboratory for experimentally verifiable facts. A topic of such richness and complexity merits a complete chapter in itself.

REFERENCES

1. Adler, A. *Problems of Neurosis*. London: Kegan Paul, Trench Trübner and Co., 1929.
2. Bettelheim, B. "Individual and mass behavior in extreme situations," *J. Abn. Soc. Psychol.*, 1943, *38*, 417–452.
3. Cameron, N. *The Psychology of Behavior Disorders*. Boston: Houghton Mifflin Company, 1947.
4. Cohen, L. H., E. R. Hilgard, and G. R. Wendt. "Sensitivity to light in a case of hysterical blindness studied by reinforcement, inhibition, and by conditioning methods," *Yale J. Biol. Med.*, 1933, *6*, 61–67.
5. Dollard, J., L. W. Doob, N. E. Miller, O. H. Mowrer, and R. R. Sears. *Frustration and Aggression*. New Haven, Conn.: Yale University Press, 1939.
6. Gantt, W. H. *Experimental Basis for Neurotic Behavior*. New York: Hoeber, 1944.
7. Grinker, R. R., and J. P. Spiegel. *Men Under Stress*. Philadelphia: Blakiston Company, 1945.

8. Hunt, J. McV. *Personality and the Behavior Disorders.* 2 vols. New York: Ronald Press, 1944.

9. Masserman, J. H. *Principles of Dynamic Psychiatry.* Philadelphia: W. B. Saunders Company, 1946.

10. McKinney, F. *The Psychology of Personal Adjustment.* Second edition. New York: John Wiley and Sons, 1949.

11. Miller, N. E. "Theory and experiment relating psychoanalytic displacement to stimulus-response generalization," *J. Abn. Soc. Psychol.*, 1948, *43*, 155–178.

12. Noyes, A. P. *Modern Clinical Psychiatry.* Philadelphia: W. B. Saunders Company, 1934.

13. Page, J. D. *Abnormal Psychology.* New York: McGraw-Hill Book Company, 1947.

14. Rosenzweig, S. "Types of reaction to frustration," *J. Abn. Soc. Psychol.*, 1934, *29*, 298–300.

15. Sears, R. R. "Experimental studies of projection. I," *J. Soc. Psychol.*, 1936, *7*, 151–163.

16. Shaffer, L. F. *The Psychology of Adjustment.* Boston: Houghton Mifflin Company, 1936.

17. Symonds, P. M. *The Dynamics of Human Adjustment.* New York: Appleton-Century-Crofts, 1946.

9

EMOTION

RELATION OF EMOTION TO ADJUSTMENT

THE TERM *emotional* is derived from the Latin *emovere*, which means "to shake," to "stir up"; and through all the literature of the emotions, technical and popular, this note is frequently sounded. And further, though different phrasings may be used by different writers — "wasted reflexes," or "conflict of impulses" or "disorganized responses" — most of them imply some complication or involvement or faultiness in the individual's adjustment. When a friend "gets emotional" the significant thing about his condition is that he may no longer be counted upon to think and act in a thoroughly rational, sensible, normal, and businesslike way.

A college student was driving to a distant city to attend a football game. It was the Big Game of the season and represented an important event in the season's social festivities. He was accompanied by a girl whose good opinion he valued highly and whom he wished to impress with his extensive plans for a weekend of parties and amusement. They became very gay and hilarious during the course of the drive and he was silently congratulating himself on the successful arrangements he had made. Suddenly a siren sounded behind him and, when he stopped, the traffic officer reprimanded him severely and in a very insulting manner for "driving like a high-school kid." The sound of the siren and the officer's intrusion immediately destroyed both his rapport with the girl and the happy anticipations he had had. As soon as he was permitted to drive ahead, he began berating the manners of the officer and telling the girl that the police in that state were notorious for their bullying methods. During the remainder of the drive he seemed to have difficulty with his car; he grated the gears frequently in shifting, refused to let other cars pass him, and made insulting comments about every policeman who came in sight (though, of course, slowing down whenever they appeared). The change in behavior here is not very baffling. The student was frustrated by being humiliated before his girl; his expectations of favorable response from her diminished. His behavior became aggressive because of his hostility toward the policeman which he could not express directly and which kept bubbling up after the arrest.[1]

For an experimental example, let us view the behavior of some other college students when they found themselves in an annoying situation and compelled to find a way of escape. The floor plan of a quadruple choice apparatus used at the University of North Carolina is reproduced in Figure 53. Each subject was admitted at *Ent.*, and upon advancing to the point *O* found himself equidistant from four exit doors, *1, 2, 3, 4.* Three of these doors were locked; and he had to find the unlocked one to make his exit. On the next following trial that door would be locked and some other unlocked; and so on for the series of trials, no door being the unlocked one on two successive trials. The order of unlocking was settled by chance so that it could

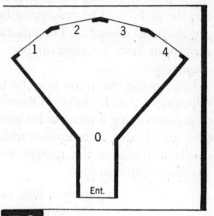

53 The Quadruple Choice Apparatus

Explanation in text. (*From G. V. Hamilton,* J. Anim. Behav., *1911, 1, 33–66.*)

never be solved; and the subject had to resort to some kind of searching or try, try again. And it is the *kinds* of searching used that form the heart of the story. They were classified into five types, as follows:

Type A: The three inferentially possible doors tried once each, the previously unlocked door being avoided. Examples (assuming 2 to have been unlocked last trial): 3–4–1 or 1–3–4.

Type B: All four doors tried, once each, in irregular order. Examples: 3–4–2–1 or 4–2–1–3.

Type C: All four doors tried in regular order, right to left, or left to right. Examples: 1–2–3–4 or 4–3–2–1.

Type D: More than one try at same door, though with an intervening tria¹ elsewhere. Examples: 1–2–3–1–4 or 4–3–4–3–2–1.

Type E: Several automatisms. Examples: 1–1–2–3–4 or 2–3–3–3–1–2.

[1] From J. Dollard, *et al.*, *Frustration and Aggression* (New Haven, Conn.: Yale University Press, 1939), pages 12–13. By permission of authors and publishers.

As the reader may judge for himself, these types of searching are ranked in order of adequacy, from *A*, the most intelligent, to *E*, the least. Now let us note the behavior of the students. When introduced into the enclosure and left to their own devices, they made choices quite predominantly in the Type *A* manner of search, as shown by the upper horizontal line of data in Table XVI. Then in another series of runs, the experimenter placed each subject under special exciting conditions. From the moment of arriving at *O* until escaping through the one unlocked door, he was subjected to (*a*) a shower, (*b*) electric shocks applied to his feet, or (*c*) the raucous noise of an automobile horn. (All three of these stimuli continued to have equally exciting value throughout the series.) The results, to be read from the lower horizontal line, are eloquent enough. The emotional responses aroused by the exciting conditions had a disorganizing effect upon the subjects' attempts to escape.

Convincing exception may be taken to our speaking of all emotion as adjustment that is faulty. Observe a person at the end of a perfect day, or one surveying a piece of his work well done. Note the serenity of him who anticipates communion with the blessed saints, or the smiles and gentle pattings of the master with his dog, or the contentment of a strolling couple in love.

> Reason, thou vain impertinence,
> Deluding hypocrite, begone!
> And go and plague your men of sense;
> But let my love and me alone.

Surely, it may very properly be claimed, these people are emotional, too, and in no especially disorganized way. True! And we must not entirely neglect this application of the term — even though on further consideration it can be pointed out that these mild forms of behavior need only be intensified to become themselves disrupting and disorganizing.

TABLE

XVI Effect of Emotional Excitement on Choosing Behavior

Conditions of the Subjects	Distribution of Reactions in Percentages				
	A	B	C	D	E
Normal, control	60	29	10	0	1
Emotional excitement	16	14	10	3	57

From J. R. Patrick, J. Comp. Psychol., 1934, 18, 178

THE PERSISTENT PROBLEM OF DESCRIBING EMOTIONS

The emotional condition of a person may be regarded from three aspects: (1) the state of mind he is feeling, (2) the physiological agitation of his bodily "insides" or viscera, and (3) his overt reactions toward other people and things. In a word: the experiential, the physiological, and the behavioral. While these three are not different processes so much as different phases, we shall do best to treat them separately at first, and to keep in mind with which of them we are dealing from time to time.

(1) Emotion Viewed as Experience

In his investigations of any realm of phenomena the scientist seeks to classify, sort out, and label the manifold things with which he deals. It is an inevitable and legitimate query for him to ask: Do emotional experiences fall into certain definite classes or types, and if so, what are these classes? Consider the wealth of names of supposedly different emotions in current use: joy, grief, mirth, ecstasy, restiveness, exuberance, wonder, fear, disgust, detestation, timidity, shame, awe, tenderness, coyness, love, lust, jealousy, pride, exultation, remorse, dread, anxiety — and on and on through a list of interminable length. For centuries thinkers have been describing and comparing the experiences referred to by such names, and have shown much ingenuity in matching them to discover differences and identities. Emotions have been divided into the strong and the weak, the pleasant and the unpleasant, those slowly arising and those suddenly arising, the egoistic and the altruistic, the sensuous and the intellectual, the subjective and the objective, the sthenic and the asthenic. All this led William James to exclaim that he "should as lief read verbal descriptions of the shapes of the rocks on a New Hampshire farm as toil through them again."

Are we then to conclude that it is fruitless to attempt any analytic study of emotions as consciously experienced? There is no denying the fact that the study of emotions springs in part from a popular interest in how the emotions "feel." Long before a person reaches the stage of appreciating music intellectually as an art-form, he welcomes the agreeable thrills it awakens in him. Poetry is above all a language of emotional experience, and one reads it with an interest in tasting the moods and nuances of feeling communicated by the poet. Practical life recognizes the desirability of increasing the number of occasions that will set up certain emotional experiences and reducing those that set up others. In the case of certain neurasthenics, esthetes, *bons vivants*, and indeed in certain classic philosophies of living, emotional states become morbidly over-emphasized. Are such matters of conscious experiencing to be given up as beyond the reach of scientific method?

W. A. Hunt has given a negative answer. During one of his lectures to a college class, he had a concealed automobile horn suddenly give forth a piercing blast. He then unrolled a chart listing fourteen adjectives, and he asked the students to note down any of these terms that described their feelings at the sound of the horn. The results for this *A* group are given in Table XVII. A year later the situation was repeated with another group of students, shown as Group *B* in the table. Finally, to compare these more immediate introspective reports with memorial retrospective reports, a third group, *C*, were presented simply with the list of fourteen terms and requested to check those which best described the feeling of being startled as they could recall having experienced it at some previous time. Inspection of the rows of data, *A*, *B*, and *C*, leads to the conclusion that it does seem possible to obtain introspective reports that possess a high degree of reliability. The same result has been repeatedly obtained by another psychologist, and Hunt himself has obtained equally reliable results for other emotions — "fear," "anger," "joy," and "sorrow." We conclude, then, that introspective approaches to emotion have their analytic usefulness, and that a classification of at least some of our emotional experiences may turn out to be a worthwhile object of scientific work.

Do the other directions of approach promise more?

TABLE XVII Percentages of Three Groups of Subjects Who Used the Common Descriptive Terms to Characterize "Startle"

(74 S's in Group A; 91 in Group B; 94 in Group C)

Group	Pleasant	Unpleasant	Bright	Dull	Excitement	Depression	Tension	Relaxation	Warmth	Cold	Ease	Strain	Dense	Spread
A	1	73	11	1	81	1	82	1	49	11	0	67	5	5
B	2	62	8	1	80	0	85	0	14	7	0	45	0	9
C	7	54	25	0	68	2	77	0	21	23	0	63	2	7

From W. A. Hunt, AMER. J. PSYCHOL., 1937, 49, 650. By permission of the author.

(2) Emotion Viewed as Bodily Changes

> Some strange commotion
> Is in his brain: he bites his lip, and starts;
> Stops on a sudden, looks upon the ground,
> Then lays his finger on his temple; straight
> Springs out into fast gait; then stops again,
> Strikes his breast hard; and anon he casts
> His eye against the moon: in most strange postures
> We have seen him set himself.

When introspectionists analyze just what they are aware of when emotional, they find that they have sensory experiences which originate beyond doubt in the activity of receptors in the viscera, the muscles, the skin. The following reports are typical:

I received a telephone call and was told of my election to Phi Beta Kappa.

My mind seemed to be a blank, that is, there seemed to be no ideas present, at least at first. Then there were kinesthetic and organic sensations in head as blood seemed to rush to head. I was hot all over and hands were moist — great emotion of joy. Organic sensations in chest, breathed fast, then it seemed as though I must say something to somebody. Wanted to burst with such an emotion of joy and as always, I couldn't keep it to myself. Head became cooler and I tried to reason with myself in terms of snatchy verbal ideas to see that I must calm down a little. Left my hairdresser and felt so good that I wanted to run. Exhilaration and still also joy.

[After a vigorous scolding another subject reported:]

Feeling of warmth arises in entire body. Biting of lips; rapid beating of heart; quivering in pit of stomach. The warmth sensations give prickly feeling in face. Then quivering in arms. I dug nails into palms of hands. Breathing came faster. Perspiration felt in palms of hand and under knees; also soles of feet were moist. Face twitched as blood came up. So angry that I was ready to hit E.[1]

Involvements of the Gastro-Intestinal System. A child of three years after his first meeting with Santa Claus stated, "I wasn't scared but my stomach was scared." Twenty-five years later he reported that when he was a Marine in a PT boat approaching the dread shore of Iwo Jima his stomach "felt like a block of cement." That the digestive organs play their part in much emotional behavior has been recognized from ancient times. And in the animal laboratories of psychology and physi-

[1] From C. A. Ruckmick, *The Psychology of Feeling and Emotion* (New York: McGraw-Hill Book Company, 1936). By permission.

ology it has become a truism. As mentioned in Chapter 3, the emotionality of rats has been measured by the frequency of their defecation.

The most striking demonstrations of the involvements of the gastrointestinal tract come from the cases of "psychosomatic medicine." Worry, especially on the part of the hard-driving, ambitious man of business — whether or not we interpret this ambition as motivated by disappointed cravings for care or for love support — will often cause peptic ulcers, the so called "Wall Street stomach." For a hyperacidity of the gastric secretion accompanies worry, and ulceration or even hemorrhages of the stomach walls result. Other emotionally-induced physical ailments are chronic diarrhea, several forms of colitis, and a form of constipation [24, 27]. Long-continued emotional alteration in the functioning of smooth muscles and glands eventuates in morphological (structural or organic) changes.

Cardio-Vascular Involvements in Emotion. Sharing the same hospital wards, or at least the same physician's office, are the patients with excessive blood pressure (essential hypertension) which has no simple organic basis in disease of specific organs, but is explained instead as a consequence or at least a symptom of anxiety or of rage. Typical cases are those of suppressed hostility, of rebellion against a dominating relative, in which one gets his blood pressure up, often without realizing why.

There are times, however, when the involvement of the heart certainly depends much less upon such individual predispositions and far more upon the stresses of the life-situations. For example, in the case of an armored brigade that had seen combat repeatedly in the African desert, more than a fourth of all the veterans who had been members of the brigade for from one to three years showed abnormally high blood pressure. It took a rest of two months to return most of the pressures to normal levels [11].

Changes in blood pressure level are measurable with the *sphygmomanometer*. This instrument, in common use in medical examinations, consists of a rubber bag connected by air tubing to a mercury manometer with a millimeter scale. The rubber bag is bound about the upper arm and inflated. When by inflation of the bag the pressure about the arm is sufficient to overcome the blood pressure within the artery, the pulse will be prevented from passing, which point can be determined by applying a stethoscope. The reading on the manometer or dial taken at this point is the peak or systolic blood pressure. As evidence of the importance of the circulatory system in major emotion, we may note that among combat veterans it is sometimes the most frequently mentioned of those physiological disturbances that are recognized introspectively.

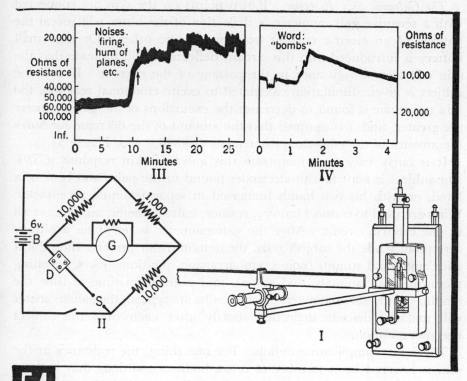

54 The Galvanometric Measurement of Emotional Reaction

I. A commonly used form of galvanometer. The amount of current passing through the instrument determines the position of a moving coil hung within the case; and riding on the latter is a small mirror that reflects numbers from the horizontal scale in front into the telescope. (For very delicate researches the Einthoven string galvanometer is often used.)

II. One arrangement of connections (Wheatstone bridge) for the study of emotion: *S*, the human subject under observation; *G*, galvanometer; *B*, battery; *D*, dial resistance; other resistances shown as coils and indicated in ohms.

III. Record of changes in resistance in a subject during an air raid over London by enemy planes. Beginning at the tenth minute of the observations she heard the noise of warning maroons, of humming aeroplanes, and of gunfire, which continued for some time.

IV. Record of changes when the same subject was given the word "bombs," no noises as in *III* being present. Note that a mere word has assumed effectiveness as an emotional stimulus. (The records in *III* and *IV* were obtained by photographic recording of the positions of a light beam reflected by the mirror of the galvanometer upon a traveling film.) (*III and IV from A. D. Waller,* NATURE, *1921,* 107, 185, *and* PROC. ROY. SOC. OF LONDON, *B, 1917, 90, 217.*)

The Galvanic Skin Response. If two points on the skin are connected with a sensitive galvanometer, a deflection of the latter will reveal the passage of an electric current from one to the other. Or if a small battery is introduced into this circuit, deflections will indicate that the skin offers some resistance to the passage of the current. If now the subject is given stimulation calculated to excite emotional reaction, the skin resistance is found to decrease: the excursions of the galvanometer are greater, and it is assumed that the amount of the decrease measures the amount of the emotional excitement aroused. (See Figure 54.)

It is fairly easy to demonstrate this galvanic skin response (*GSR*). The subject is seated, with electrodes bound to the palm and back of a hand, or with his two hands immersed in separate liquid receptacles. Wires are used to connect battery, resistor, galvanometer, and subject all in one electric circuit. After the galvanometer is set at an arbitrary zero point while the subject rests, the demonstrator presents the subject with emotional stimuli (noises, embarrassing questions, jokes, revolting pictures, small animals, and so on), and notes from time to time the readings of the galvanometer. If the results are typical, the galvanometer will make a definite deflection shortly after each time the subject becomes emotional.

There are complicating details. For one thing, the resistance at the skin is lowered by a number of other bodily conditions that are not properly called emotional, such as muscular exercise, alertness, deep breathing, concentration on an intellectual problem. And whatever the condition responsible, the measurements read from the instrument are not to be interpreted as absolute units of resistance but are entirely relative to what happens to be the subject's general level of reading in the setting at the time [7, 18].

Many other disturbances in the functioning of one's internal organs occur with emotional excitement. A military example will show a few. An examiner once participated in some twenty bombing missions over Japanese-held bases known to be well defended with anti-aircraft equipment; he rode in the cockpit just between and behind the pilots where he could make records of their physiological reactions. Table XVIII gives two typical records. As we scrutinize the data we note that when a pilot first sighted his target, when he first ran into anti-aircraft fire, and while he was driving directly over that fire, clearly marked changes were recorded in his blood pressure, in his pulse rate, and in his breathing rate, and at one time also in his rate of perspiring. The pilots' subjective statements about their reactions paralleled these objective readings.

There is much practical wisdom packed into some incidental notes

TABLE XVIII

Two Records of Physiological Reactions of Pilots
on Bombing Missions

Pilot A

Time	Situation	Blood Pressure	Pulse	Respi-ration	Other
0743	Take-off				
0800	Climbing to cruising altitude	132	96	18	
0805	Co-pilot flying aircraft	132	96	18	
0827	Formation leveled off at 9000 ft.	132	92	18	
0845	Uneventful cruising	122	86	18	
0850–	Donning of oxygen equipment, climbing				
0935	to 18,000 ft., and leveling off	122	86	18	
0937	Sighting target	138	94	22	Profuse per-spiration at palms
0941	Approaching target	138	82	28	
1003	Gliding to target	132	90	26	
1006	Over target	132	90	26	
1007	First anti-aircraft position	138	90	26	
1014	Approaching strongest anti-aircraft position	138	94	26	
1015	Over same	140	96	26	
1020	Out of anti-aircraft range	120	84	18	
1030	Returning to base	110	72	16	
1100	Returning to base	104	68	16	

Pilot B

Time	Situation	Blood Pressure	Pulse	Respiration
1135	Outward flight	122	88	
1215	Sighting target	140	100	
1230	Circling at distance, waiting for clouds to lift	130–140	120	
1250	The same	146	120	20
1300	Starting over target	142	118	
1302	Over target	140	112	
1303	Over center of target	132	108	
1304	Run completed	128	100	
1330	Returning flight	118	82	16

From E. E. Kirsch, J. AVIAT. MED., *1945,*
16, 378. By permission of editor and publisher.

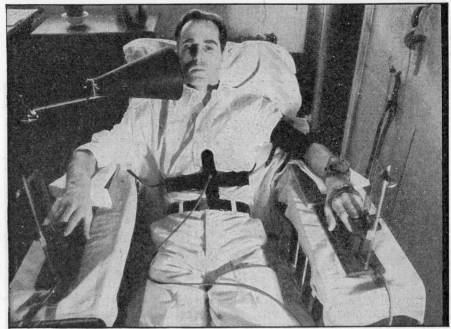

55 **Registering Physiological Changes in Emotion (Darrow's Photopolygraph)**

Several aspects of the subject's reactions can be automatically recorded. His *vocal* responses are received through the megaphone and transmitted to a sound recorder. *Involuntary movements* of his fingers, on springs, produce variations in pressure which are transmitted pneumatically through tubes to recording pens (cf. Figure 56). Changes in *respiration* are detected in changes in the pressures imparted to the *pneumograph* bound about thorax and abdomen, and also connected pneumatically with recording pens. The *pulse* is recorded as changes in pressure on the *sphygmograph* mounted over an artery at the left wrist. *Blood pressure* is recorded as changes in pressure against the air-bag or *sphygmomanometer* bound about the left upper arm, or else as changes in level of the pulse record. Both the latter instruments communicate pneumatically with recording pointers. The *galvanic skin response* is registered through a galvanometer circuit, not shown (but cf. Figure 54), connected with electrodes strapped to palm and back of the left hand. (*From P. T. Young*, EMOTION IN MAN AND ANIMAL, *Wiley, 1943. By permission of author and publisher. Photograph by the courtesy of Dr. Ralph R. Brown.*)

made by this same observer. He pointed out that close attention to one's duties, while engaged in flight over enemy positions, alleviates one's fright considerably.

Figures 55 and 56 are presented here to show a number of techniques for obtaining records of the above-mentioned physiological changes and others occurring under laboratory conditions.

Word-Association Technique. Although it is not directly a study of specific physiological changes, we should do well to note another method that has had rather better success in bringing emotional responses to light, though it has usually been employed in conjunction with the blood pressure or the galvanic skin response method. In this, the free word-association procedure, instructions are given to the subject in somewhat the following manner: "I am going to say a word aloud; as soon as you have heard it I want you to respond by speaking out the first word that then occurs to you, just as quickly as you possibly can — no matter what the word may be. Suppose that I were to say 'table' and you were to start at once to say 'chair,' or that I were to say 'hot' and you were to say 'cold' or 'summer.' I have a list of words that I will use, one at a time." The experimenter keeps accurate record of each stimulus word, of the subject's response word, and of the exact time interval between the two, as measured by a fifth-second stop watch or by a chronoscope started and stopped with voice keys.

The subject may be expected to react emotionally to certain of the words and not to others. (See Figure 54, III and IV, for evidence of the potency of a mere word.) Usually he shows suppressive processes at work: the normal or neurotic person is unwilling to divulge secrets of his past history; the criminal suspect is trying to conceal all knowledge of the crime in question. How is the experimenter to know when his subject is reacting suppressively? In such cases, the presence of emo-

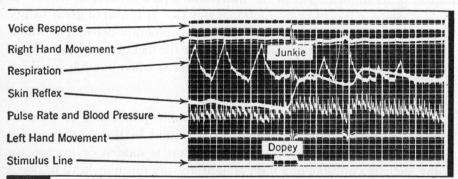

56

A Record from Darrow's Photopolygraph

A short section of a record traced by writing pens connected with the receiving instruments illustrated in Figure 55. To the word "dopey" (slang for a user of narcotics) the subject answered with "junkey" (slang for drug addict). The break in the voice line indicates the moment that the vocal response occurred. Note that all records suggest some emotional excitement associated with that response. (*From Young, op. cit. By permission of author and publisher, and courtesy of Dr. Brown.*)

tional disturbance in response to certain stimulus words, especially in connection with a fear of exposure through his verbal reactions, may interfere with the otherwise smoothly running word-reactions of the subject and produce symptoms readily recognized by the skilled operator.

Among the symptoms or *diagnostic signs* of emotionally disturbed word-associations the following have been included by workers in this field:
(1) Suspiciously long reaction time in giving the word.
(2) Suspiciously short reaction time.
(3) No response whatever.
(4) Repetition of the stimulus word itself.
(5) Repetition of a response word used previously.
(6) Strange and apparently senseless reactions.
(7) Apparent misunderstanding of the stimulus word.
(8) On a later retrial with the same stimulus, a defective reproduction of the word response given the first time.
No one of these symptoms is used by itself as indicative of emotion.

In this technique — just as in the use of instrumentation — it must be said that we are not provided with a method of determining precisely which emotional reaction pattern is in activity at a given time, but we are enabled to know when some kind is occurring, and also to know with what situations or ideas the emotional responses of the subject are bound up. And the last-mentioned advantage is of enormous practical utility in assisting a clinical examiner to get at crucial points (suppressed complexes) of habit-formation in the individual's past history, as well as to find out some of his present emotional quirks. It is also of great utility in the so-called "lie-detector" (or better, emotion-detector), which brings to the surface not the fact of lying but the fact of emotional excitement often appearing in characteristic patterns when one has just lied.

(3) Emotion Viewed as Behavior

Startle. The best example of a fixed innate patterning of a motor response of emotional character is to be found in the *startle* pattern. Immediately after a sensory stimulation that is sudden or intense (or both), such as a gunshot or a flash of light, the organism makes a response which involves muscles of the face and of almost the entire body. Employing a camera running as fast as 2000 to 3000 exposures per second and a fast clock in the field, Landis and Hunt have been able to analyze fleeting changes in a total response that is over in about a half-second. The facial part of the pattern involves first a blinking of the eyes, then a stretching of the mouth and a jerking forward of the head, as shown in Figure 57. Meanwhile there occur these other characteristic reactions: a hunching forward of the shoulders, a bending at the elbows, a flexing of the fingers, a bending of the knees, a contracting of the abdomen. These details may not all be invariably present, but the general pattern is; and the principal difference from case to case is the omission of this or that detail rather than the substitution of new and quite different details.

The general pattern is universal. It is found in all normal people, in all races, in infants as well as adults, in primates and some lower animals as well as humans, and in all clinical types of psychotic and neurotic patients excepting some epileptics. What is more, it is never completely overcome by training, for even policemen with long experience on pistol ranges were unable to inhibit the response entirely.

Rage. Rage is a universally recognizable pattern of behavior. And for good biological reason, for if there be any motion, manner, or manifestation by one animal or person that another animal or person should not be slow to recognize, it is this precursor and warning of attack. Darwin's pictures of angry animals remain classics today, for their uniformity and definiteness and identifiability as rage is convincing argument for the basic nature of the patterning. Figure 58 is a sample. Curious support is forthcoming in the convincing patterns of behavior in decorticated dogs and cats (animals which have been deprived of their highest brain parts, the cerebral cortex), for certainly any patterns exhibited then may be considered more basic.

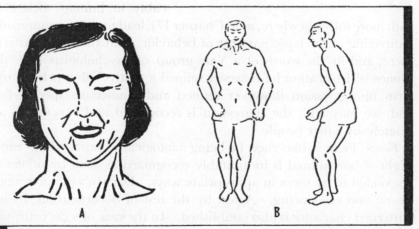

57 **The Startle Response**

Schematic representation of the facial pattern (*A*) and the more general bodily pattern (*B*). (*From C. Landis and W. A. Hunt,* THE STARTLE PATTERN, *Rinehart, 1939. By permission of author and publisher.*)

Cat 103 displayed a stereotyped reaction when the tip of the tail was pinched. This consisted of: lowering the head, raising the back, drawing the ears back, loud growling, hissing, biting, vigorous alternate striking movements of the forelegs with claws unsheathed, turning (usually to the left), erection of hair, pupillo-dilatation, retraction of nicti-tating membranes, widening of the palpebral spaces, and cardiac acceleration (from 70–100 a minute at rest to 200–250 during activity). This reaction varied from the display of rage seen in normal cats [only] in being undirected.[1]

58   **An Animal Emotion**

The pattern is identifiable and un-mistakable. (*From C. Darwin*, [8].)

With human beings we should not expect to find such stereotyped patterns, for as the infant and child grows richer in his social experience, his overt conduct toward other infants and children undergoes continual re-shaping as it evokes reciprocal conduct from them. The very processes of learning to live amicably in human society (dealt with more fully elsewhere, as in Chapter 17), lead to much suppressing and redirecting of the basic patterns of behavior. But the basic patterns are there; and in the words of a Yale group of psychologists [9], "the existence of frustration [of however refined a motive] always leads to some form of aggression [however refined and masked its specific form]"; and, we may add, the aggression is recognized and reacted to appropriately by other people.

Fear. Fear is like rage in being biologically basic. Like rage, the fright of one animal is indubitably recognized as such by others and is responded to by them in appropriate ways. Darwin's pictures again are classic and convincing. Again by the test of decortication, its innate-patterned character is also established. In the case of a decorticated cat:

The moment the loud noise of escaping steam was heard the animal suddenly retracted and lowered her head, crouched, mewed and then dashed

[1] From P. Bard, *Psychol. Rev.*, 1934, *41*, 434. Quoted by courtesy of the American Psychological Association.

off running rapidly in a slinking manner with head, chest, belly, and tail close to the floor. After blindly colliding with several objects in her path she came to rest in a corner where she crouched, mewing plaintively. During this activity and for some time afterwards the eyes were widely opened, the pupils were maximally dilated and there was some erection of hair on the back and tail. . . . A repetition of the same noise a little later produced the same striking reaction and it was also observed when a very similar noise was made by running water from a tap through a narrow nozzle.[1]

Smiling and Laughing. A unique kind of evidence for the native-patterned character of smiling and laughing is to be found in Goodenough's study of a ten-year-old child that had been both blind and deaf from birth, and hence quite isolated and unable to observe the emotional behavior of other children or adults. The girl was observed daily for several weeks; notes were made, and motion pictures taken.

On one occasion a doll had been dropped inside the neck of her dress. Her body grew tense, the eyebrows were raised, and the sightless eyes opened wide. When she had failed to retrieve the doll after some minutes of patient attempts, she ceased her groping and, with head drooping, made light whimpering sounds. Suddenly she renewed the attack, and after much twisting and jerking she got hold of it and brought it out. Then she raised both hands, threw back her head, smiled broadly, and gave out peals of laughter.[2]

Smiling and laughing, we may safely conclude, are innate emotional patterns in the human being.

Crying. The behavior of the deaf-blind child and the description of vocal sounds she made at one time point clearly to another unlearned pattern of emotional response. Every nursery and every family knows that crying appears promptly after birth — days and weeks in advance of the first smiling or laughing — and that it recurs frequently throughout the early years of life. In brief there is ample evidence of its universality and its fundamental inborn nature.

"Love" Reactions. "Love" has numerous meanings, and it is impossible at present to establish the precise denotation of this general term.

Due to the mores of the folk, the behavioral side of sexual emotion has not been subjected to experimental investigation in human beings. With lower animals, however, much has been done; and a few generalizations may be set up. Both the male and the female patterns of sexual behavior in higher animals are possible to animals deprived of their cerebral cortices, and so are on a level with rage, fear, startle, crying,

---

[1] From Bard, *op. cit.*, 439–440.
[2] This account is made still more convincing by the photographs [10].

and perhaps other emotions. As complete patterns they are notably subject to endocrine control in the white rat, for injection of the proper hormones will eventually awaken the complete mating patterns of activity in male or female animals that have not yet attained maturity or in male animals that have been castrated [4].

How, out of the primary sexual emotions love between man and woman develops is a story on which we have but little safe and sure evidence. History and anthropology and clinical cases furnish us a wealth of material, but what analyses and deductions and generalizations are to be drawn from them cannot at this moment be predicted. One thing that is fairly clear is that "romantic love" is not an emotional pattern unique in nature and universally found throughout mankind. It is not inborn. History and anthropology suggest that what Americans know as "love" and conventionally hold to be the one essential to successful marriage — a view much insisted upon in motion pictures and in popular magazines — is a particular acquired integration of emotional segments traceable largely to the ideal of knightly chivalry formulated in the Middle Ages; for it is a pattern almost impossible to find in the behavior of men and women in Hebrew, Greek, Roman, Levantine, Chinese, and even in much contemporary European society.

Conclusion as to Classification. We cannot hope to achieve an exhaustive list of the basic emotional behavior patterns, but the foregoing will serve to suggest that the project of identifying and classifying "the emotions" is best furthered if we keep in the forefront the behavioral viewpoint — the roles that the emotions play in the inter-individual biological life of organisms.

Theories Regarding the Three Views of Emotion

For more than sixty years debates have raged over variations of the question: When a person becomes emotional which happens first: (1) his experiencing of emotion (E), or (2) the visceral physiological changes (V) or (3) his overt responses to the environment (O)? Common sense and the early psychologists usually put them in the order, E, V, O; William James in 1884 argued persuasively for what came to be called the James-Lange theory that V really preceded E; while Cannon and Bard much more recently have put forth claims that suggest something like an O, $E + V$ order. Much evidence of many sorts has been advanced, but as the matter has in no true sense been settled, it would seem unwise to burden the pages of an introductory textbook with a rehearing of the arguments [3, 6, 15]. The sounder position is that we recognize the interdependence of the three views, the *oneness* of what we call "emotion."

THE GENETIC DEVELOPMENT OF EMOTION

Some Maturational Sequences Observed

The emotional behavior of infants in a Montreal hospital was carefully observed and recorded daily over a period of four months. The investigator, Dr. Banham-Bridges, observed sufficient uniformities from infant to infant, in the ages at which various emotions were first noted, to warrant drawing a developmental diagram like that shown in Figure 59. In the newborn, it seemed, there was only one kind of emotion, an undifferentiable and general agitation or "excitement." In the course of the early days of the infant's life, the observer could begin to make out a difference developing in its excitement, a "distressed" as over against a "delighted" excitement. With later observations through the first year, further differentiations could be detected, as can be seen in the figure. Notes were taken on the attendant circumstances; and it was concluded that the character of the development was much determined by the particular events and experiences in the routine daily round of feeding, washing, dressing, and sleeping. On the other hand, the maturational factors were not completely ignored; and the successive appearances cer-

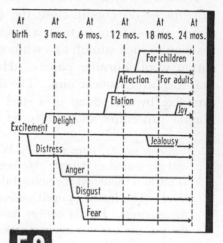

59 **Emotion in Infants**

The approximate ages of differentiation of the various emotions during the first two years of life. (*Adapted from K. M. Banham-Bridges,* CHILD DEVELOPMENT, *1932, 3, 340.*)

tainly remind us of the genetically determined developmental sequences we have already noted in chapter 4, in respect of motor traits.

This view — that the baby's emotional behavior manifests new forms in a pretty well established order for much the same biological reason as the developing seedling puts forth stem, then leaf, then blossom, then seed — is bolstered by a study of visual and motion pictures of blind and seeing children. Many of the facial patterns of emotional response of the blind turned out to be identical with those usually called smiling, laughing, anger, sulkiness, annoyance, and sadness in seeing children of the same ages. True, the blind children's expressions tended to show less muscular activity as they grew older; but the consistency and accuracy with which different judges rated the expressions of both blind and seeing children offers good evidence that these facial expressions do occur and do develop without learning [25].

Emotions Are Subject to Training

When we turn to the question of the effective stimuli or occasions for arousing emotional responses, the part played by experience is not to be minimized. The pioneer work of Watson on *conditioning* continues to be the measure of all other work in this area [26].

Watson selected a child eleven months of age as the subject in an experiment on conditioning the fear response. The child had been reared almost from birth in a hospital environment and showed no fear reaction to such stimuli as a white rat, a rabbit, a dog, a monkey, masks, cotton wool, burning papers. He reached for practically everything that was brought near him. The fear pattern of behavior was, however, excitable by the sound of a steel bar struck sharply just behind him. For the procedure and results, let us follow the experimenters' notes.

Eleven months, three days. 1. White rat suddenly taken from the basket and presented to Albert. He began to reach for rat with left hand. Just as his hand touched the animal the bar was struck immediately behind his head. The infant jumped violently and fell forward, burying his face in the mattress. He did not cry, however. 2. Just as the right hand touched the rat, the bar was again struck. Again the infant jumped violently, fell forward, and began to whimper. In order not to disturb the child too seriously, no further tests were given for one week.

Eleven months, ten days. 1. Rat presented suddenly without sound. There was steady fixation but no tendency at first to reach for it. The rat was then placed nearer, whereupon tentative reaching movements began with the right hand. When the rat nosed the infant's left hand, the hand was immediately withdrawn. He started to reach for the head of the animal with the forefinger of the left hand, but withdrew it suddenly before contact. It is thus seen that the two joint stimulations given the previous week were not without effect. He was tested with his blocks immediately afterward to see if they shared in the process of conditioning. He began immediately to pick them up, dropping them, pounding them, and so on. In the remainder of the tests the blocks were given frequently to quiet him and to test his general emotional state. They were always removed from sight when the process of conditioning was under way. 2. Joint stimulation with rat and sound. Started, then fell over immediately to right side. No crying. 3. Joint stimulation. Fell to right side and rested upon hands, with head turned away from rat. No crying. 4. Joint stimulation. Same reaction. 5. Rat suddenly presented alone. Puckered face, whimpered and withdrew body sharply to the left. 6. Joint stimulation. Fell over immediately to right side and began to whimper. 7. Joint stimulation. Started violently and cried, but did not fall over. 8. Rat alone. *The instant the rat was shown the baby began to cry. Almost instantly he turned sharply to the left, fell over on left side, raised himself on all fours, and began to crawl away so rapidly that he was caught with difficulty before reaching the edge of the table.*

The attachment of the fear response to the white-rat stimulus operated, moreover, as an attachment to several other objects that formerly did not function as stimuli to this response. The child now reacted violently to a rabbit, a dog, a sealskin coat, cotton wool, a hairy mask. A lack of specificity, a *general* character, to the $S \longrightarrow R$ relation was thus demonstrated, the R excited by a certain specific S being also excitable by many other S's having certain visual stimulus qualities in common with it.

Finally, it is important to note that the conditioned reaction persisted over a full month's interval, although in not quite its original intensity.

Many Fears Are Acquired

One corollary from the above experiments has extremely practical bearings. If a child is afraid that "the goblins'll git" him, that is evidence enough that a misguided parent or ignorant nursemaid, thoughtless teacher or bullying brother, has been trying to control him by deliberately attaching his fear response to the "goblins" — or to darkness, to the attic, to the big policeman, to the old black man — and has then been calling up such stimuli to cow him into submission when obedience was not promptly forthcoming. It may be well to develop in the child a sense of caution with reference to traffic in a busy street or to contagious diseases or any of the many conditions and situations of life in which danger actually lurks; but the cultivating of such attachments to essentially harmless and even nonexistent things is indefensible. As a matter merely of physical hygiene, it is to be remembered that fear, like rage or any other emergency type of emotion, is antagonistic to the healthy body-developing processes of the organism. And when the reactions become so violent as to turn into "tantrums," grave consequences may be entailed to the poise and nervous equilibrium and even to the sanity of the man or woman in the making.

Conditioning Is a Useful Key to Much Emotional Life

What was true for fear is equally true for other emotions. We have here a key to the interpretation of all sorts of irrational likes and dislikes, pet peeves and preferences, manias and phobias, and the innumerable big and little emotional attachments we find in ourselves and in other persons. One adult of the writer's acquaintance experiences an almost uncanny warmth and friendliness toward pink chinaware, which can be explained by his having had his porridge and cereal from a pink bowl during his infant years. Another confesses to a dread of houses with arched windows, an aversion traceable to the shape of the windows in a mouse-trap he now recalls from his fourth year, from which captured mice would be released on the lawn as game for the excited dog and even more excited children.

Every clinical psychologist is constantly running into symptoms which have no sensible or rational explanation, except as things that have been acquired by his patients through little more than accidental associations.

Retraining an Emotional Response

If, then, a child's fears may be a serious and even a dangerous factor in his development, psychology, after having shown definitely how fears can be built up, bears the obligation of showing how they can be eliminated. Considerations of mental health in children and in adults dictate that such a question has far more than merely academic interest.

Some useful principles are to be derived from the investigations made by Jersild and Holmes into the ways and means by which parents have helped their children to rid themselves of fear [16].

1. *Removing the cause.* Parent holds hand of child afraid to go to sleep alone; does not let him see animal or policeman he fears. Result: successful in only 10 per cent of the cases reported.

2. *Ignoring the fear.* Changing the subject when child talks about death; paying no heed to his fear of dark room. Result: successful in only 17 per cent of the cases.

3. *Examples of fearlessness in others.* The parent wades ahead into the waves; has the child watch brother ride on the noisy vacuum cleaner. Result: successful in but 33 per cent of the cases.

4. *Verbal reassurance.* The parent explains that the dog really is not dangerous; that the thunder and lightning are simple natural phenomena; that dangerous wind-storms happen only in Kansas. Result: successful, when used alone in 41 per cent of the cases.

5. *Passive association* of feared thing with an unfeared thing; strange nun smiles at him; old, wrinkled person makes him a toy; mother plays piano for him during thunderstorms. Result: successful in 50 per cent of the cases.

6. *Graded presentation.* Mother begins cutting child's hair in the barber shop and lets barber finish; child given a smiling mask first before the scary

ones, or a soft-sounding alarm clock before the Big Ben. Result: successful in 75 per cent of the cases.

7. *Growing familiar with it on his own accord;* no urging. Friendly dog left in yard where it can be approached; ugly masks left lying about house; feared slide left standing in playroom. Result: successful in 82 per cent of the cases.

8. *Promoting skill in dealing with it.* Coaching in how to out-smart a dangerous imaginary dog; making the dark closet a center of some games; showing how to mount and control wheeled toys. Result: successful in 90 per cent of the cases.

As scientific findings, these descriptions of collected incidents leave much to be desired, of course. Under each heading, the characterizations are anything but precise; the cases are not arrayed in any strict quantitative way; and many of the incidents undoubtedly involved more than a single principle. Yet there can be discerned favorable weightings in the direction of *gradualness* of approach to the feared object of the child's *own accord*, and especially in ways of *acquiring skills* by which it may be gotten under control. And, it is here submitted, these points are of suggestive value in connection with other problems of control in the quest of a healthy emotional life.

AFFECTIVITY

The Pleasant-Unpleasant Dimension

Viewed subjectively, emotional life has always been recognized as pervaded by a certain polarity, *pleasant-unpleasant.* This unique character of conscious experience needs only to be named to be recognized. The terms *pleasantness* and *unpleasantness* do not denote any independent experiences or processes, but are used as names for the qualities considered in the abstract. These qualities of human experience, though certainly distinct from each other, appear each in varying degrees; so that taken together they form a continuum or *dimension.* And this dimension is one, regardless of the more concrete details of one's many experiences. A drink of lemonade when one is moderately thirsty; the sight of a child cruelly beaten; the realization that one has completed a good job; a long wait in a queued-up line at a ticket window; the sight of a carelessly speeding autoist; the sounds of the *Siciliana* sung off-stage by a tenor; the sight of the names "Dachau" and "Lidice"; the finding of a five-cent piece; the rhythm of a Shakespearian passage — all such events in a person's experience could be assigned by him to various points on the same P-U scale.[1] They are "agreeable-disagreeable" in different degrees.

Some Dependent Relationships

This *hedonic* or *affective* character, as it is called, is an extremely unstable and inconstant one, as anyone can testify if he will note how the agreeableness of a favored dish varies with each successive helping. In that particular case the variations are correlated in an obvious way with variations in appetite. Other relationships of a dependent nature have had attention in the experimental laboratory. Of these we may mention two that involve easily measured stimulation variables.

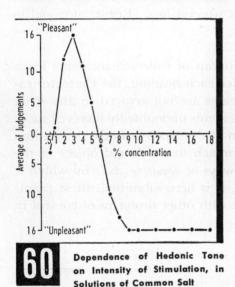

60 Dependence of Hedonic Tone on Intensity of Stimulation, in Solutions of Common Salt

Eight observers, in two sittings, judging on a scale: "very pleasant," "pleasant," "indifferent," "unpleasant," "very unpleasant." For each degree of salt concentration, shown horizontally, the judgments were pooled to furnish one index of *P–U.* (*From Saidullah, "Experimentelle Untersuchungen uber den Geschmacksinn," ARCH. GES. PSYCHOL., 1927, 60, 477.*)

Hedonic tone varies with *intensity* of stimulation. A slight pinch of salt added to a glass of water may make the water just perceptibly salty, but neither pleasant nor unpleasant; that is, it affects the taste indifferently. Let a few more grains be added, and the taste experience will take on a certain amount of pleasantness. But let further intensifications of the salt stimulation be made and — though the sensory quality of saltiness as such will undergo no change — the affective character will, and abruptly. Figure 60 from an Indian authority reveals this phenomenon. We may generalize it as follows: In all forms of sensory stimulation there is likely to be a certain optimal range of intensity, which will occasion

[1] The conscious experiences of pleasant-unpleasant have been the object of analytic attack for decades. Can they not be further analyzed? A theory much in the limelight of contemporary discussion is Nafe's belief that the feeling of "pleasant" is further reducible to bright points of experience of the general nature of a very mild thrill, and vaguely localizable in the upper part of the body, while "unpleasant" is a duller, heavier sort of pressure experience localizable in the lower part of the body [21]. As the reader will admit, only after pretty specialized training is one equipped to pursue this introspective kind of inquiry; and we cannot follow it further here.

a pleasant character to the experience; while supraoptimal intensities will excite unpleasant, and infra-optimal intensities either unpleasant or neutral.

Hedonic tone varies with *repetition* of stimulation. It is commonly accepted that as one hears a piece of music over and over again it is likely to change in its P-U character — and the direction in which it changes may indeed be taken as a rough index of its artistic value. This is well borne out in an experiment at Vassar College in which orchestral recordings of four grades of musical quality were repeated five times in succession. After each presentation the subjects were asked to rate the musical themes on a five-point scale. From these ratings, the investigators picked out the number of times the 220 judges assigned the top rating to each of the themes on each of the five successive presentations. Figure 61 brings out strikingly not only that with repetition the P-U character changes, but that for themes of recognized artistic merit there is a gain in pleasantness while for those of questionable artistic merit there is a corresponding loss. The reader will think of many phenomena of daily life quite outside the field of music to which a generalized form of this principle will apply. "Familiarity breeds contempt" — for certain things. Others "improve upon acquaintance."

Methods of Impression

As the Vassar research will suggest, the affectivity studied may take the form of esthetic appreciation.

Man's appreciation of the beautiful is subject to study and analysis as truly as any other natural phenomenon. Even quantitative investigations are possible. To be sure, a person's reaction to a work of Rembrandt, Milton, Chopin, or Saint-Gaudens is not yet subject to detailed psychological description; and the experimentalist must limit himself to modest beginnings with colors, lines, rhythm beats, or tonal combinations. But this is also true of the scientific study of any complex phenomenon. The procedures of experimental esthetics are, essentially simple.

The artistic properties of an object are not something to be found by examining the object itself but by noting the human reactions to it. If the esthetic value of a given work of art is to be determined, show it or sound it along with another or others, and then note the directions and amounts of preferences. These are the *Methods of Impression*.[1] Scientific studies have dealt, for the most part, with pictures, musical compositions, and poems; and they have taken the typical experimental form of

---

[1] So called by contrast with the *Methods of Expression*, a term applied to the instrumentations described on pages 207 ff.

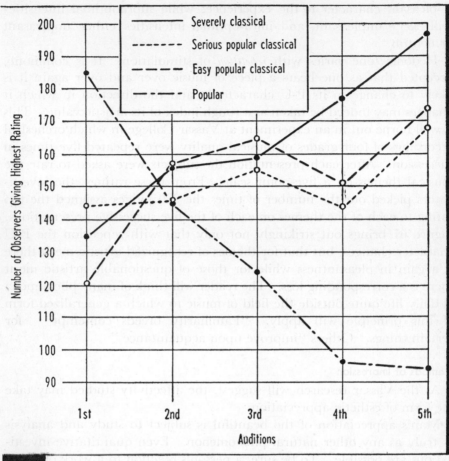

61 Effect of Repetitions on Pleasantness of Music

(From M. F. Washburn, M. S. Child, and T. M. Abel, in M. Schoen, THE EFFECTS OF MUSIC, Kegan Paul, 1927, pages 204 ff; after Beebe-Center. By permission.)

analyzing the complex subject-matter into simpler parts: iambic versus trochaic rhythms, balanced versus unbalanced masses, complementary versus non-complementaty color combinations, the curve versus the straight line — these are typical. One famous discovery was Fechner's. Of many shapes of rectangle shown, his observers consistently preferred the "golden section," in which the two dimensions of the figure are in the ratio 21/34 or approximately .62.

There are two time-honored methods of impression. Suppose some eight or ten objects are to be ranked as to their hedonic value. In the original procedure of Fechner, known as the *Method of Paired Comparisons*, the investigator displays the objects two at a time, and records the subject's preference between them. When each stimulus-object has been paired once with every other one, a totaling of the number of preferences each stimulus has received furnishes the final order of choices. In the *Method of Order of Merit*, the subject is supplied with the whole set of materials; and he is to arrange them into a row or sequence to show which one he prefers most, which next most, and so on. Simple though the two procedures seem, they present many pitfalls; when, for example, in the P-C Method the order of the paired presentations needs to be worked out with statistical insight. Perhaps indeed their great merit lies in the fact that they are adaptations of methods in everyday use from time immemorial, but now rigorously standardized and purified of many of the sources of error that creep into the judging of needlework, babies, jellies, bathing beauties, and Poland China hogs.

Affectivity and Values

Through the centuries men have sought out the organic correlates of the P-U experiences. We need not go into them; but there is a point in realizing that nearly all of them have some explicit or implicit reference to the organism's *favorable* or *unfavorable* relation to the object in question. Pleasantness is felt in the former case, unpleasantness in the latter. The polarity may be traced back to the primitive opposition, noted by Aristotle, between approaching and withdrawing — a phenomenon easily seen in the ways in which the amoeba or the earthworm or the fish react positively or negatively to the objects and conditions facing them. Here, it may be, is the primordial basis for that polarity of "good" and "bad" that pervades all human life and culture, differentiating into the ethically, esthetically, economically, politically, and socially good and bad (see pages 163 ff).

REFERENCES

1. Banham-Bridges, K. M. "Emotional development in early infancy," *Child Develop.*, 1932, *3*, 324–341.
2. Bard, P. "On emotional expression after decortication," etc., II, *Psychol. Rev.*, 1934, *41*, 424–449.
3. Bard, P. "The neuro-humoral basis of emotional reactions," in C Murchison, ed., *A Handbook of General Experimental Psychology*. Worcester, Mass.: Clark University Press, 1934.
4. Beach, F. A. "Sexual behavior of prepuberal male and female rats treated with gonadal hormones," *J. Comp. Psychol.*, 1942, *34*, 285–292. Beach, F. A., and A. M. Holz, "Mating behavior in male rats castrated

at various ages and injected with androgen," *J. Exp. Zool.*, 1946, *101*, 91–142.

5. Beebe-Center, J. G. *The Psychology of Pleasantness and Unpleasantness.* New York: D. Van Nostrand Company, 1932.

6. Cannon, W. B. "The James-Lange theory of emotions," *Amer. J. Psychol.*, 1927, *39*, 106–124.

7. Darrow, C. W. "The equation of the galvanic skin reflex curve: 1," *J. Gen. Psychol.*, 1937, *16*, 285–309.

8. Darwin, C. *The Expression of the Emotions in Man and Animals.* London: Murray, 1872.

9. Dollard, J., *et al. Frustration and Aggression.* New Haven, Conn.: Yale University Press, 1939.

10. Goodenough, F. L. "Expression of the emotions in a blind-deaf child," *J. Abn. Soc. Psychol.*, 1932, *27*, 328–333.

11. Graham, J. D. P. "High blood-pressure after battle," *Lancet*, 1945, *248*, 239–240.

12. Hebb, D. O. "Emotion in man and animal: an analysis of the intuitive processes of recognition," *Psychol. Rev.*, 1946, *53*, 88–106.

13. Hunt, W. A. "The reliability of introspection in emotion," *Amer. J. Psychol.*, 1937, *49*, 650–653.

14. Hunt, W. A. "Recent developments in the field of emotion," *Psychol. Bull.*, 1941, *38*, 249–276.

15. James, W. *Principles of Psychology.* New York: Henry Holt and Company, 1890. Chapter XXV.

16. Jersild, A. T., and F. B. Holmes. "Methods of overcoming children's fears," *J. Psychol.*, 1935, *1*, 75–104.

17. Kirsch, R. E. "A physiological study of aviators during combat flying," *J. Aviat. Med.*, 1945, *16*, 376–384.

18. Landis, C., and W. A. Hunt. "The conscious correlates of the galvanic skin response," *J. Exp. Psychol.*, 1935, *18*, 505–529.

19. Landis, C., and W. A. Hunt. *The Startle Pattern.* New York: Rinehart and Company, 1939.

20. Lund, F. H. *Emotions: their Psychological, Physiological, and Educative Implications.* New York: Ronald Press, 1939.

21. Nafe, J. P. "The pressure, pain, and temperature senses," in C. Murchison, ed., *A Handbook of General Experimental Psychology.* Worcester, Mass.: Clark University Press, 1934. Pp. 1037–1087.

22. Patrick, J. R. "Studies in rational behavior and emotional excitement: II," *J. Comp. Psychol.*, 1934, *18*, 153–195.

23. Ruckmick, C. A. *The Psychology of Feeling and Emotion.* New York: Mc-Graw-Hill Book Company, 1936.

24. Saul, L. J. "Physiological effects of emotional tension," in J. McV. Hunt, ed., *Personality and the Behavior Disorders.* New York: Ronald Press, 1944.

25. Thompson, J. "Development of facial expression of emotion in blind and seeing children," *Arch. Psychol., N.Y.*, 1941, *37*, No. 264.
26. Watson, J. B., and R. Rayner, "Conditioned emotional reactions," *J. Exp. Psychol.*, 1920, *3*, 1–14.
27. Wolff, H. G. "Emotions and gastric functions," *Science*, 1943, *98*, 481–484.
28. Young, P. T. *Emotion in Man and Animal.* New York: John Wiley and Sons, 1943.

10

SENSORY FUNCTIONS

INTRODUCTION TO THE THREE FOLLOWING CHAPTERS

WE HAVE BEEN STUDYING the behavior of human (and sub-human) beings as total organisms. At times we have analyzed conduct into some simpler components, even down to reflex arcs; but our eye has been on the person (or animal) as a whole — integrated, self-regulatory, and in contact and interaction with his environment at many points. He has developed from a single cell, and his growth has been the growth of a body with delicately interdependent parts. His activities have been concerned with the adjustment of his whole self to conditions of life.

Such a viewpoint too rigidly maintained may lead to vagueness, however, and we need to know more precisely how the particular parts work. We shall, therefore, carry out an analysis suggested in Chapter 2, and give attention in turn to the functioning of the particular sensory mechanisms, the particular motor mechanisms, and the main types of neural or organizing mechanisms.

When this survey is completed we shall return to the viewpoint of a man-as-a-whole, and proceed to consider the more elaborate and refined developments of his behavior throughout the remainder of the book.

SENSITIVITY IN GENERAL

The Importance of Studying Sensory Phenomena

There can be no expression without impression, no response without stimulation. A man does nothing, is not active in any manner involving the effectors studied in the last chapter, unless in some way he is being influenced by energy-changes, occurring inside or outside of him, which play upon his receptors — provided we except a few cases of smooth muscle and gland excitation by hormones. The student interested in the phenomena of human nature and in their prediction and control must have some definite knowledge as to how men are sensitive to influences: to what kinds of forces or influences they are sensitive; at what degrees of intensity; and at what places on or in the body the influences must be applied. Many are the practical questions that turn upon such facts. What are the most effective colors for switch lights and street-crossing signals? Can all men see them equally well? What is the best form of illumination for a factory? How fine a difference can the average pilot detect in the directions of the motion of his airplane when it is enveloped in clouds? Do different pilots vary much in this regard, and can such variations be measured and tested? How good an "ear" and what kind of "ear" must one have to become a successful violinist? What are the essentials of a good musical tone? Just what is the nature of the difference of tones which proceed from various string, wood-wind, and brass instruments? In what way does the rolling of a ship excite nausea? When one is learning to operate a typewriter, what controls the speed and accuracy of the strokes? Why is the touch method of typing recommended? In learning to hold a billiard cue or a fencing foil precisely right, what receptors are involved? To put all this in a nutshell: no attempt systematically to understand the hows and whys of human nature can be successful unless consideration is given to *the paramount role of stimulation in the initiating and in the controlling of behavior.*

Another reason for the study of human sensitivity presents itself as soon as we recognize a centuries-old motive for psychological study — the analysis of one's own personal and private conscious experience. It is a fact that the great majority of thoroughgoing inquiries into the nature of consciousness have been highly analytical in character, and have discovered as the basis of consciousness sensations of one sort or another. A person's awareness of an object perceived or of an event imagined or dreamed, the feelings of his emotional responses, and even the processes of thinking as he is conscious of them — all are held to be reducible to the primordial sensory experiences of particular colors, tastes, sounds, pressures, strains, and the like. This analysis of one's consciousness, while for the most part exceedingly difficult for the untrained, is well typified by some fairly easy and common analyses attempted by the average man. He may, for example, examine the experience which he calls the taste of lemonade to determine whether it has sourness enough or sweetness enough, or he may examine the taste of his breakfast cereal to see whether the sweetness and the saltness of the taste are properly balanced. To summarize: any systematic study of psychology from the introspective approach must recognize *the central importance of sensations* (that is, the individual's awarenesses occasioned by stimulations) *in the analysis of conscious experience.*

A third reason for emphasizing sensitivity in our survey of psychology is the fact that this division of the field has been more thoroughly worked out in its details than any other; and it would be an unfair survey indeed that failed to show the reader some of this detailed work. As it happens, the answers to many of the problems that World War II presented to the psychologist turned on correct knowledge of the serviceman's sensory capacities.

A Classification of Receptors

The facts of stimulation and sensitivity are so many and diverse that we will do well to block out the phenomena by a preliminary classification (Table XIX).

TABLE

XIX A Classification of the Receptors and Their Stimuli

Stimuli	Receptors	Classes
I. *Energy changes in environment*	*Exteroceptors*	
light	in eye	visual
sound	in ear (cochlea)	auditory
heat (and cold)	in skin	cutaneous
pressure	in skin	cutaneous
noxious conditions	in skin*	cutaneous
chemicals	in nose	olfactory
chemicals	in tongue	gustatory
II. *Changes in position and movement of organism*	*Proprioceptors*	
of parts	in muscle, tendon, joint	kinesthetic
of whole	in ear (canals and vestibule)	static
III. *General organic conditions, especially of alimentary canal and other viscera*	*Interceptors*	
emptiness or distention of a viscus, chemical substance, etc., etc.	in linings of alimentary canal and in other deep tissues	organic

* Pain receptors are found in nearly all important organs, deep and superficial. These are sometimes classified in a fourth division as the "nociceptors."

This classification of stimuli is far from being clear-cut. We know as yet too little about all the stimulating conditions in the third class. This ignorance is the result, for one thing, of a relatively great difficulty in experimental analysis; for while in the laboratory it is a comparatively easy matter to control whatever light or sound stimuli are allowed to fall upon the eye or ear, it is quite another thing to attempt similarly to manipulate the normal stimuli that play upon receptive areas in the soft organs of the bodily interior.

The stimuli here listed are the usual or *adequate stimuli* for the respective receptors. In many cases the latter are excitable by other kinds of agencies or conditions. For instance, when the eyeball is poked with the finger, the eye may be affected as if by a light; and electricity applied to the eye, ear, tongue, or skin will be respectively seen, heard, tasted, or felt. Thus the experience arising from the excitation of a given sensory nerve is said to be specific to that nerve, regardless of how it came to be excited. This is the concept of the *specific energy of nerves*, developed over a century ago by Müller and by Helmholtz, and widely accepted in some form today.

The Relative Nature of a Stimulus

In order to function as a stimulus, an agent must play upon a receptor not in absolutely constant manner but with some change or contrast. To affect hearing, for instance, a sound must be louder or softer, higher or lower, or in some other way different from other sounds preceding or accompanying it. To be seen, an object must differ from its surroundings and background. The converse of this principle is strikingly demonstrated in the camouflage of war vessels and in the protective coloration of a chameleon or a flat fish, which, by changing their coloration and pattern to correspond to those of their background of tree trunk or ocean bottom, escape the vision of predatory animals.

Associated with this point is the phenomenon of *sensory adaptation*. After continuous stimulation of a given receptor, the stimulating agent progressively becomes less effective and may ultimately have no effect at all. This is true of most classes of sensation, ranging from smell and from temperature sense, in which it is strikingly shown, to pain, in which it is hardly observable. The nose, as is well known, becomes rapidly inexcitable by the same odor if the odor is long continued; the skin receptors of cold become inexcitable after the bather is once well in the pool. One "gets used to" the stimulation, as we say.

Interaction Between Different Modalities

The foregoing classification might suggest that the different senses of man operate in complete independence of each other; and we shall for the most part respect these modality division-lines in the present chapter. But we must recognize in passing that there are solid scientific bases for such everyday phrases as those that describe off-key singing as "blue" or "sour," or feelings on the morning after as a "dark-brown taste," or for those cases of "colored hearing" in which sounds of differing pitch are seen as colored in different ways. Where such linkages of sensory experiences in one modality with those of another are extensive, the phenomenon goes by the name of *synesthesia*. For example, a student reports that all sounds of human voices seem to her as colored, the higher the pitch the brighter the color. Another finds that all chemical names have subtle taste qualities.

Numerous experimental studies support the view that the different senses are not sealed off from each other. It has been demonstrated that a laboratory subject's sharpness of vision is increased if, while viewing, he hears a whistle blowing or smells an odorous bottle held under his nose; and his touch sense is keener when a diffuse light is admitted to his blindfolded eyes. And an attribute like "brightness" is found to be equally applicable to sounds, colors, odors, temperatures, skin-pressures, and other supposedly distinct sensory fields, making them comparable and commensurable in surprising degree [10, 13]. Original musical themes that had been improvised by a number of outstanding composers after studying each of the designs of Figure 62 were matched to these designs by thirty auditors far more frequently than could have happened by chance [19].

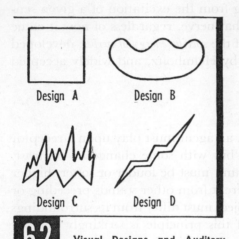

62 **Visual Designs and Auditory Patterns**

Design A   Design B   Design C   Design D

Each of several well-known musical composers, working individually, studied each design by itself for a while, then composed a theme that seemed somehow to fit it. A group of experimental auditors succeeded in matching visual to auditory pattern more often than they could have done by chance. (*From R. R. Willmann*, PSYCHOL. MONOGR., *1944*, 57, *no. 261.*)

CUTANEOUS SENSITIVITY [1]

Stimuli and Receptors

It is natural to begin our analysis of sense organs with those operating at the general surface of the body. These are relatively simple and are rather generally distributed. The skin is affected by temperature and by contact.

Let us follow a typical experiment. A small area of the skin is marked off with boundary and cross lines, and a variety of stimuli are then applied systematically to the whole area point by point. If a dull-pointed brass cylinder of the temperature 37° to 40° C. is placed in contact with the skin, it will in some places produce characteristic experiences and responses on the part of the subject: if properly instructed, he will say "warm" when it touches these points. These *warm* spots are relatively sparsely distributed. Now let a cooled cylinder of 12° to 15° C. be applied in the same manner of exploration, and at other places on the skin a clean, clear flash of "cold" will be sensed — the *cold* spots. There are on the average about thirteen cold and two warm spots to a square centimeter area. Next if we apply with gentle pressure a round wooden point we will succeed in arousing throughout most of the area experiences of "touch" or *pressure* — invariably so if we touch a hair or the skin just to the "windward" side of a hair. Finally, if we employ a rather stiff and sharply pointed bristle we will find that all parts of the area — with rarely an exception — will be sensitive to the pricking in a way that, if intensified, will evoke reflex retraction movements, and our subject will report "*pain*." A sample

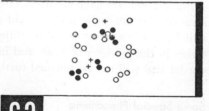

63 Map of Sensitive Spots in the Skin: Greatly Enlarged

Explanation in text.

map of the sensitivities in a small area (from the volar or palm surface of the forearm), as determined by this type of exploration, is given in Figure 63. In this diagram points where application of a warm stimulus elicits response are indicated with dots; where application of cold elicits response, with circles; where pressure fails to elicit response, with crosses. The application of a pain stimulus was effective throughout this area.

[1] The presentation of the different classes of sensitivity in the following pages will not follow strictly the order appearing in Table XIX. Simple but well analyzed classes will be presented first, and the most complex will be reserved for treatment last.

It is now obvious that within the same class of sensitivity (here, the cutaneous) different sensory functions may be included. The so-called sense of touch is not a single and simple capacity but a multiple one. On the structural side we would infer that within the skin there must be not one but several kinds of receptors, each selectively sensitive to its own peculiar type of agent — warmth, cold, pressure, or pain. Critical work [3] has, however, thrown so much doubt upon the traditionally accepted list of skin receptors that we shall not go into the matter beyond one differentiation. There are the *free* nerve-endings that abound throughout the skin, even in the epidermis — and also in the visceral organs in the body's interior (Figure 64, *A* and *B*). And in the deeper layers of the skin as well as in blood vessels, muscles, and elsewhere in the viscera, there are the *encapsulated* endings, which are probably variations upon one kind of basic structure: nerve endings that are much elaborated and are enclosed in some sort of capsule (*C* and *D* in Figure 64). We cannot say with assurance which of these subserve warm, cold, pressure, and pain experiences respectively. The fact remains that these four elemental kinds of cutaneous experience must somehow be mediated by different structures; for under certain conditions when anesthesia of the skin is reached by degrees, they will disappear in certain regular orders.

Some observers have reported a further differentiation of pressure and of pain sensory experiences into the bright and the dull kinds. The reader doubtless will be able to recognize some differences of the sort in the kind of pains he senses in the pricking of a pin and in a dull ache; but the matter is still controversial and will not be pursued further here.

Some Special Phenomena

It is not to be assumed, of course, that by ordinary agents only one receptor will be excited at a time. More commonly, many receptors of

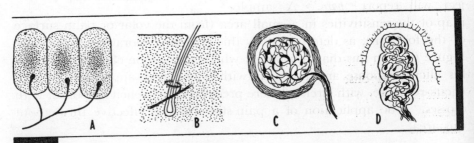

64 **Some Cutaneous Nerve Endings**

(*Redrawn from C. T. Morgan,* PHYSIOLOGICAL PSYCHOLOGY, *McGraw-Hill, 1943.*)

the same and of different types are aroused. The fact is well shown in the way immersion in water baths of different temperatures is found to excite different combinations of receptors and different qualities of experienced "feels." This is brought out in detail in Table XX. There the reader should note how at different degrees of temperature three kinds of receptors are excited in varying combinations and degrees, giving rise to experiences of qualitatively different character.

TABLE

 XX Different Temperatures Excite Different Receptors

Temperature in Centigrade	Receptors excited	How experienced
Below 10	Cold and pain	"biting cold"
15–30	Cold	"cold"
35–42	Warm	"warm"
46–50	Warm and cold	"hot"
Above 50	Warm, cold, and pain	"burning hot"

The distribution of sense organs varies greatly in the different areas over the body. A two-point esthesiometer, consisting of two dulled points of hard rubber, fixed at adjustable distances from each other and so placed on a handle as to be easily and lightly applied to the skin, is used to determine *spatial thresholds* of pressure, that is, the minimal distances that must separate two points before the subject can perceive them as distinct points. Some of these thresholds are given in Table XXI.

TABLE

 XXI Some Spatial Thresholds

Area of Body	Minimal Distance Between Two Points
Tip of tongue	1 mm.*
Tip of finger	2
Outer surface of lip	5
Palm	8
Forehead	22
Back of hand	30
Along spine	60

* These are mean values obtained by many measurements, in which the deviations are sometimes considerable.

A well-known phenomenon of cutaneous sensitivity is the rapid *adaptation* of the temperature end organs. Suppose that three vessels of water are provided at the temperatures 20°, 40°, and 30° C., respectively exciting the cold receptors, the warm receptors, and neither (the "physiological zero"). Let the left hand be held in the 20° bath and the right in the 40° bath for one minute, and it will be found not only that the excitation of the cold and of the warmth receptors gradually disappears, but also that when both hands are plunged into the "neutral" water at 30°, the left (previously in cold) shows stimulation of its warm receptors and the right (previously in warm) stimulation of its cold. Thus it is the change of temperature that is effective.

GUSTATORY SENSITIVITY

Stimuli and Receptors

In order to act upon the organism as a *taste*, a substance must be in liquid, or at least soluble, form and must be brought into contact with the "taste buds" located principally in the mucous membrane of the tongue and to a lesser degree on the soft palate and the lining of the pharynx (Figure 65). The taste buds on the tongue are embedded in some of the papillae (protuberances visible to the eye). In each of these

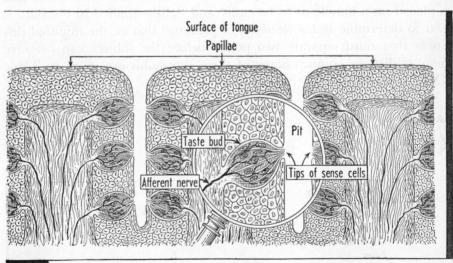

65 **A Taste Bud**

Showing its location in a papilla, its hairlike tips extending from the sensitive cells into the pit between papillae, and its nerve supply. Highly schematic. Taste bud drawn to much larger scale than are papillae.

buds the branching end of an afferent nerve is in close connection with hair cells, the hairy ends of which project out into the mouth cavity and are exposed to the substances there. The process of receptor stimulation is, then, excitation of some energy change in the hair cells caused by a substance having taste, consequent excitation of the nerve ending, and the transmission of this excitation along the afferent nerve to the central nervous system.

The sense of taste, like the sensitivity of the skin, is a multiple function. It is possible to classify all taste stimuli into the four groups *sweet, salt, sour,* and *bitter,* and their many combinations. Sensitivity to sweet substances is greatest near the tip of the tongue, to sour along the sides, and to bitter toward the back, while that to salty substances is more generally distributed.

The technique for the experimental investigation of taste is relatively simple. With camel's hair brushes or with pipettes, simple sapid liquids (liquids having taste, such as solutions of sugar and of common salt, tartaric acid, quinine hydrochlorate) are applied to individual papillae or to areas of the tongue, and the subject's verbal responses are noted. Care must be exercised to eliminate disturbing factors, particularly those other classes of stimulation mentioned in the preceding paragraph.

Some Special Phenomena

Some *adaptation* of the receptors may be observed. After continued eating of candy or syrupy food, a child may declare that a more mildly sweet food is not sweet at all; and salty ham becomes less salty with successive bites.

Contrast effects are also present. A sweet stimulation of subliminal intensity (that is, below the threshold of perception, too weak to be effective) on one side of the tongue may be rendered supraliminal (above the threshold of perception) by the simultaneous application of a sour stimulus on the other side. The same heightened effect is seen when the sour and the sweet stimuli are applied successively. Similar contrasts are obtained between sour and salt, and between salt and sweet.

An outstanding fact about taste in everyday life is that it is commonly confused with other modes of stimulation. In the process of eating, food stimulates the tongue as a cutaneous surface and ordinarily stimulates the olfactory receptors in the nasal passages to a marked degree, so that the effect of such things as hot coffee or iced lemonade is by no means an effect on taste alone.[1] For that matter, a person's

---

[1] An instructive demonstration is to have a blindfolded subject hold his nose well closed, and then to lay upon his tongue (not to be chewed) a small bit of onion and one of apple alternately, to see if he can discriminate between them.

preferences in foods may be traceable even to kinesthetic or to auditory stimulation, as when a salad or a pie crust is pronounced crisp.

OLFACTORY SENSITIVITY

Stimuli and Receptors

To furnish olfactory stimulation an agent must be in the form of, or must produce, gaseous particles which, when brought into direct contact with the olfactory membrane in the nose, will chemically excite it. This special membrane is of very limited area, not so large as a dime, and is to be found in high alcoves in the upper part of the left and right nasal passages, so that sniffing brings the substance to the membrane better than does ordinary breathing. The receptors proper are simple, consisting of afferent nerve cells with branches running out to the surface of the mucous lining and bearing fine hairs that project into the nasal passage. We have seen that there are different kinds of cutaneous and gustatory receptors; whether there are different kinds of olfactory receptors cannot be determined by use of present techniques, for point-by-point exploration is virtually impossible on account of the well-nigh inaccessible position of the olfactory membranes.

The extreme delicacy of the sense of smell is indicated by the fact that with one substance (a mercaptan) human subjects can detect a dilution in air as fine as 1/460,000,000,000 gram, a concentration far weaker than is detectable by any chemical tests. And since this is true of human beings, the following of odor trails by animals with greater olfactory sensitivity seems the less surprising.

For olfactory experiences, just as for cutaneous and gustatory ones, we might expect to be able to reduce the many thousands of different qualities of sensory experience, the thousands of different odors that man detects, to a simple analysis. But to date this has not been found possible. The relative inaccessibility of the receptive surface makes a differential presentation of substances extremely difficult. And by their very nature, the substances themselves are difficult to classify. For one thing, while the differences of odor seem at times to parallel the chemical periodic table of elements, there are many exceptions and reversals.[1] One

---

[1] To the student of chemistry it may be pointed out that Henning has postulated a chemical basis for smell classification. He has attempted to relate the different odor qualities a person experiences to different structural peculiarities of the molecules of the substances that are being smelled. Taking the benzene ring with its six carbon atoms as the most common molecule in cases of odorous substances, he has attempted to show that each odor is based on (a) the nature of the core of the molecule, (b) the kinds of atom groups substituted at any of the six places, and (c) the manner of their substitution.

attempt has been made (by Henning) to determine not elemental irreducible odor qualities but simply salient odors that will serve as reference points in a purely descriptive introspective classification. He fixed upon six such reference odors, which are shown in Figure 66 at the corners of a prism, so that all other odors can be described by being assigned to points on the surfaces of the schematic prism. Even though it does not get at elemental qualities in the sense of ingredients, at least the scheme does furnish a convenient system by which all smells can be placed in order on the basis of their resemblances. For example, the smell of onion is mostly putrid, but it is also somewhat burned, spicy, and resinous.

Some Special Phenomena

With the double olfactometer two kinds of odorous substances can be presented at the same time. This instrument consists of (a) two glass tubes curved at one end for insertion into the nostrils, and (b) over each a larger tube, lined on the inside with the odorous material and sliding smoothly so that it is possible to adjust the amount of the material exposed by it to the air that is being drawn into the smaller tube and into the nostril. One result of the simultaneous presentation of two odors is that each may cancel or *neutralize* or *mask* the effect of the other, as occurs with iodoform and Peru balsam. This principle has been hit upon in the practical employment of deodorants, as when carbolic acid is used to neutralize the odor of gangrene. On the other hand, two odors may mix or *fuse* and form a new kind of stimulation, as do xylol and turpentine. Many synthetic perfumes illustrate this phenomenon. If presented in succession, the second odor may be enhanced by the first, showing the *contrast* effect familiar in other classes of sense.

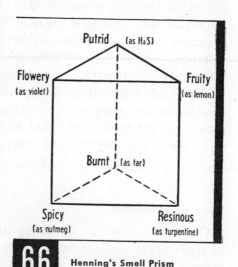

66 **Henning's Smell Prism**

A diagram for arranging different odors on the basis of their similarities to six salient odors.

Adaptation is nowhere better shown than in olfactory sensations. After continued presentation most odors show diminishing stimulus value down to total abolition; and simple laboratory tests with such substances as iodine, heliotrope, and camphor may show this to occur within from one to six minutes. In everyday life the phenomenon is common indeed. We may recoil on first entering the foul atmosphere of an overcrowded auditorium or a fish market or a dissecting room, but inevitably, if we remain a while, the odor will become ineffective. Moreover, the process may be highly specific, adaptation setting in for the one odor being constantly smelled, but not for other odors.

Reactions Aroused

The primary biological function of taste and smell is, of course, that of inspecting substances about to be taken into the digestive and respiratory tracts. The connection of these two senses with those tracts is so intimate that a strong, foul odor may upset and even reverse some of the normal processes of digestion, while another odor may powerfully facilitate them. It is true, moreover, particularly in the case of smell, that peculiarly intimate sensory-motor connections exist with other internal organs as well and thus awaken emotional reactions. Advertisers of perfumes make much of this in the descriptive names they apply, as, for instance, *"toujours fidèle,"* "seductive," "indiscreet," *"l'heure romantique,"* "irresistible," "danger," "confession," "my sin," and the like. Dr. Holmes once wrote that "memories, imagination, old sentiments, and associations are more readily reached through the sense of smell than by almost any other channel," and Kipling said that "smells are surer than sights and sounds to make the heart strings crack."

KINESTHETIC SENSITIVITY

Stimuli and Receptors

Of all the classes of sensitivity the kinesthetic (from the Greek *kinesi* — movement) is the most fundamental and the most necessary to man or animal. Man is an organism whose behavior includes the simultaneous and successive functioning of an enormous number of different action units; therefore if this behavior is to show organization and consistency, he must be so equipped that these action units can reciprocally affect one another. A contraction of a muscle at one place must in some way influence the contraction or relaxation of another muscle at some other place.

Almost anyone can close his eyes, extend his arms, and then bring together the tips of his two middle fingers. Or, after noting a small object on the table, he can with eyes closed reach out and touch it. Or he can find his way through a familiar room even though it is in total darkness. What kind of sensory cues can be the guides here? Certainly not sight nor touch, taste nor smell. The control depends upon the returns to the central nervous system of afferent impulses arising in the moving muscle-systems themselves. When a person feels that his outstretched hand has reached just far enough, this judgment is based upon his sense of just how much his muscles have now contracted. When he picks up a book and says, "That's a heavy one!" the experience he is having is essentially a sensory experience arising from the muscles that do the lifting.

The *muscles*, *tendons*, and *joint surfaces* are supplied with afferent nerve-endings originating in receptor structures (Figure 67). As a muscle contracts or relaxes, the receptors in the muscle tissue are naturally affected, and since the muscle pulls upon its tendinous connections, the receptors located in it are likewise affected. If movement occurs, the change of position of one member with reference to another to which it is joined (as forearm to upper arm at the elbow) produces a change in the location and amount of pressures at the surfaces of the joint, thus affecting receptors there also.

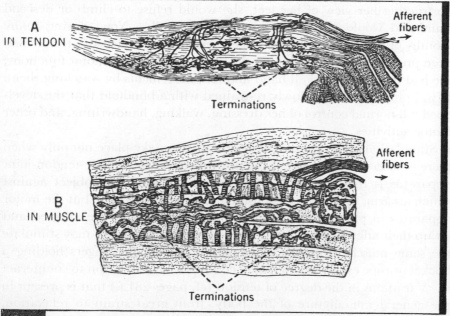

67 **Kinesthetic Afferent Nerve Endings**

A, in tendon. The tendinous bundle near the point of attachment of muscle fibers splits up into spindles, and among these the finely divided nerve branches ramify and end in plate-like expansions. *B*, in muscle. The muscle tissue is divided into many spindles, and the nerve branches wind around these spirally and circularly, and end in plate-like expansions. (*After Huber and DeWitt, and Ruffini.*)

Importance to Behavior

The manner in which the contraction of one muscle plays a part in determining the contraction of another is illustrated in so simple a performance as tapping the finger or waving the hand: *the muscular contraction that produces one movement furnishes the necessary stimulation for exciting the muscular contraction of the next movement.* Very different members may be so connected, as in walking, when the contractions in the left leg in the forward swing of the foot lead to the alternately succeeding contractions in the right. This is shown in a negative way in *tabes dorsalis*, sometimes called locomotor ataxia, wherein the diseased condition of the spinal cord blocks the afferent impulses arising from a moving leg: without this source of renewed stimulation and control the movement of the other leg is seriously handicapped, and a reeling, staggering gait is the result (see Figure 101, page 320). Or again, consider the case of K, who at eight years of age could neither dress nor feed herself, could not walk without stumbling nor go through any motor performances in a way normal to her age. All her movements were guided by visual instead of kinesthetic stimulation; and when a large collar was put about her neck obstructing her view of her feet, she would refuse to climb or descend stairs and would fall if she attempted to walk. Now, during many months of her infancy she had been seriously ill and bedfast, and had been prevented from developing the normal kinesthetic-motor functions; she had tried to control all hand and foot movements by watching them. It was only after being slowly re-trained with a blindfold that she developed full normal control of her dressing, walking, handwriting, and other motor activities.

Stimulation of the kinesthetic receptors may take place not only when there is observable movement but also whenever the muscle-tendon-joint apparatus is thrown into a condition of tension. The object against which an arm, head, or leg is pushing may be immovable, but the motor apparatus in play is doing work, so that its receptors are affected and set up their afferent neural impulses. Tension in a muscle may stimulate the same muscle, as when an increased pull on the fingers holding a bucket or rope excites an increased condition of contraction to counteract it. Variations in the degree of tension (cf. pages 281 f.) that is present in the general musculature of the body, from great strain to relaxation, give rise to variations in kinesthetic impulses sent toward the central nervous system and eventually out again to the effectors; and in this way the amount of motor activity already in process in the body has important effects upon the amount of activity to be shown subsequently. In passing, the reader should note that kinesthetic functions are not limited to those members of the body involved in grosser movements, but are essentially involved in such finer adjustments as those of the eye muscles in reading or in seeing objects as distant, and those of the laryngeal muscles in speaking aloud or to oneself. To these we will return at several points later.

In spite of the downright importance of kinesthetic sensitivity, relatively little experimentation has been done in this field, except for the *lifted-weights experiment.* In this experiment the question is raised: how fine a difference between two weights can be detected by simple "hefting" between thumb and finger? The blindfold subject is given in irregular order two weights to be lifted, one of a Constant value (for example, 100 grams), the other of varying values above or below the Constant. The Variable is increased and decreased irregularly, and the whole series of judgments by the subjects are totaled and compared to find just how much heavier (or lighter) the Variable had to be in order to be discriminated from the Constant a high percentage of times. One consistent outcome of several decades of work is the conclusion that the heavier the Constant weight, the greater must be the difference between it and the Variable; so that acuteness here is a relative matter — an instance of Weber's law, to be discussed elsewhere (pages 270–271).

STATIC SENSITIVITY

Stimuli and Receptors

Closely associated with the kinesthetic receptors are those of the semicircular canals and the vestibule of the ear. The internal ear (see Figure 68) is a tortuous cavity in the temporal bone, divisible into a central portion, the *vestibule;* an upper portion, the *semicircular canals;* and a lower portion, the *cochlea.*[1] Within this bony labyrinth lies a membranous labyrinth, roughly following the general structure of canals and of cochlea, but dividing into two large sacs in the vestibule, which are called the "utricle" and the "saccule." On the inner walls of the canals and also of the utricle and the saccule lie cells with fine hairlike filaments projecting into the liquid that is within the membranous labyrinth. About the base of these hair cells arise the afferent nerve fibers.

The immediate stimulus acting upon the hair cells consists of varying pressures of the liquid when it is disturbed by a movement of the head. By the familiar principle of inertia, when a bucket containing water is suddenly spun around or when it is jerked in any direction, the water

[1] The cochlea is quite distinct in function from the other two parts. In it are located the receptors for hearing.

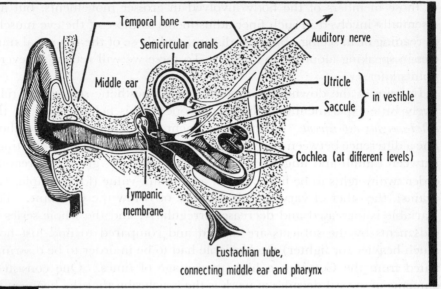

Temporal bone

Semicircular canals

Auditory nerve

Middle ear

Utricle
Saccule } in vestibule

Cochlea (at different levels)

Tympanic
membrane

Eustachian tube,
connecting middle ear and pharynx

68 **Cross-Section of the Ear**

Note that the ear consists of divisions and membranes in cavities in the bony mass of the skull.

itself shows a lag and exerts a reverse pressure on anything projecting from the wall of the bucket into the water. The same thing occurs in the canals and vestibule, where the suddenly displaced liquid presses against the highly sensitive hair-bearing cells. That the receptor cells of the semicircular canals are specially affected by *rotary* movements of the head is suggested by their peculiar arrangement — the three canals of each ear approximating the three planes of space. The relation of the canals to rotary movements can be demonstrated. If one matching pair of the canals in the two ears of a pigeon are destroyed, the bird keeps moving its head from side to side or turns somersaults sideward or backward, depending upon which pair has been damaged. It is supposed that the receptors of the vestibule are especially sensitive to changes of *rectilinear* type, especially with reference to the vertical (gravity). Deafmutes with imperfect development of utricle and saccule cannot adjust themselves to the vertical direction when swimming in deep water, and may even drown because of the absence of cues to guide their strokes toward the surface. A frog with the vestibule removed is as likely to swim upside down as right side up. It is easy to see, then, why the canals and vestibule have been dubbed "the compass of the body," and why they may with equal fitness be termed also "the gyroscope of the body."

Reactions Aroused

Stimulations of the vestibule and canals affect behavior in two ways. The first type of effect is the reflex *compensatory* movements, which are a striking feature of all disturbance of body orientation. The reader will find a curious illustration of these movements if he observes birds standing upon slightly swaying wires. With the backward and forward swings of the wire the bird will gently thrust its head forward and backward so that, when he is observed against a background, his head remains stationary. These compensatory movements have been investigated with the rotating-chair technique. When the chair begins to turn to the left and as long as the rate of turning is being increased, a subject seated in the chair with his eyes closed will show alternating movements of the eyeballs (detectable as movements of the bulges in the lids where they overlie the corneas): a slow turning or drift backward toward the right, frequently corrected by quick movements in the forward direction. Along with this there is a twisting of the trunk and a lateral straining in the legs. The subject will report, "I'm turning left." Once a constant speed of rotation is maintained, these motor readjustments decrease gradually to passivity (the adaptation phenomenon); and he will report, "Not turning at all!" Finally, upon a slowing down of the rotation, precisely the reverse compensatory movements are set up, which gradually subside after a complete stop, the subject meanwhile reporting, "Now turning right!"

Secondly, afferent impulses from the canals and vestibule play a highly significant part in the maintenance of *muscular tension*. The pigeon (already referred to) with injured semicircular canals displays, in addition to its faulty spatial adjustments, enfeeblement of general behavior: its flying is weak, its legs do not remain rigid, its whole attitude is drooping and listless. The knockout blow so well known to the boxer is one given to the jawbone, imparting such a shock to the inner ear that its afferent functions are temporarily abolished; and lacking this source of stimulation, the muscles of the previously vigorous athlete lose their tension, becoming inert and paralyzed as he lies, a helpless lump, upon the floor.

The subject himself is seldom keenly aware of the static functions, but in unusual cases of disturbance he can report them; for example, when in an elevator operated with unaccustomed changes of speed, when balancing himself on the hind legs of a chair, when dizzy from digestive upset or eyestrain, or when suffering from motion sickness induced by slow, rhythmical ups and downs of an airplane or ship.

The essential part that these two functions play in human and animal

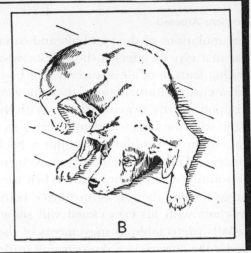

69 **Behavior Changes Following Injury to Static Receptors**

A. Dog after recovery from an operation in which the semicircular canals and vestibule of the right side were destroyed. The subject fails to make appropriate compensatory movements to right the head position. *B.* Dog after recovery from an operation in which canals and vestibule of both sides were destroyed. The subject shows loss of muscular tension over the whole body. (*From J. G. Wilson and F. H. Pike.* Philos. Trans. Roy. Soc., *Series B, 1912, 203, 127–160.*)

behavior is evident from Figure 69, in which are shown the serious alterations produced when they are abolished.

ORGANIC SENSITIVITY

Its General Importance

The original sources of the energies that set an animal or a man into action are not (as we have seen in previous chapters) solely in the environment outside him, but are to be found in great measure within him as well. In connection with the kinesthetic and static classes of sensitivity we have already identified some internal sources. There remain to be considered, however, the great soft-organ systems of the body.

Pathological cases of visceral anesthesia bring to light very clearly the importance of afferent impulses from these internal organs as the necessary stimuli in certain lines of behavior. A patient who is suffering from such anesthesia has no inner gauge operating to stop him when he has eaten sufficiently, and consequently his food must be measured out for him; nor can his bladder and bowels signal their need of evacuation.

He shows no definite attitudes toward food, such as appetite or repugnance. His general behavior exhibits little emotional influence; he is apathetic. Whatever the time-beating mechanisms within him may be, they are now ineffective as controls of his reactions, for he cannot time his day's activities except by the clock, nor on waking can he correctly judge whether he has slept one hour or ten.

It must be admitted at the outset, however, that very little can be definitely stated concerning the receptor mechanisms involved. (1) For one reason, they are so difficult or often impossible of access that experimental control of the application of stimuli is frequently out of the question. (2) Since the normal processes of digestion, circulation, and so forth are somewhat constant and regular, they seldom provide any sudden and pronounced changes of stimulus to the local receptors, such as the external world provides for eye or ear, nose or skin.

Different Forms of Organic Sensitivity

Most sensory experiences arising from the inner soft organs are so vague that they are hard to analyze introspectively. Suffocation, nausea, the sense of fullness after a heavy dinner, sex cravings, objectless anxiety — such feelings as these are as little understood as they are universal and common. In general, psychologists expect to find in them much the same elemental kinds as we are familiar with in cutaneous experience. Partly this is so because the receptive nerve-endings they have found in the tissues of alimentary canal, lungs, heart, liver, and so on, are not essentially different in type from the various cutaneous and kinesthetic ones. Partly, too, it seems to follow from the fact that the two organic qualities so far worked out — hunger and thirst — have proved to be cutaneous-like. *Thirst* is found to arise principally from the mucous lining at the back of the throat, and to be set up when that membrane reaches a condition of dryness. The thirst stimulations disappear whenever the membrane is sufficiently moistened, either by the introduction of water into the system through drinking or injection, or by the local application of an acid, such as citric acid. *Hunger* (which is not to be confused with appetite for food) has been traced to vigorous rhythmic contractions of the walls of the empty stomach. The subjects of an experiment swallowed soft balloons attached by rubber tubing to recording devices, and these were inflated in the stomach so that movements of the latter would be pneumatically conveyed to the recording instruments (see Figure 40, page 143). During the first three to five days of a fast, the hunger contractions became gradually weaker until they practically disappeared. It is reasonable to suppose that none of the forms of organic sensitivity involves the functioning of any unique type of receptor.

On account of the scantiness of our information we can only roughly classify the rich number of different sources of afferent impulses. Nausea is probably associated with a reversal of the peristaltic movements of the *digestive* tract. From the *respiratory* system arises suffocation. From the *circulatory* arises heart panic, and so forth. From the *sex apparatus* arises sex appetite in its various phases. From the *distention* of many *hollow organs*, stomach, colon, bladder, and others, arise impulses akin to kinesthetic or cutaneous pressure. From tonic conditions of the *smooth musculature* itself probably come afferent streams of impulses having much influence upon the general attitudes and energy of the body. From many, but not all, tissues and organs arise impulses of the nociceptive, or *pain*, type.

From these few notes it may be gathered that very much of the motivation of a person — what makes him "go" — is traceable to these organic afferent impulses. Already we have seen (in earlier chapters) that the typical situation for setting an organism into activity is one in which environmental conditions are unfavorable to its internal needs. We are now in a better position to see that these unsatisfied internal needs set up stimulations which arouse efferent impulses to the active organs, muscles and glands.

AUDITORY SENSITIVITY

Stimuli and Receptors

Hearing is a result of stimulation by vibrations of air, typically, but also by other material media, such as the bones of the head, water, and so forth; and these vibrations may fall between the extreme limits of frequency of 20 and 20,000 cycles per second, at the outside.

Diagrams of the ear are offered in Figures 68 and 70. Vibrations of the air passing up the external canal set into vibration the *tympanic membrane* or eardrum. By means of the system of levers formed by the three small bones of the middle ear the vibrations of the eardrum are transmitted to a membrane stretched across a window of the inner ear, thus communicating the oscillations to the liquid filling the cavities of the inner ear, including the cochlea. The cochlea is a tapering cavity winding spirally through the bone for two and a half turns, and longitudinally divided into canals by a bony shelf and membranes. Along one of these canals (the cochlear) stretches the *basilar membrane* bearing the organ of Corti and its hair cells, about which are to be found the endings

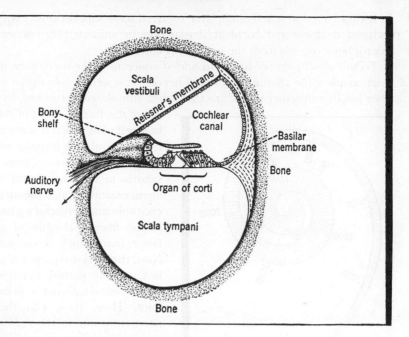

Bone

Scala
vestibuli

Reissner's membrane

Bony
shelf

Cochlear
canal

Basilar
membrane

Bone

Auditory
nerve

Organ of corti

Scala tympani

Bone

70   **Diagram of a Cross-Section of a Coil of the Cochlea**
Explanation in text.

of afferent nerve fibers. It is supposed that what occurs is that vibrations of the liquid of the inner ear and the cochlear canal excite these hair cells in some indirect manner, and that these in turn set up the chemical changes in the nerve endings, which, as neural impulses, take an afferent course along the *auditory nerve* to the brain — thence, of course, to pass out along efferent nerves to effectors for initiating and controlling action.

Theories of the Auditory Mechanism

Much experimenting has been devoted to the question of just what mechanisms in the cochlea make possible differential responses to the ten thousand different pitches of sound heard; and a variety of hypotheses have been advanced. Helmholtz's theory is historically the most famous. The basilar membrane, he pointed out, contains transverse fibers which vary in a continuous way, suggesting a progressive tuning from high to low, like the strings of a piano. Assuming the principle of sympathetic vibration, Helmholtz supposed that each particular vibration of the liquid of the cochlear canal sets into oscillation some particular region of fibers of the basilar membrane, and this in turn excites the hair cells in the immediate neighborhood and the afferent nerve endings there. Modern versions of this *place* theory, that pitch depends upon place in the cochlea that is activated, have received some support from experimentally induced deafness and cochlear destruction in animals [12], as well as from microphone records from the cochlea (Figure 71).[1]

To this a *volley* theory has been added concerning the method of neural conduction along the afferent (auditory) nerve. It is well known that a given nerve fiber has its refractory period, so that when stimulated, let us say, by the bending of the fine filament of the so-called hair cell with which it is connected, the fiber transmits an impulse and then remains inactive for a time (in thousandths of a second) until it becomes again excitable; and the alternation of excitable and refractory phases sets up in the fiber a rhythm of conduction faster than which it cannot conduct. Now, the wave-frequency of a high tone is known to exceed the frequency at which any single nerve fiber can conduct. How, then, can the auditory nerve transmit to the central nervous system the effects of such high tones? But the auditory nerve is composed of a very great number of individual fibers; and like a drummer who beats a tattoo with both sticks alternately, producing a total effect twice as rapid as the beat of either stick alone, so the composite nerve can with its individual fibers conduct a variety of impulses of different frequencies but so spaced as to reproduce in the central nervous system a total effect duplicating the complex stimulation impressed upon the sense-organ end [18].

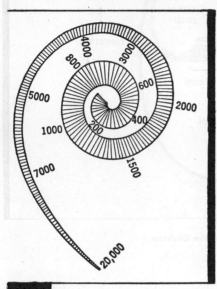

71 Map Showing Localization of Different Tonal Frequencies in the Cochlea

A mapping of the basilar membrane of the human ear.[1] (*From O. Stuhlman,* An Introduction to Biophysics, *John Wiley and Sons, 1943. By permission of the author.*)

In this connection a curious fact was brought to light. When electrical action potentials (cf. pages 287 ff.) were led off by wires from the auditory nerve of an anesthetized cat and conducted to a distant room, it became possible to hear from an amplifier stationed there a faithful report of all the sounds occurring in the room in which the cat was placed; even intelligible conversation could be heard.

[1] When the ear is stimulated by sound, minute electrical potentials can be detected by electrodes placed at various points on the cochlea. With different frequencies of sound stimulation, different points on the length of the cochlea will give off the maximal potential. By determining the point where there is recorded the greatest potential for each sound frequency, a map can be drawn.

Two Physical Variables in Sound Stimulation

Every day's experience is full of sounds of extraordinary variety. The roar of a high-balling freight train, the piercing shriek of its whistle, the gentle sounds from a lightly strummed guitar, the full-bodied tones from a cathedral organ, the rasping voice of the sideshow barker, the crackle of distant lightning, the chatter of children's voices — can so wide a variety of sounds be reduced to a few basic dimensions?

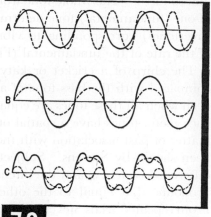

The vibrations of air that produce sound in the human ear differ from one another in two elemental ways: in *frequency* or *length* and in *amplitude* or *intensity* (Figure 72). A person's ability to react appropriately to different sounds depends in the first instance upon his capacity to discriminate between them in these dimensions. Discriminations that are based primarily on variations in frequency are known as *pitch* differences; those based primarily on variations in amplitude, as *loudness* differences. In music, the sounds are organized in terms of pitch differences (along with different intervals between them) to form melody, and changes

72   **Variations in Wave Formation**

In *A*, the continuous line represents a greater wave length and lower frequency than the broken line. In *B*, the continuous line represents a wave of greater amplitude. In *C*, the continuous line represents a complex wave that can be analyzed into two wave frequencies as represented by the broken lines.

in loudness furnish variations in emphasis and accent. When sounds of all wave lengths are produced at once, as by an airplane, the resulting sound is sometimes given the name "white noise," analogous to the white light which is compounded of all the colors.

Other Phenomenal Dimensions to Sounds as Heard

Still another way in which sounds as we consciously hear them vary from each other is in their *timbre*. This is the attribute which distinguishes the sounds from different kinds of instruments of a symphony orchestra — strings, woodwinds, brasses, and different individual pieces within each of these choirs; and it marks much of the difference between human voices. Timbre variations are traceable to variations in the *composition* of the physical waves. The wave composition can be analyzed into the *fundamental*, by which its assigned pitch is established, and its *overtones* or *partials*. Resonant bodies vibrate in parts as well as in wholes. A stretched metal string, for instance, when plucked will vibrate not only in its whole length but also in two segments, in three, in four, and so on. This can be demonstrated easily by damping (gently touching) a full-sounding string at its half-way point, third-way, quarter-way, and so forth. The whole tone from such a string has a complex makeup of one (fundamental) tone determined by the string's length, plus others (overtones) corresponding to vibration rates that are simple multiples of the rate of the fundamental (Figure 73).

The chirp of a cricket or katydid seems "small" and "pinched" as compared with the bass tone of an organ or the roll of distant thunder even when all these tones are equal in loudness. Certainly, as we experience them, tones have a spatial or *volume* character. This is not a mere matter of past association with the sizes of the producing sources, as has been shown by Stevens. Subjects were given alternately two tones of different frequency, and the intensity of one was varied until the subject pronounced it equal to the other in its apparent bigness or volume. From repeated trials Stevens was forced to the conclusion that the volume is a genuine attribute of a tone, and that it increases with the intensity and decreases with the frequency of the tone [14]. Here we have a psychological dimension, a fact of experience, to which no physical parallel is found. But it is a phenomenal fact.

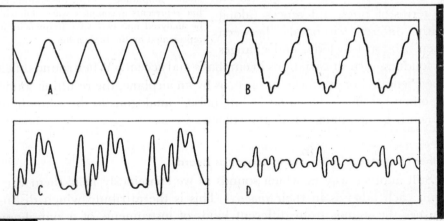

73   **Sound Wave Forms as Produced by Different Instruments**

A, tuning fork. *B*, violin. *C*, oboe. *D*, bass voice. (*From D. C. Miller*, THE SCIENCE OF MUSICAL SOUNDS, *Macmillan, 1916;* SOUND WAVES, *Macmillan, 1937. By permission of the publishers.*)

When air vibrations are non-periodic and irregular or are less than two full vibrations, they produce *noises* rather than *tones*. The vast majority of sounds ordinarily heard are of this character: the pattering of rain and the hissing of wind, the puffs of an engine and the rattle of wheels, the rustle of a newspaper and the clatter of dishes, and all the wide range of rumbles and sputters and snaps and pops.

Heard sounds — like experiences in other sense modalities such as odors — have a number of other phenomenal characterizations: "brightness," "density," and so on. We have not space here, however, for their presentation.

Discriminating Intensities

A sound, to be heard at all, must have sufficient intensity or loudness, must exceed its "stimulation threshold" or lower limit. This limit varies considerably for sounds of different vibration frequencies, the ear being most sensitive to sounds in the middle pitch range, from about 800 to about 4000 double vibrations (cycles) per second. With an instrument called the audiometer an individual's sensitivity with each ear to sounds of various frequencies — that is, the intensity point where he just can hear each sound — can be determined and plotted to give an overall picture of his hearing ability.

The physicist-engineer measures the intensities of physical sounds in relative terms, in terms of the ratio between sound-intensities. For this purpose, he has adopted the unit, the *decibel* (db). The number of decibels between two tones is equal to ten times the logarithm of the ratio of the energies of the two tones.[1] If tone B is generated by a physical energy just 10 times as great as that generating tone A, tone B is said to be 1 bel (or 10 decibels) louder. If tone C is generated by energy just 10 times that generating tone B — and therefore 100 times that generating tone A — it is said to be 1 bel (10 decibels) louder than B, and 2 bels (20 decibels) louder than A. Now, if we use as basis for comparison the physical energy required to make a sound just barely audible, we can state the physical loudness of any given sound as so many decibels above this threshold. Examples: the sound of a slight rustle of leaves is

---

[1] The reader may need to remind himself of the meaning of a "logarithm." Consider the progression:

$$10^1 = 10$$
$$10^2 = 100$$
$$10^3 = 1000$$
$$10^4 = 10,000$$

As the exponents increase arithmetically, 1, 2, 3, 4, the values increase much more rapidly. The 1, 2, 3, 4, = the logarithms for 10, 100, 1000, 10,000.

about 10 db; that of the whisper, less than 20; the noise of a busy office may be 40 db; a conversation is 50 or 60; a pneumatic drill, 80 db; a boiler factory may be 100 db; and an airplane engine, 100 to 120. One of the many useful psychological applications of the decibel unit is the measuring of street or factory noises at various places, in campaigns for abating such noises as a nuisance.

Audibility of Vowels and Consonants

Wartime studies of interphone conversation has brought out the fact that one's ability to understand speech is often improved by weakening the lower pitches of the tonal complexes. This is consistent with the well-known fact that in a certain type of hearing loss common in old age (Figure 74), useful hearing of conversation is impaired by reason of the loss of sensitivity to high frequencies only. In contrast with vowels,

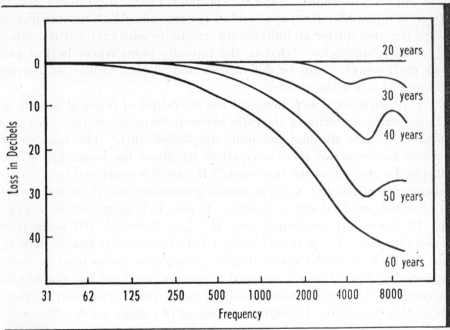

74 **Loss of Sensitivity to High Frequencies with Age**

The audiogram obtained at 20 years of age is taken as the basis of comparison. A subject is tested for that intensity which he just can hear (his *stimulation threshold*) at each of a number of sound frequencies at which the audiometer is set. The audiogram is made by plotting the readings from the audiometer. (*From C. T. Morgan,* PHYSIOLOGICAL PSYCHOLOGY, *McGraw-Hill, 1943, after C. C. Bunch,* ARCH. OTOLARYNGOL., *1929, 9, 625–636.*)

the sounds of most consonants (*sh, f,* etc.) are of very high pitch; and as the reader can verify for himself, vowels without consonants (what children call "hot-potato talk") make much less sense than consonants without vowels [6].

Some Interrelations of Sound Stimulation

If two tones that are nearly identical in pitch are sounded together, there will be a pronounced *beat* or swell in loudness occurring at regular intervals, with as many beats per second as the difference in number between the cycles of one tone and those of the other. Two forks set at 435 and 437, for example, would produce two beats per second. This is purely a physical, not a physiological, effect, arising as it does from interactions of external sound waves and not of nerve processes; and it is due to alternate reinforcement and interference between the two lengths of air waves, as they occur in the same and in opposite phases.

If the two original tones sounded together are more widely separated in pitch, they may set up in the hearing apparatus excitations similar to those producible by additional sound stimuli of other frequencies. These are called *combination tones*.

Quite the most elaborate and complex uses for which man has organized sound stimuli are in music. In those simultaneous and successive pitch patterns that are called harmonies and melodies the frequencies of the component tones turn out to be related to each other in certain mathematical ratios. The octave, for instance, shows the following ratios of vibration frequency to C:

C	D	E	F	G	A	B	C_2
1	9/8	5/4	4/3	3/2	5/3	15/8	2

With the insertion of intermediate tones, still other intervals are provided. Some of these intervals are much employed and preferred in music because they produce harmony or *consonance*, and certain others are actually avoided because they produce *dissonance*. Precisely what is the basis of consonance and dissonance? Many have sought to identify it in terms of some physical characteristic of the sound waves produced. The matter is controversial, and too technical for us here. But whatever the physical basis for these musical preferences of man, it is certain also that the part played by *habituation* is great. A person may be trained to regard as consonant certain intervals between tones that do not readily fuse, especially the "sevenths"; and such clean fusions as the "octave," the "third," and the "fifth" come to have low musical value for experienced auditors. Getting used to certain intervals undoubtedly has an influence upon one's preferences among tone-combinations, as is evident when we compare European music with Chinese, the classical German school with the ultramodern Russian, or the likings of an untrained child with those of a seasoned concertgoer.

VISUAL SENSITIVITY

The Stimuli

The energies that fall upon the visual apparatus of man and awaken in him the act of seeing take the form of light vibrations that range in length between 400 mμ (violet) and 760 mμ (red) (mμ = 1/1,000,000 mm.)[1] These are the stimuli in the narrowest sense, but it is common to apply the term also to the objects from which the vibrations are transmitted or reflected. A child acquires adjustments not so much to the light waves as to the sources from which they come; he comes to react not to brightness and to colors in themselves but to the milk bottle and the nurse's face.

In contrast to the effluvia of smell or the sound waves of hearing which can go around corners, a significant characteristic of light waves is that they are transmitted only in straight lines, even after they have been reflected or refracted. On this account, they serve as cues by which the active organism can accurately orient itself with reference to its spatial relations. Thus the receptor of sight is developed as an organ with its own delicate motor adjustments, so that sensitivity to fine differences in the direction and distance of stimulating sources may serve as the control for the subject's motor reactions in space.

The Receptors

The eye may well be compared to the photographic camera. In the latter there are necessary: (A) a light-proof box to shut out all rays but those from the object to be photographed; (B) an aperture through which the selected rays are admitted; (C) a diaphragm controlling the size of this aperture; (D) a lens to bring the admitted rays to a proper focus; (E) a sensitive plate upon which the focused rays are projected and in which they set up photochemical changes. Analogous parts are found in the eyeball as shown in Figure 75.

The innermost coat of the eyeball wall, the *retina*, is the receptive mechanism proper. It consists of several layers of cells (Figure 76). The layer that is sensitive to the action of light rays is made up of *rods* and

---

[1] Shorter waves are found in the ultraviolet rays, X-rays, and cosmic rays, and longer ones in the infrared and radiant heat rays and the waves used in radio broadcasting. Man is sensitive to none of these, except to heat waves, which affect cutaneous receptors.

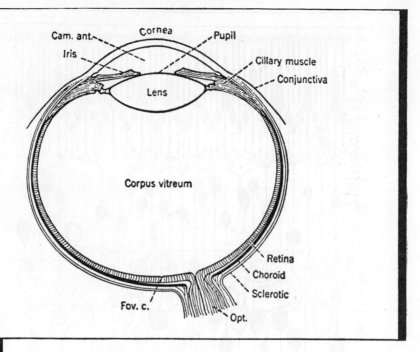

75

Cross-Section of the Eyeball

The wall (*A* — see text) is composed of three coats, the sclerotic, the choroid, and the innermost delicate retina. At the front the wall is transparent (the *cornea*). Behind it the circular window or *pupil* (*D*) is controlled by the blue or brown *iris* muscle (*C*). Light admitted through this window is focused by the *lens* (*D*) upon the retina (*E*) as upon a camera plate. The lens is adjusted for near and far objects by the ciliary muscle. *Corpus vitreum*, the vitreous humor filling the main chamber, as the *aqueous humor* fills the anterior one, *Cam. ant.*

cones and lies toward the periphery in such a way that the rays projected back through pupil and lens to the retina must pass through the other layers of cells before reaching the rods and cones. When light falls upon this last layer of cells, it sets up some chemical change, which in turn sets up a neural process, and in this manner afferent impulses are originated that pass out of the eye and then along the optic nerve toward the brain.

Some points about the anatomy of the eye explain certain peculiarities of vision. In ordinary daylight the objects seen most clearly are those in the center of the visual field, the light waves from which are projected upon the center of the retina at the *fovea*, where the cones are very great in number (about a million to a square one-tenth of an inch). Under twilight or night conditions, however, objects a little to one side of the

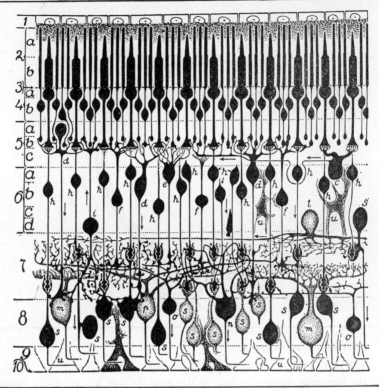

76   **Scheme of the Retina**

Note the different types of cells (neurons) and the variety of relationships and interconnections of their tips (synapses). The lower edge of the figure represents the layers lying toward the interior of the eyeball; the top edge shows the long, narrow *rods* and the shorter, thicker *cones*, which point outward away from the interior of the eyeball. Light admitted into the eye through pupil, lens, etc., has to pass through layers *10, 9, 8,* etc., before falling upon the sensitive tips of rods and cones in layers *2a* and *1*. (*From S. L. Polyak,* THE RETINA, *University of Chicago Press, 1941. By permission of the publishers.*)

center will be more easily seen — as when a gazer finds it best to turn the eye a little to one side in order to see a very dim star — and these off-center stimuli fall upon areas of the retina where the rods are relatively greater in number. This is consistent with the view (the "duplex theory") that sensitivity to differences of low brightnesses is limited to the rods, while that to high brightnesses and to colors is limited to the cones.

In one region of the visual field the eye is blind (the *blind spot*), for here the layer of rods and cones is interrupted to make room for the exit of the optic nerve. The fact is easily demonstrated; see Figure 77.

77   The Blind Spot

Hold this figure about a foot in front of the right eye, close the left eye, fixate the cross, and note whether the disk can be seen. It may be necessary to rotate the page a little and to change its distance, but eventually a point will be found where the eye is blind to the disk.

The side-by-side arrangement of the sensitive cells (rods and cones) of the retina in a mosaic-like surface upon which the light waves fall might mislead us into assuming that their action is of a punctate character, each cell acting independently of the others.   This notion is strengthened by a knowledge of how acute are the resolving powers of the eye, for one can discriminate two seen points no further apart than 1 minute (1/60 degree) of angular distance.   Yet the way in which the retina operates is not so simple. Note that the individual cells are closely compacted: the smallest ray of light admitted into the eye will fall upon not one but many cells. Note especially the interlacing of fibers between different retinal cells (Figure 76, layers 5 and 7). The processes that occur in certain stimulated rods and cones are not absolutely local and limited; rather, they interact with processes of neighboring rods and cones. Accordingly, any area of the retina is not an aggregate of discrete points but a *field*.[1] What we experience in seeing, then, is not a

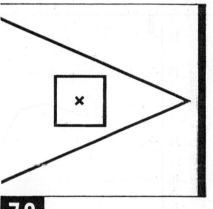

78   A Field Phenomenon in the Visual Apparatus

Fixate the cross, and note that the proximity of one pattern, the enclosing angle, produces a distortion in the other pattern, the square: the horizontal sides of the square will converge a little toward the open side of the angle (Ponzo's illusion). Gazing at separate drawings, first of the angle alone, then of the square, produces the same kind of distortion, and in greater amount. (*From W. Kohler and H. Wallach, "Figural after-effects,"* PROC. AMER. PHIL. SOC., *1944, 88, 285.*)

---

[1] This "field" notion, that the activity of a particle is determined largely by the field in which it is embedded — as in the magnetic field or the gravitational field — is of broad application throughout sensory and indeed all psychology. Note especially the treatment of Perceiving, in Chapter 16.

number of points of light but *patterns* of lights and darks, and any one of these is influenced in some degree by the others. For one illustration, see Figure 78.

Visual Acuity and Job Demands

A practical point is in order here. It goes without saying that ability to see is a necessity for doing most of the world's work. But is excellent vision required for all kinds of jobs? A moment's attention will lead us to return a negative answer to the question. And we must go further. We must recognize that of the jobs calling for good vision some demand good distance vision only, others good near vision only. Figure 79 shows the specific character of the vision demands for success in the job of assembling radio tubes. This is but one of the sensory capacities that personnel experts find a requirement for this or that specific job.

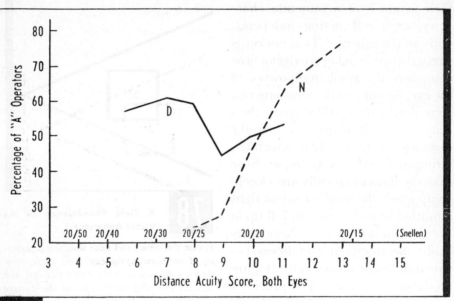

79 **Visual Acuity Scores of Good Radio Tube Assemblers**

Of 225 radio tube assemblers, 53 per cent were rated by their supervisors as "quite satisfactory" or "A." These were given tests by the personnel office for near vision and for distance vision. Curve *N* shows the percentages who were "A" workers among those scoring at different levels on the test for *near* acuity. The higher the acuity score, the greater the percentage of good workers; and for an applicant making this score, the greater the likelihood of his being satisfactory. Curve *D* shows the percentages who were "A" workers among those scoring at different levels on the test for *distance* acuity. There is no relationship between good distance vision and aptitude for this job. (*Adapted from J. Tiffin and W. F. Long. "Visual standards and job requirements,"* AMER. J. OPTOM., *1946, 23, 463–476.*)

Reactions by the Eye

We must remember that the eye is a motor, as well as a sensory, organ. Indeed, it is one of the most elaborate motor organs of which man is possessed. Besides the muscular *iris*, which regulates the amount of light to be admitted to the eye, and the *ciliary* muscle, which adjusts the lens for proper focusing, there remains to be noted the work of the six large *extrinsic muscles* on the outside of each eyeball, which rotate it in its socket (Figure 80). In binocular vision these muscles regulate the relative positions of the two eyeballs, so that a single stimulus will be projected on corresponding retinal points, drawing them inward if the object is near and returning them to parallel if it is distant. But whether a man uses two eyes or one, the remarkable mobility with which his eyeball rolls about — glancing here, there, and everywhere, scanning print with jerky movements across the page, examining a Grecian urn or a street car advertisement with veerings and shiftings that baffle all but a cinematograph — is, once mentioned, well enough recognized by the reader to call for no further elaboration (see also Figures 112 and 163).

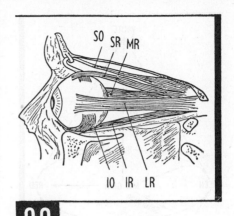

80 **Muscles of the Eyeball**

SO, superior oblique; *SR*, superior rectus; *MR*, median or internal rectus; *IO*, inferior oblique; *IR*, inferior rectus; *LR*, lateral or external rectus.

Three Variables in Light Discrimination

Discrimination of one light stimulation from another is in two physical dimensions. Vibrations of light, like those of sound (Figure 72), may vary as to *amplitude* or *intensity*, as to *length* or *frequency*. Then there are resultant differences as to *complexity* or *composition* (that is, number and character of component vibrations).

(1) First, as to differences in the intensity of light. All human and animal organisms possessing eyes are able to distinguish light-dark or *brightness* differences, no matter what their other visual defects; and man must rely upon this difference solely under conditions of twilight illumination. All stimuli discriminated in terms of light-dark range from the high extreme of illumination, "white," to its opposite, "black." Seeing in terms of brightness differences is the principal part of seeing, as is

shown by the satisfactoriness of most black-and-white photographs and photoplays, in which the absence of color is hardly noted at all.

(2) Sensitivity to differences of wave length only, that is, color vision or the ability to distinguish *hues* (what is ordinarily meant by "colors"), is more limited in several ways. Fewer animal species have demonstrated it; some human individuals show special disabilities (color blindness, to be discussed later); and the retinas of all individuals are insensitive to wave-length differences in certain areas (retinal zones, discussed later).

(3) Discrimination of light stimuli in terms of the differences in their composition has not been so extensively explored, but it is certain that these differences in *saturation* of colors as seen have an important share in determining the esthetic reactions to such objects as paintings, natural scenery, houses, and dress goods. Light is called well saturated if the component vibrations are fairly homogeneous in their frequencies, poorly saturated if they are very heterogeneous; for example, light of 472 trillion vibrations per second with little admixture of other frequencies would be called a "pure" or "clear" or well-saturated "orange" and is colorful; whereas if it is mixed with vibrations of many other frequencies it approaches what would be called "gray" and is lacking in color or chroma. In Figure 81 is presented a much-used scheme for representing these three directions in which different stimuli of sight vary from one another.

81 Scheme for Representing the Three Variables of Sight

Differences of *hue* are represented as ranged about the periphery of the plane circle; differences in *saturation* as distances on radii out from the vertical core (neutral gray); differences of *brightness* as vertical distances above-below this plane. For illustrations, positions are assigned to a poorly saturated orange of medium brightness (x) and a well-saturated pink (y).

In passing we may recognize that there are still other ways of distinguishing color experiences. The yellow of a painted flat surface certainly looks different from the yellow of a flame, even though the two be equated for brightness, hue, saturation. The blue of the open sky looks different from the same blue of a glass through which we are gazing, and again from the same blue in a neon sign, or the blue of a fog, or the blue of a cord held in our hands. These and other *phenomenal* varieties of color experiences seem to be dependent upon the apparent texture of what we are looking at or upon our ability to localize it [11]. They do not, however, throw doubt on our threefold list of color attributes so far as it goes; for in all cases we have differences of hue, of brightness, of saturation.

Some Special Phenomena of Color Vision

For half a century psychologists have given a great deal of attention in their experimental research to problems of sensitivity to the wave lengths of light, and certain phenomena of color vision have been determined in great detail. In this discussion, space permits only brief mention of a few of these phenomena.

If lights of two different wave lengths (two different colors) are projected upon the same retinal surface, a new excitation is there set up and the individual sees a new color. The usual technique for producing this *retinal fusion*[1] is with the color wheel, a spindle upon which are mounted interlapping paper or cardboard disks that are revolved so fast (at least forty times per second) that before excitation of the retina by one of them has subsided excitation by another is set up; the result is the same as if the stimulations were simultaneous. An inertia of the retina is thus involved. (Figure 82.) Titchener has enunciated three laws of color fusion. (1) For every color there can be found another (*complementary*) which if "mixed" with

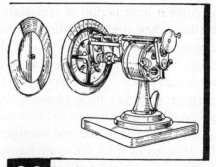

82

Color Wheel for Mixing Colors

The disks are interlapped and mounted upon the shaft of the motor. For comparative purposes smaller disks may be combined at the same time as the larger. The instrument here illustrated has the additional advantage of permitting adjustment of the ratio between the disks while the wheel is in motion.

---

[1] This phenomenon must not be confused with that resulting from a mixing of the pigments themselves on a palette or in a bucket. For example, if blue paint and yellow paint be mixed in that physical manner, each absorbs some of the wave frequencies of light, reflecting the rest. What is left after this double absorption may be a green, instead of the gray that results from superposition of the two colors on the retina. The latter is a physiological phenomenon.

the first in the right proportion will produce a gray.   Thus a slightly
purplish red when mixed with a slightly bluish green will excite the
retina just as a gray would do.   (2) The mixture of any two colors
that are not complementaries will give an intermediate color, which
varies in saturation with the nearness or remoteness of the two colors
to each other in the wave-length series.   A red and yellow revolved
together produce the same retinal effect as would an original orange
disk.   (3) If two color mixtures which match each other are combined,
the new combination will match either of the original mixtures.

A striking phenomenon is that called *simultaneous contrast*.   Any color
stimulus falling upon a limited region of the retina tends to induce in an
adjacent region an effect similar to that of its complement.   If a blue
field is presented to the eye with a strip of gray alongside or across it,
the retinal excitation induced by the gray strip will have an effect the
same as that of the complementary of blue; that is, the gray will look
yellowish.   Gray on purple will appear yellowish green; a medium bright
gray on dark green will appear a bright red; a blue strip on yellow will
appear a more saturated blue.

After a long period of stimulation by a given brightness or color, the
retina, when the stimulation is removed, is affected as if by the complementary brightness or color.   This phenomenon is called *successive contrast*, and also is described as *negative after-imagery*, or better, negative
after-excitation.   After gazing at the lock on a window frame and then
turning the eyes to a blank wall, a person is likely to see the visual
pattern of the lock with the reverse arrangement of brightnesses; or after
gazing at a red figure and turning to a gray background, the retina will
be affected as if by the same figure except that it now appears as green.

But the first after-effect of retinal stimulation is a *positive after-image*.
This is one essential of color fusion, as hinted above.   It is demonstrated
by whirling a lighted stick in a circle in a dark room, by gazing at an
incandescent electric lamp for a few seconds and then turning it off, and
so forth.   A period of time is required after the removal of stimulation
before the complete effect of the stimulation subsides.

Even the normal retina, as has been suggested, is not sensitive to all
colors throughout its extent, but varies from differential sensitivity for
all colors at the center, to that for none at the edge of the field of vision.
This variation appears in concentric *retinal zones*, as shown in Figure 83.
Ordinarily a person is not aware of this.   (Why?)

Introspective Analysis of Light

It will be remembered that cutaneous sensations may be reduced to

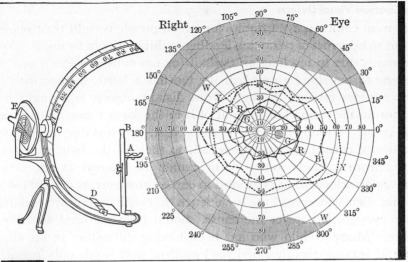

83 A Perimeter

The subject's chin is placed on the rounded chin-rest, *A*, which is so adjusted that one eye is directly over the semicircular top of rod *B*, the other eye being closed. A small hole through the axis at *C* serves as a fixation point. The color stimulus is moved on a carriage along one circular arm, *D*, toward or away from the center. The arms rotate, so that all meridians of the visual field can be explored. On the back of plate *E* (which rotates with the perimeter arms) is fastened a paper disk, and on it are recorded the points along each meridian where the given color appears or disappears. A sample record disk is presented at the right, showing one subject's areas of the visual field sensitive to green, red, blue, yellow, and white or gray, respectively.

four elemental sensations, taste to four, and the like. We may therefore ask: Can all the "sights" that one experiences be reduced to elemental sensations? We find an answer in the work of introspective psychologists. The colors of the solar spectrum vary by fine degrees from red through orange, yellow, green, blue, and indigo to violet; and to these must be added the non-spectral purple. Careful scrutiny of these colors-as-seen leads to the judgment that some of them seem to partake of others (as orange seems to be reddish but also yellowish), but a few seem to be unique and irreducible, namely *red*, *yellow*, *green*, and *blue*. These are therefore called the psychologically *elementary* sensations of color. To them are added the two elementary sensations of brightness, *black* and *white*. All visual experiences are then said to be produced by the compounding or fusing of two or more of these elementary six.

Some Common Visual Defects

The most common eye troubles for which people consult their oculists turn out to be errors of refraction leading to difficulties in focusing. *Near-sightedness* is due to too long an eyeball (or too convex a lens), and *far-sightedness* to too short an eyeball (or too flat a lens), so that with the ciliary muscles relaxed the light from distant objects is brought to a focus not on the retina but in front of it in the former case or back of it in the latter. Equally common is *astigmatism*, which is due to imperfect curvature of cornea or lens or eyeball, so that all the light rays being received from a single source point cannot be focused at one retinal point. Spectacles are lenses ground to correct these errors of light refraction, and their widespread use is evidence that such defects are common.

Poor eyesight, whatever the cause, should be recognized as early as possible. Many a child who has been having difficulties in his school work and is consequently rated backward or dull needs only reseating in his classroom or perhaps an oculist's examination and treatment to give him the opportunity to show what he really can do.

Color-weakness came to the popular attention during World War II as never before. For the armed services then recognized, as the civilian railway and harbor employment services had done earlier, the critical importance of ability to read colored signals; and they set standards of ability in color discrimination as a prerequisite for admission to training as a commissioned officer. And these tests ambitious young men were eager to pass. Out of this state of affairs two notions about weakness in discriminating colors became widely accepted — but not scientifically established. One was that color-blindness was something an individual did or did not have, and that it was easily brought to light by simple tests. The other was that many cases of so-called color-blindness were remediable, or at least improvable to a degree that made intensive coaching and persistent color-gazing exercises successful in getting the rejectee through his second examination. In actual fact, color-weakness is a variable impediment; that is, some persons show it to a pronounced degree, others to a lesser extent. It is primarily a structural defect, a difference in the very anatomy of the retina; yet it is susceptible to influences, such as from tobacco smoking. Estimates of frequency vary, but it is fairly safe to say that less than four per cent of the male and less than one-half of one per cent of the female population are so seriously handicapped as to be called color-blind.

Theories of Color Vision

The above-described phenomena point to the fact that while physical light itself varies in its wave lengths by all gradations, the effects aroused in the retina and its nervous connections in man seem to be analyzable into a few elementary processes excited there. Certain facts are known about color vision, but these facts are complex and apparently contradictory. How can they be related? It is in answer to this question that theories of color vision have been evolved. Although several have been proposed, no single theory is completely satisfactory. It would seem sensible here to mention only the two most famous ones [2].

The *Young-Helmholtz* theory posited three kinds of receptive cells in the retina: one specially affected by light waves producing *red*, a second specially affected by those producing *green*, a third by those producing *blue*, but each responsive in some degree to all light waves. This has always been well regarded by physicists; and, after having been almost superseded for a time by the Hering theory, it now seems to be regaining favor with psychologists, at least as the point of departure for new theories.

The *Hering* theory seems most in accord with facts and phenomena such as we have been presenting. It asserts that in the rods and cones are three distinct kinds of structures. One kind is set into chemical activity by green and by red light [1] in antagonistic ways (anabolic and catabolic, respectively); another is in similar manner made active by blue and by yellow light; and a third, by black and by white as well as by all the other colors.

SOME QUANTITATIVE PROBLEMS

Thresholds of Sensitivity

Most of the problems about human sensitivity are originally of a qualitative character. The following are examples. What kinds of stimulation are effective at the skin, or on the tongue, or on the periphery of the retina, or along the enteric canal? If the olfactory membrane is exhausted for response to heliotrope, what other odors become ineffective at the same time? What is the relationship between tones x and y that makes them more harmonious than tones x and z? Does the after-excitation remaining from eye stimulation by a given wave length bear any special relation to the latter? The qualitative problems in any field of science tend, however, to become increasingly quantitative, more and more a question of precisely how much. And so it is with the above and similar queries.

Quantitative refinements of sensory problems date from 1860, when Fechner summarized elaborate investigations that he and others had been making. In the first half of the nineteenth century it had become increasingly evident that the study of human nature could not be

---

[1] The green selected by Hering would ordinarily be called a bluish green, and the red, a slightly purplish red.

soundly prosecuted merely by the armchair method of comparing anecdotes and personal experiences, but that it must be closely linked with
physics, physiology, and mathematics. Accordingly, a few scientists
undertook to measure certain phenomena in human nature, especially
along the line of sensory thresholds.

A receptor, like any other mechanism, has a certain amount of inertia;
that is, it requires a certain degree of stimulation to be awakened into
activity. A clock tick in an adjoining room may be too weak to excite
the ear, a star too faint to affect the eye, a snowflake too light to excite
the pressure receptors on the back of the hand, for they may all be below
the necessary intensity, or "below the threshold." Just what is the
minimal intensity that a given stimulus must have in order to be sensed?
This is the question of the *stimulation threshold*.

The inertia of a receptor, like that of any other mechanism, is further
revealed in its failure to react to infinitesimal gradations of intensity;
when it is already in activity, the receptor requires a certain amount of
increase of stimulation before it will be set into any increased activity.
The ear hearing a large orchestra playing ensemble will not be sensitive
to the increase of sound that results when one more violin joins in. The
tongue tasting coffee sweetened with three lumps of sugar will not be
differently affected if a quarter lump more is added. Just what is the
minimal increase of intensity that a given stimulus must have in order
to be sensed as "just perceptibly more"? This is the question of the
difference threshold.

Weber's Law

While working on the difference threshold for the cutaneous and kinesthetic senses, Weber discovered a significant relation between increases
of stimulus and increases of receptor excitation (and increases of the
experienced sensation). This may be cast into the formula

$$\frac{\Delta St}{St} = K$$

in which Δ = "discriminable difference of," St = intensity of the stimulus, and K = a constant holding for a given stimulus (sight, hearing,
and so on). The law may be stated: *The increase of a stimulation necessary
for the subject to discriminate it as an increase bears a constant ratio to the total
preceding stimulation*. This law has been found to hold in various sense
fields, and it furnishes us with a ready explanation of some everyday
phenomena. The same star that is visible at night is invisible in the
daytime, for its own light is not enough, when added to that of the sun's,

to be discriminable by the visual apparatus. A voice is strong enough to be heard under conditions of quiet, but when it is added to the noise of a machine shop it forms an increment too slight to be discerned. If a man is carrying a bucket weighing twenty pounds, an added half pound may make no difference to him, whereas if to a two-pound bucket the same half-pound addition is made, he will promptly react to the difference. To be sensed *as* an increase, a stimulus must be increased relatively; a small original stimulus needs but little added, a large one, much. This relative increase remains much the same for any one sense, but may be quite different in different senses, as Table XXII shows.

Exhaustive investigations of Weber's law have forced modifications of it as a general law. (1) It holds principally for changes in intensity of stimulation, and not usually for other sorts of changes — such as a change in color or wave length. (2) It holds well through the middle sections of intensity in the different senses, but not in the extremely high and extremely low intensities. (3) It varies (to a small degree) with the individual, and within the same individual at different times and under different conditions. Nevertheless, this principle, enunciated in 1831, deserves attention, as the first clear achievement in rendering psychology quantitative [7].

The Psychophysical Methods [1]

The precise determination of a sensory threshold is by no means so easy a process as might be supposed. It is necessary for both experimenter and subject to exercise particular care throughout long series of repetitions of some seemingly simple performance on the part of the subject. Also a definite and rather elaborate order of presentation of stimuli must be planned out in advance.

TABLE XXII — Values of K in Weber's Law

	Commonly Assigned	Limits
Visual	1/100	1/65–1/195
Kinesthetic	1/40	1/20–1/100
Cutaneous: pressure	1/20	1/10–1/30
Cutaneous: temperature	1/3	1/3–1/4
Auditory	1/5	1/3–1/8
Olfactory	1/3	1/3–1/4
Gustatory	1/3	1/3–1/4

[1] The reason for this name, being based on an outgrown metaphysics, need not detain us. It is still universally employed — with no metaphysical implication.

Suppose one were working to find the stimulation threshold of a sound. In one series the stimulus is first presented at an intensity well above the threshold (easily heard) and by repeated changes reduced until it is well below the threshold (cannot be heard at all); then from the latter point the stimulus is increased in intensity back again to a point well above the threshold. In both series of changes the subject is instructed to react positively as long as he can sense (hear) the stimulus and negatively as long as he cannot. The two series must be repeated frequently. Also, it is often well to reverse the order of stimulus changes within either series, for the purpose of checking such factors as the subject's expectancy of reaching the threshold and so making too prompt a report of it, or his continuance in a set manner of reacting and so making too late a report of it. Moreover, there are a number of incidental disturbing factors to be guarded against, so that all in all this is an exercise that will reward only the careful and the industrious investigator.

Again, if one were seeking to determine the difference threshold for kinesthesis, the experiment of the lifted weights would be used, which is to be described below.

It is not content so much as technique which has maintained interest for nearly a hundred years in these sensory threshold problems. These experiments have been particularly valuable in developing and refining statistical procedures in many different areas. Whenever the question is that of determining *at just what point* in a series of changing values a certain phenomenon occurs, these methods are applicable. The following questions are examples of the kind that may be profitably explored through the psychophysical techniques: Just how far out on the lateral side of his field of vision can a person see green? Just how many digits can the average adult repeat backward after one hearing? Just how many objects can one take in at one instant's glance? At just what age will the average child show some understanding of human relations in a picture and not simply enumerate the persons in it?

It has been well said that psychophysics helped much in winning World War II. A soldier could not squeeze a trigger effectively without the finest trained integration of sensory data coming in from his eyes and his muscles. When it came to the skillful operation of anti-aircraft guns, the piloting of bombing planes by night, the accurate receiving of radio messages or of radar echoes, the recognizing of enemy planes, or the hearing of speech over the interphone of a noisy plane, the ultimate limits of human sense capacities were frequently demanded. And it became notably recognized that in the designing of new machines the psychophysicist's accurate determinations of what is humanly possible and feasible had to be taken repeatedly into account [16].

A knowledge of these methods is invaluable to the student who wishes to develop insight into the pitfalls of experimental procedure. For psychology this is basic training!

There are three most-used standard methods of threshold determination. One is the *Method of Average Error*, in which the subject (S) himself adjusts the Variable stimulus to make it apparently equal to the Standard stimulus, the amount of his errors from trial to trial being averaged and called the threshold. Examples: (*a*) S is to move a slide on the left arm of a horizontal (Galton) bar to make it look to him the same distance from the middle as is a standard slide on the right arm of the bar; (*b*) S is to adjust a rheostat so that the gray light at one ground glass window is apparently of the same brightness as that at another window.

The Method of Minimal Changes is one in which the experimenter (E) now manipulates the Variable stimulus, changing it gradually through all degrees until S reports that it apparently is just equal to the Standard stimulus; and the errors are averaged. Examples: (*a*) Little by little E slides the weight on a tuning fork to bring its tone nearer and nearer to that of another (Constant) tuning fork, S to judge just when they are identical; (*b*) E gradually increases the brightness of the darker of two windows, S to judge when the two windows are apparently of equal brightness.

In the *Method of Constant Stimuli* E has a definite number of definite values of the Variable. E pairs each in irregular order with the Standard stimulus, calls upon S to decide in each case whether the second-presented is greater than, equal to, or less than the first-presented. Examples: (*a*) S may be asked to compare by "hefting" them weights of 88, 92, 96, 100, 104, 108 and 112 gr. with a Standard weight of 100 gr.; (*b*) S may be asked to compare the sound of forks varying .5, 1, 2, 3, 5, 8, 12, and 17 cycles below the Standard with the Standard tuning fork.

TABLE
XXIII

Data from a Lifted Weights Experiment

Judgments	Weights of the Variable								
	84	88	92	96	100	104	108	112	116
Times Variable is judged "heavier" than Standard	0	1	6	20	38	55	82	98	100
Times Variable is judged "equal" to Standard	1	4	21	31	36	32	11	1	0
Times Variable is judged "lighter" than Standard	99	95	73	49	26	13	7	1	0

A moment's consideration will make clear to the reader the necessity for the development of statistical procedures in handling the results, especially when the third-named method is employed. Suppose that a subject comparing various graduated weights with the 100-gram Standard makes the rather typical judgments entered in Table XXIII (page 273).

Just where is the subject's threshold? These data assume more meaning when plotted, as in Figure 84. Incidentally, we note one thing about the general form of distribution curve for each of the three kinds of judgments: the curve for judgments of "equal" resembles the bell-shaped curve of normal error, while the others assume the "ogive" or S-shaped curve and reversed-ogive forms for cumulative chance distribution. And now to find the degree of sensitivity for our hypothetical subject in lifted weights at the 100-gram standard. We draw a horizontal line at the level of 50 per cent of judgments; and where it intersects the lines for judgments of "lighter" and of "heavier," we drop vertical lines to the base, noting the points on the base. We find that the weight of Variable where the subject would be exactly 50 per cent correct in judging it

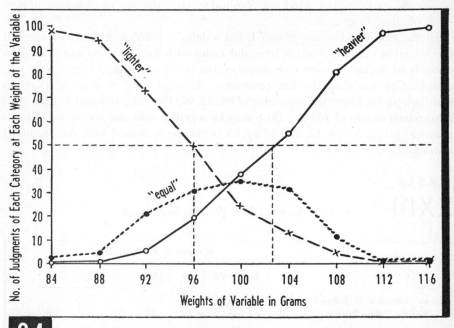

84 **Threshold Determination for Lift Weights**

The Variable weights, indicated on the base line, were presented, in pairings with the Standard in a double-chance order: (1) sometimes the *S* was presented first, the *V* second, at other times this was reversed; (2) the order in which the nine Variables were used was by chance.

"lighter" is at the value 95.9 grams (the *lower threshold*); and we find by similar interpolation that he would have been correct in 50 per cent of his judgments of "heavier" at the weight 102.8 grams (the *upper threshold*). Finally we see that the difference between the two thresholds is 6.9 grams, and we find this useful as a measure of his discriminating ability at the standard weight of 100 grams.

A CONCLUDING VIEW OF RECEPTIVE PROCESSES

Let us now summarize the roles played by the different classes of receptors in the life economy, in the light of the preliminary descriptions and analyses of human and animal behavior we have set forth in earlier chapters. The primary sources of human and of sub-human behavior are to be found in the metabolic processes occurring within the body and especially in the inadequate relations of external conditions to these processes. The *interoceptors* are the sensitive organs most directly implicated here. Next, the organism when it gets into action proceeds to make some change in its environment. In this the *exteroceptors* act the part of advance guards through which the specific characters of the surroundings play upon the body and modify the directions of movements. Further refinement of the movements is secured through the coordinations made possible by the *proprioceptors*.

A simple illustration lies at hand in the behavior of a hungry child. The empty stomach sets up interoceptive impulses which initiate motion and locomotion: the child goes after food. The direction in which he goes is determined by the smell or by the sight of cookies or oranges, the sight of doorways, and by other exteroceptive stimulations. The maintaining of his general bodily positions and the effective reaching for and taking hold of and eating of a cooky or an orange depend upon his proprioceptive organization.

REFERENCES

1. Bartley, S. H. *Vision.* New York: D. Van Nostrand Company, 1941.
2. Boring, E. G. *Sensation and Perception in the History of Experimental Psychology.* New York: Appleton-Century-Crofts, 1942.
3. Dallenbach, K. M. "The temperature spots and end-organs," *Am. J. Psychol.*, 1927, *39*, 402–427.
4. Davis, H. *Hearing and Deafness.* New York: Rinehart and Company, 1947.
5. Evans, R. M. *An Introduction to Color.* New York: John Wiley and Sons, 1948.

6. Fletcher, H. *Speech and Hearing*. New York: D. Van Nostrand Company, 1929.

7. Garrett, H. E. *Great Experiments in Psychology*. Revised edition. New York: Appleton-Century-Crofts, 1941. Chapter 15.

8. Guilford, J. P. *Psychometric Methods*. New York: McGraw-Hill Book Company, 1936.

9. Jenkins, W. L., and L. J. Stone. "Recent research in cutaneous sensitivity," *Psychol. Bull.*, 1941, *38*, 69–91.

10. Karwoski, T. F., and H. S. Odbert. "Color-music," *Psychol. Monogr.*, 1938, *50*, No. 222.

11. Katz, D. *The World of Colors*. London: Kegan Paul, French and Trubner, 1935.

12. Kemp, E. H. "A critical review of experiments on the problem of stimulation deafness," *Psychol. Bull.*, 1935, *32*, 325–342.

13. Ryan, T. A. "Interrelations of the sensory systems in perception," *Psychol. Bull.*, 1940, *37*, 659–698.

14. Stevens, S. S. "The attributes of tones," *Proc. Nat. Acad. Sci.*, 1934, *20*, 457–459.

15. Stevens, S. S., and H. Davis. *Hearing*. New York: John Wiley and Sons, 1938.

16. Stevens, S. S. "Machines cannot fight alone," *Amer. Scientist*, 1946, *34*, 389–400.

17. Titchener, E. B. *Experimental Psychology*. New York: The Macmillan Company, 1901. Vols. I and II.

18. Wever, E. G., and C. W. Bray. "The nature of acoustic response," *J. Exp. Psychol.*, 1930, *13*, 373–387.

19. Willmann, R. R. "An experimental investigation of the creative process in music," *Psychol. Monogr.*, 1944, *57*, No. 261.

20. Woodworth, R. S. *Experimental Psychology*. New York: Henry Holt and Company, 1938.

MOTOR FUNCTIONS

11

PSYCHOLOGY, we have said, is primarily the scientific study of human nature. Human nature, we have said, is primarily a question of how the human being behaves. And behavior in its first intention, so to speak, is a matter of activities. The first things we can know about any person, before we can go into analysis of his deeper-lying possibilities and potentialities, are the ways in which he acts. In the preceding chapters it should have become evident that a psychological interest in prediction and control is one involving, first of all, inquiries as to how, when, and why a man does this or that, acts thus and so, desires, seeks, accepts, rejects — in a word, why he moves.

If we were to make a psychological study of the motorist, for example, we should expect to begin with a survey of just how he does things with feet and hands: the way he pushes in this pedal, pulls out that dashboard lever, turns this large wheel, throws the gear-shift lever, and turns head and eyeballs sharply this way and that. So with the businessman at his desk: we may see him reach over and pull out a file of papers, riffle through them with fingers and thumb, lay one flat on his desk, seize a pen and make ink marks with it, press a call-button, make sounds by using his voice, and all the while be moving his eyeballs (and even his head) left-right-up-down in a bewilderingly rapid and continual play of motion. To be sure, all such activities are but the resultants of energies playing upon our motorist or businessman, as well as of complicated energy-changes that have been going on within his body, and they are but a small part of the whole story; yet in an analysis of motor functions we may well begin with these more observable phenomena and

277

work our way backward to the processes that precede and determine them.

Now, activities of these sorts are primarily the functioning of striped muscles. These are the tissues at work in the acts of eating, walking, listening, sewing, talking — in fact in nearly all the activities of a person that are externally observable. Hence we may profitably learn at least the bare essentials of the striped muscle processes, first in the gross, then in somewhat finer detail.

Distribution and Arrangement of the Striped Muscles

The striped muscles, to which we have already had some occasion to refer, constitute from a third to a half of the total mass of the organism; there are over six hundred of them all told. Their function of moving a part of the body is typically performed by pulling on levers. The bony skeleton furnishes a framework, consisting mainly of systems of levers upon which the body is hung and stretched; and it is through the manipulation of these levers by the muscles attached to them with tendons that the body changes its positions and postures.

An Example. Every boy knows the biceps because he has felt it dozens of times to estimate his growing strength. It is located just above the elbow and to the front of the humerus bone of the upper arm, and it plays the simple but enormously important role of raising the lower arm. That performance may be part and parcel of behavior processes of a very wide range: the lower arm may come up sharply at the buzzing sound of a mosquito, or it may snap up in a military salute; it may go up in response to a barked command out of the darkness to "stick 'em up!", or it may be making the first movement of manipulating a cocktail shaker; it may be the preliminary to striking a piano keyboard, or it may mark only the transferal of a spoonful of oatmeal to the mouth. But whatever the total performance in which the biceps participates, the raising of the arm is one and the same mechanism when it is considered locally and in isolation. Let us analyze this with the aid of Figure 85.

The upraising of the forearm and hand is accomplished by the contraction of the biceps muscle. This round, spindle-shaped mass is attached at one end to a bone of the shoulder, and at the other to one in the forearm. When it shortens, it draws the forearm and hand toward the shoulder. The elbow joint serves as the fulcrum.

The conditions that can excite this contraction are several: a sharp blow, a sudden stretch, certain chemicals, electricity, a sudden temperature change; but the normal excitation is a neural impulse received via motor (efferent) nerve fibers from the central nervous system — and

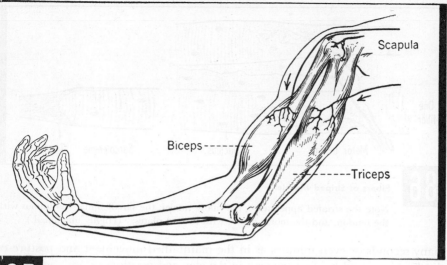

Scapula

Biceps ------

------Triceps

85 A Typical Motor Unit

The two muscle-groups, biceps and triceps, operate the lower arm as a lever with the elbow serving as the fulcrum. Their modes of innervation and reciprocal action are described in the text.

resulting from processes that may be traced back to activated receptor organs. The energy changes coming in from the nerve serve to excite energy changes in the muscle. This *innervation*, as it is called, of the biceps is indicated in Figure 85 by a line running to the biceps, with an arrowhead to show the direction of the efferent impulses.

The Nature of Contraction

The story of a simple contraction includes first a "latent" period, which is the interval between the time the neural impulse is received and the beginning of contraction; then comes the contraction, at first slow, then rapid, then slow; finally there is a relaxation. The duration of latent period, of contraction, and of relaxation is in each case a matter of hundredths of a second, the whole operation frequently occupying less than one-tenth of a second. However, the simple twitch type of muscle contraction is the exception rather than the rule. Barring a few extremely simple reflex actions, the excitations received via motor nerves are multiple rather than simple. They appear at a rate varying greatly for different fibers, but average around fifty per second. They reach the muscle fibers in a succession or volley which is so rapid that before one contraction has ceased another has been aroused; and the result is a single continuous pull maintained for as long as the excitations continue. This may be a matter of a fraction of a second, as in most of the arm-raising illustrations used above, or of

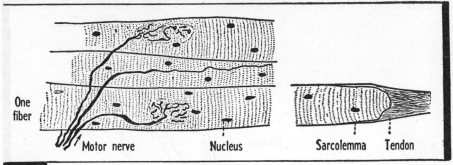

One fiber   Motor nerve   Nucleus   Sarcolemma   Tendon

86   Fibers of Striped Muscle

Note the striated appearance, the many nuclei, the sarcolemma, continuous with the tendon, and the motor nerve, with its end plates. (Highly magnified.)

many seconds or even minutes as in the maintained movement and posture of slowly raising and holding the arm in the elevated position.

The *all-or-none* principle is found to hold in the operation of the individual muscle fiber. It contracts either to its fullest extent or not at all. Hence the intensity of the pull exerted by the muscle as a whole is dependent not upon the intensity of neural excitation per fiber but upon the number of different fibers excited.

Antagonistic Relations of Musculature

To return to our example of the biceps, this muscle when it shortens to draw up the forearm is not merely pulling up a dead weight; it is pulling against the triceps (see Figure 85 again). The latter muscle is found to the back of the upper arm; and because it is attached by tendons to bones at the shoulder and to one in the lower arm, it operates to pull the lower arm in the downward direction. The biceps, then, tends to flex the arm, the triceps to extend it, the two usually working in coordinated fashion. Thus the upward sweep of the hand is often arrested at some given point, as in saluting or in lifting a glass to the mouth; this stoppage is made more definite by the timely innervation of the triceps — over the efferent nerve supply indicated in the figure by another line. This antagonistic arrangement of the muscle systems is common enough throughout the body; the muscles are so paired as to check and control each other; and it is by their opposed but concerted pulls that finely controlled movements, as the engraver's or the surgeon's, are made with such precision.

One connecting link is necessary to this story. How does it come about that toward the end of one excursion the muscles then receive innervations whose effect is the reverse of those just preceding? We must now recognize a further muscle and nerve relationship, one of the sensory or afferent type. In and on the muscle fiber there lie also the sensitive ends (receptors) of *afferent* nerves. (Not shown in Figures 85 and 86 but to be seen in Figure 67, page 243.) It is essential to remember that when a muscle is thrown into contraction, this change of the condition in the muscle tissue, as well as in the tendinous tissue to which it is attached, is an adequate stimulus to excite sensitive nerve beginnings that are found there and in the joints, and so to generate neural impulses running away from the moving member and toward the nervous centers (cf. pages 242 ff.). Bearing in mind these two kinds of nerve supply, the efferent and the afferent, we should now be able to understand how a movable member can by its own movements elicit still further movements by "circular reflexes" via the nerve centers. An upstroke of the forearm itself furnishes neural stimulation leading to a downstroke; the downward movement arouses impulses leading to an upstroke; and so on.

Muscular Tension

The contractions of which we have been speaking are to be viewed against a background of some degree of continuous contraction that is always present to some extent in the muscles. At no time are they absolutely inert. The local chemical conditions of the tissue itself seem to keep it in some mild degree of contracting state; but in addition we are to recognize a continuous flow of motor impulses going out over the nerves. When these innervations are received in heavy volleys, the muscle is excited to the contractions that are ordinarily noted as movements of the arm or finger or other body-part, or at least as noticeable muscular strains.

If we were to trace these tension-maintaining neural impulses backward to their origins, we should find them originating in the afferent impulses coming into the central nervous system from certain receptors. (1) They come to a significant degree from the muscle-tendon-joint apparatus itself, which amounts to saying that the muscle re-excites itself through a continuous series of weak reflexes. (2) Also important are the receptors in the labyrinth of the ear; for interference with their afferent impulses will impair the organism's ability to sit up or stand (cf. page 248). (3) The greater vigor of movement displayed by anyone in cold weather points to the cold receptors in the skin as contributing their part. (4) The slashing, dashing movements of the person or animal emotionally aroused in fright or rage argues for a tie-up with the visceral segments of response and hence of deep interocepters, perhaps through release of brain centers related to the activation of visceral patterns.

The role of these muscular tensions or "tonus" in determining human behavior is tremendous and must not be overlooked.

(1) For one thing, gross *postural reactions* are maintained by these continuous contractions. Aiming at a target, listening to a lecturer, computing at the accountant's desk, feeding any industrial machine — all such performances depend upon the supporting tensions of muscles in legs, trunk, and neck.

(2) Again, a general tonus makes for excitability or irritability in the muscles of the whole body, so that upon receipt of any definite stimulation one's reactions are more prompt and more intense than they would be otherwise. It is a condition of readiness, *alertness*. With muscles on the *qui vive*, a man responds the more quickly and vigorously; as, for example, after he has been aroused from his drowsiness by a cold shower bath, or after the football coach has warned him to be on his toes. And this greater readiness is found in psychological functions of higher order than gross muscular activities; for various kinds of so-called mental work, such as continuous adding or mirror drawing or memorizing, are facilitated by tensions in general musculature. There are limits to this favorable effect, of course, for when the tensions exceed a certain optimal degree they may retard the performance. Moreover, even when the muscular-tension condition does speed up work, it is quite likely to reduce precision.

(3) So much for tensions in the musculature generally. We must further recognize that the degree of tonus waxes and wanes in different ways for *different muscle groups*. The degree to which it furthers or hinders a given performance varies with the physical and functional closeness between the muscle-groups that are tensed and the muscle-group engaged in the active performance.

These three experimentally derived principles are recognized — or at least practiced — by any golf professional, voice coach, dancing master, or rifle instructor.

> There is one very bright hope for those who find themselves habitually tense and excitable. If such people can acquire inhibitory control and coordination of their activities in the face of a hyperactive postural substrate, they may come actually to excel more phlegmatic individuals; if they can learn to harness their machine, it should produce not only *more* intellectual goods but also goods of *finer quality* than a sluggish machine. Many of our most successful men are dynamos of neuromuscular energy behind their surface of exterior calm. They are apparently separated from certain inmates of our state asylums by a rather narrow line. They have learned to coordinate and control rather than to dissipate and abuse.[1]

[1] From G. L. Freeman, *Sci. Mon.*, *N.Y.*, 1938, *47*, 167.

Progressive Relaxation

The reverse of tension is relaxation. But though clinicians — and many laymen as well — recognize its importance to mental health, complete relaxation is not easy to achieve.

> I found, [says Jacobson] as others have found previously, that an individual might lie on a couch apparently quiet for hours, yet remain sleepless and nervously restless. Even as he lay there, he might continue to betray signs of mental activity, organic excitement, anxiety or other emotional disturbance; he might breathe irregularly, fidget and start, with restless movements of the eyes, fingers or other parts, or perhaps with an impulse to unnecessary speech. These signs might occur occasionally or frequently and might be quite obvious to the observer or require close inspection. When attention is once called to the matter, it is evident that such rest at best is not complete; following it, the patient often fails to seem refreshed, retaining his symptoms and complaints of nervousness, fatigue or other ills.[1]

To achieve complete relaxation Jacobson advocates training. This involves first the careful moving of one muscle and another, so that the subject can familiarize himself with the kinesthetic sensory experience induced by each. The large muscle-groups are studied first, such as those that lift the hand or move the foot; and later the finer ones, as those that operate the eyelids and eyeballs. Having practiced systematically and frequently, the subject becomes better able to spot the residual tensions that linger when he is supposedly at rest. He will then see to it that they are released. Many persons testify that sleep is more readily induced by this method than by counting sheep or engaging in other thought-routine. There are many busy men, also, who report that they secure a pick-up of energy in spare minutes by this voluntary relaxing of muscular tensions.

Coordinations of Muscles

Suppose the reader at this moment were to reach for a pencil lying eighteen inches from this book. His "hand reaches for it," he might say. But on examination it is clear that an enormous number of muscles are sharing in this act. The angle at the elbow widens; biceps and triceps cooperate. The upper arm is raised from the shoulder, with the massive deltoid playing the principal part. All five fingers are extended, each being pulled by its own combination of muscles in the forearm. The trunk of the body shares in the reaction by leaning forward; and a great number of separate muscles are involved. The head is tilted upward

[1] From E. Jacobson, *Progressive Relaxation* (Chicago: University of Chicago Press, 1938).

on its cervical axis; this is done by a concerted shortening of several back muscles. The eyes turn toward the object, and a delicate coordination of the six muscles of each eyeball takes place. Other muscle movements, also, could be mentioned.

The advantages secured to the organism by this teamwork, coordination of its muscles, may be reduced to three: *strength*, *speed*, and accuracy or *precision*. That a combination of pulls may make a stronger total pull is readily seen; but in many cases the particular combination that will give the maximum power is not evident to the worker, and he is likely to continue lifting loads from the ground with the musculature of his back rather than of his legs, for example, or to sing *forte* with an extravagant expenditure of breath. Somewhat the same point may be made with respect to speed. The speediest boxer is by no means the one with the most strength, but rather the one who has the nicest organization of pulls by various muscles in forearm, upper arm, shoulder, trunk, and legs, all of which require great precision in timing. As for precision or accuracy in performance, it too is essentially a matter of economy. He who can lay a brick with six or eight coordinated movements in succession, instead of fifteen or eighteen, is the skillful worker. So likewise is he who can perform with one circular motion rather than two angular ones. Precision is also a matter of balance. When one undertakes to drink a glass of water, too strong use of the deltoid muscle will toss the water over the head, too strong use of the pronator muscles will empty it on the floor, too strong use of the elbow flexors will strike the glass against the face.

In laboratory studies these three characteristics — strength, speed, and precision — have been found to have a *general* application. That is, they do not hold for specific motor units, as the right-thumb-and-first-finger, say, or the left foot, but are found true for many or all the musculatures of a given person. If Mr. B. shows higher than average steadiness in thrusting a stylus into a series of holes, he is likely to show higher than average steadiness in rifle target shooting; but his hand and arm that proved so steady in the stylus-thrusting would not be likely to be above-average with respect to speed of stylus-thrusting. In the analytic study of motor abilities, then, one should expect to find similarities in these general characteristics regardless of the musculature involved, rather than any grouping of abilities about anatomical units [16, 18].

Motor Ability Tests

For laboratory measurements of the above-mentioned characteristics of muscular activity — strength, speed, and precision — much use has

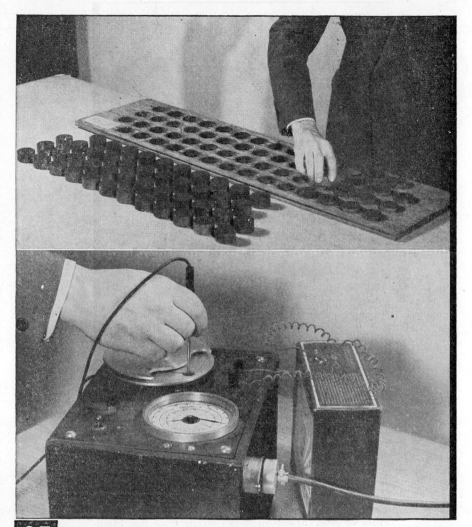

87

Some Tests of Motor Coordination in Industry

A. Arm and hand dexterity (speed and precision), Minnesota model. Subject is to pick up the blocks and place them in the holes, total time being recorded for the 58 placings. *B.* Hand precision, Purdue model. Subject is to punch the stylus into each hole of the base plate as it is uncovered by the rotations of the covering plate, without touching stylus to either plate. The total amount of such contact is automatically registered. (*From D. G. Paterson,* Minnesota Mechanical Ability Tests, *University of Minnesota Press, 1930; J. Tiffin,* Industrial Psychology, *Prentice-Hall, 1946. Photos by courtesy of the authors.*)

88 **Testing Complex Coordination in the A.A.F.**

Each candidate sits facing three double rows of
lights. His task is to manipulate his stick and
rudder to change the position of a green light appearing in
each of the three rows to match the position of a red light
in each row. When the three green lights have been made
to match the red ones simultaneously for one-half second, a
new pattern of red lights appears. The candidate's score is
taken as the number of settings he completes in a specified
length of time. Mashburn model arranged for four candidates. (*Photo by courtesy of Dr. Glen Finch and Colonel William H.
Powell, Jr.*)

been made of such simple instruments as the *hand dynamometer*, the *tapping
board*, and the *three-hole test*. In testing applicants for industrial jobs, it
has been found useful to devise still other instruments. Some of those
most widely used in industrial personnel work for testing the arm, hand,
and finger movements are shown in Figure 87. Such tests have been
tried out as selective devices in connection with many industrial jobs,
but it is impossible to determine by theoretical analysis alone which test
is a suitable criterion for the particular job. Packing matches into boxes

may require speed, but to assume that any simple speed test will help to separate those who will make speedy match-packers from those who will not is dangerous thinking — and costly for any industrial manager who allows an untrained person to set up as a personnel expert on such grounds. On the contrary, every test must be painstakingly validated by a comparison of its findings with foreman's ratings of individual workers, with production records, or some other objective criterion of the true individual differences among the examinees.[1]

THE DETECTION OF ACTIVITIES OF MUSCLES

Introduction

When we observe a human being we note what he is doing, what his actions and postures are; and in a sense this resolves itself into what his muscles are doing. Now, a great deal of muscular activity goes on in so minimal a way that it cannot be observed by ordinary methods. It is implicit. Particularly is this true of activity during functions of much psychological interest such as paying attention, thinking hard, and the like. Without instrumentation, with only naked-eye methods, we should be forced to remain in a state of ignorance analogous to that of the physiologist and zoologist before the microscope was discovered or that of the astronomer before Galileo discovered the telescope. Accordingly, the development of techniques for bringing out into the open the obscure and the minute processes occurring in human behavior must be recognized as of first importance. These techniques are of many types. For the present, however, we shall confine ourselves to a technique that is designed to detect and measure one of the most delicate phenomena.[2]

General Nature of Action Potentials

It has long been known that whenever a muscle is thrown into contraction (or thickens) or whenever neural impulses pass over a nerve, a wavelike electrical change (action current) passes through the tissue concerned. Suppose, for instance, that an isolated muscle or nerve fiber be stimulated near one end, as shown in Figure 89. A wave of excitation in the form of a difference of potential that is negative with

[1] Refer to Chapter 5, pages 105 ff.
[2] Since this phenomenon is found in neural as well as in muscular tissue, we may find it convenient to refer to the former at places in the discussion that follows, even though more specific descriptions of neural tissues and their general functions must be postponed to a subsequent chapter.

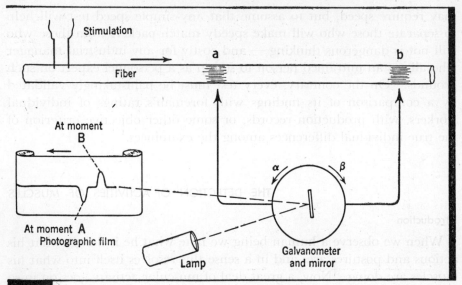

89 Arrangement for Registering Electrical Potentials from an Active Muscle or Nerve Fiber

The simple galvanometer here indicated is ordinarily replaced by more sensitive instruments. Explanation is given in the text.

respect to the rest of the fiber will pass from the stimulated point along the fiber. This is detected simply by attaching electrodes from a galvanometer at points *a* and *b*. At the instant *A*, when the excitation passes point *a*, a current will be revealed by the galvanometer in the direction indicated by the arrow α; at instant *B*, when the excitation passes point *b*, a current of opposite direction β will be revealed. A permanent and continuous record can be obtained photographically. Let a beam of light be reflected from the mirror of the galvanometer upon a traveling film, so that a deflection caused by a current flowing in the α direction will be recorded as a drop in the light beam and therefore in the light-line on the film, and a deflection of opposite β direction will be recorded as a rise in the beam and in the line. Then the successive passing of points *a* and *b* on the muscle (or nerve) fiber by a single wave of excitation of that tissue will appear as a diphasic tracing on the film. If desired, a time line can be produced by a regularly oscillating light beam from another source playing upon the upper part of the film; and a measurement of the time relations involved is in this manner rendered simple.

In this description we have assumed that the tissue being studied is a single fiber (cell). As a matter of fact, the studies made in psychological laboratories have been upon muscle masses or nerve trunks, consisting of many, even hundreds of distinct fibers. Since it is certain that different fibers may differ greatly in their characteristic manners of energy propagation (in frequency and in intensity), the wave form along a bundle of fibers will vary in its complexity with the number of fibers composing the trunk.   For example, when a pianist is striking the keys, any action current picked up from the contracting triceps participating in the movement will be a complex one.

For simplicity's sake, in presenting the general notion of action currents we have mentioned the use of the ordinary mirror galvanometer.   In practice, however, the moving parts of that instrument have too much inertia for prompt

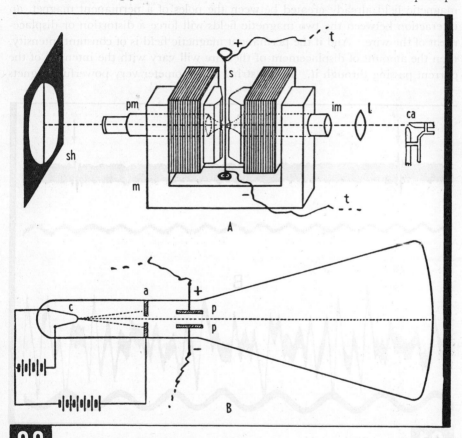

90   **Apparatus for Recording Action Potentials**

A. Einthoven string galvanometer. *m*, magnet; *s*, string; *ca*, carbon arc light source; *l*, lens; *im*, lens system for forming image of light source at string; *pm*, lens system for projecting image of string on photokymograph; *sh*, shadow of string in projected image; *tt*, leads from the living tissue, as muscle or nerve. *B*. The cathode ray tube for oscilloscope. *c*. hot cathode; *a*, anode; *p, p*, one pair of deflection plates; *t, t*, leads from the living tissue. (*From G. R. Wendt.* Arch. Psychol., *N.Y., 1938, pages 34, 36. By permission of the author.*)

and delicate responsiveness to very rapid oscillatory changes of potential. With much more sensitive instruments it is now possible to obtain faithful reproductions of potential changes as minute as a few millionths of a volt and with a frequency of many thousandths per second. Galvanometers in which the mirrors used are almost microscopic in size have been used in much experimental work in this field. Two other instruments that are frequently used may be outlined here for the student who is interested.

(1) The *string galvanometer* (Figure 90, *A*) operates on the principle of the electric motor. When an electric current is passing through a wire, it induces a magnetic field about the wire. If, then, the wire is suspended within another magnetic field already created between the poles of a permanent magnet, an interaction between the two magnetic fields will force a distortion or displacement of the wire. And if the permanent magnetic field is of constant intensity, then the amount of displacement of the wire will vary with the intensity of the current passing through it. In the string galvanometer very powerful magnets

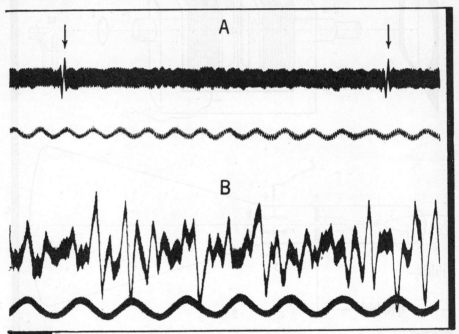

91 **Oscillograph Records of Muscle Contractions**

A. A slight contraction of a single motor unit (a group of muscle fibers innervated by a single nerve fiber). The electrodes were hypodermic needles inserted through to the muscle. The rate of the discharges was about 9 times per second, of which 2 are shown. *B.* A contraction of a muscle as a whole. The electrodes were placed on the skin surface over the muscle mass. Many motor units were discharging asynchronously, the total frequency being some 400 to 500 per second. In both *A* and *B* the time is indicated in 1/100 second by the wavy line. (*By courtesy of Dr. L. E. Travis.*)

are used and the wire or "string" is mounted and centered between them. The ends of the wire are then connected with leads from the living tissue, so that minute changes of electrical potential in the tissue will produce changes in the position of the suspended wire; and by being placed in the path of a beam of light, the wire will project a highly magnified shadow of itself on a traveling photosensitive record. Modern instruments have been developed in which pens write on a continuously moving paper tape and thus record changes of the sort discussed.

(2) The general physical principles of the *cathode ray oscilloscope* are similar to those of the ordinary radio or electron tube. (See Figure 90, *B*.) Some of the electrons flying off a hot cathode pass through an aperture of the anode, and form a stream that falls upon a screen at the end of the tube. On its way this stream passes between two pairs of deflection plates, one pair horizontal and one vertical; and the changing states of the electrical field created by these plates deflect the stream in various ways. To these plates the action potentials from the muscle or nerve are communicated (after being very greatly amplified). In this way, any change of electrical potential in the tissue deflects the stream of rays as they play upon the screen. The wave form is visible to the eye, and can be photographed. (See Figure 91.)

We shall have several later occasions to refer to the phenomenon of action potentials.

THE SMOOTH MUSCLES

Their General Role

The behavior of a man toward the people and objects about him is not limited to activities involving his striped musculature only. When the motorist sees a child dart suddenly across his path, what he does is not completely described in terms of slamming in clutch and brake pedals, throwing his steering wheel over to one side, and the like, for there is also a sudden pallor, and soon a cold sweat, a dry mouth, a loss of appetite. Similarly, the temper of the fighting man appears not simply in the clenching of his fists and swinging of his arms, but also in the widening of his eyes and dilation of their pupils, in the reddening of his face and neck, in a certain noticeable bristling of his hair, perhaps in tears of helpless rage. Certainly these phenomena are of sufficiently deep psychological concern to interest us in the mechanisms at work. As in the preceding section, we must here limit attention to the end-segments, the effectors. In such components of human behavior as we find in the startled or angry man, there is a striking participation of smooth muscles, duct glands, and ductless glands. We shall take them up in that order.

It is not only in the exciting, dramatic moments of emergency that these effectors are at work. The process of living is a process of continuous internal functions — circulation, digestion, excretion, and the like — and the outward conduct and performances of the most staid individual in his most staid moments are intimately dependent upon these internal operations.

Distribution and General Function of Smooth Muscles

Smooth muscles are to be found in the walls of the so-called hollow viscera of the body — such as the arteries and veins, the esophagus, stomach, and intestines, the passages and ducts of the genital and urinary organs, the bronchi, and the ducts of certain glands, and also in the skin in connection with hairs.

92 Smooth Muscle Tissues
Cross-section of an artery, showing smooth inner coat, *a;* muscular layer, *b;* and outer connective tissue coat, *c.*

Generally speaking, these muscles are disposed in the hollow organs in two typical ways, *longitudinal* and *circular*. Figure 92, shows circular muscle tissue *b* in a cross-section of an artery. Its contracting and relaxing produce constriction and dilation of the blood vessel, thereby decreasing or increasing the bore of the blood vessel. This muscular control of the diameters of the different blood vessels in the whole body results in a control of the direction in which the excess supplies of blood are sent — to striped muscles and to lungs, to digestive apparatus, to sex apparatus, to brain, to skin, and so forth; and this phase has prime importance in the mechanics of the body machine.

Sphincter muscles are of the circular type, and are found at various openings, as of the bladder, the rectum, the iris of the eye, and a few glands, such as the sweat glands.

In general, the smooth type of muscle tissue is intimately involved in the maintenance — and in the disturbances — of vital processes of the more vegetative sort, for example, alimentation, excretion, circulation. These become of considerable psychological interest as important components of emotional response.

THE DUCT GLANDS

The Essential Nature of Glands

Many glands are important organs of response, whether in the smooth-running placidity of an easy-going day, in the precipitant haste of excitement, or in the lethargic heaviness of depression.

Glandular tissue is built out of cells that have become specialized for the function of secreting or excreting. Every cell in the body may be thought of as making constant exchange with the blood and lymph stream. The latter acts as a common carrier, transporting nutritive and other substances to the cell and bearing away the waste and other products given back by the cell. The *secreting* cell (1) receives certain substances from the blood, (2) remanufactures them, or at least isolates parts of them, and (3) delivers these products to other tissues for which they are useful, either by reshipment via the blood and lymph stream (as in ductless glands), or by direct transmission through a duct (as in duct glands). The *excreting* cell performs much the same function, except that its products are for elimination from the organism, being waste products of cells throughout the body.

Distribution and General Function of Duct Glands

A duct gland consists typically of hollow chambers, or alveoli, which are lined with the secreting type of cells. These receive their raw material from the blood capillaries and exude their products into the chambers, from which they are conveyed by the duct to some opening at a surface, as the skin or the mucous lining.

At this point we need hardly do more than enumerate the more important duct glands. Along the alimentary canal many are to be found. There are three pairs of *salivary* glands supplying the mouth, and many *gastric* glands in the walls of the stomach; there are those in the walls of the *intestines* providing the intestinal juices, and there are the large *liver* and the *pancreas*. The combined function of these glands is primarily that of food-digestion, but it includes also both lubrication of the alimentary canal for the onward movement of its contents and elimination of waste products from the blood. Duct glands on the outside of the body include the *lachrymals*, which furnish liquid for the eye; the *sweat* and the *sebaceous* (oily) glands, which condition the skin by excreting waste products from the body and regulating the temperature; the *kidneys*, which are perhaps the greatest excretory organs in the body; the *sex* glands, which serve for reproduction.

But these are functions having special reference to the internal metabolism of the body. In what ways are the duct glands involved in the psychological story of man-and-his-environment? By way of anticipation, let the reader consider the roles played by one or another of these duct glands in some types of human behavior: (1) They act as organs of *direct response* when, for instance, the sight of an audience causes a dry mouth in the amateur actor, or when sounds of a burglar downstairs make the householder break into a cold sweat, or when the receipt of a telegram marked with the warning star arouses tears. (2) They act as occasions or sources of *self-stimulation* when a dyspeptic Carlyle writes a bitter *Sartor Resartus*, or when the sex-urge impels to mating. (3) In addition, glands often play a considerable part in *social* behavior; for tears shed in another's presence are well calculated to stimulate that other person to some kind of response. Each of these psychological roles of duct glands we have had, or shall have, occasion to describe more fully elsewhere in this book.

THE DUCTLESS (ENDOCRINE) GLANDS

Introduction

Certainly one of the outstanding traits of the human living organism is the mutual dependence within it of part on part, so that, far from being a mere agglomeration, it manifests considerable unity: it is an individual. And since much of the character of a person's behavior toward the things and the people about him depends upon the degree to which this organization into an individuality has been achieved, integration is a key word in psychology.

How is this interconnection of organ with organ secured? First, mechanically: through mere juxtaposition and also through connective tissues; second — and this is more striking — through chemical agencies. But the quickest in action is the neural interconnection; and when in later chapters we analyze the behavior of a man, we shall have occasion constantly to keep in mind the integrative action of the nervous system. For the present, however, our attention should be given to the chemical interconnection.

The chemistry of the human body is just beginning to be understood in all its enormous complexity. Discoveries of the importance to life of the different vitamins, of the maintenance of proper acid-alkaline balance, of the necessity of supplying minute amounts of calcium, iodine, and so on, when certain glandular organs are defective — these are giving us some realization of how astonishingly subtle are the chemical interrelations of the internal environment. The human being is an organism balanced chemically upon a knife edge. Let this equilibrium be ever so slightly disturbed and the result may be fatal to him. And even if he escapes death, he may be physically misshapen, he may be an idiot charge upon the community, or he may be a permanent hospital patient with fits of depression alternating with periods of manic excitement and overactivity

The ductless or endocrine glands — our fourth type of effector endorgan — are so strikingly connected with normality or abnormality in human behavior that writers of fiction have not been slow to seize upon them as dramatic material. And even some writers with more technical aims have let their anticipations outrun scientific assurance, and have taken to naming different types of human temperament after different endocrines. The student will do well, therefore, to be cautious in dealing with generalizations in this field.

The endocrines are glands having no special outlet. Each is well supplied with motor nerves, mostly from the autonomic division. Their remanufactured products are placed

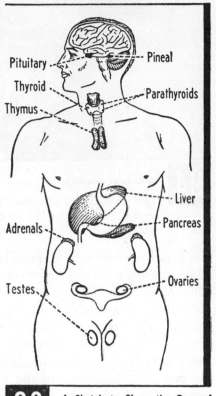

93 A Sketch to Show the General Locations of the Principal Ductless Glands

back in the blood and lymph stream, and conveyed over the body. These products, called *hormones*, are very complicated chemically. The general locations of the different endocrines are indicated in Figure 93.

The Thyroid Gland

The most definite information about the effects of internal secretions on human physique and human behavior is that obtained from investigations of the thyroid and its secretion *thyroxine*. This organ consists of two lobes, one on either side of the windpipe, connected by a narrow neck, the whole gland averaging about 5 cm. by 6 cm. in size, but varying greatly.

It has been known since about the sixteenth century that failure of

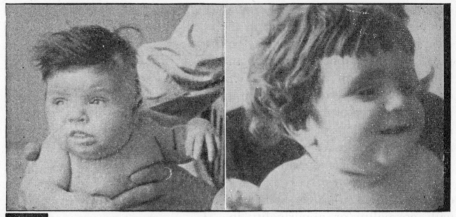

94 **A Case of Cretinism**

Left: At the age of 34 weeks. *Right:* The same infant after 42 weeks of thryoid feeding. (*From A. Gesell, C. S. Amatruda, and C. S. Culotta,* AMER. J. DIS. CHILD., *1936, 52, 1117–1138. Photos by the courtesy of Dr. Gesell.*)

this gland to develop is responsible for the conditions of arrest both in physical growth and in the development of behavior known as *cretinism.* The victim of the disease is characteristically dwarflike in appearance. He is stunted in height, but obese, with protruding abdomen; the head is short and broad; the skin is dry and scaly, loose and wrinkled; sex organs fail of normal development; the hair is dry, coarse, and brittle (see Figure 94, *left*). But what interests us more in a psychological way is the general sluggishness in the patient's activity toward things about him, and a sluggishness in development of this overt behavior as the child grows older. His apathetic facial expression suggests well a deficiency in intelligence, which is frequently so grave as to be classed as idiocy. His emotional life is almost colorless. Such unfortunates are absolutely incapable of meeting the demands of life around them; they cannot take care of themselves and must be placed in special institutions. Every large colony for the feeble-minded has its cretins.

Atrophy of the thyroid tissue in childhood or adult years produces much the same effects (*myxedema*). Loss of hair, puffy dry skin with fatty masses evident in places, brittle nails, and other structural changes accompany a deterioration in behavior traits. The person appears slow of movement and lacks interest in things around him. Often he is emotionally depressed, and in adapting himself to situations he is sluggish and inefficient, owing to his increasingly faulty memory and his retarded thinking — a condition that sometimes leads to delusions and other psychotic ("insane") disturbances. Sterility may develop also.

How is this compound effect to be understood? A key notion is that thyroxine is a "catalyzer" — a substance that accelerates a certain chemical change without being changed itself — and that this facilitates the chemical break-down of waste products of metabolism throughout the body so that they can be eliminated (at the kidneys, lungs, and skin). If this breaking-down process is arrested, then the waste products cannot be properly eliminated from the organism; they will serve only to clog the normal processes of the whole living machine. With this key concept the reader is in a position to understand each of the above-mentioned disturbances in physique and in behavior.

So much for hypofunctioning (less-than-normal functioning) of the thyroid. As someone has said, while a pinch too little of thyroxine spells idiocy, a pinch too much spells raving delirium. Marked hypertrophy or overdevelopment may give rise to "exophthalmic goiter" [1] (see Figure 95, *C*). Among the manifestations of the latter are: rapid heartbeat and high blood pressure, protrusions of the eyeballs, precocious development of the sex characteristics, elongation of the skeleton; and withal a nervous excitability and busyness of general conduct that knows no rest nor relaxation. At times the patient is low-spirited and anxious, at others cheerful and smiling, but always he resents being thwarted or contradicted. This condition also may become exaggerated to psychotic proportions.

Medical treatment in cases of hypothyroidism has assumed the form of feeding the patient with thyroid tissue or extract taken from other animals; and sometimes with fair success. Some defective children have been brought up to normal — and maintained there when the feeding was kept up (Figure 94, *B*); though improvement in mental ability is less common than improvement in physical traits. Myxedema patients may in some cases show an almost equally dramatic change under the treatment (Figure 95, *A* and *B*).

The Adrenal Glands

These two organs are located one on each of the kidneys — with which, however, they have nothing to do. Each is a compound of an internal *medulla* and an enclosing *cortex* of different structure, and they should be treated as two distinct endocrines.

The secretion of the *cortex* seems to influence all the cells of the body. When it fails, the individual grows weak, restless, irritable, and uncooperative; then when it is artificially supplied, his enthusiasm and energy

---

[1] This is not the most common form of goiter (colloid goiter), which is of less significance, medically and psychologically.

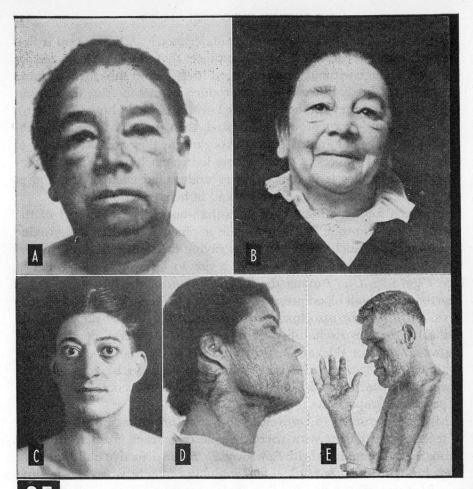

95 Some Physical Abnormalities Associated with Endocrine Imbalance

A. A myxedema patient before thyroid treatment. *B.* The same patient after treatment. (Photos from the Thyroid Clinic of the Massachusetts General Hospital.) *C.* Hyperthyroidism — exophthalmic goiter. (From the Thyroid Clinic of the Massachusetts General Hospital.) *D.* Adrenal cortex — masculinity associated with cortical tumor. (*From G. Blumer, ed.,* BEDSIDE DIAGNOSIS, *vol. 3, Saunders, 1929. By permission of the publishers.*) *E.* Anterior pituitary — acromegaly. (*From L. F. Barker, ed.,* ENDROCRINOLOGY AND METABOLISM, *vol. 1, Appleton, 1924. By permission of the publishers.*)

are restored. There is indication that it is closely associated with the activity of the sex glands. There have been reported cases in which sex maturity in infants or children, and also masculine physique and behavior in older females (see Figure 95, *D*), are associated with excessive growth of the adrenal cortex, especially with a tumor. The active substances are collectively known as *cortin*.

The secretion of the *medulla* has been prepared synthetically and is called *epinephrin* or *adrenin*. Its effects upon various tissues of the body assume much psychological importance and have attracted attention. In general it may be said to play an important part in a man's behavior when prompt and vigorous activity is called for in emergencies — the *alarm reaction*. In several ways that are too detailed for us to follow here, it serves to support the muscles called upon for action: by stimulating the liver to release some of its stored sugar into the blood stream for transportation to the muscles; by speeding up the heartbeat and at the same time raising the blood pressure; by reducing the activity of the smooth muscles of the stomach and intestines and so slowing down digestion; by increasing the release of the oxygen-carrying red corpuscles into the blood stream from the spleen. The effect of these and other changes associated with them is to enable the person to react more vigorously and with much more endurance; his digestive and certain other vegetative processes may be stopped, but his outward conduct is more emphatic; for example, his legs run faster, his fist hits harder. The significance of this change in the demeanor of man or animal we have already considered as a phase of his emotional reactions; and the description on pages 151 and 326 should be read at this point.

The Pituitary Body

The pituitary (also called *hypophysis*) is really composed of two independent bodies, an anterior and a posterior lobe. The whole structure is about the size of a very large pea and fits into a small pocket in the bony floor of the cranium in the very center of the head. Though connected with the brain stalk, it has nothing to do directly with brain functions. It is important in the activation of the body.

In the *anterior lobe* we are confronted with a truly remarkable organ, one that has earned the nickname of "the master gland." It is not known for certain how many separate hormones are secreted by it; there may be only two or three. But it is established that somehow, through derivatives or otherwise, the master gland performs at least seven specific and distinguishable kinds of regulating functions on other glands and on the body generally. Let us review them briefly.

(1) The most striking role of the anterior pituitary is that of growth-promotion. The hormone bears an important relation to the nutritive condition of the body during growth, particularly promoting the growth of the skeletal structures and connective tissues. This is shown only too well when the secretion is excessive in early life and results in *gigantism* with the elongated skeleton and massive bones at the extremities which are noticeable in certain boxers and basketball players as well as in some of the personnel of circus side shows. If the hyper-secretion takes place after maturity, the long bones do not become longer, but the shape of the face as well as that of chest and hands and feet gradually changes (*acromegaly*) (see Figure 95, *E*). The bony ridges over the eyes grow more prominent, the nose more bulging, the jaw heavier; an increased ruggedness of the features suggests the facial look of the gorilla, or better, that of the classic character Punch. Mental and temperamental abnormalities are often but not invariably shown. Frequently the person cannot get hold of himself; is morose or irritable; is unable to concentrate or to sleep well; suffers memory losses; has noticeable loss of sex drive. On the other hand, undersecretion of these same hormones may produce *dwarfism*, a condition in which there is a reduction in scale of size without great disturbance of proportion nor usually any serious mental abnormality. (These cases are not to be confused with that type of dwarf who is normal in head and trunk but telescoped down in his arms and legs — a physiological disorder not well understood.) It should be added that some investigators have found a high percentage of psychotic adults and of problem children to be handicapped with defective pituitaries. The gland may be of first importance psychologically.

The other controlling functions of the hormones from the anterior pituitary need only be mentioned. These hormones (2) promote growth and activity of the thyroid gland, (3) regulate the secreting function of the adrenal cortex; (4) advance the development of the gonads, involving several different effects on the operations of the ovaries or of the testes; (5) promote the activity of the mammary glands — and incite such maternal behavior as nursing and nest-building by lower animals; and (6) serve as a diuretic, increasing the production and discharge of urine as a great avenue of waste discharge. As for the psychological effects, each of these glandular kinds of functions has mental and emotional aspects that have been mentioned elsewhere as characteristic, and need not be repeated here.

From the *posterior lobe* is secreted a hormone — possibly one, possibly four — that affects the activity of the smooth muscles much as does adrenin, though not in exactly the same way. The blood pressure is heightened, the heart rate slowed, and the contractions in the intestines, the bladder, and especially the uterus are increased. The extract pituitrin has well-known use as a tonic for the uterine muscles in childbirth. Thus the tonus of smooth muscles, so necessary to the life functions, is maintained by the posterior lobe; its atrophy produces sluggishness in these functions.

The Sex Glands, or Gonads

The primary organs of sex are the testes in the male and the ovaries in the female, which in their reproductive functions are not dissimilar to duct glands. The testes produce the spermatozoa and the ovaries the ova or eggs.

The gonadal hormones of the male are called *androgens*, the principal one being *testosterone*. Their overproduction leads to precocious maturity or to excessive sex drive; their underproduction, to a persistently infantile condition. Loss of the testes results in changes in temperament that are well known in the ox, the gelding, and the capon; and there is reason to suppose that similar changes occur in the human eunuch, though here the emotional-social complications are so pronounced that it is hard to know how much of the person's alteration in temperament and behavior is directly the effect of changes in his hormonal supply.

Most of the hormones of the female are loosely grouped under the name *estrogens*. The whole story of the physiological processes involved in reproduction is a complicated one in the female, as is readily seen if we bear in mind that the female mammalian organism not only (*a*) must produce the ova but (*b*) must then nourish the embryo and fetus and later (*c*) must nurse the young. The collaboration of hormonal processes that prepare the ovaries, then the uterus, and then the mammary glands for this procession of remarkable functions is quite too complicated a story for us to follow out here. It must suffice us to note that the estrogens have in general a *feminizing* function that parallels or complements the *masculinizing* function of the androgens, in being responsible for the secondary sex characteristics that differentiate woman from man.

As it happens, however, both androgens and estrogens are produced in both the male and the female organisms. We are therefore compelled to recognize that the two sexes are not two hard-and-fast types. Whether the male shall be excessively masculine or rather effeminate in his looks and in his behavior, or the female excessively feminine or somewhat masculine, is apparently determined by the relative strengths of the androgens and the estrogens. It is interesting also to find that in the life-cycle of the same individual the ratio of the one to the other is probably the factor responsible for the changes from the more feminine childhood temperament to that of the more masculine one of youth and adulthood, and finally to the more feminine characteristics of later maturity.

The *secondary sex characteristics* include many traits of physique and of activity. First, there are the well-known differences in height and weight. Male and female differ also in body shape or contours, the former showing more angularity and the latter more curved lines. They differ in voice. The distribution of hair on the body, including the beard, and the development of mammary glands are further contrasting traits. Differences in characteristics of a more psychological nature have hardly been demonstrated. There *may* be some differences in the fundamental nature of striped muscle-skeleton coordinations; and there *may* be inborn emotional and temperamental differences. On the other hand, in the traits involving fine implicit habit formations and activities — memory, intelligence, reasoning capacity, and the like — no differences are demonstrable at all. The whole question of innate sex differences is complicated by the fact that the childhood training of a boy is in marked contrast to that of a girl, so that it is almost impossible at present to rule out the effects of environment in the explanation of why Jack and Jill behave so differently on certain occasions. To say, for instance, that woman has more of an instinct of tender care and man more of a pugnacious instinct is nonsense, as is also the assertion that man uses his reason while woman uses her intuition. This matter has received our attention in Chapter 5.

One thing certain is that the gonads have much to do with motivating the organism, as has already been shown in Figures 41 and 42 (pages 144 and 145).

The Pancreas

Besides acting as a duct gland concerned with digestion, the pancreas acts also as an endocrine organ through the internal secretions of the small islets of Langerhans found scattered through the body of the organ. The *insulin* secreted by these islets has lately played a dramatic role in the medical treatment of diabetes mellitus.

The Liver

The liver, too, has endocrine functions. For one thing, it changes into glycogen the sugar that has been absorbed into the blood from digested food. Further it stores up this glycogen; then later, on emergency demand, transforms it back into sugar and returns it to the blood stream. Thus the liver ultimately fulfills the function of supplying readily available energy to working muscles. We have considered this as an important phase of emotional behavior in Chapter 9. Fighting and fearing both involve these changes; and unless we know something of the changes, we cannot fully understand fighting and fearing.

Interdependence of the Endocrines

We have now surveyed the ductless glands one by one. The qualifying words, "it seems," "probably," "may be," so frequently used in describing the functions of a given gland, should serve to remind us that these many different endocrines really act in an interlocking way. We might almost refer to them collectively as "the endocrine system," so intimate is their interdependence in stimulating one another, controlling one another, compensating for one another. Consider these examples: (1) The atrophy of the ovaries after the menopause leaves the thyroid without its former counterbalance and a hyperthyroid condition ensues; this awakens overactivity of the adrenals with a train of symptoms. (2) Hyperthyroidism may be traceable to underactivity of the pituitary or to overactivity of the adrenals. (3) The pancreas opposes the pituitary, and the adrenals oppose the pancreas. (4) The development of the sex glands we have seen to be possibly advanced or held in check by the pituitary, the pineal, the thymus, the adrenal cortex, the thyroid. And a number of different controls of other glands we have seen to be attributed to the anterior pituitary. Balances and counter-balances! When we consider this amazing complexity of interrelations and bear in mind the technical difficulties involved in experimental work on such delicate structures and substances, we do not wonder that endocrinology is a much-delayed branch of knowledge, important though it is to the understanding of man and the reasons for his behavior.

In general, we may say that knowledge of the operations of ductless glands is important in several ways to a psychological analysis of human nature. (1) These glands are of prime importance in the general development both of physique and of behavior. (2) They have great influence upon the person's general efficiency at a given time. This includes (a) proper interaction of organ with organ inside the body, and (b) adequate support of overt reactions toward people and things outside. (3) They play significant roles in emotional behavior. It should not surprise us, then, to learn that many forms of nervous and mental disorders are now being treated with glandular extracts.

A consideration of even these sketchy accounts of how a person's intellectual, emotional, and physical development depends upon bodily factors as causes, how his temperamental characteristics and behavior toward people about him are to a large extent the outcome of his physical conditions, should help to induct the reader into the scientific and impersonal attitude toward his fellow man.

REFERENCES

1. Barker, L. F., ed. *Endocrinology and Metabolism.* Vol. 1, ed. by R. G. Hoskins. New York: Appleton-Century-Crofts, 1924.
2. Beach, F. A. *Hormones and Behavior.* New York: Hoeber, 1948.
3. Bennett, G. K., and R. M. Cruikshank. *A Summary of Manual and Mechanical Ability Tests.* New York: Psychological Corporation, 1942.
4. Corner, G. W. *The Hormones in Human Reproduction.* Princeton, N.J.: Princeton University Press, 1942.
5. Courts, F. A. "Relations between muscular tensions and performance," *Psychol. Bull.,* 1942, *39,* 347–367.
6. Davis, F. C. "Methods of measuring muscular tension," *Psychol. Bull.,* 1942, *39,* 329–346. "Motor effects of strong auditory stimuli," *J. Exp. Psychol.,* 1948, *38,* 257–275.
7. Denny-Brown, D. E. "On the nature of postural reflexes," *Proc. Roy. Soc.,* series B, 1928, *104,* 252–301.
8. Freeman, G. L. "The optimal locus of 'anticipatory tensions' in muscular work," *J. Exp. Psychol.,* 1937, *21,* 554–564; "The optimal muscular tensions for various performances," *Amer. J. Psychol.,* 1938, *51,* 146–150.
9. Gasser, H. S., and H. S. Newcomer. "Physiological action currents in the phrenic nerve. An application of the thermionic vacuum tube to nerve physiology," *Am. J. Physiol.,* 1921, *57,* 1–26.
10. Gesell, A., C. S. Amatruda, and C. S. Culotta. "Effect of thyroid therapy on the mental and physical growth of cretinous infants," *Amer. J. Dis. Child,* 1936, *52,* 1117–1138.
11. Ghiselli, E. E., and C. W. Brown. *Personnel and Industrial Psychology.* New York: McGraw-Hill Book Company, 1948.
12. Hoskins, R. G. *Endocrinology.* New York: W. W. Norton and Company, 1941.
13. Jacobson, E., and A. J. Carlson. "The influence of relaxation upon the knee jerk," *Am. J. Physiol.,* 1925, *73,* 324–328.
14. Jacobson, E. *Progressive Relaxation.* Chicago: University of Chicago Press, 1938.
15. Max, L. W. "An experimental study of the motor theory of consciousness. I. History and critique," *J. Gen. Psychol.,* 1934, *11,* 112–125. "II. Method and apparatus," *J. Gen. Psychol.,* 1935, *13,* 159–175. "III. Action-current responses in deaf-mutes during sleep, sensory stimulation, and dreams," *J. Comp. Psychol.,* 1935, *19,* 469–486.

16. Paterson, D. G., *et al.* *Minnesota Mechanical Ability Tests.* Minneapolis: University of Minnesota Press, 1930.
17. Schneider, E. C., and P. V. Karpovich. *Physiology of Muscular Activity.* Third edition. Philadelphia: W. B. Saunders Company, 1948.
18. Seashore, R. H. "Experimental and theoretical analysis of fine motor skills"; R. H. Seashore, C. E. Buxton, and I. N. McCollom, "Multiple factorial analysis of fine motor skills." *Amer. J. Psychol.*, 1940, *53*, 86–98, 251–259.
19. Werner, A. A. *Endocrinology.* Philadelphia: Lea and Febiger, 1942.

12

NEURAL ORGANIZATION

OF BEHAVIOR

GENERAL IMPORTANCE OF THE NERVOUS SYSTEM

THE MUSCLES AND GLANDS of an idiot may not be greatly defective, and his eyes, ears, skin and muscular sense organs may be almost as good as those of the average person; but with his pitifully inadequate connecting mechanisms he remains nothing but a grimacing, twisting, monkey-like human body. A man can hardly boast of much nimbler fingers than the ape's, much better vocal parts than a parrot's, more acute distance vision than the eagle's, nor a keener sense of smell than the dog's; yet his capacities for surviving under complex or novel conditions by adapting himself to them or reshaping them to fit his own needs are enormously greater — just because his fingers and voice and feet, his eyes and nose and skin and muscle senses, are so much more richly interconnected. However excellent his motor organs and his sense organs, they will profit him nothing if he is not well equipped with connections for them. In our attempts to comprehend the behavior of a person we shall be helped considerably if we have a general overview of the principal system by which he as an organism is integrated, and by which his actions are rendered consistent and serviceable.

How Can We Explain These Cases?

(*A*) After drinking some wood alcohol a student lost his sight, though it was found that his eyes were really not injured at all.

(*B*) In a street brawl a man received a cut in his arm above the elbow; and upon recovering consciousness found that he could not move his hand nor get any feeling from it.

(*C*) A Cleveland lad of nineteen dived off into a new place in the water and did not come up. When dragged out, he was conscious but was unable to feel his legs and feet or to move them.

(*D*) A Los Angeles boy, ill with polio, lost all ability to move his legs but did not lose sensitivity in them.

(*E*) A victim of locomotor ataxia gradually lost ability to walk or to make other coordinated motions of his legs, though he could still move them.

(*F*) Careless Jack happened to touch a hot radiator; his hand jerked itself away before he was fairly aware of the contact.

(*G*) A patient at a state hospital who has "softening of the brain" (paresis) cannot say "Methodist Episcopal" and can no longer·walk or write his name.

(*H*) Nellie, a girl with a very small pointed skull, has never developed beyond the behavior of a four-year-old.

(*I*) A blow on the left side of a young woman's head resulted in a total loss of feeling in her right hand and arm.

(*J*) A student reports that after hours of despondency he was surprised to experience a change to the opposite emotions.

(*K*) During World War II a soldier was shot in the head just above the ear, the bullet shattering the bone but not entering the brain. He showed no loss of movement or of sensitivity; but he made mistakes in enunciation, and did not respond to any words addressed to him.

(*L*) After an auto accident a man in New York state did not know what to call such things as chairs and tables and did not know what they were for; yet he could see them and could even draw pictures of them.

(*M*) An intelligent laborer in a Pittsburgh steel mill was injured in the forehead by flying metal. After recovery he surprised his friends by playing very crude and almost cruel practical jokes on them constantly.

(*N*) Some monkeys that had had parts completely cut out from both sides of their brains later regained their locomotion (lost through the operation) and even acquired a high degree of skill in handling things.

(*O*) A laboratory investigator found that upon his severing one or the other of two nerves of an anesthetized cat the pulse rate would either speed up to nearly 300 beats per minute or slow down to barely 30.

(*P*) A Mrs. Madison, who had been depressed and anxious in all her waking hours and even in her dreams, became happy and relaxed after a surgeon's knife was thrust through the left side of her cranium.

These are all cases of irregularity in actions, thoughts, or feelings; hence they are of psychological interest. All of them depend for their explanation upon knowledge of the central nervous system, its structures and functions. To understand many things psychological, then, we must know rudiments of things neurological. The brief survey our space allows us in this book may not bring us the keys. to all such cases as those, but it will at least orient us so that we shall know where to look for more detailed facts.

THE NATURE OF NEURAL TRANSMISSION

Its General Character

We have already learned that neural tissue furnishes the basis for inter-connections within a person's body and therefore underlies the integrations of his behavior toward the world about him. In a Western motion picture, the sight of the desperado (stimulation of eye) will arouse in the hero a split-second response of drawing and firing in a beautifully coordinated set of arm, wrist, and finger movements. In an orchestral performance, sight of baton and of musical notes, plus sounds of other instruments, can promptly set up in the player the appropriate movements of fingers and hands on keyboard or strings. As the grocer hefts the sack he is filling, the sensory effect on muscle and skin receptors evokes the vocal reponse "ten pounds." The stenographer, at each variation of the voiced sounds to which she is attending, manipulates her pencil to form a hook, a shading, or a line in her notebook. All such phenomena are dependent upon neural connections between the stimulations and the responses.

What is the character of these connections? In contrast to the transportation of materials from place to place in the lymph and blood stream, we have here a transmission of energy-changes of the connecting medium itself. The nerves are not tubes through which a substance is conveyed, but solid protoplasmic threads that propagate disturbances from end to end. What, more precisely, is the nature of this propagated disturbance? In spite of the awe with which nerve and brain are popularly regarded, they are products of natural evolution in a natural world. They are not mysterious; they are protoplasmic, and the only intelligent attitude is to seek out a more precise knowledge of their functions and structure.

About neural transmission some matters of physics and chemistry are now well known. A resting nerve is like any other tissue in that it consumes a certain amount of oxygen, gives off carbon dioxide, produces heat, and manifests electrical changes. When the nerve becomes active, these small physiological changes are increased in degree.

The disturbance that passes along neural tissue is not like the continuous flow of water in a pipe nor the continuous flow of electricity in a simple conductor like a copper wire. Instead, it is more comparable to a stream of machine-gun bullets, a stream of interrupted firings that follow rapidly upon each other. Most important for the detection and study of these volleys of activity are the electrical changes or *action potentials*. We have already dealt with the technique for observing them in connection with muscle tissue (see pages 287 ff.), and therefore will confine ourselves at this point to the fact that each neural impulse can be registered as a wave. If these waves are registered and measured as they pass along a nerve, we learn accurate details concerning the impulses themselves — their frequency, their intensity, and their complexity. We now turn to some of the facts discovered by this and other techniques.

Some Salient Characteristics

First and last, it must be remembered that a nerve is a bundle of individual fibers (each an individual cell called a *neuron*, with elongated branches), and that its activity is a composite of the activities of the various fibers. Furthermore, the component fibers of a nerve are not precisely alike, and in fact, certain differences in the way they are activated are an important part of the story.

When a given fiber is excited at all it is excited to its maximal degree. This is known as the *all-or-none* principle, similar to the principle already mentioned in describing the action of muscle cells. It is familiar enough in a general way, as in the fact that a given charge of gunpowder will explode with one specific amount of violence regardless of whether the agent that sets it off is a small match or an acetylene welding torch.

Each fiber has its own *threshold of excitation*, that is, the minimum intensity that an excitation must reach in order to call it into action at all. From this it is easy to understand that when an excitation of a given physical intensity is applied to one end of a nerve, it may throw into action some but not all the component fibers, depending upon their thresholds.

Again, each fiber has its own *refractory phase*. Immediately after it has transmitted an impulse, a fiber will remain for a brief fraction of a second inexcitable and non-conductive. This is what gives to neural transmission its interrupted character and determines the *frequency* with which the successive impulses follow upon each other. And in different fibers there are different frequencies, so that one and the same excitation applied to the end of a nerve trunk may arouse in the various fibers composing the trunk varying rates of rapid-fire conduction.

We are now prepared to answer a central question concerning the

nerve-as-a-whole: In one and the same nerve how can there be gradations of intensity in conduction if the all-or-none law holds true? The
evidence points to a double answer. (1) The intensity of nerve activity
is a matter of the *number of separate fibers* that are participating. The
higher the strength of the exciting agent, the more individual units are
thrown into activity by it. (2) The intensity of the disturbance has
been found definitely to depend also upon the *frequency* of the impulses.
In one and the same fiber, the higher the strength of the exciting agent,
the more rapid will be the succession of impulses aroused by it.

The Physical Nature of the Neural Impulse

The membrane theory is the best of the several theories that have been advanced to explain precisely what occurs when a neural impulse passes. According to this theory, a nerve fiber is thought of as surrounded by a thin membrane
with a difference of electrical potential existing between its outer and inner surfaces, being positive on the outside and negative on the inner (that is, it is
"polarized"). The neural disturbance or impulse is thought of as *a wave of
temporary depolarization between these surfaces that passes along the length of the fiber.* In
Figure 96, the potential differences (+ and −) of the passive nerve's membrane
are shown reduced (depolarized, neither + nor −) at that point where the
impulse is at a given instant. This depolarized condition propagates itself as
follows: the neural tissue quickly recovers its equilibrium and restores its polarized state, but meanwhile in the next adjoining segment of the fiber (to the right
in the figure) there is induced a similar depolarizing (through a local electric
current represented by the arrowheads); and so the succession of upset-and-
restored conditions moves progressively along.

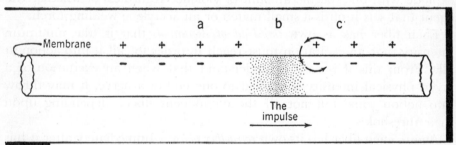

96   **The Membrane Theory of Neural Transmission**

In the resting state the outer membrane of a nerve is polarized: positive ions on
outside and negative on inside. When the nerve is activated, the precise point
where the impulse is at a given instant is depolarized (*b*). This sets up a local
electric current (arrowheads) that is counter to the polarized condition in adjoining parts of the membrane (*c*) and so reduces it. At the same time the upset condition at *b* is being quickly recovered from, as has already occurred at *a*. This continuous succession of induced depolarization and spontaneous recovery moves as a
rapid current down the fiber. (*After Lillie.*)

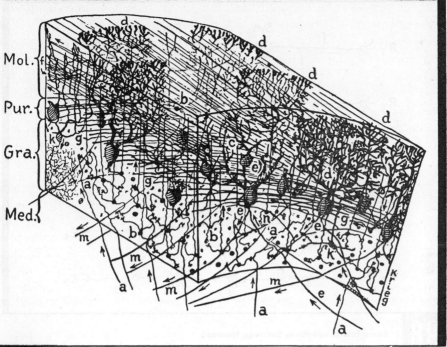

97

Phantom of Small Block of Cerebellar Cortex, to Show Relations Between Neurons

a, mossy fiber; *b*, granule cell; *c*, bifurcation of granule cell axon; *d*, Purkinje cell; *e*, climbing fiber; *f*, basket cell body; *g*, basket cell axons; *Gra*, granule layer; *h*, stellate cell; *k*, Golgi I cell; *m*, Purkinje cell axon; *Med*, medullary center; *Mol*, molecular layer; *n*, Purkinje cell collateral; *Pur*, Purkinje cell layer. (*From W. J. S. Krieg,* FUNCTIONAL NERUOANATOMY, *Blakiston, 1942. By permission of the publishers.*)

The Neuron

We must pause in our study of functions to take better note of the essential structural elements involved. What is neural tissue?

It is built out of individual cells, microscopic in size. In the differentiation of the multiplying cells in the body of the embryo, the nerve cell becomes distinguishable from all others by its long branches. A great variety of neurons is to be found here and there throughout the nervous system, all with certain characteristics in common (see Figure 97). First, each has a *cell body* which is the nutritive center of the cell. From this cell body run processes or branches of two sorts: the *axon*, frequently very long, and the *dendrites*. The axon is single, but it itself has branches; and the dendrites, which may be in any number, are usually so ramified as to present a tree-like appearance (hence their name). These two

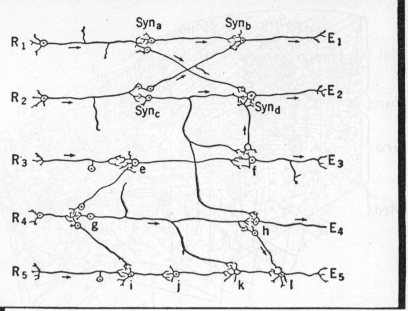

98 **Some Interconnections Between Neurons**

Schematic diagram showing many possibilities of connection between receptors and effectors through many alternative synaptic junction points between neurons. Discussion in text.

sorts of branches have different functions based on a difference in their structure. Impulses, in their passage through the cell, first enter at the tip end of some dendrite, are then conducted along this and through the cell body, and finally pass out along the axon and some one of its branches to a tip end where they induce a change in an adjoining neural or muscular fiber. A most important feature is the richness of interconnections between numerous neurons that is furnished by the branchings of their axons and their dendrites (see Figure 98). This, as we are to see later, is the very basis of the organization of behavior.

BASIC PRINCIPLES IN ORGANIZATION

The Problem Stated

Provided now with some comprehension of what neural activity is *per se*, we are ready to face a question confronting all students of the nervous basis of behavior. The way in which a person acts *changes* from time to time. This is strikingly true of John Doe as a baby compared with the same John Doe as a man. Consider his acts of eating, of handling such an object as a pencil, or of using his voice, in infancy and again later: his actions become remarkably altered with the years, and not only in respect to the particular motions he makes but also in respect to the stimulating circumstances under which he comes to make them. Through the years of his development (as we have seen in Chapter 4) maturing and learning conspire to remold his behavior. But his muscles and his sense organs have not been greatly changed. We seek therefore to know about the changes in his nervous system.

Again, even within a short quarter of an hour, John Doe's manner of acting may show a variety which is, on the face of it, puzzling enough. Toward one and the same office-boy or baseball player or roommate he may show at first an attitude of approbation, only to shift a little later to a posture of challenge. In some instances the shift appears to grow out of a change in the externalities of the social situation: the other person may have done something to disappoint and irritate him. In other cases the shift may seem to result from a change in John Doe's own internal condition: his digestion has gone wrong or he has had bad news or he has been reminded somehow of an unpleasant incident that took place a month or a year ago. But whether the antecedents be extra- or intra-organic, a marked shift in his behavior may take place within a few minutes. What is happening in his nervous system?

These long-time or short-time alterations in what a person does and how he does it involve still another point. Note that a shift in the way a person acts is a shift *from* one and *toward* another given line of action. The primary fact, then, is this; a person's behavior is always in some degree directed in some line or direction. On the physiological side, when a certain stimulus releases activity or initiates activity, the commotions it excites in the neural pathways do not travel in all directions and excite all the muscles in equal degree.

In a word, a person's activities seem at all times to be more or less directed, and the transmission of neural impulses is always more or less *channeled*.[1] It is this channeling and rechanneling that now presents itself as a problem to us.

In the preceding section we concerned ourselves exclusively with the nature of the impulses passing over a given nerve or nerve fiber. We

[1] By channeling we do not refer to single, local, and highly specific neural fibers to be found in a single anatomical place, but rather to great functional systems. For example, the fibers running from the touch end-organs to the brain ascend mostly in the ventral spinothalamic tracts, but some of them ascend in the dorsal funiculi, and at least the former include both crossed and uncrossed fibers. All these together may be considered as a channel. There is, then, recognition of the fact that a high amount of correlation exists between anatomy and function, but allowance is made for some variation in details.

must now enlarge our scope to include the interconnection of different nerves to form innumerable alternative pathways. Figure 98 hints at a few of the ways in which neurons are laid in end-to-end relations throughout the nervous system, with special emphasis upon the alternative ways in which these relations are offered. For illustration, assume that a stream of impulses is excited at the receptive point R_2. What directions through the nervous system will it take: (1) over the synaptic junctions c and b and to effector E_1, (2) over synapses c and d to E_2, (3) over c and f to E_3, or (4) over c and h to E_4? What relations between each neuron and the next succeeding one are the determining factors? Here we pass into the realm of physiological theories rather than physiological facts.

Theories of Selection of Pathways

Best known is the theory of *different synaptic resistances*. Where two neurons (axon of one and dendrite of other) lie in end-to-end connection (at a synapse), a resistance is offered there to the passage of impulses from neuron to neuron. These resistances, at various synapses, differ greatly in degree; and a volley of impulses will follow the line of least resistance. The differential existing between the synaptic resistances at b, d, f, and h (in Figure 98) is what determines whether the neural disturbances excited at R_2 will discharge finally into E_1, E_2, E_3, or E_4. The route which provides the lowest resistances will be the one followed. Putting it quite generally: what a person will do in a given situation all depends upon the differences of resistances at his synapses.

Simple though it is, much criticism has been directed against this theory, and others have been advanced, among them the theory of *different nerve (and muscle) rhythms* or frequencies. In an earlier paragraph it was stated that each nerve fiber has its own refractory period and frequency, that is, its own rhythm at which it will transmit impulses of a given intensity. The whole nerve, moreover, will have its preferred frequencies of transmission based on those of its component fibers. The theory of different rhythms assumes that, to awaken a given nerve, a stream of impulses brought up to it by another nerve must be of a certain corresponding rhythm. A disturbance of a given frequency which is propagated over the neuron running from R_2 will naturally pass on into that neuron which is most susceptible to being excited at the same frequency (or a multiple or sub-multiple thereof). In a figurative sense, then, the channels that will be taken by impulses in transit through the nervous system are those channels that are most in tune with it and with each other.

Another latter-day theory is that of *different excitation thresholds*. Different fibers (and different nerves and muscles, too) differ as to the time-factor necessary in the exciting stimulus. There are those who contend that for an impulse to pass from one neuron to another neuron (or muscle fiber) the latter must be of the same excitability as the former. In Figure 98, then, if the fiber conducting impulses from R_2 has a certain index of excitation, the impulses will more likely be carried further by a next-lying neuron which has an excitability index of the same order.

The Theories Applied

These theories of "which pathway" bear upon the question of changes in behavior — the matter raised in the first paragraph of this section. For any condition whatever that operates to modify the resistances at any synapses, or to modify the refractory periods of any fibers, or to modify their excitability thresholds, will necessarily alter the routes to be taken by impulses in transit, and so will alter the precise way in which the person will react to one and the same stimulating agent.

The preceding discussion of how the neural impulses pass through the nervous system must be accepted with caution. It is necessarily an oversimplified one, and it neglects three qualifying points.

For one thing, in spite of the fact of one-way conduction across a single synapse, the volleys of impulses passing through the complicated routes of the nervous system do not invariably proceed in the general receptor-to-effector direction. Certain neurons may lie in such a manner as to complete closed circuits, so that some of the impulses may be carried backward from a later synapse to an earlier one (see Figure 99). Recurrent or *self-perpetuating* neural activity can in this way continue even in the absence of any fresh afferent impulses [18].

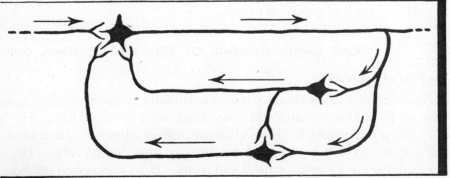

99 Diagram of a Closed Self-Reexciting Chain of Neurons

(*After Lorente de Nó,* J. Neurophysiol., *1938, 1.*)

Furthermore, neurons seem to be endowed with capacity for long-continued spontaneous activity of rhythmic sort. The waves of electrical changes that take place in the brain (see pages 336 ff.) occur in such independence of any incoming afferent impulses as to indicate that they are actually self-generated in the neural tissues [20].

In the third place, neurologists have expressed doubts that separate nerve fibers, running side by side and each apparently as insulated as the individual wire of a telegraph cable, are indeed so completely insulated. And it seems credible enough that a neural (electrical) process in one fiber may induce alterations in the states or processes of neighboring fibers, analogous to the "cross-talk" sometimes encountered in telephony.

These three points suggest that the nervous system is not to be likened to a switchboard and that the known complexity of psychological facts is eventually going to be matched by an equal complexity of neurological facts. But at the same time the notion of the sensori-motor arc serves as an anchor that we dare not throw away.

It should now be plain that any theories concerning the routes taken by neural discharges lie at the base of most psychological problems. For one thing, the theories offer interpretations of "learning" and "habit" as well as of "maturation" and "development." Further, they suggest interpretations of "attitude" and "attention," of "set" and "directing tendency," of "memory" and "recall," of "associations" and "thinking." Research in neurological laboratories may perhaps ultimately demonstrate the final truth of one or more of them; and the detailed working out of the contributing factors will ultimately be of great aid to the psychologist.

But we whose primary interest is really in the behavior and experience of human beings, as such, must return to the broader problems concerning the behavior of people as people.

SOME SIMPLER SEGMENTS OF BEHAVIOR: THE SPINAL CORD

The Point of Approach

Any case of human conduct is an enormously complex affair. Take that of John Doe walking and conversing with Richard Roe. He is swinging a walking-stick. He is glancing at shop windows. He is smoking a cigar. He is breathing a bit heavily from his exertion. He is maintaining erect posture of head and trunk. He is considering the topic of the conversation — war in China. He is recalling a newspaper head-line. Indeed, hardly an end could be found to the large and small aspects and segments of the total phenomenon we call "John Doe taking a walk with Richard Roe." However, if we are to seek an understanding of such a phenomenon as this, we must not leave it in the large but must approach it analytically, with artificially simplified examples.

Example: The Knee Jerk and Its Dependence upon Other Processes

If a person is seated so that his leg hangs free from the knee down, a smart tap administered just below the knee cap will elicit a prompt kick. A simple-looking act: simple enough to be called a reflex. Essentially it involves two groups of nerve fibers, an afferent group running from the skin receptor to the spinal cord and an efferent group which takes up the impulses there and passes them back out to the muscle that jerks the leg. Figure 100, *a* — *b*, shows the route schematically. As we describe it, however, this is an artificial abstraction from the facts. Back in the 1880's it was learned that this kick movement will be augmented if, at the time the blow is struck, another sensory stimulation such as a pressure on the finger or a sharp sound, be applied to the subject simultaneously. To represent the neural base of this phenomenon, other lines appear in the figure, suggesting possible pathways of influence. The *spinal cord* is now revealed as playing a double role: (*a*) as furnishing immediate *connections between afferent and efferent* neurons involved in simple acts, and (*b*) as furnishing a highway in the form of *tracts of fibers that connect higher and lower afferent and efferent neurons at many different levels*. It also appears that the *brain* parts, too, play the latter role, though with more intricate connections involved.

But the intimate relationship between one segment and another of a total response is shown by further data on this "simple" knee jerk. The influence upon it by the extraneous stimulus at the finger or the ear depends in a most surprising way upon the precise time interval between this type of stimulus and the tap stimulus. The reinforcement is greatest when the two processes are practically simultaneous; if the incidental process precedes the tap on the knee by an interval of 0.4 seconds, the reinforcement amounts to nothing; with longer intervals between the stimuli reinforcement changes to inhibition and the amount of kick is actually diminished below the normal; with an interval of one second the inhibiting influence tends to disappear; and after 1.7 seconds the kick ceases to be affected by the other process at all and is normal.

The very nicety of the relations found between the two variables — time interval and degree of *reinforcement* or *inhibition* — is certainly arresting. Why, in the first place, should the transit of impulses aroused in a finger or in the ear influence a simple movement in a very different part of the body? Granting this influence, why should it be at times positive

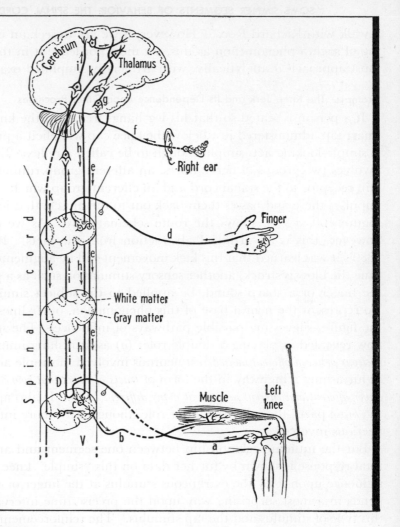

100 A Simple Reflex Arc and Some Complications

The knee jerk as a reflex involves neurons *a* and *b*, which are connected at one level of the cord by an intermediate neuron *c*. The reflex act is influenced, however, by many other neural processes, such as impulses initiated by pressure on finger, conducted along afferent fibers *d* and the descending fibers *e*; or impulses initiated by a sound at the ear, passing along afferent fibers *f* and *g* to a relay point (thalamus), where the impulses pass over to the descending fibers *h*, and are transmitted to the proper level of the cord to reinforce impulses out along *c* and *b*. A further complication of the knee jerk reaction may be brought about by voluntary action. The incoming afferent impulses from *a* also pass up ascending fibers *i* to the sensory projection cortex of the cerebrum; then via association neurons *j* to the motor projection area; thence down the descending tract fibers *k*. (Figure very incomplete. Relative proportions are not preserved. Each fiber represents many of its kind actually in operation. *V* = ventral aspect, *D* = dorsal.)

and at times negative? Why, finally, should this effect be so nicely graduated and dependent upon fine differences between time intervals under
1.7 seconds? We must confess that we do not know the explanation in
neural terms. We can only remain impressed with the delicate relationships that surround even the simple knee jerk.

But there is a still wider range of factors to be considered. If the person is asleep, his knee jerk disappears, and even in a passive waking state
it remains small; whereas if he is excited or irritated it becomes markedly
increased. If he has just had flashed before him a word he dislikes, the
kick is decreased. Even more generally, a daily rhythm is discoverable,
for the amount of the reflex is lowest when the subject is just out of bed
and at the close of an afternoon of standing and talking; it is highest just
after breakfast and just after lunch. It seems, then, that *the knee jerk is
increased and diminished by whatever increases and decreases the activity of the
central nervous system as a whole.*

One point further. The knee jerk can be trained. It has been found
that if either of the stimuli referred to above (a sound or a pressure on the
finger) is repeatedly presented to an experimental subject just before the
tap is delivered to the knee, eventually the mere presentation of the sound
or the pressure *alone* without the tap will evoke the knee jerk in a reflex-
like way, that is, quite without the subject's intention or even expectation of so responding.[1]

From this examination of one simple segment isolated artificially we
can conclude: *Any neural impulses spreading through the nervous system may,
under certain conditions, affect and be affected by any other impulses spreading
through. And to speak of a reflex is to speak of an artificial abstraction, useful but
not complete.*

Some Simple Impairments Involving More Complex Processes

By this time we have come to recognize the significance of the spinal cord as
an integrating avenue through which sensory and motor processes of different
parts of the body are related. The manner in which these processes are impaired
in two well-known diseases is instructive. In the more serious cases of poliomyelitis the patient upon recovering from the disease itself is incapable of carrying out certain activities that call for the use of certain muscles, especially those
of the legs. The muscles themselves waste away. Now, post-mortem examinations of the spinal cord reveal that the germs of the disease have destroyed many
of the cell-bodies of the efferent nerves leaving the spinal cord at this level (Figure 101, *A*). The lesions may be confined to a small region on one side the cord
or may involve both sides for a great part of its length. What has happened is
the destruction of an efferent channel.

[1] This is the phenomenon of conditioning. See pages 421 ff.

In tabes or locomotor ataxia a paralysis is again present, but in a different form. The patient finds it difficult to walk or to stand; and sometimes only by watching his foot can he lift it properly to mount a ladder. If he closes his eyes and tries to touch his forefinger to his nose, the hand may fail utterly to find the nose. If he attempts to feed himself with eyes closed, he is likely to spill his food on his clothing. What is wrong? Upon examination the patient may show ability to move his arms and legs to their fullest extent and vigorously. The impairment, then, is not in the motor pathways. Rather it is in the sensory, in the kinesthetic; and in fact, microscopic examination brings to light degeneration (due to disease germs) of ascending afferent fibers in the dorsal parts of the cord (Figure 101, *B*). With these afferent channels from the muscles interrupted, the patient has no incoming kinesthetic impulses to start and stop the moving muscles and so to control them. (Cf. discussion of this kinesthetic control of movement, pages 244 f.)

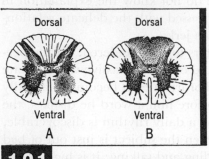

101 Destructions of Neural Tissue in the Cord Associated with Impairments of Behavior

A. Typical region found destroyed in *poliomyelitis.* The cell bodies of motor neurons in the left ventral horn being destroyed, movement of the muscles of the left side normally innervated by them is rendered impossible. (A motor paralysis.) *B.* Region found destroyed in *tabes dorsalis.* Ascending afferent fibers in the dorsal part of the cord are destroyed. Afferent impulses aroused at moving muscles, tendons, and joints, cannot reach the brain to play their part in stimulating (controlling) muscular movement. (A sensory paralysis.)
(*From S. I. Franz and K. Gordon*, PSYCHOLOGY, *McGraw-Hill, 1933.*)

In conclusion, we may say that a man is dependent especially upon his spinal cord not only for the central connections necessary to many of the simpler segments of his activity (reflexes), but also for the afferent and efferent functions involved in more complex kinds of activity as well.

The Structure of the Spinal Cord

Before leaving the subject, we should have a more definite anatomical description of the spinal cord. It is a long tube with greatly thickened walls, extending two thirds of the way down the inside of the vertebral column (Figure 102). Between the bony vertebrae, spinal nerves emerge from the cord, coming off on each side by a ventral motor root and a dorsal sensory root. Two million fibers are said to make up these nerves.

In cross-section the cord presents a characteristic picture with its butterfly-shaped gray matter and the surrounding white. The gray matter is composed mainly of cell bodies. The white matter is composed

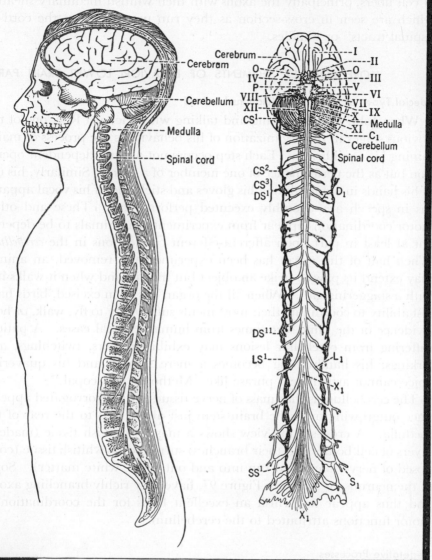

Cerebrum

Cerebrum

Cerebellum

Medulla

Spinal cord

I
II
O — O — III
IV — V
P
VIII — VI
XII — VII
CS¹ — IX
X
XI — Medulla
C₁
Cerebellum
Spinal cord

CS² —
CS³
DS¹ — D₁

DS¹¹ —
LS¹ — L₁
X₁

SS¹ — S₁

X₁

102   The Central Nervous System as a Whole

On the left it is seen from the side in position in the vertebral column; on the right, exposed and seen from the front. The 12 cranial nerves are designated by Roman numerals. The spinal nerves are designated in part: C_1, the first of the 8 cervical; D_1, the first of the 12 thoracic; L_1, the first of the 5 lumbar; S_1, the first of the 5 sacral; X_1 (lower figure), the coccygeal. Ganglia and connections of the autonomic division are shown in solid black: CS^1, CS^2, CS^3, superior, middle, and inferior cervical ganglia; DS^1–DS^{11}, thoracic ganglia; LS^1, the first lumbar ganglion; SS^1, the sacral ganglion.

of cell fibers, principally the axons with their whitish medullary sheaths, which are seen in cross-section as they run up and down the cord in "spinal tracts" or bundles.

MORE COMPLEX SEGMENTS OF BEHAVIOR: LOWER BRAIN PARTS

Special Types of Motor Coordinations Involved

When John Doe is walking and talking with Richard Roe, one of the obvious stages in the organization of his behavior is the process of maintaining his equilibrium.   Each step occurs not as an independent operation but as the performance of one member of a team.   Similarly, his use of his hands in manipulating his gloves and stick and of his vocal apparatus in speech are smoothly executed performances.   These and other motor coordinations appear from experiments on animals to be dependent at least in part upon afferent-efferent connections in the *cerebellum*. When half of this organ has been experimentally removed, an animal may extend its paw to strike an object but miss it, and when it walks it is with a staggering gait.   When all the organ has been excised, birds have lost ability to coordinate their movements sufficiently to fly, walk, or hop. Evidence of the same sort comes from human clinical cases.   A patient suffering from cerebellar lesions may exhibit tremors, twitchings, and jerkings; his handwriting becomes a mere scrawl; and his quavering voice cannot articulate a phrase like "Methodist Episcopal."

The cerebellum is that mass of nerve tissues with a corrugated appearance outgrowing from the brain stem just above and to the rear of the medulla.   A cross-section view shows a mass of grayish tissue (made of layers of cell bodies and their branches) surrounding whitish tissue (composed of nerve fibers that run into and out of the white matter).   Some of the neurons, as shown in Figure 97, have very richly branching axons, and thus appear to furnish an excellent basis for the coordination of motor functions attributed to the cerebellum.

Vegetative Processes

Let us return to John Doe as he is walking and conversing with Richard Roe.   We realize that certain visceral processes are going on steadily: he is breathing, his heart is beating, his dinner is being digested, he is perspiring a little, and the like.   These operations may strike the reader at first as being purely physiological and as unrelated to either the man's outward conduct or his inward experiences.   Nothing could be more false.   The afferent impulses arising from one's internal organs probably contribute an important share to his awareness of his own identity, his own self; for in pathological cases, anesthesias and other disorders of the viscera are often at the bottom of feelings of alienation and feelings of lost identity.

The neural bases of the vegetative or life-maintaining functions involve more than the spinal cord. Many of the organs referred to — lungs, heart, throat, stomach, and numerous muscles and glands elsewhere — have afferent and efferent fibers running into the *medulla* and the *hypothalamus*. The former may be seen as a swollen part of the cord and in structure only a more complicated version of it. Its greater complexity furnishes the delicate and elaborate interconnections of incoming and outgoing nerve processes essential to the functioning of the organs mentioned. It is essential to the proper interrelations between organs, and between them and more overt behavior. The hypothalamus is a name applied collectively to several bodies [1] lying at the base of the thalamus and of the cerebrum.

Emotional Aspects of Behavior

There are more dramatic ways in which these various physiological processes mentioned above are of psychological importance. Suppose, for instance, that the topic of the conversation has veered to something touching closely on the personal interests of John Doe and he becomes, as any observer will say, "angry." What is involved in this "anger"? Not only will his stride change, and his manual gestures and pitch of voice, but his breathing will be obviously heavier, his face flushed from an accelerated circulation. If the observer could apply registering technique from the laboratory, he would discover profound changes of digestion, of perspiration, and numerous other physiological functions. Doe himself, if he will stop to examine his own feelings now or in retrospect later, will realize that his "insides" are somehow working differently (cf. pp. 207 ff.)

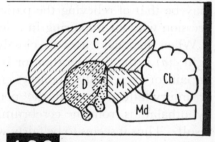

103 Longitudinal Section of Mammalian Brain

C, cerebral hemispheres; *D*, diencephalon; *M*, mid-brain; *Md*, medulla; *Cb*, cerebellum. The light dotted portion of *D* is the supposed locus of neural connections for emotion. (*From W. B. Cannon, "The mechanism of emotional disturbance of bodily function,"* NEW ENGL. J. MED., *1926, 198, 877–884.*)

[1] They include the optic chiasm, nervous part of the hypophysis (pituitary), infundibulum, mammillary bodies, and others.

Two principal kinds of evidence point to the hypothalamus (Figure 103) as the most important site of those connections responsible for emotional changes in behavior.

(1) Several different authorities have reported finding lesions in the hypothalamus on post-mortem examination of patients who had manifested strange deviations from the normal in their emotions only. Some had lost all emotional expression on one side of the face without losing ability to move the same muscles voluntarily; some had become extremely apathetic, with a fatuous serenity of attitude and a complete indifference to insults and jibes. On the other hand, there have been cases that showed over-reaction to the least emotional provocation (such as moderate warmth, tickling, or pricking), going off into long roars of laughter or into one weeping spell after another. A cat whose hypothalamus has been specially stimulated by a needle-type of electrode will raise its back and lash its tail, crouch and growl and draw back its ears [19].

(2) Evidence comes also from the surgical operation known as prefrontal *lobotomy*, in which neural fibers connecting the thalamus and some parts of the frontal lobe of the cerebrum are severed. The result may be that of relieving the patient of his anxiety or of his chronic depression without impairing in a serious way his intellectual abilities [7].

When these evidences are closely analyzed, more specific facts come to light: (*a*) if the degeneration or injury affects the hypothalamus itself it impairs or even totally abolishes emotion; whereas (*b*) if the degeneration or injury affects instead the neural pathways running down to the hypothalamus from the cerebrum, great exaggeration of emotion is the result. Thus it seems to be fairly well accepted that while the hypothalamus furnishes pathways and interconnections that throw into play the visceral and somatic segments of a man's behavior which form a part of such reaction patterns as fear or rage, these processes are held in check by impulses discharging into the hypothalamus from the cerebral cortex. Injure the hypothalamus, and emotional behavior is reduced; injure the pathways of inhibitory impulses from the cortex or injure the cortex itself, and emotional behavior may run riot [2, 4].[1] This is a matter of high interest to students of human nature, for it gives physiological support to the well-known view that the more primitive emotional aspect of a man's life is subject to domination and control by his more evolved and civilized intellectual side.

[1] The evidence presented is clinical and experimental. But little anatomical working-out has been given the neural fibers involved; hence no detailed diagrams of them will be furnished in this book. Moreover, this view has not gone unchallenged in neurological quarters [1].

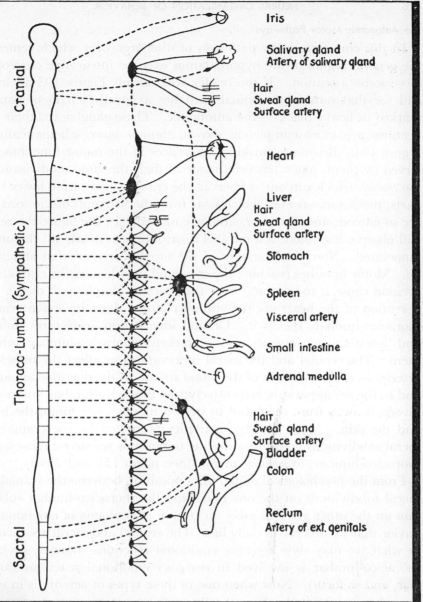

Cranial

Thoraco-Lumbar (Sympathetic)

Sacral

Iris

Salivary gland
Artery of salivary gland

Hair
Sweat gland
Surface artery

Heart

Liver
Hair
Sweat gland
Surface artery

Stomach

Spleen

Visceral artery

Small intestine

Adrenal medulla

Hair
Sweat gland
Surface artery
Bladder

Colon

Rectum
Artery of ext. genitals

104 The Autonomic Division

The central nervous system — brain and spinal cord — is represented at the left (brain merely suggested by the anterior segments). No afferent nerves and no efferent nerves to striped muscles are shown: only efferent nerves innervating smooth muscles and glands. They all operate in relay manner, some synapsing at the *sympathetic ganglia* near the cord, others near the muscle or gland. (From P. Bard, *after* Cannon, in C. Murchison, *editor*, HANDBOOK OF GENERAL EXPERIMENTAL PSYCHOLOGY, *Worcester, Mass.: Clark University Press, 1934.*)

The Autonomic Motor Pathways

In this connection, the pathways of discharge over which centers in the general region of the hypothalamus exercise integrative control deserve some attention. If the reader will consult Figure 102 again, he will see that outside the spinal cord lies a parallel chain of ganglia, marked in heavy black — the autonomic. These ganglia and their connections are more completely shown, though more schematically, in Figure 104. Because of striking differences in the motor functions subserved by them, much has been made of their threefold subdivision into the *cranial*, which run out as fibers in the cranial nerves from lower brain parts; the *thoracico-lumbar*, which issue from the segments of the cord that are so named; and the *sacral*, similarly named. In the figure the reader will observe that there is a parallel distribution to nearly all the organs innervated. Now, the character of the supplies is somewhat antagonistic. Motor impulses reaching the eye-pupil muscle over the cranial subdivision cause it to contract; over the thoracico-lumbar, to dilate. Innervation of the heart via the cranial channel slows its action; via the thoracico-lumbar, speeds it. Cranial innervation accelerates stomach and intestinal movements and secretions; thoracico-lumbar inhibits them. The cranial and the sacral innervations so affect the muscles of arteries as to divert much of the blood stream to the digestive apparatus and to the sex apparatus, respectively; the thoracico-lumbar innervation diverts it away from these and to striped muscles: the lungs, the heart, and the skin. More broadly, activities promoted by the cranial and sacral subdivisions tend to *conserve* the organism's resources; those by the thoracico-lumbar, to *mobilize* them. (See pages 151 and 299.)

From the psychological angle, this opposition between the cranial and sacral subdivisions on the one hand and the thoracico-lumbar subdivision on the other gives us a key to certain phenomena of emotional behavior that we observe in daily life. The cranial and sacral are involved in what we may style *appetitive* emotional reactions (hunger, sex); the thoracico-lumbar is involved in *emergency* emotional reactions (anger, fear, and so forth). Now when one of these types of activity is in sway, the other is inhibited. Fear throws sexual functions out of gear; thus arise nervous and psychic causes of impotence. Rage or anxiety may seriously impair appetite for food; hence the meal hour, of all times, should be kept free from animosities, worries, and griefs. A full stomach with digestive operations well established fortifies a person in a measure against the development of anti-social attitudes toward his neighbors. For as many a wife knows, the man who has dined well may be that much the more surely counted upon for sociable and amiable conduct.

Two misunderstandings must be avoided. The antagonism is not uncoordinated; that is, the two systems do not act independently but are brought into correlated activity by the hypothalamic centers. Moreover, those centers are supposed to be under the influence of the cerebral cortex, as was mentioned above; and so the demands being made upon the living organism by external agencies will determine to a large extent what rearrangement of the internal functions will be set up.[1]

THE HIGHEST TYPES OF BEHAVIOR: THE CEREBRUM

Introduction

In our example of the behavior of John Doe, the segments and aspects so far described have been the more obvious, visible, and overt. In nearly all regards, moreover, they can be found about as well in lower mammals as in man. But the reader will properly protest: So far we have not really gotten to the more distinctively human capacities that John Doe can exercise. What other animal could talk with a friend about Manchukuo and Spain, about John Marshall and Disraeli, about atomic energy or the star Aldebaran? Or — more modestly — what other animal would glance at shop windows mindful of the approach of Christmas; or casually remark of new vehicles passing, "The new Cadillac," or "The new Ford"; or debate with himself, "Dare I invite Roe home for dinner tonight?" These are higher capacities which from time immemorial have been called "reason" or "intellect." The modern psychologist would have some qualms about the use of these terms, for he would be mindful of the enormous role that the non-rational and irrational really play in anyone's life; yet he would accept them as limiting terms, that is, as describing unusually high degrees of functions that have more modest names, such as "perceiving," "recognizing," "abstracting," and other manifestations of "intelligence." In all of these the man is *adjusting himself to larger complexes and relationships between present situations and physically absent or represented ones.* This is far more than his reflex and emotional equipment would make possible alone. In these functions he quite outdistances even his nearest relatives among other animal forms. Looked at in another way, man's capacity *to readjust, to learn,* seems almost incommensurable with the capacities of other animals.

The neural basis for intelligent behavior is unquestionably the cerebrum. In certain types of feeble-mindedness the defect is clearly traceable to some deficiency in growth of these parts. In the microcephalic, for instance, an abnormally small cranium indicates a pitifully inade-

---

[1] Much of this has been stated or implied in Chapter 9, on Emotion.

quate cerebrum; while in many other types post-mortem microscopic examinations have brought to light greatly inferior numbers of neurons in the most highly evolved layer (the "supra-granular") of the cortex. Again, it is well established that in some types of psychoses ("insanities") the deterioration in the patient's thinking and general behavior is associated with degeneration of these neurons through certain agencies such as old age, chronic alcoholic poisoning, or the germs of syphilis.

It may prove helpful, in considering the cerebrum, to emphasize the enormous complexity of its pathways and of their synaptic interconnections. What does this mean for stimulus-response connection possibilities? Says Herrick:

> If it were possible to find an educated man who knew nothing of electricity and had never heard of a telegraph or telephone, and if to this man was assigned the duty of making an investigation of the telegraph and telephone systems of a great city without any outside assistance whatever, and of preparing a report upon all the physical equipment with detailed maps of all stations and circuits and with an explanation of the method of operation of every part, his task would be simple compared with the problem of the

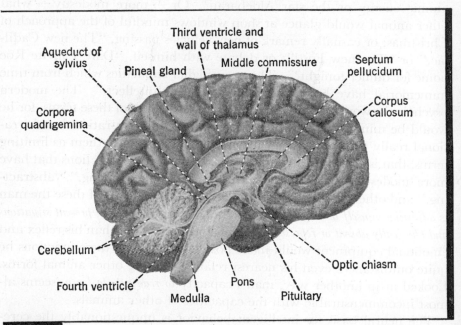

Third ventricle and
wall of thalamus
Aqueduct of
sylvius
Pineal gland
Middle commissure
Septum
pellucidum
Corpora
quadrigemina
Corpus
callosum
Cerebellum
Optic chiasm
Fourth ventricle
Pons
Medulla
Pituitary

105 Vertical Median Section of the Brain, Showing the Left Half

The cerebrum is the great convoluted mass filling more than half the picture. (*J. B. Watson*, PSYCHOLOGY FROM THE STANDPOINT OF A BEHAVIORIST, *J. B. Lippincott, 1929*.)

neurologists. The human cerebral cortex alone contains some 9280 million nerve-cells, most of which are provided with long nerve-fibers which stretch away for great distances and branch in different directions, thus connecting each cell with many different nerve-centers. The total number of possible nervous pathways is, therefore, inconceivably great.[1]

The Gross Structure of the Cerebrum

The cerebrum overtops the whole nervous system, filling the bony cranium (Figures 102 and 105). It is partly divided by a deep longitudinal fissure into a right and a left hemisphere and these are joined by a broad band of white matter called the corpus callosum. The surface is much convoluted by fissures. The gray matter on the outside forms a "bark" or *cortex* about three millimeters thick, and contains several layers of neurons and their fibers, of varying shapes and sizes, forming synaptic interconnections of inconceivable complexity. The large masses of white matter beneath the cortex are composed of great fibers (axons). These axons connect the cortex with lower centers of the nervous system, connect the two hemispheres, and connect the various parts of the cortex of the same hemisphere.

Projection and Association Functions of the Cerebrum

The various receptors and effectors of the body are connected with the cerebral cortex via the sensory and motor tracts of the cord and the brain stem. These fibers *project* the sense and motor organs upon the cortex in the geometrical or photographic sense of a point-to-point correspondence between the one and the other (Figure 106, *A*). This implies that every given sense or motor organ is in connection with some particular portion of the cortex.

It was a chance observation on a battlefield of the Franco-Prussian War that started the careful experimental investigations of this problem. Fritsch, an army surgeon, happened to apply an electric current to a surface of the exposed brain of a wounded soldier, and noticed thereupon the twitchings of certain muscles. At once he and Hitzig took up laboratory research on similar phenomena in dogs, and they succeeded in demonstrating that certain special areas of the cortex were in direct connection with certain functional units of muscles of the *opposite* side of the body. Many succeeding investigators have added to the facts; and today fairly consistent views have been arrived at by different methods, so that a certain amount of the surface of the cerebrum has been marked off into

[1] From C. Judson Herrick, *Introduction to Neurology* (5th ed.; Philadelphia: W. B. Saunders Company, 1931). By permission of the publishers.

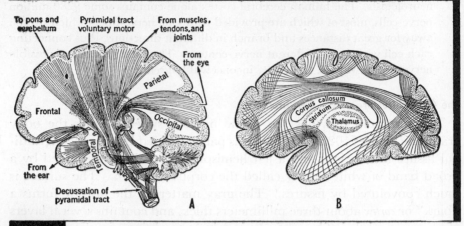

106 **Principal Systems of Fibers in the Brain**

A. Projection fibers, furnishing connections between the higher and lower brain
centers, and via the cord between the brain parts and peripheral organs (receptors and effectors). *B. Association* fibers, furnishing connections between
various regions of the same cerebral hemisphere. (Not shown are the *Com-
missural* fibers which furnish connections between right and left hemispheres.)
(*From N. L. Munn,* PSYCHOLOGY, *Houghton Mifflin, 1946, page 47; after Starr. By
permission.*)

sensory and motor projection areas, that is, those general locations where
afferent fibers from particular receptors first reach the cerebral cortex,
and those where efferent fibers leave it to conduct to particular effector
groups. These are represented in Figure 107.

But we have not seen how these motor and these sensory projection
centers are connected to each other in order to complete the transit of
neural impulses from the receptors, in which they originate, out finally
to the effectors.

The matter may be briefly introduced as follows. The general areas
just in front of and just behind the fissure of Rolando are not purely
motor and purely sensory, respectively, but are to be taken as forming a
large *general sensory-and-motor area* [22], with what might be styled two
poles, the anterior one being chiefly motor, the posterior one chiefly
sensory. The sensory and motor projection areas representing the same
parts of the body are in close relation each to each; and connections of a
fairly direct sort between afferent and efferent channels are thereby provided, making possible the simpler forms of human activity. But we
must note two elaborations that make possible more complicated reactions.

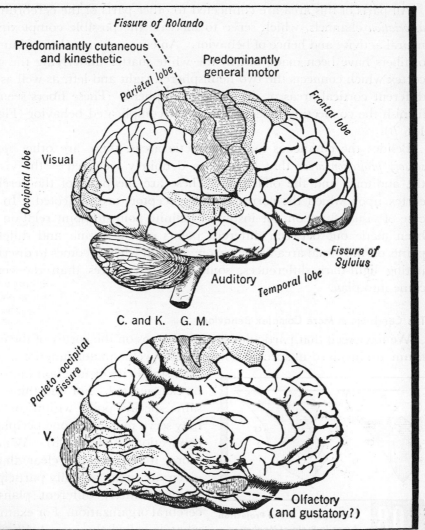

Fissure of Rolando

Predominantly cutaneous
and kinesthetic

Predominantly
general motor

Parietal lobe

Frontal lobe

Occipital lobe

Visual

Fissure of
Sylvius

Auditory

Temporal lobe

C. and K.   G. M.

Parieto - occipital
fissure

V.

Olfactory
(and gustatory?)

107   **Areas Localized as the Cortical Terminations of Sensory and Motor Projection Tracts**

The upper figure shows the outer surface of the right hemisphere; the lower
figure the mesial surface of the left hemisphere. The sensory areas are marked
by vertical shading, the motor by horizontal shading. The doubtful or partially sensory and motor areas are dotted. The association and unknown areas
are unshaded. The surface of the hemisphere is roughly divided up by three
fissures (Sylvian, Rolandic, parieto-occipital) into four lobes (frontal, parietal, occipital, temporal): which fissures and lobes help in specifying the precise
localities of the functions mentioned. It may be added that the longitudinal
or median fissure is the one dividing the two hemispheres, and that the olfactory
area is on the hippocampal lobe. (*From Pillsbury*, FUNDAMENTALS OF PSY-
CHOLOGY, *Macmillan, 1934; after Campbell, Flechsig, and Cushing.*)

All parts of this area are connected to other parts of the cerebrum by *association* channels, which serve to increase the possible complexity of neural activity and hence of behavior. An enormous number of bundles of fibers have been made out in the white matter underlying the gray cortex which connects the two hemispheres, right and left, as well as the different cortical areas of the same hemisphere. These fibers seem to furnish the connecting links necessary for complicated behavior (Figure 106 *B*).

Besides the cutaneous and kinesthetic areas, there are other *special sensory projection areas* that have been definitely localized — the visual, the auditory, and the olfactory. These are the parts of the cerebral cortex upon which the corresponding receptors are projected. In the case of visual function, for instance, definite point-to-point relation has been made out between different points on the retina and different points on the visual area of the cortex; though when it comes to discriminating light-dark differences, some lower structures than the cortex come into play.

The Cerebrum in More Complex Behavior

We have seen that particular localized areas on the cortex of the cerebrum are involved in specific sensory and specific motor functions. But such simplicity of function must not be exaggerated. For one thing, the same specific point within an area may serve more than one peripheral connection (Figure 108). What is more, it has become clear that a given area may actually participate in two entirely different plans of cerebral organization. For example, what is called the *area striata* plays a part both in the projection functions of vision and in the associational activities at the core of learning a complex maze habit.

Some classic studies that helped to establish that fact deserve our attention. Lashley was interested to know to what extent an animal's learning and retention of such habits as those employed in learning mazes and problem boxes — which are far more complex than simple

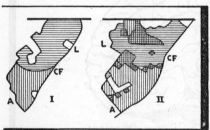

108 **Overlapping Motor Projection Areas in Brain of Monkey**

CF, central fissure of Rolando. *A:* in areas marked with vertical lines artificial stimulation elicited movements of arm; *L:* in areas marked with horizontal lines, movements of leg; in areas marked with both, stimulation elicited *either* arm or leg movements. I and II = two monkeys. (*From Franz, in S. I. Franz and K. Gordon,* PSYCHOLOGY, *McGraw-Hill Book Co., 1933, page 235.*)

responses to simple stimulations — are dependent upon its cerebral cortex. Working with white rats that were under anesthesia, he opened the cranium of each and destroyed some part of the cortical tissue. From rat to rat, he varied the size and location of the lesions, so that in one or another animal every part of the cortex had been destroyed. After it had fully recovered from the operation, each animal was tested on its ability to learn a simple problem, such as the running of a maze or the more delicate act of opening a latched door by a skilled manual operation, such as pressing a lever to unlock the catch (Figure 109).

The learning rates of the different animals were then compared with the amounts and loci of their cortical losses from the operations. The results showed clearly that the greater the area of brain damage the more retarded the rats' learning. This was true for both the simple and the more skilled acts, the coefficients of correlation being .86 in the case of the maze, and .48 to .72 in the case of the latched door.

But the results showed, further, that the learning of a habit was as much retarded by an injury in one cortical area as by a similar-sized

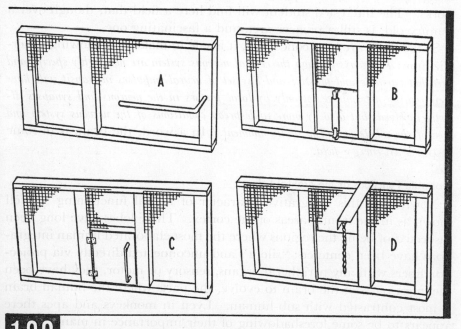

109 **Latch Doors for Study of Cortical Functions**

Four types of problems used with rats. *A*, simple lever; *B*, paper strip; *C*, spring door; *D*, pull chain. (*From K. S. Lashley, "Studies of cerebral function in learning. XI," Comp. Psychol. Monogr., 1935, 11, no. 52, p. 9. By permission of The Johns Hopkins University Press.*)

injury in another. That is, *the learning did not depend so much upon the integrity of any particular area of the cortex as upon the total quantity of cortical tissue left intact.* This does not mean, however, that specialized parts of the cortex are interchangeable, such as that those concerned with vision are interchangeable with areas not concerned with vision.

A significant incidental point bearing on the nature of cortical functioning lies in the effect that the loss of cerebral tissue had upon the manner in which the animals attacked their latch-box problems. For they failed to display the variety and adaptiveness we always see in the behavior of normal animals: they wandered more aimlessly about; they showed a more limited variety of exploratory acts; when they did happen to undo a latch they simply continued thereafter to repeat the original movements without modifying them into smoother and more economical skills.

Experimental investigations and scattered clinical studies into how the acquisition and retention of motor habits depend upon the functioning of the brain have multiplied greatly; and the rich literature of this field brings out varying conceptions of the precise way in which the cortex works. The interested student will find here a field that, though over a century old, is still a pioneer area and a fascinating one.

So far as we are here concerned, it is safe to make the following generalization: *Pathways through the central nervous system are not highly specific and fixed but variable and plastic; and any set of neural impulses in transit will have their routing determined not only by local factors in the neurons and synapses directly involved, but also by more widespread conditions of the nervous system and even of the whole organism at the moment.* In a word, the brain is in some respects an *energy field.*

Probable Functions of the Frontal Lobes

Nowhere is this integrative character of neural functioning so well shown as in the frontal areas of the cortex. These lobes have long been suspected of being the regions where the most elaborated human integrations have been centered; "silent" and unconnected directly via projection fibers with any peripheral organs, sensory or motor, they have been the latest parts of the brain to evolve, the parts where the human brain is most contrasted with sub-human. Even in monkeys and apes there appears to be some foreshadowing of their importance in man. Jacobsen and co-workers surgically removed parts of the animals' frontal lobes, testing them before and after on a "delayed reaction" problem which took the following form. A monkey would first be taught to reach at once for that one of two inverted white cups under which food had just been placed by the experimenter. This learned, he was subjected to a delay by having a sliding door dropped between him and the cups, to be raised again after an interval of perhaps fifteen or more seconds. Thus delayed, the unoperated animal was able still to reach for the correct cup, but the operated was unsuccessful oftener than could be attributed to chance. The frontal lobes, consequently, may be said to be essential to the animal's ability to organize his movements over a period of time. Without them he is unable to recall cues that he has recently experienced and to make a postponed reaction to them in the face of new incoming stimulations [10].

A recent clinical case, in which a human being suffered considerable loss from both frontal lobes as result of surgical operation for tumors, extends this conception of how those lobes function, and in directions that confirm a substantial body of opinion growing through a century of clinical observations. The patient, a member of the New York Cotton and Stock Exchanges, survived the operation and for several years conducted a somewhat successful life. But he was a changed man in many ways. Though apparently as intelligent as ever, he showed traits of childishness, irritability, rudeness to others, self-glorification, lack of inhibitions. When he observed a newspaper left slightly disarranged, he would storm, "Where the hell do you think you are that you can throw the papers all around the house?" Then only a moment later he would tell a funny story. In a word he showed impairment of *restraint*.[1] Aside from such social-emotional relations his intellectual operations revealed a loss which became evident after continuous observation. A short sample of his conversation will illustrate:

> *Clinician's question:* Wilson got us into the war.
> *Patient's answer:* Well, he couldn't keep us out of it. After what they did on the ocean, we couldn't stay out.
> *Q.:* What did they do?
> *A.:* Sank the Lusitania.
> *Q.:* Was that sufficient cause to go to war?
> *A.:* We're not too proud to do anything in this country. We can do anything as well as any other country and probably better.
> *Q.:* Why did we go to war?
> *A.:* Ill treatment by foreign nations. No respect was shown to this country.
> *Q.:* Elaborate.
> *A.:* It needs no elaboration. It's a very compact statement that tells all

[1] Compare with the findings of C. P. Richter and associates (*Amer. J. Physiol.*, 1939, *126*, 158–161, and elsewhere) that extirpation of the frontal lobes leads to very greatly increased spontaneous activity in cats, rats, and monkeys.

that I mean to tell. And we helped win the war by a long majority. [He smiles.] [1]

For an intelligent man, that is a somewhat disjointed and unorganized way to talk. Similarly, on his psychological tests the patient showed himself limited in ability to tie many simpler thought elements together into more complex ones. Impairment of *complex synthesis*, then, was a second major result of frontal lobe loss.

These two broad traits, restraint and synthesis, become key principles in the development of character and of effective intelligence, as the discerning reader can see in some later chapters. Hence the frontal lobes are indeed the loci of highest psychological development. The scientific study of these parts is still being pursued in an active way and there is evidence that some of the phenomena seen as resulting from operations on the frontal lobes may be attributed to the scar tissue which forms after the operation.

Electroencephalography

We have had occasion to refer to electrical potentials that are to be obtained from active muscular and neural tissues (see especially pages 287 ff.). Now, since the brain is a vast concentration of neural tissues, we should naturally suppose that electrical potentials would be set up by activity there. And such is the case. When pairs of electrodes attached to the head are placed in circuit with exceedingly delicate registering apparatus (such as those mentioned on pages 289) and amplified a half-million times or more, rhythms of electrical discharge can be detected (Figures 110, 111). When a person is resting quietly, an *alpha* rhythm of

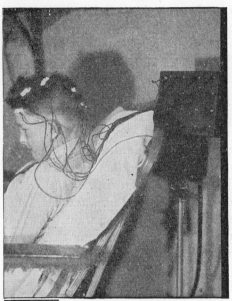

110 **Electrodes Applied for Obtaining Electroencephalograms**

From electrodes attached to the scalp and ear lobes, wires conduct the minute potentials to voltage and power amplifiers. The amplified potentials activate writing pens which inscribe continuous records on moving tape, much as is shown in Figure 163. (*By courtesy of Dr. Donald B. Lindsley.*)

[1] From R. M. Brickner, *The Intellectual Functions of the Frontal Lobes*. New York: The Macmillan Company, 1936. By permission of the author.

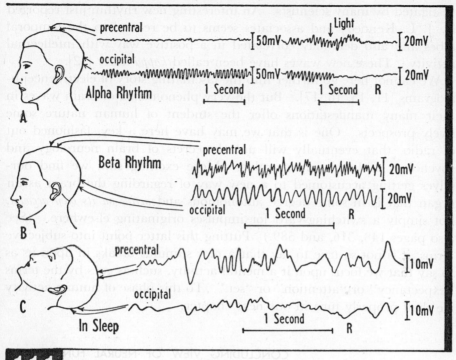

111

Alpha, Beta, and Irregular Rhythms

Note the general differences in frequency, amplitude, and regularity; and how the record obtained depends upon the part of the cranium (brain) to which the electrodes are attached. (*From G. Kreezer*, AMER. J. PSYCHOL., *1938, 51, 747. By permission of author and editor. After Jasper and Andrews.*)

about 10 per second is detectable, especially in the occipito-parietal region, coming from the synchronized activity of many cell-bodies. This rhythm is markedly changed if he falls into deep sleep; and it may largely disappear, is said to be "blocked," if he is alerted by stimulation from light (and to some extent from other sensory sources), or if he gives close attention to anything. And again, the rhythms are disturbed when the subject is frightened or anxious or embarrassed. It therefore appears that these alpha waves may be important indices of what is going on in a man, both intellectually and emotionally; but at present the matter is still too complicated for any simple statements to be made.

Meanwhile other rhythmic characteristics of brain waves have been identified, including the *beta*. Some rhythms recorded from the cortex are faster than the alpha rhythms and some are slower. The exact significance of this whole *spectrum of frequencies*, as it has been called, in relation to behavior or brain diseases is at the present time being investigated by many scientists. An interesting new rhythm just reported by J. L. Kennedy and associates seems to be related to the temporal lobes and also definitely correlated in a positive way with intellectual activity. These new waves have been called *kappa waves* [12].

We cannot here go further into the fascinating story of electroencephalograms [11, 13, 16, 17]. But the very phenomenoa of brain waves in their many manifestations offer the student of human nature some lively prospects. One is that we may have here a key, fashioned out of radio, that eventually will unlock secrets of brain neurology and psychology hitherto impenetrable. More exciting still, we find ourselves getting accustomed to a new way of regarding the brain as an organ that is in some degree autonomous and *active on its own account*, not simply a switching-yard for impulses originating elsewhere. (See also pages 148, 316, and 589.) Putting this latter point into subjective terms, it is not so true to say that a new stimulus breaks in upon us as to say that we focus upon it a mental activity, such as goes by the terms "expectancy" or "attention" or "set." To this phase of human activity we shall properly turn in our next chapter.

CONCLUDING VIEW OF NEURAL FUNCTIONING

Our survey of the nervous system in this chapter has minimized anatomical details. These the interested reader can find in numerous physiological and neurological texts. To place the subject in general perspective, let us trace again the analytic process by which we arrived at the study of the nervous system. Psychology, we have said, is a study of behavior, that is, of how a person lives and moves under the life conditions in which he finds himself. This interaction between organism and environment is, however, obviously dependent upon two sets of variables: the environmental conditions, social and non-social, and the variables of the person himself. If $B = f(PE)$, as we have previously had it formulated (page 26), then P and E alike call for scrutiny as co-determiners of behavior. P, on his part, is an animate organism with certain tendencies to self-maintenance and adjustment; but analyzed further, these depend upon his bodily organs and structures. The organs and structures most directly involved in adjustment are the receptors through which he is stimulated, the effectors by which he responds, and the system of interconnectives between the two.

It is appropriate, then, to gather up and generalize the substance of the present chapter as an answer to some such query as: How can we have a better understanding of psychological problems through what we have learned about the nervous system as a codeterminer of behavior?

From our survey we must now realize that neurology is likely to aid psychology more in general points of view than in detailed explanations of particular cases. Suppose, for instance, that a particular individual John Jones says, "The square of 6 is 36." The precise why and wherefore of this performance is not to be stated as the particular activity of a particular group of neurones at one particular locus in the brain, since it is impossible at present to observe experimentally and control in fine detail the infinitesimal and infinitely complex neural impulses occurring in any instance of human behavior. Our knowledge is indirect; it comes only from the post-mortem examination of the cases the clinician happens to run across or from the experimental examination of sub-human forms. Knowledge of the nervous system does not always throw light on details of response, but such knowledge is of basic importance in understanding the general characteristics of behavior.

(1) We can see that the architecture of the nervous system determines the level or grade of behavior on which a person can act, the adequacy with which he can take care of himself. Comparisons of one animal with another, examination of pathological human cases, and operative procedure on animals combine to furnish us with a general picture of how the character of a person's adjustments to his problems depends upon the integrity of the whole nervous system and upon the normal operation of some of its evolving parts.

(2) Through a review of available knowledge of neural process we have provided ourselves with some general principles of function and integration that will, if properly appreciated and employed, serve as explanatory keys to a number of problems of human conduct and thinking. In the expositions of psychological phenomena to follow, we shall not have space to return repeatedly to these fundamental neural principles; but the alert reader should be able to identify the operation of such principles as "threshold," "refractory phase," "inhibition," "re-enforcement," and the like.

(3) And even though we may not have space in this book to trace out details, there will be several psychological topics in our later chapters that imply or assume functioning of delimited parts of the brain, and which, if they are to be completely understood, will demand some consideration of the cerebrum in particular. Such topics include learning, perceiving, language, abstract thinking, thinking in general, and fatigue.

Finally, our study of neural functioning would have been in vain had it not served to purge the reader of some lurking popular superstitions.

The nervous system is not mysterious; nor is the cortex the residence of daemons.

This completes a series of three chapters in which we have studied directly and analytically some of the particular organs that are involved in the various forms of human behavior described previously and subsequently. After Chapter 9 we paused in our study of man-as-a-whole to take special note of the ways in which his afferent, central, and efferent functions are carried on. We now return to our broader viewpoint.

REFERENCES

1. Arnold, M. B. "Brain function in emotion," *Amer. Psychologist*, 1947, *2*, 344–345; "Physiological Differentiation of Emotional States," *Psychol. Rev.*, 1945, *52*, 35–48.
2. Bard, P. "Emotion," in C. Murchison, ed., *Handbook of General Experimental Psychology*. Worcester, Mass.: Clark University Press, 1934.
3. Brickner, R. M. *The Intellectual Functions of the Frontal Lobes*. New York: The Macmillan Company, 1936.
4. Cannon, W. B. "The James-Lange theory of emotions," *Amer. J. Psychol.*, 1927, *39*, 106–124.
5. Cobb, S. "Personality as affected by lesions of the brain," in J. McV. Hunt, ed., *Personality and the Behavior Disorders*, vol. I. New York: Ronald Press, 1944.
6. Crafts, L. W., *et al. Recent Experiments in Psychology*. New York: McGraw-Hill Book Company, 1938.
7. Freeman, W., and J. W. Watts, *Psychosurgery*. Springfield, Ill.: C. C. Thomas, 1942.
8. Gibbs, F. A., and E. L. Gibbs, *Atlas of Electroencephalography*. Published by the authors: 1941.
9. Herrick, C. J. *An Introduction to Neurology*. Fifth edition. Philadelphia: W. B. Saunders Company, 1931.
10. Jacobsen, C. F., *et al.* "Studies of cerebral function in primates," *Comp. Psychol. Monogr.*, 1936, *13*, No. 63.
11. Jasper, H. H. "Charting the sea of brain waves," *Science*, 1948, *108*, 343–347.
12. Kennedy, J. L., *et al.* "A new electroencephalogram associated with thinking," *Science*, 1948, *108*, 527–529.
13. Kreezer, G. "The electro-encephalogram and its use in psychology," *Amer. J. Psychol.*, 1938, *51*, 737–759.
14. Krieg, W. J. S. *Functional Neuroanatomy*. Philadelphia: Blakiston Company, 1942.
15. Lashley, K. S. *Brain Mechanisms and Intelligence*. Chicago: University of

Chicago Press, 1929. "Studies of cerebral function in learning: XI," *Comp. Psychol. Monogr.*, 1935, *11*, No. 52.

16. Lindsley, D. B. "Electroencephalography," in J. McV. Hunt, ed., *Personality and the Behavior Disorders*, vol. II. New York: Ronald Press, 1944.

17. Loomis, A. L., E. H. Harvey, and G. Hobart. "Electrical potentials of the human brain," *J. Exper. Psychol.*, 1936, *19*, 249–279.

18. Lorente de Nó, R. "Analysis of the activity of the chains of internuncial neurons," *J. Neurophysiol.*, 1938, *1*, 207–244.

19. Masserman, J. H. *Behavior and Neurosis.* Chicago: University of Chicago Press, 1933.

20. Morgan, C. T. *Physiological Psychology.* New York: McGraw-Hill Book Company, 1943.

21. Papez, J. W. "Structures and mechanisms underlying the cerebral functions," *Amer. J. Psychol.*, 1944, *57*, 291–316.

22. Penfield, W., and E. Boldrey. "Somatic motor and sensory representation in the cerebral cortex of man as studied by electrical stimulation," *Brain*, 1937, *60*, 389–443.

23. Ranson, S. W., and S. L. Clark. *The Anatomy of the Nervous System.* Eighth edition. Philadelphia: W. B. Saunders Company, 1947.

13

TEMPORARY SET; ATTENDING

IN THE BROADEST possible perspectives, how may we group the manifold factors that determine just how a person acts or what he experiences? What causes Johnny to thrust out his lower lip when Jackie lays hold of his electric train? Why does the absent-minded professor forget most of the items on his grocery list? Why in the spring does a young man's fancy take a turn for the worse? Why do Joe and Jane College work for diplomas?

Four Determinants of Behavior in General

(1) To begin with, there are of course the *genetic* and *congenital* factors, such as we recognized quite explicitly in Chapters 3 and 4. They are the purely biological groundwork, the raw materials.

(2) The genetically given core of the individual is played upon by *environmental* forces, by the conditions of life; and very much of the human story consists in the acquisition of habits and attitudes, skills and interests that have been and are being learned. To the factor of learning we shall give some technically detailed attention in Chapters 14 and 15.

(3) These two complementary groupings of determinants furnish the personal background. However, in describing any given case or occasion, we are likely to take note first of the *present stimuli* and *situation*. Thus it is that the particular energy of light or the vibrations basic to sound and other forms of stimulation as they activate the organism have often received the major attention of psychologists. These factors are considered analytically in Chapters 10 and 16.

(4) With these three groupings of determinants our analysis is still incomplete. Let us suppose that we have before us a pair of identical twins, John and Joe, who have been reared together, who have shared alike the same family benefits of food and protection and intellectual stimulation, who have had the same childhood diseases at identical times, and so on; in brief, for illustration's sake, a pair of identical twins who have had identical experiences. Further, we shall suppose that they are now both facing the same present stimulus-situation — both gazing at an enlistment poster. On the counts of genetics, experience, and stimulation, their responses should be the same. But let us introduce a variable in a fourth category of determinants. Let us suppose that John has just received a smile from a friendly coed, that Joe has just learned of his failure to win a scholarship. A differential has been introduced; John and Joe will not react to the poster in identical ways. Crucial determinants, then, of just what a person is going to do, are to be sought in the *immediately preceding* moments, as well as the long-term, continuing, individual conditions.

Some Examples from Daily Life

See the sprinter on his mark as he awaits the starting gun: any sudden sound or the sight of a quick movement made in his vicinity will start him off. The elusive open-field runner in the football stadium counts on the phenomenon of temporary set on the part of an opposing tackler: he runs as if to pass directly within the latter's clutches, and then, at a nicely judged instant, abruptly alters his course or momentarily slows his pace, so that the tackler is caught unprepared for this new situation and lunges ignominiously into the sod. Similarly, the batter at the plate, after watching and perhaps swinging at two or three fast balls, adjusts his movements to this speed and is likely to swing too soon on a slow pitch.

More subtle forms of predisposing adjustment are easily found. Let a person whistle or sing an air in a certain key, and unless he is practiced in such shifts, it may be difficult for him to change to a different key when he is halfway through and complete the melody without error. The popularity of many a short story rests in part upon the author's cleverness in getting the reader well started on one train of thought, and then toward the end introducing a novel turn that catches the reader off his guard and leads to an unforeseen outcome. It is the essence of most laughter-evoking situations that some new aspect excites a sudden shift in the spectator's or auditor's general adjustment.

In a jury trial, many a juror reaches a definite opinion about the case early in the trial and interprets all the later bits of evidence in the light of that opinion; others may show the same effect to a lesser degree, in that the weight they attach to any new testimony is influenced in a measurable amount by all their preceding judgments [17]. Bias is early established and hard to change.

Examples from the Experimental Laboratory

Again and again through the hundred and fifty years of experimental psychology, the effects of a person's temporary set on his acts or experiences have forced themselves upon the attention of scientists in many connections.

"Set" enters strikingly into the classic *lifted-weights* experiment (page 245), wherein the subject is asked to heft one block and then another, and to judge whether the second is heavier or lighter than the first. Now, it turns out that any single judgment he makes is all too likely to be markedly affected by the judgments he has just been making in preceding trials. After he has been hefting a constant weight and a variable weight, one and then the other in different pairings for a number of times, he finds himself often ready to render his judgment upon lifting the first weight only of a new pair, without lifting the second. Something called an "absolute impression" has become temporarily established in him.

A more colorful instance comes from the *word-association* technique (pages 212 ff). Instruct a subject to give you "opposites," say, or "subordinates" of the stimulus words you are to announce. As the exercise proceeds and he gets well into it, the particular kind of word-associates he gives will continue to be selected by your instruction, yet without his reminding himself each time that he is to give an opposite or a subordinate. What is the control? It must be some temporary predetermination in him that continues to operate unconsciously.

The *reaction-time* experiment has given emphasis to the phenomenon of "set" because it plays a critical role in such reactions (pages 35 ff). The subject may be instructed, for example, to release a key as soon as he hears a given sound. But it becomes necessary for the experimenter to present a warning signal shortly before the real signal is to be sounded, so that the subject may be properly set. What is more, the interval of time by which the warning precedes the signal must be varied to some extent from trial to trial; for if it remains constant the subject soon becomes set to react to the time interval itself and so to give falsely quick reactions ("jumping the gun").

These are samples of the scientific occasions when investigators simply have been forced to take cognizance of the subject's condition of the moment as a potent influence on when and how he will react.

TWO CHARACTERISTICS OF TEMPORARY SETS

In instances such as those described above, two characteristics seem to stand out.[1] For one thing, we note in all cases some form of *perseveration*, some persistence or inertia. Something in the way of a carry-on or hangover of one's immediately preceding manner of responding, perhaps some persisting verbal formulation, dominates one's behavior during succeeding moments. In short, a person tends to continue.

In the second place, we note in every case some kind of *differential readiness*. One movement, word, idea, is more ready to appear than others that have the same advantage so far as past experience or present stimulation-details are concerned.

(1) Perseveration

This influence of a perseverating set can be demonstrated experimentally even in *simple voluntary movements*. College students at the University of North Carolina, working as individual subjects, were once asked to tap at a rate that was convenient and natural for them. When this rate had been reliably determined for each person in three trials of 100 taps each, the experimenter had him tap at a much slower rate (one-half as fast) under guidance by a metronome. This done, he was again asked to tap at his convenient natural rate. It turned out that this second "natural" rate was slower than the first "natural" rate. Then, with other student subjects, the experimenter followed a reversal of the speed conditions; that is, after their natural rates had been determined, the subjects were required to tap as rapidly as possible for a period, then again at their convenient natural rates. This time the second "natural" rate was faster than the first. Both procedures, then, showed that after working at an externally imposed rate, there was some carry-over or perseveration of this speed even when the subject was quite free to work as he pleased [14].

Perseveration, in a sense, is to be found in one's *motives*. If an activity well begun should be interrupted, there is set up in the person a strong tendency to resume that activity if and when the opportunity offers. An experiment made by one of the students of the psychologist, Lewin, is a case in point. Children, after being well started in clay modeling,

---

[1] Psychologists may still maintain that a single concept-name like "set" is but a tag for a conglomerate of heterogeneous experimental facts [6], and indeed something of the same sort has been said of the term "learning." However that may be, it strikes the present writer that there is need to recognize temporary predeterminations more explicitly and to seek any marks they may have in common [3].

sketching, painting, or other interesting tasks, were interrupted before finishing and transferred to other activities of equal intrinsic interest. But at the first opportunity many of them went back to their original tasks [10].

The tendency to continue what and as one has begun, rather than to shift to some other operation or mode of procedure, is to be observed in *problem solving*, and even when the operations or procedures are highly particularized. This will be demonstrated to the reader directly if he will engage in a simple task. Let him first prepare a worksheet by copying off Table XXIV on a large sheet of paper. Each line poses a general

TABLE XXIV

Copy for Worksheet

Problem	To Obtain	How Use These Pint Measures?		
Sample	20 pints	49	25	2
Sample	32 pints	7	24	49
A	100 pints	21	127	3
B	99	14	163	25
C	5	18	43	10
D	21	9	42	6
E	31	20	59	4
F	20	23	49	3
G	18	15	39	3
H	25	27	76	12
I	22	18	48	4
J	6	14	36	8

problem: *How to obtain a stipulated volume of water by use only of three specified empty jars for measures?* To solve the first sample problem, he will find that he must first fill the 49-pint vessel (underscoring that number on his worksheet as hinted in the table), then pour from it enough to fill the 25-pint vessel once and the 2-pint vessel twice (drawing arrows on his sheet to show these cross-pourings), thus leaving the required 20 pints in the first vessel handled. The solution for the second sample problem is also shown in the table. In this general manner the reader may proceed to solve the other problems in order. When finished — and not before! — let him turn to the footnote on page 348.

The persistent character of the way one can be set appears in deductive *formal reasoning*. Which of the following arguments is sound, which unsound? (Solve them quickly!)

A

If all *x*'s are *y*'s,
And if all *z*'s are *x*'s,
Then all *z*'s are *y*'s.

B

If some *x*'s are *y*'s,
And if some *z*'s are *x*'s,
Then some *z*'s are *y*'s.

C

If no *x*'s are *y*'s,
And if some *x*'s are *z*'s,
Then some *y*'s are not *z*'s.

It is likely that the reader will judge incorrectly the soundness-unsoundness of at least one, and maybe two, of the deductions. Two of them were incorrectly judged by a majority of the Columbia University students tested. The errors seemed to stem from an unwitting carry-over of a general impression of "negation" or one of "particularity," which had been set up by the form of the first two statements of an argument, and which dominated the way of reading the third as a conclusion. (See footnote, page 348.)

The dead weight of a temporary set sometimes makes itself manifest by *impeding shifts* from one task to another. Students can testify that this perseverating effect of an occupation can become a positive drag. It is experienced on a day of quizzes when, after thinking and writing for an hour or so on Elizabethan poetry, the student must quickly adjust himself to thinking and writing on integral calculus, and then perhaps to questions on the coal-tar derivatives or on utilitarianism as a social philosophy. Many instructors, too, confess that they cannot make the shift from lecturing to administrative duties to laboratory research and back again to lecturing without losing much time in changing from one task to another. Each requires a warming-up period [7].

Under some conditions of physical handicap this burden on shifting set stands out clearly. It is one of the symptoms of what we call "being tired." And when men have been given batteries of psychological tests under conditions of depleted oxygen such as are to be met with at high altitudes, they seem to lose not so much the ability to handle each test but the ability to shift quickly from one test to another [12]. (Also cf. page 670.)

(2) Differential Readiness; Attention

In Chapter 10 it was noted that each of the different receptors with which man is equipped is sensitive to agencies only as these play upon it in some few limited types of energy-change (such as sound only, pressure only). It is sensitive to these agencies, moreover, only within limited ranges of each type of energy. Sensitivity is selective, and the receptors are well called "analyzers" of the environment. This, however, is but the beginning of the story. Were an organism to react invariably to each and all forms of stimulation, were the neural excitements that are engendered at all the different receptors to find their ways open to as many separate motor units, the organism would consume its whole life-time in making a mere diffusion of energy discharges through all its effectors. Quite to the contrary, a characteristic obvious enough in all animal and human behavior is its pointedness, its selectiveness. The conditions set up for the moment determine that the organism will be-have in a differentiating manner, at one time responding to this source of stimulation and at another responding to that.

In most cases this *selectivity* is of a preparatory nature. The cat looking at the mouse, the audience turned toward the speaker, the diner deli-cately taking a sip from his demitasse, the workman looking and reaching toward the approaching half-assembled structure on the conveyor-belt, the marine rifleman steadily watching a certain spot among the rocks — each is a picture of readiness for further stimulation and action. Even he who is suddenly startled by an explosion will reveal in his very move-ments much reorienting in a new direction (cf. pages 214 f.).

Note regarding the reader's solutions to problems in Table XXIV, page 346. He will most likely find that he has solved all the problems, from *A* down, with exactly the same operations. If so, let him re-examine the last two problems: has he solved them in the simplest ways? Interpretation: a few acts of solving established a temporary set; and this temporary set over-directed the later solutions [11].

Of the arguments (syllogisms) on page 348: *A* is sound, *B* and *C*, unsound. They were incorrectly judged by 9 per cent, 74 per cent, and 60 per cent of the students, respectively [15].

When a person has assumed a temporary set that facilitates his responding to some particular stimulus or stimuli, that set goes by the name of attending or attention. Consider the military command of "Attention!" What is aroused on the soldier's part is a certain stance, a fixed position of arms and hands, a poise of head, even a certain directing of the eyeballs; this posture is designed to render the soldier more sensitive to the next commands heard and more prompt in their execution — and by the same token, less sensitive and reactive to other stimuli, whether extra- or intra-organic.

The preparatory nature of attention is convincingly seen in the *motor aspects*. Ernst Mach, the physicist-psychologist, after describing how an attentive auditor can analyze complex musical sounds into their elementary sounds, says of the process:

> It is more than a figure of speech when one says that we "search" among the sounds. This hearkening search is very observably a bodily activity, just like attentive looking in the case of the eye. If, obeying the drift of physiology, we understand by attention nothing mystical, but a bodily disposition, it is most natural to seek it in the variable tension of the muscles of the ear. Just so, what common men call attentive looking reduces itself mainly to accommodating and setting of the optic axes.[1]

> Galton once observed an audience of fifty persons, listening to a long and tiresome lecture. The number of movements clearly discernible in the audience was very uniform: forty-five a minute, or say an average of one movement for each person. Several times, the attention of the audience having been aroused, the number of movements decreased by half; besides they were less extended, less prolonged, sharper and more rapid.

> Attention . . . is not an indeterminate activity, a kind of "pure act" of spirit, acting by mysterious and undiscoverable means. Its mechanism is essentially *motory*, that is, it always acts upon the muscles, and through the muscles, mainly under the form of inhibition . . . the person who is unable to control his own muscles, is incapable of attention.[2]

For one thing, as we have just seen, the act of paying attention is an act of *adjusting the receptive mechanisms* for the better sensing of the necessary stimuli. This phase of attending is so well recognized and so prominent a feature that in polite social circles a really indifferent listener may affect a tilt of head and a fixity of gaze that will do very well to simulate a complete concentration upon the speaker's words, when in reality he may actually be listening to the sound of another voice at

[1] Quoted by William James, *Principles of Psychology* (New York: Henry Holt and Company), I, 436 n.
[2] Th. A. Ribot, *The Psychology of Attention* (1889).

the table or may be occupied with his own thoughts. Likewise, it is an old device of the schoolboy who is well prepared on the day's lesson to let his gaze wander so that the teacher, mistaking these motor signs for inattention, will be sure to call upon him.

In Chapter 10 we found that receptors have, closely associated with them, effector mechanisms which aid them in receiving stimulation. The eye furnishes an excellent example, with its external muscles pointing the eyeball toward the source of light, the ciliary muscle focusing the lens, and the *sphincter pupillae* controlling the amount of light admitted. So with the other receptors: contact stimulations of the skin awaken active feeling or palpation; slight sounds cause a turning of the head and a tensing of the *tensor tympani* muscle; light odors evoke a sniffing; sapid liquids, licking; poorly discriminated weights, hefting; and so on.

Support for these more local adjustments of receptors is furnished frequently in those *diffuse muscular tensions* that are an inalienable part of the picture of the attending person. These contribute to the total result of enhancing the stimuli in question negatively by serving to reduce the number of competing stimuli. "Attention" may be thought of as two words, "a tension." In fact, the degree of one's muscular tension is experimentally found to vary with one's alertness; and it can be used as an index of the latter. An experimental subject was assigned a pursuit or tracking task that simulated the lookout work of the air pilot, truck driver, or ship helmsman: he was to keep watch on a moving target and to operate by hand a control stick in such manner as to keep a pointer following the target (a task not unlike that illustrated in Figure 88, page 286). Muscle action potentials were led off from electrodes placed on the forehead to an oscilloscope. When these potentials dropped to a dangerously low level, a red warning light went on, to which the subject was to react by releasing a pedal with his foot. The graphic results showed that the three variables — muscular tension, speed of reaction, and efficiency in the tracking task — all varied concomitantly [8].[1] A somewhat similar relation of variables is seen in the reaction-time experiment, for the higher the muscular tension the quicker the reaction [4]. In other words, alertness on a job demanding watchfulness (accuracy and promptness in perceiving and in reacting to changing conditions) is intimately related to the striped muscular tensions.

Certain changes in *respiratory* and *circulatory* functions often contribute a share to the more adequate reception of stimulations. Rapt attention is said to be breathless attention; and several laboratory investigators

[1] The student may form a better picture of this experimental set-up by refreshing his knowledge of apparatus through reference to Figures 88–91, 163.

have noted accelerated pulse rate and breathing rate when the subject is attending closely.

Subjective Observation of the Process of Attending

The selective character of attending is particularly well observed by the person himself. That to which he attends appears to him *clearer* as well as more *intense*. It is sometimes spoken of as being at the *focus* while the rest of the situation (real and imagined) is said to be at the *margin*. For illustration, suppose the reader, at the very moment of perusing this page, is stimulated by the odor of smoke. To this he is likely to remain inattentive: he is long used to cigarette-smoking in his room, and the presence of the odor now remains dimly in the hazy background of his experience. It remains there, that is, until some peculiarity about the odor, some other-than-usual quality of it, draws his attention (as we commonly say it) away from the content of the book. As the odor becomes clearer under this scrutiny, he suddenly says, "Why, that's not tobacco smoke, that's wood smoke! Is the place on fire?" Now occurs a complete transformation in his experience. That which had been focal, the argument of the text, recedes into dimness or goes out altogether. That which had been only marginal now becomes focal; and the reader's experience is that of a rapid procession of highly definite sensory and imaginal events — of flames, of smoke, of people shouting and running, of an upheaval even within his own chest and abdomen and tightenings of his whole musculature.

Or, for a less dramatic example, let the reader listen to a chord struck on the piano. He may hear it as a familiar chord from, say, Rachmaninoff's famous *Prelude*. But if he will attend in a different way, he will be able to single out this or that particular note. As each is singled out it comes to him apparently intensified a little, and certainly more definite and describable than it was when he was attending to the chord as a chord.

WHAT FACTORS DETERMINE THE DIRECTION OF ATTENDING?

The Problem Stated

Let us suppose that the reader is at this very moment in such a study-situation as the following. He is sitting at his desk in his dormitory room, reading and taking notes on his textbook. Consider the many other sources of stimulation bombarding his senses. Besides the book and notebook there is in his field of vision a pin-up picture on the wall.

To his ears come sounds of voices participating in a lively bull session
a few doors down the corridor, as well as the blaring music from a
thoughtless freshman's radio and the grinding gear-noises of a cavalcade
of automobiles starting up with the green light at the crossing. His skin
receptors are assailed by the coldness of the draft from the window, by
the hardness of his unpadded chair, and by the tight pressure of a neck-
band shrunk by the college laundry. Stimulations of intra-organic sorts
are not lacking: he is hungry and ready for a snack; his leg muscles cry
for a stretching; and a trace of the morning's headache still lingers. And
this merely begins to catalogue the multitude of stimulations playing
upon the student; yet happily we find him reacting to and aware of
none of them but the book and notebook. He is set — thanks to the
announcement of a quiz on the morrow — in such a way that the text-
book is a prepotent stimulus — its threshold is lowered.

But suppose that the student does interrupt his reading to gaze at the
pin-up picture, or to listen in on the lively conversation down the hall,
or to discard his hard chair for a more comfortable one, or to throw
aside the book and hunt up something to eat. What are the factors that
gave that particular stimulus its advantage?

Physical Factors

As stimuli, things and people undoubtedly have varying attention-
getting values, depending upon certain attributes that they possess. Of
these, *intensity* is at once to be recognized as of high importance. A
loud noise or a blinding flash of light or a vigorous slap on one's shoulder
is a fairly reliable stimulus for forcing the subject to reset himself. The
ballyhoo man and the hawker, the automobile horn and the locomotive
whistle, the brilliant electric sign and the searchlight, the black newspaper headlines and the heavily inked advertisement of a fire sale —
these are all cases in point. Other things being equal, the more intense
a stimulation, the more likely it is to attract attention.

Another obviously effective attribute is that of *extensity* or size (really
reducible to intensity). Other things being equal, the larger a stimulus,
the more likely it is to be noticed. The principle was long ago hit upon
by the advertisers: a full-page insertion attracts more attention than a
half-page or quarter-page, large signboard than a small one. Is it safe
to assume, however, that the effectiveness of the advertisement increases
in direct ratio to its size: that a full page gets four times as much attention as a quarter page? One of the many experimental attempts to
answer this question is illustrated in Figure 112. On a card the size of
a standard magazine page were mounted five pictures of nearly identical

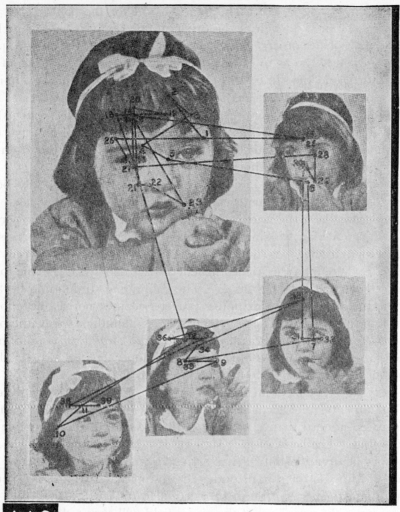

112 Eye Movements in Looking at Pictures of Different Sizes

By projecting upon the card the eyeball photographs of a person looking at it, it was possible to map the points of fixation of visual regard, from *1–2–3*, etc., to *37–38–39*. Note the number of fixations for the large and for the small pictures. (*From H. F. Brandt*, AMER. J. PSYCHOL., *1940, 53, 569. By permission of author and editor.*)

content. Four were of a certain size, and the fifth measured four times that area. Each subject looked at the card for ten seconds, while the movements and fixations of his eyes were recorded photographically, and later projected and drawn upon the card. The total time any part of the card had been directly regarded was then used as the measure of

its attention-getting power. The fixation-time for the picture that was
four times the area of each of the others totaled only twice as much as
that for each of the others. To check other variables, the picture-posi-
tions were rotated so as to exhibit the large one in each quarter of the
card in turn, and the same ratio prevailed each time. It was obtained
again when geometric designs were used in place of pictures. This
suggests the so-called square-root principle (diminishing returns) in
advertising: to get two times as much attention the area of an advertisement must be increased four times, and to get three times the attention
it must be increased nine times.

A second subspecies of intensity is *duration and repetition*. By being
repeated a stimulus may be greatly strengthened in effectiveness. An
incident from the writer's experience will suggest others of the sort to
the reader. A man walking just ahead of the writer called across an
avenue to a friend. As the first call awakened no response, it was
repeated; whereupon the friend turned, and hurriedly said, "Ah, Jones,
I didn't hear you the first time!" The subliminal stimulation became
supraliminal. A quietly dripping faucet becomes noticeable enough
when long continued. The advertiser makes abundant use of the principle of repetition. But again, under some practical conditions a
principle of diminishing returns seems to operate, for two or three
insertions a month may give few more returns than one.

A very different physical factor from that of intensity is involved in
the fundamental biological principle that a *moving* object is far more
likely to be noticed than a still one. Illustrations of this principle are
easy to find. The beast of prey stalking its victim moves so slowly that
it escapes observation until it has arrived within striking distance. An
insect crawling on the skin or under the resting hand will alert a person
with an effectiveness out of all proportion to its size. The flitting of a
mouse across the periphery of the visual field will turn a dozing cat into
an alert hunter. Castaways on a desert island, upon sighting distant
smoke or sail, tear off their shirts and wave them vigorously back and
forth, so that the ship's lookout may be sure to notice them. Many
electric signs are operated by switching devices that produce illusions of
motion to attract attention from the passerby. The waving of a red
flag gets attention in cattle not by virtue of the redness but by virtue of
the motion. Many a weak and helpless animal, on the other hand, has
for its most effectual defense a death feint (e.g., playing 'possum), which
renders it so motionless that it may escape the notice of its enemy.

Closely allied to movement are the factors of *change* and *contrast*.
Undersea explorers say that when all other objects are moved uniformly

113 **Camouflage of a Gun**

A. Modern anti-tank gun, before camouflage, quite noticeable (attention-attracting) by virtue of contrast with its background. *B.* The same gun, after camouflage. Less noticeable because irregular silhouette and folk painting are in less contrast with the surroundings. (*From R. P. Breckenridge,* Modern Camouflage, *Rinehart, 1942. Photos by courtesy of the publishers.*)

under the pressures of a constant water current it is the still fixed object that attracts attention. The steadily ticking clock may receive no notice until it happens to stop, when the very cessation of the stimulus arouses attention. The protective mimicry of the flatfish and the chameleon, of the mantid, the walking-stick and the tree toad, by which they change quickly to resemble their backgrounds, renders them virtually invisible and hence safer from a predatory foe. The skillful speaker knows how to hold attention by judicious changes in the pitch of his voice.

Camouflage

Camouflage is the military art of concealing by *not* attracting attention. In a sense, therefore, it exploits many of the objective factors of advantage in attracting attention — but in reverse. The infantryman is taught to cover a sun-reflecting helmet; glass roofs of factories are painted over; civilians blackout their windows. The reflection of starlight in a river remains a major source of concern in defending a nearby city against bombing. These are matters of *intensity*. The infantryman learns also to keep with small groups rather than large ones, to crouch and reduce his own visible size, in short to reduce his *extensity*. Any *movement* is to be avoided, or if necessary is to be made slowly. A principal factor to be offset is *contrast*. Observe Figure 113. The gun, originally highly noticeable because very different from its surroundings, is lost in the protective camouflage. The introduction of dummy roads and of faked gas tanks, planes, and factory roofs serves to make the true objects less noticeable, because less unique by contrast. Attention may be misdirected by use of decoys, such as the false causeway and false harbor in Figure 114; and similarly the dazzle-painting of a ship's hull serves to mislead the aim of submarine gunners.

Personal Factors

A living man or animal is not the mere sport of energy conditions external to himself. The conditions obtaining within have their own share in directing his orientations and posturings. For example, the organism's past experience operates in the form of acquired manners or directions of paying attention — what we may call *attention habits*. In the middle of the night the physician will often hear the telephone or the door bell although his wife will not; while on another night the wife will be awakened by the crying of one of the children but the husband will sleep peacefully on. A telegrapher often nods at his desk, but let his particular call signal come over the wire and he is quickly alerted. So, too, the well-trained nurse is able to sleep on her cot in the patient's room heedless of outside noises, until some turning movement of her

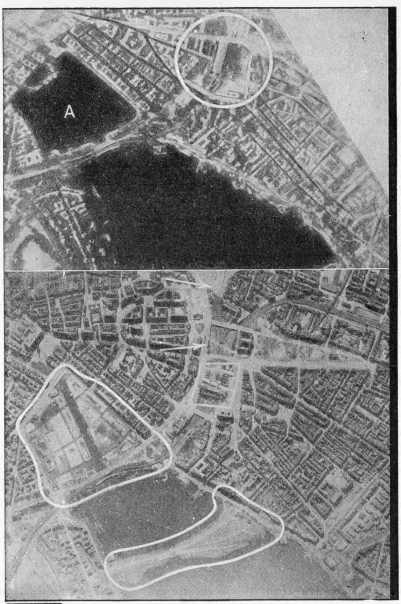

Camouflage of a Harbor

114

Upper. Harbor of Hamburg, before camouflage. Important military installations in inner harbor, marked "A," were noticeable to airmen and hence endangered by bombing.

Lower. The same harbor, after camouflage. The inner harbor has been "moved" 600 yards by means of a painted cloth, stretched on rafts, and by constructing a new causeway as a decoy (distractor). The important railway station (in square) has been camouflaged by dummy roads painted across its roof, and the tracks disguised to some degree by paint (see arrows). (*From R. P. Breckenridge,* MODERN CAMOUFLAGE. *Rinehart, 1942. Photos by courtesy of the publishers.*)

patient arouses her at once. And anyone, however well he has learned to disregard office conversation around him, is brought to with a jerk when his name is mentioned.

Attention habits of a *negative* character — habits of disregarding — are of great importance to human efficiency. One eventually learns to sleep in spite of the noise of elevated trains outside the window or of the wheels and trucks under the Pullman sleeper. The clicking of a dozen typewriters or the banging of a dozen hammers, all assaulting the auditory mechanisms of the new clerk or workman, become with time decreasingly effective, until he has grown quite negatively adapted to them, and they no longer compete with the stimuli appropriate to his work. He may even grow so adapted that the sounds become facilitating stimuli, actually furthering his proper work on ledger or drill press, so that during overtime hours when the office or shop is quiet his work suffers.

All such habits of attending are functions of the past experience of the individual. But conditions of the present also have much to do with determining which way a man will attend and to what. Even the long-trained attention habits of an art lover will become sidetracked when fatigue becomes intensified by prolonged walking and standing about in the Metropolitan Museum. Illustrations need not be multiplied. On earlier pages the importance of one's present temporary set in directing one's attention has been exhibited many times.

When is a "Distraction" Distracting?

Some persons claim that on a job demanding close attention they are hindered greatly by the sounds from a nearby radio; others claim they are helped. There are creative workers who must get far from the madding crowd in a MacDowell Colony or in a private cabin built on a lonely mountain; and there are others who write their editorials, plays, or lectures amid the hurly-burly of Manhattan or of the Chicago loop. The truth is that any attempt at a "psychology of distraction" would face a dismaying number of complications. We have canvassed above some of the factors that determine attention; and that is but the beginning of the analysis. As just hinted in our examples from daily life, so it is in scientific experimental work on the problem: Whether certain given sounds, sights, or other stimulations will divert or confuse a man's efforts depends upon who, when, where. Broad generalized laws on the subject are unsafe. Guessing at one complication we could ask: Is a person's belief on the question — one way or the other — likely to influence the effect on him of incidental stimulations? Would the factor of *suggestion* — that little-thief-in-the-woodpile that has to be checked in experiments on the effects of drugs, coffee, tobacco, and numberless other things about which the individual has his own convictions — be important here, too?   Let us go to the laboratory.

Students at the University of Minnesota volunteered to serve as subjects in an experiment which they knew in advance to be one on the effect of distractions.   For his concentrated work each subject did continuous oral adding; to an announced number he was to add 6, then 7, then 8, then 9, then 6, then 7, and so on, until interrupted at the end of thirty seconds with a new announced number; and so on for twenty consecutive times.   Ten of the problems were performed under normal conditions, ten in the presence of extraneous stimulation in the form of music (the order of the two-conditions being of course systematically varied, to eliminate the effect of the variable of order).   The subjects in the control group went to work after receiving preliminary instructions and seeing graphs purporting to represent earlier findings that *did not suggest what* the effects of distraction were expected to be.   No pre-experimental set was established in them.   Those of another group were informed that this was to be an experiment to check earlier work that had consistently shown *facilitation* under extraneous stimulation, the facilitation being exhibited to them in the form of fictitious red and black curves.   Conversely, subjects of a third group were told that earlier work had indicated the retarding effect of distraction and were shown curves purporting to represent *interference* throughout.   Finally, a preliminary talk and graphed scores were presented to a fourth group in a manner to indicate that an inhibitory effect on early trials would be expected to *change* to a facilitating one on later trials.

What of the actual scores made under the four conditions?   The outstanding characteristic of the data was a general conformation to the type of suggestion given to the respective groups of subjects.   Most of those to whom facilitation had been suggested showed facilitation in their own work; those to whom interference had been suggested showed interference; and those to whom initial-interference-then-facilitation had been indicated showed initial-interference-then-facilitation [1].

Here, then, we have a criticism of a good many artificially set up experiments, and a clear warning against hasty generalizations on the effects of distraction.[1]

Let us pause at this point to note that we have now come full circle. We have in this last experiment an example of how one may be temporarily set, of how the set will perseverate, and of how it will influence what one does.

---

[1] This is not to deny the value of a few of the best-controlled studies, such as that on noise-distractions to be reported in Chapter 22, pages 667 f.

IS BEING–SET A UNIQUE PHENOMENON?

The intellectually inquisitive reader may be unsatisfied with the largely descriptive accounts of temporary sets presented in this chapter. What *is* it to be set? To what simpler or to what already familiar psycho logical concept can they be reduced? These are still moot questions; and the present writer will merely bring in some relevant considerations.

How Is Temporary Set Experienced?

Let us start with a description from Titchener, considered America's most thorough introspectionist.

> I am sure that when I sit down to the typewriter to think out a lecture, and again to work off the daily batch of professional correspondence, and again to write an intimate and characteristic letter to a near friend, — I am sure that in these three cases I sit down differently. The different Aufgaben [tasks] come to consciousness, in part, as different feels of the whole body; I am somehow a different organism, and a consciously differ- ent organism. Description in the rough is not difficult: there are different visceral pressures, different distributions of tonicity in the muscles of back and legs, differences in the sensed play of facial expression, differences in the movements of arms and hands in the intervals between striking the keys, rather obvious differences in respiration, and marked differences of local or general involuntary movement. It is clear that these differences, or many of them, could be recorded by the instruments which we employ for the method of expression, and could thus be made a matter of objective record.[1]

This analysis of how one consciously experiences his own temporary sets assigns prime importance to the kinesthetic contributions, and therefore to motor activities. To be set is to be in action. But in what kind of action?

In the hope of getting at the matter on the physiological level, psycholo- gists have advanced several physiological theories. Some have directed atten- tion to two kinds of muscles or even of muscle-fibers, the phasic (prompt-acting) and the postural (slow-acting); and they have tried to identify the phenomena of set with the functioning of the latter, which furnishes a general substratum for the actions-in-particular [2, 5]. Some have traced close relationships be- tween the characteristics of sets and those of the action potentials of muscles [4, 5]. Others have sought explanation of set in neural terms — in the cere- brum. For example, since a person is slower in making reaction to either of

[1] From E. B. Titchener, *Experimental Psychology of the Thought Processes* (New York: The Macmillan Company, 1909), pages 180–181. By permission of Mrs. Titchener.

two signals than to one alone, it is argued that the mere readiness of his muscles is not the only factor in the person's readiness to react [13]. We have already noted (page 315) that the arrangement of neurones in the cerebrum provides for perseveration through closed circuits.

Set and Organized Performance

Whatever the physiological bases, let us raise a behavioral query: Within the totality of a person's activity, what is the relation between the preparatory set and the act performed? In such cases as the sprinter on his mark or the reaction-time subject with finger on his key, his set is in essence a partial activating of the specific response that is to be made, a response that awaits only a signal to be released in full. In other cases, as when the pianist strikes a few preliminary notes in the key in which he is about to play, or as when the experimenter asks his subject to be ready to respond to the signal-words with opposites, what is placed in readiness is something more general than the specific responses of playing the opening phrases of the musical number, or of saying "cold" to "hot" and "white" to "black." *Thus readinesses are of different degrees of generality.*

This point will be clarified if we look more closely into the matter of shifting from one set to another. Earlier in the chapter we noted in many ways how the perseverative nature of being-set prevents easy shifting from one class of actions to a very different class. This has been put under experimental scrutiny at Columbia University. Students were required to (a) add each of the many pairs of digits printed consecutively in one column, (b) multiply each pair in a second column, (c) then alternately add, multiply, add, and so on, all the paired digits in the third and fourth columns. For half the subjects the order was (c) before (a) and (b). Again, to tap other operations, the subjects were timed in (a) naming fifty consecutive colors shown on a sheet, (b) then naming fifty geometrical forms similarly printed on a sheet, and (c) naming colors and forms printed alternately. In both kinds of tests the (c) operation, which involved shifts, took a bit longer on the first trials. But with practice, the subjects improved in shifting between the separate tasks, and at the same general rate as they improved in each task alone. It appears that ability to assume a more comprehensive set was formed through practice, a set which prepared and enabled the individual to do the shifting between component tasks [7].

At this point we shall be further helped by a principle to be given more attention later (page 368): the *hierarchical* character of habits. Adding is a habit; adding 6 and 8 is a more specific habit; doing simple arithmetic (using $+$, $-$, $\times$, $\div$) is a more general habit; handling figures (as versus words) is a yet more general habit. A similar hierarchy of habits or abilities in ascending order is: naming the green colored squares; naming colored squares; naming things printed in rows on paper (forms, letters, and the like); looking at a spot and saying something about it.

Applying the above reflections, we see that the phenomena of being-set are not new or unique. The perseverative character is reducible to that universal trait of any process, its *inertia*, its tendency to continue in the absence of an agency or condition to divert or stop it. The directive character results simply from the fact that *more general members of the habit hierarchy are activated* (as to do these examples or to name these colors) or even the specific response itself (to release this key).

Summary

While we need no new concepts or unique psychological functions to explain it, the fact of temporary predetermination is one that must be recognized and dealt with constantly in seeking to understand the why's of a man's behavior. And it is of very great practical concern, as will appear.

REFERENCES

1. Baker, K. H. "Pre-experimental set in distraction experiments," *J. Gen. Psychol.*, 1937, *16*, 471–488.
2. Dashiell, J. F. *Fundamentals of Objective Psychology.* Boston: Houghton Mifflin Company, 1928.
3. Dashiell, J. F. "A neglected fourth dimention to psychological research," *Psychol. Rev.*, 1940, *47*, 289–305.
4. Davis, R. C. "Set and muscular tension," *Indiana Univ. Publ. Sci. Ser.*, No. 10, 1940.
5. Freeman, G. L. "The problem of set," *Amer. J. Psychol.*, 1939, *52*, 16–30.
6. Gibson, J. J. "A critical review of the concept of set in contemporary experimental psychology," *Psychol. Bull.*, 1941, *38*, 781–817.
7. Jersild, A. T. "Mental set and shift," *Arch. Psychol.*, 1927, *14*, No. 89.
8. Kennedy, J. L., and R. C. Travis. "Prediction and control of alertness: II," *J. Comp. Physiol. Psychol.*, 1948, *41*, 203–210.
9. Knott, J. R. "Some effects of mental set upon the electrophysiological processes of the human cerebral cortex," *J. Exp. Psychol.*, 1939, *24*, 384–405.
10. Lewin, K. *A Dynamic Theory of Personality* (trans. by Adams and Zener). New York: McGraw-Hill Book Company, 1935.

11. Luchins, A. S. "Mechanization in problem solving," *Psychol. Monogr.*, 1942, *54*, No. 248.

12. McFarland, R. "The psycho-physiological effects of reduced oxygen pressure," *Res. Publ. Assn. Nerv. Ment. Dis.*, 1939, *19*, 112–143.

13. Mowrer, O. H., N. N. Rayman, and E. L. Bliss. "Preparatory set (expectancy) — an experimental demonstration of its 'central' locus," *J. Exp. Psychol.*, 1940, *26*, 357–372.

14. Rethlingshafer, D. "Measurement of a motor set," *J. Exp. Psychol.*, 1943, *32*, 75–81.

15. Sells, S. B. "The atmosphere effect," *Arch. Psychol.*, 1936, *29*, No. 200.

16. Titchener, E. B. *Experimental Psychology of the Thought Processes*. New York: The Macmillan Company, 1909.

17. Weld, H. P., and E. R. Danzig. "A study of the way in which a verdict is reached by a jury," *Amer. J. Psychol.*, 1940, *53*, 518–536.

18. Woodworth, R. S. *Experimental Psychology*. New York: Henry Holt and Company, 1938.

14

LEARNING AND REMEMBERING

THE VERTICAL DIMENSION

As WE HAVE OCCUPIED ourselves with various phenomena of human nature in the preceding chapters, we have had to neglect a most important dimension running through most of them. We have looked at the phenomena cross-sectionally for the most part: we have described them as occurring at a given moment or during a brief interval. It is high time that we enlarged such a limited view. We turn, then, to the making not of cross-sections but of longitudinal or vertical sections.

Broadly speaking, of course, the longitudinal dimensions of human life embrace both (a) growing and maturing and (b) exercise and practice. Major attention has already been given to the former in Chapter 4. In any case, without practice, maturation has been found of limited account; and what is more, practice is the more directly controllable and controlled variable in human living, and is consequently of greater experimental importance in the study of the human mind.

Learning is Habit Building

The all-pervasiveness of learning and the effects of learning throughout the daily life of any person are certainly impressive. Consider the ubiquitous character of "habits." In common speech this term is used with primary reference to *overt* learned performances, such as throwing, dancing, handwriting, typewriting, speaking, singing, manners of eating, listening to music, and so on; but the more technical uses of the word apply it also to implicit (internal, covert) forms of learned performances. There are the various employments of *silent speech* in so-called mental arithmetic, or in reading to oneself, or in telling oneself what one does not care to speak aloud. We have already noted the formation of habitual *emotional* reactions: a child's fear of bugs or of the dark, one man's love for his work, another's extreme self-esteem, still another's super-patriotism. Again, we have noted the organizing of habitual ways of *attending* as well as of *perceiving:* how one man notices the street-car advertisements while the other studies his fellow men; how a husband may appraise analytically the wines served at a dinner while his wife directs her critical appraisals at the guests' clothes. Still more general habits are the *attitudes* that reveal themselves in the man who shows consistent prejudices against those of alien races, or who is for his town or his profession right or wrong. Habits, then, are of all sorts. Some of them are movements that can be observed a block away. But some are hidden inside a person, private activities that may go on without detection by the keenest eye. Or again, habits may be anything from the specific and nearly invariable motions of a handshake to such broad and inclusive manifestations as a general theory or even a philosophy of life.

"Memories" are "Habits"

In popular speech the words "habit" and "memory" are used as if they connoted two quite different human functions. In a general way, habit is used to refer to a non-verbal act — or series of acts — that involves some movements of the skeletal or visceral muscles, or both, like bicycling or using knife, fork, and spoon; while memory has been applied to the acquiring and retaining of words and other implicit and explicit symbols, and of conscious experiences. Habit is the modification and improvement of overt behavior; memory, the acquisition of new modes of activity in which muscular action is at a minimum. But though both words have survived in technical as well as popular psychology, the distinction must not be overworked. Many an act of motor skill has been learned with the aid of verbal cues and instruction furnished by another or by oneself (examples: golf, automobile driving, using a calculating machine); and there is hardly any activity of remembering that is not based on some kind of muscular movements, if only of the vocal apparatus (examples: calling a man's name, taking an examination, testifying in court). What is more, the facts and findings concerning "memories" hold with equal weight for "habits," and vice versa. In the present discussion, therefore, this verbal distinction will be largely ignored.

Three Problems in Learning

The various questions we shall ask about learning fall conveniently into three groups, which correspond to roughly marked stages in the whole process of learning. First, it is obvious that when we say any reaction has been learned, it must have been first *acquired* at some past time, recent or remote, and that it does or can function again at a later time. It has been acquired and can be *recalled*. But what of the meantime? Many hours, days, or years may elapse between the earlier occasion, when the reaction was first aroused and fixed, and the later date when it is rearoused. Clearly, the reaction as a reaction-possibility has somehow been *retained* through the interval. It has been potentially there. Accordingly, our inquiries will revolve about acquiring, retaining, and recalling, respectively. At each stage of inquiry there are many practical points useful to the student in his daily work and living; but here as elsewhere (in psychology as in other sciences) the technical treatment is to be devoted to the experimental findings, and their application to this and that concrete problem must be left largely to the thoughtful and resourceful student.

ACQUIRING

The Rate of Acquiring a Habit

How shall we measure a person's learning? The primary question will be how rapidly he learns; and to measure this rate we must adopt units. For the known variable it is customary to take specified and controlled amounts of practice, usually stated in terms of length of practice, period and number of periods. For the unknown variable, to be tabled and plotted against the known variable, usually either or both of two criteria are employed: speed, stated in terms of either amount of work per unit of time, or amount of time per unit of work; and accuracy, stated in terms of the number of errors made, or of the general scoring of the character of the work done. (In plotting graphically, the known variable is always indicated by distance from O on the horizontal or x axis; the unknown by distances on the vertical or y axis.) Some sample curves are shown in Figure 115. Note that the scoring methods used determine whether the curve is a rising or a falling one.

It will be noted that most of the curves show a *negative acceleration*, a slowing down in the rate of improvement. That is, as the number of trials increases, the amount acquired per trial decreases. These studies have been almost exclusively on overt functions or functions in some single type of work. Thorndike, who gave a thorough analysis of learning curves, had the following to say on the point:

> Negative acceleration of any great amount is far from being a general rule of learning. On the contrary, it may well be that there are some func-

tions, such as amount of knowledge of history . . . or of fiscal statistics, where, by any justifiable score for "amount of knowledge," the rate of improvement in hour after hour of practice would rise, giving a pronounced *positive* acceleration. Each item of information may, in such cases, make the acquisition of other items easier.

One obvious characteristic of the learning curves is their saw-toothed irregularity. The irregularities may be long or short. These short-time *fluctuations* represent the fact that the efficiency of a performance is affected by all sorts of factors: distraction by extraneous stimuli, changes in the learner's interest and effort, changes in his practice methods, altered physiological condition and health, and the like. The reader can easily add a dozen other factors that would be important here if he bears in mind changes in the external environment, changes in the subject's intra-organic condition, and changes in his attitude toward the work. Anything, we may safely say, that bears upon one's efficiency at a given time would help or hinder his progress in acquiring knowledge or skill.

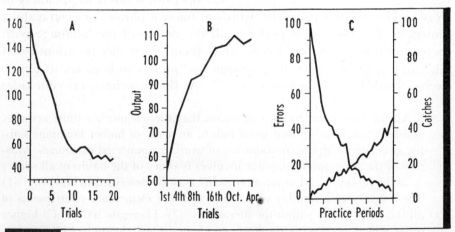

115

Sample Learning Curves

A. Mirror-drawing. Improvement in tracing a diagram that is seen inverted in a mirror, in the course of 20 trials, is measured in terms of reduction in both errors and time. *B. Typesetting.* Improvement on the job is measured at various intervals in units of work accomplished. *C. Ball-tossing.* Improvement in tossing and catching two balls with one hand is measured day by day in two ways: as decrease of errors committed; and as increase of successes in catching. (*Adapted from I. Lorge,* Teach. Coll. Contr. Educ., *1930, No. 438;* H. D. Kitson, Univ. J. Bus., *1922, 1;* Peterson, J. Exp. Psychol., *1917, 2.*)

Example: Learning to Telegraph

An early quantitative study of improvement in a human function is that of Bryan and Harter on *telegraphy*. Student telegraphers were tested each week on their rates of sending or receiving messages in the Morse code of dots and dashes, and their rates were plotted. Figure 116 shows some typical receiving curves. The subject was tested each week on (*a*) his rate of receiving letters not making words, (*b*) his rate of receiving letters making words but not sentences, (*c*) his rate of receiving letters in words and sentences. If we examine the curves closely we see that they check very well with the testimony of many experienced operators who had reported: "(*a*) At the outset one 'hustles for the letters.' (*b*) Later one is 'after words.' (*c*) The fair operator is not held so closely to words. He can take in several words at once, a phrase, or even a short sentence. (*d*) The real expert has all the details of the language with such automatic perfection that he gives them practically no attention at all," and in taking down the message he "prefers to keep six to ten or twelve words behind the instrument." As the experimenters conclude:

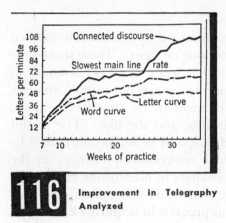

116   **Improvement in Telegraphy Analyzed**

Explanation in text. (*From W. L. Bryan and N. Harter*, Psychol. Rev., *1899, 6, 350.*)

> All the facts point to the conclusion that the telegrapher must acquire, besides letter, syllable, and word habits, an array of higher language habits, associated with the combination of words in connected discourse. Mastery of the telegraphic language involves mastery of the habits of all orders . . . a hierarchy. . . . *A hierarchy of habits* may be described in this way: (1) There is a certain number of habits which are elementary constituents of all the other habits within the hierarchy. (2) There are habits of a higher order which, embracing the lower as elements, are themselves in turn elements of higher habits, and so on. (3) A habit of any order, when thoroughly acquired, has . . . psychological unity. The habits of lower order which are its elements tend to lose themselves in it, and it tends to lose itself in habits of higher order when it appears as an element therein.

It would be a mistake to assume that different levels of habits are organized one after the other: letters being learned first, then words, then phrases and sentences. The parallel rises of the three plotted curves correspond rather to the testimony of all operators that the letter-habit, the word-habit, and the sentence-habit all show improvement *simultaneously*, if not equally; and from the earliest practice, they all gain fastest when practiced together in connected discourse. In practical daily life it is a fairly general rule that one should not break up a complex act with the intention of drilling the dislocated parts separately and reassembling them later. Every teacher of handwriting, dancing, swimming, tennis, and even golf knows well enough that it is far better to tackle the whole performance early and count upon the elimination of inefficient moves here and there by special attention from time to time, now to this and now to that. Most notably, the modern methods of teaching reading in the elementary school show this recognition of the importance of developing the simpler and the more complex habits together, for no longer does the child have first to learn all his letters one by one, then isolated words, "cat," "rat," "cow," etc., then short sentences containing these; rather, from the first he practices reading as a total, meaningful, organic kind of process.

Some Principles of Economy in Acquiring

Our knowledge of factors that help and hinder in learning has reached respectable proportions, thanks to the work of many experimental investigators. Ebbinghaus initiated the studies of this type in 1885 with his monograph *Ueber das Gedächtniss*. His technique was so remarkable and his findings were in many ways so well verified by later workers that in the following pages we shall accord him the lead.

The kind of performance he studied was memorizing, "learning by heart," in which the learner reads material over and over until he can repeat it unaided, the total time spent in reading (at uniform rate) furnishing the score. For the material to be learned, he sought to eliminate chance disturbing factors and also to provide units of measure by devising nonsense syllables (each a vowel placed between two consonants), drawn by chance as from a hat and then combined into series of various lengths. Each syllable series was to be learned as a whole, so that the subject could repeat it all verbatim.

The fact that Ebbinghaus had no apparatus makes his procedure all the more important. Using himself as subject and drawing his materials quite in chance order, he established the most constant possible experimental conditions throughout the learning: (1) The separate series were always read through completely from beginning to end. (2) The reading and the reciting of a series took place at a constant rate set by a metronome making 150 strokes per minute. (3) After the learning of each series a uniform pause of 15 seconds was made. (4) Association of syllables by mnemotechnic devices was avoided. (5) Concentration of attitude on the task was maintained as far as possible. (6) Care was taken that the objective conditions of life during the period of the tests were so controlled as to eliminate too great irregularities.

Ebbinghaus employed the savings method for testing.[1] The number of repetitions necessary to enable a subject to make one complete reproduction of the series was noted; and after an interval of time the series would be relearned and the time saved in the relearning noted.

Since Ebbinghaus, various kinds of apparatus have been devised by later investigators in order to standardize the presentation of the stimuli. It can readily be appreciated that a precise timing of the duration of each exposure is important.

(1) For the relearning of a 12-syllable series at a given date, Ebbinghaus found that 38 repetitions distributed over the three days just preceding was as effective as 68 repetitions made on the one immediately preceding. The conclusion drawn from this, that *distributed practice* is more effective than *massed practice*, has been amply borne out by many other studies done since.

For example, college students memorized lists of nonsense syllables of three different lengths arranged in two different ways. In the one arrangement they were allowed only 6-second intervals between presentations of the list (called massed practice); in the other they were allowed 2-minute intervals (distributed practice). The data in Table

TABLE

XXV

Distributed versus Massed Practice

Mean Numbers of Trials Required to Memorize Nonsense Syllable Lists of Different Lengths to the Criterion of One Perfect Recitation

Method of Practice	Number of Syllables in List		
	8	11	14
Massed	7.0	11.6	17.1
Distributed	5.9	9.4	12.1

From C. I. Hovland, J. Exp. Psychol., 1940, 27, 272.

[1] Several other methods of memorizing and testing for retention have been employed by different investigators. Cf. Whipple [23], pp. 151–152; Woodworth [26], chap. II.

XXV tell the story of the greater effectiveness of spacing the trials for lists of all three lengths, though especially for the longest. Two implications of this study are borne out by other researches. One is that some kind of spacing gives better results than massing, whether the habit practiced is learning nonsense or meaningful verbal materials, manual skills such as running stylus mazes, mirror-drawing, or even puzzle solving. The other implication is that the more difficult the task to be mastered, the more impressive is the advantage of distributing the practices.

Probably no principle of learning is more obviously practical in its application. It is one of the reasons why cramming has always been looked upon as a poor method of study. To take a single instance, at one army camp recruits undergoing training to become radio operators were being drilled at it for 7 hours a day. When the drill time was reduced to 4 hours a day, the men learned just as rapidly, as measured day by day — not to mention the improvement in their morale [24].

One offsetting factor, however, is the fact that the postural set or *Einstellung*, so important in grasping thoughtful material, may require much time to establish, and it may often be more advantageous for the student to continue study for some time, once he has gotten well set.

(2) To determine the relative rates at which *rote* and *meaningful* materials could be memorized, Ebbinghaus used stanzas from Byron's *Don Juan*. He found that each stanza (consisting of 80 syllables) required an average of less than 9 repetitions, whereas the same number of nonsense syllables in a series would have required between 70 and 80 repetitions. In other words, expressed as a ratio — meaningful: nonsense : : 9:75. One moral of this, of course, is that one does well to look for meaning even in relatively meaningless material.

(3) Another point recognized by Ebbinghaus was the importance of *rhythm*. He tried to prevent this from being a disturbing factor by adopting a constant rhythm in his readings. Experiments by others have tended to show that complete suppression of rhythmic vocalization actually renders the memorizing task almost impossible for certain individuals. The practical value of rhythm in memorizing has always been obvious enough — as shown by the young children who fall into a sing-song manner when rehearsing to speak a piece.

(4) *Reciting* — that is, attempting to reproduce material vocally — is quite effective. One investigator who was practicing on series of nonsense syllables tried out twelve different combinations of readings and prompted recitings, as shown in the following table:

TABLE

XXVI   The Value of Attempting to Recall

Read-ings	Recit-ings	Read-ings	Recit-ings	Read-ings	Recit-ings	Read-ings	Recit-ings
6	0	6	5	6	10	6	15
11	0	11	5	11	10	11	15
16	0	16	5	16	10		
21	0						

From E. Meumann, THE PSYCHOLOGY OF LEARNING. *New York: Appleton, 1913.*

Of these he found the most economical method to be the combination of six readings with fifteen recitations. A dramatic finding, perhaps; yet in its direction, at least, one that has been verified by others. In the memorizing of piano music — to take a very different kind of perform-ance — it has been found that keyboard practice is much facilitated if it is interrupted midway by a four-minute purely mental rehearsal of the finger movements with the eyes closed [13]. The meaning of this seems to be that an active attitude on the part of the subject aids rapid acquiring.

Importance of the Subject's Motivation and Attitude

After his reading of Chapters 7 and 13, it will be clear to the reader that the way a person acts in any particular instance is a function not only of his environment, and of his more overt manner of attack, but also of his motivation and of the degree and direction of his orientation and mobilization *at the time.* Letting O stand for a subject's organic conditions of motivation and set, we may revise our familiar formula to read: $S \times O \longrightarrow R$. The student may now ask what conditions, on the basis of the available evidence, the subject himself should control in order to facilitate the acquisition of knowledge and habits.

(1) Attending to the material is not enough; it must be attending with the *intent to learn* it. As said above, an active attitude is demanded: the learner must go after it!

The psychologist E. C. Stanford once wrote that he had read in his family the form of Morning Prayer of the Episcopal Church no less than five thousand times in the course of twenty-five years, yet that he was unable to recall the prayers unaided. One prayer of 124 words required 44 promptings to learn; another of 146 words, 38 promptings; another of 158 words, 27 promptings [14].

The principle that it is beneficial for the learner actively to participate in the learning process carries over strikingly to applied fields. During World War II servicemen were at first taught the military phonetic alphabet ("Able" for A, "Baker" for B, "Charlie" for C, etc.) by passively looking at each letter and its phonetic equivalent. But learning rates were definitely speeded up when the men were instructed to call out the phonetic equivalent when each letter appeared.

Now the intent to memorize, while it certainly makes for more effective retention, may be almost absent in some cases. There are many interesting anecdotes in the literature attesting that people often absorb and later recall incidents and details of which they are not aware at the time of exposure. And there are experimental studies to support this general point. We may mention a single case [19]. One at a time a dozen magazines were exhibited before a group of college students, who were told that they would later be tested on their memories for the names of the magazines and for the order in which they had been presented. At the time of the test, however, they were asked to recall many other details as well, such as

> What was the picture on the *Country Gentleman?*
> From which cover was a piece torn from the bottom right-hand corner?
> Was the girl on the *Red Book* a brunette or a blonde?
> Of which magazine were you told the name as it was shown to you?

The students were able to answer many of these questions regarding incidental details, and it turned out that those individuals who had better memories for the direct materials tended to have better memories for the incidentals also.

But let us not mistake: our original point remains true here. Those facts which the subjects intentionally learned were very much better recalled than the others. Moreover, it has recently been shown that incidental learning is not purely haphazard, for explicit instructions strengthen memory for certain related categories. For example, subjects instructed to remember the details of content in a story read to them will show better incidental recall for general comprehension than for details of wording or of presentation. We may interpret this point more broadly as showing how one's sets to learn may be of varying degrees of generality [12]. (Cf. page 361.)

The general principle simply cannot be overemphasized for the student. Certainly his reading of a book has only a fraction of its value if done passively. He should actively attack it, address questions to it, ask himself questions about it. Summer fiction, "movies," and other forms of entertainment contribute their share to the breeding of passive habits of attending — although an alive thinker can profit by such things without letting his wits slumber.

(2) A dozen or more investigators have measured the effect upon grade school, high school, and college students of letting the students *know the results* of their practice from time to time; and it was almost unanimously favorable. There is little to be said in favor of mere blind practice. We may ascribe this effect to the facts (*a*) that the learner by knowing how he is getting on is enabled to check on his right and his wrong procedures and so more rapidly select the one and eliminate the other, and (*b*) that the rises and falls in his score serve as stimuli to emotional responses of reinforcing character.

Practical applications of this rule are numerous. During World War II, the standard Army method of training gunners — merely to give them verbal instructions and coaching before, during, and after their gunnery practice — was called into question. Trainees working on the 40-mm. gun which was aimed by two men, one to track the moving target horizontally, the other vertically, were divided into three groups. Those of one group were instructed verbally. In the second group, the men of each gun-pair coached one another in turn. For the third group, a telescope check-sight was mounted on the gun, and by watching through it an instructor could sound a buzzer whenever a gunner was aiming off his target. The men of this third group were also told the scores they made on each course.

The performance scores of the three groups are presented in Figure 117. For each trial of each group the average percentage of misses is plotted. At the start, the three groups were equal in ability to keep gun on target; but as practice continued the trainees given knowledge of results through the check-sight reached a much better level of performance than did those of the other groups.

In another type of military training, the learning of the international Morse code, improvement was speeded by having men post their scores, construct their individual learning curves, and so keep accurate records of their progress [24].

(3) Since so much learning is socially directed, it is an inevitable question whether one learns best under others' *praise*, under their *reproof*, or under neither. Certainly factory, business office, and schoolroom procedures cry aloud for facts here! But it is not a simple matter to isolate the variable, as is clearly shown by the outcome of a more recent investigation in which the social and physical conditions were varied from group to group. Code substitution work was assigned to

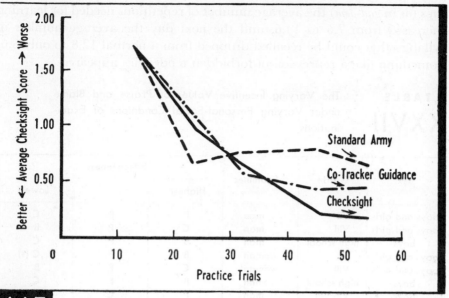

117 Improvement in Anti-Aircraft Gun-Aiming as Affected by Knowledge of Results

Explanation in text. (*From C. W. Bray*, PSYCHOLOGY AND MILITARY PROFI-
CIENCY, *Princeton University Press, 1948. By permission of author and publisher.*)

boys and to girls in the seventh-grade classes, to boys and to girls in
eighth-grade classes, to boys in high school classes, and to men in college.
Some of the tests were administered by a man, the others by a woman.
Thus there were four varying conditions: the age of the examinees, their
school grade, their sex, and the sex of the examiner. Some of the individual members of each group of subjects received praise for their work
(*P*), others received words of blame (*B*), while the remainder received
neither (controls, *C*). What of the findings? They were utterly inconsistent, as can be seen from Table XXVII, where the present writer has
attempted to tabulate an analysis of the graphs appearing in the original
report. Clearly the relative value to learning of such social incentives
as these depends upon the personal circumstances to an impressive
degree. And we are here again reminded of the grave difficulties that
beset the psychologist, the many variables he must reckon with, in his
attempts to isolate and measure aspects of human nature so often glibly
phrased in everyday speech.

(4) Furthermore, the *emotional reaction* aroused by the *learning material*
itself must be recognized. For instance, in an experiment in which
nonsense syllables were memorized in pairs, when the paired syllables
were such that they suggested words with salacious or sacrilegious mean-

ings (as in *gad-dem*) the average number of repetitions needed for learning increased from 7.6 to 14.6, and the next day the average number of syllables that could be recalled dropped from a normal 12.8 to only 8.0. Something like a repression of forbidden tendencies appeared.

TABLE XXVII The Varying Incentive Values of Praise and Blame under Varying Personal-Social Conditions of Examinations

Sex	Grade	Examiner	Effectiveness		
			Highest		Lowest
boys and girls	VII	man	P	B	C
boys and girls	VIII	man	C	P	B
boys	high school	man	B	P	C
boys and girls	VII	woman	B	P	C (?)
boys and girls	VIII	woman	C	P	B
boys	high school	woman	B	P	C
boys	VII–VIII	man	P	C	B
girls	VII–VIII	man	B	P	C (?)
boys	VII–VIII	woman	C	P	B
girls	VII–VIII	woman	B	P	C (?)
boys	college	man	B	P	C (?)

P = praised group,   B = blamed group,   C = control group

From H. O. Schmidt, PSYCHOL. MONOGR., *1941, 53, No. 240. By permission.*

The student who has read Chapter 8 will not be surprised at the assertion that the emotional involvements of an earlier experience may have much to do with facilitating or blocking learning and recall. This is a cardinal point in the doctrine of psychoanalysis; and in a simplified form it has been asserted by many outside that faith. We tend to *remember the agreeable* and to *forget the disagreeable* — so the claim runs. Does this assertion have scientific support? One of the better planned pieces of experimental evidence appears in a study employing both normal and abnormal subjects. From case histories and clinical notes, there was assembled a list of 15 things which had proved distinctly disturbing and troublesome to psychoneurotic and psychotic patients. Included were such items as "failing always," "fearing poison," "disliking folks," "crying frequently." To balance these, 15 more items were gathered which had proved acceptable and agreeable, such as "thinking clearly," "gaining affection," "becoming important," "liking folks." Finally, 15 more were assembled which were neither particularly acceptable or unacceptable. These three lists of 15 phrases each were then used as memorizing material by a group of psychoneurotics and by a group of normals, each of whom learned the lists once, then relearned them 16 days afterwards. From the data in Table XXVIII it

TABLE XXVIII Learning and Retention for Pleasant, Unpleasant, and Neutral Items

Subjects	Items	Trials Required to Learn Originally	Trials Required to Relearn 16 Days Later
Abnormal S's	Pleasant	9.9 ± .82	3.6 ± .26
	Neutral	6.5 ± .65	4.4 ± .25
	Unpleasant	9.4 ± .60	7.0 ± .55
Normal S's	Pleasant	9.7 ± .63	3.0 ± .29
	Neutral	4.2± .19	4.4 ± .34
	Unpleasant	8.8 ± .42	6.9 ± .41

From A. A. Sharp, J. EXP. PSYCHOL., 1938, 22, 407.

is clear (a) that the emotional character of the meaning of the verbal material interfered with its being memorized in the first place, (b) that the unfavorable emotional character was an interfering factor in its being recalled later, and (c) that these effects were observed in psychoneurotic and normal alike.

Interrelations Between Habits

Given one habit learned, what will be its effect upon the learning of another habit? Theoretically we can predict that the former may facilitate the latter, may inhibit it, or may have no effect.

(1) The first relationship mentioned was the assumption underlying the formal discipline theory of education, which preoccupied educators for some centuries: education was seen as a process whereby the mind-in-general somehow received a general disciplining from the intensive pursuit of certain particular academic subjects, and this beneficial training was supposed to carry over into any field to which the student then turned his trained mind. Inevitably such a broad and vague claim — advanced in the interest of certain school subjects — was challenged by the ever-inquiring psychologists; and after the critical experimental work of Thorndike and Woodworth in 1901 [21], skeptical reaction led almost to pouring out the baby with the bath, to rejecting belief not only in a vague mental discipline but also in any specific carry-over effects from habit to habit or from situation to situation. After all, it may be argued,

any kind of learned memory or other habit inevitably implies some transferability to new situations, else there simply is no learning!

The great rash of experimental studies on transfer that has broken out in the last three decades has led to some consensus, which we may attempt here to formulate. (*a*) Where the details of *stimulus-content* and of *procedure* (such as letters and words, digits, addings and subtractings, fractions, particular facts of geography and history) are common to both the old familiar situations and to the new one, a person will ordinarily be able to transfer his old skills successfully. (*b*) The same is true for *special procedures* he has learned (such as ignoring distractions, allowing for constant errors, using a dictionary or a slide rule). (*c*) Further, it is a sound educational objective to learn *generalized* rules or *principles* or ideals so that they may be applied in new fields and problems.

Let us take up a research which will exemplify correct experimental designing of a transfer experiment, will illustrate the value of generalized principles, and will give the reader some practical hints. Woodrow was

TABLE

XXIX   The Experimental Design for a Transfer Experiment

Group	Initial Test	The Practice	Final Test
Control	Six memory fields	none	Six memory fields
Practice	Six memory fields	Practiced memorizing poetry and nonsense syllables: without special instructions (twice weekly for 4 weeks)	Six memory fields
Training	Six memory fields	Practiced on same poetry and syllables but also spent some of their time listening to rules and their demonstration (for same total time as Practice group).	Six memory fields

The Rules Studied by the Training Group

1. Practice not piecemeal but by wholes.
2. Test yourself actively.
3. Employ rhythms and groupings.
4. Attend to meanings and symbolic representations.
5. Keep alert and concentrated.
6. Have confidence in your ability to memorize.
7. Use secondary associations and mnemotechnics.

From *H. Woodrow*, J. EDUC. PSYCHOL., *1927*,
18, *159–172. By permission of the author.*

interested to see what effect persistent practice on two narrow kinds of memorizing (learning poetry verbatim and nonsense syllables by rote) might have upon one's ability to memorize a variety of things (listed in Table XXX). Three equated groups of college students were arranged, and were employed as shown in Table XXIX.

Inspection of the results in Table XXX brings out some interesting

TABLE XXX

The Results of a Transfer Experiment

End Tests Used	Group	Percentage of Gain or Loss Between Initial and Final Tests
Rote poetry	C	−33
	P	−29
	T	−11
Rote prose	C	+29
	P	+26
	T	+51
Facts (prose substance)	C	−5
	P	−5
	T	+13
Historical dates	C	+29
	P	+38
	T	+88
Vocabulary, Turkish-English	C	−1
	P	+3
	T	+55
Memory span, consonants	C	+7
	P	−6
	T	+20

From H. Woodrow, J. EDUC. PSYCHOL., 1927, 18, 159–172. By permission of the author.

points. If we compare those subjects who simply practiced rote memorizing throughout the four weeks of training with those who did not practice at all during that time, we see that the former show little if any carry-over benefit from their labors. On the other hand, the persons who had invested some of their time and attention in studying the general principles of economy in memorizing were able to show a great profit, in a considerable transfer to the other memory fields.

(2) One habit that is learned may not, after all, have a positive effect on the learning of another: it may have a neutral effect, or even a negative effect. There is, for instance, the well-known phenomenon of *interference*. Münsterberg noted that if he changed his watch from the left vest pocket where it was usually carried to the right trousers' pocket, he made a number of false movements when he wished to know the time, although he could soon get habituated to the new reaching reactions required. Then, after returning the watch to its original place in the left vest pocket, he again made a few false movements. Everyday illustrations of interference abound, and the reader will be able to cite instances from his own experience in changing from one kind of clothing to another or in driving a make of car to which he is not accustomed.

It is a general finding that the interferences that seem striking when one or both habits are in their initial stages of formation tend to disappear as the habits become well fixed. For this reason most colleges will not permit a student to begin his study of two foreign languages in the same year.

An interesting attempt to explain in $S \longrightarrow R$ terms just when the effect of one habit on the forming of another is likely to be positive or to be negative, takes the form of the rule that when a new stimulus is to be connected with an old response, positive transfer results; when an old stimulus is to be connected with a new response, interference results [4].

RETAINING

Once a habit has been acquired, what about its permanence? Forgetting is an all too familiar process, and everyone can probably hazard hazy estimates regarding the factors involved. But here, fully as much as in discussing the process of acquiring, we must seek scientific evidences, take quantitative results first, then some qualitative points. Obviously, retention is never observed directly but studied only in recall. And it is well to bear in mind that inability to recall something at a given time does not mean that its retention is wholly lost.

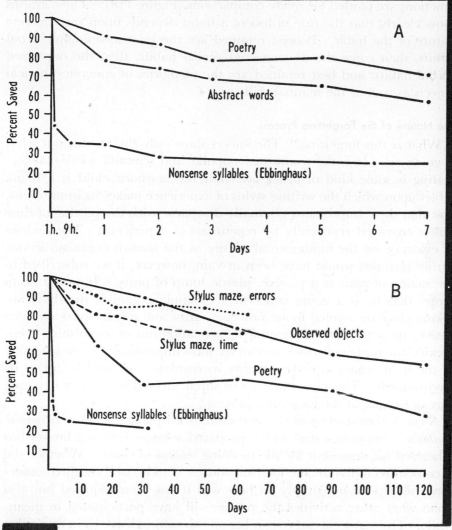

100
90
80   A
70   Poetry
60
50   Abstract words
Percent Saved
40
30
20   Nonsense syllables (Ebbinghaus)
10

1h. 9h.   1   2   3   4   5   6   7
Days

100
90   B
80   Stylus maze, errors
70
60   Observed objects
Percent Saved
50   Stylus maze, time
40   Poetry
30
20   Nonsense syllables (Ebbinghaus)
10

10 20 30 40 50 60 70 80 90 100 110 120
Days

118

Some Curves of Retention for Different Kinds of Material

(From O. Williams, J. Exp. Psychol., *1926, 9, 373; Ebbinghaus, op. cit.; C. Tsai,* Comp. Psychol. Monogr., *1924, 2, 6; J. A. McGeoch and P. L. Whitely,* J. Educ. Psychol., *1926, 17, 422; 1928, 19, 477.)*

The Rate of Forgetting

Working with his series of nonsense syllables, Ebbinghaus found that the process of forgetting went on in a definitely measurable way. His results are included in the two accompanying graphs, which are drawn on different scales, and in which retention curves for a variety of learned functions are plotted for ready comparisons (Figure 118). These graphs show clearly that the rate of loss of a habit depends upon the concrete nature of the habit. Poorest retained are the least meaningful verbal habits, then come the disconnected verbal habits, then the organized verbal habits, and best retained are the memories of concrete physical objects as well as the manual skills.

The Nature of the Forgetting Process

What *is* this forgetting? The curves show only the results, not what is going on. It is the traditional popular and scientific view that forgetting is some kind of *fading out:* that the newborn child is a blank tablet upon which the writing stylus of experience makes its impressions, and that these impressions gradually disappear with the passing of time unless engraved repeatedly by repetitions of experience. The reviews of evidence on the fundamental nature of the human organism in our earlier chapters would have been in vain, however, if we subscribed to the notion of man as a passive, plastic lump of putty. It would be to forget that he is a going concern, a dynamic organism in which are taking place uncounted living processes, gross and subtle, local and pervasive, these processes operating in a relationship of astonishing complexity, the upshot of which we can see most impressively as the tendency of the total organism or personality to regulate itself and adjust to its environment. This view needs to be supplemented by a more dynamic way of looking at the forgetting process.

A cue is furnished us in the well-established phenomenon of *retroactive inhibition.* Suppose a student has prepared a lesson well or a lawyer has rehearsed his argument for the morning session of court. Whether the classroom recitation or the forensic address is to be well recalled tomorrow will depend not simply on how well it has been acquired but also upon what other activities the person will have participated in meanwhile. The many careful researches on this subject leave us in no doubt: what one will retain over an interval of much interpolated activity will show impairment as compared with what he will retain over an interval of rest. This difference, moreover, will vary in its magnitude with differences in the nature of the interpolated work or rest, retention being best of all after an interval of sleep (see Figure 119).

For us at this time, the point is that what is responsible for the loss of a learned function is clearly not a passive fading away on its own part, but some active interference with it, *an inhibition of it by other functions that are going on.* Forgetting, in a word, is not simply a passive fading out but is a phase of the subject's active life.

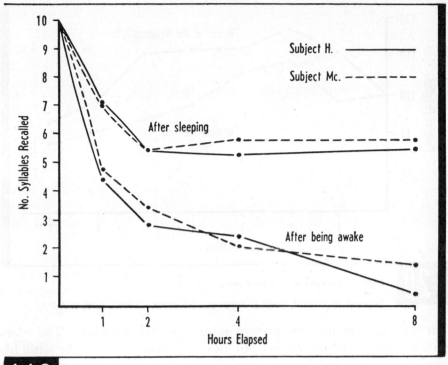

119 Average Number of Syllables Recalled After Intervals of Sleeping and of Being Awake

(From J. G. Jenkins and K. M. Dallenbach, AMER. J. PSYCHOL., *1924, 35, 605–612.)*

A curious discovery that further invites speculation as to the interacting play of learned processes and interferences is given the name *reminiscence*. This is not to be confused with the popular use of this word, but refers to improved recall after a delay following the original learning. School children memorized sections of poetry, though not to complete mastery, and were called upon to repeat them immediately after, and again after an interval of time (different groups of children being called upon at the different intervals). Let the children's ability to recall immediately be represented as 100 per cent; then their abilities to recall after the set intervals can be represented as relative to that. From Figure 120 it appears that they were able to recall the poetry better after intervals of one or a few days than they could immediately after learning. It must be admitted that such observations are exceptions to the general rule of loss of memorized material with passage of time.

Still another factor responsible for man's forgetting is the way in which his memories are altered in the very process of recalling them, so

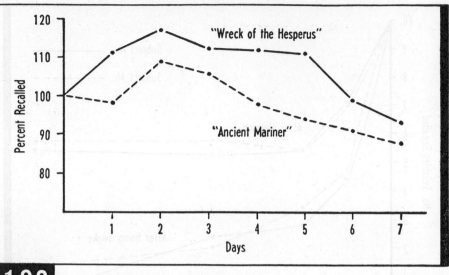

120 Reminiscence in Memory for Poetry

(*From P. B. Ballard*, Brit. J. Psychol., Monogr. Suppl., *1913*, 1, *No. 2.*)

that they may fit into the present pattern of his behavior. The "forgotten" things are not wiped out but are changed to fit in with his dominant moods and intents now. This takes us into the problems of recalling, which will be elaborated in the next section.

When all is said, however, we must remember that neural change is basic to learning, and the persistence of this neural change must somehow be recognized even though cellular activity is, as we have noted, always in a living and dynamic state.

Is a Habit Once Acquired Ever Lost?

It is interesting to ask whether or not a habit once acquired is ever entirely lost. Evidences against any such total forgetting seem to come from different sources. The accelerated form of curves for the *reacquiring of old habits* is in point. Outside the laboratory, too, this is to be seen in the surprisingly short time often taken by an adult to relearn some of his high school or college subjects which he supposed he had entirely lost. Consider the experiment in which selections of Greek drama were read aloud to an infant daily, with changes of selections every three months, from the age of 15 months to 3 years. When the boy was $8\frac{1}{2}$ years old he was set to learning these passages as well as new equal-length passages of similar material. The surprising result was that in every case the selections to which he had been exposed in his infancy were now learned (relearned) considerably faster than were any of the new ones [5].

A second way in which an apparent forgetting may not be a real and total loss is manifested in the way the training that a person has once had helps almost mysteriously *in learning new tasks*. The fretful freshman may wonder why he has so many required courses to take in subjects of which he is certain to forget the major part in the course of two or three years. But it is almost a certainty that those thousand-and-one bits of habits once acquired will continue to exert their influence in determining his point of view, his background, his *Anschauung*, to a degree distinctly noticeable and important. Indeed, this kind of transfer is the very essence of culture.

William James sums up the implications of this in his inimitable way:

> Let no youth have any anxiety about the upshot of his education, whatever the line of it may be. If he keeps faithfully busy each hour of the working day, he may safely leave the final result to itself. He can with perfect certainty count on waking up some fine morning, to find himself one of the competent ones of his generation, in whatever pursuit he may have singled out. Silently, between all the details of his business, the *power of judging* in all that class of matter will have built itself up within him as a possession that will never pass away.[1]

It is here that one sees the value of the hunch. It is here, too, that one should seek explanation for the intuitive wisdom with which the long-experienced practitioner sometimes mystifies the tyro. Many a family physician has become adept at diagnosing the common diseases at a glance; and there is salty truth in the story of the retiring judge who advised his successor about to graduate from bar to bench, "Don't be afraid to render your judgments: they will usually be right; but be careful in announcing your reasons: they will often be wrong."

Finally, we must not overlook the many kinds of unusual *recall under special conditions*. In the hypnotic state, for instance, or in the course of well-conducted psychoanalytic interviews, old forgotten memories have frequently been reawakened by the clinician; so that this becomes a therapeutic means of approach to those cases where a neurotic condition has its origin in a long-repressed incident (cf. discussions in Chapters 8 and 20). The crystal-gazer, upon reaching a sufficient degree of concentration may seem to observe in his glass ball scenes that he fails to recognize but that on a check-up turn out to be forgotten previous experiences. The anesthetic hand of an hysterical patient may automatically proceed to jot down old things once known but no longer recallable by the less dramatic processes of full waking thought. And if the tales be

[1] W. James, *Psychology* (New York: Henry Holt and Company, 1890), I, 127.

true, many a person drowning or falling from a height has lived to report most striking rehearsals of long-forgotten incidents under the stress of his emergency.   In a word, the traces of forgotten items of experience may not be totally lost beyond any reawakening but may only be *unavailable* to the ordinary efforts of recall.

REPRODUCING

Reproducing is a Way of Reacting

The measure of retention is recall, and the value of a person's learning inheres in his capacity to set at work again segments of behavior established formerly.   If recalling be an act, it cannot be an unstimulated response any more than an effect can be uncaused, but it must have its initial excitation in some extra- or intra-organic event or condition. Suppose a person finds himself repeating "Ich weiss nicht was soll es bedeuten."   This may be due to his having seen or heard the word "Heine" or even "Heinrich"; or he may have heard a snatch of Silcher's music, or only a certain tapped rhythm; or he may have heard the Rhine mentioned, or "mermaid" or "siren."   The name of an instructor, who once read the poem aloud or sang it in its musical arrangement, may have been heard or may have been pronounced by the subject himself in his soliloquy; or someone resembling the instructor may have passed on the street.   Or again, a revival of the particular emotional mood in which the poem had formerly been read might now effect a revival of the poem itself.   The speaking of the sentence has, in short, been a part of so many and so subtle events that the precise stimulation evoking its recall may be beyond detection.

The stimuli to recalled reactions, then, are many and fall into many types.   *Socially produced stimuli* are common — the words of the dinner-table conversation provide a potent and rich supply of stimuli to many a spoken or unspoken "that reminds me."   There are the *physical stimuli* of the world about: a certain type of headgear, a familiar train whistle, the string on one's finger (a placed "reminder"), a calendar, the pressures on foot and hand of pedals and steering wheel, moonlight on water, or, as in the case of Leonard Merrick's Conrad, a faint whiff of the peculiar perfume one's sweetheart wore in the long ago.   Then there are the *organic and emotional conditions;* such as the hunger that causes Arctic explorers to be musing continually — whether awake or asleep — about bountiful tables that they have formerly seen.   Some children, when given free word-association tests and picture-interpretation tests just before their meals responded with significantly more food-meaning answers than did children of a paired group who were given the same materials just after their meals, as shown in Table XXXI. Again, there

TABLE
XXXI   Appetite and Recall

Associations	Group	Number of Food Responses Before Meal	After Meal
Word-Associations	A	8	3
	B	2	2
Picture-Interpretations	A	7	4
	B	8	2

From R. N. Sanford, J. Psychol., *1936, 2, 134–135.*

is the reawakening of old reactions by stimulations via auditory and kinesthetic pathways from the *subject's own words, gestures, and bodily postures.* The following is an example of this last. The writer's ten-year-old son, who had been a great fan at university athletic events, was once being shown how to tie a better four-in-hand, when he cried, "Wait a minute, wait a minute, let me!" The rhythm of this speech rearoused some well-integrated cheering activities he had frequently performed in concert in the bleachers; and he stepped over to the mirror, calling over the above words to the tempo and beat of a college cheer, accompanying it with motions of a cheer leader, and finishing up with a drawn-out "Wait — wait — wait." Then there is Proust's protagonist who happened to step backward onto uneven flagstones and was thereby reminded vividly of a day in Venice when he had stood on the uneven flagstones at Saint Mark's — "and with that sensation came all the others connected with it that day, which had been waiting in their proper place in the series of forgotten days, until a sudden happening had imperiously commanded them to come forth." [1]

There is no recalling, then, without some kind of present stimulus. Or, to turn this statement into a more practical form, if you want a person to recall some former activity, you should supply an appropriate stimulus — one that is connected to that activity by previous experience, or contains an element that is so connected.

[1] From *Remembrance of Things Past* ("The Past Recaptured," trans. by Frederick A. Blossom. New York: Random House), II, 992.

A Phase of Adjustive Behavior

The whole truth is not yet told when we speak of a man's recalling as reacting. He is indeed so active in this reacting that he makes contributions of his own. The unintended falsification of memory at the very moment of recall is a well-recognized phenomenon in everyday life — and one not limited to the witness stand, nor to children, either.

A technique for getting this phenomenon under scrutiny is to have subjects who have been exposed to a situation or story attempt to reproduce it after different intervals, and then to compare their accounts for any definite trends of change. Sir Frederic Bartlett of Cambridge University, England, had students read a tale from American Indian folklore; then at various intervals (ranging from fifteen minutes to ten years) they were asked for reproductions. The experimenter made no quantitative count of details lost, but was interested rather in a qualitative analysis of what happens to the material in the recalling. He did notice a simple forgetting, in that stories were simplified by the dropping out of proper names, definite numbers, and the like. But he observed at the same time some tendency to elaborate the story by transforming some items into more familiar ones or even by inventing and inserting new ones. We are interested here to note that what was particularly well retained was the subject's reactions to the general plan, scheme, form, order, arrangement, and that omissions were mostly of items unessential to this general form, while the inventions and transformations were usually quite in harmony with it. Of this we are assured by the

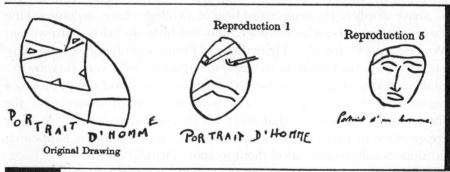

Reproduction 1

Reproduction 5

Original Drawing

121   **Changes Occurring in Reproduced Material**

The original primitive drawing was shown one observer who redrew it from memory to show to a second observer, he to a third, and so on. Both elaboration and simplification are in the direction of a schematic form current in the group of subjects. The figure becomes thus easier to handle. (*From F. C. Bartlett,* REMEMBERING, *Cambridge University Press, 1932, 178. After Philippe. By permission of the author.*)

evidence: when a person is originally reacting to a (story) situation, he is reacting not simply to its details in piecemeal fashion but also to the whole general pattern or configuration; and when recalling that experience *he recalls it primarily as a general pattern or configuration*, and his errors are errors in harmony with it. Indeed, Bartlett found that the distorting of recalled details to fit the general scheme often proceeded to the point of naïve rationalizations in which definite reasons were furnished by the subject for new items he had quite unwittingly introduced.

The process of memory changes toward a more familiar form is graphically revealed in Figure 121.

From the above it is clear that recalling is not mere reproducing, it is usually some *process of adjustment* that the individual is making to *some problem* at the time, one in which his *personal interest* is to some extent enlisted.

Some Objective Determinants of Recall

The richness of human experience is such that any sight, sound, or other stimulus may be capable of arousing any of several very different reactions. It is a commonplace that the one appropriate response to an automobile horn, to a request for a loan, or to a proposal of marriage is sure to be determined by many coincident and qualifying circumstances: who is concerned, where and when the stimulation occurs. And so it is with the re-exciting of an old habit: that one of the reactions formerly coupled to the stimulus which will now be called forth depends upon many things.

For over a century, certain factors, *secondary laws of association*, have been considered as among the conditions that determine which of many possible responses is the one most likely to be reinstated. These secondary laws of association, which were originally the fruit of everyday observation, have since been corroborated in the laboratory. They are as follows. *Other things being equal:*

(1) The $S \longrightarrow R$ connection or series of connections most frequently exercised is the one most apt to be operative later (the law of *frequency*). Of the various faces seen in pictures or in life, a person is most likely to recognize the one he has seen oftenest. The right rather than the wrong way of spelling "occasion," of writing the product of "11 times 12," of speaking the lines of a play, depends for its proper selection, and especially its fixation, upon this law of frequency. This is the gist of the old saw that practice makes perfect. Paderewski is said to have insisted, "If I leave off practice one day, I know it; if two days, my friends know it; if three days, everybody knows it."

(2) The most recently used function is the one most apt to be re-aroused later (the law of *recency*). The student does special reviewing just before his examination. The lawyer concentrates on his brief just before a case is to be called up. One can repeat in full a conversation of yesterday, but a conversation of a year ago only by snatches and distortions, or not at all. (We have taken note of a seeming exception to this principle in the phenomenon of "reminiscence.")

(3) The first $S \longrightarrow R$ function used is most easily reinstated later (the law of *primacy*). One is often able to give a better account of the happenings during his first day in college or his first day in the new business office, remembers better his first medical case, his first ocean or air voyage.

(4) The function organized with the greatest *intensity* is the one most likely to reappear later. Every teacher, whether in factory or in school, knows that his pupil's overt and implicit reactions that are made attentively have a greater recall value than those performed in a perfunctory manner. To this end the instructor may adopt various devices for enhancing the stimuli: raising the voice, lowering it, using diagrams, using red chalk, using motion pictures, and so on. The learner, for his part, may employ various ways of intensifying the original stimulation, such as taking a concentrated attitude toward the lecture, book, or experiment. *Emotionalizing* the reaction to a stimulus seems often to strengthen its readiness on later recall. For months after a child's death the parents may be quickly and excessively reactive to any situation containing elements in common with earlier experiences with the child. The lovelorn is excitable by stimuli in any way conditioned by or associated with the sight and sound of his loved one, often to the well-nigh total exclusion of any other kind of behavior.

These four classic laws have been experimentally confirmed even to different *degrees* or *kinds* of frequency, of recency, of primacy, and of intensity. A lecturer once read aloud to ten different groups of college students a fictitious biographical sketch containing seventy items; and they were immediately to try to reproduce it. The first items had of course the advantage of primacy, and the last, of recency. (In changing from group to group the lecturer switched the order of the particular items to control the variable of differences in their content.) Some of the items were given the advantage of frequency by being repeated immediately or later in the recital. Some of them were intensified by devices of word or hand.

In Table XXXII the results for all groups are reproduced in percentages. The frequency of recall of the items falling in the middle part of the biography, and having no reinforcement by repetition nor intensification, is represented as 100 per cent. The reader will note by casting his eye down the columns that all but one of the particular methods of applying the four laws did strengthen the recall above the normal standard. He will also discern interesting and important differences in the effect of variations within each of the four methods.

TABLE XXXII	Advantages for Recall of Primacy, Recency, Frequency, and Intensity

Middle neutral (taken as normal)	100%
Primacy	
the 1st item	175
the 2nd item	163
the 3rd item	135
Recency	
the 68th item	123
the 69th item	119
the 70th (last) item	128
Frequency	
given 3 repetitions	197
given 4 repetitions	246
given 5 repetitions	315
Intensity	
followed by "Did you notice that?"	154
spoken slowly	79
accompanied by a bang of the fist	115
accompanied by a gesture	118
in louder voice	126
followed by a pause	143
preceded by "Now get this"	191

From A. T. Jersild, J. Exp. Psychol., 1929, 12, 62.

Incidentally, this study illustrates neatly the second great office of the experimental method in the advancement of knowledge: not only does it check and verify everyday observations, but it goes on to work out the detailed conditions, the qualifying circumstances. Instead merely of following up popular experience, it goes on ahead.

(5) Research experiences lead us to add a fifth law to these classic ones, that of *identity of setting and context*. Investigators of animal behavior, especially Carr at the University of Chicago Laboratory, found that after a white rat had learned to run a maze successfully, any change

made in some detail of the general environment (even though not an alteration in the true path that had been learned) affected the rearousal of its habit. The animal might hesitate, or even momentarily lose its way. The alterations were of various kinds: the illumination of the room was slightly increased or decreased or was switched from artificial light to daylight; or the experimenter stood in another place; or the maze was rotated on its pedestal so that its direction was changed; or the maze was moved to another part of the room; or some very slight detail inside the maze was altered. So potent did such incidentals prove that precautions to control them have now become part of the standard laboratory procedure.

In human investigations the point is no less well demonstrated. One recalls memorized materials most completely when the general surroundings are the same as on the occasions when he first acquired them: the same room, the same time of day, the same experimenter or experimenters present, even the same pervading laboratory odors. The same holds true for the narrower environmental conditions called *context*. One of Carr's students had Chinese and American subjects learn word-pairs, some of them being printed on cards that bore extraneous words in smaller type which the subjects were to disregard. When these incidental words were changed, it became more difficult to recall the essential word-pair. The subjects were also given faces and names to be learned in changing contexts. Twenty-four pictures of human faces cut from popular magazines were pasted with new names on postcards, some of these being picture postcards which then served as visible context. The results in Table XXXIII exhibit a definite trend in the

TABLE XXXIII	The Effect of Changed Context on Recall Number of Names Correctly Given to Pictures After 48 Hours

Context	Subjects	
	A B C D E F	O P Q R S T
Unchanged	6 2 8 5 6 7	8 6 5 7 7 10
Changed	3 0 3 4 5 9	3 8 7 3 4 5

The pictures used with unchanged contexts for subjects A to F were used with changed contexts for subjects O to T; and vice versa.

From S. Pan, J. Exp. Psychol., *1926, 9, 486.*

direction of the importance of stable context in promoting good recall.

The facilitating effect of unchanged surroundings has found amusing illustration in the established habits of certain famous writers. Balzac had to put on a monk's costume when he sat down to write; Buffon donned his cuffs and dress coat; Joyce felt it necessary to dress entirely in white like a surgeon. To these cases we may add others. There is Saroyan's fictitious character, private Wesley Jackson, who could not play his trombone for his buddies until someone had found him a straw hat. The boy in the little red schoolhouse lost his leadership in spelling after his rival had filled up the knot hole in the floor into which he had habitually thrust his toe. A young preacher assigned to deliver a well-learned sermon before his college literary society begged for a stand, table, desk or anything that could play stand-in for his usual pulpit, else he could not remember his phrases.

> An individual lived for several years in China and laboriously acquired the ability to speak the Chinese language. Upon his return to this country for a couple of years' vacation he found to his dismay that his ability to speak and understand this language had practically disappeared by the end of this time. Naturally he expected that a considerable amount of effort and time would be required to relearn the language, but to his surprise he found that he was able to speak the language quite fluently upon his return to China. . . . There is the old story of the Irish porter who misplaced a package while drunk and was able to recall its location during a subsequent period of drunkenness.[1]

(The disturbing effect of unusual surroundings on one's ability to think is illustrated again on page 483.)

Subjective Determinants are Important

Closely related to objective context is the subject's set. Out of all his learned repertoire, just which response a person is likely to revive on a given occasion depends upon what he is set for, what determining tendency may be uppermost, what he is expecting.

Place before a number of school children the problem

$$\frac{36}{17}$$

and simply ask them to "do" it, and you are fairly sure to get three very different responses: 53, 19, and 612. Each is a correct enough answer which has been drilled as the R to such S's. Each, however, was acquired in a certain context of material, when the pupil was doing a certain

[1] From H. A. Carr, *Psychology* (New York: Longmans, Green and Company, 1925).

kind of thing and was thereby set to continue that kind of thing. The reactions leading to the answer 53, for instance, were originally acquired when adding happened to be the order of the day. If a teacher, then, would test whether a pupil can multiply the two numbers 36 and 17, it is not sufficient to place these two visual patterns before him. He must be prepared to multiply — either by being given the verbal signal "multiply this," or by being occupied previously with multiplying — so that when he addresses these new figures he is primed, oriented, set in the right direction.

Important in a person's set is his *mood of the moment*, and this is indeed an important determinant as to which old habits will reassert themselves. The Dead March from *Saul*, Chopin's Marche Funebre, the last movement of Tschaikowsky's Sixth Symphony, come more readily from the fingers or the throat of the musician who is steeped in sorrow than does Anitra's Dance, March of the Sardar, or the last movement of Beethoven's Ninth. So, too, the man who is in love is more likely to repeat snatches of lyrical, springtime verse than lines from some solemn epic. Such illustrations remind us that the emotional segments of the whole motor attitude are there and are operative. Emotional congruity is a determining factor in recalling.

Experimental results confirm these general observations of the strong influence of a person's present set and mood upon the rearousal of his habits. Subjects were once provided with printed lists of skeleton words whose missing letters they were to supply. Some of the lists were headed with a statement that "the following are names of familiar fruits," or "of American authors," or "of domestic animals." Other lists were not described further than as miscellaneous nouns. The exact time required for each person to complete each list was noted, and a comparison was drawn between the average time for the classified and for the unclassified lists. For every one of the 28 individuals, the average for the classified was found to be shorter than for the unclassified, the group averages being, respectively, 36 sec. and 1 min. 15 sec. The establishing of a set in some particular direction, as in that of naming fruits, or authors, or animals, not only dictated which previously acquired response would be reproduced but also facilitated its reproduction. A preliminary orientation or set, we may conclude, aids definitely in recall.

The Scientific Study of Testimony

So important is the subjective determinant in recall that it has always furnished a most serious practical problem in the evaluation of legal testimony. Not only is the average man subject to errors, but even the trained reporter may frequently betray his own limitations either in observing or in recalling an event.

Consider for example the following court case, as reported in the *Raleigh News and Observer*. A Mr. Dietz was charged with the killing of a Mr. Kelly, in broad daylight, on a public street, in plain view of numerous witnesses.

> On motion of the defense Judge Shaw ordered all witnesses excluded from the court room until they had testified; and some wide discrepancies in testimony developed. No two witnesses saw the shooting alike. Some said four shots were fired, others six. Some said Kelly rushed Dietz before any shots were fired, others that Kelly stood still and retreated under fire. None seemed to have seen Dietz back into an automobile driven by Mrs. E. A. Gregory, until that lady, who had been scared nearly out of her wits, told about it. Some say Kelly held an auto plate in his left hand; others saw nothing in either hand. Mrs. Gregory saw something shiny like nickel in his right hand.

Some fifty years ago, Stern initiated research on the reliability of report by using *Aussage* or testimony experiments. One has come to be known as the "dramatic incident" method. In one case he says: "My lecture was interrupted by the entrance of a gentleman who spoke with me and took a book from the bookcase, the performance having been exactly studied beforehand in all its details. The members of the seminar gave but little attention to what was going on. A week later they were required to report upon what had taken place." As frequently used by scores of teachers since, the event may contain much action, sound, and fury, so that the effect of distracting and emotion-arousing elements of the situation may be observed.

The many investigators of testimony agree that the more immature the subject, the more unreliable the report. For one thing, his suggestibility is greater. A young child on the witness stand, we can be assured, is of exceedingly doubtful value to any court. Other factors that enter in to distort testimony are a low level of general intelligence, the subject's emotional attitudes, the emotion-exciting character of the event in question, and the nature of the questions in the examination and the cross examination. These are but a few of many psychological points about human fallibility that, as experimentally demonstrable and measurable facts, are bound to be increasingly recognized in the legal process of seeking the truth about an event that is in question.

Some Special Difficulties in Recalling

A man who has never shown distress when seeking to rearouse an old reaction is as fortunate as he is rare. It seems to be the portion of humanity that sometimes when occasion arises for the prompt use of a certain part of a man's former equipment, that part stubbornly refuses to be recalled. On his first night the budding actor may hear the cue for the speech that he has learned by heart, and yet be able only to stutter and shiver before the sea of upturned faces. The overanxious young host, upon presenting an old friend to a different circle of acquaintances, may suddenly and unaccountably forget his old friend's name, though he has spoken it readily enough dozens and hundreds of times. A student recently told the writer that at his own wedding reception he had been unable to recall his bride's name.

What causes such irregularities in human performance? In the case of several, it is fairly obvious that emotional complications are at the root of the difficulty. We have already seen that many grosser emotional reactions operate to block the smooth-running activities of more delicate and elaborate reaction mechanisms. The more primitive and lower-center processes, taking their right of way, inhibit later acquired and higher-center processes. *Intense emotion*, particularly fear, will then block attempts to recall such delicately organized activities as the language responses — will render negative the effects of stimuli to them. Anxiety over an examination often renders an otherwise well-informed person partially helpless, so that he sets down answers which on cooler reflection he knows to have been wrong.

In the same class with these recognizable emotional blockings is the less dramatic *interference by antagonistic habits*. Skillful speakers can be overcome with confusion when a certain phrase just uttered has the power to start them off on two different lines of serial reaction, and the set and context are not sufficient to determine the recall of one alone. The difficulty observed in introductions, mentioned above, is of this type also. Let a person start asking himself, "Now let's see, shall I be able to speak each name properly or shan't I?" — and this question is given so undue an amount of his attending that the naming reactions become displaced (inhibited). The trouble, then, is in allowing too many antagonistic stimuli to be operative.

> The centipede was happy quite until the toad in fun
> Said, "Pray, which leg comes after which?"
> This raised her doubts to such a pitch
> She fell distracted in the ditch,
> Unable now to run.

Another form of failure in recall has been stressed by the psychopathologists. In cases when a subject may be unable to recall a name or a number, analysis of his past life and the conditions under which the desired reaction was once acquired or with which it had later been conditioned may bring to light a somewhat more complicated causal explanation. Suppose a scene, a story, a form of socially forbidden behavior, to be of a character so strongly emotional as to arouse an avoidance reaction by the subject. By conditioning, the avoidance or repression may come to function as the regular R to any S that may have been in any way connected with the original avoided situation. The substitute R has become the habitual way of dealing with such occasions. The original R has been forgotten, or, as the psychoanalysts prefer to say, "repressed." We may well recall the cases of forgetting by repression given on pages 191 ff.

RECOGNIZING [1]

As a Test of Memory

The degree to which a particular learned mode of reaction has been retained up to a given time may be tested by the method of recognition. A series of stimuli (for example, nonsense syllables, digits, geometrical designs) once presented to the subject for memorizing are subsequently presented again in conjunction with other stimuli to see how many of the first series he can identify in the second. It is a universal result of experiments that the subject can recognize many items that he has been unable to reproduce by direct recall. So too in everyday life, countless are the musical airs, the passages of prose or poetry, the names of acquaintances that one can identify promptly upon hearing or seeing them, but few are those that one can resurrect without special and elaborate aids. The unhappy public speaker searching for his word would recognize it instantly were someone only to whisper it to him.

Ability to recognize correctly is another aspect of memory that is important from a legal standpoint. The identification of suspects by injured parties or by incidental witnesses is at times taken as sufficient evidence for conviction; and it is unfortunate that the authorities take too little account of the errors so easily committed. For instance, to have a witness identify by indicating whether a single person or a single thing presented before him is the one in question is little more than worthless on account of the powerful suggestive effect, and whenever possible he should be called upon to pick out the man or object from a group of similar persons or things.

[1] Properly speaking, recognizing is a phase of reproducing, but as some special studies have been directed to this phase alone, and as one may at times recall without recognizing, we may follow the precedent of treating it as involving a fourth set of problems.

Age Differences

It has commonly been believed that one's neural connections change in some way through the years of childhood, and that thereby one's basic memory capacity and learning ability are increased. The evidence, however, is certainly ambiguous. Consider, for instance, the results of a research in which children of different ages were tested for their ability to learn poetry and also to memorize nonsense syllables. The results as plotted in Figure 122 show that the older the child, the

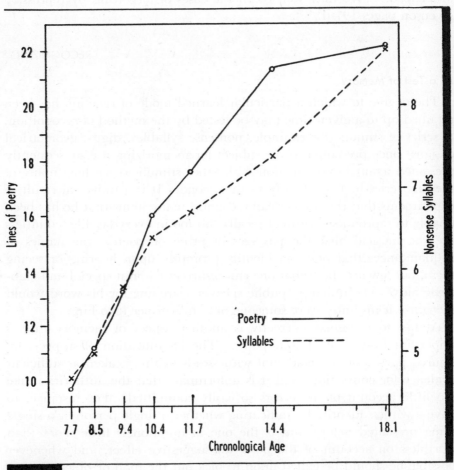

122 Age Changes in Learning Ability in Childhood

(Stroud and Maul. Data from J. B. Stroud, Psychology in Education, *Longmans, 1946. By permission of author and publishers.)*

greater is his learning of both meaningful and relatively meaningless material. To what shall we attribute such improvement with age? To increasing *retentiveness* of the neural tissues? Or to improvement in *habits* of attending and *methods* of memorizing? Or again, can we explain it in terms of greater familiarity with the materials, greater *knowledge* as a basis for understanding? There is scanty evidence on which to choose among the three explanations, although psychologists are inclined to discount the first in favor of the other two.

What quantitative changes in learning and remembering may be expected to come with *maturity* and declining years? In one investigation in California, three age-groups of 40 subjects each (young, middle-aged, and old) were asked to learn two motor and three verbal tasks. The motor tasks (pursuit) consisted of (*a*) trying to keep the end of a pointer in contact with a small brass button mounted on a revolving phonograph disk, the contact being necessary to close a circuit and rotate the disk (score taken in number of rotations in a given time); and (*b*) doing the same, but watching disk and hand as reflected in a mirror. The verbal tasks were to memorize (*c*) lists of paired-associates (man-boy, etc.); (*d*) lists of nonsense equations ($E \times Z = G$); and (*e*) false multiplications ($3 \times 5 = 25$). The data obtained are presented in Table XXXIV

TABLE
XXXIV   Age Changes in Learning Ability After Maturity

Mean scores of three age-groups in learning new tasks of more and less congruence with old established habits. The scores for the young group are taken as 100%.

Test	Young (12–17 yrs.)	Middle-Aged (34–59 yrs.)	Old (60–85 yrs.)
Motor learning			
a. Direct vision	100%	98%	84%
b. Mirror vision	100	96	53
Verbal learning			
c. Paired associates	100	92	82
d. Nonsense equations	100	80	48
e. False multiplications	100	72	47

From F. L. Ruch, J. GEN. PSYCHOL., *1934, 11, 277.*

as ratios between the results of the different age-groups. Thus, considering the mean score for motor learning by direct vision on the part of the young as 100 per cent, the score of the middle aged was 98 per cent and the score of the old, 84 per cent. As we scrutinize the data we perceive little decline in learning ability at middle life, but a considerable one after 60 years. An interesting difference appears between the ability of the old to acquire habits built directly on previously established habits and their ability to acquire habits that contradict and are presumably interfered with by the established habits. Here as elsewhere we are reminded that the fate of a learned item or act depends not so much upon change in it itself as upon its relations to other items and acts, old and new.

Artificial Mnemonic Systems

Everyone is familiar with certain simple artificial devices that aid in recall: "Thirty days hath September" for the number of days in the month; "Wash-Ad-Jeff-Mad-Mon-Ad-Jack" for the presidents; "frip" for the objective determinants of recall, and the like.

The student of mathematics can easily learn the value of π (pi) to the thirteenth decimal place by memorizing the doggerel:

> How I wish I could determine
> Of circle round
> The exact relation
> Arkimedes found,

and then setting down the number of letters in each successive word: 3.1415926535895.

The gunner can keep straight the three symbols W (width of target in yards), M (width in mils), and R (range in thousands of yards) by repeating the word, $WORM$; then translating: W Over RM or $\dfrac{W}{RM}$.

The student of psychology and neurology is helped in recalling in order the names of the twelve cranial nerves — the olfactory, optic, oculomotor, trochlear, trigeminal, abducens, facial, auditory, glossopharyngeal, vagus, accessory, and hypoglossal — by repeating to himself the lines:

> On old Olympus' topmost top,
> A fat armed German viewed a hop.

Such devices are useful for dealing with material that does not lend itself to logical analysis or fall into any meaningful order.

Sound Memory Training

What is to be recommended as rational training? Memory capacity is not "the memory" which, like a biceps muscle, can be strengthened by repetitious exercise. Improvement must come by training in the *ways* of learning, the technique. If formal memory training is to be advocated in the schools, let it not be the study of this or that particular subject in which disciplinary potencies are thought peculiarly to reside, but instruction and guidance in the best methods of studying. Here there is nothing to be added to the principles already enumerated and discussed in this chapter. Many of the points made, for example, on the acquiring of habits and on the recalling of habits, have been put forward not simply as scientific facts or laws but also as rules of economy and utility; and the student eager and conscientious and persistent in adapting them to his individual needs will be abundantly rewarded. But as we saw exemplified in a transfer experiment (pages 378 ff.), there is no short cut, no royal road.

REFERENCES

1. Ballard, P. B. "Oblivescence and reminiscence," *Brit. J. Psychol. Monogr. Suppl.*, 1913, *1*, No. 2.
2. Bartlett, F. C. *Remembering.* Cambridge, Eng.: Cambridge University Press, 1932.
3. Bills, A. G. *General Experimental Psychology.* New York: Longmans, Green and Company, 1934. Part III.
4. Bruce, R. W. "Conditions of transfer of training," *J. Exp. Psychol.*, 1933, *16*, 343–361.
5. Burtt, H. E. "Experimental study of early childhood memory," *J. Genet. Psychol.*, 1932, *40*, 287–295; 1941, *58*, 435–439.
6. Ebbinghaus, H. *Memory* (trans. by Ruger and Bussenius). New York: Teachers College, Columbia University, 1913.
7. Hovland, C. I. "Experimental studies in rote learning theory, VII," *J. Exp. Psychol.*, 1940, *27*, 271–284.
8. Jersild, A. T. "Primacy, recency, frequency, and vividness," *J. Exp. Psychol.*, 1929, *12*, 58–70.
9. McGeoch, J. A. "The vertical dimensions of mind," *Psychol. Rev.*, 1936, *43*, 107–129.
10. Meumann, E. *The Psychology of Learning.* New York: Appleton, 1913.
11. Myers, C. S. *Text-Book of Experimental Psychology.* New York: Longmans, Green and Company, 1911. Chapters XII, XIII.
12. Postman, L., and V. L. Senders. "Incidental learning and generality of set," *J. Exp. Psychol.*, 1946, *36*, 153–165.
13. Rubin-Rabson, G. "Studies in the Psychology of memorizing piano music, VI," *J. Educ. Psychol.*, 1941, *32*, 593–602.
14. Sanford, E. C. "A letter to Dr. Titchener," in *Studies in Psychology*, Louis N. Wilson. 1917.

15. Schmidt, H. O. "Effects of praise and blame," *Psychol. Monogr.*, 1941, *53*, No. 240.

16. Schulze, R. *Experimental Psychology and Pedagogy* (trans. by R. Pintner). London: George Allen and Unwin, 1912. Chapter VIII.

17. Seashore, H., *et al.* "A comparative study of three methods of teaching code." (OSRD, 1944; Publ. Bd., No. 12–167.) Washington, D.C.: U.S. Dept. of Commerce, 1946.

18. Sharp, Agnes A. "An experimental test of Freud's doctrine of the relation of hedonic tone to memory revival," *J. Exp. Psychol.*, 1938, *22*, 395–418.

19. Shellow, S. M. "Individual differences in incidental memory," *Arch. Psychol.*, *N.Y.*, 1923, *10*, No. 64.

20. Stroud, J. B., and R. Maul. "The influence of age upon learning and retention of poetry and nonsense syllables," *J. Genet. Psychol.*, 1933, *42*, 242–250.

21. Thorndike, E. L., and R. S. Woodworth. "The influence of improvement in one mental function upon the efficiency of other functions," *Psychol. Rev.*, 1901, *8*, 247–261, 384–395, 553–564.

22. Thorndike, E. L. *Educational Psychology*, vol. II. New York: Teachers College, Columbia University, 1913.

23. Whipple, G. M. *Manual of Mental and Physical Tests.* Second edition. Vol. II. Baltimore: Warwick and York, 1915.

24. Wolfle, D. "Military training and the useful parts of learning theory," *J. Consult. Psychol.*, 1946, *10*, 73–75.

25. Woodrow, H. "The effect of type of training upon transference," *J. Educ. Psychol.*, 1927, *18*, 159–172.

26. Woodworth, R. S. *Experimental Psychology.* New York: Henry Holt and Company, 1938. Chapters II, III, IV, VII, VIII, IX.

15

LEARNING AS ADAPTIVE BEHAVIOR

THE BIOLOGICAL VIEWPOINT RESUMED

IN THE PRECEDING CHAPTER we studied learning as a phase of human living. We have given major attention to the kinds of learning usually called memory and motor skill, for they are of most immediate practical concern to the college student or professional or business or industrial man. To integrate our knowledge of learning with other psychological topics, however, and to see its relation to the whole picture of man engaged in living his life, we should assume the broader biological perspective.

Many of the principles of learning, in fact, have been derived from experimental studies of other animal forms than *Homo sapiens*. As in other areas of psychology, here again it is extremely helpful to note phenomena as they are manifested more simply in the living of lower animals.

A Method of Survival

In the competition between animals for place on this earth and for food and other materials of subsistence, a competition which we have seen to be the story of life at all levels of physical and psychological organization, we can discern several principles of survival — several ways in which individuals of a species are enabled to maintain life and live long enough to reproduce their kind, so keeping that species extant. The simplest principle is *fecundity*. So great is the toll exacted by climate, disease, and predatory animals that only those types of life can be perpetuated that reproduce their kind in excess numbers. One conger eel lays fifteen million eggs; and although nothing like fifteen million ever hatch and grow into adults, out of so many the chances are enhanced for some to survive. This simple numerical method of surviving is the main reliance of very low animal forms. Of Nature it has been said:

> So careful of the type she seems,
> So careless of the single life.

Another principle of survival is seen to some degree throughout the animal kingdom. Other things being equal, that particular animal type has a better chance of surviving that is *well adapted* to its conditions of life. The diving beetle has fully retained its terrestrial mode of respiration, but has an improved means of carrying air with it when diving. The dull color of the field sparrow enables it to escape the view of the hawk, and at the same time helps it approach its own prey undetected. The color of the coat of the Arctic fox, white in winter and grayish brown in summer, adapts it similarly to aggressive activities.

In the vertebrates, especially the mammals, and most especially the Primates, another principle of animal survival comes to the fore. Other things being equal, that species which is *adaptable* or intelligent and can learn has the advantage over others and will eventually outstrip them. Moreover, if the species is adaptable enough, the other conditions need not be equal, for great disadvantages of slow rate of reproduction or poor inborn adjustments to the details of the surrounding world may be more than counterbalanced by an individual's readiness to change its front, to find new ways out of difficult conditions, and to refrain from committing again old and dangerous errors.

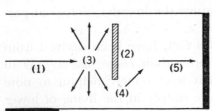

123 Diagram of Adjustive Behavior Leading to Learning

1, the organism is motivated to respond in the direction 5; when blocked, 2, it makes varied and excess reactions, 3, until by some reaction, 4, it surmounts the obstacle and is readjusted. On later occasions the organism is likely to meet the situation by making the successful response, 4, more and more directly.

Of the three principles mentioned (fecundity, being natively adapted, and being adaptable) the third is plainly the most advantageous. It means economy of individual lives, so that birth rate and death rate may both be reduced to a minimum. In the long run it means also a superior mode of meeting the conditions of life. If only they are variable and resourceful, quick to mend their ways and prompt to seize any new advantage, a few individuals can get the upper hand of an innumerable horde of hidebound and too-machine-like creatures. That is the basic reason for man's dominance. His outstanding trait is his incomparable capacity to profit by experience, to change his environment, and to change himself.

Let us recall our earlier analysis of the adjustment process with the help of the diagram again (Figure 123). A motivated person or other organism (1), upon encountering an obstruction or difficulty (2), shows excess and varied activity (3), until one of his variant ways of acting chances to take him around his difficulty (4) and a goal or a more nearly optimal situation is obtained (5). It is now relevant to observe an additional feature of much behavior of this sort. When the person *again* encounters much the same difficulty, he tends to hit upon and utilize the appropriate solution (4) more readily and with less fuss and confusion. And when the situation is repeated *on succeeding occasions* the individual's process of adjustment shows *an increased directness and effectiveness, an economy of effort and of time.*[1] A *habit* has been established; that is, *a response or response-pattern has been developed as a result of previous experience.* Our problem now is to study at close hand this improvement phenomenon.

THE TRIAL–AND–ERROR BASIS OF LEARNING

The most elaborate studies of animal learning have been carried out with vertebrates. The English biologist, Lloyd Morgan, had earlier pointed out that to build up a psychology of animals by collecting and analyzing anecdotes about them was an unscientific procedure. After detailing certain cases of remarkable performance by his own dog, Tony (as opening a gate at will, or waiting for the rebound of a ball), he had shown that the real explanation of the performance lay in its genesis, in the earlier habit formations of the dog. And those habit formations were a matter of "varied trial-and-error with the utilization of chance successes." [2] This insight gave the cue for American investigations, and laboratory study of how animals form habits was begun.

The three principal types of habit formation in lower animals studied

[1] The reader will not confuse "learning" with other sorts of modification of behavior, such as "fatigue," which is a temporary reduction of capacity to respond after continued exercise, and "sensory adaptation," which is a temporary adaptation to a stimulus or situation so that it is no longer effective. The differentiating mark of true learning, we may say, is the test of time.

[2] Again the basic dialectic of all natural progress, which we have noted before (for example, as in Chapters 2 and 3) and shall meet again (as in Chapter 19): *variation* and *selection.*

in the early years by American comparative psychologists were *manipulation* habits, *discrimination* habits, and *locomotor* habits. Let us survey these briefly for two reasons, namely: (1) each type of habit is still being utilized today in one or another investigation, in more elaborate form; (2) each line of early investigation, when taken with critical refinements later introduced, will direct our attention to some fundamental characteristics of the learning process.

The Problem Box Method

Thorndike introduced the problem box as a device for observing how an animal that one sees undoing a lock, lifting a lever, ringing a doorbell,

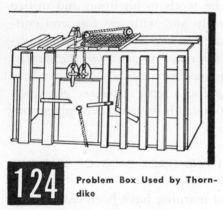

124   **Problem Box Used by Thorndike**

(*From E. L. Thorndike, "Animal intelligence,"* PSYCHOL. MONOGR., *1898, 2, No. 4.*)

or performing some other apparently remarkable stunt, actually comes to have such a manipulating ability at his command. His method was to put a very hungry cat or dog into a box from which it could escape only by doing some simple act, such as pressing a lever, pulling at a loop of cord, or stepping on a platform. Food was placed outside the box to insure that the animal was well motivated, and its behavior was then closely observed. A record was kept of the time the animal was in the box before it performed the necessary act. The general arrangement of the door and some of its fastenings, used one at a time, may be understood from Figure 124.

A learning curve was drawn to show changes in the amount of time taken by the animal in successive attempts to escape. In Figure 125 is reproduced a sample of Thorndike's curves. Distances on the abscissa represent the order of the trials, distances on the ordinate the amounts of time taken. From the more or less gradual and irregular slope of the curves Thorndike argued that the animals came to do things quite by accident, by chance, rather than by anything like understanding. This certainly accords with his observation of their behavior:

> When put into the box the cat would show evident signs of discomfort and of an impulse to escape from confinement. It tries to squeeze through any opening; it claws and bites at the bars or wire; it thrusts its paws out through any opening and claws at everything it reaches; it continues its efforts when it strikes anything loose and shaky; it may claw at things

within the box. . . . The vigor with which it struggles is extraordinary. For eight or ten minutes it will claw and bite and squeeze incessantly. . . . The cat that is clawing all over the box in her impulsive struggle will probably claw the string or loop or button so as [accidentally] to open the door. And gradually all the other nonsuccessful impulses will be stamped out and the particular impulse leading to the successful act will be stamped in . . . until, after many trials, the cat will, when put in the box, immediately claw the button or loop in a definite way. . . . Cats would claw at the loop or button when the door was open. . . . Cats would paw at the place where a loop had been, though none was there. The reaction was not to a well-discriminated object, but to a vague situation, and any element of the situation may arouse the reaction.

From E. L. Thorndike, "Animal intelligence,"
PSYCHOL. REV. MONOGR. SUPPL., *1898, 2, No. 4.*

Here we have a description of the way an animal learns which in more general terms may be taken as an account of the main features of any animal learning, at least as viewed by the early comparative psychologists. A few salient points of this behavior deserve our examination.

(1) The animal is definitely *motivated*. It is seeking to gain something or to avoid something. We may say it is, however blindly, *goal*-directed.

(2) The motivated animal facing the problematic situation displays *random* and *variable* kinds of reaction, which seem to occur in a wholly fortuitous manner.

(3) In the course of repeated trials there occurs a process of *selection*. Certain of the random responses (usually those successful in the sense

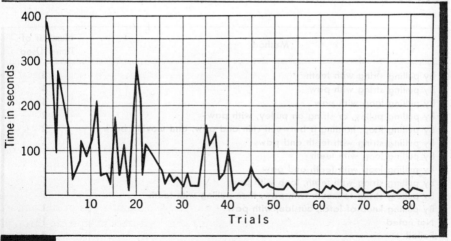

125 **Curve to Show Rate of Learning by an Animal in a Problem Box**

(*From E. L. Thorndike, "Animal Intelligence,"* PSYCHOL. MONOGR., *1898, 2, No. 4.*)

of advancing the subject toward his goal) tend to be repeated and *stamped in*, while others (usually those unsuccessful in advancing the subject to his goal) tend to be *dropped out*.

(4) Eventually an effective habit becomes established, in which the animal makes a *definite movement* or *set of movements*, which are the motor aspect of the habit.

(5) This habitual movement or pattern of movements is made to a *particular stimulus* or *stimulus-pattern*.

That is the general picture. As we look briefly at the different types of experimental investigation as illustrated in pioneer researches we shall see all these principles exemplified in general.

Then, as we take note of later investigations that have utilized this and other techniques, will the picture of learning remain so easily sketched, the analysis so elemental? Adams, for instance, repeating Thorndike's work and using a duplicate of the box shown in Figure 124, got clear evidence that the cat's random fumbling was *not purely* random and undirected, that the established habit was not so specific and simple, and that it was not directed to one simple stimulus. Consider one example. The cat "Ace" achieved some success in making her escapes, in the course of thirty-one trials, but her solutions were found to be varied, as shown in Table XXXV.

TABLE

XXXV   Different Methods of Escape Used by the Same Animal

Method	Number of Times Used
By pulling string with teeth	8
By pulling string with paw	4
By pulling loop with paw	4
By pulling pulley, or string on pulley, with paw	2
By pulling loop, holding it between chin and paw, and moving back	2
By pulling string with teeth and paws	1
By pulling loop with teeth	1
By pulling loop with teeth and paw	1
By pulling string with teeth, loop with paw	1
By pulling string to mouth with paw, then pulling with teeth	1
By pulling knob of latch, outside, with paw	1
Not noted	1
Failed	4
Total	31

From D. K. Adams, COMP. PSYCHOL. MONOGR., 1929, 6, No. 27.

The Discrimination Method

To settle the question whether a certain organism is able to see or hear or otherwise sense a particular kind of stimulation, when it cannot tell you, Yerkes developed a procedure of determining whether it could react to the stimulus in a discriminating manner. To test the capacity of the dancing mouse to discriminate differences of color-hue, he devised the apparatus represented in Figure 126. The hungry animal, upon being introduced at *A* and admitted through *I* to *B*, had then to choose either the right or the left compartment. One was illuminated with red light, the other with green, by transmission of light from the adjustable lamps *L L*. The filters *R G R* were arranged on a slide to permit easy reversing of the right-left positions of the two colors, and so to avoid the forming of a position-habit. If the mouse entered the correct compartment (e.g., red), it was allowed to pass through a side door out to its food reward in the side alley; but if it entered the incorrect one (e.g., green), it received a light electric shock as punishment. Yerkes was not able to establish the fact of color vision in the dancing mouse, but he found that it was able to react correctly to differences of brightness in the two signals. With white rats, other investigators were able to demonstrate ability to learn to choose correctly between certain simple geo-

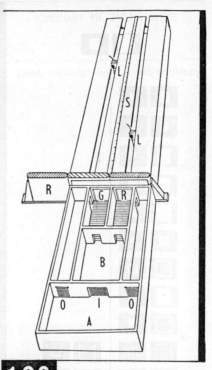

126 Discrimination Apparatus

A. Nest-box. *B.* Entrance chamber. *R,R.* Red filters. *G.* Green filter; *L,L.* Incandescent lamps in light-box. *S.* Millimeter scale on light-box. *I.* Door between *A* and *B.* *O,O.* Doors between alleys and *A.* (*From R. M. Yerkes,* THE DANCING MOUSE, *Macmillan, 1907.*)

metric forms, e.g., between a circle and a star of equal area and brightness, or between an equilateral triangle with the apex up and one with the apex down [10].

It has become certain in the course of further work with rats, and more so in work with monkeys, that when we speak of an animal's choosing "a circle" or "a star" or "a triangle" we are not to assume that it is reacting to one very specific circle, star, or triangle, as might have seemed to be implied above in point 5, page 408. Observe the "figure-on-ground" stimuli in Figure 127. A Java monkey was trained always to choose and pull in by a string a box that bore the smaller of the two white rectangles shown at the top (regardless of whether it was to the right or to the left of the box bearing the larger rectangle). It was then tested for a number of trials with each of the pairs illustrated below the training pair. In all the cases of pairs shown on the left of this figure, the monkey continued to react positively nearly every time to the smaller of each pair of signals. Only when presented with the two pairs shown on the right did it fail to do so. The conclusion is clear: a learned reaction to a stimulus is not a reaction to that exact and precise individual stimulus but *to a certain generic class or type of stimuli.*

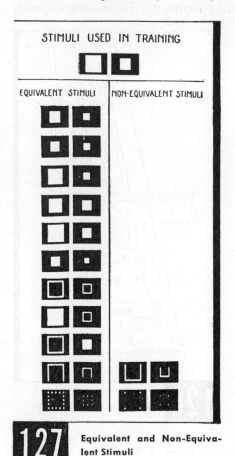

STIMULI USED IN TRAINING

EQUIVALENT STIMULI   NON-EQUIVALENT STIMULI

127   **Equivalent and Non-Equivalent Stimuli**

Based on results obtained in "figure-ground" experiments with monkeys. (*From H. Klüver,* BEHAVIOR MECHANISMS IN MONKEYS, *University of Chicago Press, 1933. By permission.*)

Further, it is demonstrated that a learned reaction may be not to a stimulus as one lone isolated thing, but to it as standing in some kind of *relationship* (here: the relation of "smaller-than").

The Maze Method

A third device used early in the analysis of animal learning, and destined to become one of the commonest of all laboratory instruments, is the maze. Essentially a maze consists of a series of complicated pathways and blind alleys among which the subject must find his way to reach his goal, usually food or escape. The progress of his learning is rated in terms of the reduction in the amount of time taken to get from the entrance to the goal-exit, and of the reduction of errors made by straying into blind alleys or going the wrong direction on the true path.

128 **The Maze at Hampton Court Palace, England**

When the plan was adopted for laboratory mazes, only right-angle turns were used.

In the earliest observations on how an animal learns the true path, the mazes used were adopted from the complicated design of hedgerows in the garden of the Hampton Court palace (Figure 128). But the lack of uniformity in the lengths and shapes of the blinds made this a poor measuring instrument; and much better standardized forms are in current use. For work on different animals and on humans a great variety of mazes have been devised. Some are shown in Figures 129 and 130. Learning curves for the maze have the same general features as those for problem boxes.

An early theory of how an animal learns a maze habit was that the various twists and turns the animal must make at different points are first learned separately in piecemeal fashion and then get linked together. According to this theory, the well-trained animal, upon entering the first alley, simply follows out a well-trained set of running movements down the first alley, a well-trained set of turning movements at the alley-turn, and so on through the succeeding segments of the whole maze (cf. our point 4 on page 408 above). Later research, however, has shown this theory to be quite false. In the case of rats in a maze that offered twenty possible routings from entrance to exit (Figure 131) it was observed that the typical rat did not fixate any particular route. On the contrary, once it had found food the first time, it learned to

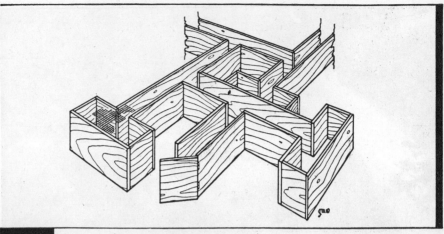

129 Detail of Construction of a Maze of a Much-Used Simple Type

Alleys are built of boards to be painted black and covered with wire mesh.

adjust to the space situation by running in the general direction of the exit, so that in a series of trials it followed a variety of different, but equally short and errorless, routes from entrance to exit. Some of these routes included particular segments that it had never before traversed. An important characteristic of habit-forming is now suggested by these and other recent experiments. To the definition of "habit" furnished

130 A Foot Maze in Use

(From W. Brown, "Auditory and visual cues in maze learning," UNIV. CALIF. PUBL. PSYCHOL., 1932, 5, 115–122. Photo by courtesy of Dr. Brown.)

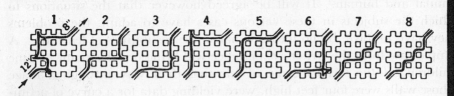

131 An Open-Alley Maze Learned as a Flexible Habit

The tracings are records of the first runs made by one subject. In five of these eight runs the animal took routes that included segments that had never been taken before. (*From J. F. Dashiell*, COMP. PSYCHOL. MONOG., *1930*, 7, *No. 32.*)

on page 405 we should now add a modification. A habit is *not an ironclad fixed and immutable pattern of activity* but is *a mode of adjustment capable of some modification* to fit circumstances; within limits it is *flexible* [21].

It was also formerly assumed that whether the subject, on its very first trial, would turn right or left, upon encountering a choice-point, was entirely a matter of chance. Much emphasis was laid upon the supposedly fortuitous and random character of the first reactions. But upon analyzing animal and human behavior in mazes, later workers have been able to show that even the initial behavior at a choice-point is not truly a matter of chance. For one thing, it is a function of the spatial arrangement of the immediately preceding alleys. For another, it is a function of certain very general reaction-tendencies in the subject. A human subject, after making correct left-right choices in the order *LLR*, will next choose a right turn 70 per cent of the time [6]. As for rats, their choices of paths have been found to fall into certain categories: alternating *RLRLRL*, or left-going *LLLL*, right-going *RRRR*, or making at the later choice-points the same turn as made at the first one [30]. And one investigator noted that his rats in the course of many trials seemed to shift from one systematic kind of choosing to another — much as if they were trying them out as "hypotheses" [17]. Certainly we are forced to recognize that we are dealing with the complications of live organisms, not the simplicities of a marble in a pin-ball machine. There is *no pure chance* in the way an animal or person seeks his goal.

LEARNING FACILITATED BY OBSERVATION

A Neglected Aspect

The experimental methods of studying learning have yielded rich returns in bringing to light certain fundamental marks of all learning, animal and human.   It will be agreed however that the situations to which the subjects in these various cases have to adapt, the problems they have to solve, by no means exhaust the possibilities of learning.   A simple case from the writer's experience will bring out this point.   Some children, at the serious game of learning their way through a maze whose walls were four feet high, were yielding data for a curve of acquisition quite similar to those obtained for white rats and other subjects. However, when a variation was introduced by permitting one bright ten-year-old, before her first trial, to stand on a raised platform and to look carefully and thoughtfully over the arrangement of the walls, she turned in a totally different performance.   Upon being admitted to the maze she went through it without error.   Her learning curve showed an abrupt drop!

The experimental methods described in the preceding pages are hardly adequate for studying all cases of animal learning, to say nothing of human.   Where the subject is afforded more opportunity to survey the field before him, to perceive or take in wider aspects of it all, he is given an opportunity to make a more intelligent response.   The doublings and other cunning tricks of dogs and foxes, the stalking of the human huntsman himself by the Bengal tiger or the formidable Indo-Chinese Gaur, and many less dramatic performances that have their place in the memoranda of naturalists, all seem to be inadequately brought out by the experimental procedures we have so far surveyed.

The importance of allowing the subject to react to the whole field of stimuli, and to the lay-out and relations that are observable there, was recognized in the earlier investigations on monkeys and apes by Hobhouse in England [15], Yerkes in America [31], and Köhler in Germany [16].   We can do no better than to quote some of the vivid descriptions by Köhler and to reproduce some pictures by Yerkes (Figure 132).

Tool-Using

Köhler had unusual opportunity to make intensive observations on chimpanzees while practically interned during World War I at an anthropoid station on one of the Canary Islands.   He reported numerous occasions of the following types [16].

> Nueva was given a small stick with which she scraped around on the ground of her cage.   Fruit was placed outside her cage just out of her reach. In vain she reached repeatedly, then set up characteristic beseeching and whimpering cries, until, some seven minutes later, "she suddenly casts a look at the stick, ceases her moaning, seizes the stick, stretches it out of the cage, and succeeds, though somewhat clumsily, in drawing the banana

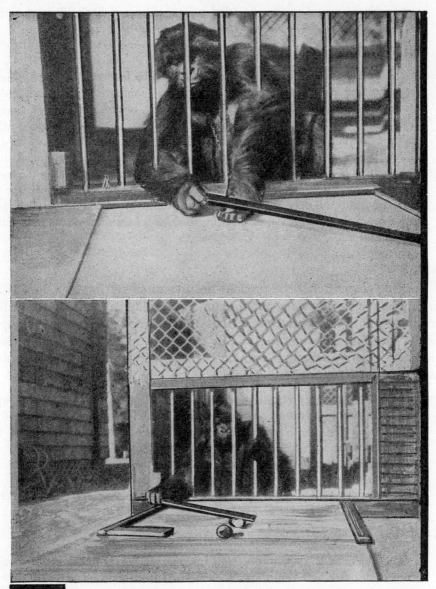

132   **Ape Learning to Use a Stick as a Tool**

(From R. M. Yerkes, " The mind of a gorilla," GENET. PSYCHOL. MONOGR.
1927, 2. Nos. 1–2. By permission of the author.)

within arm's length." Two days later, deprived of her stick when food was again placed out of reach, she tried to pull it toward her with rags, with straws, and with her drinking bowl.

Still more striking are the following cases:

(a) Sultan, having had his attention drawn to food out of reach, "approaches the bars, glances outside, the next moment turns round, goes straight to the tree, seizes a thin, slender branch, breaks it off with a sharp jerk, runs back to the bars, and attains his objective . . . one single quick chain of action." (b) Sultan, being allowed to play with two sticks of different size so that the end of one can be just fitted into the end of the other, "first of all squats indifferently . . . then he gets up, picks up the two sticks . . . and plays carelessly with them. . . . He pushes the thinner one a little way into the opening of the thicker, jumps up and is already on the run toward the railings . . . and begins to draw a banana towards him with the double stick."

Building

Erecting structures to be used as the means of getting at a lure is a form of activity with somewhat the same psychological character. Fruit was hung out of an animal's reach, and the animal was forced to adopt special methods for obtaining it. In the initial test, the food objective was nailed to the roof and a wooden box was left standing some distance away. Again Köhler tells us:

All six apes vainly endeavored to reach their objective by leaping up from the ground. Sultan soon relinquished this attempt, paced restlessly up and down, suddenly stood still in front of the box, seized it, tipped it hastily straight towards the objective, but began to climb upon it at a (horizontal) distance of half a meter, and springing upwards with all his force, tore down the banana . . .; from the momentary pause before the box to the first bite into the banana, only a few seconds elapsed, a perfectly continuous action after the first hesitation.

On a later date two boxes were left handy.

The objective is placed very high up, the two boxes not very far away from each other and about four meters away from the objective; all other means of reaching it have been taken away. Sultan drags the bigger of the two boxes towards the objective, puts it just underneath, gets up on it, and looking upwards, makes ready to jump, but does not jump; gets down, seizes the other box, and pulling it behind him, gallops about the room, making his usual noise, kicking against the walls and showing his uneasiness in every other possible way. He certainly did not seize the second box to put it on the first; it merely helps him to give vent to his temper. But all of a sudden his behavior changes completely; he stops making a noise, pulls his box from quite a distance right up to the other one, and stands it upright on it. He mounts the somewhat shaky construction.

The persistent pursuit of the objective involves variations of procedure that are not merely repertoire reactions appearing in more or less random fashion as the expression of exploratory excitement, but are directed explicitly at the boxes while at the same time the original set is maintained toward the ultimate objective, the food. From Köhler's descriptive account it is apparent that there was often an abruptness with which on the original occasion the animal's behavior became all at once reoriented and systematized about the getting-or-fixing-stick-and-reaching-out-and-scraping-food-inward or the placing-of-box-on-box-and-climbing-upon-them-and-reaching-toward-fruit. There is here surely some degree of perceiving of the *relation of means to objective*, some grasping, if only upon seeing them in a line, of a *connection* of stick-and-banana or box-and-banana, a seeing of each as part of a *configuration* or *Gestalt*.

As we analyze these concrete examples there emerge certain marks of behavior similar to those adopted by one writer or another as criteria of learning by *insight*.

(1) The animal is reacting to the *situation-as-a-whole*, not merely to some detail.

(2) More definitely, it is responding to certain *relationships* within the situation-as-a-whole.

(3) The relationship most significantly determining its behavior is that between a *means* and the *end* or goal.

(4) The subject, we may say, is *restructuring* the field, it is "taking in" or apprehending or *perceiving* it.

(5) The *suddenness* of change in the subject's total behavior which frequently is seen is indicative.

To these we may add the statement (6) that in insightful learning we observe an *integrating* or *reintegrating* of *part-processes* into a *new total pattern*, these part-processes having been provided by *previous experience*. Psychologists of the Gestalt school of interpretation have severely discounted the role of previous experience and have exalted the role of the present situational factors instead;[1] but the importance of the former has been exhibited interestingly in a recent experimental study.

Previous Experiences Essential

Six chimpanzees that had been under detailed observation from birth

[1] We shall have much to say of this matter in our treatment of Perception.

in the Yale Laboratories, and that were known never to have had contact with sticks, were given the hoe problem represented schematically in Figure 133. (*A*) Given a full thirty minutes, four of the subjects failed utterly: they did not reach through the bars to pick up the hoe-shaped stick and with it rake in the bit of fruit. Indeed, for some of them the stick was only a nuisance that lay in the way. (*B*) The apes were turned out into their open-air enclosure into which a dozen straight sticks of varying lengths had been strewn; and for three days they were allowed to play at large. The animals at first would pick up the sticks and hold them in their hands, even when reaching for other objects with the same hands — but without using the sticks to get those objects. In time they came to use the sticks as functional extensions of their arms, perhaps to poke each other provocatively. They were not seen to use the sticks for sweeping distant objects into reach. (*C*) When returned to the cage and tested again with the hoe-problem, the behavior of the chimps now became markedly different from what it had been in the initial test. Whereas originally only two of the six had used the stick in any fashion as an instrument for overcoming the distance of the food-lure, now every one of them was able to solve the problem with no difficulty at all. Once the basic pattern of using a stick to extend one's armreach had been hit upon and established, the animals were capable of employing sticks in a wide variety of ways. What had at first been just another object lying on the floor was now recognized and used as a potential means to the end.

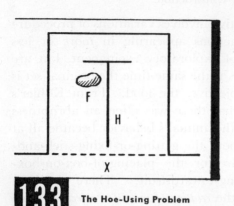

133 **The Hoe-Using Problem**

Can the chimpanzee at *X* solve this problem by reaching through the bars, taking hold of the hoe *H*, and with it drawing in the food *F*? (*From H. G. Birch, J.* Comp. Psychol., *1945, 38, 372.*)

The Methods Applied to Children

The same types of problem situations as set for animals were soon applied to children. One useful series of problems is described in the sketches and legends of Figure 134.

Important differences between animal and child came to light. It will be easy to appreciate these if we consider excerpts from one experimenter's records of children on somewhat similar problems [2].

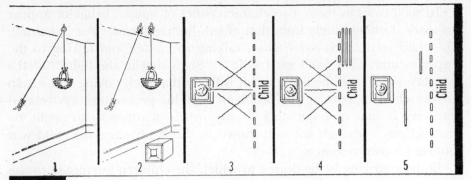

134

1. (Viewing from behind.) A basket containing an animal cookie is suspended above the child's reach at the end of a red string, which runs through a black ring in the ceiling and down again to another black ring that was placed over a simple hook in the wall well within the child's reach.

2. The basket with lure is hung out of reach by a string which ended where it is tied to a ring in the ceiling. Another string tied to another ceiling ring ends in a hook similar to the hook in 1. Two boxes were left nearby.

3. (Viewing from above.) Beyond a railing lies a box out of reach bearing a picture and containing a cookie. Fastened to it is a red string the other end of which touches the railing. Four other strings lie in crossed manner with ends also touching the railing.

4. The box and strings are laid as in 3 except that none of the strings touch the box, and there are provided on the child's side of the barrier three sticks, any of which was long enough to reach the box.

5. The box with cookie and also a long stick lie beyond reach, and a short stick lies inside the barrier. The solution: securing the long stick with the short one and pulling the box in with the former.

(*Adapted from descriptions in Matheson, E., "A study of problem solving behavior in preschool children," *CHILD DEVELPM., 1931, 2, 242–262.*)

Girl, 40 months old. Problem: toy outside, stick on floor inside.

First trial. Subject handled the stick and talked about it before instructions were completed and then dropped it, trying to climb out of the pen to get objective; tried to reach objective by leaning over the top of pen, by stretching for it between the bars; sought an exit, repeating over and over, "I can't get birdie"; asked experimenter to move objective closer; stepped on stick, looked down at it, and began to walk around. Subject picked up stick, banged with it on the wall, and threw it down; looked around and again tried to reach objective as before and by pushing her legs out between the bars. Subject appeared tired, and trial was terminated.

Second trial. Subject stretched for objective through the spaces, first with right hand and then with left, shouting, "Today, I can get him"; tried to climb out and again reached through the spaces. Subject stepped on stick, *pounced down on it*, and used it for obtaining objective, which she had inside the pen in a short time. Repeated the performance for fun.

Same child. Problem: broom replacing stick on floor.

First trial. Subject picked up broom at once and swept objective in deftly.

In such cases as these, two characteristics of human behavior appear to mark it off strikingly from that of sub-human forms. For one thing, the child used much *verbalization*, talking to himself and talking to the experimenter. ("I can't get birdie"; "She's tied to the light?" "It's too far away," and the like); and it is likely that such talking was a help to the child in refining his problems and his procedures. A related capacity is that of responding to the words of others — to profit by instructions — though not well shown in this study since the child was put on his own resources.

Equally striking is the degree to which the children attempted to use *social aids*. Direct verbal requests ("You swing the dolly"; "May I have the other stick?"), indirect seeking of guidance (glancing at experimenter's face before continuing with a new method), and emotional appeals (whimpering or crying) — many and sundry such incidental social items are found through the running accounts.

> *Boy, 42 months. Problem: suspended toy.* Subject tried to reach objective with both hands, repeating, "I can't reach it"; came to experimenter, repeating this chant, almost with a sob. Receiving no assistance, subject began to cry, and trial was terminated with the promise that subject should have another opportunity to reach objective.

Finally with the children, other types of *emotional response* and general *personality characteristics* were often of importance in aiding or hindering the solution.

Some Practical Applications

On the basis of observations of children's responses to problem situations such as we have described, some useful suggestions have been pointed up [20]. As these have wide application to the teaching and directing of problem solving — and hold for adults as well as for children — a few may be worth mentioning at this point.

(1) A child should be encouraged as early as possible to be self-reliant when he faces new problems arising in daily routine.

(2) He should be taught to keep calm when minor difficulties challenge him.

(3) He should be taught the importance of carefully looking about, keenly scrutinizing what he faces.

(4) He should be encouraged to keep at it, to persevere.

(5) He should be encouraged to vary his manner of trying to solve a problem.

All are pointers for adults as well, most especially the last.

Insight in Human Adults

Adaptive behavior as problem solving certainly permeates the higher mental processes of man. It is central to our understanding of the nature of his thinking; and most scientific studies of the operations of thought are simply more elaborate analyses, with more complexity of language or other symbols. We shall do better, then, to postpone our inquiries concerning insight in adults until later chapters (Chapters 16 and 19).

THE CONDITIONED RESPONSE

At the very opening of the present century, Pavlov at Petrograd and Bekhterev at Moscow were calling attention to an aspect of animal (and human) learning which we have largely neglected in this chapter. As laboratory physiologists, they were narrowing their investigations to the simplest possible examples of learning.

Pavlov's Experiment

Working with the dog, Pavlov made an incision through the animal's cheek, carrying the end of one of the salivary ducts through to the outside, and by a system of tubing led off the saliva to a point where the quantity that the dog secreted in, say, a thirty-second period could be measured. The animal was first trained to stand quietly in a room free from all distracting stimulations while the experimenter sat in an adjoining room with electric or pneumatic control of all stimuli and with a periscope for watching the animal (Figure 135).

The procedure of formal training or conditioning was as follows (with variations). With the dog alert and attentive to the usual food source, some extraneous stimulation was given him before the food appeared — sound of a metronome or buzzer or bell, pressure or irritant applied to the skin, a flash of light, or other stimulus to which the dog did not make a salivary response, however much he might prick up his ears or show tension in neck and leg muscles or change his breathing or make other negligible responses. Shortly after this incidental or *conditioned stimulus* (*CS*), the original or *unconditioned stimulus* (*US*) of food was presented, whereupon the animal made the usual eating responses, including a copious flowing of saliva, as an *unconditioned response* (*UR*). However, through frequent repetitions of the situation, with the sound or contact or light presented each time just before or along with — and so being *reinforced* by — the food, the conditioned stimulus eventually developed potency to arouse when given alone the salivary response as a *conditioned*

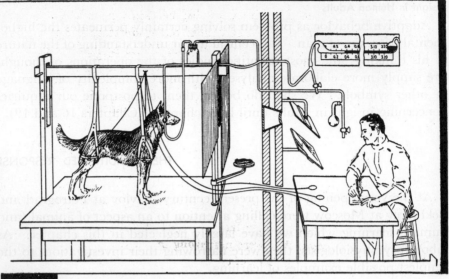

135 **Pavlov's Arrangement for a Salivary Conditioned Response in the Dog**

In this figure the incidental stimuli to be employed are tactual, at shoulder and hip, and are under control at the experimenter's table. (*From I. P. Pavlov,* LECTURES ON CONDITIONED REFLEXES, *International Publishers, 1928.*)

response (*CR*). A general principle suggested by this finding might be worded: "If a stimulus that is effectively arousing a given response is frequently preceded or accompanied by an ineffective neutral stimulus, the latter may itself acquire power to arouse the given response: it becomes a substitute stimulus to that response." A neat principle this is — one which implies a simple switching or duplicating of connections to attach a new stimulus to an old response or an old stimulus to a new response. And in terms of this simple formulation, conditioning has long been considered a key to unlock many complicated problems of human nature.

Interpreting the Pavlov Experiment

The apparent simplicity of Pavlov's work is, however, deceptive. Let us re-read his own words to get his whole direction of approach and interpretation, for it is in line with the biological viewpoint implicit in learning as we have surveyed it to this point.

> The strong carnivorous animal preys on weaker animals, and these if they waited to defend themselves until the teeth of the foe were in their flesh would speedily be exterminated. The case takes on a different aspect

when the defence reflex is called into play by the sights and sound of the enemy's approach. Then the prey has a chance to save itself by hiding or by flight. . . . The animal must respond not only to stimuli which themselves bring immediate benefit or harm, but also to other physical or chemical agencies — waves of sound, light, and the like — which in themselves only *signal* the approach of these stimuli. . . .

A great number of all sorts of stimuli always act . . . as temporary and interchangeable signals for the comparatively small number of agencies of a general character which determine the inborn reflexes. . . . This is the only means by which a most delicate adjustment of the organism to the environment can be established. To this function . . . we gave the name of "signalization." . . .

Visual, auditory, and even pure olfactory properties of our objects, *per se* . . . remain without any influence on the salivary glands; for they, on their side, possess no business relation, so to speak, to these properties. In our psychical experiments [however] there appear before us as [possible acquired] stimulators of the salivary glands not only such properties . . . but absolutely all the surroundings in which these objects are presented to the dog, or the circumstances with which they are connected in real life. For example, the dish in which it is presented, the furniture upon which it is placed, the room, the person accustomed to bring it, and the noises produced by him — his voice, and even the sound of his feet. . . . In the psychical experiment the connection of the objects exciting the salivary glands becomes more and more distant and delicate. Undoubtedly we have before us an extreme degree of adaptation.[1]

Let us now attempt a more adequate definition of conditioning than that mentioned above. *If an indifferent, neutral stimulus is presented one or more times along with or just before an adequate stimulus to which the organism is reacting in an appropriate way, the neutral stimulus may acquire potency to arouse much the same kind of appropriate behavior. It thus becomes a signal standing for the original stimulus.*

The Motor Form of Classical Conditioning

Bekhterev was studying essentially the same phenomenon at Moscow, though called by him "association reflexes," and involving defensive muscular reflexes in dog and man (Figure 136). From an electric shock (*US*) the foot is retracted — a native, biologically adequate response (*UR*). Just before applying the shock, Bekhterev sounded a bell (*CS*), which originally had aroused only a milder and more general sort of behavior. Repeating this combination a number of times he eventually

[1] From I. P. Pavlov, *Conditioned Reflexes* (New York: Oxford University Press, 1927 by permission); *Lectures on Conditioned Reflexes* (New York: International Publishers, 1928).

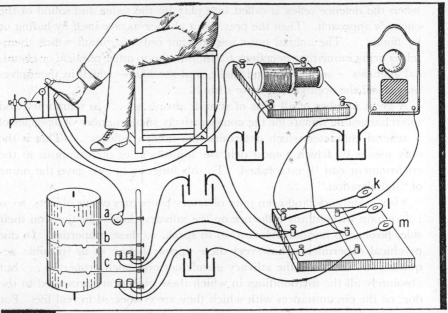

136 **Bekhterev's Arrangement for a Motor Conditioned Response in Man**

Explanation in text. (*From V. M. Bekhterev,* GENERAL PRINCIPLES OF HUMAN REFLEXOLOGY. *International Publishers.*)

trained his subject to the point where the foot was withdrawn automatically upon sound of the bell (*CR*).

This general technique has been rather thoroughly employed in America in Liddell's laboratory at Cornell, on such animals as the sheep, goat, pig, dog, and rabbit. What the animal learned to do was to make a defensive flexion of its foreleg (*CR*) at sound of a buzzer (*CS*) before an electric shock (*US*) was delivered there. Figure 137 presents kymograph tracings at two stages in the learning process. On the first presentation, immediately following the buzzer sound (*CS*) only a head movement and a change in breathing occur (as parts of attention-giving orientation to the buzzer); then when the shock (*US*) is received, a vigorous movement of the leg appears (*UR*). On the eleventh presentation, immediately following the buzzer (*CS*) a full leg movement (*CR*) occurs, along with the head and respiratory changes. In effect, the *CS* now serves as a warning signal; and the *CR* may be looked on as part of a whole preparatory response whereby the animal seeks to defend itself in a way appropriate to the situation.

We must take note that the *CR* is often not qualitatively the same reaction as the *UR*. The conditioned leg tensing by the sheep, cat, or other animal assumes a neater, simpler, more precise movement than the violent jerking that appeared when a shock was received. A rat had jumped a fence with a jerky, hasty, frantic scramble when it received a shock; after it had become conditioned to jump the fence at sound of a loud buzzer, it did so with clean movements, neatly clearing the fence without hesitation or haste or wasted energy [28]. And so it is with many other cases, both animal and human: conditioning is not simply a business of switching, hitching, and unhitching sensory or motor units [14].

Instrumental Conditioning Methods

The adjustive value of the *CR* is heightened considerably when the experimental set-up gives the subject a chance to escape a punishment or to obtain a reward by making that response. This is just what is done in the two variations of procedure called *instrumental conditioning*,

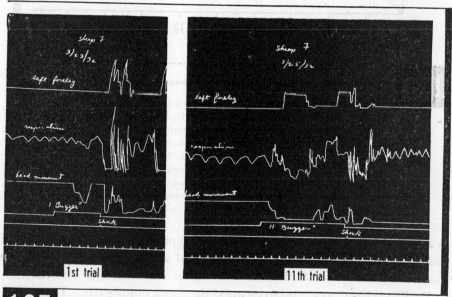

137

Acquiring of a Preparatory Response (CR) by a Sheep

The smoked drum records are read from left to right. The continuous tracings record simultaneously. Reading from bottom up: time in seconds, the timing of shock and of buzzer, then the occurrences of head movements, of breathing changes, and of movement of the foreleg. Discussed in text. (*From H. S. Liddell, W. T. James, and O. D. Anderson, COMP. PSYCHOL. MONOGR., 1934, 11, No. 51. By permission.*)

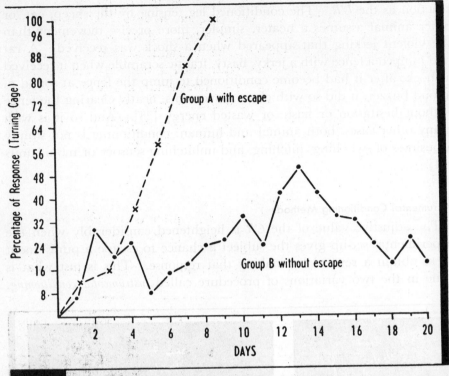

138   **Conditioning of Guinea Pigs with and Without Escape**

Guinea pigs in a rotating cage were given a shock after a tone had been sounding for two seconds. The animals in Group A could avoid the shock by rotating the cage, which broke the circuit. Those of Group B could not escape the shock in that manner. Eventually the animals of Group B reacted a little by rotating the cage but more by "sitting tight," holding the breath, and tensing the muscles against the shock to come. On the other hand, the animals of Group A rapidly established the CR of rotating the cage, since this response was of biological value to them. (*From W. J. Brogden, E. A. Lipman and E. Culler*, AMER. J. PSYCHOL., *1938, 51, 110.*)

in contrast with the *classical* or Pavlovian type. In Culler's laboratories much the same arrangement of harness and apparatus was used, except that, when the animal lifted its foot upon receiving the CS, the foot came off a contact grid and so escaped the shock completely. Figure 138 shows that the increased biological value of reacting in a way that escapes punishment makes for more rapid learning.

Probably the most dependable of all the CR's with human adult subjects is the conditioned *eyelid* response. A puff of air delivered to the eyeball (US) elicits a reflex wink (UR); and mild auditory, visual, or cutaneous stimulation may be used as the CS. The fundamental simplicity of the essential processes coupled with the possibilities of refined instrumentation for photographic recording make this a useful technique; and in fact a number of refinements and specialized phenomena of conditioning, which are too subtle for treatment here, have come to light in the course of investigations on the air puff–eye wink *CR*.

The "Skinner box" furnishes a second variation for studying in considerable detail a reward-obtaining *CR*. (See Figure 139.) The hungry animal has the opportunity to learn to get food by performing a new simple movement. It must learn to react to the sight of the lever (and to the general enclosure) by pressing the lever, this response occasioning a new stimulus, a food pellet, to which the animal will respond by eating. Schematically: the behavior segment *CS* (lever) $\rightarrow$ *CR* (pressing the lever), is followed by and reinforced by the behavior segment *US* (food) $\rightarrow$ *UR* (eating); and the promptness with which the hungry animal performs the first-mentioned behavior segment is a measure of the degree to which conditioning has been established.

139   **A Section of a Skinner Box**

The animal is to learn to depress the lever, which automatically releases a pellet of food into the pan.

The Skinner box has become an extremely useful instrument for exploring the time relations and intensity changes of the various phenomena in conditioning, for controlling extraneous factors, and for permitting more precision in the use of quantitative formulations.

At this point the thoughtful reader may have been struck by two points. We have before us an acknowledged experiment in *CR* learning. But in its initial stages the learning is indistinguishable from trial-and-error learning. Then again, in the quick way the change of behavior takes place, it is indistinguishable from learning by insight. Thus we are reminded that *the processes of learning may be experimentally approached from three different sides.*

Some Special Phenomena and Principles

So far we have limited our attention largely to the general fact of the conditioned response (*CR*), and to some of the types of technical set-up that bring it out clearly. Out of the very abundance of researches by Pavlov and the many Russian and American workers inspired by him, an impressive series of special points has been developed; and it is to the eternal credit of his keen intelligence that most of these points have been confirmed by other investigators, whatever their laboratory techniques and whether using animal or human subjects.

These principles form the bulk of current discussions of conditioning by psychologists; and they have importance in our understanding not alone of learning but also of human behavior in general. Their peculiar interest and value lie in their highly analytic biological character. We shall not have space for much more than a listing of the more significant ones that have not already been alluded to in foregoing paragraphs.

The *CR* in its early stages is aroused by *general* and *non-specific stimuli*. In one investigation [3], along with a shock stimulus applied to the wrist that aroused a galvanic skin response (*GSR*), a tapping stimulus was applied to the shoulder, until the subject was trained to the point where the shoulder-tapping served as an effective substitute stimulus for the *GSR*. After this was well established it was found that the same sort of tactile stimulus would be effective if applied at the small of the back, on the thigh, or on the calf of the leg; but it *decreased* in degrees of effectiveness with remoteness from the point originally conditioned. The conclusion follows that the *CR* was really established not simply to a tactual stimulus at one particular local point on the shoulder but to that general sort of tactual stimulus applied to the skin generally. Taken in conjunction with Klüver's experiment on equivalence of stimuli (page 410) and with many studies on dogs, this experiment leads to the broad statement that any *CR* in its early stages typically is a response *to a general type of stimulation*. Analogues of this principle abound in everyday life: if snapped at by one dog, a child fears all dogs; a person who has learned a musical tune in one key perceives the same tune in another key; the word "cat," to be recognized, need not always be printed in the same size or face of type. This point will prove to have a considerable theoretical value for us.

On the motor side, also, the simplicity of the *CR* has been much exaggerated, as we have seen. In reality, there is in the beginning a *reaction* of almost the *whole organism*. This was well suggested in Figure 137, where the effect of the conditioned stimulus, a buzzer, is seen not only in foreleg movement but also in change of breathing and in the position of the head. When a human subject is being conditioned to raise his finger off a grid at sound of a bell, his *CR*'s are at first likely to include a jerking of the whole arm, a wrinkling of the brow, even a vocal grunt. And who knows how many other participating reaction segments might be brought to light out of the total conditioned response if still other instrumentation were employed? It certainly is clear — as was found in the Duke University Psychology Laboratory [33] — that the apparent simplicity of *CR* learning is really due to the experimental restriction of observation to a single component of the total behavior of the animal or human.

CR's are formed that are not only excitatory but *inhibitory* in their action. Several types of inhibition were worked out by Pavlov and have been found also in human subjects.

(1) When a *CR* is frequently repeated but never again coupled with the original stimulus (no reinforcement), it may appear to lose its conditioned effect, to undergo *extinction*. This is not a true wearing out, however, for after a

rest period of a day or week or even a year it may spontaneously reappear and in partial strength.

(2) What is more, this extinguished state is often set aside by some new extraneous stimulus that appears to release the reflex from a kind of inhibition. In other words, we have an example of inhibition of an inhibition, or *disinhibition*.

(3) A third kind of inhibition is found in the process of *differentiation*, in which the non-specific and general nature of the stimulus when first conditioned becomes more and more narrowed and refined upon continued training. This phenomenon was exploited early by the first American psychologists to work with conditioning. A reflex retraction of the hand after the subject has been conditioned to a red light is likely to appear also at sight of a green one; but if the shock is used only when the red is shown and never with the green, the retraction to the latter will die out. A retraction conditioned to a tone of 256 cycles per second will appear also at a sound differing from it by only 6 cycles; but after frequent shocking with the former and never with the latter, the nervous system will be trained to respond with the hand to the former only, not to the latter.

Still other phenomena of conditioning seem to depend upon some kind of time-recording in the animal or human. If in the training series a constant time interval is introduced between the incidental stimulus and the normal adequate one, the conditioned responses will finally come to appear at that same interval of time following the incidental stimulus and in the absence of the adequate one. This delay phenomenon can be made to appear either at a constant interval after the beginning of an incidental stimulus that continues and is overlapped by the adequate one (the *delayed* or *retarded CR*), or at an interval after the cessation of a short-lived stimulus that does not continue (the *trace CR*).

Now for a final principle. From one *CR*, a *secondary CR* can be formed by accompanying a newly effective stimulus with a second neutral one. For example, a human subject that had been trained to withdraw the hand at a tactile stimulation formerly coupled with an electric shock was further conditioned to a metronome-ticking after the latter had accompanied the tactile stimulation but without the shock. In other words, the metronome became substituted for the tactile *S*, as the latter had already become substituted for the shock. With dogs, this building up has been carried as high as the fifth order; and it is claimed that for an indefinite building of *CR* on *CR* the one great essential is sufficient energizing of the individual throughout. Consider a simple illustration from the story of habit-on-habit building in the education of the human being.

"(A) Contact with candle-flame → withdrawal: original unconditioned.

(B) 'Look out!' (spoken): first order conditioned.

(C) 'Look out!' (printed): second order conditioned.

(D) Wet paint: third order conditioned.

(E) Achtung! fourth order conditioned.

(F) Sterile surgical field: fifth order conditioned.

The process continues step by step: $A + B$ eventuates in a negative response to the warning cry, "Look out"; $B + C$ gives the printed words "Look out" similar negative value; $C + D$ keeps the child from sitting on wet paint; $D + E$ gives avoiding significance to the German warning, *Achtung*! $E + F$ finally makes the child careful of a sterile field. . . . The factors which serve to keep these responses alive are . . . such things as parental stimulation, the code among playmates, emulation and rivalry, the rewards and penalties imposed by social discipline — all the many incentives commonly used to promote learning in children" [11].

The *CR*, even after having been well-established, remains a *flexible habit* (cf. page 413), for its specific form may change adaptively with a change in the circumstances. Human subjects had been conditioned to make an involuntary withdrawal movement of the finger with the flexor muscles at sound of buzzer; then when the hand was turned over the involuntary withdrawal was executed by the extensor muscles [29]. In either case the fingers came off the electrode; and we see that the *CR* was not an invariable movement of an identical action unit but a more useful response because adjustable to the change in the situation that the organism was facing.

"Personal" Factors Important in Conditioning

Pavlov had frequently pointed out that much of his success in training the dog's alimentary response to a *CS* was conditioned on "personal" factors. In the first place, there are the individual differences between the different animals, some dogs yielding excellently to the training procedures while others made poor subjects. All workers have noted this same general point. Some have made interesting comparisons of different animal species; some have found surprising differences between human subjects.

In the second place, Pavlov insisted that the subject must be in a condition of alert readiness. This likewise has been a universal finding; and with human subjects the matter has been much further pursued. After the early years of puzzlement, when would-be demonstrators of he *CR* phenomenon were baffled to find that they could not obtain the standard results from many subjects, research has been directed more and more to the unraveling of mental complications. Razran and others have localized a major difficulty in the *attitude* or set of the person about to be conditioned: how get the proper amount and direction of the all-important expectancy?

It is essential that the subject cooperate. He should neither attempt to outsmart his experimenter nor try to hurry up what he takes to be the expected results. Some experimenters have found it advantageous to explain clearly to the student-subject the purpose of all the wires and tubes and other apparatus; others prefer to give an explanation but one that directs the subject's attention away from the crux of the problem. To sophisticated subjects some investigators assign some mental occupation (as continuous reading or calculating or tapping when *CS* appears) so that their thought processes do not participate too actively in the process of conditioning. Certainly the role of "personal" factors is a rich field for useful research [12, 26].

Verbal Conditioning

Not only the overt reactions of duct glands and striped muscles but also implicit and autonomic responses of endocrines and smooth muscle tissue have been trained into *CR's*. The pupillary reactions of the eye, the *GSR*, the vasomotor control of blood supply to the hands, and other actions involving the autonomic division of the nervous system have been found amenable to training. There are other physiological changes. One is the production of excess white blood corpuscles after the skin is scratched — the scratching being a former accompaniment of the injection of cultures. Another is the "blocking of the alpha rhythm" (the disappearance of that particular wave form from the electroencephalogram, which, as we have seen on page 337, occurs when a person changes from a quiet resting condition to alert concentration, as on a light signal). This is shown in Figure 140 *A*.

An especially significant feature is that several of the kinds of changes we have just listed have been gotten under voluntary control, that is, have been conditioned to implicit verbal stimuli. An interesting example is recorded in Figure 140 *B*. The blocking of the alpha rhythm was brought about in this way. The subject repeated subvocally the word "block" and pressed a switch button at the same time. The circuit closed by the switch turned on a light (*US*) which promptly blocked out the alpha frequency from the electroencephalogram being recorded from the subject's head. Now the experimenter in an adjoining room was able to break this light circuit so that the voluntary stimulus (saying "block" and pressing button) could occur without the light reinforcement. Before the training trials, the saying-block-and-pressing-button (*CS*) had no effect on the alpha rhythm; but after the training that double act was followed by a depressing of the rhythm, occurring sometimes in advance of the button pressing. Voluntary blocking of the rhythm was thus established.

Some Everyday Applications

After the foregoing technical discussions it will help us to see the woods

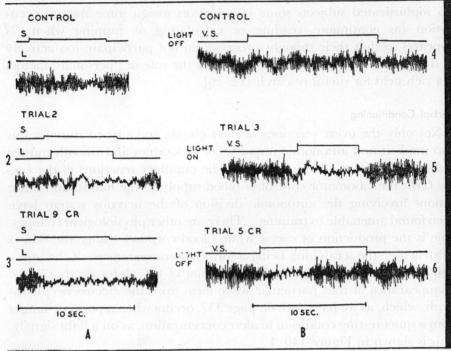

CONTROL
S
L
1

CONTROL
LIGHT OFF   V.S.
4

TRIAL 2
S
L
2

LIGHT ON   V.S.
5

TRIAL 9 CR
S
L
3

TRIAL 5 CR
LIGHT OFF   V.S.
6

10 SEC.
A

10 SEC.
B

140   Voluntary Conditioned Blocking of the EEG

The alpha rhythm (cf. page 337) appears best when the subject is awake but resting quietly and inattentively. The rhythm is blocked (disappears from the tracing record) when the subject is stimulated by a light. This blocking of the alpha and its conditioning are shown in *A*. *1*: Sound alone produced no appreciable effect on the alpha rhythm. *2*: Light produces a blocking. *3*: After repeated presentations of sound with light, the sound alone has acquired power to block the rhythm.

Further conditioning of the blocking is shown in *B*. A voluntary stimulus was provided by having the subject repeat subvocally the word "block!" and simultaneously press a button. The wiring of the latter was under the experimenter's control so that it would or would not throw on a light. *4*: At first the voluntary stimulus had no effect on the rhythm when no light was thrown on with it. *5*: Blocking effect was obtained whenever the voluntary stimulus did involve a light. *6*: After a number of trials, the voluntary stimulus produced a blocking of alpha in the absence of any light.

S = sound; L = light; V.S. = voluntary stimulus (word).

(*From H. Jasper and C. Shagrass, J. Exp. Psycol., 1941, 28, 373–388, 505–508. By permission.*)

instead of the trees if we note some concrete examples of learning as conditioning.[1]

(A) At the slam of the gate to their corral, the chickens come running. (B) At the sounds, "Here, Gyp!" the dog dozing on the front lawn jumps to his feet and heads around the house for the back door, where he finds the cook ready to offer him a bone. (C) At sight of master-carrying-gun the quiet house dog changes at once into a vibrant impatient hunter. (D) A child under the writer's observation, who had heard others cry "hot" when he was near a steam radiator by which he was slightly burned, always drew back at hearing that word wherever he might be.

Consider cases of emotional behavior. (E) Before and after tonsilectomy a boy was given examination and treatment by a white-coated shiny-instrument-wielding physician. For a year and more thereafter he was terrorized by the very sight of a barber wearing his white coat and manipulating his nickeled clippers and scissors. (F) This fear reaction was eventually overcome by a barber who set a bowl of goldfish near the child, directing his highly interested attention to them, and saying "fish," meanwhile working upon the boy's hair unobtrusively and casually. (G) Later the child, upon hearing the word "fish" or "haircut" or "Dayton's" (the barber's shop) spoken aloud would smile, and with a hand describe circular gestures accompanied by rising and falling vocal inflection (mimetic of the swimming of the goldfish). (H) A college student relates that once he greatly enjoyed Chopin's Marche Funèbre, but that ever since he heard it played in a certain naval hospital whenever the body of an unfortunate sailor was being removed for burial, he has been unable to react to it with anything but extreme depression. (I) And who does not still react with a touch of dread to the mere words "Lidice" or "Dachau" or "March of Death" or "Iwo Jima"? (J) The writer acknowledges a strangely warm, almost affectionate liking for pink willow-pattern dinner ware, which he can trace back to childhood lunches eaten from a pink plate. (K) In good contrast is the case of Arnold Bennett, who once wrote of a sudden dejection that came upon him whenever he saw anything pink; eventually he was able to trace it to the pink-colored almshouses of the English countryside. The reader may well recall the conditioning of an early emotional reaction as related by Watson and Rayner (see pages 220 f.). Such cases show how emotional attachments can be acquired in the most nonlogical ways, and afford a key to many of the little phobias and manias and pet likes and aversions that manifest themselves in astonishing array in the life of every person.

[1] The reader would do well to analyze these cases into appropriate S's and R's, and their respective connections.

Nor is the matter essentially different when the responses acquired are of less emotional and more intellectual types. (*L*) A common procedure in teaching a child to read is to point out to him some printed word, as C A T, at the same time pronouncing the word aloud, in the expectation that, as he has already learned to speak such a word upon hearing it, he will now be able to substitute the new visual for the familiar auditory stimulus, and so be enabled to read the print. (*M*) The remembering of a melody, of musical notes in a serial arrangement, is based upon earlier neural changes in which the vocal production of each successive note was conditioned to the auditory or to the proprioceptive afferent impulses of the note produced just before it. (*N*) The office worker soon becomes so accustomed to the sounds of the clicking typewriters and adding machines that, should they be abruptly suspended, he might find it extremely difficult to concentrate on the job before him, for his reactions have become conditioned in part to these sounds.

THE ROLE OF MOTIVATION IN LEARNING

Drive and Incentive in Maze Learning

If there are to be "trials" and "errors," "successes" and "failures," the subject must *try*, must be actively seeking. Out of the laboratories of the University of California (to name but one place) have come a number of clean-cut demonstrations of how an animal's motivation will accelerate or retard its learning of such problems as the maze. We shall cite one of those studies.

Rats were once trained to choose the proper path around a square maze, to run it with speed, and to avoid useless wandering. Two groups of subjects were run, with the usual feeding at the goal, for 10 consecutive daily trials. (*A*) Then on the 11th day and each day thereafter, the rats of the experimental group found no food in their goal boxes, but had to wait until they had been transferred back to their nest cages to receive it. (*B*) On the 23d day, the experimental group received no food at all, even in their cages. (*C*) On the 25th day, as an added variation, the experimental animals received a double portion of food, which they had not entirely consumed by the time they were started on their 26th run. The reader will note in Figure 141 the effects of goal-postponement, goal-removal, and goal-excess on the way the rats subsequently used the habit they had learned. He will also note that the animal's degree of hunger was a potent factor.

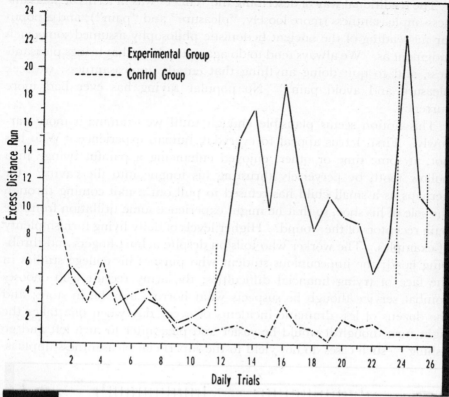

141 **Some Effects on Maze Performance of Changes in the Reward**

Reward for Experimental Group: trials 1–10, food in goal box; trials 11–22, food in cages; trials 23 and 24, no food in goal box or cages; trial 25 double feeding. The reward for the control group (food in goal box) remained unchanged throughout. (*From R. H. Bruce*, UNIV. CALIF. PUBL. PSYCHOL., *1930, 4, 208.*)

The Problem of the Selecting Agent

A fundamental thing about the simplest trial-and-error learning, as well as about more insightful adjustments, is that improvement of performance depends upon a selection of some only of the many alternative possibilities of response. The accomplished individual turns this button and not that, turns right and not wrong, chooses the correct signal and not the incorrect. Just what leads him to make those particular choices? For one thing, the consequences to which the various kinds of responses led during preceding trials must somehow be a critical factor in determining what responses shall appear in succeeding trials. This has been formulated by Thorndike as the *Law of Effect* and in its more general formulation is hardly to be challenged.

The traditional way of describing the "effect" was in terms of pleasant-ness-unpleasantness (more loosely, "pleasure" and "pain"); and a popular misreading of the ancient hedonistic philosophy assumed some such judgment as, "We always tend to do again anything that brings pleasant-ness, and to quit doing anything that entails unpleasantness: we seek pleasure and avoid pain." No popular saying has ever had more currency.

This notion seems plausible enough until we examine it more narrowly. First, let us appeal to everyday human experience. Who has not, at some time or other, enjoyed enhancing a painful twinge in a hollow tooth by perversely thrusting his tongue into the cavity? Or perhaps as a small child has refused to pull out a nail coming through the sole of his shoe, so that he might experience some titillation from the pain receptors of the wound? Higher levels of daily living furnish plenty of examples. The worker who toils on despite aching fingers and throbbing head; the impecunious student who pursues his college studies in the face of trying financial difficulties; the army recruit who chooses combat service though he suspects what horrors may be in store; and the dozens of less dramatic incidents of every day when one takes the right turn though it would be easier and pleasanter to turn left and go fishing — such cases do not yield to the superficial pleasantness-unpleas-

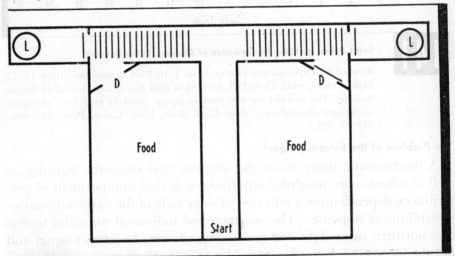

Food   Food

Start

142

A Light Discrimination Box

Used for training white rats to choose the lighted alley. The lamps *LL* were lighted in irregular order; and door *D* on the lighted side was left open, while a shock was turned on in the floor of the opposite or wrong alley. (*From K. F. Muenzinger*, J. Comp. Psychol., *1934, 17, 268. By permission.*)

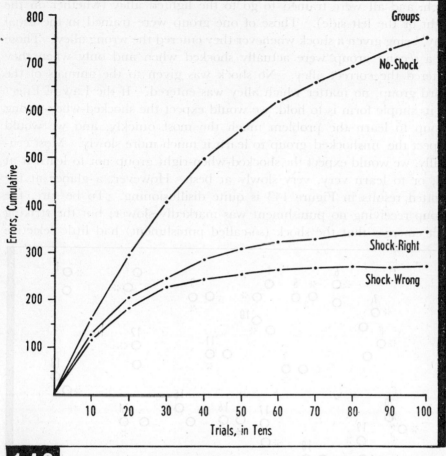

143 Cumulative Error Scores for Rats Learning Under Different Conditions of "Punishment"

Here the number of errors made by the animals of a group in each trial is added to the total of errors made by them in all previous trials; so that increased rate of acquisition of the habit is represented not by a drop in the curve but by its tendency toward a horizontal flattening out. (*From K. F. Muenzinger, J.* COMP. PSYCHOL., *1934, 17, 272. By permission.*)

antness formula.   Finally, to prove that such exceptions are not limited to man, one could cite the faithful dog that continues in spite of lacerations to fight off the beast attacking his master when retreat and escape would be easy enough.

Experimental proof is easily obtained.   Muenzinger at the University of Colorado trained rats to make habitually the correct discrimination between a lighted alley and an unlighted alley in a simple discrimination box (Figure 142).   The animals were divided into three groups, 25 in each, and all were trained to go to the lighted alley (whether on the right or the left side). Those of one group were trained in the usual way, being given a shock whenever they entered the wrong alley. Those of a second group were actually shocked when and only when they entered the correct alley. No shock was given to the animals of the third group, no matter which alley was entered. If the Law of Effect in its simple form is to hold, we would expect the shocked-when-wrong group to learn the problem much the most quickly, and we would expect the unshocked group to learn it much more slowly. Most crucially, we would expect the shocked-when-right group not to learn it at all, or to learn very, very slowly at best. However, a glance at the plotted results in Figure 143 is quite disillusioning. To be sure, the group receiving no punishment was markedly slower; but the striking fact emerges that the shock (so-called punishment) had little selective

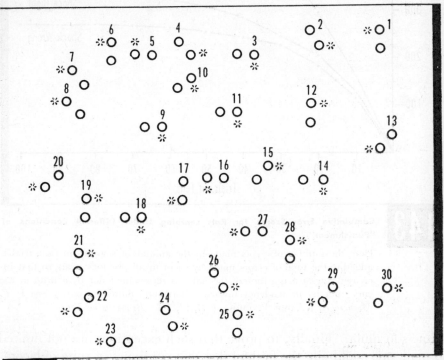

144 A Punchboard Maze

The subject is to learn by inserting a brass stylus which is the correct hole of each pair, beginning at pair no. 1 and continuing through to pair 20. Trials are repeated until the subject makes no error at any of the twenty choice-points The asterisks marking the correct holes do not appear on the maze. (*From E. C. Tolman, C. S. Hall and E. P. Bretnall, J. Exp. Psychol.., 1932, 15, 602. By permission.*)

value. Let us note that the animals were hungry and were seeking food: their fundamental hunger-food motivation remained the dominant element in their learning.

Findings consonant with these have been obtained on human subjects working at another kind of maze problem (see Figure 144). Different subjects were to learn the correct holes in the series of choice-points under different conditions of punishment:

    I. a shock received at both right and wrong holes;
   II. a shock received at wrong holes only;
  III. a shock received at right holes only.

Result: no significant difference was obtained between any two of the groups in the rates of learning the problem.

We may generalize the evidence and arguments by concluding that that version of the Law of Effect which assumes that the effective rewards and punishments are the ones *incurred immediately* upon entering a particular alley, turning a particular button, or approaching a particular visual signal, is too superficial. It neglects the *relation* of each particular act to the *total performance*. More serious still, it neglects the relationship of each act to the *fundamental motivation* of the subject in his learning. The Law of Effect still holds, but we must broaden our notion of "effect."

Some Recent Learning Theories

Less naïve interpretations of what goes on in learning have been advanced in recent years. The student interested in the more explanatory phases of our subject will find the current discussions of considerable value, revealing as they do different systematic backgrounds for the different learning theories [13, 22].

The *sign-significate theory* of Tolman conceives of learning as involving cognitive elements or bits-of-knowledge. When a rat learns to take regularly a certain maze pathway, or a dog learns to lift his forepaw at sound of a buzzer, or a child comes to say "cat" when he sees the visible marks C A T — in each case the subject has learned to follow *signs* (the maze stimuli, the buzzer, the letters "C A T") to a goal (by turning right or left, lifting the forepaw, saying "cat," respectively). Thus the subject learns meanings, not movements; and as he repeats this experience he learns that the signs signify things to come, that is, he learns sign-significate relations. If the dog lifts his paw after he hears the buzzer, he avoids shock. Then he develops an expectation of avoiding shock. In popular terms, when one has learned something, he has come to recognize a new or a special feature of his environment as invested with special "come-on" meaning.

The *stimulus-response contiguity theory* of Guthrie may be called another association theory, but it differs from the foregoing as emphasizing the contiguity or togetherness of appropriate stimulus and appropriate response. When the rat, dog, or child comes to make his correct response he does so because the critical to-be-learned stimulus complex and the to-be-made response have occurred together once or many times. The rat is running the pathway while he is seeing it; the dog is raising his foot while he is hearing the buzzer; the first-grader is vocalizing the right throat-sounds while looking at the printed letters of his primer. Within this theory, it can be seen, the movement-produced kinesthetic sensory cues must have a central role of play. The true cue being learned is not the stimulus as set up and measured by the experimenter; instead, that cue gives rise to movements which in turn occasion (kinesthetic) stimuli, and it is these stimuli that fill the gap between stimuli and responses. This may be styled a behavioristic associationism.

Both the foregoing theories may be said to emphasize the contiguity of two things. Emphasis is laid on the $S \rightarrow R$ mechanisms and on the simultaneous occurrence of certain items — S_1 and S_2 or S and R. The *reinforcement theory* of Hull takes in a wider range of phenomena. It lays emphasis upon the fact that the learning occurs in a motivated subject, the association between S and R being determined by their relationship to the subject's drive and a reward (drive-release). Responses to stimuli in the presence of drives will be strengthened (learned) if those responses lead to *reward;* weakened (extinguished) if they do not. The rat gets its hunger satisfied after choosing the right alley; the dog saves himself a shock by lifting his paw; the child's interest in learning to read or his desire to do as teacher says (or both) is satisfied when he enunciates the correct word. The reinforcement theory has led to highly precise formulations of many of the principles and phenomena of habit-forming.

The student need not be too much concerned over the controversial character of these theories of learning — and of others that we have not mentioned. It is sensible and true enough to recognize that they emphasize different things and really supplement each other [9]. These principles are in essence only elaborations of the conception of learning as a phenomenon of organismic adjustment to environment. The psychologist looks forward to the day when all partial, single-viewpoint theories will become successfully incorporated into one complete and completely satisfactory system of learning principles. Until then we should remain empirically interested in learning wherever and however manifested.

Looking Forward

Our survey of the yieldings of typical experimental researches, to which so many of the pages of this chapter have been devoted, should have enriched the conception of organismic adjustment and provided us with an equipment in the fundamentals of learning. It has also pointed the way ahead for our inquiries into the more subtle forms of human adjustment, by suggesting in advance many of the problems that are to be attacked — the nature and role of "perceiving," of "social behavior" and "verbal behavior," of "generalizing," and of "thinking." There is no more helpful approach to each of these problems than from the notion of the learning and readjusting organism which in its higher evolved stages has developed these more elaborate capacities.

REFERENCES

1. Adams, D. K. "Experimental studies of adaptive behavior in cats," *Comp. Psychol. Monogr.*, 1929, *6*, No. 27.
2. Alpert, A. "The solving of problem-situations by preschool children," *Teach. Coll. Contr. Educ.*, 1928, No. 323.
3. Bass, M. I., and C. L. Hull. "The irradiation of a tactile conditioned reflex in man," *J. Comp. Psychol.*, 1934, *17*, 47–66.
4. Bekhterev, V. M. *General Principles of Human Reflexology*. New York: International Publishers, 1928.
5. Birch, H. G. "The relation of previous experience to insightful problem-solving," *J. Comp. Psychol.*, 1945, *38*, 367–383.
6. Brown, W., and J. Buel. "Response tendencies and maze patterns as determiners of choices in a maze," *J. Comp. Psychol.*, 1940, *29*, 337–399.
7. Bruce, R. H. "The effect of removal of reward on the maze performance of rats," *Univ. Calif. Publ. Psychol.*, 1930, *4*, No. 13.
8. Dashiell, J. F. "Direction orientation in maze learning by the white rat," *Comp. Psychol. Monogr.*, 1930, *7*, No. 32.
9. Dashiell, J. F. "A survey and synthesis of learning theories," *Psychol. Bull.*, 1935, *32*, 261–275.
10. Fields, E. "Form discrimination in the white rat," *J. Comp. Psychol.*, 1928, *8*, 143–158.
11. Finch, G., and E. Culler. "Higher order conditioning with constant motivation," *Amer. J. Psychol.*, 1934, *46*, 596–602.
12. Grant, D. C. "The influence of attitude on the conditioned eyelid response," *J. Exp. Psychol.*, 1939, *25*, 333–346.
13. Hilgard, E. R. *Theories of Learning*. New York: Appleton-Century-Crofts, 1948.
14. Hilgard, E. R. "The nature of the conditioned response. I," *Psychol. Rev.*, 1936, *43*, 366–385.
15. Hobhouse, L. T. *Mind in Evolution*. Second edition. New York: The Macmillan Company, 1915.
16. Köhler, W. *The Mentality of Apes* (trans. by E. Winter). New York: Harcourt, Brace and Company, 1925.
17. Krechevsky, I. " 'Hypotheses' versus 'chance' and the genesis of 'hypotheses' in rats," *Univ. Calif. Publ. Psychol.*, 1932, *6*, 27–44, 46–64.
18. Jasper, H., and C. Shagrass. "Conditioning the occipital rhythm in Man," *J. Exp. Psychol.*, 1941, *28*, 273–288; "Conscious time judgments

related to conditioned time intervals and voluntary control of the alpha rhythm," *ibid.*, 503–508.

19. Liddell, H. S., W. T. James, and O. D. Anderson. "The comparative physiology of the conditioned motor reflex," *Comp. Psychol. Monogr.*, 1934, *11*, No. 51.

20. Ling, B. C. "The solving of problem-situations by the pre-school child," *J. Genet. Psychol.*, 1946, *68*, 3–28.

21. Luh, C. W., and N. C. Shen. "Direction orientation in mice," *Yenching Stud. Psychol.*, 1933, *1*, No. 3.

22. Moss, F. A. *Comparative Psychology*. Revised edition. New York: Prentice-Hall, 1942. Chapters 6–11.

23. Muenzinger, K. F. "Motivation in learning," I, *J. Comp. Psychol.*, 1934, *17*, 267–277; II, *J. Exp. Psychol.*, 1934, *17*, 439–448.

24. Pavlov, I. P. *Conditioned Reflexes*. New York: Oxford University Press, 1927.

25. Pavlov, I. P. *Lectures on Conditioned Reflexes*. New York: International Publishers, 1928.

26. Razran, G. H. S. "Studies in configural conditioning," II, *J. Exp. Psychol.*, 1939, *24*, 95–105.

27. Skinner, B. F. *The Behavior of Organisms*. New York: Appleton-Century-Crofts, 1938.

28. Warner, L. H. "An experimental search for the 'conditioned response,'" *J. Genet. Psychol.*, 1932, *41*, 91–115.

29. Wickens, D. D. "The transference of conditioned excitation . . .," *J. Exp. Psychol.*, 1938, *22*, 101–123.

30. Witkin, H. A. "The rat's systematized habits of response in a non-problem situation," *Psychol. Bull.*, 1937, *34*, 708–709.

31. Yerkes, R. M. "The mental life of monkeys and apes," *Behav. Monogr.*, 1916, *3*, No. 1.

32. Yerkes, R. M. "The mind of a gorilla," *Genet. Psychol. Monogr.*, 1927, *2*, Nos. 1–2, No. 6.

33. Zener, K. "The significance of behavior accompanying conditioned salivary secretion . . .," *Amer. J. Psychol.*, 1937, *50*, 384–403.

16

PERCEIVING

A PROCESS OF ORGANIZING OR CONSTRUCTING

IN THE PRECEDING CHAPTER the point has been made that much of the process of learning is the coming to apprehend or structure correctly a thing or situation. We turn now to a closer examination of this apprehending.

In the first place, the behavior of an animal or person perceiving or apprehending something is not by any means simply the passive receiving of sensory excitation: the perceiver *supplements* and *interprets* that excitation. When the pilot spots on the ground another airplane that looks familiar, he is likely to report the guns on it in the usual places for that type of plane, whereas in fact the plane he is looking at may have no guns at all. It is he, the perceiver, who has added them. The concert listener may continue to "hear" the pianissimo tone from the violinist's A-string so long as the performer continues his bowing motions, even though they be out of contact with the string: it is the perceiving listener who supplements the sights with the sounds. Or consider the first-grade child who announced that she was going to draw a man, then produced Figure 145. How did she come to put in the extra eye? The answer is found in the general observation that young children draw not what is sensorially presented to their receptors, the images on their retinas, but what they apprehend as "there." Assuredly, what this particular child (or anyone!) perceives when she looks at a man's profile in any ordinary way is not a one-eyed man but a two-eyed man: the mere sensory excitation is enriched, interpreted, supplemented. When it comes, then, to putting down on paper what she sees, she is naïve enough to put down

443

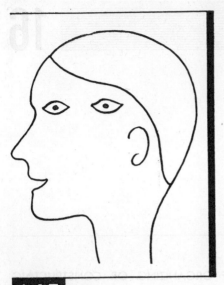

145   **Drawing of a Profile by a Young Child**

The child has drawn not simply what meets the eye but what she usually perceives when looking at a person from the side: a two-eyed person. In the drawing she fails to correct for the unconscious supplementing.

what she does perceive — and not the sophisticated reductions which a few lessons in drawing would have taught her. So, too, for other modalities of sense. If a person hears a certain noise in another room he may recognize his dog, though so far as he is concerned the noise is all that is physically "there." We apprehend more than meets the eye or ear.

Children sometimes turn ambiguities of interpretation into puzzles, as in Figure 146. This may take a cutaneous form in "blind man's buff" or an auditory form in such riddles as "The man rode across the bridge and Yettie walked."

A correct way of perceiving is often a real achievement, for in a sense it is a personal construction. One who hears only some of the bells from the carillon tower may find himself facing the problem of "Just what is that melody?" Or when driving a strange road at night, he may puzzle, "Just what is that looming bulk ahead?" He may hear or see a succession of wrong constructs before he gets what he accepts as the right one. And it is worth noting that each construct far exceeds the poor array of tones or the sketchy blurs which were the contribution of the stimuli themselves. Laboratory analysis of this process of constructing has shown that where the presented material is at all resistant, the process may reveal three phases. To begin with there is (1) the *sensory* phase, largely descriptive, in which the subject identifies his data in terms of their mere size, number, placing, and the like. There is (2) the *exploratory* phase, wherein by trial-and-error he musters suggestions as to what they are all about, sometimes experiencing blocks and difficulties that make him impatient and aggressive, and sometimes finding his material reversing itself in tumultuous ways; until in (3) the *interpretative* stage, the sensory stuff has yielded itself to the perceiver's designs, be they ever so extravagant and highhanded, and the perception is at last constructed [6]. These three phases doubtless overlap and interpenetrate a good deal in most cases; but such descriptions will remind the reader that the process of perceiving, too, is adjustmental in its basic nature. (Two protocols from this study have been used above on pages 24 f.)

The Organizations Are Transposable

A person reacts primarily to the relationship and not to the particular items related. The organization or pattern which he apprehends is often independent of the absolute character of the stimulus-detail: the principle of transposability. One who has learned the air of "Swanee River" or the leitmotif of "*Die Preislied*" is able to recognize it in whatever key it may be played and even, within limits, regardless of the tempo.

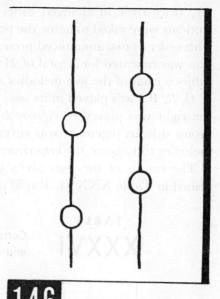

146   **A Puzzle: What is It?**

The answer is furnished in a footnote on page 476.

This everyday observation was reinforced by a simple experiment using the piano melodies shown in Figure 147. To college students the ten melodies were played, each being presented with its corresponding let-

147   **The Melodies Used in the Transposing Experiment**

Explanation in text. (*From K. Leeper and D. O. Leeper*, J. GEN. PSYCHOL., *1932, 6, 363. By permission of the authors.*)

ter, twice over in changed order; then on the third presentation the students were asked to name the proper letter upon hearing each melody. This order of two announced presentations and one recognition presentation was repeated for a total of 21 presentations. Now, for one group of subjects each of the five melodies appearing in the figure on the left (*H*, *J*, *O*, *R*, *W*) was played in its *same key* throughout, while each of those on the right was played in *different keys* on successive trials. (For another group this arrangement was reversed for the left-hand and right-hand melodies to balance the experimental controls.)

The results of the tests given on the successive third-trials are furnished in Table XXXVI. Rapid inspection and comparison of columns

TABLE XXXVI
Correct Recognitions of Constant and of Transposed Melodies

Trial	Constant mean score	Transposed mean score	$\dfrac{M_c - M_v}{SE_{diff}}$
3	.68	.78	− .81
6	1.34	1.18	1.18
9	1.59	1.50	.60
12	1.68	1.38	2.13
15	2.05	1.86	1.74
18	2.19	2.28	− .68
21	2.37	2.27	.73
All trials	11.92	11.25	1.31

51 subjects in one group; 57 in the other

From R. Leeper and D. O. Leeper, J. GEN. PSYCHOL., 1932, 6, 364. By permission.

2 and 3 bring out only differences that are very small and not always in the same direction; and in column 4 none of the critical ratios approaches the value of at least 3, which is necessary to indicate that the difference found is a reliable and certain one. We may therefore conclude that changing the *absolute* qualities of the details of stimulation while leaving the pattern unchanged does not affect one's recognition of a melody.

DETERMINANTS OF PERCEPTUAL ORGANIZATION

What things determine the way in which a man will perceive what is before him? What are the factors that shape his perceptions?

(1) Some Primary Configural Tendencies

Suppose that the reader were to listen to a series of taps sounded at equally spaced intervals, all alike in intensity and other qualities. He would find that he could not long hear them simply as an undifferentiated succession. For the pure series breaks up. The individual sounds group themselves into some kind of rhythm, some kind of recurring accent by twos or threes. And further, minor groupings frequently combine into more inclusive ones with primary and secondary accents. This is the psychological basis for the temporal rhythms of poetry and of music. The auditory field of discrete stimulations undergoes inevitably some kind of structuring, some insistent organizing, even when the discrete stimulations are quite homogeneous. Then let some objective variations appear among them and the organization becomes more striking: if every second tap-sound is louder, a twofold rhythm is compelling; if a longer time interval follows every third sound, a threefold rhythm appears. Note that this structuring occurs not in consequence of what the perceiver has learned nor of what he is set for — though his set might make one rhythm more likely to appear than another. It is simply *given* him. It is due to some *organizing processes of sense-organ or neural conductors or nerve centers or of the bodily organism generally.* In everyday phrase, it is "natural" to hear the accents. More generally, it is natural to hear or see or otherwise perceive certain kinds of totals; the baby does, anybody does, and in spite of himself.

As in a field of auditory stimulation, so this configural tendency holds in other fields of sense. Gazing at the starry night sky, the spectator will see not just a star-studded dome (Figure 148). The longer he gazes the more definitely does his visual field arrange itself into patterns and constellations — the Milky Way, the Great Bear, the Pleiades — as well as relations of dominance and subordination between the more brilliant planets and first-magnitude stars, on the one hand, and the many fainter third- and fourth-magnitude stars about them, on the other.

A few of the simpler principles that operate in the primary organizing of a visual field may be taken from Wertheimer's classic study [21].

Suppose, he says in effect, a person is facing a row of dots like those in Figure 149, *A*. He will treat them not as so many individual items but as *a row*. Suppose, next, that some of these items are absent, as in *B*. Inevitably he will perceive the row as broken up into the groups *ab/ de/ gh* and not as broken into *a/ bd/ eg/ h*. The *nearness* of stimulus details, then, is one thing that directs the way the organism patterns them.

Suppose, however, the row is constituted of different characters, as

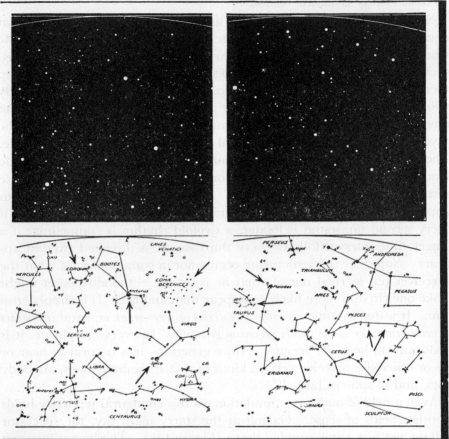

148 Some Primary Configural Tendencies in Viewing the Sky

Note that at first glance either field does have a certain single character:
it is "*a starry sky*," and is not perceived as "this star plus that star plus a third
star," etc. Then certain constellations begin to make their appearance as
segregated structures. The operation of the following primary organizing
tendencies in the human observer may be noted: *Proximity* — shown in seeing
as one constellation the Pleiades, or Taurus. *Similarity* — in seeing Coma
Berenices as a single mass, "Berenice's hair." *Continuity* — from the string of
seven stars at the left in Pisces the observer continues to the right and takes
in the loop of stars, to form head of fish. *Closure* — the loop of Corona tends
to complete itself in a crown. *Better figure* — the stars of Taurus in rough
V-formation suggest the well-shaped head of a bull. *Uniqueness* — Arcturus
or Spica stands out by virtue of this quality. The reader will find such organizing principles as these operating more vividly as he contemplates an actual
sky. (*From K. McKready,* A Beginner's Star-Book, *Putnam, 4th ed., 1947.*
By permission of the publishers.)

in Figure 149, *C*. Now the items automatically group themselves *ab/ cd/ ef/ gh*. Or better, suppose them to be arranged in several rows, as in *D*. Now they fall into vertical arrays, the rows giving place to columns. The factor of *similarity*, then, is another basis of organization.

The dots or lines in *E* group themselves as *ac/ b*. This is called the principle of *continuity*, for it seems that with the *a* segment the *c* segment is more continuous than is the *b* segment.

Another principle is exhibited well in an example suggested by Koffka. In *F* the tendency of an observer is to treat the configuration not as a set of three lines forming two angles, nor perhaps as the representation of a narrow-mouthed vessel, but as an unclosed triangle. Similarly, *G* is more likely to be taken for a broken circle than a pair of arcs. There is a tendency, it seems, for the organism to complete a configuration. This tendency, called *closure*, is notably seen in the way we look at drawings, as Figure 150.

Still another primary principle is *uniqueness*. This point is illustrated by the perceptions of a jay bird that had been trained to push over an inverted flower pot to get its food. Whenever the pot used for the bait stood in the segregated position "+" in any of the presentations reproduced in Figure 151, the bird had no difficulty in going to it directly; but if the pot used was any of the others, it was forced into random searching.

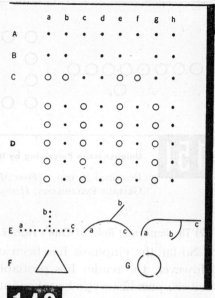

149 Some Primary Configurational Tendencies

Described and analyzed in the text. (*After Wertheimer*)

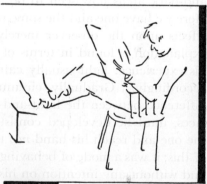

150 Example of Closure: Reading the Sports Page

What the reader perceives is more than the few lines actually presented to the eye (which may be better appreciated if the picture be turned upside down). What he perceives is more complete, more closed up. (*From S. I. Franz and K. Gordon, PSYCHOLOGY, McGraw-Hill, 1933.*)

151

Uniqueness in Perceiving by the Jay Bird

Described in text. (*From M. Hertz in W. D. Ellis (ed.), A* Source Book in Gestalt Psychology, *Harcourt, Brace, 1938.*)

(2) The Important Role of One's Habits

So far the emphasis has been on primary structurings in perceiving. However, the reader has probably had some qualms. Is not the perceiver's past history to be taken into account? Most assuredly it is. This is vividly brought out by Figure 152. Holding the picture so that the word "Lehigh" is easily read, observe the larger light-and-dark areas which are roughly circular in shape. What do they seem to be? Look also at the small light-and-dark spots. What are they? Next, invert the picture so that the word is upside down. What are the larger light-and-dark areas now seen to be? And how do the small spots appear? Here we have one and the same physical figure producing quite opposite effects upon the observer merely by being rotated 180 degrees. The explanation is found in terms of his experience, that is, his habits. In his experience, light usually came from above and shadows were cast accordingly. Gradually circumstances compelled him to learn the difference between the light-and-shadow of convex and of concave surfaces, until he developed consistent tendencies to place his hand *upon* the one and reach his hand *into* the other. Not that he ever was aware of this; it was a mode of behaving that became established unconsciously and without any intention on his part.

When the letter *V* was being made into a symbol of hope by the underground people suppressed by the Nazi terror, the tapped-out sound of the Morse code equivalent, – – – ⎯, was heard by many not as the intended letter but as the rhythm of the first motif in Beethoven's Fifth Symphony. Music-hearing habits prevailed.

It is told that Sir Arthur Sullivan, the composer-member of the famous Gilbert-Sullivan team, after having imbibed several glasses of port one afternoon, set out with a companion to go to tea at a house where he

152 **The Effect of Old Habits in Reacting to Lights and Shadows**

Explanation in text (*C. H. Stoelting Co.*)

had been only once before. Upon reaching the street, Sir Arthur could not remember the number.

"Never mind," he said, and systematically walked up to every door in turn, to give its boot scraper a gentle kick with his boot.

"Here we are," he said at last. "E flat." [1]

One of the ways in which the influence of the factor of past experience on the interpretation of a stimulus-complex has been brought into the laboratory for quantitative treatment is by the study of the phenomenon of *constancy*. We tend to perceive objects in their normal — that is, most habitual way — in spite of alterations in the particular stimulus conditions. The colors or the sizes in which we have most commonly had experience with a thing will tend to be preserved, whatever the actual colors and sizes now presented to the eye. The usual or constant or normal way of perceiving it in the past will influence the way of perceiving it now. When one looks at the top of a rectangular table, even

[1] From the *Golden Book.*

though he realizes that the four angles presented to his retinae are not right angles, he is likely to underestimate the amount by which they differ from true right angles. Or again, upon entering a room illuminated by a fluorescent bulb or a photographer's ruby lamp, one may see various objects — flowers, pictures, one's own hands — in startlingly abnormal colors at first, but quickly the normal modes of apprehending assert their dominance, and the objects are then seen as normal again.

For this constancy effect, it is necessary that the perceiver be aware that the unusual conditions *are* unusual. If seen only through a small aperture, a flat-surfaced piece of coal lying in bright sunlight is likely to be taken for "a light gray something," even a "white paper"; but if it is more generously exposed so as to evoke the coal-recognizing habits of the individual, the "light gray" will give place to "black." And the resolute efforts of the most sophisticated person will effect only a partial correction, a partial approximation to the "light gray" [3].

This point has been quantitatively studied in the following standard experiment (see Figure 153). Upon two color rotators, R_1 and R_2, are mounted black and white paper disks, their ratios adjustable to produce on rotation any desired intensity of gray. A shadow screen *SS* placed between the two rotators cuts down the illumination coming from a window on the right so that disk R_2 is shaded. The subject sits at X behind a reduction screen *RS*, which cuts off all sight of anything but a reduced area of each disk visible to him through holes in the screen. He is instructed to match the gray of R_1 to that of R_2 by manipulating a device (not shown in the figure) to control the ratio of black-white mixture on R_1. In one classic case [10], while R_2 was kept a pure white (360° W, 0° B), the adjustment of R_1 set by the subject was found to be: 4.2° W, 355.8° B). Then when the reduction screen *RS* was removed to permit view of rotators, shadow screen, illumination source, and all, the subject made his matching adjustment of R_1 at no less than 116° W, 244° B. In a word, the shaded disk *when seen to be shaded*, retained to a surprising degree its normal or usual character of whiteness. And this general phenomenon will repeat itself in either direction as the reduction screen is introduced or taken away. It seems that the organism somehow quite unwittingly corrects for unusual conditions present. It tends to perceive things in a constant manner, that is, as they normally (most commonly) are. And this, obviously, is the operation of past experience.

The part played by a person's established habits is exhibited well in cases where the familiar stimuli are encountered in radically changed organization, producing breakdown of the responses and necessitating their reorganization. In one case, an investigator mounted a pair of

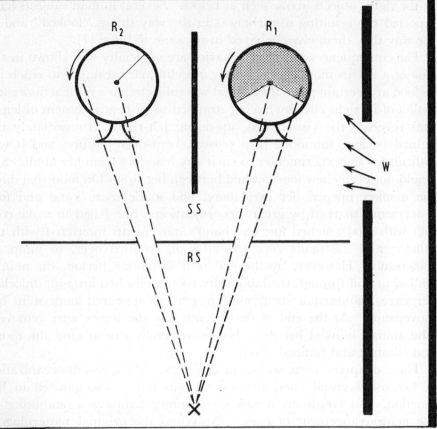

153 Arrangement for Measuring Brightness Constancy

Explanation in text. (*After D. Katz,* AUFBAU DER FARBWELT, *Barth, 1930.*)

small eartrumpets on his head, but crossed the tubes so that each receiving trumpet conducted to the ear on the opposite side of the head. He writes of one of the resulting incidents:

> While walking along the sidewalk I heard the voices of two ladies and their steps approaching and overtaking me from behind on the right. Quite automatically I stepped to the left making more room for them to pass. I looked back and found that I had stepped directly in front of them. My automatic reaction as well as the localization was reversed [22].

Even more confusing have been the consequences of radical disturbance of the patterning of visual cues, when lenses that rotate the visual field 180 degrees have been worn so that objects on the left were seen at the right, objects above seen as below. Several human subjects have reported the resulting disturbances in the way things "looked" and in the way they themselves behaved in response to them [7].

The consequences for overt behavior are especially well shown in the case of a rhesus monkey [8]. After a preliminary training to reach for its food at a certain place the animal was subjected to a radical disorganization of its sight cues by having strapped to its head a system of lenses that reversed the visual field, up-down, left-right. Immediately the animal became immobile in a passive, bent-over posture, and it was difficult for the experimenter to elicit any reactions from her at all. She would not even chew food pushed between her lips. On following days, the monkey opened her eyes more, and made more hand and foot movements, marked by great incoordination. She failed to make contact with food reached for; one hand's movements interfered with the other's; and she made repeated attempts to turn over, to jump, to somersault. However, by the end of a seven-day period, the animal walked at will through the laboratory rooms, climbed around, unlocked her cage, mounted a shelf, and in general appeared normal in her movements. At the end of the seventh day the lenses were removed. The animal blinked her eyes, but immediately ran around the room, and climbed and jumped about.

Three chapters, then, we see in this story. (1) Upon disorganization of her usual visual cues, the animal was badly disorganized in her reaction. (2) Gradually a new set of motor habits was established to the new arrangement of cues. (3) When the original patterning of stimuli was restored, the nine-year-old long-established perceptual-motor coordinations were readily available.

It is consistent with this that Lashley and his associates have shown that chimpanzee infants raised for months in the dark do not readily acquire normal visually controlled behavior when they are finally brought out into the light, even though their eyes are undamaged.

(3) One's Temporary Set as Determining How He Perceives

In other connections we have had occasion to recognize that what direction one's attention takes depends not only on his long-established habits but also on the temporarily maintained attitudes or postures called sets that may have possession of him at the time. This same principle comes out again as we regard a person's observing-acts from the point of view of how the attended-to field becomes meaningfully organized. A simple experiment will illustrate this everyday, obvious point.

Old Woman   Composite
                  (-from Boring)

                                    Young Woman

Pirate   Composite   Rabbit

154 Ambiguous Figures Used to Study Influence of Temporary Set

Explanation in text. (*From R. Leeper*, J. GENET. PSYCHOL., *1935, 46, 62. By permission of the author.*)

An ambiguous *composite* figure (Figure 154) was displayed on a screen to student subjects, who were to write down what they saw. These served as the control group. A second group of subjects were first shown one or the other of the *single-phase* drawings derived from the ambiguous or composite one. (One sub-group were shown the single-phase drawings of old woman and rabbit respectively; the other sub-group, the young woman and the pirate.) Then they were shown (with no explanations) the composite figures and were asked for descriptions, as had been done with the control subjects. A third group were given only verbal preparation beforehand by being told, "You will be shown a drawing of a young woman's head" [or "an old woman's head," or "a man's head," or "a rabbit sitting up"]. Each hint was elaborated with verbal details.

Did the preceding way of regarding a pattern of stimuli carry over as

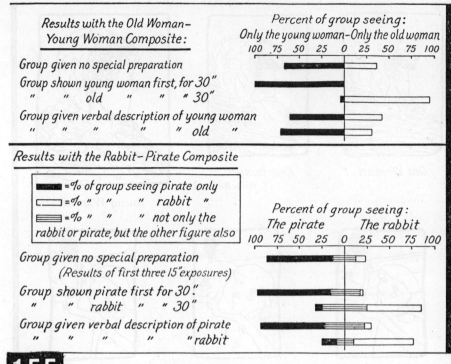

Results with the Old Woman-
Young Woman Composite:

Percent of group seeing:
Only the young woman-Only the old woman
100 75 50 25   0   25 50 75 100

Group given no special preparation
Group shown young woman first, for 30"
    "   "   old   "   "   " 30"
Group given verbal description of young woman
    "   "   "   "   " old   "

Results with the Rabbit-Pirate Composite

▬▬▬ = % of group seeing pirate only
☐ = % "   "   " rabbit "
▤ = % "   "   " not only the
rabbit or pirate, but the other figure also

Percent of group seeing:
The pirate   The rabbit
100 75 50 25   0   25 50 75 100

Group given no special preparation
    (Results of first three 15" exposures)
Group shown pirate first for 30".
    "   " rabbit   "   " 30"
Group given verbal description of pirate
    "   "   "   "   " rabbit

155 Graphed Results Obtained with the Ambiguous Figures

(*From R. Leeper, Ibid., 66. By permission.*)

a predisposition that influenced the way of regarding a later pattern?
The graph in Figure 155 gives us an affirmative answer in quantitative
terms.   Other influences being equal, what a person is set to perceive,
he is more likely to perceive than anything else.

(4) The Influence of One's Values

We must take cognizance of still deeper determining factors in the
perceiver's make-up.   In our account of the part played by the three
foregoing factors in shaping one's perceptual organization, we might
seem to have treated man or animal simply as an intellectual or as a
behaving machine.   But he is a living organism with urges, wants,
needs, values, goals.

In a recent study, two groups of ten-year-olds — one composed of
children from wealthy families, the other of children from poor families
— were given the task of adjusting the size of a disk to make it look
equal in size to various coins in turn — a penny, a nickel, a dime, a
quarter, and a half-dollar.   The disk was a visible patch cast on a

ground-glass screen by a light shining through an iris diaphragm which could be varied in diameter from ⅛ inch to 2 inches as the subject turned a knob. Holding the coin in his left hand and manipulating the knob with his right, each child tried to match the size of the lighted patch to the size of the coin. A control group then was put through the same tests, but using no coins, only gray cardboard disks of corresponding sizes.

The data obtained are best put in terms of the amount (in percentage) of difference between children's estimates of the size of a valued object (a piece of money) as compared with their estimates of the size of a relatively worthless object (a piece of cardboard). In Figure 156, *A*, the difference is quite considerable. "Money looks big to the child." Further, that difference depends upon the child, or, more accurately, upon his economic background; for in Figure 156, *B*, we see that the overestimation of the size of the coins is far greater on the part of the children from the poorer families. Present results of this experiment, then, make it seem that "Money looks especially big to those who need it most."

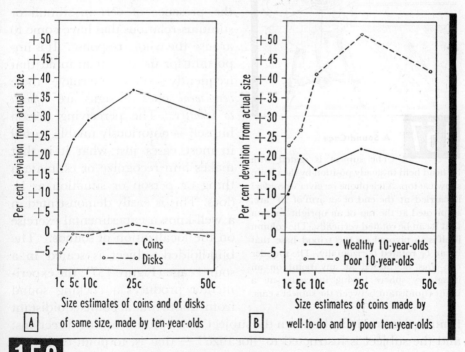

156 One's Values Influence His Judgments of Coins

(*From J. S. Bruner and C. C. Goodman, J. ABN. SOC. PSYCHOL., 1947, 42, 33–44. By permission of authors and editor.*)

The ways in which a person perceptually organizes his heard, seen, smelled, felt, and otherwise sensed stimulations is much more than a sense-perceptual matter. It may be fundamental to or symptomatic of his whole personality [18]. That is the assumption of those who employ the Rorschach type of examination device (see pages 634 ff.). And it is coming to be recognized as a cardinal principal in the understanding of social psychological phenomena [12].

EXTENSIONS OF THE MEANING OF "CUES"

Reduced Cues

The response called "perceptual" depends, as we have seen, upon the presence of certain stimuli or stimulus-relations that have come to arouse the whole response. It is important for us to bear in mind that frequently — if not as a rule — these *very weak* cues or signs are *difficult to identify*. The perceiving person himself is notoriously unable to tell in most cases just what it is that makes him recognize or estimate a thing or person or situation as he does. This is easily demonstrated in a well-known experimental exercise on the localization of sounds. The blindfolded subject is seated in a sound cage (Figure 157); the experimenter produces a clicking sound from time to time at points equidistant

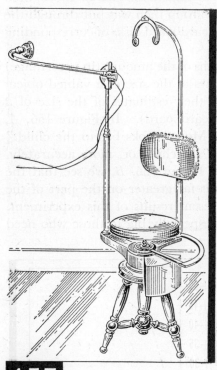

157 **A Sound Cage**

The subject is seated with his head held in steady position by the clamp shown at top. A telephone receiver (sounder) is carried at the end of an arm of 90° arc, so pivoted at the top of an upright column that it can be rotated vertically. The column itself is so pivoted on the tripod base that it can be rotated horizontally. The sounder can thus be placed at any point on an imaginary sphere having its center at a point equidistant between the subject's ears.

from a point midway between the subject's ears but in varying directions; and the subject is instructed to "localize" — that is, to point each time toward the source of the sound. Errors of as much as 180 degrees are not uncommon. A striking feature is that in no case can the subject tell *just how* it is that he localizes a given sound as from such and such direction; he is at a loss to specify the characteristics of the sound by which he was directed; he cannot by analysis identify the cues. The sound "just came from that direction," and that is all he can say. However, objective controls bring to light the true conditions at work. Earphones have been connected by air tubes to a source of sound that can be instrumentally controlled so that the sound waves transmitted to each ear can be varied in several of their physical attributes. By comparison of the subject's correct and incorrect localizations, it can be demonstrated that differences in the sound, as it falls upon the right and upon the left ear, cause the difference in his judging. Further, these differences may be in the time of reception, in the timbre, in the intensity, in the cycle-phase, or in the complexity of the tone. They are differences that the subject cannot consciously detect, yet they guide his localizing. With none of them present he is helpless. This principle of catching stimulation at differently placed receivers simultaneously is utilized in the sound direction finder that has been much used in military installations. One is shown in Figure 158.

158 **An Army Sound Locator**
Detecting the direction of a sound by utilizing differences in the way it falls on the two ears is made more accurate by use of an apparatus which has larger and more widely separated "ears" (horns), and which has separation between horns in both horizontal and vertical directions. Tubes lead from the horns to the operators' ears. (*From the* INFANTRY JOURNAL. *Photo by courtesy of Colonel Joseph I. Greene.*)

A physician who had had years of general practice once assured the present writer that frequently as he first stepped into a sickroom he would be possessed by a conviction that the patient's illness was of a certain particular order, then after careful diagnosis would find the conviction confirmed. And he maintained that he was often quite unable to say what it was about the patient that had shaped his guess. But he was not guessing; he was being guided subtly by perceptible signs too weak to be explicitly recognized by him.

The principle is well illustrated by a tale from the A.A.F. In some of the training centers in England students were at first instructed to learn to recognize a plane in an analytic way: by spotting in turn its

*w*ings, its *e*ngine, its *f*usilage, its *t*ail. But this w-e-f-t method was eventually found inferior to that of observing a plane as a whole, and — so
runs the story — the initial letters were then said really to mean "Wrong
every fool time."

Some horses at Elberfeld were once greatly celebrated for their feats
in tapping out sums, square roots of numbers, and the like, when such
problems were posted on a board in front of them; yet when no one was
present who knew the problem or the answer, the animals failed. Evidently, in the course of tapping out their answers, these acutely impres-
sionable animals were prompted or checked by the unintentional gestural
or vocal responses of the person knowing the correct solution.

The performances of certain human wonders are of the same order.
The mind-reader may announce one or another fantastic explanation
of his ability to tell what another person is thinking about. But his
true cues are really his dupe's slight gestures and changes of facial
expression — a complex and subtle ensemble of fine muscle reactions —
if not, indeed, certain words uttered by the subject which serve to
correct and direct the vague trial-and-error talking of the mind-reader.
Mind-reading is muscle-reading. In a similar way the intelligent salesman
perceives that it is time to close his interview. Something about the
movements of the auditor's eyes, or the fingering of his blotter, or his
way of sitting backward in his chair, or glancing at his papers or at his
office force — something, though he cannot say just what it is, tells the
salesman that it is time for him to go. It is the operation of such reduced
cues that often leads to the intuition or what is colloquially called the
hunch, and gives some basis to the claim that even a guess has a certain
value.

Symbolic Cues

If there is any one thing most outstanding in the life of mankind it is
surely this: that far from being limited to the here and now man's world
is extended to include past history and future time, mythology and fairy
tales, China and the Antipodes, and even other planets and suns and
the vast interstellar spaces. With all such remote things he can deal.
Or rather, with their representations he can deal. No living man, of
course, has ever seen Cortez, though he can roundly condemn that free-
booter and plunderer; no child really ever hopes to see or hear Snow
White or Hansel and Gretel or even supposes that they ever were in
flesh; the temple of the Lamas and the snowy peaks of Everest will never
be seen by most of us; and the new planet Pluto was discovered mathematically by scientists before they ever saw it. How has such an

extension of his world been rendered possible to man? In a word, by *symbols*.

We may define a symbol as *an object or a response that becomes a representative substitute for some other object, response, or situation.* It is reacted to directly, but only in this recognized relationship of sign-and-thing-signified. The sign may in fact be something utterly distinct in all sensory qualities from that for which it stands. The printed word "ORANGE" cannot be eaten, but it can throw the child reader into preparatory attitudes appropriate to that for which it is a sign. What is more, in this case reacting to the black-marks-on-white is not reacting to some larger whole of which they are a part, as would be the case in recognizing a motor car by its noise or a burning pudding by its odor or an orange by the feel of it in a Christmas stocking. The child is responding to something with which the pattern of black marks has been artificially associated and for which it then has come to function as a substitute. It is not a full and complete substitute, to be treated exactly as the original object or situation would be treated; it is always handled as in-relation-to that other. "Words," Hobbes puts it, "are wise men's counters, they do but reckon by them; but they are the money of fools." But even money is only symbolic material, until it becomes sought after by the miser on its own account purely, for its touch and sight and clinking sounds.

Dealing with symbols, or symbolic behavior, as we may call it, develops characteristically under *social* conditions, and has both active and receptive aspects. As communicative relationships between man and man evolve beyond the level of brute cries and ejaculations and pushings and shovings, and as cooperative attacks upon third objects are hit upon, the ability to deal with things not in their first intention but as instruments or signs of other things becomes of first importance. Now man can signal to a fellow-man concerning something the first can observe or has observed, so that the latter, taking the word or gesture or other signal for the fact or thing itself, can behave appropriately thereto. A *symbolic response* by one is perceived as a *symbolic stimulus* by the other.

The advantages are obvious. The printed symbol "ORANGE" is in a more convenient form than the visible, odorous, palpable, piece of fruit; it may, so to speak, be packed away in a smaller space; it is not liable to chemical disintegration and is replaceable if lost. In like manner, the interchange of commodities, of wealth, of real estate is made possible between men seated in offices remote from the material itself. The stock speculator can handle sugar, thousands of pounds of it, buying it with thousands of dollars and selling it for thousands of dollars — and all with merely a ticker tape and a telephone. If symbols have become the chief means of economic exchange between man and man, they have also become the great means of interstimulation and response in other ways, making possible the highly organized society peculiar to *Homo sapiens*.

We must postpone further analysis of symbolic behavior and genetic aspects of its development to the special treatments of Social Behavior and of Language Habits (Chapters 17 and 18). Meanwhile, let us note here that in this *capacity to perceive symbols* we find only *an extension of* the fundamental *capacity to be affected by and responsive to relationships*, in this case the relation of the-sign-and-the-signified.

ILLUSORY RESPONSES

Introduction

To err is human, and to be misled by appearances, equally so. Man's life is one in which he is continually forced to handle and respond to things, people, and happenings upon very slight and partial stimulation from them; and, furthermore, even his manner of responding to quite rich and adequate stimuli varies much under the influence of context and pre-established set. It is only to be expected, therefore, that often-times his particular perceivings may lead him astray. Everyone is subject to illusions.

Illusion, Hallucination, Delusion

Even in learned circles these three terms are frequently used in confusing ways. For the sake of clarity let us understand just how each is used in technical psychological discourse. An *illusion* is a misinterpretation of stimulation, a misleading perception, but usually recognized as such. In *hallucination* the error in perception is so great that the object is lacking or is fantastically misrepresented. Illusions are constantly experienced by the "normal" person, whereas hallucinations seldom are experienced except in unusual states, as delirium tremens or high fever, or by "abnormal" people. *Delusions* are false beliefs, usually of a degree to be counted as morbid or pathological and maintained by the person against any rational criticism.

Dreams are like hallucinations of waking life, except that, being experienced during sleep, and recognized by the dreamer on awaking as unreal, they are not taken as symptoms of mental disorganization.

Hallucinations and delusions, much more than illusions, are commonly symptomatic of motive-trends in pathological conditions. Dreams may or may not be symptomatic. (See pages 195 f.)

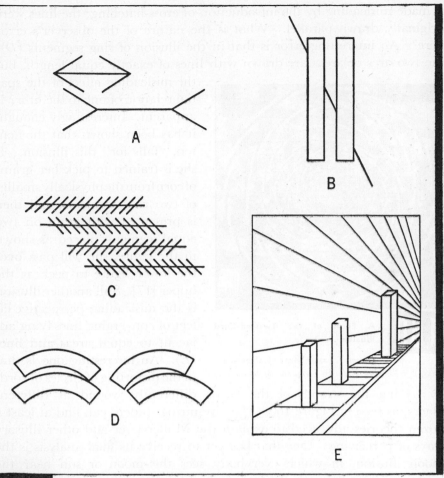

159 Some Optical Illusions

A. Müller-Lyer; *B*, Poggendorff; *C*, Zöllner; *D*, ring segments; *E*, perspective.

Optical Illusions

Probably the most famous of illusions is that produced by the Müller-Lyer design (Figure 159, *A*). The two base lines are of equal length, but after the attachment of small inward-turned and outward-turned lines at their ends they are taken to be of unequal length. Many variations of this illusion have been devised. Another well-known misleading design is that of Poggendorff (*B*), in which the continuity of a line is interrupted by strips of narrow width laid across it at an angle. The reader will readily discover what effect is given to the character of the line. In the Zöllner figure (*C*), the value of lines as indicators of direction is made misleading by the introduction of cross-hatching; the lines were originally drawn parallel. What is the nature of the observer's error here? An interesting error is that in the illusion of ring segments (D): the two arcs or areas are drawn with lines of exactly equal length, but the misleading effect of the spatial relation of one to the other is apparent. Interestingly enough, it has been shown that the hen, too, "falls for" this illusion. If she is trained to pick her grains of corn from the physically smaller of two ring segments, and then is presented with grain on two equal segments placed as shown in the figure, she will pass over the lower figure to peck at the upper [17]. Still another illusion is the misleading perspective effect of converging lines lying adjacent to equal areas and lines (E). An interesting one is that of the distorting of circles of cords

160 A Form of the Twisted-Cord Illusion

(From J. Fraser, Brit. J. Psychol., 1908, 2, 320, plate VII. By permission of the editor.)

by having the strands of the cords differently wound at different places, as seen in Figure 160.[1] The inquiring student can find at least a dozen theories advanced to explain the Müller-Lyer and other illusory ways of perceiving. One that has yet to receive its final analysis is the moon illusion, in which everybody sees the moon or sun near the horizon as much larger than when high in the sky. That this is not merely a matter of physics is easily shown. Let the reader lie on his back on a table, head toward the horizon moon, and hanging over the table edge; or let him stoop over and look at the horizon moon between his legs: it will be seen much shrunken [1].

The Proofreader's Illusion

In learning to read language one learns to react to larger and larger patterns of stimuli. Once these large higher-order habits are organized, they tend to be arousable by various particular stimuli forming a usual frequent part of the whole stimulus-pattern. It follous, then that a word-perceiving act should often be arouseable when not all detials of that word are actully stimulating" The printed word may be misspelled,

[1] The reader may need to trace out these circles to be convinced.

by omission or insertion or transposition of letters, or in other ways; spacing may be superfluous or omitted; punctuation marks may be improperly introduced or left out. But the reader, set for the meanings and silently speaking whole words in response to the few cues that do fall upon the center of his retina, reads confidently on with hardly an interference or trip on account of the printer's errors. (In one of the preceding sentences seven different errors have intentionally been permitted. How many of them attracted the reader's attention?) In the effort to print books perfectly, proofreaders are employed whose chief duty it is to scan the page and keep set to respond to all printers' errors. Yet so inveterate are a reader's habits of responding not piecemeal but to patterns of stimuli that even the professional proofreader has his illusions. Not even the most experienced can attain one hundred per cent accuracy.

The Phi-Phenomenon

One more illusion deserves our attention both because of its common occurrence and because of its importance to recent psychological history.

The enormous success of moving pictures is based upon their power to arouse an illusory perceiving of action. The screen, although actually in darkness many times per second, is able to stimulate the audience much as do the continuous movements of actors in person — arousing and holding attentive postures, touching off emotional tendencies, exciting thinking behavior. The situation presented is discontinuous and the observers are not actually looking at objects in motion; but the successive pictures obtained by instantaneous photography follow each other so rapidly, while their actual shiftings in this succession before the projector is being concealed by a shutter, that the same responses are elicited as though the scenes of things and people were actually moving.

This phenomenon has long been familiar to the laboratory worker. Since 1912, however, it has assumed a new importance in the psychological world on account of a closer analysis given it and an interpretation which marks that year as the beginning of the *Gestalt* movement. Wertheimer demonstrated the phenomenon as follows. Two black lines were shown on a white background in rapid succession, the first vertical, the second horizontal, as in Figure 161, *a* and *b*. If a fairly long interval of time, say 150 milliseconds (thousandths of a second), is allowed between the two flashes, the two lines will be perceived successively as *a* then *b*. If the interval is cut extremely short, to around 20 ms., then the two lines will be seen simultaneously and forming a right angle. If, however, the interval is adjusted between these two lengths, at somewhere about 60 — 90 ms., then still a third manner of perceiving is aroused: the vertical *a* line will be seen moving over to the horizontal *b* line in a sweeping motion, as indicated by the arrow in *c*. This Wertheimer has called the phi-phenomenon.

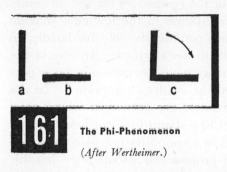

161 The Phi-Phenomenon

(After Wertheimer.)

Space forbids our telling in detail all of the intensive analyses which have been made of this event. One analysis employing illuminated slits on black lines has brought out the fact that other conditions than (1) time-intervals determine whether the phi-type of perception is aroused. They are (2) the spatial distance between the slits, and (3) their brightness. These three are intimately interdependent so that as one is varied one or both the others must be changed also if the phi effect is to be preserved. Some fascinating varieties in this effect itself have been produced. Under certain conditions the subject can be made to see one line pass behind the other, or one to pass to the other and back again, or one to pass in the opposite of the usual direction, or to approach and recede from the observer. The phenomenon has been produced by tactual stimulation also, the subject perceiving the movement on the skin, or, in a curious variant of the experiment, perceiving a movement from the first-touched spot up into the air and in an arc over to the other spot.

More important for general theory is the conclusion to which we are led: *The perceived movement is not made up of separately perceived lines* a *and* b *or of these and intervening lines: it is a unique and indivisible event.*

The foregoing survey of the illustrations of misperceiving and their analyses offers us a basis for a generalization. In all cases of illusion we can find one or more of the following causal factors responsible: long-established and *deep-rooted habits* of response; the person's *present set*, posture, expectation, the context in which the stimulus is found; and, occasionally, *peculiarities of the sense-organs*.

SOME SPECIAL EXPERIMENTAL PROBLEMS

Spatial Relations

None of the problems of human behavior have been so extensively examined in experimental laboratories as the problems of perceiving, and the studies of space perception have easily led in number. When the stimulations from an agent provoke a person or animal to turn directly toward it, or to treat it as something large or something small, or something near at hand or far away, what is it about these stimulations that is the determining thing?

Along with the kinesthetic, the *visual* mode of stimulation is most important and most used by man in the guidance of his movements in space. The retina of the eye is so refined that when two points of light are separated by only one or one and one-half minutes angular distance they can be discriminated as two points. Add to this the astonishing delicacy of the various muscles of the eye, and it is easy to see that localizing the directions and gauging the extents of objects presented to vision should be quite acute.

Cues to Visual Perceiving in the Third Dimension

"I can remember," wrote Helmholtz in his *Physiological Optics*, "as a child passing by the spire of the garrison church in Potsdam and seeing people on the balustrade, whom I took to be dolls. I asked my mother to take them down for me, believing she could do this by merely reaching up with her hands. I remember the incident so well, because it was this mistake which taught me the law of perspective, that is, the diminution of size with distance." A favorite problem for psychological analysis arises from the fact that a man can make adequate judgments of objects at various distances through sight alone. Consider that the retina is essentially a two-dimensional, although curved, surface, and that differences of physical distance in stimulus-objects cannot be directly projected upon this, since distance lies in the third dimension. How, then, can an object which stimulates the retina at a given set of points on this two-dimensional surface be reacted to as near and as far? In

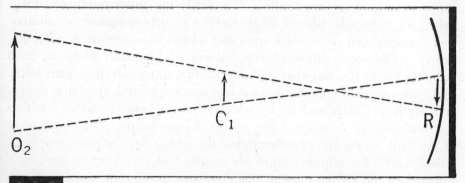

162 **Distances and the Retina**

The projection of light on the sensitive plate of the eye (R) from objects of different sizes but at different distances $(O_1$ and $O_2)$ may be identical.

Figure 162, it is shown that so far as the retina itself is concerned there can be *no difference in the area stimulated* by objects 1 and 2, though one is much farther from the retina than the other. If they are to be distinguished, some other stimulus-characters must be present for the organism to use in learning to react to them as near and far. What are these cues?

Three aspects already mentioned are (1) relative *height* in the visual field, (2) *interposition* of one object before another, and (3) *apparent size*. (4) *Clearness* is another cue. An object appearing as a dim, vague mass is taken to be further away than one with a clear-cut, distinctly detailed figure. This is a principle of "aerial perspective." Still another cue in this same class is (5) *color*. Light waves transmitted through a long distance of atmosphere, especially if it is hazy, are so affected that the original clear values are distorted; trees that are green when near at hand appear to be bluish on a distant mountain. In the example analyzed in Figure 152 the principle of (6) *lights and shadows* was found to be involved. The adequate handling of objects in terms of their depth and solidity is especially dependent upon usualness and normality of shading. Again, when the seeing person is moving through space, whether on a tricycle or on a railroad train, the relative positions of the eye with reference to objects seen are altered decidedly. A distant tree or house will continue to stimulate the retina from a given direction, while objects nearer the person enter, move across, and leave his field of vision. (7) *Apparent motion* (change of direction of stimulation) is, then, another cue to adaptations to objects both near and far.

All of the foregoing seven principles are used in those arts that seek to produce the same effects as visible scenes: painting, the stage, photography in motion picture studios. To clarify his understanding of these principles the reader himself might draw a picture designed to imitate a three-dimensional scene, with trees and houses indicated at varying distances. The explanation of the flatness of Egyptian sculpture and painting lies in the fact that the artists failed to use all these principles.

As was noted in Chapter 10, the eye is not merely a receiving organ. It is equipped with muscles by which it can accurately adjust itself to differences in the distance of the sources of stimulation. (8) The *focusing* of the lens, which allows definition of the image (in the photographer's sense), varies for objects within about fifty feet of a person; and, as a function of the ciliary muscle, this gives rise to afferent kinesthetic impulses to which spatial reactions can become attached. The same may be said for kinesthetic impulses arising from (9) the *convergence-divergence* of the eyeballs in binocular vision. The six muscles attached to each of the two balls cooperatively produce in varying degrees a certain turning-in of the eyes so that the stimulations from the objects, whether near or far, will fall upon the centers of both retinae. In binocular vision another cue is provided. Owing to their different positions in the head, the two eyes take different pictures of the object being looked at, the one from a position a little to the right, the other from a little to the left. Consequently, when a solid object, such as a book, a pencil, or a tree-trunk, is being regarded it presents to one eye a view of the front and a little around the right side; to the other eye, a view of the front and a little around the left side. Thus, as cameras placed a short distance apart will have their films exposed to slightly different aspects of the same object, so with the eyes and their retinae. The amount of overlapping of the two views varies with the distance, up to a mile or more. (10) The *double images* produced in this way furnish a cue of great reliability for the finer afferent control of behavior in space.

Doubtless the reader is surprised to find all these factors analyzed out of his visual perceiving of depth: he had seldom if ever been aware of them. Precisely so. They illustrate most happily the participation of reduced cues in normal perception — cues to which responses became attached more and more accurately back in his early infancy.

Temporal Relations

The living organism must adjust itself not only to things in space but to things in time; it must be able to time its own reactions adequately to seize the prey, or to dodge the blow. Man's life, in its complexity of organization, has forced upon him elaborate conditionings of his behavior to many sorts of time factors. Dressing, fixing the furnace, catching the 7:49 for the city, getting to work, stopping for lunch, returning to the office, all the activities of the day's and night's routine are based upon nice adjustments of a man's personal habits in point of time. To be sure, much of this is controlled by repeated reference to standard time indicators, clocks, watches, and factory whistles, which are attuned to the movements of celestial bodies (the most constant of phenomena); but even so, without some ability to tell time himself a man would be fatally handicapped. In special interests, as in music, the perception of time intervals is necessarily extremely delicate, and it is one of the objectives of special training.

Through the years a great number of experimental investigators have devoted themselves to problems in estimating short time intervals. They have measured individuals' ability to reproduce an interval they have just heard tapped off, or their ability to judge whether the second of two such intervals sounded in close succession is longer or shorter than the first. In consequence, the literature is full of generalizations of the results obtained. Yet, regrettably, these many generalizations are so conflicting in so many ways, that this is not an appropriate place to attempt to summarize them. For the student of methodology they do supply a rich field of problems in experimental designing, in the standardizing of conditions, objective and subjective, and of procedures to be followed [11].

What, now, are the cues operative in time-perceiving? If we neglect sunrises, mill whistles, clocks, and other external guides, we must seek the occurrences to which activity is timed in terms of intraorganic changes. This is shown with especial certainty in the surprising ability of some people to tell the precise hour, by day or by night, without any deliberate computation, and also in the ability of many to awaken exactly at a given hour, though usually with some loss in depth of sleep [15]. Now, certain physiological processes have well known rhythms, respiration, heartbeat, digestion, striped muscle phasic changes, and so on; and evidence is accumulating that more profound and more general chemical processes in the body furnish rhythms that are independent of exteroceptive stimulations. (1) Is the ability of the body to respond appropriately to a given interval traceable to some kind of quantitative summating of such rhythms, so that when a certain number have occurred the total effect serves as the stimulus? We know that a person's judgment of certain intervals is modified by the amount of muscular and visceral strain maintained, as in prolonged orientation and waiting, and the resultant afferent restimulation. (2) Is the time-perceiving ability in general due to some qualitative changes in organic conditions, which operate as the stimulus? [1] There may be other cues; it is still much of a problem.

Reading as Perceiving

Of peculiar interest to the student is that type of perceiving he employs much of the day and every day, reading. It is an exceedingly complex process, as the years of training in school eloquently testify, even if we neglect its highly symbolic nature and view it on its motor side. If we stand directly behind one who is reading and observe one of his eyeballs by reflection in a small mirror held just below it, we will note that the eye moves from left to right not with a steady sweep but with alternating

---

[1] Compare the method described by Plautus:

> When I was young, no time-piece Rome supplied,
> But every fellow had his own — inside;
> A trusty horologe, that — rain or shine —
> Ne'er failed to warn him of the hour — to dine.

jerks and pauses, then swings back from the extreme right to the extreme left to start the next line of reading.   During the actual moving of the eye nothing can be distinctly registered on the retina and anything like reading is quite impossible; so that the eye's work as a receptor is done during the fixation-pauses.   This peculiarity of the eye-movements in reading was first discovered in 1879 and has been abundantly examined and confirmed since.   With refinement of apparatus (such as that shown . in Figure 163 or that described in [19]) detailed facts and principles have been brought to light, and these have been useful for testing and for making diagnoses of readers, as well as for prescribing proper kinds of printing.   There have been misguided efforts to make poor readers into good ones by simply training them to make more adequate eyeball movements.   But that is putting cart before horse [4].

A general way of stating some of the findings is as follows.   The fixations vary around 5 or 6 for lines 100 millimeters long, if the reading matter is easy, but more if it is difficult.   The number of words seen per pause averages about 2. The eye does not sweep from very beginning to very end of line, but leaves "indentations."   Color-hue has little effect on legibility, the important thing being brightness contrast between the type and its background.   Words in lower case are more easily read than words in all capitals.   Many other equally definite points have also been made out.

It is easy to see that practical applications can be made not simply to schoolbooks but to telephone directories, advertisements, road signs, and automobile license plates.

But, we now must ask, *how is reading possible?*   In the course of the eye's jerky movements and few fixations as it travels over a line, how can it be effectively stimulated by all the elements of that line?

(1) In the first place, we need only be reminded that a person attends to a stimulating situation *not piecemeal but as a pattern* or a whole — not as individual, component stimuli, but as a situation.   For example, in brief exposures (as on the tachistoscope) two or three short words can be read as easily as three or four letters; and the reaction time for reading aloud letters that have no connection is about twice that for reading aloud letters that make words.   The fact that there are five or six eye-fixations to the line, then, does not mean sensory exposure to that number of letters, but to that number of large segments of the line.

(2) In the second place, we must bear in mind that the words simply touch off trained *speech habits*, habitual *sequences*.   The enunciation of a series of words may lead almost inevitably to a certain concluding phrase: "Senator Sorghum will not again run. . . ."   "Of the people, by the . . ." "Virtue is its . . ."   "There ought to be a law . . ."   "The land of the

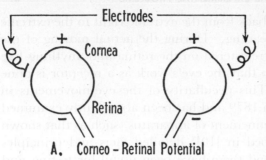

Electrodes

+ Cornea +

Retina

A. Corneo – Retinal Potential

B. Placement of the Electrodes

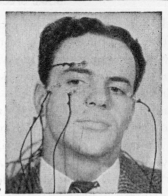

C. Ink-writing Polygraph

163 A Method of Recording Eye-Movements

A. There is a polarity of electrical potential between the front and the back of the eye, the former being positive, the latter, negative. Electrodes mounted on the skin near the eye and leading through amplification to a recording device will reveal changes in the direction of the polarity-potential (which way the eye points).

B. Four electrodes shown in place. Those at temporal side of both eyes pick up the electrical shifts associated with horizontal eyeball movements; those placed above and below an eye, the shifts associated with up and down movements.

C. The potential changes led from the pairs of electrodes operate oscillograph-controlled writing pens, inscribing on a moving tape.

(*From L. Carmichael and W. F. Dearborn,* READING AND VISUAL FATIGUE, *Houghton Mifflin, 1947. Reproduced by permission of the authors and publishers.*)

free and the home . . ." In reading, the visual patterns of the printed page touch off speech habits which supplement visual stimuli.

(3) But the reader is not merely a bundle of habits. He is a going concern. Perhaps he is in the midst of a story, and eagerly anticipating later developments: the stimuli from the printed page serve now as hardly more than "stop" and "go" cues for his pressing progress, or better, as *signposts* of direction which give him the cue to turn down one or another avenue of his prospective thinking. This activity of the reader is easily seen in his hop-skip-jump manner of glancing down a newspaper column. Who reads every word? Whole sentences, whole paragraphs are skipped, and yet the informed reader, recognizing this phrase and that one for symbols of large organizations of his experience (high-order habits), is able to integrate the whole account into a sufficiently connected story, a story in the perusal of which he was truly half reader, half teller.

Esthetic Perceiving

Man's appreciation of the beautiful is subject to study and analysis as truly as any other natural phenomenon. Even quantitative investigations are possible. To be sure, a person's reaction to a work of Rembrandt, Milton, Chopin, or Praxiteles is not yet subject to detailed psychological description; and the experimentalist must limit himself to modest beginnings with colors, lines, rhythm beats, or tonal combinations. But this is also true of the scientific study of any complex phenomenon [16].

To determine the esthetic value of a given object of art, show it or sound it along with another or others, and then note the directions and amounts of preferences — the Method of Impression.[1] For, by the very nature of it, the artistic properties of an object are not something to be determined by examining the object itself but by noting the human reactions to it. For the most part, scientific studies have dealt with pictures, musical compositions, and poems; and they have taken the typical experimental form of analyzing the complex subject-matter into simpler parts: iambic versus trochaic rhythms, balanced versus unbalanced masses, complementary versus non-complementary color combinations, the curve versus the straight line — these are typical.

A classic study made by Fechner some seventy-five years ago pertained to the esthetic values of spatial proportions. Displaying to his subjects rectangles of differing proportions, he secured their choices of the most

---

[1] So called by contrast with the Methods of Expression, a term applied to the uses of instrumentations described on pages 207 ff.

pleasing and the least pleasing to look at. The accompanying partial summary of his findings points to the ratio .62, or approximately 21/34, as the "golden section," as it is called.

Ratio of width to length	1.00	.83	.80	.75	.69	.67	.62	.57	.50	.40
Percentage of times chosen as best	3.0	0.2	2.0	2.5	7.7	20.6	35.0	20.0	7.5	1.5
Percentage of times chosen as worst	27.8	19.7	9.4	2.5	1.2	0.4	0.0	0.8	2.5	35.7

And studies made since, in the arts, in advertising, and elsewhere, have on the whole verified his conclusion.

Some points relevant to the topic of esthetics are to be found in the last section of Chapter 9, above.

THE PLACE OF PERCEIVING IN THE LIFE ECONOMY

Handicaps of Poor Perceiving

What does it profit a man (or other animal) to be able to respond to the things about him perceptually? He makes responses to environmental stimuli, and to intra-organic stimuli. But if he were allowed only a capacity to respond to them as physico-chemical energies which excite his receptors, his activity would be limited to a primitive array of simple reactions to what is explicitly and immediately present. In infancy, he might, like a clam, make some invariable defensive movement when a shadow fell upon the sense organs; but he could not learn to open his mouth if the shadow were cast by an approaching nurse, to laugh and "pat" if it were made by a Scottie's bulk, or years later to reach forward, pull down, finger and inspect the object that blocked off the light. A similar limitation of man's possible reactions to sounds as physical sounds only would debar him from more than a turn of the head or a meaningless, distraught behavior in the presence of symphonic music, a friend's voice, or the whistle of an approaching locomotive.

The disabilities entailed by an incapacity to build up and use perceptual reactions may be glimpsed by considering the case of profound idiocy. Idiots cannot adjust themselves adequately to their living conditions. If left alone, they would in many cases quickly die. When they are able to feed themselves they are likely to eat anything and everything, including refuse from the garbage pail. The seeing or hearing of something that has been repeatedly an agent of pain may not function for them as a pain signal at all. Many do not learn to respond to certain interoceptive stimulations, and fail to attend to the calls of nature. An oscillating object such as a swing excites no anticipatory behavior, as they walk right into trouble. The same feeding attendant who has thrice daily entered their field of vision may not excite their salivary and gastric glands or their facial and vocal muscles — he is but a visibly moving mass. In fine, although the idiot of low mentality has eyes to see and ears to hear and may in general be receptive to all the usual modes of external and internal stimulation, his responses are not habits appropriately adjusted to the whole objects and whole situations in his world. The raw stimuli fail to touch off any of the larger organizations of activity.

Looking Forward

In the present chapter we have given more direct attention than we have hitherto to the fact that human beings concern themselves not with isolated and abstracted stimulus details but with whole objects, persons, situations, and facts; and we have turned our efforts in the direction of analyzing the controlling factors and the detailed problems involved. And now, having clarified the notion of reacting-to-relationships, we are equipped to come to grips with the higher thought processes. In unraveling them we shall find ourselves dealing again with relationships, especially those of symbolic character. Thinking, in fact, has frequently been characterized as "manipulations of symbols."

However, in that attack we shall be greatly re-enforced by a better knowledge of the social situations out of which symbolic behavior evolves. Hence we shall devote our next two chapters to a survey of psychological problems in social life, and especially in language. And meanwhile, several problems in those fields are interesting and important on their own account.

REFERENCES

1. Boring, E. G. "The moon illusion," *Amer. J. Physics*, 1943, *11*, 55–60.
2. Bruner, J. S., and C. C. Goodman. "Value and need as organizing factors in perception," *J. Abn. Soc. Psychol.*, 1947, *42*, 33–44.
3. Brunswik, E. *Experimentelle Psychologie in Demonstrationen.* Springer, 1935.
4. Buswell, G. T. "Remedial reading at the college and adult levels," *Suppl. Educ. Monogr.*, 1939, No. 50.

5. Carmichael, L., and W. F. Dearborn. *Reading and Visual Fatigue.* Boston: Houghton Mifflin Company, 1947.

6. Douglas, A. "A tachistoscopic study of the order of emergence in the process of perception," *Psychol. Monogr.,* 1947, *61,* No. 287.

7. Ewert, P. H. "A study of the effect of inverted retinal stimulation upon spatially coordinated behavior," *Genet. Psychol. Monogr.,* 1930, *7,* Nos. 3 and 4.

8. Foley, J. P., Jr. "An experimental investigation of the effect of prolonged inversion of the visual field in the rhesus monkey," *J. Genet. Psychol.,* 1940, *56,* 21–51.

9. Fraser, J. "A new visual illusion of direction," *Brit. J. Psychol.,* 1908, *2,* 307–320.

10. Gelb, A. "Colour constancy," in W. D. Ellis, *A Source Book of Gestalt Psychology.* New York: Harcourt, Brace and Company, 1938.

11. Gilliland, A. R., J. Hofeld, and G. Eckstrand. "Studies in time perception," *Psychol. Bull.,* 1946, *43,* 162–176.

12. Krech, D., and R. S. Crutchfield. *Theory and Problems of Social Psychology.* New York: McGraw-Hill Book Company, 1948.

13. Leeper, R., and D. O. Leeper. "An experimental study of equivalent stimulation in human learning," *J. Gen. Psychol.,* 1932, *6,* 344–375.

14. Leeper, R. "A study of a neglected portion of the field of learning — the development of sensory organization," *J. Genet. Psychol.,* 1935, *46,* 41–75.

15. Omwake, K. T., and M. Loranz. "Study of ability to wake at a specified time," *J. Appl. Psychol.,* 1933, *17,* 468–474.

16. Peters, H. N. "The experimental study of esthetic judgments," *Psychol. Bull.,* 1942, *39,* 273–305.

17. Révész, G. "Experiments on animal space perception," *Brit. J. Psychol.,* 1924, *14,* 387–414.

18. Rogers, C. R. "Some observations on the organization of personality," *Amer. Psychologist,* 1947, *2,* 358–368.

19. Tiffin, J. "An eye-voice camera for clinical and research studies," *Psychol. Monogr.,* 1937, *48,* No. 215, 70–77.

20. Tinker, M. A. "The study of eye movements in reading," *Psychol. Bull.,* 1946, *43,* 93–120.

21. Wertheimer, M. "Untersuchungen zur Lehre von der Gestalt," *Psychol. Forsch.,* 1923, *4,* 301–350.

22. Young, P. T. "Auditory localization with acoustical transposition of the ears," *J. Exper. Psychol.,* 1928, *11,* 399–429.

The sketch in Figure 146 is supposed to represent a bear climbing a tree.

17

SOCIAL BEHAVIOR

MAN AS A SOCIAL BEING

UP TO THIS POINT, we have found it convenient to discuss man as though he were isolated from the complexities of the society of which he is in fact a part.   Except for an incidental qualification and an occasional reference, we have given no attention to the contribution of social environment to the making of the man.   And this contribution has been enormous.   Here, then, let us make good our comparative neglect of the social factors by giving them special attention.

The life of a man is that of a person among persons.   As a new-born infant, he is placed in a crib, nursed, and tended by another human being.   Through childhood and youth he is a dependent object of solicitude to his parents and other adults, and a frequent object of favorable or unfavorable treatment from associates nearer his own age.   As he approaches adulthood, he gradually assumes obligations toward the people about him, in his own family, in the family he acquires, in his church or lodge, in his profession or business, in his town and state.   So constantly present and constantly sensed is this social aspect of his environment that even in childhood the major portion of his interest and aims is cast in terms of his relation to others; and throughout life the principal stresses or strains, the episodes of maladjustment, are but the difficulties of adapting to other human agents.

The values that men live by also assume a predominantly social character.   Not only do they include a person's satisfaction in the approbation or the envy or occasionally the fear that is manifested by others toward him as an individual; they include also his actual seeking of the welfare of these others. In many a sub-human form the biological principle of regulation or adjustment becomes extended to include more than the one organism to be regulated or adjusted: it is the group. In human life, likewise, this extension of the sphere of interest is striking. Educating one's children, purchasing life insurance, carrying home one's pay envelope, contributing to the community chest or to a Friendship Train for Europeans, supplying food and clothing for strikers, and similar prosaic actions are primarily motivated by some kind of interest in others.

The Urgent Need for Research in Social Psychology

The remark has often been made that man's scientific and technological discoveries and knowledge in regard to physical and biological nature have outrun his knowledge of himself. Today, as never before, we have become conscious of the Machine; and it is almost a commonplace assertion that the woes and ills of our Western civilization are due in large part to a too-rapid development of mechanical discovery and invention and a too-slow development of knowledge about mankind. Certainly the world is out of joint. It is high time, then, that scientists turned to a more intensive study of psychological and social phenomena, applying to them not theories only, nor general observations, but the experimental techniques that have proved so fruitful and epoch-making in other fields.

With World War II, America awoke to the need of psychological study of men in groups, in masses, and in publics; and lately even a technological institution established a research center for the dynamics of the group.

INTERSTIMULATION AND RESPONSE

Analysis of Social Behavior in These Terms

Man-in-the-mass is really *men*-in-the-mass, and the behavior of each of these men is a matter of stimulation and response. His behavior in a social situation is not essentially different from his behavior in the presence of non-living things. It is only more complicated. In place of one sensitive and behaving organism, adjusting itself to its environment and adjusting its environment to itself, we have two or more sensitive and behaving organisms, forced by conditions to be sensitive to each other and to behave toward each other. Nothing new is added — no new force, no new mechanism. Figure 164 shows a schematic analysis of this psychological interaction between different organisms. Let us start with an audible or visible move on *A*'s part. We will suppose that, as a wink or a sneer, a curt word or an amicable wave of the hand, it

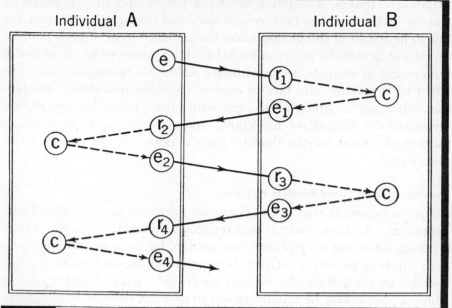

Individual **A**   Individual **B**

164

A Schematic Analysis of Reciprocal Stimulating and Responding

The broken lines represent general neural channels or general functions rather than single pathways and simple reflex arcs.

will suffice to stimulate B to some sort of reciprocal demonstration, such as a smile in response to the wink or a head-toss to the sneer, a soft answer to the sharp word, or a return wave of the hand in greeting. Air or ether vibrations act upon B's receptors r_1; and neural impulses, via centers c, arouse to action certain effectors e_1. But B's smile or toss of head, his mild words or friendly wave, may now stimulate A to further overtures. Activity of B's effectors of face, throat, hand, and so on, e_1, are heard or seen by A, as air or ether waves excite receptors r_2, and arouse some more or less appropriate reaction in turn at e_2. Further interchange of such hand, eye, face, or voice signals add no really new features to the actions in progress.

Minimal stimuli are generally involved. In dancing, the leader may be largely unaware of the slight changes in his movement of right or left hand or of the body generally, yet these serve as sufficient cues to his partner so that, without identifying or verbally noting them, she is able to follow accurately and smoothly.

The Perceiving of Social Cues

The lack of a fair amount of ability to size up or see into a social situation — that is, a situation involving people and their attitudes — usually makes a person both conspicuous and unpopular. If a man is blunt, he speaks of things that make his audience gasp; if he is tactless, he talks or acts to the injury of his friend; if he proves to be the object of amusement or ridicule, he unwittingly smirks his satisfaction over the effect he is making, and fails to observe the signs that should tell him that others are laughing at and not with him. When he does rightly recognize the attitude of his fellows and seeks to guide his conduct accordingly, what are the signs he notes? What are the cues to social perceiving?

The Perceiving of Facial Reaction Patterns

An obvious set of cues is that composite of visible stimuli called facial expression. Its importance is well recognized when it is absent. When a person is holding a telephone conversation, for instance, the quickness with which he perceives his friend's speech in all of its allusions is much lessened by his inability to see and watch the friend's facial reactions. Many a phrase may be misunderstood in its more delicate implications, and it behooves the man at the other end of the wire to make his sentences short and his meanings obvious. On the other hand, a good share of the interest maintained by an audience in a motion-picture show is traceable to the perceiving of changes in the facial reactions of the characters portrayed upon the screen.

Measuring Judgments of Facial Expressions

By adapting the general procedure followed in constructing social attitude scales (*infra*, pages 504 ff.) it has been found possible to arrange a scale for measuring an observer's ability to judge pictured facial expressions. Photographs of poses representing a great variety of emotions were sorted by students at Brown University into six piles, labeled with the names of six emotional categories. By taking account of the number of times each picture was assigned to this or that category, it was found possible to arrange the categories in a continuous order, calling the "love-mirth-happiness" category step number 1, the "surprise" category step 2, and so on, as shown at the top of Figure 165. This was possible because in addition to those pictures which had been assigned by all judges to "surprise," there were pictures assigned by some to "surprise" and by others to "love-mirth-happiness," and again pictures assigned by some to "surprise" and others to the "suffering-fear" category; and so on through all the pictures and categories. It is also interesting to note that some pictures assigned to the sixth category,

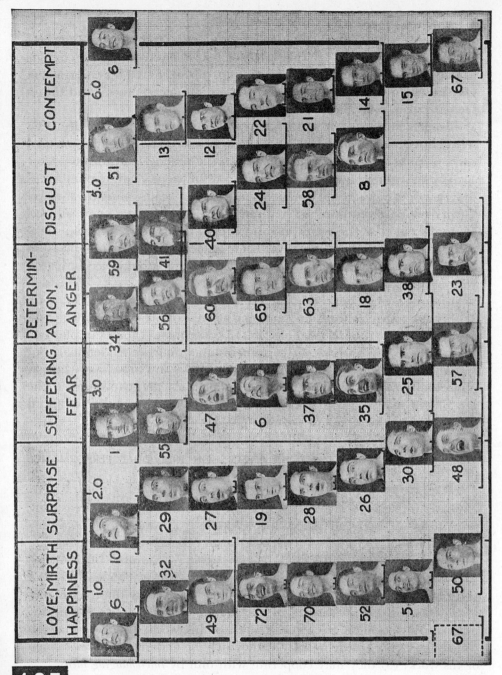

165   **A Scale for Measuring Reactions to Facial Expressions**

Pictures as assigned by a group of judges to the six categories named at the top. Each category is given a step value, shown immediately below its name (except in case of step 4). A horizontal line under each picture represents mean deviation of its assignments about its scale position. Number to left of a picture is only for identifying it; the vertical positions are only a device for spreading the pictures out. (*From H. Schlosberg, "A scale for the judgment of facial expressions."* J. Exp. Psychol., *1941, 29, 497–510. Pictures by courtesy of Dr. Schlosberg.*)

"contempt," are assigned also in varying frequencies to the first category, "love-mirth-happiness"; so that the scale turned out to be almost circular in nature. Careful scrutiny of the pictures has suggested that a principal way in which they vary is as to pleasantness-unpleasantness, and that a secondary variable may be called attention-rejection.

The general idea promises to be useful in this simple procedure. To set up a test, let carefully selected judges be asked individually to assign each picture to one or another of the six numbered categories. After such assignments have been made by a sufficiently large number of judges, each picture can be given a resulting scale-value (mean and mean deviation) based on the step-numbers. Then to test a new subject, let him sort the 46 photographs into the six categories; and his assignments can be compared with the scale-values. We can thus measure his ability to perceive facial expressions correctly — that is, as compared with assignments made by the judges.

We must bear in mind that the momentary view of a man's face is an artificial abstraction from the on-going process of his behavior which in real life is reacted to as a whole by the other-man. For example, two smiles, which are snapped at certain instants may seem identical, but actually they may be readily distinguishable by any observer who has opportunity to note their beginnings, completions, and vanishings. The use of the motion picture for getting at the recognizability of facial changes in process is full of promise [20, 8].

GROUP EFFECTS ON INDIVIDUAL PERFORMANCE

The Typical Experiment and Typical Findings

One simple experimental procedure for observing and measuring some forms of interstimulation and response is to *compare the individual's measured achievements when he is under influences from other persons present with his measured achievements when he is working alone*. A number of problems that can be handled in this way suggest themselves rather easily. We can readily see that (1) these "other persons" may play the role merely of *passive auditors* or *spectators;* (2) they may be *working alongside* him but not with any explicit reference to him or his work; (3) they may be *contestants* or rivals in the work; (4) they may be making *remarks about him* or his work; (5) they may cooperate with him by *interchanging ideas*.

In America the first experimental approach to social psychology was made along this line by Allport [1]. He arranged sessions with adult subjects in which they were given the same psychological tests under two different sets of conditions: in one they sat working as solitary individuals in separate rooms; in the other they worked together in a group seated about a common table. The work given them included tests in free chain word-association, in letter canceling, in holding attention on a reversible hollow-cube figure, in multiplying, and in writing out arguments to disprove an assertion put before them. The subjects were carefully instructed that they were not to compete even when they were working at the same table, and were not to make any comparisons of their work, nor even to discuss the results. The outcomes of work on the tests under the two sets of conditions differed in two ways. A distinct majority of the subjects exhibited a *speeding-up* on all the tests when they were in the presence of their co-workers, as compared with their work when alone.[1] To this effect the term "social facilitation" was assigned as contrasted with "social inhibition." The increase in quantity, however, was generally accompanied by a *decrease in quality*, especially in so far as the tests involved thinking. This was called a *social subvaluent* effect, in contrast to the *social supervaluent* effect if quality of work improves under the social condition.

Sir Henry Beecham tells an amusing tale that is in line with this finding of a social subvaluent. An ambitious Parisian lady once assembled some forty poets, musicians, painters, and designers, at forty individual tables in one large room, to see whether the very proximity of so many fertile brains might not produce inspirations at heights hitherto unimagined. The results were of quite another sort. Under such circumstances, not one of the geniuses was able to turn out anything less humdrum than something he had seen in a shop window that morning or heard in a cabaret the night before.[2]

The reader may wonder if the effects Allport found were due to a certain amount of rivalry that crept into the attitude of the co-workers. The answer is found in the study of one of Allport's students, who had subjects working at a printing task under two sets of conditions. Objectively the conditions were the same: the subjects worked at the same table and with the same types of materials. Subjectively, however, the conditions were different, for at some sessions the subjects were instructed not to work competitively, at other sessions to work competitively. And

[1] The student interested in methodology may wish to note that Allport — and most others in this field — did not work with group averages of scores made in the different situations but with the *number of individuals* showing faster or slower work, better or worse performances, in each situation. A social influence is often more validly measured by counting the number of persons affected in a given direction than by averaging the degrees to which all are affected. Certainly many practical social processes assume the former measure; voting is one example.

[2] *A Mingled Chime* (New York: G. P. Putnam's Sons, 1943), pages 176–177.

all twelve subjects did faster and poorer work under the latter condition. It seems clear that the attitude of rivalry can be voluntarily assumed or voluntarily eliminated to a very large degree.

That the "social" character of a situation is as much a subjective as an objective fact was shown in another way by the present writer, who found that Allport's social facilitation and social subvaluent effects could be obtained by having the subjects work at the *same time in separate rooms*, with a common set of starting-stopping signals, and comparing the results with their work done in these rooms at different times [7].

Much research has been done in this general area. Though there has been lack of agreement in some details obtained by different investigators — due, we can be sure, to the difficulty of controlling the perplexing number of variables inherent in group situations with their inter-stimulating individuals and to the subjective character of many influences — some trends are discernible.

(1) As more persons participate in a situation, there is most likely to be an increase in speed of performance, along with a decrease in *quality and accuracy*.[1]

(2) In most cases there is an observable *leveling effect*. The poorer individual workers improve when in a group, while the superior ones do less well. The group becomes more homogeneous.

The Effects of Discussion

Freedom to discuss — in assemblage, in speech, in teaching, in the press, on the radio — is a jealously guarded human privilege which liberal-minded people regard as basic to all rights. And back of the individual-right principle there indubitably lies the conviction that human progress is, sometimes at least, advanced by discussion. True, there are skeptics. There are those who claim that many an official pow-wow is staged primarily to allow the more volatile individuals to blow off steam, that often a governmental fact-finding conference is a problem-killing device; that most four-o'clock meetings of the executives of a big business are called to build up *esprit de corps* and merely turn into yes-men affairs. But the abiding faith in deliberative and parliamentary processes characteristic of democratic peoples does have support not only in public events but also in scientific findings.

In 1924, Bekhterev first obtained students' perceptual judgments on the time intervals between tapped sounds, their ethical judgments on a

---

[1] Cultural setting furnishes a backdrop for this finding. On performance tests of general intelligence, Yakima Indians moved more slowly than did whites — and they made fewer errors [14].

picture of a boy receiving a beating for stealing apples, and their creative judgments on how to memorialize a Russian poet. In each case, the individual judgments were read aloud to the group, and some informal voting on various items was permitted. The progress of voting revealed clear changes in the direction of the judgments; and taken all in all, the work of the group was not only in the direction of greater accuracy (as in the time judgments), but was also in the direction of greater creativeness (as in the memorials).

Just what is it in the course of a so-called discussion that makes for advance? Is it the pro and con *arguments* by which one individual convinces another? We have commonly assumed that this is the primary and the effective function of discussion. But that assumption overlooks the incidental but vitally important *presentation of different viewpoints*. It would be rash to assert that argument never achieves its purpose, that he convinced "against his will is of his own opinion still," and that logical argumentation makes no converts; but the practical recognition of the value of a mere pooling of ideas is supported by some experimental results [31].

The Opportunity to Vary

In an American study [12] students of four different college classes were assigned as a test the estimating of the number of beans in a sealed glass jar. Some time later each was tested on this again. In the intervals between the first and second tests, the four classes were allowed different opportunities for discussion, as follows. In the case of Class D, the members were not allowed to consult and discuss with each other at all. Between the first and second tests only 57 per cent of them showed improvement in their estimates. In the case of Class B, small groups were made up by the instructor so as to include in each group only individuals whose original estimates were in close agreement; each group then discussed the problem among themselves. Between their first (pre-discussion) tests and their second (post-discussion) tests only 50 per cent of them improved in their estimates, a result no better than that obtained in the case of the non-discussing class, D. In Classes A and C similar small discussion groups were made up, but these included individuals in each group whose original estimates had shown wide diversity. Improvement in estimating from pre-discussion to post-discussion tests was now found in 77 per cent and 74 per cent of the individuals, respectively. This much is clear: whatever the role of the give-and-take arguing that went on, a cardinal influence upon each individual was his knowledge of how the other individuals' opinions differed from his own.

Hence his opportunities to vary — and so perhaps to improve — were increased.

Another sort of verification of the general principle comes from a later experiment in which not the range of individuals but the increased range of possible answers furnished by the experimenter gave the advantage [29]. College students served as subjects in two sub-groups. Sub-group A worked as individuals in sessions 1 and 4, and together as a cooperating group in sessions 2 and 3; sub-group B followed the reverse program. The task included easy and hard sentence completions, one-line and three-line limericks, easy and hard vocabularies, and crossword puzzles; and they varied considerably in range of possible responses. To illustrate: one completion test supplied five choices, while another furnished none and so was unlimited. The general finding was that better results were obtained on those test-forms that allowed the wider range of choice.

Let us pause to recognize a recurrent theme. Group discussion and group thinking may be looked upon as another case of a fundamental biological logic operating upon a high plane. The cardinal principles of organic evolution we saw to be Variation and Selection. The cardinal principles of learning we again have seen to be Variation and Selection. The cardinal principles in the individual's effective thinking we have seen and will see again to be Variation and Selection. And now on the societal plane, we recognize the same principles of advance especially when brought out in the white heat of discussion.

SOCIALIZATION OF THE INDIVIDUAL

Introduction

In Chapter 4 and elsewhere we have seen enough of the newborn infant to recognize that it is a non-social organism. Neither social nor anti-social, its activities have nothing to do with other people, and have no reference to them. It reminds us of Victor, the wild boy of Aveyron, who when first captured, "was destitute of all means of communication and attached neither expression nor intention to his gestures or to the movements of his body." The baby's outcry is not an appeal; its first smile — when it is old enough to achieve one — is not addressed to the face above it; its struggling is not away from, nor its kicking aimed at, the hands that minister to it. How does it become socialized — a person among persons — a "he" instead of an "it"? We have already noted (pages 78 ff.) that in the process of his biological maturing he comes to differentiate among the sources of stimulation playing upon him, to know personal from impersonal, to recognize familiars from strangers, and the like. But we want to know more about him than these sensory-perceptual-motor phases, to go deeper into his make-up, especially as it is affected by his social environment. *How does he assume those habits that are socially desirable and that enable him to live as a member of aggregations of people, sensitive to stimulations he receives from them and responsive to the demands of group life?* How do the group standards become his standards, that is, become *interiorized?* An adequate answer to such questions would demand a volume or more in itself. Becoming socialized is a matter of years, for it is one ever-present aspect of the individual's development. It is a matter, too, of many factors, many causes.

The Basic Personality Structure is Socially Molded in Infancy

Since it is out of the question for us to attempt a complete survey, we must be content to pick out a few characteristic features that have received attention from one or another quarter by one or another scientific method and at one or another age-period in the life of the individual.

We turn first to the social influence that is most fundamentally effective, the family, and to the most formative years, infancy. Now, in spite of the superlatives in the preceding sentence, we are referring to an area of psychological inquiry that is very difficult of scientific analysis, description, measurement. To obtain knowledge about the infant's intimate relationships to his mother and others, psychology must rely mainly upon two sources: (1) the work of the ethnologists who have lived among primitive peoples, and (2) that of the clinical psychologists and psychiatrists who have been called in when things have gone wrong with families or individuals in our own society. The progress and outcome of investigations in both these observational fields depends, far more than does laboratory work, upon the subjective judgments of the observer, upon the keenness and appositeness of his discernments, and upon the soundness and the logically compelling nature of his interpretations. We shall be careful to follow recognized authorities.

One of the more illuminating concepts in the contemporary studies of personality and culture is what Kardiner and Linton call the *basic personality structure* of a people [13]. The manners and methods of caring for the wants and tensions of the infant and child eventually generate definite attitudes on his part toward his parents and others. These attitudes become habitual and automatic, and thus a basic structuring of his personality is established. Then, as he grows up, his value-systems and ideals (honesty, heroism, success, beauty, respectability, skills) reflect the manners of his upbringing; and as he rounds out and extends his material world with ideological, religious, poetic, mythological constructions, he inevitably projects (expresses) himself and his basic personality trends into them.   All the individuals of the culture have these basic features in common, whatever personal idiosyncrasies each may develop.

With the Comanche Indians of the southwest United States, maternal care was solicitous and consistent. The infant was fed and looked after whenever he cried; he was allowed to sleep undisturbed; he received no punishments beyond warnings; he was given careful training in his toilet habits; and he was gradually and carefully weaned at the appropriate age. Such treatment, calculated to establish a pattern of regularity and promptness, is unlikely to occasion stresses and tensions in the child's experience. There is a significant emotional side to the story, too. The baby received much fondling, was played with and caressed and made an important object of his mother's ministrations. This kind of handling tended to encourage emotional responsiveness on his part, and it encouraged a sense of stability and security. Through it he learned that he could count on his mother, on the other members of the family-group, and on himself. He had opportunity to develop a well-integrated feeling of self, or "ego," to acquire a status that was definite and sound.

The Alorese of the East Indies furnish a very different picture. With them, parental care was sporadic and undependable. The hungry baby might be fed and cared for when he cried — or he might not, depending upon the whim of whoever was left near him. He received no systematic training in how or when to relieve bladder and bowel and in associated habits of cleanliness; his rest and sleep were happenstance matters; his weaning from the mother's breast was accompanied by slaps and rough pushes; and he might be alternately scolded or petted for the same kind of conduct. He had small chance to learn how to care for himself, and certainly little experience on which to base expectations of aid from others. Furthermore, little affection was bestowed on the child, nor was he solicited to make affectionate responses to others. Accordingly, he had no basis for learning friendly give-and-take, and he developed a suspicious, fundamentally hostile attitude toward the world at large. At the same time, no sense of his own personal security was built up, no-self-assured status, no healthy ego-appreciation.

We turn now to more objectively controlled observational researches on later ages of the individual.

Determinants of Social Participation in Nursery School Children

Any kindergarten child or any parent knows that different individual children vary considerably in the amount of sociability they show. But "vary considerably" is a vague expression; and it has been recognized that we should have means for measuring the degrees of difference, if only with large steps. At the University of Minnesota a method was applied which has proved useful for this purpose and has been adapted by others to a variety of problems. This is the method of *repeated short-time-sample observations*.

During the free play hour of a nursery school each individual child was observed for one minute on each of a number of days. His behavior was recorded on a printed schedule in such a way as to show how much of the minute was taken up with behavior that could be classified in each of the following categories: "Unoccupied" (not playing at all), "Solitary" play (with toys different from the other children's), "Onlooker," "Parallel" play (beside rather than with the others), "Associative" play (together, as following one another, or borrowing), "Cooperative" play (where all work toward a common goal in organized manner, as in games). Figure 166 should help us to appreciate the differences between these categories. They may be taken as different steps or degrees of social participation, increasing in the order of mention.

One thing that comes out strikingly, as much from the score sheets as from direct observation, is the really great amount of individual differences. In Table XXXVII the present writer has placed in closer juxtaposition a few striking cases. However, these are only seven cases selected for their contrasts out of a total of forty-two; and the group as a whole showed sufficiently definite trends to warrant two generalizations. By assigning to the several categories weights ranging from −3 to 3, a given child's behavior on a given day — and so on all his days — could be stated in numerical degrees of social participation. These numerical

TABLE XXXVII Showing the Percentage of Each Child's Observed Play Time that Was Spent in Each Type of Social Participation

Child	Unoccupied	Solitary	Onlooker	Parallel	Associative	Cooperative
J4	....	6.2	15.0	27.0	27.0	25.0
N3	....	1.2	1.2	8.0	33.0	57.0
I3	....	6.2	3.4	15.0	37.0	39.0
N2	....	30.0	3.4	32.0	20.0	15.0
K2	11.0	23.0	38.0	20.0	7.0	1.0
D1	12.0	9.0	6.0	62.0	8.0	2.0
B1	2.9	30.0	10.0	50.0	7.0	1.4

Adapted from M. B. Parten, J. Abnorm. Soc. Psychol., *1932, 27, 257.*

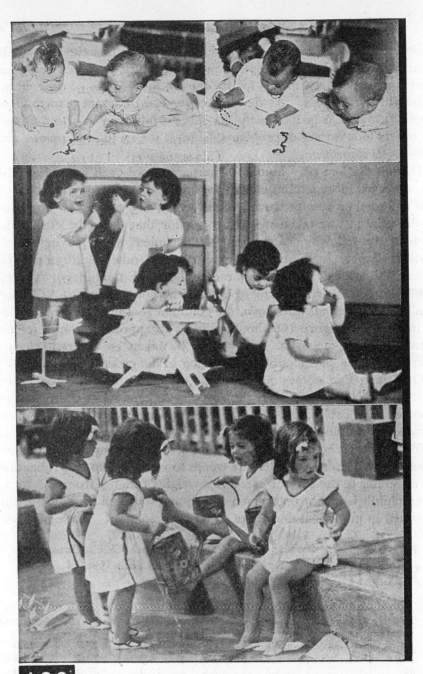

166   **Different Types (Degrees) of Social Participation**

The Dionne quintuplets. The two cases at *10 months* are readily classified as parallel and onlooker types. Those at *20* and *37 months* furnish examples of other types between various pairs of the children. (*From W. E Blatz,* et. al, "*The early social development of the Dionne quintuplets,*" UNIV. TORONTO STUD., CHILD DEVELPM. SERIES, *No. 13, 1937.*)

values could then be compared with other measurements of the child. The following relationships appeared. (1) The older the child the more likely he was to play in the highly organized groups (Associative and Cooperative), and the relation between age and social participation for the whole group was represented by a correlation coefficient of .61 ± .08. (2) *Intelligence* level, too, was related to social-participation scores, at least to the small extent indicated by an r of .26 ± .11. Both age and intelligence, then, are factors in the child's degree of social participation.

Dominative versus Integrative Behavior

Once children get to playing associatively and cooperatively, one can see further differences of kind appearing. One way of characterizing child-to-child adjustive relations is by contrasting what has been called "domination" with "social integration."

Dominative behavior is rigid and inelastic. The dominating person has his mind made up, his goals settled. Consequently, he does not yield to differences inaugurated by another, is not seeking better cooperation with his fellow nor trying to find a common denominator for mutual understanding. Examples: Jimmy reaches for the toy locomotive with which Joe is playing, and plays with it himself. (No pugnacity nor teasing here: simply a blind thoughtlessness.) To Frances' "Let's make a tunnel," Doris answers, "No. I want to make a house there."

Socially integrative behavior, by contrast, is marked by flexibility, by a yielding or modifying of one's own plan or activity, not through submissiveness but through a willingness to discover common purposes with others. Examples: Joe gets a car to hitch to the locomotive Jimmy took from him so that the boys can play together. Frances remarks, as a follow-up: "A tunnel up to the house would be fun, wouldn't it?" Behavior of this elastic kind tends to bring out the differences between individuals and so to advance mutual understanding and hence social integration.

Even in the kindergarten age this contrast in behavior has been observed and measured, at the University of Illinois [2]. Children were taken in pairs to a room where they were allowed to play five minutes in a sand box with toys. Each individual child was paired at random with five other children; and as he played, the observer watched through a one-way-vision screen and kept detailed tally of his actions and reactions to the other child, classifying them as of the dominating (inflexible) or the integrative (flexible) type in one or another degree. When all these ratings were assembled and treated statistically certain interesting generalizations were indicated.

(1) Dominative behavior on one person's part induces domination in one's companion.   ($r = .68 \pm .02$)

(2) Integrative behavior induces integrative behavior in one's companion.   ($r = .82 \pm .01$)

(3) Domination is not only different from integrative behavior, but is unrelated to it; for, in resisting another's dominating overtures, one may simply ignore the other and withdraw to continue about one's own business.   Domination, then, does not arouse integrative behavior in any significant amount, nor does integrative behavior arouse the dominative (both r's $= -.10 \pm .02$).   To use an adult historical illustration, the American Indians responded to the dominating attitude of the ever-encroaching white man by migrating to other hunting grounds, as long as any remained.

It has been suggested that the dominating individual, by not yielding to differences in his social environment, is trying to preserve his own status, is resisting change in himself.   To use a term that is all-important nowadays, he is insecure.   On the other hand, he who can be flexible and yielding at this point or that, for the sake of a broader or more distant objective, is enjoying a sense of *security*.   This lets one accept other people as they are, with all their differences; and so the effective interplay and integrating of personalities is advanced.

Effects on the Individual Child of Political Atmospheres

As the individual conforms more and more to the modes of acting, feeling, and thinking of the people about him, the effect upon him and his ways may be both subtle and surprising.   The interest and initiative he takes in his work, the playfulness or seriousness with which he deals with others, the degree of cooperation and teamwork between him and his mates — these and other aspects of his behavior are often determined to a marked degree by the "social climate" he moves in, by the sort of leadership to which he is subjected.

This was interestingly brought out in a University of Iowa experiment by Lewin and his students [17].   Some ten-year-old boys had been organized into clubs to work on soap carving, airplane building, and other manual constructive projects.   An adult leader was assigned to each club.   These leaders were rotated every six weeks, and they assumed in rotation very different roles as leaders, so that each club was exposed to each leader-person and to each type of leadership.   When acting as an *authoritarian* leader, the adult took it upon himself to decide everything, to dictate who should do what and when and how and with whom.   His instructions were definite and final.   Suggestions from the boys themselves seldom were adopted.   (In this as in the other roles, all the adult leaders were careful not to be antagonizing or unpleasant.)   The *democratic* leader put all matters of plan and project up to the boys themselves for discussion and collective decision.   When technical advice was needed, the leader did not set himself up as sole expert but suggested two or three alternative procedures from which the boys could choose.   The boys were free to work with whomever they chose.   The third kind of leader created a *laissez-faire* atmosphere.   He participated very little in the activities or in the talk, supplying information when asked, but otherwise content to be an onlooker.

After some days the ways in which the boys played began clearly to be affected by the character of the leadership and political atmosphere. Under the authoritarian regime, the boys became most efficient workers so long as the leader was present, but when left to their own resources their work disintegrated.   Morale was plainly highest in the democratic atmosphere, as was shown in several ways.   It was in the democratic groups that friendly remarks from boy to boy were recorded most frequently.   It was there that the highest ratio of "we" to "I" pronouns occurred in conversation.   Under the democratic conditions there were decidedly the fewest remarks expressing discontent, and by far the greatest degree of organization and cooperation in the manual work itself.   All the autocratic-group members voted to stop; most of the democratic-group members voted to continue.   What is well called a spontaneous cohesion characterized the democratic groups.   If we bear in mind that the same individual boys composed the groups that were put in rotation under each of the three kinds of leadership and atmosphere, we can appreciate the considerable degree to which each individual's morale and social behavior and initiative in his work was the product of his surroundings.   And, incidentally by extension to adults and to the international scene we are reminded to be critical of loose talk about the essential German or Japanese or Russian soul, as if referring to something genetically determined.

Effects on the Individual Adult of Group Ideology

The molding of individual conduct into discrete group patterns may result also from discrete ideologies that happen to develop.   A case in point was reported from a camp in Italy of eight hundred displaced persons who had recently been in concentration camps or in partisan groups.   Upon arriving at the camp, these persons furnished a homogeneous picture of aggressive behavior that was aimless and chaotic. Everyone was ready to quarrel with anyone over any trifle.   As they were all Jewish, the general idea of Zionism was prevalent. But soon there took shape two groups, between which there was progressively less and less contact. One group was fascist in its political philosophy, and developed into a military organization with a hierarchy of leaders who gave and took orders. The second group was socialist in its philosophy; it evolved into a collective, with general meetings called to discuss major issues. And the individual members came to reflect this difference in their personal relations. Members of the fascist group continued to be quarrelsome and aggressive — and emotionally unstable generally. Members of the socialist group, by contrast, seemed to become more emotionally stable, more thoughtful about social problems, and definitely less aggressive. Ideologies led to group-formation; and group-characters shaped individual characters [9].[1]

The Influence of the Majority and of Experts

Turning to another mode in which one's personal-social surroundings influence his behavior, we may note the role of prestige. The general assumption that a person is genuinely influenced in his opinions by what he learns to be the opinions of the *majority* of other people, and by what he learns to be the opinions of *experts* in the field, is supported by an experiment with adults, not college students in a laboratory but a non-campus public. An attitude scale was developed (cf. pages 504 ff.), and with the help of some clergymen, administered to members of several Protestant churches. Seven phases of religious attitude were covered by the scale; they are listed in the first column of Table XXXVIII. About one month later, the same blanks were given again to the same respondents in a second series; but now they were divided into three sets. In one set every item had a circle drawn around the alternative that had been marked most frequently by the subjects in the first case (majority opinion). Another set bore similar markings to indicate the alternative for each item that had been most frequently marked by a group of twenty clergyman who had been asked to serve as experts. The third set bore no circles, and was designed to serve as the control (comparison) set which would show how many changes in opinion between the two series might be expected of a normal population unsubjected to the above influences. The three sets were distributed in a random manner among those who had responded in the first series.

By means of code identification marks it was possible to compare the

---

[1] The critical reader will perhaps wonder how effectively genetic and other basic differences between the two groups of persons were ruled out. Here, as elsewhere in social psychology, it is important that inborn and early-life factors be not underestimated.

TABLE XXXVIII Attitude Changes under Majority and Expert Influences in Comparison with Controls

Category	Major-ity Mean	Con-trol Mean	Differ-ence	Criti-cal ratio	Expert Mean	Con-trol Mean	Differ-ence	Criti-cal ratio
1. Doctrines	5.6	1.7	3.9	7.3	5.7	1.3	4.4	6.7
2. Education and science	4.9	1.6	3.3	5.2	4.1	1.2	2.9	3.3
3. Pacifism	4.1	1.8	2.3	4.2	4.4	1.7	2.7	4.7
4. Social aspects	3.6	1.6	2.0	4.0	3.8	1.3	2.5	3.8
5. Industry and politics	4.8	1.8	3.0	5.3	4.4	1.5	2.9	4.5
6. Preachers and preaching	3.5	1.6	1.9	3.6	4.4	2.1	2.3	5.1
7. Religious observance	4.5	1.5	3.0	5.2	3.6	1.7	1.9	3.8
Total	4.3	1.7	2.6	12.7	4.3	1.5	2.8	11.2

From H. E. Burtt and D. R. Falkenberg, Jr., J. ABN. SOC. PSYCHOL., 1941, 14, 274.

responses on the two series made a month apart by the same individuals, and to measure the amounts of change, if any, in their expressed opinions. The alternatives on each item had been assigned values from 0 to 6 (the higher the value, the more "liberal" the indicated opinion), so that each individual's attitude on each category could be represented by a single number, the average of the items. The obtained results are brought together in the table. It is to be read as follows: In the fifteen items of the scale bearing on "Doctrines," the subjects in the group who were informed of the judgments previously made by the majority changed their attitudes on the average 5.6 scale units in the same direction. The people of the control group changed their opinions on this same item only 1.7 scale units. The difference of 3.9 scale units, supported by a critical ratio of 7.3, is clear evidence of the weight of the majority influence. On the same item, the weight of expert influence is shown by an average shift of opinion in the same direction as the experts' by 5.7 scale units, which is 4.4 units more than the uninfluenced changes of the controls. As the reader can see by inspecting the differences and their critical ratios, both kinds of influence were weighty in every category.

COOPERATION AND COMPETITION

Was Grotius on the right track when he claimed that there is an involuntary impulse in men that compels them to seek communion and association with fellow men; or was Hobbes nearer the truth in holding that in a state of nature every man's hand would be raised against his neighbor? If there be one basic and at the same time most urgent set of psychological questions about human nature and human society, surely it is that pertaining to man's cooperativeness and his competitiveness. A consideration of this morning's news items will bring this point home to us. In column one, perhaps, we read of a strike of workmen in a local plant; in column two, the results of a world series baseball game; in column three, a meeting of a consumer's union in the next town; in column four, news from a battlefront in the Balkans; then, accounts of a Methodist church supper, of a home talent play at the Little Theater, and of a Saturday night affray in a tavern. Throughout the minor dramas of daily life, the person-to-person relations seem almost always to take the form of striving for one's objectives either *with* others or *against* others. On the broadest of political and economic stages, also, these apparently antithetic motives seem to play central roles; and the ideologies of whole peoples may emphasize the one or the other, so that the international scene is dominated by contrasts between politico-economic systems that stress the virtues of cooperation and those that stress the virtues of competition.

The social psychologist witnessing such manifestations of human nature, inevitably comes to ask: *Is the human being by original nature instinctively cooperative or is he instinctively competitive?* Are these two kinds of behavior based on *specific biological drives?*

Before we look at the evidences, we should note one thing: pure cooperation and pure competition are rarely encountered. Consider, for example, a tug-of-war between labor and management. It is a contest between the laborers on the one hand and the owners and managers on the other (competition). But the laborers are banded together in unions where uniformity and concerted action is paramount, under leadership elected for the benefit of each and all (cooperation). Going further back to the daily work of each one, we find them individually in rivalry for promotions and more satisfying job assignments (competition). So with the other party to the main conflict. The employers' associations (cooperative) are made up of individual manufacturers or businessmen who hold that "competition is the life of trade" and that "prosperity depends upon free enterprise." Again, out at the ball park the shortstop, second baseman, and first baseman make a clever double-play: they cooperate on that play to defeat their collective competitors. And so on through the manifold activities of living. It is seldom possible to label human behavior as unqualifiedly cooperative or competitive. One type of behavior may predominate but will almost always contain some elements of the other.

Anthropological Evidence

One of the criteria for an innate human trait is its universality. Is it to be found among all peoples regardless of differences of geography and of race? What data can the anthropologists furnish the psychologist here? Their accounts of a dozen or so primitive folk have been set side by side for comparative study of this very aspect of their cultures [23]; and we shall have space for brief summaries of two, the Zuñi and the Kwakiutl, both Indian peoples of North America and of very similar biological stocks.

The Zuñi Indians of New Mexico are a people of peaceful and industrious life, skilled in agriculture, herding, weaving, and the fashioning of jewelry. They are rich, but this wealth is not matter for individual rivalries or enmities. Ownership is defined by use; and one may call his own as much of the land as he can keep under cultivation. Though the sheep are owned by individuals, kinsmen pool their flocks, and cooperatively herd, lamb, and shear the animals. So with personal property. The silver and turquoise ornaments, the beaded and tooled moccasins, though individually owned, are freely loaned; and one may wear another's clothing and jewelry to the feast with no loss of prestige. And the same condition holds for wealth in general: the richer give more than the poorer to the religious festivals, but they acquire no prestige by doing so; and if they give a bountiful feast, much more is made of the good so done to many than of any increased reputation earned by the giver.

In other than property customs, Zuñi are similarly non-competitive. They may put on ceremonial four-mile foot-races, but no betting is involved, and the name of the winner is not even announced. They may hold a stick-kicking contest over a twenty-five mile course to bring rain, but the winning team gains no particular personal prestige, and consistent winners may even be barred.

The Kwakiutl Indians of British Columbia also are a wealthy people,

167 **Is Primitive Man Cooperative or Competitive?**

Explanation in text. (*From M. Mead,* COOPERATION AND COMPETITION AMONG PRIMITIVE PEOPLES, *McGraw-Hill, 1937.*)

but they look upon their canoes and copper plates and blankets and fish oil as means of acquiring individual prestige. Everyone must own material goods in abundance if he is to maintain any considerable rank. And "to own" means exclusively to own and exclusively to display, even to the conspicuous waste and wanton destruction of goods. This economic attitude comes to flower in their "potlatch" ceremonies, where they give away blankets and coppers on a grandiose scale; and a rival who cannot return such gifts with interest at the end of the year — even to a hundred per cent — is crushed with the loss of social status.

These two primitive societies, and eleven more, have been compared diagrammatically by arrangement on a triangle, as shown in Figure 167. The midpoint of each side of the triangle represents the most intense development of that emphasis — competitive, cooperative, or individualistic — while points nearer the angles stand in more intermediate position. We see that, so far as their social systems go, these peoples differ in respect of these traits by varying degrees, and that there is no anthropological basis for assuming that either cooperative or competitive tendencies are genetically prior. Certainly the criterion of universality fails.

> The Arapesh eat little flesh;
> They live secure, but futile.
> They're not competitive or harsh,
> As are the Kwakiutl.

> The Eskimos are doughty foes.
> Their wives they're always beating.
> Bathonga buy their wives with hoes
> And will not stand for cheating.

> Bachiga think that food and drink
> Should come from lone endeavor.
> The Zuñi, herding sheep in peace,
> Cooperate forever.

> Samoans feel the great ideal
> Is helping one another.
> Ojibwas try to stand alone,
> And no one loves his brother.

The Maori loan whate'er they own
To Kingdom Come from now;
But interest rates are very high
Among the Ifugao.[1]

Experimental Evidence

Whether a group of people is more cooperative or more competitive depends, we have just been shown by the anthropologists, upon the culture. We can carry this general point further. Experimental psychological work shows us that it depends upon particular situational factors.

In one research, groups of children from six different school classes were set to the task of doing examples in addition (e.g., 3 and 5; 6 and 9; 7 and 4) as fast and as accurately as possible for two-minute periods. The examples were furnished on seven sheets of paper. Before starting on a sheet, each child was to indicate on it whether he wanted the score he would make on it to be assigned to himself or to his group. The groups differed at different times in their make-up, in the following ways:

(1) *The School Class.* Each child when not working for himself alone, was working for the class-as-a-whole (but not in competition with any other class). This served as the control for comparing the other situations.

(2) *Arbitrary Groups.* The experimenter divided the class into halves, which were then asked to try to outscore each other.

(3) *Partners.* Each child chose one other to be his partner, and the contest became a contest between the various partnerships.

(4) *Choose-up Teams.* Two captains were elected by the class, and they chose the ones to be on their respective teams. The teams then were to compete with each other.

(5) *Boys versus Girls.* All the boys were placed in one group, all the girls in the other; and the two groups were then to compete.

What was the relative value of each kind of group-situation as furnishing incentive to work? A simple measure was available to the experimenter. In connection with each of the above-named situations, each child had assigned some of his work sheets to himself and some to his group as he might prefer. Was there any difference in the ratio of these self-assigned and group-assigned sheets with differences in the group involved? Table XXXIX shows clearly that, taken as a whole,

[1] From A. F. J., *J. Abnorm. Soc. Psychol.*, 1939, *34*, 415. Quoted by courtesy of the American Psychological Association.

And as an illustration of a difference in two highly civilized cultures, one is reminded of a story about the Shah of Persia, who, after an hour at the English Derby, remarked in bored tones: "Everybody knows that one horse can run faster than another. What does it matter which one?"

TABLE

XXXIX   Cooperative versus Competitive Spirit in Different Group-Situations

Type of Grouping	Sheets assigned to			
	Self		Group	
	Number	Per cent	Number	Per cent
Class	6.48	93	0.52	7
Arbitrary groups	4.66	67	2.34	33
Partnerships	4.19	60	2.81	40
Teamwork	3.95	56	3.05	44
Boys vs. girls	2.12	30	4.88	70

From J. B. Maller, "*Cooperation and Competition,*"
TEACH. COLL. CONTR. EDUC., 1929, No. 384.

the school children were most highly motivated to work cooperatively when the boys were pitted against the girls, next most highly when working with a group chosen by a fellow pupil elected by the children themselves to be their leader; and that they were least motivated to cooperative endeavor when they had no say about the make-up of the group but were arbitrarily assigned.

As a general conclusion we may infer that "competition" and "cooperation" are not terms that have absolute meanings: they do not have absolute values to the individual person. To him it makes a difference with whom or with what organization he is to do the cooperating or the competing. We may further note that the relative incentive values of the different group-situations refer to American school children, not to Samoans, Maori, or Ojibwas. They depend upon one set of cultural values. Relativity within relativity! "Human beings by original nature strive for goals, but striving with others (cooperation) or against others (competition) are learned forms of behavior." "Neither one nor the other can be said to be the more genetically basic, fundamental, or primordial" [22].

Prototypes of Environment-Determined Cooperation and Competition in Lower Animals

If we needed further evidence that cooperative and competitive behavior are in high degree products of the culture — or, more broadly, of the conditions of living — we have it apparently coming from a curious direction. Animals below the Primates can be put under situations that make them either "cooperative" or "individualistic."

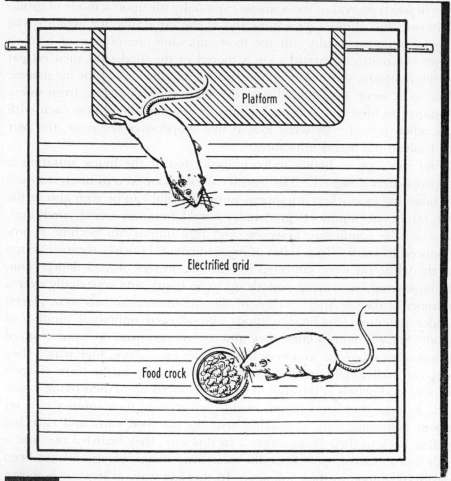

168 Cooperative Behavior Acquired by Rats

Explanation in text. (*Adapted from W. J. Daniel*, J. COMP. PSYCHOL., *1942, 34 361–368. By permission of the author.*)

In a series of experiments at the University of North Carolina, white rats were placed under a specially-designed social condition. The animals were dropped in pairs into the enclosure shown in Figure 168. They quickly learned to escape a shock from the floor-grill by running to a tilting platform which, when pressed down, broke the circuit and so terminated the shock. But the animals were hungry; and sunk in the floor of the box was a food cup which they could reach only by getting down off the platform. The situation would have compelled a single rat to go hungry or to accept the severe shocking to get his food.

But in pairs, several of the animals eventually hit upon a mode of group behavior that allowed for eating and at the same time for avoiding the shock. One rat would visit the food cup while the other was holding down the platform, would seize a morsel of the food, and then retreat to the platform, thus effectually releasing the other to go for his morsel. And so it went, one animal and then the other changing from safety platform to food cup and back again, in regular alternation each with the other animal. By what looked like cooperative behavior, the pair had solved the practical problem.

But rats can be highly individualistic, too, if the living situation is appropriately designed. The instinctive behavior seen in many animals of hoarding food when it happens to be plentiful can be seen also in the rat, but in only a minor degree under usual laboratory colony conditions. Change the conditions, however, and this animal can become a pronounced hoarder. In a series of experiments [11] newly-weaned young of the white rat were subjected to extreme degrees of food deprivation, being starved for varying periods up to 36 hours, and repeatedly over a number of days. After 15 days of this treatment, the rats were placed under the usual colony conditions and allowed unlimited supplies of food. Some 5 months later, they and control rats from the same original litters were subjected to a very limited diet for 5 days, after which they were all individually given hoarding opportunities in the form of open cans of food pellets at the ends of runways moved up to their living cages. The animals that had suffered food-deprivation in their infancy now set about hoarding, that is, making trips to the food cans and carrying pellets back to their living cages. In this way, they hoarded two and a half times as many pellets as did their litter-mates which had not been deprived of food in their infancy. In this one way, at least, it is shown that infantile experiences form an effective determinant of adult individualistic behavior.

A Graphic Representation of Interpersonal Attitudes

Put a number of individual persons into one area — whether a playground, a prison, a battalion of infantry, or a new town — and, no matter how homogeneous a population they may appear to form at the start, sooner or later lines of cleavage will begin to appear. Degrees and shadings of attraction-repulsion inevitably develop between the component individuals; and so groupings come to be precipitated out of the original solution. Moreno [24] originated a convenient graphic method of representing these interpersonal relationships which furnish the groundwork for spontaneous groupings. See Figure 169.

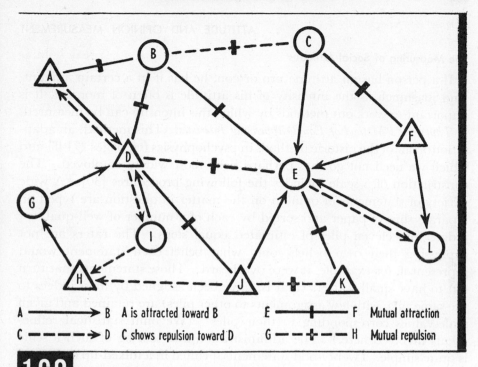

A ⟶ B A is attracted toward B   E ⊢ F Mutual attraction

C ⤏ D C shows repulsion toward D   G ⟍⊢⟋ H Mutual repulsion

169 **Sociographic Structure of a Third-Grade Room**

Plotted from answers to questions asked each child: "Which boy(s) or girl(s) would you like [not like] to work with?" Boys are represented by triangles; girls by circles. (*After Moreno.*)

In one interesting application of his method there was obtained a picture of women's friendships in a whole community [19]. In a New England village every housewife was canvassed. She was asked many questions regarding church, occupation, magazines taken, club membership, and the like, and (quite casually and confidentially) the names of her best friends in the community, those with whom she exchanged "social" visits. The responses were plotted on charts. A study of correlated factors indicated that the friendship-lines in the community seemed to be along the lines of similarity of occupation (though not economic status), church membership, and cultural interests, while blood-relationship and geographical proximity seemed unimportant.

The same graphic method can easily be elaborated. Girls living in a residence hall have been asked for their preferences in roommates; children of a schoolroom, their preferred seatmates; members of a flight squadron, the men they would like to have fly beside them; and often the individuals have been re-grouped at periodic intervals along the lines of their indicated likings and dislikings.

The Measuring of Social Attitudes

If a person has an attitude pro or con, he has it in a certain amount. And inasmuch as the intensity of his attitude is often of moment, it is important to work out methods by which this intensity can be measured.

Thurstone's Method of Equal-Appearing Intervals. This method, an adaptation of one of the historic methods in psychophysics (cf. pages 271 ff) into which we need not go, has perhaps been most widely employed. The construction of a scale includes the following procedures [30]. A wide variety of statements of opinion on the matter in question are typed on separate slips of paper and sorted by each of a number of well-qualified judges into eleven piles of estimated equal steps. The raters are not expressing their own beliefs, only what belief each statement would represent if, for example, it were overheard. Those statements that turn out to have small scatters (that is, have been assigned by most judges to the same pile, with few assignments to other piles) are retained and given scale-values corresponding to their piles. (We omit statistical refinements involved here.) The administration and scoring of such a scale is quite simple. Twenty-odd statements, printed in a mixed-up order and without their scale-values, are handed the subjects whose opinions are being sought; and each subject checks those statements with which he agrees. Later his score is read off as the median scale-value of the checked items. For instance, in a study of attitudes of different people on the then moot question of prohibition, a few of the statements used and their scale-values when scored, were as follows:

It is absolutely immaterial whether we have prohibition or
    not. (5.5)

The Eighteenth Amendment should be repealed. (10.2)

Possession of intoxicating liquor in any form should subject
    the individual to punishment. (1.4)

Prohibition should come as a result of education, not legisla-
    tion. (6.4)

Scales have been worked out for the measurement of attitudes on a great number of social issues: birth control, communism, evolution, God, war, the Chinese, and very many others. As a tool they have served well in many investigations of the influences that shape attitudes. A clear-cut early example of their use was an experiment to ascertain the effect of a single motion-picture show upon children's attitudes toward the Chinese. First the children of two towns were given an attitude test on the Chinese; then a week later those of one town were shown a film depicting Chinese culture in a favorable light while those of the other town were shown one that presented China unfavorably; and finally the attitude test was again administered to both groups. The results were convincing; the attitudes of the children were changed in the two towns, toward the more favorable and the less favorable extremes, respectively.

Likert's Method of Five-Step Responses. Another technique, considered as sound as Thurstone's, and labor-saving in construction as well, is Likert's method, whereby the subjects indicate one out of several ways of answering to each statement of opinion [18]. For example, two items in an "International Scale" appear in the following form (except that the numerical values did not appear):

19. A person who loves his fellow men should refuse to engage in any war, no matter how serious the consequences to his country.

Strongly Approve	Approve	Undecided	Disapprove	Strongly Disapprove
(5)	(4)	(3)	(2)	(1)

20. The United States should have the largest military and naval air fleets in the world.

Strongly Approve	Approve	Undecided	Disapprove	Strongly Disapprove
(1)	(2)	(3)	(4)	(5)

Each subject was to check the one response to each item that represented his reaction to it. The items used were selected from a number tried out on a several hundred preliminary subjects, those statements being retained which were found to be highly correlated each with the total score on all the items. When such a scale has been administered to a population in question, the scoring amounts to the totaling of all the checked numbers.

Do the recipients of governmental relief come to feel themselves pauperized? What does the typical Japanese think of democracy since the occupation? Do the college years weaken religious faith? Do men and women view the career woman differently? Are a Northerner's feelings on the Negro question changed by a short residence in the South? Is pacifism now a dead issue? Do a person's views on capitalism seem to go with his views on moralistic questions? How effective are newspaper editorials in shaping readers' views? Do people of different religious affiliations agree on what are the gravest menaces to American life? What does Americanism mean to the American people? These are samples picked at random from the wide areas of live social inquiry to which the measurement of people's attitudes is applicable.

The Polling of Public Opinion

At this point in our study of psychology we may properly broaden our survey to touch briefly upon public opinion and upon a type of methodology in measuring it of which the present-day reader has become keenly aware, a methodology in whose development psychologists have had an active share. A simple definition of "public opinion" is that of James Bryce: the "aggregate of the views men hold regarding matters that affect or interest the community." Public polls have come to assume many forms, but for convenience we may roughly group them into consumer research and opinion research. Consumer-research polls are conducted by or for large commercial firms who seek to determine more precisely the demands of the consumer public so that they can point up their products to meet them. Opinion-research polls are typically carried on by agencies which seek to determine what people are thinking on noncommercial public issues of the day.[1]

The general notion of an opinion poll is familiar. In essence it is the *questionnaire* technique applied to a *sample of the population* which is taken as adequately representing the whole. It has taken several concrete forms [3].

The *mail questionnaire* has some obvious advantages such as convenience, cheapness, and wide geographical coverage, but its one great disadvantage for most polling purposes is that it fails to get at a representative sampling of the general population. The now-famous *Literary Digest* presidential straw vote of 1936 failed for that very reason. The ballots were mailed to people whose names were listed in telephone directories, or to lists of automobile owners. In consequence, answers received at the magazine's counting rooms were from only the upper half, economically speaking, of the people who were to vote in November.

The *telephone interview* has some of the advantages just mentioned for the mail ballot, but it too is automatically selective in its respondents.

The *personal interview* is found to be the soundest means of contact. Dangers still lurk, however [10].

The reader-psychologist will recognize at once that the person of the

---

[1] Among the best-known agencies in America are: the American Institute of Public Opinion (Dr. Gallup's), *Fortune* magazine, the Office of Public Opinion Research (at Princeton University), the National Opinion Research Center (at the University of Denver), the Psychological Corporation (Dr. Link), the Bureau of Agricultural Economics (of the U.S. Department of Agriculture), and the recently established Survey Research Center (at the University of Michigan, Dr. Likert).

TABLE XL

Relationship of Interviewers' Bias and Respondents' Opinions, in Towns of Different Sizes

Size of Place	Percentages of "Yes" answers obtained		Difference
	by "Yes" interviewers	by "No" interviewers	
Over 100,000	49	51	−2
2,500 to 100,000	58	46	12
Under 2,500 and rural	65	44	21

Question: Do you think that the United States Navy should be used to convoy ships carrying war materials to Britain? (From a 1940 survey.)

From H. Cantril, GAUGING PUBLIC OPINION (Princeton, N.J.: Princeton University Press, 1944), 112.

interviewer himself introduces a human variable that may not safely be overlooked. Will an interviewer who would himself answer "yes" to the question be more likely to get positive answers than an interviewer who would answer "no"? Table XL gives evidence that such a result is to be expected. Even with experienced questioners there is a subtle influence from the interviewer's bias. The way to control this factor is for the director of a poll to arrange for an equal number of interviewers who reflect bias in opposite directions and so cancel out this factor.

Two other major considerations present themselves. The sample population must be an *adequate sample*, must truly represent the whole population. No reliable pollster, for example, would interview only postmen and policemen to make up his quota of working men and only waitresses as his quota of working women. For once it is borne in mind that the general population is not homogeneous, the reasons for *stratified* sampling are obvious. First, the total population to be studied is analyzed into its various classifications or strata, and the size of each stratum is determined. When the sample is made up, it must contain the same proportions drawn from the different strata, based on sex, age, education, race, religion, political preference, income level, occupation, state of residence, rural versus urban, or other classifications that might presumably affect the returns. That polling techniques have not yet been perfected to a point where all sampling errors are avoided, seems to be the lesson to be drawn from the failures in prediction made by most of the best-known polling services in the presidential election of 1948.

The sample must be on a scale large enough to represent the population fairly. Roughly, the degree of confidence the pollster has in results from his sample increases as the square root of the *size* of that sample; e.g., a sample increased from 100 to 400 persons (4 times) would be about 2 times as adequate. A formula is commonly used to determine the standard error of the proportion used:

$$\sigma = \frac{p\,q}{N}$$

in which σ = the standard error of the percentage, p is the percentage of instances in which a given answer has been obtained within the sample, q is 1.00 minus p, or the percentages of instances when a different answer was obtained, and N is the number of persons asked. Thus the formula takes into account both the size of the sample and its variability.

Another major consideration is the *form* of the *questions* to be used. Shall they be dichotomous ("yes" or "no"), multiple-choice ("which do you think. . . ?"), or open-end ("what do you think about. . . ?")? A choice here depends upon the stage which the study has reached, the open-end questions being best for preliminary work. Then there are general precautions that are relevant to any form of questions: they should be unambiguous; should not be involved or long; should be as concrete as possible; and should conform to other rules that the present reader can readily suggest.

We have not, in the foregoing paragraphs, afforded the reader very concrete pictures of organized polling questionnaires and their results. It is more important that he get some impression of the increasingly careful and complicated safeguards being demanded of opinion polls nowadays. And he should bear in mind further that little has been said about statistical formulae and procedures that are employed in truly scientific polling.

THE INDIVIDUAL USE OF SOCIAL SITUATIONS

Reaction-Getting Habits

In our frequent returns to the fundamental concept of the organism's adjustments to, and of, its environment, we have not usually characterized its environment in particular. But the fact is that the individual lives among other human beings, so that the problems of his life are problems of adaptation to these others and by means of them. We have already noted the fact that children, when facing difficult problems that are set up experimentally, often call upon other people for aid in getting the suspended ball or the barred-off doll (pages 420 f.); and the elaboration of this in later childhood and adult life is one of the central features of the socializing of the individual. But let us first look to its phylogenetic antecedents.

When Köhler's apes were seeking the out-of-reach banana (p. 416 f.), one of them sometimes pushed or pulled the experimenter or the keeper over to a position under the lure so that it might climb him and so reach the objective. The man was treated like a box. This is hardly social behavior.

Bekhterev tells the story of a pigeon he once observed, which, "flying round a horse's head, at first frightened the horse by the whirring of its wings and thus made him spill grain from his nose bag. Led by this casual experience, it repeated the trick several times and for the same purpose." The pigeon was plainly utilizing the horse. But it was not using him as a mere physical object: it was *getting reactions out of him, reactions useful to itself.* It had developed a *reaction-getting habit.*[1]

Consider also a description of a rather common chimpanzee mother-baby relationship. At first, the mother controls her young by physical force, drawing it suddenly back from danger and clasping it to her breast, vocalizing excitedly meanwhile. After many repetitions of this behavior, the baby learns to leap into its mother's arms, at first when her hand is extended to seize it, and later at a mere gesture on her part suggestive of the seizing movement, or at a slight squeal. The mother has gotten social control of her baby now, by the mere device of eliciting desired responses from it. She uses it as a reactive organism for her own end — and end that is, to be sure, concerned with the good of the baby in this case, but still an end or adjustment of hers.

Here we can with profit return to our diagram of the adjustive sort of behavior (Figure 5, page 26), but with an amplification to include the fact that much successful adjustment is made through using other people. (See Figure 170.) Let *1* again represent the on-going activity of our original subject *A*, and let *3* again indicate the encountering of some difficulty or hitch (*2*) arousing *A's* excited and exploratory behavior. Now, let the reaction *4* be such as to stimulate *another* person or animal *B* to make the response *4-b*, a response that in one way or another removes the hitch or difficulty (in the above examples: horse spilling oats, baby chimp leaping to its mother). Then we can represent the satisfaction of the original motive again as *5*. Instead of avoiding or

---

[1] Chimpanzees will tease chickens, dogs, each other. And the present writer will not soon forget that chimp which pursued and tossed sand at him as he dodged to right and left before its cage.

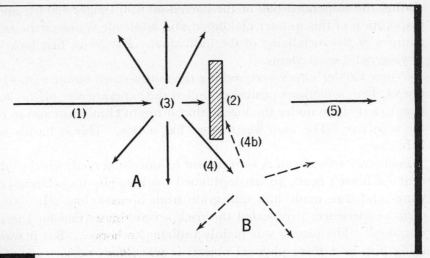

170 Diagram of Typical Animal Behavior in which Stimulation of Another Animal and its Reactions Furnish the "Way Out" (Compare with Figure 5)

removing the obstacle himself, subject *A* stimulates subject *B*, who removes it. It is an adjustive process in exactly the same sense as before, except that the intermediation of a social reactive object is now involved.

This sort of phenomenon is to be seen constantly in human society. It is expressed in the phrase, "getting a rise out of him." Some of the more dramatic illustrations that present themselves to the clinical psychologist are appropriate here. Take the following cases: the adult who has her way, when facing ugly situations, by the habitual device of copiously weeping or hysterically fainting or screaming and scolding; the confirmed toady ingratiating himself and fawning; the persistent bulldozer and bluff; and the four-year-old child who develops there action of vomiting as his habitual way out of disliked assignments. One and all, they have found how to get others to do things for them by the familiar process of trial-and-error. Once upon a time, finding themselves in a difficulty and reacting this way and that, they chanced to do something (to weep or faint or scold, to fawn or bluff, or even to vomit) that aroused from people near them just the kind of behavior that removed the disliked restraint. They didn't *have* to go to school, to give up the coveted toy, or to eat the spinach. And the rest is merely the story of fixation of this successful way of adjustment as a tool or weapon to be used on all obnoxious occasions.

Learning to Make Abbreviated Social Stimulations

In the case of the chimpanzee mother referred to above, it was to be noted that she developed control over her young merely by a gesture or a warning cry.   Another illustration from animal psychology will re-enforce the point and give us a further hint as well.   In over fifty species of birds, from sparrow and canary to flamingo and gray goose, it has been observed that there is a definite order of precedence between any two individuals, a definite "peck-right" [27].   Bird A can peck or threaten to peck bird B without being pecked in return.   The "right" is ordinarily determined after one encounter.   On that occasion A has inflicted pain on B; whereupon occurs a change in B's neuromotor organization that is simple enough.   The situation in which B's cutaneous receptors were receiving the intense pain stimulation, thus arousing his own withdrawal movements, included also such incidental stimuli as the sight of A's ruffled feathers, high-held head, or angry face and eyes, and the sound of his pugnacious squawking.   It is easy to see that on later occasions the re-presentations of A's ruffled feathers or angry squawk will become potent to excite the complete act of withdrawal by B. Henceforth, A need only ruffle up or give one warning squawk to control B's responses satisfactorily.   A relationship of this sort often furnishes the psychological basis of a whole social order. A pecks B, B submits to A but pecks C, C pecks D, and so on; furnishing a pretty complete hierarchy.   The whole group can derive a definite structuring from the building up of these interindividual stimulations and responses carried no further than the merest gesture and vocal sound.   Many a boys' gang becomes similarly structured.

Of course, it is in the human that we would expect to find and do find the most elaborate developments of social control through abbreviated reactions.   And they can be traced to early years.   Preyer found his infant son turning away his head when he had had enough of feeding, and then later shaking his head in the same general manner when a negative response was aroused to any presentation or demonstration by another person.   Similarly, what began as an actual pushing away of things he disliked evolved into the more refined head and arm gesture of rejection that we see in older children and adults to wave other people aside or indicate to them, "No!"

A suggestion as to the natural history of the military salute provides a neat illustration of successive abbreviations [16]:

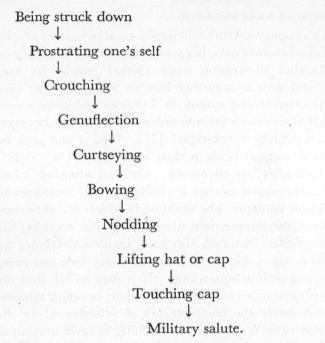

Being struck down

↓

Prostrating one's self

↓

Crouching

↓

Genuflection

↓

Curtseying

↓

Bowing

↓

Nodding

↓

Lifting hat or cap

↓

Touching cap

↓

Military salute.

When a boy draws back his hand and threatens a younger brother, or when he cries aloud and gets attention from friendly quarters, or reaches toward the ground and so sets a dog in fleeing retreat, we cannot fail to see that he has picked up, or learned, the trick of letting an abbreviated reaction do duty for a complete one in socially stimulating others. Given a drive and an environment which does not satisfy that drive until a change is produced by the action of another person B, the response aroused from the subject A need be only an abridged one. B has previously learned to perceive social cues, that is, to recognize the whole reaction from this partial act of A and will readjust his behavior accordingly; and A will have hit upon and fixated this device by trial-and-error as an adequate adjustment on *his* part when the whole situation arises. The mere threat to act thus and so is now the selected and fixated line of activity with him.

It is by the medium of language, however, that the most potent, most delicate, and most versatile forms of social influence are made possible. The use of language is so important that we shall devote a special chapter to its presentation (Chapter 18).

REFERENCES

1. Allport, F. H. *Social Psychology*. Boston: Houghton Mifflin Company, 1924.
2. Anderson, H. H. "Domination and integration in the social behavior of young children in an experimental play situation," *Genet. Psychol. Monogr.*, 1937, *19*, 341–408.
3. Blankenship, A. B. *Consumer and Opinion Research*. New York: Harper and Brothers, 1943.
4. Bühler, C. "The social behavior of children," in C. Murchison, ed., *Handbook of Child Psychology*. Worcester, Mass.: Clark University Press. 1933.
5. Burtt, H. E., and D. R. Falkenberg, Jr. "The influence of majority and expert opinion on religious attitudes," *J. Soc. Psychol.*, 1941, *14*, 269–278.
6. Daniel, W. J. "Cooperative problem solving in rats," *J. Comp. Psychol.*, 1942, *34*, 361–368.
7. Dashiell, J. F. "Experimental studies of the influence of social situations on the behavior of individual human adults," in C. Murchison, ed., *Handbook of Social Psychology*. Worcester, Mass.: Clark University Press, 1935.
8. Dusenbury, D., and F. H. Knower. "Experimental studies of the symbolism of action and voice," *Quart. J. Speech*, 1938, *24*, 424–435.
9. Fensterheim, H., and H. G. Birch. "The influence of group ideology on individual behavior," (Abst.) *Amer. Psychol.*, 1947, *2*, 317.
10. Gallup, G. *A Guide to Public Opinion Polls*. Princeton, N.J.: Princeton University Press, 1944.
11. Hunt, J. McV. "The effects of infant feeding-frustration upon adult hoarding. . . ," *J. Abnorm. Soc. Psychol.*, 1941, *36*, 338–360.
12. Jenness, A. "Social influences . . . the role of discussion . . .," *J. Abnorm. Soc. Psychol.*, 1932, *27*, 29–34, 279–296.
13. Kardiner, A., R. Linton, *et al*. *The Psychological Frontiers of Society*. New York: Columbia University Press, 1945.
14. Klineberg, O. "An experimental study of speed and other factors in 'racial' differences," *Arch. Psychol.*, 1928, *15*, No. 93.
15. Krech, D., and R. S. Crutchfield. *Theory and Problems of Social Psychology*. New York: McGraw-Hill Book Company, 1948.
16. Krout, M. H. "The social and psychological significances of gestures," *J. Genet. Psychol.*, 1935, *47*, 385–412.
17. Lewin, K., R. Lippitt, and R. K. White. "Patterns of aggressive behavior in experimentally created 'social climates.' " *J. Soc. Psychol.*, 1939, *10*, 271–299.
18. Likert, R. "A technique for the measurement of attitudes," *Arch. Psychol.*, 1932, No. 140.
19. Lundberg, G. A., and M. Steele. "Social attraction-patterns in a village," *Sociometry*, 1937, *1*, 375–419.

20. Lynn, J. G. "An apparatus and method for stimulating, recording and measuring facial expression," *J. Exp. Psychol.*, 1940, *27*, 81–88.

21. Maller, J. B. "Cooperation and competition, an experimental study of Motivation," *Teach. Coll. Contr. Educ.*, 1929, No. 384.

22. May, M. A., and L. W. Doob. "Competition and cooperation," *Soc. Sci. Res. Council Bull.*, 1937, No. 25.

23. Mead, M. *Cooperation and Competition among Primitive Peoples.* New York: McGraw-Hill Book Company, 1937.

24. Moreno, S. L. *Who Shall Survive?* Washington, D.C.: Nervous and Mental Disease Publishing Company, 1934.

25. Murphy, G., L. B. Murphy, and T. M. Newcomb. *Experimental Social Psychology.* Revised edition. New York: Harper and Brothers, 1937.

26. Parten, M. B. "Social participation among pre-school children," *J. Abnorm. Soc. Psychol.*, 1932, *27*, 243–269.

27. Schjelderup-Ebbe, Th. "Social behavior of birds," in C. Murchison, ed., *Handbook of Social Psychology.* Worcester, Mass.: Clark University Press, 1935.

28. Schlosberg, H. "A scale for the judgment of facial expressions," *J. Exp. Psychol.*, 1941, *21*, 497–510.

29. Thorndike, R. L. "On what type of task will a group do well?" *J. Abnorm. Soc. Psychol.*, 1938, *33*, 409–413.

30. Thurstone, L. L., and E. J. Chave. *The Measurement of Attitude.* Chicago: University of Chicago Press, 1929.

31. Timmons, W. M. "Decisions and attitudes as outcomes of the discussion of a social problem," *Teach. Coll. Contr. Educ.*, 1939, No. 777.

18

LANGUAGE HABITS

GENERAL IMPORTANCE OF LANGUAGE HABITS

MAN has been called the talking animal. Throughout childhood and maturity, language maintains a central place in any person's equipment. A surprisingly large part of one's life involves speaking or listening to speech, writing, or reading. If the oculist were to forbid any reading whatever, while the otologist closed up the ears and the laryngologist banned all efforts to talk, any patient would be in for a thoroughly miserable time, no matter how well he might be otherwise. What an impoverished life would be his! We may pity the G.I. who, when asked by his buddy who had just received a letter if he could "read writin'," had to answer, "No, I can't even read readin'!" But at least his experiences since childhood had equipped him with hearing and speaking habits with which to keep in practical contacts with his fellows.

Let us pause to consolidate our groundwork before advancing. Speech is first of all a business of social communication. From an anthropological angle its primary usefulness is obvious enough. If communication is destroyed, any work dependent upon cooperative activity becomes as the mythical Tower of Babel. The organization of peoples into empires and kingdoms would have been impossible with deaf-mutes. It is almost inconceivable that a speechless people could carve a totem pole, with its implication of magico-religious practices, or could erect pyramids like those of Maya or of Egypt. And without speech how could man have developed systems of counting, or preserved tribal histories, or worked out astronomical calendars? It is language, then, that has made possible all cultural achievements in their more complex forms.

515

Language Originates as a Mode of Social Control

What is implied in preceding paragraphs deserves to be made more explicit. It is a common popular supposition that the primary function of language is to *express thoughts*, to serve as a kind of outlet for what is "in the mind," to bring out into the open what is being enacted on one's mental stage. True, in time, when the child is older or the human group more sophisticated, speech will be used more and more for that purpose, but its original and basic ends are more immediately practical. One of the fundamental situations in which language arises is that in which several individuals are engaged in concerted action; and the *utterances* of the different persons *guide and control their fellows*. For example, during a fishing expedition by Malinowski's Trobriand Islanders,

> short telling exclamations fly about, which might be rendered by such words as: "Pull in," "Let go," "Shift further," "Lift the net"; or again technical expressions completely untranslatable except by minute description of the instruments used, and the mode of action. . . . The structure of all this linguistic material is inextricably mixed up with, and dependent upon, the course of the activity in which the utterances are imbedded.[1]

The point is easily grasped if we approach language from an understanding of infant crying. The very young baby does not cry to acquaint nurse and others with his feelings or state of mind. At very first, his crying is impulsive, a segment of the natural instinctive response to pain or discomfort — as natural as the jerk of the most uncommunicative and dignified patient when his nerve is touched by the dentist's probe. A bit later the baby begins to learn through conditioning the *reaction-getting* value of a cry: it brings someone, it gets attention. It is not a description or representation; it is a summons. Only some considerable time later does the child come to use his vocal sounds to describe or represent something.

We may trace the origins of language still farther back, biologically. Communication among animals is either of the instinctive-outcry or of the reaction-getting sort. And even the reader, as he observes his pet dog's sounds and motions, rarely asks himself what Tige is thinking about, what pictures are in his head, but rather what he is about to do or what activity of his master he is soliciting.

It is out of this matrix of interstimulation — animal, child, or group — that language arises, when the human organism achieves some *symbolizing* power.

[1] From E. A. Esper, "Language," in C. Murchison, ed., *Handbook of Social Psychology* (Worcester, Mass: Clark University Press, 1935).

Language and Other Symbolizing Develops into Thought

Language has been recognized for decades by psychologists of many different persuasions as intimately and subtly linked with man's most delicate and elaborate forms of activity — his thinking. We shall have abundant occasion in the following chapter to expand this conception. When the human being communes with himself, takes counsel with himself — note the phrases! — he is still using language-like processes. However silently and inconspicuously, he is talking and signaling to himself.

LANGUAGE AND OTHER SYMBOLIC SOCIAL BEHAVIOR [1]

Language and Gesture as Indirect Stimulus

We have now to note the development of a phase of socially stimulating behavior of first importance. In the preceding chapter our examples and analyses have, for the most part concerned reactions by B to A's stimuli, in which B's behavior has more or less direct reference to A and A's actions. But in much human intercommunication the activity of B has nothing to do with A directly. *It has to do with a third object.*

When one enters into vocal or gestural conversation at the dinner table, for instance, by far the larger number of the sounds and movements he makes will arouse on the part of his right-hand or left-hand neighbor not responses to him personally and directly so much as toward other things: "Please pass the salt," "Have we ice cream for dessert?", "Did you hear the concert last night?" and the like. So, too, at the baseball park: most vocal signals between bleacherites — above the level of "Down in front!" — are likely to be favorable or derogatory references to the players out on the field, not to the immediate parties to the conversation: "We wuz robbed!", "Kill the umpire!", and other strange sound patterns. Again, in the classroom the vocal and other demonstrations of instructor or of student are far more elaborate than the mere physical give-and-take of two individuals, for their remarks and notes have abundant signification to third objects of discourse. An intercollegiate debate differs strikingly from a boxing or wrestling match in this same regard: whereas the man in the ring makes overt movements toward his adversary and responds more or less effectively to that adversary's overt movements, the debater does not make a physical attack upon the other disputant nor ward off threats of his opponent's bodily approach. Instead, he makes sounds and motions that refer his opponent

[1] The reader should not fail to refresh his knowledge of symbolic behavior by reading again pages 460 ff.

and his audience to third objects and events, objects and events that may actually be thousands of miles distant or hundreds of years away or even entirely fictitious; and it is respecting those objects and events that his opponent must in his turn make appropriate response. "Was Old World culture transported across the southern Atlantic to form the basis of the ancient Inca and Maya civilizations?" "Will the next war exterminate populations by atomic fission?" "Was Hamlet mad?"

As the reader will readily appreciate, new dimensions have now been added to the life and activities of men. No longer are they limited to the here and now, but transcend space and time.

There is no mystery in this, however, and no essential departure from the proposition that psychology is a matter of organismic behavior analyzable into stimuli and responses. Let us try an analysis in these terms. Let a stimulus X, which does not directly affect person B, stimulate A (S_a) to make a communicating or signaling response (R_a) to B; then this may operate as a stimulus (S_b) to the latter person, and excite in him a reaction (R_b) appropriate to the unsensed X. Let us fill in concrete details.

Huckleberry Finn (A) appears in the alley, and, under the stimulating conditions of weather and habit and a possible sight (S_a) of the old swimming hole (X), holds aloft two fingers (R_a), to which (S_b) Tom Sawyer's prompt response (R_b) of "goin' swimmin' " is the answer. Or, on another day, Tom may signal with a crook of a thumb the imminence of Auntie, and his chum will disappear (Figure 171). A lecturer (A) has occasion to point (R_a) to a map that he sees (S_a); thereby directing the attentive postures (R_b) of his audience (B) toward the map (X). Or, a stranger (X) appears in Batouala's camp, and by the latter's drumming (R_a), his tribesmen for miles around (B) are prepared (R_b) for this new turn of events.

In each of the cases the stimuli are symbolic. Two fingers can in no conceivable way be a derivative or abbreviation of swimming or of the pool. A jerked thumb bears no likeness to and may never have been formerly spatially connected with Tom's aunt. The lecturer's extension of arm has nothing especially in common with a map. The thump-a-thump of the mid-African's drum in no way sounds like a stranger.

There is another aspect of the problem. The object or event referred to *may be one not actually in the immediate environment* of the person oriented to it. For instance, Tom Sawyer is probably not in sight of the pool or of people going in that direction. Tom's aunt may be doing her scowling behind a fence or a kitchen door out of Huckleberry's sight. The lecturer's map may be on a side wall visible to the auditor only after

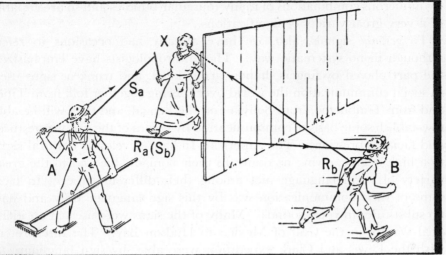

171 **Symbolic Social Stimulus Arouses Reaction to Absent Object**

Tom (A) signals by hand gesture (R_a) in direction of Auntie (X), who is invisible to Huckleberry (B); and the latter reacts to this signal stimulus (S_b) by retreating (R_b) from this "absent stimulus" (X).

rotation in his seat. Batouala's distant tribesmen may not be able to see or hear the stranger. Yet in each episode the party of the second part is led to make an adjustment to a stimulus that was indirect.

Methods of Signaling

The anthropologists, in their study of the earlier and simpler forms of human culture and relationships, describe several distinct methods by which one individual person has gotten into $(S$ and $R)$ communication with others by using symbols. For one thing, there is the *whistling* of messages. In many parts of Africa explorers have noted "conversation" in the form of whistling from some distance. The arrival of one visitor was announced by relays in this way to an official forty miles away. There is the *drumming* of messages, again in Africa. Every white man takes his drummer, and officials moving up or down stream have their drummers to announce their mission to the natives along shore.

The employing of *facial* reaction patterns has already been dealt with in the present book. That it should have been hit upon and fixated as a device in controlling others is small wonder. It forms a striking and readily observed part of total emotional reactions, and, since emotional behavior generally concerns other people, this device is likely to obtain and hold their attention. Then, too, the facial patterns are determined by numerous combinations of many muscular bundles and so are capable of a very great variety of significations.

To *gestural* signals, also, we have already had occasions to refer, although in no systematic way. The anthropologists have emphasized the part played by fingers, hands, arms, head, and trunk as signs used in social communication the world over. Bring together folk from Tibet and from Timbuctoo, from Bolivia and the Bengal, and they will be able to establish some basis of communication by means of the simpler gestures and facial expressions. The American Indians developed gestural signs to a high degree, owing no doubt to their nomadic life and to the great variety of vocal language met among their different tribes. In fact, some of their communication was by this sign language only and had no substitutes in vocal sounds. Many of the signs were used in an identical way from the Gulf of Mexico to Hudson Bay. The interpreters with the Lewis and Clark expedition were able, by sign language, to converse fluently with all the tribes encountered in their long journeys through the Northwest. Much the same signs are employed by deaf-mutes in civilized society; so that once when a small company of Ute Indians were brought to converse with a number of students in the National Deaf-Mute College at Washington, there was a surprising degree of common understanding. Some of the obvious signs used by the Red Man and readily understood are sketched in Figure 172.

Gesture language has, of course, been used by other peoples than the American Indians; and it is even said that the massacre of foreigners in the "Sicilian Vespers" revolt of 1282 was plotted throughout the island, even to the precise day and hour, without the use of a single spoken syllable. This seems not impossible if we bear in mind that the total number of differential gestures involving arm and fingers is estimated to be as high as 700,000 [11], and that the Cheyennes alone used 7000.

> Action is eloquence, and the eyes of the ignorant
> More learned than the ears.

In earlier years, the teaching of the deaf in America was built upon this natural sign language. Manual communications were systematized and more or less standardized. Since the 1860's a rival system of instruction has developed, known as the oral method, in which the deaf child is taught to talk and to read the lips of others. Furthermore, the development of the electronic hearing aid has enabled teachers to utilize with profit the residuum of hearing to be found in nearly all "deaf" children. Much emphasis is naturally put on drill in articulating, on producing the movements involved in consonants and vowels. One advantage of

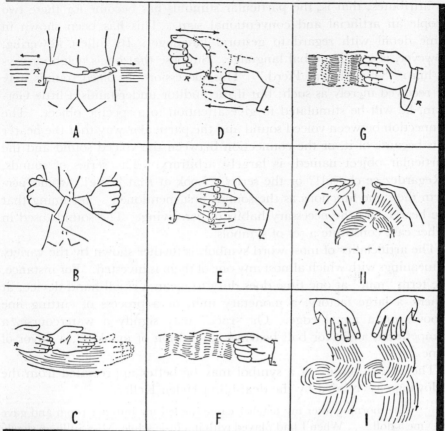

172   **Indian Sign Language**

The nine manual signs are employed to represent the following meanings (in a different order): fast; fight; fish; fond; house; hot; hungry; snake; snow. The reader should be able to pair each of the signs with its meaning. (Correct pairings are furnished in a footnote on page 524.) (*From William Tomkins,* UNIVERSAL INDIAN SIGN LANGUAGE; *published by the author, San Diego, 1931.*)

this oral method is that it gives the hard-of-hearing child more opportunity to communicate with people of normal hearing by utilizing the latter's own medium.[1]

Word Signals Are Highly Symbolic

The manner in which one person stimulates another person often takes the form of setting up a stimulus to which the other has already learned to react as though it actually were something else totally different in all

---

[1] Dr. C. V. Hudgins, in a letter to the author.

its attributes; that is, the particular stimulus has become for these two people an artificial and conventional sign. This has been shown in some detail with regard to gestural language. Its fullest flowering, however, is seen in verbal language. Suppose that one's neighbor says to him: "Sehn Sie das Pferd." This succession of voiced sounds may be received merely as such; but if the auditor understands a little German, he will be stimulated to give attention to a specific object. The connection between voiced sound and the particular way that the hearer acts because of it, or the connection between the voiced sound and the particular object named, is largely arbitrary. The series of sounds, "Regardez ce cheval!" or the series, "Look at that horse!" would perform the same functions as the sounds first mentioned — assuming that the hearer had the necessary habits of perceiving. The sounds used in either case constitute a set of symbols.

The artificiality of most word symbols is further shown by the variety of meanings with which almost any one of them is invested. For instance, the term "mill" at one time does duty to mean a small hand device; at others, a large factory, a monetary unit, or a process of cutting fine grooves on a metal edge. Or "race" may signify a watercourse, a competition, a slot for ball bearings, a division of mankind, a flavor of wine.

The precise nature of a symbol may be better appreciated from the following case related by the deaf-blind Helen Keller.

> The morning after my teacher came she led me into her room and gave me a doll. . . . When I had played with it a little while, Miss Sullivan slowly spelled into my hand the word "d-o-l-l." I was at once interested in this finger play and tried to imitate it. . . . Running downstairs to my mother I held up my hand and made the letters for doll. I did not know that I was spelling a word or even that words existed; I was simply making my fingers go in monkey-like imitation. . . .
>
> [One day my teacher and I] walked down the path to the well-house, attracted by the fragrance of the honeysuckle with which it was covered. Someone was drawing water and my teacher placed my hand under the spout. As the cool stream gushed over one hand she spelled into the other the word *water*, first slowly, then rapidly. I stood still, my whole attention fixed upon the motions of her fingers. Suddenly I felt a misty consciousness as of something forgotten — a thrill of returning thought; and somehow the mystery of language was revealed to me. I knew then that "w-a-t-e-r" meant the wonderful cool something that was flowing over my hand. That living word awakened my soul, gave it light, hope, joy, set it free! There were barriers still, it is true, but barriers that could in time be swept away.[1]

[1] Helen Keller, *The Story of My Life* (Boston: Houghton Mifflin Company).

Other Forms of Language

If space allowed, it would be interesting to review the historical rise of other signaling methods that developed from speech. Written language, of course, has been of incalculable importance in the life of civilized men of all times. By writing down his talk an individual can effectively communicate with others in distant parts and in coming ages. The development of written language is usually said to have had four stages. (1) First came the *pictographic*, in which the inscribed character is some sort of pictorial representation of the thing referred to. There was no relationship between such writing and the *sounds* one made in oral speech when referring to the same object. See Figure 173. (2) In time, these pictures became increasingly simplified and *schematic*, more and more conventionalized and less pictorially representative of the object or relationships symbolized (*hieroglyphic*). Among the Peruvians, the concept of hearing was early represented by a picture of a man with very large ears; then by only a head with large ears; and later by large ears only; until finally the schematic lines lost their obvious picture character entirely, and were only conventional strokes. Such characters are familiar to us in modern Chinese. (3) These hieroglyphics came also to stand for the sounds made in the vocal naming of the objects. They became *phonetic*. They were not essentially different in psychological character from the modern rebus or the modern game of charades, wherein a picture of an object or action (as a "bee" for the verb "be," an "inn" for the preposition "in," or an "eye" for the pronoun of the same sound) stands for the sound of the name applied to it and not for the object at all. (4) Eventually, with a vocal language developing on its own account, the written language underwent a change of the greatest conceivable importance when it became entirely phonetic. All its characters were then reduced to the representations of sound elements, and an *alphabetic* array of consonants and vowels was produced.

The elements of the written languages with which we are familiar are not direct symbols of the things meant. They are, rather, symbols of the vocal sounds made when the things are referred to in speech. In the preceding sentence, for instance, not a word as a pattern of marks even remotely looks like that to which it refers, but each depends upon its ability to arouse a speech reaction formerly learned in connection with it. It would be interesting also to make a survey of the evolution of number systems and number notations — through the Roman, in which quantities were indicated by fingers and thumbs in *I*'s, *V*'s, and so forth, to the Arabic and decimal system permitting the astonishing elaboration we find in higher mathematics.

173   Pictographs

The characters in these pictographic stories are arranged in a spiral formation, the course of the spiral being from right to left, starting from right center and reading backwards. *

Interpretation of pictographic story in Figure 173. An Indian trader by the name of Little Crow went on a journey. He traveled for three nights until he came to a river. The reason he traveled at night was because he was in enemy country. At the river he secured a canoe, camped there that evening, and at sunrise the next morning started down the river and traveled two suns (days). He now traveled in daytime, because he was in friendly territory. He was an Indian trader in shells, which were used for wampum and ornamentation. At the end of the fifth day's travel he reached the village where the shells were obtainable. He rested there for three days in conference with the chief, and as a result he traded for a large amount of shells, and at sunrise on the fourth day he loaded his canoe and started down the river and traveled for two days. On the second day a storm came up, with rain and lightning. He saw the lightning strike a tree and set it afire. As a result of the storm he became sick, so he searched and found some medicinal plants and waited there a couple of days until he felt better. He then traveled at night and hid away in the day time. He knew that the country abounded in game because he heard foxes and wolves. He finally reached home, though some days late. Twenty braves of the tribe came out to meet him, including their chief, Standing Bear. Their hearts were glad as a result of his safe and successful trip, and they all had a very sociable time.

(*From W. Tomkins,* Universal Indian Sign Language; *published by the author, San Diego, 1931.*)

Interpretations of manual signs in Figure 172 on page 521: A, hungry; B, fond; C, fast; D, fight; E, house; F, snake; G, fish; H, hot; I, snow.

We should find much that is psychological if we followed this avenue into the field of *semantics*, that is, the science of linguistic meanings, the study and classification of word-significations and of the changes that occur in them [8, 12, 5, 7]. But enough material has been presented for the reader to see that, as written means of social interstimulation have evolved, some familiar psychological processes have been at work. Throughout this development there has been a tendency to simplify to the mere rudiments that are necessary. There has been a constant standardizing or conventionalizing of the signals (an aspect of social conforming). And there has been evident the human capacity and propensity to get away from the limitations of concrete particulars by abstracting and generalizing common aspects for more independent and universal use.

However artificial a word symbol is, it does not become so standardized in a single meaning that it is not heavily dependent upon its contexts. In learning a language one must learn far more than a vocabulary of single words to be strung together in this and that sequence. Even synonyms never mean precisely the same thing. When the beginning student of a foreign language attempts translations by adopting the first equivalent given for each word, he may be dealing with recognizable synonyms, but the resultant melange must often be a sore trial to his instructor.[1]

Two significant non-language forms of symbolizing on paper are the *number system* and *maps*. With a little attention, the reader can appreciate how very important these forms have been to both ancient and modern life. The conduct of any kind of business, for one thing, depends to a very high degree upon the use of numbers. Maps are important to commerce, essential to the conduct of a military campaign. In the technical work of engineer or navigator or artilleryman, high aptitude in both kinds of symbols is an absolute requirement. But one does not need to have been a paratrooper, for example, to have had plenty of experiences

[1] The effect must be like that on the English reader of the following essay on "The Banana" reputed to have been written by a foreign-born schoolboy. Most of the words are literal translations, but they are the wrong synonyms.

"The banana are constructed in the same architectural style as sausage, difference being skin of sausage are habitually consumed, while it is not advisable to eat wrappings of banana.

"The banana are held aloft while consuming, sausage are usually left in reclining position. Sausage depend for creation on human-being or stuffing machine, while banana are pristine product of honorable Mother Nature.

"In case of sausage, both conclusions are attached to other sausage; banana, on other hands, are attached one end to stem and opposite termination entirely loose. Finally, banana are strictly of vegetable kingdom while affiliation of sausage often undecided."

when a few lines and dots and circles on a piece of paper meant, if not actual escape from peril, at least a considerable saving of time, worry, and gasoline. The highly symbolic nature of the aid given by maps is apparent when we recall that the marks on paper do not look at all like the landscape itself.

All this implies development not simply in words as such but also in their meanings, in ideas or concepts. We shall have much to say about concepts in the following chapter (on pages 568 ff., especially pages 580 ff.)

A GENETIC APPROACH

Do Lower Animals Use Language?

To this question most authorities return a negative answer. In the most conventional view, at least, no animals can employ symbols as social stimuli — that is, as *signals*.

For nearly twenty-five years it has been conceded that raccoons, cats, dogs, and other forms definitely below the primate level do carry on some kinds of symbolic processes. This has been demonstrated experimentally by the delayed reaction technique, in which the subject manages to react to a stimulus that he has been shown but which is physically absent from his present environment. In that case, it is argued, he must be reacting to some intra-organic process which represents the absent stimulus. In chimpanzees symbol recognition appeared when these animals learned to use poker chips as tokens with which to obtain food from a vending machine [14]. They learned to seize and use any white token, which procured a grape from the machine, but not to bother with brass ones which brought forth nothing. Later they learned when hungry to pick out the black tokens, which alone procured food, but when thirsty to pick the yellow ones which procured water. The tokens, it is clear, had become partial substitutes for food or water, not in the sense of simple conditioned stimuli, either, but in the sense of symbols that indicated or pointed to the ultimate reward.

Again, field observations have called attention to the variety of vocal cries by which monkeys and gibbons [1] call to their mates and evoke from them responses appropriate to the conditions. When an offspring has fallen, the mother's wail gets the attention of the males. When disturbed by an enemy, human observer, or airplane, the males of the clan emit barking roars which prompt the others to grow quiet and hide. On the march, the leading male sounds a metallic cluck that serves to start, speed up, and direct the followers. While engaged in play the youngsters make reciprocal chirps and squeals that keep each other oriented and active. If this fighting-play gets too noisy, a nearby male adult may utter a grunting sound that stops the play. In short, vocal sounds clearly play their part in group coordination, control, and integration, by inter-individual stimulation.

The fact remains, however, that no substantial proof has been advanced for any sub-human animal's ability to combine these two functions, that is, to use symbolic processes for social stimulation. They do not use language.

The Human Infant's Repertoire of Vocal Sounds

The learning of language, like the learning of activities generally, starts from a capital of acts and tendencies already on hand. Hence we first ask: What is the infant's original equipment in sound production? It is by no means complete, of course, on the first day of life; and the problem becomes that of the times of initial emergence of the different sounds.

The first vocal sound of the infant is the birth cry. Speculative thinkers have called it various things from *himmlische Musik* to a wail of protest against being ushered into this world of sin; but as scientists we shall be content to describe it as the vocal part of the first act of drawing breath. The cry is purely reflex action, possibly excited by pain stimulation by the air newly drawn into the lungs.

During the first few months the crying of the infant becomes differentiated — or at least becomes more easily discriminable by attendants. Preyer and others have noted the wail of hunger, the monotonous cry of sleepiness, the sharp loud cry of rage, the high-pitched yell of pain, and the crow of delight. These are reactions of the *emotional* order, forming parts of innate patterns of response. They are aroused mainly but not wholly by intra-organic conditions.

With increasing frequency other vocal sounds come to be made by the baby, especially if he is healthy; these are sounds of a more *random and playful type*. Again the source of stimulation is principally intra-organic, and such babblings and cooings are often called "spontaneous" reactions. The organs of speech are a new-found toy. Now, however, the reactions are not made to such specific stimulating conditions as are those mentioned in the preceding paragraph, nor do they have their places in organized action-patterns. As mere energy overflow through motor outlets not forming a part of definite reaction circuits, they take many forms of laryngeal, epiglottic, lingual, labial, and palatal adjustments.

During the first month the sounds that are made are mostly *vowel: â, ōo, ă,* and so forth, and they may be heard both on inspiration and on expiration. Some observers report next the appearance of *nasal-gutturals* such as *ngâ, ng-gng, mgm.* Finally appear the distinctly *consonant* sounds. Of these, *p, b, d, m,* and *k* are by all observers reported among the first to be heard, and *l* and *r* among the last. These points are of interest for two considerations. The last two sounds are apparently most difficult of precise enunciation in a given language when they are attempted by an adult who is a stranger to that language. Because the group including *p, b, d,* and *m* comprises the earliest distinct consonant sounds, these determine the character of the first syllables spoken by the infant: *da, ma, pa, ba.* It is no accident, then, that the first words that the child comes to use are variations of the polysyllables, *da-da, ma-ma-ma, pa-pa, ba-ba-ba-ba.*

In short, the newborn baby does not present a full equipment of vocal sounds; and he must await the processes of his organic maturing. It is a developmental matter. This is suggested in Table XLI, which summarizes Gesell and Thompson's findings of some of the vocal and related items of behavior in infants observed in the Yale clinic. For each of the bits of behavior listed at the left, the percentage of the infants who manifested it at each successive age-stage is given. For example, cooing appeared in none of their infants at 4 weeks of age, in 3 per cent of them at 6 weeks, in 42 per cent at 8 weeks, in 88 per cent at 12 weeks, and in 76 per cent at 16 weeks. At the last-named age the vocalizing of *ma* or *mu* emerges and grows in frequency for a while.

The number of sounds that ultimately appear is astonishing. One can hear all the vowels and consonants, diphthongs, aspirates, sub-vocals, nasals, German umlauts and tongue trills, French throaty trills and grunts, and even the Welch *l.* And these syllables are rehearsed in grotesque mixtures.

Learning Vocal Habits

The repertoire of sounds that become available to the infant from time to time furnishes the raw material for his building-up of certain habits of vocal reactions which are adaptive. It is a matter of common observation that babies, even before they are able to use words as such, are able to satisfy their wants through the medium of one or another sort of vocal sound. The crying reaction, if it invariably brings the too-indulgent nurse and parents on the run, will become selected and fixated as an easy solution: this will then appear in any and every situation that is uncomfortable, no matter how slight the degree of discomfort nor how advisable it is that the baby be left alone. He will cry when left by himself, when in the dark, when another child happens to possess a

TABLE
XLI

The Maturing of Vocal Behavior

*Behavior Items	Weeks of Age														
	4	6	8	12	16	20	24	28	32	36	40	44	48	52	56
1. Face brightens ..	40	68	..	..	..										
2. Chuckles	0	0	36	42	24										
3. Smiles	22	65	96	100	100										
4. Laughs	0	0	7	31	88										
5. No vocalization heard	45	31	21	15	28										
6. Vocalizes small throaty noises .	84	72	3	4	4										
7. Vocalizes ah-uh-eh......	40	96	82	96	67										
8. Coos	0	3	42	88	76										
9. Blows bubbles ...	0	0	3	42	44										
10. Gurgles	0	0	10	42	56										
11. Vocalizes da					0	7	7	18	59	64	63	62	69	67	59
12. Vocalizes ma or mu					5	11	26	43	47	51	60	52	60	64	64
13. Two syl., 2nd rep. first, ma-ma, ba-ba, etc.....					14	11	7	25	66	70	80	83	86	79	91
14. Makes "d" sound					0	7	22	21	66	64	69	62	88	67	73
15. Makes "m" sound .					5	11	26	43	47	58	63	55	60	64	64
16. Makes "ē" sound (at end of word)					0	4	7	7	16	12	14	35	46	48	64
17. Makes "b" sound					9	4	15	14	22	24	32	41	32	57	64
18. Says no word ...					100	100	100	93	88	79	66	31	23	12	5
19. Says one word or more........							0	7	12	21	34	69	77	88	95
20. Says two words or more........							0	4	0	3	3	28	34	67	86
21. Says three words or more											0	10	26	40	68
22. Says four words or more												0	7	9	26	36

All percentages over 50 are set in italic figures.

From A. Gesell and H. Thompson, INFANT BEHAVIOR; ITS GENESIS AND GROWTH *(New York: McGraw-Hill Book Company, 1934).*

toy he is interested in, when anything desired is out of reach or out of
sight. Such crying is one side of the spoiled child's habitual make-up.
Even articulated words may have this routine and mechanical character.
The writer once noticed that a child of two years, who was playing
with her older sisters some distance from home and mother, mechanically murmured "mamma" in protest whenever she was imposed upon
by the other children.

In the light of the discussion in the preceding chapter, we can see how
this acquiring of a vocal habit is the learning of a mode of social stimulation, of reaction-getting. It is, for the child, only one of several possible
reactions; yet through the stimulated ministrations of others, it brings
about a satisfactory adjustment, and therefore becomes selected and
fixated as the habitual response to be made under the given set of circumstances. When "mamma" herself is brought by the uttering of that
word or by a cry or a coo, we need not suppose that the presence of the
mother is necessarily the objective of the activity, but rather that the
uttering, crying, or cooing is a way out of trouble.

Learning to React to Words as Stimuli

Meanwhile the infant is learning also to make appropriate responses
to verbal signals made by others. As is repeatedly observed, his understanding of simple words in the spoken language of adults — that is, his
appropriate reaction to them — precedes by some time his ability to
make and use such sounds himself. Most of the infant vocabularies
furnished in psychological literature are confined to word responses; but
any parent can supply lists of words to which a child made the right
response with eye, face, hands, and body, several months in advance of
attempts to articulate the words himself. The hearing vocabulary is
acquired much in advance of the speaking vocabulary.

The process of learning to suit one's action to the other person's word
is a simple matter for us to analyze. We need only bear in mind the
principle of conditioning. Let "bottle" be clearly enunciated with each
feeding, or "kitty" with each presentation of a cat, and the stage is
clearly set for the child's behavior in response to those words heard alone.

Learning to Speak Words

When the child has learned to recognize words and to behave appropriately in response to them, how does he come to make such verbal
sounds himself? There was a time when such a question was answered,
as it seemed, simply and easily, by invoking the term "imitation": it
was explained that the baby merely imitates the words he hears. But

"imitation" as an explanatory concept has been discredited. If babies did have a tendency to imitate all the sounds and words about them, the wonder would be not how quickly they acquire speaking vocabularies but how slowly, for during month after month the babblings of the baby resemble in no way the sounds that are spoken to it. Someone has remarked that the baby does not imitate the adults but the adults imitate the baby, and this observation has an element of truth.

How does the vocal repertoire of an infant become made over into word-speaking habits? If it is borne in mind that vocal reactions are reactions in the same sense as are blinking the eye, grasping with the fingers, kicking, or wiggling the toes, it will not be hard to see that habits of speech are built up as are other types of habits.

(1) For one thing, speech may be thought of as *trial-and-error learning*. It is a story of random articulation, with selection and fixation of correct speech-patterns when they are hit upon. When the baby first chances to sound "da-da," the action is hailed as a real achievement by the social environment of fond and admiring relatives. As a matter of fact, the infant just happened to make those sounds; he was making other sounds as well. But if every occurrence of this particular reaction is accompanied by pettings and applause, it is easy to suppose that the essential conditions are provided for a selecting and fixating of the "da-da" or "daddy" reaction. So with the developing of certain other well-integrated sound-patterns: "mamma," "bye-bye," "kitty," "baby," "ball," and the rest. These sounds come to be made more and more especially in certain situations and in connection with bodily efforts to handle certain things. Let the random sounding of "ball" or of "doll" or of "papa" be frequently accompanied by the appearance and approach of certain highly stimulating objects, and the stage is set for the selection and fixation of these very responses. Thus the social environment, by granting or withholding the objective sought by the child, provides the positive or negative incentives in his trial-and-error efforts at a talking control over things around him.

The syllables *ma* and *da* (or *pa* or *fa*) are the roots of the words signifying "mother" and "father," respectively, in English, French, German, Latin, Greek, and Sanskrit; yet the Chilians say *papa* for "mother" and the Georgians say *mama* for "father," and among various peoples the sound *dada* may signify "father," "cousin," or "nurse." Whatever meaning a given pattern of sounds happens to have in the vernacular of a group will determine the meaning built up by the infant: *papa* will, when enunciated by an English baby, bring the father running, but when sounded by the Chilian it will bring the mother. The former

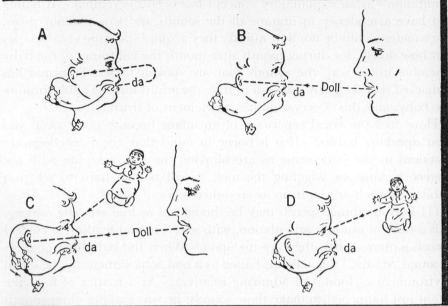

174   The Circular-Reflex Theory of the Development of Language Habits

A. Random articulation of syllables; then fixation of them as circular responses by conditioning. When the baby articulates a syllable, for example, *da,* he is receiving auditory stimulation from the sound he makes at the same time that he is receiving kinesthetic stimulation from his vocal apparatus. In time the auditory stimulus of hearing *da* spoken by himself evokes the motor response of saying *da:* a circular reflex is formed. The very sound of the syllable leads to his saying it over and over.

B. Sound of *da* articulated by another becomes substitute for sound of *da* articulated by himself. Another person, by repeating some of the baby's own syllables, can get him to say them again in response to that other person's voice. This is the so-called "imitation."

C and *D.* Sight of object frequently accompanying sound of *da* becomes stimulus for articulation of the syllable. A doll, having been presented frequently at the same time that the syllable *da* is articulated by another person, the baby's response now becomes conditioned to this new stimulus; and eventually he comes to say *da* whenever that doll is seen. He is now said to "name" the doll.

(*From F. H. Allport,* SOCIAL PSYCHOLOGY, *Houghton Mifflin, 1924.*)

baby will in time use the device thus hit upon when he is seeking his father, the latter when seeking his mother.

(2) An additional explanation of how the infant, after merely making sounds, comes to speak words has been advanced in terms of the *conditioning* experiments. Allport has made a clear statement of this view with an illustration as reproduced in Figure 174. The principle of the

circular reflex — a reflex in which the response serves to renew the stimulus and so leads to a repetition of the same response — is a well-established one; and it is abundantly shown in infantile "lalling," the reiteration of *muh-muh-muh-muh*, *bup-bup-bup*, *goo-goo-goo-goo*, and the like. In fact, many of the infant's words are of this double-syllable character — the fixation of these repetitive articulations — as seen in *bow-wow*, *choo-choo*, *papa*, and *mama*.

Developments in Speech

Once he has mastered the speaking of a few words, a child's improvement through the next half-dozen years is a rich field of study. In everyday life we seem to see several ways in which children's speech improves as they grow older; and scientifically controlled observations have verified and measured the improvements in each of these directions. Though

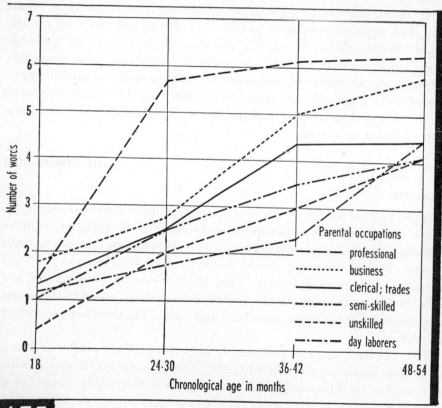

175   **Paternal Occupation and Length of Sentence Used by Children**

(From D. McCarthy, Univ. Minn. Inst. Child Welf. Monogr., 1930, No. 4., p. 56. By permission of the publisher.)

space forbids much more than naming them here, we may note that with increasing age during the years of infancy and early childhood the following changes have been definitely established [9]:

> An increase in number of words uttered: greater loquacity or talkativeness.
>
> An increase in size of vocabulary: more words at the child's command.
>
> An increase in the joining up of isolated words into sentences; and in the length of the sentences.
>
> An increase in the complexity of the sentences used: more compound and complex sentences, more dependent clauses, etc.
>
> A decrease in the relative number of nouns used and an increase in the relative number of adjectives, adverbs, pronouns, conjunctions, and prepositions.

Out of the many quantitative findings that have established the foregoing points, one deserves special mention. It is reproduced in Figure 175. The relationships shown or implied there should touch off a number of queries about the conditions that really determine language improvement. What are the true causes in operation? One generality is certain: the acquiring of language habits is a socially controlled enterprise at every stage. Other people furnish not only the models for speech but the stop and go signs as well, for the slightest ridicule acts as a keen whip to direct or to correct.

SELF–STIMULATION

Introduction

In the first section of the present chapter we have had opportunity to realize the significance to life in human society of the capacity to make symbolic responses that will serve in turn as symbolic stimuli to one's fellows. Society otherwise would never have evolved beyond the level of swarms and flocks and herds. But the fact was also hinted that the individual man, by reason of his ability to symbolize, is able to transcend the limitations of the immediate here and now. That is a high-sounding assertion.

First and foremost, it is profoundly important for the reader to grasp the notion that a person can stimulate himself. An excellent scientific introduction to this point is afforded by some interesting details of a learning experiment conducted on children and apes. A subject was given the problem of learning always to choose (in order to get food) that one of two boxes that had on it a figure with a cross in the center and not a half-moon or circle or triangle or other negative stimulus.

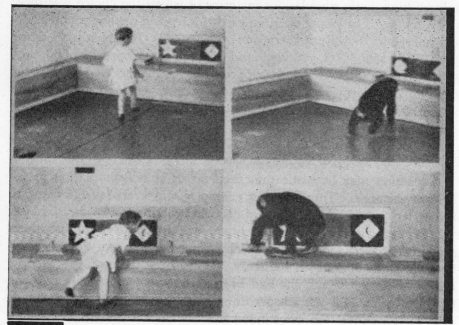

176 Self-Stimulation in a Discrimination Problem

In order to obtain food, child or chimpanzee was to learn always to choose that one of two boxes that bore a small cross in the center of the figure (the positions of correct and negative boxes being exchanged in irregular order). Both children and chimpanzees developed means of stimulating or signaling to themselves as an aid in the discriminating (described in text). (*From L. Gellermann, "Form discrimination in chimpanzees and two-year-old children," J. GENET. PSYCHOL., 1933, 42, 3–27, 28–50.*)

(See Figure 176.) Both the chimpanzees and the two-year-old children learned to make the correct discrimination after long series of trials. But what interests us is the *way* they learned it, or rather, helped themselves to learn it. The chimpanzees, after a hundred or so poor trials, were seen to bring their faces up very close to the figures on the boxes and then to trace the outline of the figures with the back side of their crooked fingers or even with the tips of their forefingers. Then, soon after they showed this sort of behavior, they succeeded in mastering the problem. What shall we make of this? It is reasonable to follow the experimenter and assign to this tracing behavior a definite symbolic significance, and, we would add, a self-stimulating significance. When facing this problem, an ape, finding it difficult to master the difference between the foodless box and the food box merely by the visual characters on them, would follow the outlines with his hand and thus give himself kinesthetic stimulations in terms of which the choice was more easily made. The young children used this tracing method much as did the apes; but they went them one step better. To the correct figure they finally said, "Yes, yes, yes," and to the negative ones, "No, no, no," this utterance followed by the appropriate taking or leaving. In the experimenter's words, "These verbal responses served as instructions administered by the children *to themselves* on how to react to the particular stimuli concerned."

Some Everyday Modes of Signaling to Oneself

A reaction may be made that then serves as self-stimulation in the field of memory. The following example from everyday life came to the writer's attention when one of his colleagues had occasion to ask his wife for her scissors. For a moment she was unable to recall just where she had left them; then after stretching out her left arm sideways and backward, she announced suddenly, "Why, I left them on the window sill!" At first, it seems, she had been able to remember only that she had previously laid the scissors down with a certain arm-movement; then on executing the same movement again she set up kinesthetic afferent currents that rearoused the whole situation-response. Other illustrations of this general point abound on every hand. The absent-minded man deliberately places a string on his finger as a means of stimulating himself later. The musician often finds it convenient to beat time with his foot, the rhythmic responses of that member helping to direct the tempo of fingers or voice.

Facial reaction patterns as well as bodily postures and gestures perform this self-stimulating function at all ages. A girl's rehearsals of coyness before her mirror and a boy's attitudinizing as a great baseball pitcher are terminated abruptly upon the sound of a footstep: such use of social reactions is here really private in character, in that the stimulating individual and the responding individual happen to be combined in one and the same human body.

As another variety of self-stimulation, consider the girl who is busily at work at her typewriter when the buzzer summons her for dictation. She may not stop typing instantly; she may continue to the end of the sentence or of the page. But in the meanwhile she has maintained an orientation that was set up at sound of the buzzer — a slight turn of head or of feet toward her employer's door, a raising of eyebrows or lifting of chin — and this postural reaction eventually becomes a directive stimulus which is effective the moment a pause in her typing is reached.

Self-signaling with drawings is another activity clearly in point. A map may be sketched for oneself and not for the eyes of another person at all. It may be a memorandum for the future location of hidden treasure — or for a projected automobile tour.

It is in the use of language, however, that we can find the most effective and refined modes of self-control. Private uses of written language well illustrate this point. The broker makes a few scratches on his pad so that later he can follow up the deal he has just made. "Sug peas porterh 2#" a busy man may scribble on a card, as he leaves the house to go to the grocer's; or "meetg bd direct PS&W 4 Tues" he may write upon his desk pad. In both cases he is providing signals to stimulate himself later.

Oral language is used to serve this same *memorandum* function. The chauffeur repeats to himself the words heard at the filling station: "Where car track turns keep straight on one block, then turn left two, then right one, then to third house on right," and at appropriate moments he suits the actions to the words. The merchant unlocking his safe at 8 A.M. repeats silently its combination: "Spin right; left to 32; right to 18; left around past that and on to 55; to right and open!" Or simply: "32 — 18 — 55." The engineer or the pharmacist memorizes his formulas, the law student his definitions and rules, in order that, as later occasion may demand, he can say these over again and so have his behavior adequately regulated.

Aside from this memorandum function of private speech that is memorized, there is the enormously significant role played by *talking to oneself* in the carrying forward of a more or less continuous train of behavior. This function is well illustrated in simple arithmetical computation. When a school child first adds a column of figures, he often articulates as explicitly and fully, as "6 and 4 are 10, 10 and 7 more are 17, 17 and 5 are 22, 22 and 9 are 31. So the total is 31!" As each particular vocal act is performed, the precise character of the response is a stimulus partly determining the next response, that one the next, and so on.

A more complicated form of the same procedure is the *soliloquy*. When a man talks to himself, his spoken words provide stimulations which do more than determine his subsequent language reactions alone, as in the case of continuous adding. They often arouse nascent reactions of a visceral and somatic nature.[1] Much of the speaking in a monologue

[1] That words can serve as effective (conditioned) stimuli to emotional behavior is apparent at once upon examination. Emotional reaction to language can be traced back to the original learning of word symbols in childhood. Often one prefers to say or

is habitual — word order in sentences, superficial transitions from one word or phrase to another, and other manners of speaking now well automatized by repeated use. Once some of the words are spoken, however, they operate via auditory and kinesthetic afferent neural pathways as potent stimuli to perceptual readjustments from time to time — so that in the course of a short soliloquy the speaker is thrown into a succession of different attitudes awakened (as a result of established habits) by the auditory and kinesthetic afferent impulses arising from the words he utters. The most dramatic part of Hamlet's famous soliloquy is a case in point:

> To die; to sleep;
> No more; and by a sleep to say we end
> The heart-ache and the thousand natural shocks
> That flesh is heir to. 'Tis a consummation
> Devoutly to be wish'd. To die; to sleep; —
> *To sleep? Perchance to dream!* Ay, there's the rub;
> For in that sleep of death what dreams may come,
> When we have shuffled off this mortal coil,
> Must give us pause . . .

The first of these lines may well have been uttered in fairly straight-away and smooth-running fashion. The whole set of the speaker is of a single type continuously maintained; and we may say — with apologies to Shakespeare! — that the language spoken is of routine enough sort for a character supposedly equipped with such a vocabulary of word- and phrase-habits. When Hamlet utters the phrase "to sleep," its frequent associate, "to dream," is next aroused, and this in turn acts as a stimulus to excite a new perceptual set, and word-associations congruous with it. These new words have a startlingly different emotion-arousing value, and the soliloquizer proceeds on a new series of speech reactions.[1]

Abbreviation of Speech to Implicit Forms

When a person talks to himself, the conditions of his social environment

write "abattoir" rather than "slaughterhouse" or "shambles," although all these terms refer to the same thing: the difference is in their values as emotion-arousing stimuli. The arts of the poet, of the prose writer, of the orator, of the lecturer, depend in varying degrees upon ability to choose verbal signals that will nicely call out from the reader or auditor just the emotional responses sought.

[1] This explanation may seem a bit complicated. The difficulty is that so many of the principles of serial habits, of set, of perceiving, are concentrated in this example. It is not a simple one. But the writer is confident that any reader familiar with the principles developed in earlier chapters of this book can work his way through a natural scientific explanation of this dramatic incident along the lines suggested. And it should be clearer still after our analysis of Thinking (Chapter 19).

often lead him to hit upon a more and more restrained and reduced manner of speaking. When he is learning to read, his vocal reactions are loud and pronounced; but as his facility increases, he is encouraged by others to read more quietly. His voice is disturbing to other pupils at work or to other readers about the family table. It would be an unsocial act to shout his lesson, like the pupils of the ancient Chinese memorizing schools. From loud speech he learns perforce to shift to *sotto voce*, later on to whispering, still later to inaudible throat, tongue, and lip movements, and finally he may reach that stage of speaking in which all his reading reactions are both silent and invisible. Few people do reach this last stage, however, as the student can verify for himself by watching readers in libraries and street cars. These stages, by the way, are not well marked, but go along more or less together. Time and circumstance as well as the nature of the material to be read may dictate whether one shall read aloud, quietly, or silently.

An illustration from arithmetic will serve us again here. On the one hand, the third- or fourth-grade child adds slowly and with obvious difficulty, voicing the names of the successive sums attained. On the other, the expert clerk is so practiced in the performance that we can observe scarcely any signs of his work other than the vertical excursions of eye and finger and the jotting down of the final result. Between these two extremes lies the vast majority of human beings for whom the casting up of a short column of one-place numbers is easy enough. But when confronted with a long list of figures running into the millions or even with a scorepad of a substantial evening's play, they resort to whisperings and even to counting aloud with accompanying tappings of pencil and noddings of head.

When speech has been reduced in intensity to the point of being implicit rather than overt, it is nevertheless still speech. Much mystery has been needlessly attached to the speech that may be going on silently within a person. Just because it is inaudible and invisible to an attentive neighbor, we need not jump to the conclusion that some new non-physical process of some new non-material entity is at work. To call this silent speech a "psychic" process, or a working of "the mind," explains nothing, and in fact merely adds to the problems which we must explain.

The reality, the actuality of motor activities that have become implicit, such as gesturing or speaking, is really so cardinal a point in our understanding of higher processes that we may well postpone it for separate and fuller treatment in Chapter 19.

SOME DISORDERS OF LANGUAGE FUNCTION

Introduction

In preceding sections of this chapter we have seen that the language functions are of absolutely fundamental importance to the human being both in his social relationships and in his individual private behavior. Perhaps no other physiological loss — not blindness nor deafness, lameness nor paralysis — would easily compare with the total impairment of one's language mechanisms. They are, therefore, of primary concern to us.

They are of exceedingly great interest, also, by reason of the fact of their very great complexity. Learning to say "cat" — and mean it — is an achievement possible only to humans. It involves the teamed and integrated cooperation of a vast range of mechanisms. It exemplifies the highest type of integration of almost the entire organism, in which motor structures that ordinarily subserve various different functions now operate together as a beautifully unified whole. Figure 177 shows the grosser details of the mechanisms.

Stuttering

An affliction of speech that seems nearly always to be psychological in character, and that occurs in at least one per cent of the population, is stuttering. The reader is doubtless acquainted with some of the symptoms of this disorder. Frequently the victim is given to a repetitious sounding of some of his consonants or syllables or words. Sometimes he shows a blocking or excessive delay between his words or phrases. (This latter form is sometimes termed "stammering," but the distinction is probably not important.) Superficially, the condition may be easily described as a lack or loss of teamwork or timed integration of the various mechanisms of speech. Perhaps the expiration movements of thoracic and of abdominal muscles are diametrically opposed; perhaps expiration is interrupted by short inspiratory movements; there may be tremors of lips or of jaw or of the abdominal musculature; there may be pronounced spasms in the larger breathing muscles or in finer muscles of articulation; or any of a dozen other types of poor integration of the whole speaking equipment.

The more fundamental nature of stuttering is not so easy to state. In fact, today there are several rival theories in the field; and on a first approach to the topic, it seems wisest not to commit ourselves but to get acquainted with those interpretations advanced by the more authoritative spokesmen. We can at least try to group them [4, 2].

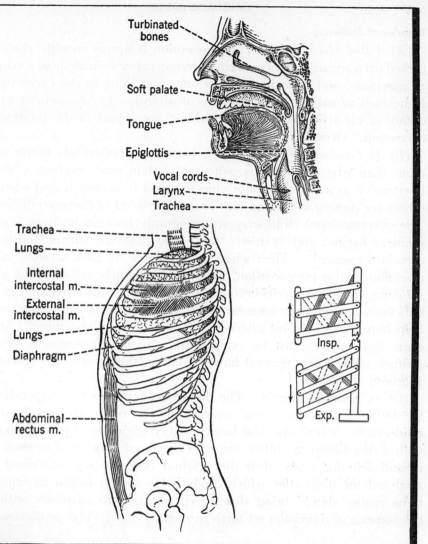

Turbinated bones

Soft palate

Tongue

Epiglottis

Vocal cords

Larynx

Trachea

Trachea

Lungs

Internal intercostal m.

External intercostal m.

Lungs

Diaphragm

Abdominal rectus m.

Insp.

Exp.

177 The Speech Apparatus

I. *Inspiration.* The external intercostal muscles contract, pulling the ribs, which are hinged to the vertebrae, upward and outward (as shown in the mechanical model); and the great diaphragm muscle contracts, lowering its dome. In this manner the cubic contents of the chest are increased, and air is drawn in through the trachea, mouth, and nose.

II. *Expiration.* The internal intercostals contract, pulling the ribs downward and inward (see mechanical model); and the muscles of the abdominal wall contract, pressing the contents of the abdomen against the diaphragm, which is now relaxed upward. Thus the cubic contents of the chest are decreased; and air is forced up through the trachea, mouth, and nose.*

* In the production of small speech-units (syllables) expiration is principally the result of quick ballistic movements of the external intercostals; while in the "breath

Theories of Stuttering

(*A*) *A Bad Motor Habit*. This conception is simple enough: the child picked up a wrong way of speaking, perhaps after hearing it in a relative or playmate, and what he needs is only retraining in the correct way. Rehearsals of material, with plenty of attention by the patient to the details of his articulation and breathing, are a part of the program of correction. (Russell; Dunlap)

(*B*) *An Emotional-Social Habit*. A stutterer can often talk better when alone than when with others, when calm than when excited, when he is attentive to something quite objective and impersonal, and when no others are present to remind him by look or word of his usual difficulty. The overemotional child may stutter simply because he is at a given moment excited and "rattled" (and who does not stutter a little on certain occasions!). Then when other people by look or word direct attention to this phenomenon, making him acutely self-directed in his thinking, a vicious circle becomes established. Stuttering makes him self-conscious; self-consciousness makes him stutter. Plainly, the way to help him is to direct his interests and his attention elsewhere. At the same time, there must be established a more self-confident general attitude as well as a general habit of taking things calmly. (Fletcher; Johnson; Solomon)

(*C*) *An Emotional Conflict*. The disturbances of a person's speech may be symptomatic of a conflict among his less observable motivational tendencies. A boy who had been terribly frightened by an encounter with a dog began to stutter the next day, and continued to show this impediment for years until the original occasion was described and analyzed for him, after which analysis his speech began to improve. (The reader should bring this interpretation into harmony with the phenomena of repression set forth in pages 191 ff.) The psychoanalysts

---

groups" of several syllables (phrases) expiration is principally the work of the abdominal muscles.

Voiced *tone* is given to air in expiration when the two elastic vocal cords are drawn together, constricting the air passage upward through the larynx. The air sets the cords (which act like reeds in a musical instrument) into vibration, and these in turn impart their vibrations to the expelled air. The *pitch* of the voice is dependent upon the degrees of nearness and of tension in the vocal cords, which are adjusted by some nineteen different muscles. *Resonance* is furnished by the chest cavity and by many cavities and chambers in the head. *Consonant* sounds arise from friction of the breath with different mouth parts: with the lips for the sounds of *b*, *p*, *w;* the lips and teeth for *v* and *f;* the teeth alone for *s*, *z*, *j;* the forepart of the tongue for *d*, *t*, *l;* the middle or sides of the tongue for *g*, *k*, *qu*, *r*, *x;* and tongue and teeth for *th* and *sh*. The nasal consonants are produced with all expiration through the nose but with lips and tongue coöperating — in *m*, *n*, and *ngh*. The consonants of other languages than English require still other adjustments.

have carried the notion further, basing each particular disorder upon some particular complex, especially one of erotic character, or upon a basis of general anxiety. (Blanton; Coriat; Despert)

(D) *A Congenital Personality Type.* The emotional difficulties, (B) or (C) above, are best understood as based upon, peculiar to, and expressions of individual inborn predispositions to emotional instability. This is a genetic emphasis, as contrasted with an environmental emphasis. (Robbins; Greene; Despert)

(E) *Imperfect Cerebral Dominance.* Movements of the right half of the body are controlled most immediately by impulses from the left half of the cerebrum, and vice versa. The speech functions seem to be centered on the same side as are those of the preferred hand or foot: in right-handed persons in the left hemisphere; in left-handed persons, in the right hemisphere. Now, suppose that a left-handed child, whose speech centers have already become established in the right hemisphere, is forced to practice his handwriting, eating, throwing, and other uni-manual movements with his right hand and so with his left hemisphere. His cerebral functions will then be uncertainly divided and the lack of integration of the delicate neural mechanisms will produce a disordered speech. (Orton; Travis; Bryngelson)

(F) *A Biochemical (Metabolic) Condition.* Some investigators have found that the stuttering person's blood contains more calcium, sugar, and inorganic phosphates, but less potassium and protein, than does the blood of the person of normal speech. And there are others who emphasize some kind of endocrine imbalance. (West; Kopp)

It is well that we are not forced to choose from among these interpretations, for evidences can be found for each. Two considerations should be advanced, however. (1) It is probable that stuttering arises out of distinctly different causes in different individuals. (2) It is more than likely that these interpretations overlap a great deal; for example, a forced change of handedness (E) may set up emotional stress and strain (B) even to the point of severe conflict (C); a child that has fallen into the easy habit of imitating a stuttering adult in the home or neighborhood (A) is certainly likely to be laughed at in school (B).

A warning note should be added for practical reasons. The very lack of a finally accepted scientific explanation of stuttering has encouraged the development of all sorts of schools of treatment, some motivated by the soundest of clinical aims (but in which every therapist uses his own system), others profiteering at the expense of desperate victims. Many stutterers can testify to having studied in several of the latter "cures," all of which advocated different favorite methods, and all of which were making money.

Aphasias

A class of language defects totally different from the foregoing, and quite clearly dependent upon anatomical bases, is that in which the symbolizing function of language, the very heart of it, suffers impairment. The complete use of language involves four types of function:

	SENSORY OR RECEPTIVE	MOTOR OR EXPRESSIVE
Using sound	...Hearing (with understanding)	........Speaking
Using light	....Reading	.......................Writing

Whenever any of these is impaired through lesions of the brain, the result is called aphasia in a narrower use of the term.[1] It refers to those impairments that affect the organizations involved in language, not to the loss of ability to use the sense organs or motor organs concerned.

From Figure 178 a general notion may be obtained of how the simpler aphasias have been localized in the cerebral cortex. In 1861 the French surgeon Broca worked with a patient whose only disability was that he could not talk, though he could communicate meanings by gestures and signs and seemed intelligent enough in every other way. What is more, he had control over the muscles of mouth, larynx, and thorax: he simply was unable to use them to convey any meanings. An autopsy brought to light a lesion in a certain part of the frontal lobe. A little later Wernicke plotted an area in which he had found lesions associated with patients' inability to understand the speech of others but no inability to hear sounds in general. Such a patient is sometimes able to duplicate the sounds of others' speech, parrot fashion, but is unable to adjust himself to their character as symbols, until he has had them written down or has received old habitual kinesthetic stimulations from his own voiced repetitions. In the reading type of aphasia the affected person may see

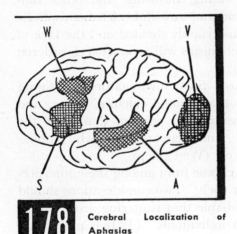

178 Cerebral Localization of Aphasias

S (including Broca's area), where lesions impair ability to speak in words and sentences. *A* (including Wernicke's area), where lesions impair ability to understand words heard. *W*, where lesions impair ability to write words. *V*, where lesions impair reading ability.

---

[1] There is still some tendency to use the word to cover all kinds of loss of symbolic functioning.

a word clearly enough — may be able to trace it with a pencil — yet be incapable of perceiving it as a unit. Or, though able to read the isolated words "The," "bread," "is," and so on, in the sentence, "The bread is on the table," he may be quite unable to get the sense of the sentence as a whole. The writer once observed a mild form of this disorder in a head-injured person who, when reading aloud, consistently read out the opposites for words his eyes actually saw. Commonly, impairments of both the receptive and the expressive functions are involved together [13].[1]

It has been maintained by Goldstein that an important characteristic of some aphasic disturbances is impairment of the patient's ability to *categorize*, that is, of his ability to recognize an object as belonging to a class and to abstract and generalize that property by which it is classified. A patient who is shown a pocketknife may be able to handle it and use it for whittling but be quite helpless when asked to name it, to give it the class-name "knife." This ability is so central a process in thinking that we shall later take it up again in more detail (pages 573 ff.).

As we have seen in our anthropological and genetic surveys in the present chapter, a truly enormous amount of social life is carried on through stimulating others with symbols and reacting in turn to the symbols of others. But we have also seen that communion with oneself, self-guidance and self-control, are made possible by the use of symbolic stimuli and responses of more or less implicit degrees. It is to the phenomena of a human organism directing himself by providing his own stimuli that we now turn.

REFERENCES

1. Carpenter, C. R. "A field study of the behavior and social relations of howling monkeys," *Comp. Psychol. Monogr.*, 1934, *10*, No. 48; "A field study in Siam of the behavior and social relations of the gibbon," *ibid.*, 1940, *16*, No. 84.
2. Despert, J. L., co-editor. "Symposium on stuttering," *The Nervous Child*, 1943, *2*, No. 2, pp. 85–198.
3. Esper, E. A. "Language," in C. Murchison, ed., *Handbook of Social Psychology*. Worcester, Mass.: Clark University Press, 1935.
4. Hahn, E. F. *Stuttering: Significant Theories and Therapies*. Stanford University, Calif.: Stanford University Press, 1943.

[1] The student interested in aphasias should by all means consult Head's re-classification along logical or semantic lines [6]. He might also consider new evidences of localization [10].

5. Hayakawa, S. I. *Language in Action*. New York: Harcourt, Brace and Company, 1942.

6. Head, H. *Aphasia and Kindred Disorders of Speech*. 2 vols. New York: The Macmillan Company, 1926.

7. Johnson, W. *People in Quandaries*. New York: Harper and Brothers, 1946.

8. Korzybski, A. *Science and Sanity*. Second edition. Lancaster, Pa.: Science Press, 1941.

9. McCarthy, D. "Language development in the preschool child," *Univ. Minn. Inst. Child Welf. Monogr.*, 1930, No. 4. Also Chapter 10 in L. Carmichael, ed., *Manual of Child Psychology*. New York: John Wiley and Sons, 1946.

10. Nielsen, J. M. *Agnosia, Apraxia, Aphasia*. Second edition. New York: Hoeber, 1946.

11. Paget, R. *Human Speech*. New York: Harcourt, Brace and Company, 1930.

12. Pronko, N. H. "Language and psycholinguistics: a review," *Psychol. Bull.*, 1946, *43*, 189–239.

13. Weisenburg, T., and K. E. McBride. *Aphasia. A Clinical and Psychological Study*. New York: Commonwealth Fund, 1935.

14. Wolfe, J. B. "Effectiveness of token-rewards for chimpanzees," *Comp. Psychol. Monogr.*, 1936, *12*, No. 60.

THINKING

19

IN OUR EARLIER SURVEY of the phenomena and principles of learning (Chapter 15) we recognized that much learning is of the nature of problem solving. We saw that insight into significant relationships, whether suddenly achieved or slowly arrived at after much implicit trial and error, was the crucial thing. And we noted in descriptive ways how different species of animals and especially human beings of different ages revealed ability to solve problems of varying degrees of complexity. But our descriptions there were limited largely to the problematic situations and to the overt reactions made upon them; we made no real analysis of what goes on inside the reacting person, but have postponed until the present chapter a treatment of *thinking*. Thinking is the inside story of problem solving on its higher levels.

Thinking is Problem Solving with Symbols

When a man is thinking, what is he doing? Surely he is doing something. A person deep in thought may present an appearance of great immobility; like Rodin's figure, he may be sitting still with chin on hand and elbow on knee. But no human observer mistakes such a pose for an inert state like sleep. Any intelligent five-year-old knows that something is going on inside this man. What is going on?

For one thing, when a person is thinking he is making some kind of indirect or mediate reaction upon the object or situation which confronts him. When one thinks about tomorrow's dinner or about an absent friend, it is easy to see that the thinking is going on in the absence of the physical object of the thought.

547

But further, the indirect response may be made in the presence of the thing itself. Consider the behavior of a child or animal which actively and overtly deals with such a thing as a puzzle-box. It manipulates the box with hands or paws, while shouting or crying. Now consider the action of a man who looks hard at the puzzle-box, perhaps keeps his hands in his pockets or perhaps scratches his head, and ponders. He may even close his eyes, but something is going on within that man. He is treating that thing in some fashion, acting in regard to it, dealing with it, and yet not in any overt way. One characteristic of the activity which we call thinking is that it deals with symbolic processes. (For the meaning of "symbolic" see pages 460 ff. and 521 ff.)

The Essential Process Is an "S ⟶ Implicit R (S) ⟶" Function

In all cases it is apparent that when one thinks about a thing his reactions toward it, whatever they are, are not direct reactions. He does not engage in direct and actual manipulation of the thing of which he is thinking. The object or person may be present or may be absent, but in either case the first move of the thinker is to deal with it not overtly, but indirectly. This indirection is plain enough where the use of tools is involved; that is, where the subject turns some of his direct behavior toward the tool instead of toward the object. Indirection, moreover, is the only way in which we can conceive of successful behavior when the subject acts without tools. When a person of our acquaintance shows that he has in some manner been thinking previously about the situation, person, or thing he is now overtly addressing, we are forced to the assumption that he has been doing something when he was thinking about it.

In these different cases it is possible to describe what goes on in the organism in terms of *responses that are set up and that serve in turn as stimuli. Implicit reactions now operate as cues.* As a formula the description would read, "$S \longrightarrow$ implicit R $(S) \longrightarrow R$." And this is no new notion. Emotion, we have seen, is an intra-organic reaction of a sort that in turn influences and determines overt behavior. Attending is primarily a response that prepares for and facilitates overt reactions of particular sorts. In the process of perception, the subject is thrown by some aspect of a situation into some anticipatory set (largely implicit) that orients him for a certain type of conduct with reference to that situation. In thinking, then, a situation arouses some implicit reaction, and that reaction in turn arouses a new implicit reaction, until sooner or later the implicit reaction arouses overt behavior.

It is illuminating to refer here to the treatment of self-stimulation (pages 534 ff.). We have seen in that connection that a person can make a response that stimulates *himself*, and then be affected by his reaction as a new stimulus to himself, just as he can react to another person's reaction (Figure 164). This is especially true of language. Some previously cited illustrations are worth keeping in mind here, especially (*a*) using a silently spoken word or phrase as a memorandum, (*b*) soliloquizing or thinking aloud just as if in verbal interchange with a second person, (*c*) thought-work in adding. An analysis of the last-named process will now prove rewarding.

Suppose that a person not adept at the task is adding the columns of figures to the left. Starting up the right-hand column, he will be talking to himself after this manner: "9 and 4 is 13. 13 and 8 is 21."

56
73
18
34
69

Now, how does he come to say "21"? It is not a response to any such figure on the page. Nor is it simply concocted irresponsibly by the person. It is a response to (*a*) the previously enunciated "13" and to (*b*) the visible "8." If he had not previously made the "13" response he would not now make the "21" response. In brief, the person's *response* "13" now serves as a *stimulus* to *himself* which excites (along with an exteroceptive stimulus, "8") the next following response. He is responding to his own response.

Thinking during addition operates under a high degree of support and control from exteroceptive cues. It ought to be easy for the reader to broaden the illustration to apply to thinking performances where exteroceptive cues are at a minimum or wholly absent.

Coming to closer grips with our problem we may profitably look at a few concrete studies of thinking, noting in each case what features of behavior are thrown into relief.

Do Animals Employ "Overt Thinking"?

Lower animals have been observed apparently trying out alternative acts before actually performing any of them. When a rat faces a choice-point in a maze, he may stop mid-way between the two alleys and swing

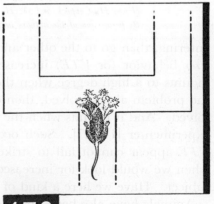

179 Vicarious Trial-and-Error Behavior in the Rat

his head first towards one alley, then towards the other, and again back and forth, before he finally enters one of them (Figure 179). At times he may approach the entrance of one alley and point his whole body for

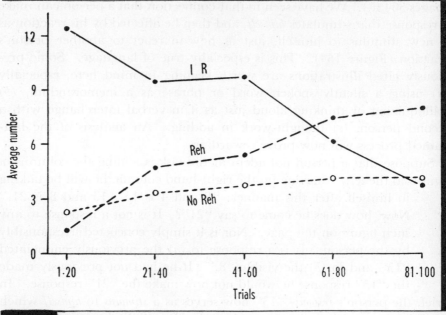

180 The Rate of Learning a Conditioned Response as Affected by the Making of Responses Between Trials

I R   The occurrence of interval responses.
Reh   The occurrence of *CR's* in animals making the interval responses.
No Reh The occurrence of *CR's* in animals not making interval responses.
(*From H. Coppock and O. H. Mowrer,* Amer. J. Psychol., *1947, 60, 611–612
By permission of the authors and the editors.*)

entering, then go to the other and do the same. This *vicarious trail-and-error* behavior (or *VTE*) increases and decreases in curious ways. It mounts to a high degree when the animal's errors grow few and he has the problem almost solved, then diminishes markedly after it is clearly solved. And it mounts when the problem is made more difficult by the experimenter [19, 27]. Such occasions when increased and decreased *VTE* appear cannot fail to strike us as closely corresponding to those when we would look for increased and decreased thinking by a human subject. Have we here a kind of "overt thinking"?

Animals have also been observed to behave as though practicing for a new performance by first acting out or rehearsing what they are trying to learn to do. In a study of conditioning, white rats were to learn to act as follows. A change in illumination (from one light to two lights or vice versa) was followed in five seconds by a shock from the grill on which the animal was standing. The animal could avoid this shock by reaching out and touching with his forepaw a steel bar. While the rats were learning to make this conditioned response, they would often reach out to the bar even when no light-change was being presented; that is, they seemed to rehearse the act they were to learn (Figure 180, *IR*). Significantly, this frequent reaching and touching seemed to have a functional value for the learning, for the animals that so behaved learned this act as a conditioned response to the light-change more rapidly than did other animals in boxes where the bar was removed between the conditioning trials (Figure 180, *Reh* and *No Reh*). The inter-trial responses appeared to function as practice, as a form of "overt thinking."

Some Experiments on Human Thinking

(*A*) *A Problem of Combining Past Experiences.* To young children Maier, of the University of Michigan, gave two separate kinds of training in order to see whether they could then combine them to solve a problem. A full-sized maze was assembled in the form of a swastika, with a small room or booth at the end of each of the four diverging runways, as appears in Figure 181. For Experience I, a child was allowed the free run of the interior of the whole maze so that he might get well acquainted with the alleys and booths. For Experience II, he was conducted around on the outside by a devious route to one of these booths and allowed to drop a penny in a musical toy to elicit a tune. Getting this tune in this particular booth furnished him his second experience. Having had these two unconnected experiences, the child was then given a test. After he had found a planted coin somewhere outside the apparatus, he was permitted to enter the maze by a different booth with the objective of going to the musical toy. To do so

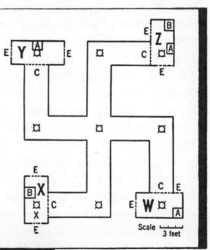

181 Maze Used as Test for Reasoning by Children

W, X, Y, Z indicate the four booths, all differing in recognizable details: entrance-exits (*E, E*), kinds and locations of chairs (*A, B*), location of overhead light. A curtain (*C*) shuts off view of booth's interior from the alley. (*From N. R. F. Maier,* "*Reasoning in children*," J. COMP. PSYCHOL., *1936, 21, 357–366.*)

directly he had now to *combine* his two experiences. Most children younger than six years were unable to do this; but with increase of age more and more of them succeeded.

The point of the foregoing example is worth generalizing. By combining two given facts or experiences, the thinking person achieves something new. And any student of logic can recognize this as the mental event that is so abstractly cast into the form of the traditional syllogism of deductive thinking:

> All x is y;
> All y is z;
> Therefore, all x is z.

Put in this way, barren of concrete denotations, the formulation looks ultra-simple. Why does it play such a role in intellectual history? For one thing, it has been found a most useful rack upon which to hang and stretch any step in argumentation, to see whether there may be any holes in it. Any text in logic will furnish examples of subtle fallacies to which human beings are liable, and which can be brought to light by re-casting arguments into syllogistic form. Moreover, it has been experimentally shown that the human thinker often makes serious errors even in manipulating such abstract symbols as these. Thinking cogently is no easy thing! (See page 347.)

(B) *The Radiation Problem.* The combining aspect of thinking just brought out is not usually a mere hitching together; it is more a growing together. And the attainment of a solution may be said to have much of the *closure* characteristic that we have noted in the perceiving of a thing or situation (page 449). The original gap yawning between the present given conditions and the sought-for goal becomes closed as the problem is resolved. Does this closing-up occur all at once and nothing first, as one single event; or is the gap narrowed in consequence of better and better conceptions of the problem and what it entails, that is, by increasing insights? To examine such questions as this, Duncker propounded the following thought-test to students in a German university [6]: "Given a human being with an inoperable stomach tumor, and rays which destroy organic tissue at sufficient intensity, by what procedure can one free him of the tumor by these rays and at the same time avoid destroying the healthy tissue which surrounds it?" One of the longest and most involved series of hunches given one after another by a single thinker was substantially the following.

1. Send rays down the esophagus.
2. Desensitize the healthy tissues by a chemical injection.
3. Expose the tumor by operating.
4. Decrease the intensity of the rays while on their way.
5. Swallow something opaque to the rays to protect the stomach walls.

6. Alter the location of the tumor. — How?
7. Introduce a drainage tube.
8. Move the tumor toward the exterior.
9. Vary the intensity of the rays.
10. Adapt the healthy tissues by previous weak use of the rays.
11. Somehow use diffuse rays . . . dispersed rays . . . stop! Send broad and weak bundle of rays through a lens adjusted so that the tumor lies at the focal point.
12. Send weak rays from different directions to converge on the tumor.

It is interesting to note that we can divide those hunches into certain groups. Proposals 1, 3, 5, 7, and 8 have in common the avoidance of contact between rays and healthy tissues; 2 and 10 involve immunizing the tissues; while 9 and 11 involve reduction of the radiation intensity on the way. The tentative solutions group themselves according to their "by-means-of-which," their functional value. It is clear, then, that the final solution is not reached by a single step from the original setting of the problem; on the contrary, the principle arises first, and the goal is reached after the principle has been made more and more concrete. Put otherwise, the problem solving usually proceeds not as a simple one-by-one try-out of several discrete proposals; but as *closer and closer refinements of the problem* — a *narrowing of the gap* between the given and the goal.

Sometimes the solution arises from the nature of the goal, by the thinker's grasp of principles inferred from that goal; sometimes the solution is reached by working from the given conditions. To illustrate, in the above problem one may think of the esophagus because a free path to the stomach is already being sought. But it may also happen that during a planless inspection of what is given in the situation, one may stumble on the esophagus which in turn suggests the free-path function. We may say, then, that the closure may eventually occur "from above" or "from below."

(*C*) *A Complication-of-Designs Problem.* Now for a more elaborate problem in which insightful solution must wait upon successive observations, inferences, and deductions.

In an experiment with Wellesley College students, Heidbreder used tasks that were novel, though utilizing simple materials. Each subject first learned to write within each of six designs the particular small symbol or sign for it. They are shown in Figure 182, *A*. The subject was then shown a card bearing two or more such designs with no particular instructions, except that she was to write on the card some one of the signs. As soon as she had marked a card she was asked: "Tell me every-

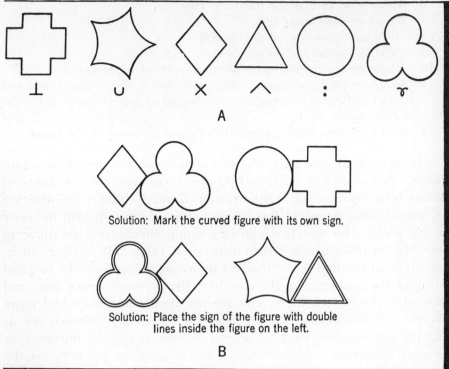

Solution: Mark the curved figure with its own sign.

Solution: Place the sign of the figure with double lines inside the figure on the left.

B

182 Materials for a Thinking Experiment

A. The six basic designs and their signs. *B.* Two of the many problems set. (*From E. Heidbreder, "An experimental study of thinking,"* ARCH. PSYCHOL., *1924,* **11,** *No. 73.*)

thing that 'went on in your mind' from the time you saw the card to the time you marked it''; and a verbatim record was kept of these reports. Then the subject was told whether her response was right or wrong. Another trial followed with a somewhat similar combination of other designs, to be marked on the same principle; and so on through a series, until the subject had hit upon the correct response, could state the rule, and marked several cards accordingly. A new series was then begun. Two such series, with their principles of solution, are furnished in Figure 182, *B.*

What was the general way of attacking such problems? A sample subject's report given at one juncture was as follows:

> First I noticed the double lines and thought that ought to have some-
> thing to do with it, but I noticed that one of the double figures was marked
> and the other wasn't, so I didn't get anything out of that. Then I started

thinking about curves and noticed that both marked ones were curved, but I knew it wouldn't be just marking the curve because we've had that and that would be too easy. Besides that didn't do anything with the double lines and I felt that they ought to come in somewhere. Then I noticed that one of the curves was marked with the sign of the other figure and all of a sudden I thought that if the curve had double lines you gave it its own sign and if not you gave it the sign of the other figure. That's the way I marked this one; but I'm not awfully sure that's right because now I see that both marked ones are on the left, so it might be marking the ones on the left. Oh! Always put the sign of the double figure inside the one on the left — or maybe inside the one that's curved. This one that I've marked will bring that out because I marked the curve and it's on the right. I mean it will show whether it's the curved figure or left figure that gets the mark. I'm pretty sure you use the mark of the double figure.

Reports of this sort furnished excellent confirmation of the experimenter's objective scores and time records. From the two together she characterized in the following way the thinking behavior that went on. The subject actively threw herself into the task, trying one or another *hypothesis*, each response being a specific enterprise based upon past experience and the present problem. Each hypothesis was *inferred* from the sujbect's preceding experiences. (The logician would call this a process of *induction*.) Then the subject turned about to check on this guess by considering its consequences (the process of *deduction*) and by seeing whether they squared with her further experiences. If her action turned out to have been correct she would repeat, whereas if it was incorrect she would change her hypothesis and try another. Here we can discern *trial-and-error* behavior, but on the level of *implicit symbolic* (frequently verbal) responses, each hypothesis being a kind of trial, *a new way of formulating a general principle.*

In this survey of a few typical experimental studies we have noted certain salient features of thinking activity that deserve mention again in a summary statement. Thinking is problem solving in which symbolic processes, especially language, are utilized so as to develop the hidden meanings or implications of a situation and of one's goal, in order to bring them successfully together and thus solve the problem. There may be much trial-and-error, with different hypotheses set up and their consequences examined. And the process of the thinking is of the nature of interstimulation and response within one and the same individual.

VARIETIES OF THINKING RESPONSES

Two Extremes

So many are the different ways in which a person manifests thinking responses, so many are the types of situations arousing them, and so complicated are the contributing factors in each case, that a complete canvassing of the different modes and orders of thinking is quite beyond the scope of this book. Nevertheless, the mention of a few will serve to exhibit something of the variety that must be recognized.

The most *routine* type of thought sequence is the mere repetition of well-learned chains of implicit responses. Going silently over a familiar air from the opera; recalling to oneself the formula for computing a circle's area from its radius; calling up all sorts of rules, principles, formulae, definitions, tables, literary passages — such serial reactions need no analysis here. Thinking of this sort is excited by particular needs in uncomplicated situations, and appears often with apparent irrelevance to objective conditions, as a sort of energy-manifestation. Such a simple meaning is implied in a frequent popular use of the word "thinking." It needs no special elaboration here, for in many places throughout our survey we have referred to processes of this character. The word-association technique, for instance, furnishes an excellent approach. When the associations are "free," the word-responses that appear in answer to the word-stimulus reveal something of the thought-habits of the subject, the main tracks and the particular switchings along which his trains of thought are likely to take their courses.

The least routine thinking is done when one is *reasoning*. This behavior is aroused in a complicated situation which calls for some characterization or formulation by which the individual may be guided, and this formulation is not easily arrived at. Reasoning is thinking in its most explicit, its most articulated form, as seen in the experiment reported on pages 554 f.

The Principal Stages in Reasoning

According to Dewey's famous analysis [4], a complete act of reasoning would include five steps. Not all five always appear distinctly in everyone's reasoning but they are at least implied.

(1) *Maladjustment.* Some crux or difficulty obstructs the motivated person. It may be a practical problem for him, like a waste-pipe that is stopped up, a distant city that must be reached by some one of several routes, an error in the day's balance sheet, the soil of a field that demands

special treatment for raising a certain crop, or a party that must be given for one's house guests. Again, the difficulty may be a theoretical question, like the identity of the real murderer in a detective story, or the authorship of the Apocrypha, or the causes of a war, or the boundaries of the universe.

(2) *Diagnosis.* The difficulty is located and defined by discrimination and insight. Precisely what is the source of the trouble? The man who buys the bottle of patent medicine because he is not feeling well is on much the same level of diagnosing as the college girl who fails in chemistry and admits to her counselor that she does not know whether the trouble lies with her laboratory work, her notebook, her reading of the text, or her understanding of the lectures. A first requirement in a good reasoner is an ability to discern and go to the heart of the matter. As has been said before in these pages, when one is facing a situation that is urgent he must face the difficulty in as clear-cyed a manner as possible. He must try to locate the crux of the matter, as precisely and narrowly as he can. The physician calls this diagnosing; but the lawyer, too, must perform this function for his client, and the businessman for himself and his partners. Ability to put one's finger on the sore spot, to go to the root of the matter, is the first intelligent step toward a solution.

(3) *Hypothesis.* To any but the most stupid people, various suggestions, guesses, conjectures, will occur in the form of nascent or tentative activities that may promise to solve the difficulty. Tentative formulations or concepts appear in the cogitations of a lawyer, an engineer, a physician, a manufacturer, a tradesman, or a chef. "Is this a case of . . . or a case of . . . ?" Now, this phase of reasoning is more or less adventurous. The step is taken not as a directly determined consequent of the immediately preceding (as when one says "34" after "27 and 7"), but is a trial, a "flyer." This inductive leap, as the logicians call it, depends not upon a person's logical consecutiveness in thinking but upon his fertility, his spontaneous and seemingly irresponsible originality. On the other hand, simply because the new idea or hunch or inspiration seems often to pop up uncaused by the immediately preceding train of thought, we are not to assume that it is uncaused. It is, of course, a function of the particular individual, and arises somehow from the deeper groundwork of his habits and attitudes which have longer histories than this particular episode. What controls its arousal now? That is an interesting question; and the whole problem of inspiration is fascinating enough to warrant further discussion in another part of this chapter (pages 562 ff.).

(4) *Deductions.* Once a suggestion for solving a difficulty has occurred

to a man, he will examine it carefully — unless he is the snap-judgment sort of person who goes off half-cocked and at any tangent. His inspirations may come to him best in irresponsible fury, but he must check them in critical phlegm. He must follow out their bearings, must deduce their consequences. "*If* I do this, then what will happen?" "*If* this is the real fact, then what about *x* and *y* and *z*?"

Here is the point where the formalized logic of the philosopher has its application. His syllogism (see page 552) is a device for explicitly setting forth the involved concepts and their relations so that their cogency may be directly ascertained. Compare the two following:

(*A*) Bubbles are appearing on this liquid in my test tube.

When sulphuric acid is poured on copper, bubbles will appear on the surface.

Therefore, the contents of my test tube are sulphuric acid and copper.

(*B*) All animals having jointed dorsal columns are vertebrates.

This specimen has a jointed dorsal column.

Therefore, this specimen is a vertebrate.

For a clear-cut example of deductive reasoning in which each step is seen to follow clearly upon its predecessors, the reader should turn to geometry and its succession of propositions.

(5) *Observations or Experiments.* The purely subjective check made by deduction often needs the support of an objective check, either by literally trying the hypothesis out, or by watching for further instances to see if it will fit them. Does it square with the observed facts?

Finally, at the conclusion of his thinking, the thinker is ready for action again; and if his interpretation or solution has stood the tests of consistency in step 4, and of validity in step 5, it will become his cue for further conduct or for further thinking.

Applied to the Psychologist's Work

These five steps are easily illustrated in the work of the psychologist. The experimentalist has his scientific problem (1); he tries to formulate it precisely (2); he sets up a hypothesis — though he may not always state it explicitly at first (3); he draws the deductions which would follow from it (4); and he conducts the experiment itself as the "payoff," to see whether the deductions and in turn the hypothesis are warranted by what he finds in his results. To make sure, he may have to analyze the results with statistical tools. If he finds the results to be reliable and to confirm the hypothesis, he has made a scientific discovery.

The clinical psychologist, too, follows much the same general order of thinking, though his ultimate interest is centered not in the discovery of a general law but in the welfare of his individual patient. The patient's problem sets his problem (1); the clinician resorts to various diagnostic methods (2); and he tentatively thinks of this and that hypothesis which might explain the patient's difficulty (3); he tests this out by further probing, perhaps re-formulating it (4 and 5). The therapy to be chosen depends upon the decision.

So too with the industrial psychologist. The management has a notion of something wrong (1); the psychological consultant tries to sharpen the focus and to locate more particularly what is wrong (2); he combines understanding of practical needs with his training in analyzing people and in analyzing jobs to consider just what ought to be done (3); certain procedures will accordingly suggest themselves (4); his first procedures are likely to be tentative, and he will watch most carefully the results he seems to get before he is ready to make his final report to the management (5).

Other Varieties of Thinking Responses

Between these two extremes of routine repetition on the one hand and logical reasoning on the other, there lie, of course, all degrees of difference. There is the free *thought-play* of the person who is resting or indulging in activity uncontrolled by any exigencies. In this, one specific response follows another with a minimum of influence from emotional or attentional sets and a minimum of habit. The fancies indulged in by the young child, the mind-wandering of the peasant seated with a pipeful of tobacco at the evening fireside, the inconsequentiality of drowsiness, all exemplify this type of thinking response. Here is the source, too, of much of the fancifulness of poetry, music, and other types of constructive free play.

More nearly resembling full reasoning but still lacking important checks is *autistic* thinking. A person who is maladjusted to his situation may set up implicit trial-and-error processes, and in time chance upon a formulation of his difficulties that satisfies the motives impelling him; but because this is done without adequate control by social perceptions, he gets out of touch with actualities. It is all very well for the poverty-stricken man to talk to himself about what he would do if he had millions, or for a Cinderella to plan elopements with her prince; but in such cases mental health depends upon maintaining the capacity to perceive correctly and to recognize that such thought-about situations are not really actual situations.

The Central Importance of Directive Tendencies

When an animal or person is making visible efforts to surmount an obstacle, he shows much trial-and-error, perhaps of vicarious nature;

yet he remains persistently oriented. In a similar way the procedure of
a person who is busy thinking may veer this way and that; but there is
in it always a *persisting direction that dominates the whole performance*. Cases
described earlier in the chapter furnish examples. The subjects who
were working on the radiation problem tried many different attacks,
but all aimed at securing a satisfactory answer to the one given problem.
The subjects marking the designs on cards tried this, that, and the other
plan of marking; but all tried to solve the puzzle. In everyday life he
who can keep thinking consistently toward the desired end is the effective
thinker. Of what avail is it, in one of the knottier problems of life, to
be able to manifest insight and to have at hand an ample stock of knowledge but to be unable to keep working on the specific problem? Effective
thinking is *nachdenken*, "thinking toward" an objective.

Once a man is oriented in a given direction, the maintenance of these
thought reactions has been known to intrude upon behavior suited to
his immediate physical and social environment. The preoccupied man
may step into mud puddles, lift his hat when saluting mere males, hold
aloft his walking stick when it begins to rain, or do any of the thousand
and one inappropriate acts that are attributed to absent-minded men.
Sometimes the orientation or set may be so profound that it persists
through all sorts of distracting situations, as in the case of him who
returns again and again to the original unsettled topic of conversation
after he and his friends have discussed a dozen other matters. Once
he has become set for the original problem, this thoroughgoing set is
not entirely disrupted by the occurrence of more superficial vocal,
gestural, or manual reactions that have occurred meanwhile.

The importance of a directive tendency in thinking is especially well
appreciated when it is conspicuously absent, as revealed in the following
verbatim accounts of the talk of hospital patients.

> Her thought-processes are blocked and her speech is incoherent, her
> sentences being composed of detached words and phrases which have no
> relationship to each other, except for an occasional superficial association.
> An example is as follows:
> "Losh, I don't know what it is. You see — she says — I don't know,
> I'm sure. There's Cinderella. There is a much better play than that. 'I
> don't know,' I said. He is an awful idiot. Oh dear God, I'm so stupid.
> That's putting two and two together — saying I really don't know — say-
> ing Cathie, and so I observe and — flowers. An orange, and shoe laces.
> The gaberdine skirt. Pettigrew's and the jazz-band, with cream cakes.
> She says no. They like my hair bobbed, but I'm so stupid. Contrary
> Mary. Statues at Copland and Lye's. 'Oh,' I said, 'yes, yes, yes.' I'd go

off to sleep immediately afterwards. I said, 'I know quite well.' 'Nothing,' I said. I forget all that I saw next. The next thing was — eh? The poor man's mad. They'll be chopping off our heads next, and — calendars tied with blue ribbons. Oh, dear God. Contrary Mary again." [1]

To the question, *Why are you in the hospital?* the patient replied:

I'm a cut donator, donated by double sacrifice. I get two days for every one. That's known as double sacrifice; in other words, standard cut donator. You know, we considered it. He couldn't have anything for the cut, or for these patients. All of them are double sacrifice because it's unlawful for it to be donated any more. [Well, what do you do, here?] I do what is known as the double criminal treatment. Something that he badly wanted, he gets that, and seven days criminal protection. That's all he gets, and the rest I do for my friend. [Who is the other person that gets all this?] That's the way the asylum cut is donated. [But who is the other person?] He's a criminal. He gets so much. He gets twenty years' crimi-

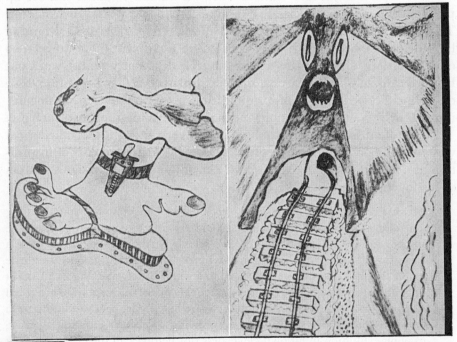

183 Drawings by Psychotic Patients

The apparent failure of directive tendencies is revealed in each drawing by the inconstancy and confusion of themes, one theme displacing another, so that the total result looks like an incoherent hodge-podge. (Kindly furnished by Doctors Anne Anastasi and J. P. Foley, Jr.)

[1] From D. K. Henderson and R. D. Gillespie. *A Text-Book of Psychiatry* (5th ed. New York: Oxford University Press, 1940), pp. 223–224. By permission of the publishers.

nal treatment, would make forty years; and he gets seven days' criminal
protection and that makes fourteen days. That's all he gets. [And what
are you?] What is known as cut donator Christ. None of them couldn't be
able to have anything; so it has to be true works or prove true to have anything, too." [1]

Whatever the directions being taken in either of these cases, they are
hard or impossible for the hearer to make out. They are easily and
frequently displaced by distracting stimuli, or by cross-currents of
thought. The same characteristics are sometimes to be observed in the
drawings of psychotic patients (see Figure 183).

CREATIVE THINKING

A Special Phenomenon in the Third Stage of Reasoning

Most experimental and clinical work on human thinking has set up
problems whose answers are, by design, foreknown to the investigator.
They are "answers" in the puzzle or quiz sense of the word. Many of
life's demands, however, are not thus cut to a pattern; there may be no
one foreordained solution to a man's perplexity, and he must work out
his own original answer. Such are the obstructions faced by him whose
daily bread depends upon his originality, whether in advertising slogans,
musical or literary composition, mechanical invention, or legal defense.

Robert Louis Stevenson, though in his very literary and allegorical
way, sets the problem for us. He describes his own moments of inspiration as coming to him in dreams and personifies the unconscious sources
of his inventions as fairy-like Brownies.

> This dreamer (like many other persons) has encountered some trifling
> vicissitudes of fortune. When the bank begins to send letters and the
> butcher to linger at the back gate, he sets to belaboring his brains after a
> story, for that is his readiest money-winner; and behold! at once the little
> people begin to bestir themselves in the same quest, and labor all night
> long, and all night long set before him truncheons of tales upon their lighted
> theatre. No fear of his being frightened now; the flying heart and the frozen
> scalp are things bygone; applause, growing applause, growing interest,
> growing exultation in his own cleverness (for he takes all the credit), and at
> last a jubilant leap to wakefulness, with the cry "I have it, that'll do!" upon
> his lips: with such and similar emotions he sits at these nocturnal dreams,
> with such outbreaks, like Claudius in the play, he scatters the performance
> in the midst. Often enough the waking is a disappointment; he has been
> too deep asleep, as I explain the thing; drowsiness has gained his little

[1] From N. Cameron. *The Psychology of Behavior Disorders* (Boston: Houghton Mifflin
Company, 1947), pp. 466–467. By permission of author and publishers.

people, they have gone stumbling and maundering through their parts; and the play, to the awakened mind, is seen to be a tissue of absurdities. And yet how often have these sleepless Brownies done him honest service, and given him, as he sat idly taking his pleasure in the boxes, better tales than he could fashion for himself. . . . I am an excellent adviser, something like Molière's servant; I pull back and I cut down; and I dress the whole in the best words and sentences that I can find and make; I hold the pen, too; and I do the sitting at the table, which is about the worst of it; and when all is done, I make up the manuscript and pay for the registration; so that on the whole, I have some claim to share, though not so largely as I do, in the profits of our common enterprise.[1]

With due allowance for the figurative manner of writing, we recognize here some of the salient characteristics of creative thought. One that has received much attention is the *sudden, unexpected* way in which many a happy idea, theme, or theory has occurred to the thinker like a bolt out of the blue. A second aspect of such inspirations is their tendency to appear when the subject is *in a relaxed condition* in which his attention, if he be awake, is on quite other and extraneous matters. A third is the seemingly *spontaneous* character of their *emergence* out of nowhere, so that not uncommonly the thinker is almost convinced that they have their authorship and origin outside himself, that he is being "inspired" in the mystical sense.

Illustrations by the score can be gleaned from literary, biographical, and scientific publications.[2] Wagner is said to have hit upon a principal theme in the overture to *Das Reingold* in his sleep. In one of the most famous instances, Coleridge awoke from a dream with the complete structure of his *Kubla Khan* ready for transcribing. Masefield tells us of his poem *The Woman Speaks* that it appeared in a fading dream, "engraven in high relief on an oblong metal plate, from which I wrote it down." Charlotte Brontë would awaken to see the progress of her tale lying clear and bright before her, its incidents being even more distinct and vivid than her physical surroundings [20].

The eminent French mathematician Poincaré has written that his mathematical discoveries were often in the nature of an "apparent, sudden illumination" when he was crossing the Boulevard, when he lay awake from effects of black coffee, when he was about to step into his carriage, and on like occasions when work had been given up. Another

[1] From *Across the Plains*.
[2] Our illustrations will be drawn from fields in which highly original ideas often appear, but it is to be remembered that the phenomenon is one of daily occurrence in the course of everyday business and domestic life. It appears on a minor scale in the multitudinous little hunches, guesses, and conjectures that are a part of one's daily thinking.

mathematician, Hamilton, made his great discovery of the quaternions while walking with Lady Hamilton "as they came up to Brougham Bridge near Dublin."

Inventors have written of their inspirations.

> I have waked out of sound sleep with a new idea. Sometimes when I am dressing or shaving or tying a shoestring. Sometimes after hours or days of sweating over the drafting table. But most often when my mind is fresh and rested and free from worry or care and when I am approaching a new subject so that I am thinking in qualitative terms.

> I studied the problem, read all I could find pertaining to it, tested experimentally all the ideas that came to me, and sooner or later the right solution would flash on my mind often at the moment of awakening in the morning after a sound sleep [23].

Scientists, too, have testified that helpful "hunches," following long periods of concentrated study, come into their consciousness at a time when they are not consciously working on the problems [10].

Creative Work Is Not Pure Inspiration

From these accounts one might gather that the process of creating is simply an irresponsible business of waiting for inspiration to come, like the ignorant man who, having heard the "call to preach," asserted that all he would have to do would be to "open his mouth and let the Lord fill it with the message." As an antidote to this romantic notion, let us note what creative thinkers themselves have to say. Interviews with many French poets and novelists bring out the fact that all of them, when hoping to do a piece of creative production, first enrich their verbal equipment, look up everything available in the field to be entered, and saturate themselves in the subject-matter they are to work up [5].

Hear a literary genius, Poe:

> Most writers — poets in especial . . . would positively shudder at letting the public take a peep behind the scenes, at the elaborate and vacillating crudities of thought — at the true purpose seized only at the last moment — at the innumerable glimpses of idea that arrived not at the maturity of full view — at the fully matured fancies discarded in despair as unmanageable, at the cautious selections and rejections — at the painful erasures and interpolations [see Figure 184] — in a word, at the wheels and pinions — the tackle for scene-shifting — the step-ladders and demon-traps — the cock's feathers, the red paint and the black patches which in ninety-nine cases out of the hundred constitute the properties of the literary actor.

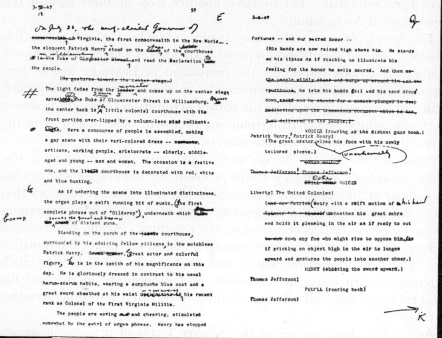

184   Trial-and-Error in Creative Thinking

Two pages from a manuscript in course of its preparation. From Paul Green's
The Common Glory, for a pageant at Williamsburg, Virginia. (*By courtesy of
Professor Green.*)

And now, an inventor:

> With few exceptions my inventions have been cold-blooded attempts to
> solve a problem presented in the course of my business. The first step is to
> give this problem and the proposed methods of meeting it a ruthless "third
> degree."

The many accounts obtainable from creative thinkers in any and all
fields agree substantially in that the story of the creative process can be
broken down into four stages, now well-recognized by all writers on the
subject: (1) *preparation,* (2) *incubation,* (3) *illumination,* (4) *verification.*
From what has already been said in this section it should be easy for
the reader to see the meaning of each stage.

Scientific Explanations

We must keep our feet on solid ground in other respects also. In a
paragraph above, three characteristics of the extreme forms of inspiration

have been set forth. Let us have another look at these against our psychological background.

The hunch or inspiration may come suddenly, we said. For this phenomenon we should be prepared. In several places in the survey made in this book (especially the treatments of Learning and of Perception) our attention has been caught by the suddenness with which many an insight is gained. This abrupt acquisition of insight is shown in the imagining or verbal formulating of absent objects, just as in the perception of physically present objects.

Again, we said that the happy suggestion frequently bobs up when one is not consciously occupied with the problem but is doing something else, or nothing at all. Now, we have seen in our treatment of Memory that successful recall is dependent upon an absence of interfering associations set up by excessive concentration on the recalling. Again, the common feeling of being fresher in the morning is due to a lapse of the thought-sets of the night before, which had kept one's thinking too much determined. In states of relaxation, and notoriously in dreams, the removal of prosaic and sober inhibitions results in a refreshing freedom of fancy.

As a third characteristic of the extreme forms of inspiration we remarked the apparent independence of the subject himself. He often seems quite passive; and the idea enters as if from without — as if from a Muse. But it need only be urged: who has the inspiration? Coleridge's dream-delivered *Kubla Khan* came to Coleridge, not to Newton nor Wagner nor Whitman; and indeed the sources of that remarkable poem have been traced back by thorough research to twenty-five years of Coleridge's note-taking based on his reading and travel experiences. Similarly, the physician does not experience insights into legal tangles nor the lawyer into engineering projects. Inspirations, in short, come from the thinker himself. "Tartini heard the devil play a wonderful sonata," said Doctor Holmes, "and set it down on awakening. Who was the devil but Tartini himself?" If this is the truth of the matter, two points of practical counsel would seem self-evident. Let him who would seek originality in his work bear in mind that a broad, thorough, extensive knowledge and competence in the field is the soil from which brilliant ideas spring. And let him realize that it is usually *after* a period of *intense application* to and complete absorption in his problem that novel and fruitful insights are awakened.

One further consideration now seems demanded. How is it possible that the relevant idea should come when the thinker is not consciously thinking about the matter at all? Such a question, however, could be asked only by one who had not been with us in the treatment of many points and topics throughout the present book. It has been shown often that performance — whether of overt muscular, or verbal, or thinking order — appears at the appropriate time without any specific beckoning. A suddenly demanded act of dodging a missile, a response on a word-association test, a recall of appropriate answers to a quiz — these, so far as the subject's awareness is concerned, just appear. And as in the final emergence, so in the incubation: rational processes commonly go on in a person without his being aware of them.

Can One's Originality be Increased?

Certain teachers of creative writing deny that they can increase the originality of their students, protesting that their hope of service is simply to see what the students do and help them to prune their products. On the other hand, a certain school which advertises widely has long maintained, on the basis of what evidence one does not know, that it can actually teach people to become original.

Whether they may be considered evidence on that question we shall not attempt to judge — but there are data to show that students pursuing different curricula may differ in their ability to show originality when tested for it. Recently a number of professional artists, a group of college students majoring in art, and a group of unselected college students, were individually given four tests of ability to re-combine familiar ideas in creative ways. The tests were the following:

I. Subject was to compose as many sentences as possible, in a given time, from a group of 10 words.

II. Subject was to form as many letters as possible in a given brief time from 3 straight lines, 2 straight lines, 1 straight line, and 1 curved line.

III. Subject was furnished with 20 words and was to construct a story using them in the same order; he was to be scored on the number used in the time allowed.

IV. Subject was furnished with 10 wooden blocks and was to construct as many pieces of home furnishings as possible in the time allowed.

The data are worth presentation in the accompanying Table XLII. The total scores indicate that for dealing with language material and notably for handling spatial shapes, both novices and professionals in art are superior to their non-art intellectual equals when constructive or creative thinking is demanded. Do art students acquire originality in the course of their training, or does the study of art attract original thinkers? The evidence, of course, does not help us to decide. If there were available valid measuring instruments (tests) of originality which

TABLE XLII Scores in Creative Thinking by Artists, Art Students, and Non-Art Students

Parts	Professional Artists N = 30		Art Majors N = 25		Unselected Students N = 48	
	Mean	S.D.	Mean	S.D.	Mean	S.D.
I. Sentences	17.7	7.2	21.9	7.6	18.0	4.2
II. Letters	12.5	1.9	13.2	1.0	6.7	1.8
III. Short story	11.4	4.1	7.3	2.5	9.1	3.2
IV. Furniture	18.4	7.8	13.9	9.1	3.4	2.7
Total Score	60.5	12.3	56.4	15.1	37.6	7.0

From V. R. Fisichelli and L. Welch.
J. APPL. PSYCHOL., *1947, 31, 280.*

could be administered to students before and after such training, a start could be made toward answering such a question.

An incidental query: Is originality a trait that tends to reveal itself in any line of thinking, as the data of the table suggest? Before we can hope to get evidence, we need to develop a wide variety of tests of creativity in a wide variety of activities, to apply these tests, and then to determine what degrees of correlation obtain between them. Eventually this would seem to call for the application of methods of statistical analysis (cf. pages 131 f.) to see whether some such factor as "originality" or "creativity" will come to light. A fallow field indeed!

From a practical and public-spirited point of view, it seems obvious that research into methods of instruction specifically shaped to encourage the development of creativeness in thinking is a crying need. Compared to what we know about how to pass on to others what is already known, our knowledge of how to promote originality is in a state of pathetic infancy.

CONCEPTUAL THINKING AND ITS DEVELOPMENT

The Development of Concepts in Childhood: Causality

Two children walking along a country road at night were startled by a peculiar whitish thing rushing at them with low whistlings and cracklings. They had just turned to flee when one of them, recognizing something about the object as familiar, cried out: "Oh, it's nothing but a newspaper in the wind!" That settled it: they knew newspapers! In like manner, the problems a person meets in life are in most cases problems calling for some insight, some perceiving of them in such a way as to rearouse habits which will furnish the meaning or cue leading to effective readjustments in those cases.

The potentialities and probabilities of things must be correctly understood; and such practical understanding turns upon answers to that question universally asked by child and by adult, "Why?" Some careful studies have been directed at the way in which the child's own answers to the "Why" sort of question, his concept of *causality*, change as he grows older.[1] Let us note one or two.

Children of school-age from the third grade through junior high school were once quizzed in two ways. (1) Some demonstrations were shown them. *Examples:* A jar was placed over a lighted candle: "Why does the candle go out?" A square open box containing a penny was whirled in a vertical circle by means of strings attached to opposite corners: "Why doesn't the penny fall out?" A horn with keys was blown: "Why does it make different sounds when I push down different keys?" (2) Some questions about phenomena common to a child's experience were asked. *Examples:* "What makes the wind blow?" "What makes the rainbow?" "What makes frost on the windows in winter-time?" "How is it you can see yourself in a mirror?" [3]

The children's answers were scrutinized by a number of raters; and though the raters varied in their judgments, they obtained evidence that the answers fell for the most part into some four classifications, and that these classifications were indicative of maturity-stages. The most naïve explanations, and those most frequently offered by the youngest children, were merely *phenomenistic* — using only superficial contiguities in space or time, as "Pebble sinks in water because it is white." Somewhat more advanced were the *dynamic* and *animistic* explanations — based on some notion of forces (sometimes live ones) within an object that make it do what it does. Then there were the *mechanical* explanations — based on the contact and passing on of the action from object to object, as "Pedals make the bicycle go." Explanations of the highest class, and those most frequently offered by the older children, involved *logical deduction* — based on fuller appreciation of all factors present, as "Water flows from one tube to another because it can go equally well

[1] This question of how men fashion unto themselves notions of causality comes close home to any student of psychology or any other natural science. Just when does he have a true explanation of a phenomenal event in terms of its necessary antecedent and attendant circumstances — of which it is a dependent variable? A common fallacy was recognized centuries ago in the *post hoc ergo propter hoc: A* follows after *B*, therefore *A* is caused by *B*.

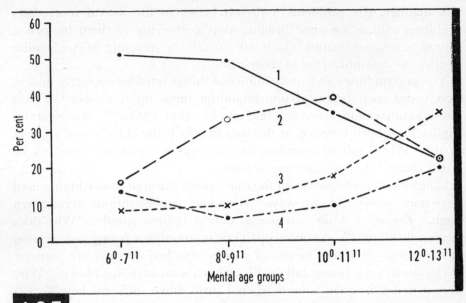

185 **Percentage of Cases in Each Two-Year MA Period Falling into Each State of Concept Development**

The concept stages are shown as numbered in the text. (*From R. W. Russell, J.* Genet. Psychol., *1940, 56, 358. By permission of author and editor.*)

in both directions." Here enter physical concepts of density, relative weights, and so on. In these children's answers, then, is a sort of developmental history of the human being's attempts to understand his world, as reflected in more and more adequate concepts of cause and effect.

A genetic sequence appears also when one of the foregoing classifications is further broken up. Piaget, a Swiss psychologist, found that children's notions of causality could be assigned to four developmental stages [21], as follows. Stage 1: *Everything* is animated, is alive. Stage 2: Whatever *moves* is alive. Stage 3: Whatever *moves of itself* is alive. Stage 4: *Plants and animals* are alive. When American children of different ages were asked whether such things were "alive" or "not alive" as stone, knife, river, clouds, lightning, dog, bug, tree, grass, and the like, it was found that their answers fell fairly easily into that fourfold classification. And the expected maturity changes appeared (see Figure 185). Further, these changes were the same regardless of whether the children had been reared in city or in country, in the North or in the South.

The four stages have been found to hold for Zuñi and Navajo Indian children; and also to hold for feeble-minded subjects of equivalent mental ages. They seem, therefore, to reflect the process of biological maturing.

From Sounds to Meanings

Recent investigations of semantic conditioning have shown us another aspect of this genetic story. We have previously noted (on pages 410 f. and 428 f.) that when a response has become conditioned to a stimulus it is actually conditioned to a wide range of stimuli of the same type or class. This is true of being conditioned to words and their meanings. If a person has become conditioned to make a salivary or a GSR (pages 209 f.) response to a specific word (with a buzzer sound, say, utilized as unconditioned stimulus) then he will be found to make the same response in less intense degrees to other words related to the specific one in several ways. The response is to a *generalized* stimulation. And the degrees of this generalization to words of varying relationship are found to vary with the intellectual maturity of the subject. This is shown in the results of a study summarized in Table XLIII. There it is made evident that the younger children tend to react to words in their superficial sensory characters — that is, to how words sound or look; but as they grow older they react to them more for their meanings. We can see also some evidence to confirm earlier findings that young children think in terms of differences more than in terms of likenesses, but change in that regard as they mature.

Table XLIII   Developmental Changes in Semantic Conditioning

Category	Example	7–9 years	10–12 years	13–15 years	17–20 years
Same word	Close — close	100%	100%	100%	100%
Homophone	Close — clothes	72	29	25	19
Antonym	Close — open	63	43	32	37
Synonym	Close — shut	58	26	45	53

From B. F. Riess, J. Exp. Psychol., *1946, 36, 147.*

From Concrete to Abstract

The maturing child's concepts do not simply change in qualitative manner; they change in scope and inclusiveness, too. From very concrete meanings and understandings, he advances to more and more abstract ones. From the handling of this doll and that block, and verbal mention of this doll and that block, he progresses to talk about dolls-in-general, blocks-in-general.

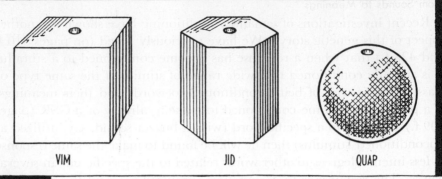

VIM   JID   QUAP

186 **Beads Used for Concert Formation by Children**

Each shape of bead was given the name shown below it. (*Adapted from L. Welch and L. Long*, J. Psychol., *1940, 9, 61.*)

This developmental change was shown in work at Hunter College with children of ages ranging from 42 to 83 months. Taking one child at a time, the experimenter got the child's attention directed on one of three wooden beads of a certain shape (see Figure 186) while he pronounced the name (a syllable) that was supposed to go with it. After the different blocks had each been so presented, the child was asked to name the blocks when they were shown him in a mixed-up order. This exercise and test was repeated many times, and the child's successes recorded. Then he was presented with a number of beads in the three general designs, and was asked: "Put all of the *QUAP* on this side of the table and all of the *JID* on the other side." Only 21 per cent of the children under four years of age could do this; but 67 per cent of the five-year-olds and 100 per cent of the six-year-olds succeeded. The ability of the child to handle objects conceptually shows, then, different levels. By elaborating the tests, the investigators discovered that the different levels of inclusiveness or abstractness suggest a hierarchical arrangement, with the maturer and more abstract ability being inclusive of the less abstract. An excellent illustration familiar to everyone is available in the child's knowledge of arithmetic (see page 580).

There is another and highly important character to this development. Not only does the child come to handle things in larger and larger groups or classes: he comes to perceive and react to and talk about their *qualities* considered quite apart from their thing-character. When he compares the sweet*ness* of a lollipop held in his left hand with the sweet-*ness* of an ice cream cone in his right, he is now dealing with an *abstracted* quality.

Some Clinical Cases Illustrating Loss in Abstract Thinking

As is true in so many instances, the presence and nature of abstract thinking can be better recognized when contrasted with its absence. Some clinicians hold that in the mental disorder known as schizophrenia (pages 611 ff.) many patients exhibit a weakening of the ability to think in abstract concepts and a regression to thinking of objects merely in terms of their individual, concrete character. To put these clinical observations under more experimental control, a block-sorting task was assigned to schizophrenic patients as well as to a number of healthy controls. Figure 187 shows the materials, which consisted of wooden blocks varying in four respects: in color, in shape, in height, and in size. On the under side of each was one of four syllable-names. Regardless of color or shape, *LAG* had been written on all the tall large blocks, *BIK* on all the flat large ones, *MUR* on the tall small ones, and *CEV* on the flat small ones.

All blocks were scattered on the table in front of the subject. He was told that there were four different kinds of blocks, that each kind had a name, and that his task was to find and to separate these four kinds. The examiner turned up a block and read its name, then asked the subject to pick out all the blocks that he thought might belong to that same class. Typically the subject proceeded by putting together all

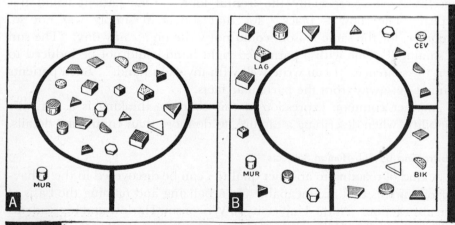

187

Blocks Used for Concept Formation by Patients

A. Beginning of the experiment when the subject is asked to pick out all the blocks which may be *MUR*. *B.* The solution of the problem by finding the principle of classification in terms of height and size of the blocks. (*From E. Hanfmann and J. Kasanin, "Conceptual thinking in schizophrenia," NERV. MENT. DIS. MONOGR. SER., 1942, No. 67. By permission of the authors.*)

blocks of the same color or all of the same shape as the sample one, whereupon the examiner would turn over one of them to show by its name that this block really did not belong. The subject continued trying. If at length he discovered those features of the blocks to which the names referred, he was able to finish the task of correctly grouping the four kinds.

Analysis of the results brought out wide variations. At the lowest or "primitive level" the block-choosing was extremely concrete, for the subject failed to grasp the relation between a block-characteristic and a syllable-name; and he grouped together individual blocks that had some similarity, doing this quite impulsively and without any searchings among the blocks. At the highest or "conceptual level" the task was correctly grasped from the start: the subject started assembling groups that represented true categories, at once discarding the basis of the grouping whenever he saw it to be inconsistent with the naming.

Here, then, we seem to have evidence for what some clinicians have emphasized as characterizing the schizophrenic's thinking: his inability to get away from concrete particulars and to think abstractly, an inability to *categorize*.[1]

Goldstein has found that loss of ability to think in categories is a mark of many of his brain-injured cases. Accordingly, he holds that the capacity for thinking abstractly is intimately connected with an intact cerebral cortex, especially the frontal lobes. One patient could not repeat "The snow is black," for that statement simply was not so. Another, for the same reason, could not write on a rainy day, "The sun is shining." One with a paralyzed right hand could not be induced to pen the sentence, "I can write well with my right hand." Such patients cannot get away from the particular facts.

Another common expression of this concrete thinking is a patient's inability, when describing a picture, to do more than enumerate details.

Abstracting by Sub-Human Subjects

A kind of reacting to abstract qualities can be discovered in the behavior of animals that are incapable of verbalizing and naming the basis of the abstraction. At the University of Wisconsin, Harlow and his students have repeatedly exhibited this form of reaction in monkeys. First they trained an animal to find its food by lifting aside that one of three similar-colored objects presented on a *cream*-painted tray which differed from

[1] Some clinicians, as Cameron, question this interpretation of schizophrenia, preferring to emphasize the patient's isolation and his speaking a dialect with idioms not understandable to others.

188   **A Monkey Solving a Problem by Abstracting**

A. When presented with three objects on a cream-painted tray, the animal chooses that one that is odd in form. *B.* When presented with the same objects on an orange-painted tray, it chooses the object that is odd in color. (*From M. L. Young and H. F. Harlow, "Solution by rhesus monkeys of a problem involving the Weigl principle using the oddity method," J. Comp. Psychol., 1943, 205–217. Photos by courtesy of Dr. Harlow.*)

the other two in *form* (regardless of its spatial position on the tray); and in the same manner they trained it to choose that one of three similar-form objects on an *orange*-hued tray which was odd as to *color*. (See Figure 188.) When the monkeys had these responses, they were given considerably more training and eventually learned to choose, from a presentation of three objects differing as to both categories, *either* the odd-form object *or* the odd-color object, depending upon whether the tray was cream-colored or orange. The tray's color (we may say) aroused the one or the other category; and so the monkeys displayed ability to respond differentially to two attributes of the same object, to handle it as in either of two categories.

Attaining of Concepts by Normal Human Adults

Returning now from the animal, the child, and the mentally disabled, we should be interested to know how the normal human adult comes to grasp and employ concepts in his thinking. In a recent investigation an approach was made through an experiment in memorizing.

An exposure apparatus, somewhat like the model shown in Figure 189, was used. For the stimuli, one of the series of drawings shown in Figure 190 was mounted on the revolving drum of the apparatus; and the nine drawings were presented to the subject in serial order and at a uniform rate. As each one of them appeared the experimenter pronounced its syllable-name; and the subject repeated it after him, striving to memorize it so that eventually he would be able to repeat the name ahead of the experimenter and promptly upon the appearance of the drawing. When one series had been learned, the next was taken up.

Now, unknown to the subject in advance, the nine names were the names of nine concepts, three being concepts of Concrete Objects, three of Spatial Forms, and three of Numerical Quantities. The concepts and their corresponding names are furnished in Table XLIV; and the

TABLE
XLIV   Experimental Concepts and Their Names

Concrete Objects		Spatial Forms		Numerical Quantities	
Concepts	Names	Concepts	Names	Concepts	Names
Face	Relk	◯	Fard	2	Ling
Building	Leth	∝	Stod	5	Dilt
Tree	Mulp	≠	Pran	6	Mank

From E. Heidbreder, J. Gen. Psychol., 1946, 35, 179.

189   **Missouri Serial Presentation Apparatus**

Materials (syllables, words, etc.) are inscribed in vertical order and mounted on the drum, which is so rotated by a constant speed motor that the individual items are exposed one at a time behind the aperture.

| Series I | Series II | Series III | Series IV | Series V |

190 Drawings Used in Experiment on Attaining Concepts

Each drawing is given a name — which name is also that of a concept. For example, in Series I, the corresponding names are: *Ling* (2), *Fard* (0), *Relk* (face), *Pran* ($\times$), *Leth* (building), *Dilt* (5), etc. (Cf. Table XLIII.) (*From E. Heidbreder,* J. GEN. PSYCHOL., *1946, 35, 173–189. By permission.*)

reader can apply them to the series in Figure 190. By the time the second or third series was reached, most subjects could name some of the drawings on their first appearance, that is, could recognize the concepts under which they belonged.

The results seem to bear out a point that has been well observed in much other work on thinking in relationships, concepts, and abstractions: the individual discovers the concept not gradually but suddenly and all at once. Once he hits upon it, he is able to use it consistently.

Were any of the concepts easier to attain (recognize, "catch on to") than others? Final data showed that those referring to Concrete Objects were attained most quickly (on the average between the third and fourth series); those referring to Spatial Forms came next (by the fifth series); and those meaning Numerical Quantities were attained the least quickly (by the eighth series).

A conclusion or two may be drawn. In scrutinizing the materials used, we find no support for the common maxim, "Always proceed from the familiar to the unfamiliar." Nor is there warrant here for the common rule, "Always proceed from the simple to the complex." What we do see well verified is the rule, "Proceed from the concrete to the abstract." Inspection of the results shows that the more a concept possesses *thing-character* (is manipulable, is relevant to a person's motor reactions), the more readily it is grasped.[1]

Incidentally, we have in this experiment a good illustration of William James's cardinal principle of *dissociation by varying concomitants*. Suppose you wish to help a person to respond selectively to one certain color, dimension, tone, time, or other aspect of a situation. You should see to it that the aspect appears now in one combination and now in another. If *a* and *b* always and invariably appeared together and always in their same relative intensities, the person would continue to react to *a* and *b* as to one thing. The failure of either one alone to stimulate him would render impossible the forging of more specific *a*-reactions or *b*-reactions. Does a teacher wish to train a child to perceive the quality of "sphericity"? Let her give him marbles, balls, oranges, and globes to observe, all alike in being spheres but different as to colors, textures, sizes, uses, and so forth. Is he to be taught to recognize and use the numerical relation of "four"? Let him be presented with four apples, four matches, four leaves, four children; let him draw four lines, hold up four fingers, walk four steps. The Sterns tell of a child of four years who, when asked by his grandfather, "How many fingers have I?" responded, "I don't know, I can count only on my own fingers." He had not abstracted the "four fingers" from the particular setting of his own hand. Then there is James's story of the proud father who, to display one of his small son's achievements, held in vertical position a table knife, with the question, "What is that, my lad?" But no amount of persistence led the boy to vary from his stout reply, "I calls that a knife," until the desperate father recalled that he had always used a pencil in his instructions.

---

[1] Note the original motor meaning of "grasp," as well as many other terms applied to thinking: "apprehend," "catch on," "take in." It is indeed true that thinking is a kind of dealing-with.

Whereupon by substituting a pencil for the knife he elicited the answer, "I calls that perpendicular."

From these examples we can draw a further conclusion. As one of the authors we have followed above has brought out — and as many earlier observers have done — the process of deriving abstract concepts is actually a double process. It involves both *discriminating* (perceiving differences between a number of things taken together and other things) and *generalizing* (formulating a general statement of some essential characteristics of the things grouped). To realize the concept of "triangle" or "triangularity," one must differentiate triangles from other geometrical shapes; and at the same time must recognize points in common for the various triangles themselves. In other words, we see here again on the intellectual plane those complementary aspects of organic development, differentiation and integration. A three-year-old child of the writer, upon catching sight of the geology building which closely resembled the psychology building, pointed and said, "No, no, Daddy's building!"

Knowledge Consists of Hierarchies of Concepts

It should now be clear that one of the main purposes of education, the imparting of information, is the building-up of concepts. Observation of a person's behavior further reveals that these are built up in hierarchical forms. "A science," runs an old definition, "is organized knowledge reduced to a system." The subject-matter of any field of study is so organized into minor and major principles, sub-topics and topics, particular facts and general laws, that to the student it must often seem as though getting the skeleton or architecture of the study were more than half the task. A simple case is afforded by mathematics. To know arithmetic one must be able not only to identify numerals, but also to add, subtract, multiply, and divide them; to treat these four fundamental processes again as applicable to both whole numbers and fractions, then to decimals, then even to unknown quantities. But in further mathematical study, lines and areas and their transformations must be dealt with; later these are linked up with the numerical operations. And so on through the higher phases. Furthermore, as this is true of mathematics, so in some degree it is true also of any field of knowledge.

Various Kinds of Concepts

Glancing back, we can now see that a person's equipment of concepts embraces many different logical sorts. We noted that there is a human ability to note *classes* of things, things that belong together. As this classification becomes more explicit, there is discrimination and recognition of abstracted *sense qualities*, of "red," of "bitter," of "hardness." In addition, there are *non-sensible qualities* of all sorts. A thing's "density" or its "resistivity," a fellow man's "friendliness" or "hard sense" become objects of attention. Of great importance, too, are the manifold *relations* between things in the world in which a man lives, such as "above," "between," "anterior," "opposite," "incongruous."

THE INVOLVEMENT OF IMAGERY IN THINKING

Imagery in General

If we shift our approach and inquire as to the nature of ideational processes from the viewpoint of the thinker himself, we shall find that the trains of thought as he experiences them are substantially a matter of imagery. Here is a term that has played a tremendous part in the history of psychology. It is especially important in the psychology which deals with the contemplation of one's own experiences. The meaning of the term *image* is familiar enough. One can "hear" a movement in Beethoven's Sixth Symphony when no music is physically present to him; he can "see" Greenland's icy mountains or India's coral strands while he is singing in his church; he can "smell" a New Orleans French market or a San Francisco or Gloucester waterfront; and he can represent to himself what his arm muscles and his finger tips "feel" like when he is rapidly typewriting. This representative function of imaging, it is clear, is too common and everyday a phenomenon to need further identification.

So common is this experiencing of imagery that it is not surprising to find that many writers from Aristotle to the present day have taken it to be the very stuff and substance of ideational activity. The modern studies of imagery were begun in the 1880's. It was then that Galton published the results of his questionnaire addressed to people in many walks of life.

Think of some definite object [he instructed them]. Suppose it is your breakfast-table as you sat down to it this morning, and consider carefully the picture that rises before your mind's eye.

1. *Illumination.* Is the image dim or fairly clear? Is its brightness comparable to that of the actual scene?

2. *Definition.* Are all the objects well defined at the same time, or is the place of sharpest definition at any one moment more contracted than it is in a real scene?

3. *Coloring.* Are the colors of the china, of the toast, breadcrust, mus-
tard, meat, parsley, or whatever may have been on the table, quite distinct
and natural?

This study of Galton's had two outcomes. One was to emphasize the
role of imagery, even the particular modality employed by this or that
person. There were those who did their thinking predominantly in
visual terms and who were called "visiles." Similarly there were the
"audile" type and the "motile." For some decades thereafter it was
held to be practically important to determine to which image-type a
person — as a school child — was assignable, and to adjust his teaching
accordingly [16]. There are indeed gross differences between individuals.
One famous lightning calculator, Diamanchi, reported that he had to
see his figures before him transformed into his own handwriting, and
then he operated on them visually; while another, Inaudi, found that he
could not perform his feats of multiplying (say, one memorized 24-digit
number by another) whenever he was hoarse — that is, whenever he
could not get his usual vocal-motor imagery. One inventor says: "When
working out a new device, mental pictures present themselves to my
mind quite rapidly, more rapidly in fact than I can record them on
paper." And another states: "I find that my hands and fingers go
through one manipulation after another. They seem to work their own
way without being guided by visual mental pictures."
Another outcome of Galton's study was less favorable to the assumption that imagery is the stuff of thinking. He found to his astonishment
that the great majority of men of science in England and France protested
that they had no such imagery at all.

> My own conclusion [he says] is that an over-ready perception of sharp
> mental pictures is antagonistic to the acquirement of habits of highly gen-
> eralized and abstract thought, especially when the steps of reasoning are
> carried on by words as symbols, and that if the faculty of seeing the pictures
> was ever possessed by men who think hard, it is very apt to be lost by disuse.
> The highest minds are probably those in which it is not lost, but subordi-
> nated, and is ready for use on suitable occasions. I am, however, bound to
> say, that the missing faculty seems to be replaced so serviceably by other
> modes of conception, chiefly, I believe, connected with the incipient motor
> sense, not of the eyeballs only but of the muscles generally, that men who
> declare themselves entirely deficient in the power of seeing mental pictures
> can nevertheless give lifelike descriptions of what they have seen, and can
> otherwise express themselves as if they were gifted with a vivid visual imag-
> ination. They can also become painters of the rank of Royal Academi-
> cians.

This conclusion need not surprise us unduly. Does the reader claim that he can visualize a substantial word like "Constantinople"? Eyes closed, let him call off the letters in the usual spelling order; then let him call them off in the reverse order. If he has the visual image of the entire word, he should be able to pick off the letters in either, or even a mixed, order. The point is demonstrated often in the letter-square test. Let a subject memorize an array of letters like this:

X   K   D

M   V   S

J   T   L

When he has done so, he will find that he can recall the letters in the sequence in which he practiced them but not in any new sequences.

The Value of Imagery to Thinking is Challenged

Since Galton's work there have been many other signs of disaffection, especially in the studies of Binet, Woodworth, and the Würzburg school. Contemporary experimental studies bring out such facts as these: (a) the imagery employed by a thinker is for the most part irrelevant to the material being thought about and on occasion may even hinder the direct trend of thought; (b) individuals especially gifted in the ability to form images have no advantage over others inferior in this regard when geometrical problems are assigned them.

The work of a group of psychologists at Würzburg is of special importance. They, too, found imagery to be far less important to thinking tasks than was once supposed. In one experiment the subject was given the task of judging which of two lifted weights was the heavier. He would report that, while he did have sensory and imaginal experiences in connection with the weights, he could not thus account for his judgment. He did not retain the kinesthetic image of the first weight and compare it with the kinesthetic sensation or image of the second weight. The judging simply occurred, the decision was ready; and the subject had *no experiences of any imaginal or other processes that determined it.*

Even psychologists who have stoutly insisted that there are imaginal processes in their thinking have acknowledged that the actual images for abstract concepts often are extremely sketchy and sometimes so irrelevant to the meanings as to be accidental. The concept of "value," one psychologist reports, is symbolized by the image of a man putting some-

191

A Picture Used to Invoke Eidetic Imagery

(From E. Brunswik, after Jaensch. By permission.)

thing in a scale; "pride" by that of a strutting, swelling figure; "liberty" by the vague image of a hand holding a torch high; "justice" by a pair of scales [26].

Eidetic Imagery and its Place in Thinking

An ability to employ visual imagery of extremely detailed character has been brought to light in the reports of *eidetic images* [14]. Found at their best in children, these images are as vivid as direct perceptions, yet are not mistaken for perceptions. When the eidetic subject has looked briefly at a picture such as that in Figure 191, in a natural manner and without pushing himself to take in details, immediately afterward he is able to give an extraordinarily detailed account of what was in the picture, even to buttons, letters, window-details, and the like. It is almost as if the subject had a photographic copy. But with differences! It is not as intensely there as are visual after-images (see page 266), but it is more persistent. And things can happen to it: it can appear in reversed (complementary) colors; it can appear or disappear all at once or piecemeal; it may or may not get larger when projected on more distant backgrounds; parts may become animated and move off — all such happenings being as independent of the subject's intent as are after-images. (Some adult psychologists have assured the writer that they were possessed of such eidetic ability in their childhood, for example, that they could repeat almost anything from a page of news-paper.)

It is likely that this is not an all-or-none power but is simply the opposite extreme of a continuum extending from those subjects who report little or no imagery at all [18]. In any case, the lesson for us here is that such faithful imag-ing of details is not conducive to effective thinking. It may be serviceable to the young child in getting the concrete objects in his world more definitely estab-lished and fixed. But as an older child, and especially as an adult, what he needs to get on with his problems of living is above all the ability to condense and foreshorten, to organize and reorganize, to abstract and generalize.

THINKING CONSIDERED PHYSIOLOGICALLY

Thus far we have identified thinking as occurring in an organism when it meets difficulties and strives to surmount them by a rational procedure. The difficulty confronting the subject excites in him some implicit response or series of responses which eventually excites some overt forms of conduct. This outward conduct is thus not aroused directly by the situation, but is by the intermediating thought reactions which finally serve as its directing cue. These intra-organic motor activ-ities operate as substitute stimuli replacing the original extra-organic ones.

When thinking is going on, *what* is going on? And first, what motor mechanisms are operating?

What Effectors Are Involved?

(*A*) *Language Mechanisms*. Let us recognize that thinking starts from the perceiving of a situation, that this perception leads to the setting up of some implicit symbolic response, which in turn serves as a cue either to an overt response or to a new implicit symbolic response that will ultimately eventuate in an overt response to the situation. What we seek to identify, then, are effectors that can react in a manner which will furnish intra-organic cues of symbolic character.

That the speech mechanisms are thinking mechanisms *par excellence* has long been recognized by many psychologists and laymen alike. "Thinking is restrained speaking and acting," said Bain a half-century ago. "A thought is a word or an act in a nascent state . . . a commence-ment of muscular activity," said Ribot with equal insight. Writers of more philosophical interests have often said as much — if not always so accurately. "It troubles me greatly to find that I can never acknowledge, discover or prove any truth except by using in my mind words or other signs. . . . If these characters were absent, we should never think or reason distinctly" (Leibniz). "Thinking and speaking are so entirely one that we can only distinguish them as internal and external" (Schleiermacher). "Without language it is impossible to conceive philosophical, nay, even any human consciousness" (Schelling). "We think in names" (Hegel). "Reasoning, the principal subject of logic, takes place usually by means of words, and in all complicated cases can take place in no other way" (J. S. Mill). Literary men, too, have made the same point. "The word is not the dress of thought, but its very incarnation" (Wordsworth). "If I do not speak I cannot think" (Daudet).[1]

These statements, let us note, are by men who have been stimulated in large part by reading and have found their outlet in writing. They have not done their thinking in terms of pipe-fitting or cabinet-making, careful motoring, skillful boxing, communicating with deaf-mutes or with savages of unknown tongues. As we have seen (pages 461 f.), symbolic reactions are not limited to language mechanisms.

(B) *Other Musculature.* A series of researches forcefully directs attention to the striped musculature of other than vocal mechanisms [13]. In brief, it is an application of the action potential technique [2] to the musculature which was presumably involved in or related to ideational processes. The subjects had been given prolonged training in how to relax their whole bodily musculature while lying on a couch in a darkened sound-proof room. For these experiments two telegraph clicks were used. At one the subject was to begin a prescribed muscular activity, at the other to cease and immediately relax any tension that was present. Then the patterns of action potentials so obtained were compared with the patterns obtained when the subject only imagined performing the acts. (1) For instance, the subject was instructed to imagine bending his right arm. It was found that currents which were set up from electrodes placed at biceps muscle and at elbow of the right arm were similar in kind to those appearing when the arm was actually bent. On the other hand when the subject was instructed to imagine bending some other member (left arm or foot) no current was registered from the right arm. (2) When the subject was instructed actually to look upward, the action potentials set up from electrodes attached near the eyeball muscles produced the record shown in Figure 192, *1*; and when the subject was instructed to imagine the Eiffel Tower in Paris, the potentials were

---

[1] We have already had a concrete illustration of thinking as the operating of language-motor (number) processes in the case of adding. The reader will do well to re-read that account in terms of the present discussion. (See pages 549 f.)

[2] For this technique see the description on pp. 287 ff., *supra.* In the experiments here referred to, a string galvanometer with great amplification was used, producing a sensitivity to changes of a millionth of a volt. These changes were photographically recorded.

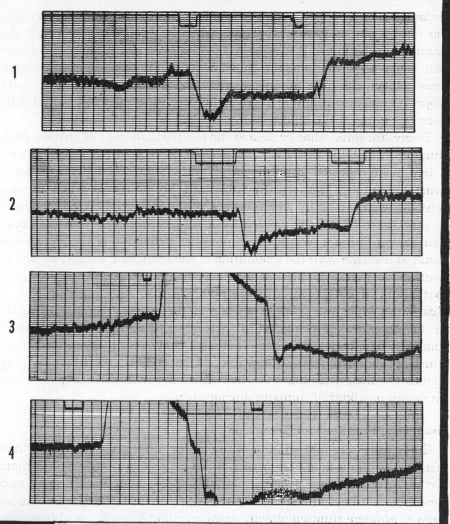

192   **Action Potentials and Ideational Activity**

1. Photographic record of potential differences *during eye-movement of looking upward*. Electrodes of platinum, covered with cotton moistened with NaCl, were placed one above right orbital ridge, the other to right of external corner of right eye. Vertical lines indicate time intervals of $\frac{1}{5}$ second. Subject was instructed, "When the signal comes, look upward." Previous to signal, the eyes were quiet, as shown by horizontal tracing of string shadow. **2.** *During visual imagining*. Conditions same as for 1; but subject was here instructed, "When the signal comes, imagine the Eiffel Tower in Paris." (Note resemblance between 1 and 2.) **3.** *During eye-movement of looking left to right*. Conditions the same. Subject instructed to look toward the right. **4.** *During visual recollecting*. Conditions the same. Subject instructed to recall the morning newspaper. (Note resemblance between 3 and 4.) (*From E. Jacobson, "Electrical measurements of neuromuscular states during mental activities. III,"* AMER. J. PHYSIOL., *1930, 95, 694–712.*)

recorded as in *2*. (3) When his instruction was to look from left to right, the record was as shown in *3*; and when it was merely to recall the morning's newspaper, it was as in *4*. The evidence is fairly conclusive that when a person imagines movements of his own he goes through these movements in a minute degree, and if he imagines some outer object he makes (in minute degree) the very movements he would if he were attending to the object itself.

There are some other evidences for the participation of striped musculature in thinking activity. The eyeball movements, as recorded with a light beam reflected from the cornea were found to be much the same when the subject was visually imagining an object as when he was actually seeing it [28]. Again, when action potentials were measured as they were led off the forearm of a subject while he was imagining that he was lifting a weight, the amount of deflection of the record was found to increase with the magnitude of the imagined weight, as well as with the degree of vividness of the imagery reported by the subject [25]. Better still, action potentials were obtained from the finger-muscles of deaf-mutes while asleep at times when no finger movements were visible to the observer. If awakened at such times, the subjects would report that they had been dreaming, whereas if they were awakened at times when no action potentials appeared, they reported no dreaming [15]. Evidently, then, deaf-mutes do their dreaming with their fingers — and dreaming is a kind of thinking during sleep.

Importance of the Cerebral Connections

In the foregoing presentation of the motor phases of thinking we have attended to the role of end organs to the neglect of central connections. Or at least we have assumed nothing more complicated than such processes as diagrammed in Figure 193*A*. The original stimulations from a problem situation playing upon receptor R_1 evoke an abbreviated response at effector E_1. This in turn serves to excite receptor R_2 (kinesthetic or other) which evokes a response at effector E_2. And so the nascent abbreviated symbolic responses continue until the thinking eventuates in an overt act, as performed by effector E_6.

Such an account fails to bring out certain characteristics of thinking behavior. Thinking behavior proceeds not in simple serial order. Unfortunately, due to three centuries of preoccupation with the trains of ideas, and the questioning of how one idea leads to the next and that to the next (as when "chalk" suggests "blackboard," "blackboard" calls up "black," "black" calls up "cat," and so on) it had come to be assumed that the physiological basis of thinking was somewhat as

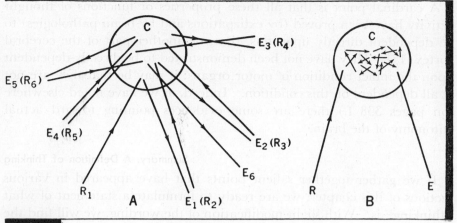

193 Two Extreme Views of the Role of the Brain in Thinking

A. An extreme motor theory. *B.* An extreme intra-cerebral theory.

sketched in Figure 193,*B.* The neural counterpart of each idea was an excitation in a local spot (cell-cluster) in the brain; and the transitions from idea to idea were referable physiologically to the passage of a neural impulse or train of impulses from cell-cluster to cell-cluster. Now this shooting around of neural currents within the cerebrum is as grossly oversimplified an account as is the story of receptor-effector arcs told above and suggested in part *A* of the figure.

Thoughtful behavior is much more complex in its organization. Often it involves temporal sequences of acts that follow upon each other faster than complete stimulus-response arcs *via* peripheral muscles and kinesthetic afferent currents could conceivably operate. Such behavior is observed in the ultra-rapid actions of the typist and the pianist, where surely there is much overlapping of $S \longrightarrow R$ sequences, and hence much condensations in the performance as a whole. Another aspect that we find characteristic of thinking is the ability to respond to a stimulus even in its absence and *after* a forced *delay* (cf. pages 547 f.). Tied up with that is the ability of a person to maintain his *set* in an original direction so that he continues to deal symbolically with the original objects of his thought in spite of all the external stimulations that bombard him. Quite impressive are those organizations of simpler symbolic functions into vastly more complex and *generalized meanings*, which are illustrated by the functions found impaired in the aphasias (pages 544 f.), or are equally well illustrated by the loss of ability to handle *abstract* meanings in certain brain damage and certain schizophrenic cases (pages 573 ff.).

A cardinal point is that all these properties or functions of thought activity have been proved (by extirpations and by brain pathologies) to be dependent directly upon this, that, or another part of the cerebral cortex [17]. They have not been demonstrated to be directly dependent upon the intact condition of motor organs; it may be that they are not at all dependent on this condition. Indeed, as we have noted elsewhere (on pages 338 f.) there are some evidences pointing toward actual autonomy of the brain.

Summary: A Definition of Thinking

If we gather together salient points that have appeared in various sections of this chapter, we are ready to formulate a statement of what "thinking" is. With slight modification of the wording, we will find the definition furnished in Warren's *Dictionary of Psychology*[1] a succinct summary of much of our treatment. When a person is thinking, it reads in substance, he is following *a course of ideational activity, symbolic in character, initiated by a problem or task he is facing, showing some trial-and-error but under the directing influence of his problem-set, and leading ultimately to a conclusion or solution.* We add a point or two. His *ideational activities are ways of symbolizing or formulating generalizations of his past experiences (concepts)* which, by furnishing *more adequate ways of viewing the situation as a whole*, further a more appropriate way of responding to it. His thinking is best understood as *a direct outgrowth of his intercommunications with others and his soliloquies,* only that now he is *stimulating and responding to himself in an implicit manner.*

When we consider the enormous economy of effort and of life and the enormous increase in precision that thoughtful behavior affords, we are prepared to believe that thinking is indeed "the most powerful tool for progress that humanity possesses."

REFERENCES

1. Brunswik, E. *Experimentelle Psychologie in Demonstrationen.* Vienna: Springer, 1935.
2. Coppock, H., and O. H. Mowrer. "Inter-trial responses as 'rehearsal'; a study of 'overt thinking' in animals," *Amer. J. Psychol.*, 1947, *60*, 608–616.
3. Deutsche, J. M. "The development of children's concepts of causal relations," *Univ. Minn. Inst. Child Welf. Monogr.*, 1937, No. 13.
4. Dewey, J. *How We Think.* Boston: D. C. Heath and Company, 1910.

[1] Howard C. Warren, ed., *Dictionary of Psychology* (Boston: Houghton Mifflin Company, 1934).

5. Downey, J. E. *Creative Imagination.* New York: Harcourt, Brace and Company, 1929.

6. Duncker, K. "On problem-solving," *Psychol. Monogr.*, 1945, *58*, No. 270.

7. Fisichelli, V. R., and L. Welch. "The ability of college art majors to recombine ideas in creative thinking," *J. Appl. Psychol.*, 1947, *31*, 278–282.

8. Goldstein, K., and M. Scheerer. "Abstract and concrete behavior," *Psychol. Monogr.*, 1941, *53*, No. 239.

9. Golla, F., E. L. Hutton, and W. G. Walter. "The objective study of mental imagery. I. Physiological concomitants," *J. Ment. Sci.*, 1943, *89*, 216–223.

10. Hadamard, J. S. *The Psychology of Invention in the Mathematical Field.* Princeton, N.J.: Princeton University Press, 1945.

11. Hartmann, G. W. *Educational Psychology.* New York: American Book Company, 1941.

12. Heidbreder, E. "The attainment of concepts: I," *J. Gen. Psychol.*, 1946, *35*, 173–189.

13. Jacobson, E. "Electrophysiology of mental activities," *Am. J. Psychol.*, 1932, *44*, 677–694; "Electrical measurements of neuromuscular states during mental activities," *Am. J. Physiol.*, 1930, *91*, 567–608; *94*, 22–34; *95*, 694–712; *95*, 703–712; 1931, *96*, 115–121; *96*, 122–125; *97*, 200–209.

14. Jaensch, E. R. *Eidetic Imagery.* London: Kegan Paul, Trench, Trubner, 1930.

15. Max, L. W. "An experimental study of the motor theory of consciousness: III," *J. Comp. Psychol.*, 1935, *19*, 469–486.

16. Meumann, E. *The Psychology of Learning* (trans. by Baird). New York: Appleton, 1913.

17. Morgan, C. T. *Physiological Psychology.* New York: McGraw-Hill Book Company, 1943.

18. Morsh, J. E., and H. D. Abbott. "An investigation of after-images," *J. Comp. Psychol.*, 1945, *38*, 47–63.

19. Muenzinger, K. F. "Vicarious trial and error at a point of choice: I," *J. Genet. Psychol.*, 1938, *53*, 75–86.

20. Patrick, C. "Creative thought in poets," *Arch. Psychol., N.Y.*, 1935, *26*, No. 178; "Creative thought in artists," *J. Psychol.*, 1937, *4*, 35–73.

21. Piaget, J. *The Child's Conception of the World.* New York: Harcourt, Brace and Company, 1929.

22. Riess, B. F. "Genetic changes in semantic conditioning," *J. Exp. Psychol.*, 1946, *36*, 143–152.

23. Rossman, J. *The Psychology of the Inventor.* Inventors Publishing Company, 1931.

24. Russell, R. W. "Studies in animism: II," *J. Genet. Psychol.*, 1940, *56*, 353–366.

25. Shaw, W. A. "The relation of muscular action potentials to imaginal weight lifting," *Arch. Psychol., N.Y.*, 1940, *35*, No. 247.

26. Titchener, E. B. *A Text-Book of Psychology.* New York: The Macmillan Company, 1910.

27. Tolman, E. C., and E. Minium. "VTE in rats," *J. Comp. Psychol.*, 1942, *34*, 301–306.

28. Totten, E. "Eye-movement during visual imagery," *Comp. Psychol. Monogr.*, 1935, *11*, No. 53.

29. Welch, L., and L. Long. "The higher structural phases of concept formation of children," *J. Psychol.*, 1940, *9*, 59–95.

30. Wertheimer, M. *Productive Thinking.* New York: Harper and Brothers, 1945.

31. Willmann, R. R. "An experimental investigation of the creative process in music," *Psychol. Monogr.*, 1944, *57*, No. 261.

20

DESCRIBING PERSONALITIES

WE MUST RETURN to the view of man-as-a-whole with which we started. In the course of our survey we have from time to time watched him from one perspective and then from another, and each time we took first a general view then made a closer examination. Frequently we have had warning that each of these partial views was itself an abstraction from the rich dynamic facts of organismic behavior. We have been frequently reminded that man's behavior arises from the interlocking interdependence of functions that makes of a person not a set of organs but one organism, and not an assortment of acts but an active life.

Man Viewed Socially

The term *personality* has a further connotation. It refers to the ways in which a man-as-a-whole presents himself to his fellow men. The word seems to have derived from the Latin *persona*, meaning the actor's mask which was chosen and worn to indicate the character that was to be played. (The same root word survives in the *dramatis personae* on one's theater program.) Hence *personality* may be taken to refer to the role one plays in life's drama, in which all the world's a stage, and all its men and women merely players. The mask had a double importance. It indicated the type of conduct that might be expected from the actor. It also served as a stimulus to other actors. Accordingly, it is interesting to find that "personality" involves the full duality of meaning for a psychological fact; it is that which characterizes a person as both a socially reactive and a socially stimulating agency.

593

Man as Behaving Consistently

Throughout all the uses of the term *personality*, whether technical or popular, there runs one logical assumption: that there is some degree of consistency in his conduct and thinking. This is the really empirical and investigable expression of the semi-mystical notion of a personality as something that diffuses through and permeates all that a man does, and that is revealed by degrees through his actions and his words.

This consistency is expected of man, whether he be considered cross-sectionally or longitudinally. After he has been observed to act thus and so under a few sets of circumstances, his acquaintances entertain fairly definite expectations of him when they find him under a new set of circumstances, so that if he fails to fit the expectation they are taken by surprise: "I wouldn't have expected that of him." But the man is also supposed to be much the same sort of individual he was two years ago, or as we knew him to be when a child. A core of continuity is expected to be maintained despite the changes induced by his growth and his experiences. "He isn't the fellow he used to be" is a verbal expression of bewilderment that illustrates this point in a negative way.

A man's personality, we may conclude, *is the total picture of his organized behavior, especially as it can be characterized by his fellow men in a consistent way.*

THE PROBLEM OF TYPES

Attempts to classify mankind into psychological types date from ancient times, definitely from the second century A.D.[1] Our purpose will be served if we limit our attention to two of the best-known recent examples that are near-classics.

Kretschmer: Morphological Types

It has long been a part of popular lore that a man's physical body-build may often be taken as indicative of his psychological make-up, especially his emotional-temperamental characteristics. Shakespeare's Caesar, for example, says:

> Let me have men about me that are fat,
> Sleek-headed men and such as sleep o' nights.
> Yon Cassius has a lean and hungry look,
> He thinks too much: such men are dangerous.

[1] With Galen (born A.D. 130) and his theory of the four emotional temperaments as attributable to the preponderance of one or another of the four bodily fluids or "humors" of Hippocrates (born 460 B.C.).

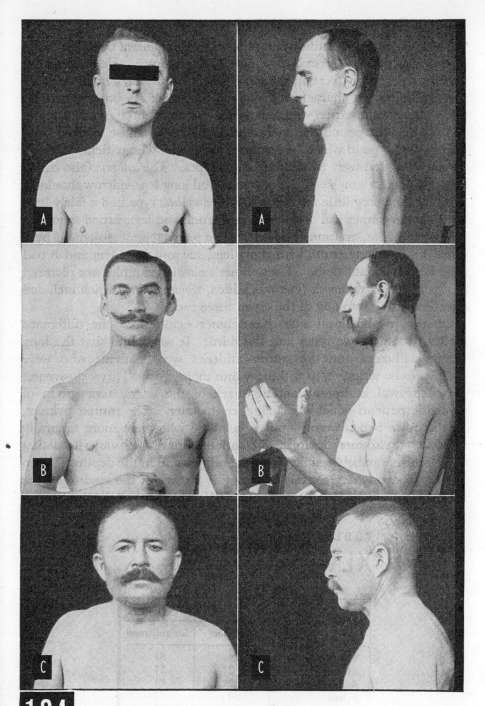

194 **Kretschmer's Main Types of Human Physique**

A. Asthenic type. *B.* Athletic type. *C.* Pyknic type. (Front and side views.)
(*From E. Kretschmer*, PHYSIQUE AND CHARACTER; *trans. by W. J. H. Sprott. By permission of George Routledge and Sons.*)

The best-known scientific attempt to verify this general belief appeared in the work of the German psychiatrist Kretschmer. He claimed (*a*) that by determining certain measurements of a person's bodily dimensions (plus certain characteristics of the surface of his body as well as of his viscera) the expert can assign him to one of three physical types, and (*b*) that the person's temperamental make-up can be inferred from the physical type to which he has been assigned. The patients in Kretschmer's hospital were classed into these types. The *asthenic* (also called *leptosomic*) had a long head, a short trunk and long legs, narrow shoulders and hips, and very little fat. The so-called *athletic* type had a fairly long head, more symmetrical development of trunk and legs, broad shoulders and narrow hips, and much muscle. The *pyknic* type was marked by a broad head, a long trunk with short legs, narrow shoulders and broad hips, and abundant flesh. (Kretschmer's classic examples are pictured in Figure 194.) A fourth type was added, the *dysplastic*, which included cases not fitting into any of the given three types.

On the psychological side, Kretschmer emphasized the difference between the first two types and the third. It was found that the long slender asthenics and the sturdy athletics were patients who were inclined to be seclusive, to withdraw into themselves. This seclusiveness or withdrawal is an outstanding mark of the *schizophrenic* group of psychotic patients which we shall take up later. The rotund pyknics, on the other hand, were found to be those who were more naturally sociable but also more inclined to emotional ups and downs, alternating in a circular way between being on the heights and in the depths. When carried to excess degree, this tendency is a mark of the *manic-depressive* (or circular) psychosis. From Table XLV, which shows the frequencies

TABLE XLV
Physical and Psychical Dispositions

Physical	Psychical	
	Circular	Schizophrene
Asthenic	4	81
Athletic	3	31
Asthenico-Athletic	2	11
Pyknic	58	2
Pyknic Mixture	14	3
Dysplastic	0	34
Uncataloguable	4	13

with which Kretschmer found one or the other psychological character in individuals of each morphological type, we can see that he did get interesting correspondences, even though his total number of cases might be thought small, and the number in the dysplastic classification to raise a question.

It is well to bear in mind the fact that Kretschmer reported these findings "as a stimulus to further research, and not as anything dogmatic." And in that aim he has succeeded. In a summary way it may be said that later attempts to verify his findings have had a dual result. When college or other normal populations have been used, no one has been successful in getting anything like his relationships of body-type and mental-type. On the other hand, some of the investigations utilizing mental hospital populations have furnished some support for the Kretschmer claims [7, 21]. How shall we interpret these two outcomes? The simplest interpretation — though not necessarily the soundest — would be that, since the patients in a psychiatric hospital represent extreme degrees of variations in personality, where there is any basis at all in human nature for correlations between certain personality traits and any other traits these correlations might be expected to become more apparent in the hospital group.

There have been other interesting and promising attempts to work out relations between broad morphological characteristics and personality characteristics [16, 20]. The best-known recent effort is that of Sheldon and Stevens. In this classification a person is described in terms of three *components of physique*, and in the degree of each: "endomorphy," or softness, roundness, fatness; "mesomorphy," or muscularity; and "ectomorphy," or thinness. A person is rated in each of these components on a scale of seven, and the combined rating determines his *somatotype*. Thus, a rating 2 — 7 — 3 would be indicative of a pronounced mesomorph. The system goes further to define three *components of temperament:* "viscerotonia" or a good digestion and what that popularly implies; "somatotonia" or vigor and assertiveness; and "cerebrotonia" or restraint and limited social interest. The proponents of this system have reported finding some high correlations between the physique and the temperament measures in their cases. A few critics, however, suspect that the claims need confirmation with more data and by other investigators; and it is fair to say that the system has not yet won a scientific position any more secure than has Kretschmer's.

The upshot of this whole question is that human physical builds and human temperamental make-ups do not seem to vary in completely independent ways; but just how these characteristics are related to each other and to some more fundamental variables too, remains a field inviting research.

Jung: Introversion-Extroversion Types

Quite the best known of modern typologies is that of the Swiss psychiatrist Jung, who suggested that men can be classed as either *extroverts* or *introverts.* The former are those whose interests are directed mostly by factual considerations, especially social life and activities broadly speaking; while the introverts are interested more in themselves and their own emotional experiences and trains of thinking. The former are more objectively interested, we might say, the latter more subjectively. As Jung used the terms it is not the contrast between the man of action and the man of thought, so much as that between the realistic and the idealistic (or imaginative, "autistic") person. Psychologists are fairly well agreed that there is some such distinction between personalities as suggested by Jung's terms. Some psychologists, however, emphasize the direction a person's interests take, some the expressing or the inhibiting of his emotions, and others the amount of his social participation. There are in the field a number of tests of introversion-extroversion which are made up of questions supposed in advance to be differentiating; but results from them have been disappointing, for in only one study has a trace of bimodality been found in the distributions of those examined. Individuals do not seem to fall neatly into the two types.

It would seem easy to classify some historic characters: the Darwins, Napoleons, and Franklins would fall clearly into a different group from that in which the Kants, Poes, and MacDowells would be found; yet where should we place the Jeffersons, F. D. Roosevelts, Leonardos, and perhaps the majority of geniuses as well as common folk? A middle class of *ambiverts* has become a recognized necessity, to include those who fall somewhere between the extremes. This class turns out to be so much the largest that when all data are thrown together no bimodality in the population appears. The types, as distinct statistical types, vanish.

Jung himself, by the way, had been forced to set up sub-types under each of his two main types. From different considerations, other reinterpretations have been suggested. Statistical (factor) analyses have been made of the question-items selected as the best ones from a number of different introversion-extroversion tests. These have been tried out on new subjects, and the conclusion has been that such tests get at not a single personality-factor to be called introversion-extroversion but a list of as many as eighteen different factors. Most important of these were: (*a*) a tendency to shrink from the environment, (*b*) an emotional sensitiveness to the environment, (c) impulsiveness, and (d) interest in oneself [8].

Some sample items used in the test were:

Do you prefer to work with others rather than alone? (Yes — No)
Do you like to speak in public?
Are your feelings rather easily hurt?
Have you ever kept a personal diary of your own accord?
Do you like to confide in others?
Do you like work which requires considerable attention to details?
Do you like to change from one type of work to another frequently?

What is the general upshot of these critical attempts to make use of Jung's psychological types? If, as someone has facetiously remarked, "there are two types of people in the world, those who divide everybody into types and those who do not," then we are clearly warned not to enroll ourselves among those of the former brotherhood. Instead of abstracting some attribute of human nature and then dividing people into two groups as being fundamentally marked and determined throughout their behavior by presence or absence of that characteristic, the part of wisdom is to inquire whether the abstracted attribute *is descriptive of this or that reaction* of Mr. X, and *in what degree.*

This is the treatment more generally accorded "introversion-extroversion" by critical psychologists in America today. It is a way of describing simply one trend-in-behavior, one trait.

Other Typologies

Typologies have been erected on still other foundations. Many are based more purely on psychiatric classification [19, 11]. Recognizing that the differences between "normal" and "abnormal" people are largely a matter of more and less, and that the abnormals have the same behavior tendencies as the normals, only to a more marked degree, they seek to describe normal individuals in terms of those types of psychiatric cases that show their characteristics in excess. We shall encounter some of these classifications later in this chapter.

Restatement of the Problem of Types; Conclusion

From our acquaintance with two well-known examples, we should now be able to see two underlying assumptions in a type-theory of human personalities.

(1) One is that there is *a certain especially revealing key trait* or characteristic which is so central and basic in the organization of any man-as-a-

whole that once we know John Doe in that trait, we will know him in many. We are familiar enough with this kind of thinking; Alexander's ambition, Jesus' humility, Benjamin Franklin's practicality, Washington's sagacity, Lincoln's humanitarianism, Theodore Roosevelt's strenuousness, Woodrow Wilson's righteousness, Franklin D. Roosevelt's debonair charm, John L. Lewis's aggressiveness — these are one-trait characterizations that suggest complete portraits. Similarly, any cartoonist shows an amusing ability to spot and play up a facial detail that, when exaggerated, seems to identify the character more patly than all the rest of his features taken together (Figure 195). These, of course, are not perfect parallels of typology, for the salient item is not systematically used for all subjects: they are not all classified, for example, as ambitious-unambitious.

(2) The other underlying assumption in a typology is that with respect to the key trait mentioned, individual *persons will tend to fall into more or less distinct groups* (types). Even when more than two types are included in the scheme, each type is differentiated from every other by the either-or dichotomy in respect to at least one characteristic.

This way of thinking, too, is familiar enough. Morally, people are good or bad; modernistic interiors are beautiful or ugly; lamb chops are expensive or cheap; this book is interesting or dull. It seems to require discipline for us to learn to judge and describe in degrees and gradations.

It will point up the issue if we look at the question statistically. In Chapter 6 we saw that in nearly all psychological dimensions the indi-

195

Cartoonists' Characterizations

Commonly used newspaper cartoonists' treatment of three famous public characters mentioned in text. Note that the details drawn are not merely pictorially clever as making identification easy but are characterologically clever as suggesting certain outstanding temperamental traits.

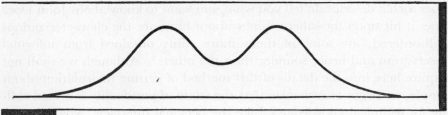

196

Bimodal Distribution Characteristic of a Population Assumed to Contain Two Types of People

Compare with the normal distributions in Figures 31 and 32.

viduals of any large, normal, unselected population distribute themselves in a quantitative way represented by various approximations to the so-called Gaussian curve. But now if a population is really divisible into, say, two types with respect to a given psychological trait, then the curve of distribution will be bimodal. This is shown in Figure 196.

Now, how are these two assumptions of a typology to be tested? (1) The first assumption calls for verification as follows. If a particular trait is claimed to be a key to the whole individual, then the claim must stand up against examination into interrelations of the trait with other traits and patterns of traits. Is it found to hang together with them so frequently as to furnish presumption of a dynamic interconnection with other traits? We shall take up this kind of investigation in our following section. (2) The second assumption of a typology demands checking to determine whether in empirically studied populations the individuals do in fact fall into distinct groups. We have already had a hint of the answer: bimodal distributions have practically never been found except in some cases of psychotic patients who were studied under clinical conditions that fell short of full experimental controls. What are offered as the names of types of whole personalities might better be considered as names for extremes of *particular* traits or *variables*.

THE PROBLEM OF PERSONALITY TRAITS

Meaning of the Term

If you were to ask a friend, employer, or former teacher of John Doe for a letter about his personality, he would be likely to write somewhat as follows:

> John is *cooperative, truthful, industrious, more optimistic* than pessimistic, a bit jerky and *impulsive in his movements,* prone to make *snap judgments,* can *take it on the chin* when razzed, is a *driver* of himself and of others, *catches on* quickly, is well *informed* on current affairs, a bit careless of his *personal appearance,* and is a little *diffident* in his address.

Does such a description tell you what you want to know about John Doe? Does it hit upon the salient things about him; are the characterizations well-ordered; are some of them more easily obtained from informal observation and hence sounder than the others? Although we shall not inquire here into the details of this method of getting information about people, we begin to recognize that the study of personality is a field calling for technical knowledge. Like the personal interview, what seems a simple everyday procedure turns out upon psychological scrutiny to be a complicated one, and one deserving careful analysis [9].

The various items mentioned in the letter above are selected ways in which one individual can be compared with others. These differentiae are called personal *traits*. Let us note a few points about them.

Each trait can be considered as *a dimension*, a matter of more-or-less, a quantitative continuum along which different individual persons are distributed at different distances, from the "extremely cooperative" through the "very cooperative" and the "cooperative," all the way over to the "extremely uncooperative." (And we can readily imagine all degrees and shadings of difference at any point.)

Each trait is a *generalization* from (presumably) several opportunities the letter writer has had to observe Mr. Doe. Mr. Doe was cooperative on this occasion and on that, though possibly not on another one. And he was cooperative with certain people, and maybe not with certain others. And perhaps the writer had been told by a third person that John Doe was cooperative. How sound, then, is the generalization? This point, as well as the preceding one, suggests practical matters of technique and procedure. We shall touch upon these later.

To the list of traits that the letter writer happened to jot down, innumerable others could be added. It has been shown that in the English language there are something like eighteen thousand terms that are used in designating distinctive personal forms of behavior [2]. How did the letter writer happen to select the few with which he characterized John Doe? Are they more striking and *outstanding* — analogous to the salient feature of a caricature? Are they more *basic* to the many others that might have been listed? The last question directs our attention to possible overlappings or relationships between the traits given in the letter from which we quoted above. For example, is the fact that John Doe is "industrious" related in any way to his "truthfulness," or to his "cooperative" spirit, or to his carelessness in "personal appearance"? Surely, we should expect to find that some of these characteristics are more closely related than are others.

Some Basic Traits of Personality

Constructing lists of personality traits has always been a popular indoor sport, and the literature of psychology abounds with the products and by-products of that sport. This is not to say, however, that such lists do not have their usefulness, nor that some are not better than others. Some good ones [as 1, page 103] have been constructed on the basis of sagacious observation and refined by logical considerations. Later and more sophisticated ones have been arrived at by applying methods of factorial analysis to the results of many correlation studies (cf. page 132), or the somewhat similar "cluster analysis" method [6]. In one review of the field, Wolfle [22] found that seven factors had been reported in three or more factor analysis studies, as follows:

> w or willful, purposive, persevering
> c or clever, with sense of humor, quick in grasping others' ideas
> s or shy
> m [1] or self-confident, dominant, "masculine"
> f or fluent, emotionally immature, cycloid
> d or depressed, worrisome
> h [1] or hypersensitive, feelings easily hurt
>
> These seven factors, and even more those which have not been described here, can have only a tentative status as traits to be included in the systematic and orderly description of personality for which we are seeking until they are confirmed by other workers.

Example: the Trait of Honesty

One of the strongest demonstrations of how specific a personality trait can be was made in a series of studies by Hartshorne and May [10] on children in many schoolroom and party situations. The children were given opportunities to cheat, to lie, or to steal — apparently without the examiner's knowledge. Here are examples. The children's answer papers were returned to them for scoring by keys, and note was made of papers handed in by them the second time with improved answers. Some exceedingly difficult puzzles that could be dishonestly solved by looking on the bottom or by lifting pieces off the board were given them to solve in a quite insufficient time. They were allowed to use coins for counters in puzzles, these to be returned apparently without being counted by the experimenters. They were asked if they had cheated.

The amount of honesty displayed by the hundreds of children tested varied with a number of factors, so many indeed that the distribution

---

[1] These letters suggested by the present writer.

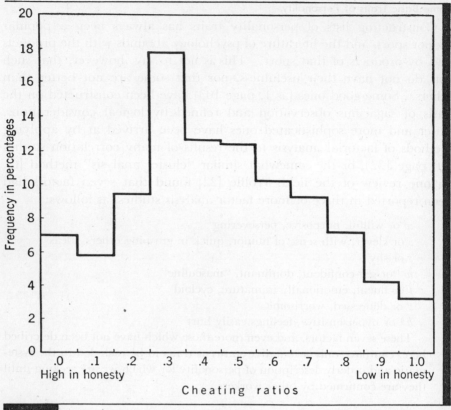

197

Distribution of 2443 Cases (School Children) of Honesty Tests

The cheating ratio = the ratio between the number of cheatings and the chances to cheat. Each child was measured on ten tests. (*Based on data from Hartshorne and May. From V. Jones, "Children's morals," in C. Murchison, ed.,* HANDBOOK OF CHILD PSYCHOLOGY, *Clark University Press, 1933.*)

of the total scores for individuals fell into a skewed Gaussian form, as appears in Figure 197. Some of the contributing factors were: the children's intelligence; their emotional stability; occupational level of their fathers; their cultural background; relationship of teachers to the children; amount of cheating done by their friends and by classmates. But such correlations are of less significance to us than is another outcome, if we want to know what a trait like "honesty" is.

Honesty or its opposite, deceit, was found to be *specific to the situation.* John X. might falsify his score on a strength test but not for a moment think of keeping a dime; Ruth Y. might cheat on her arithmetic paper but not lie about it later; and Jimmy Z. might cheat on his arithmetic paper but not on his spelling paper. The motives for cheating, lying, and stealing were found to be certainly complex. Most children, in a word, will deceive in certain situations and not in others. (All this seems a bit simpler if we but bear in mind that when a person practices deceit he is making a kind of adjustment to a difficult situation; an indirect kind, but one that in his limited experience promises to solve the problem and perhaps has solved it in the past.) "Honesty," then is not a general trait or characteristic of the child: we simply apply the same adjective "honest" to different behaviors that we think look alike.

But note that these experimenters were working with children. Perhaps the specificity of "honesty" — its holding for specific behavior situations only — was due to the immaturity of the subjects. In older people does honesty show any more generalization? And further, does it seem to go with any other traits in a whole character make-up? McKinnon tested the latter point directly, and the former point by inference [15]. He asked some graduate students to solve a set of twenty problems, working individually. On the table before him each subject had a booklet containing the solutions; and he was permitted to look at certain of the solutions but not at any of the others. Each subject was left alone, but the experimenter was able to observe his actions through a one-way screen.

Those who violated the prohibitions were identified; and then the records of their behavior in a number of ways was compared with those of the non-violators. For instance, analysis of the verbal responses made while at work at the problems showed that 31 per cent of the violators but none of the non-violators made verbal attacks on the problems ("The hardest things I ever saw," and other more colorful remarks); while on the other hand none of the violators as compared with 10 per cent of the non-violators attacked themselves ("I must be dumb!" "What a nitwit!" and the like). Analysis of overt acts shows that under the frustrating conditions the violators exhibited aggressive restlessness more often than the non-violators in scuffling the feet, stamping, kicking the table leg, pounding the fist, and so on (31 per cent as compared to 4 per cent). At the same time the violators indulged in less thumb-sucking, nail-biting, and similar behavior, than did the non-violators (48 per cent as compared to 83 per cent). As the author summarizes, "The violator reacts aggressively, the non-violator regressively." [1]

[1] The reader will find these comparisons more interesting if he will re-read relevant points in Chapter 8.

A further finding that invites reflection in connection with some points below (pages 617 ff.) is this: Of the violators 74 per cent expressed a preference for the mother, only

What was brought to light, then, was the existence of two different patterns of personality traits in the violators and in the non-violators, respectively. Honesty in the given experimental situation was part and parcel of a more inclusive pattern. It was far from being a simple character of the simple situation.

Some Opposition to the Trait Theory

Criticism of the practice of using the notion of traits, in the attempt to understand the human personality, stems from different sources. On the one hand there are those who look askance upon factor analysis methods, and who wonder whether the results, instead of throwing light on the actual organization of personality, are not merely the logical outcome of the particular tests used in the original investigations. Are the factors real abilities and determiners of some sort, these critics ask, or are they statistical fictions based on particular tests [3]? This is too complicated a field for us to enter.

On the other hand there are those who point out that this business of selecting traits to describe whole personalities overlooks the basic fact in psychology that the person is an organic whole. To sympathize with this point of view we need only remind ourselves of the story of individual development. Just as sensitivity and motility are at first general and massive, and as differentiation of more and more specific senses and movements comes about with time and maturation and exercise, so we may expect generality rather than specificity to mark the earlier organization of the individual.

SOME EXTREME DEVIATIONS IN PERSONALITY ORGANIZATION

Abnormal = Away-from-Normal

The distribution of any sizable population in almost any respect trails off into extremes where relatively few individual cases are to be found. This oft-repeated principle needs repetition here, for it is essential that the reader bear it in mind if he is to gain any adequate perspective for understanding those people who deviate in certain respects so far from the populational mean as to earn such names as *psychoneurotic* and *psychotic*. They are even as you and I — assuming that you and I are somewhere near the average of mankind. They differ only in the exag-

4 per cent for the father; while of the non-violators 36 per cent stated preference for the mother, and 29 per cent for the father. The interpretation of this finding gets pretty complicated; but the difference certainly points us toward the importance of child-family relationships in helping to shape personality make-up.

geration and pervasiveness of some traits which lead to the restructuring of many others; so that there develop in them personality-patterns that are so *maladjusted* to the actualities and responsibilities of life as to occasion some concern to their fellow men.   To present even the best-known varieties with anything like adequacy would demand all of a volume: here we have space for only a few thumbnail sketches [4, 5, 13, 17].

Let it not be forgotten that in each case we are portraying an abstract type.   What we have had to say on earlier pages of this chapter about the fluidity of human types applies here, too.   The reader will not let himself be misled by names into assuming that neurotic and psychotic people can be neatly classified and pigeonholed as of this or that pure type of mental disorder.   Each human being has his own individuality.

A few words may now be given as to causation.   Only a work devoted entirely to this area would afford the space necessary to a discussion of how each kind of disorder gets established.   We shall have to limit ourselves to superficial descriptive accounts.   Meanwhile we shall bear in mind some considerations.   (1) We know that hereditary and congenital factors play some part in furnishing the raw material out of which the person's individuality is built.   Present-day clinicians have broken clearly with a psychiatry of a quarter-century ago which assumed that various abnormal kinds of behavior simply ran in families, were matters of heredity; nevertheless, the necessity of recognizing hereditary predisposition is a starting point in the attempt to trace the genesis of a given person's difficulty.   (2) In some kinds of mental disorder the patient's physical disease history has much interpretative value.   (3) We readily recognize the significance of a person's established habits of thought and of conduct.   Indeed, very much of the re-orientation of thinking in the last two decades about abnormal behavior has been forced by a tremendous emphasis on the part played by a patient's earlier life-experiences and the trends of thinking and feeling they have established in him.   (4) Finally, the incidence of many a neuropsychiatric casualty under the stress of war has served only to reinforce the point that the degree of seriousness of any crisis one faces day by day may have much to do with whether one will surmount it.   These are four factors operating to bring about behavior that is aberrant and a source of trouble to individual man and society as a whole.

(I) The Psychoneurotic

The Hysterical Personality.   Although the term *hysterical* has a history of broad and narrow meanings, we may note certain traits as outstanding and characteristic in the type of personality so named.   The hysteric, for one thing, is extremely *unstable* emotionally. When he is seriously thwarted there are likely to be fireworks. He (or more commonly she) is likely to go into some sort of emotional blow-up; and there may be weeping or screaming or swearing or fainting away, especially if a sympathetic audience is on hand.

Another mark of the hysteric is his extreme *egoism*. All roads lead to himself; he takes most things personally and presents the picture of a spoiled child who resorts to a number of devices to get attention. In a general way, a certain psychological immaturity — a certain proneness to regression — is more marked among hysterics than among any other class of deviates. That is the general picture.

In its narrower usage the term *hysteria* has become synonymous with *conversion neurosis*, and the symptoms emphasized are those which simulate physical disease or damage but have no true organic basis. We have already had concrete cases presented in this book. Two worth consulting again are that of the soldier who lost the use of his legs and that of the man suddenly blinded (pages 180 ff.).

A classical form of hysterical conversion is presented in Figure 198. There we see that the hysterically induced anesthesias conform to certain patterns which are familiar to the patient and do *not* conform to the actual anatomical distribution of the cutaneous nerves. There are other inconsistencies, but the loss of sensitivity in the affected area is impressive enough. Even a sharp needle jab elicits no reflex jerk.

The particular symptoms assumed in conversion reactions are legion. Derangements of digestive, menstrual, respiratory, circulatory, and other organic functions are often striking. Furthermore, the disorganization may isolate a part of the personality in a way exhibited in automatic writing, wherein the writing hand, often unknown to the patient, holds the pencil and scribbles meaningful or meaningless phrases across the page. Finally the symptom may take the form of an amnesia, and this may even be productive of a multiple personality, of temporary somnambulisms or longer-lasting episodes.

It is not to be wondered that many cases of conversion neuroses furnish real problems for the courts in damage and insurance suits, for they must be differentiated from cases of anatomical damage on the one hand and from cases of intentional malingering on the other.

Anxiety Neurosis. A personality disturbance of considerable concern to the clinician is that in which the patient experiences intense emotion of fear and manifests it in externally observable tremors, cold sweating, startle, palpitating heart, labored breathing, dilated pupils, and other physiological symptoms, yet frequently can himself assign no cause for

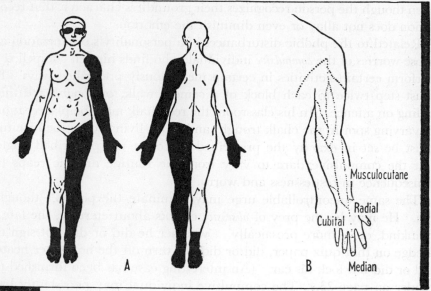

198 Hysterical Anesthesias

A. Schema of several forms of hysterical anesthesia which simulate a glove, a jacket-sleeve, a sock, and a leg of mutton. *B*. Map of the cutaneous areas served by the different nerves to the right arm. By comparing part of *A* with *B* it is seen that the hysteric's disorders bear no relation to the organic functions of nerves but correspond to popular ideas of the various organs and parts. (*From P. Janet,* THE MAJOR SYMPTOMS OF HYSTERIA, *Macmillan, 1907. By permission.*)

his fear — he is afraid of nothing he can name. The patient usually reports that thoughtful concentration on his work is impossible. Nighttime finds him irritable, discouraged, and unable to sleep well, and what dreams he has are fairly certain to be nightmares.

> She is troubled with thick-coming fancies
> That keep her from her rest.

Some clinicians claim to find evidences of underlying anxiety states in the eager-beaver activities of many a high-powered executive, reformer, politician, and other drivers of themselves and others.

Psychasthenic Personalities. In other personalities fear may attach itself to certain specified types of things. The *phobia* may be a dread of closed-in places such as sleeping-car berths; or it may take quite the opposite form, a dread of wide-open plazas or fields or oceans. It may be a dread of touching doorknobs, in particular, or a dread of dirtyness and contamination by contacts in general. Such fears are real fears; and even though the person recognizes their groundless character, that recognition does not allay or even diminish the emotion.

Related to the phobic disturbances of a personality's organization are those worries of the *compulsive* individual, who finds himself compelled to perform certain activities in certain meticulously prescribed ways. He must step twice to each block of a cement walk, or touch each third paling on a fence. In his classroom the red chalk must be placed at one unvarying spot in the chalk trough; and in his living-room the furniture must be set in exactly the prescribed places at the prescribed angles. Let the compulsive dare to vary from the routine and he reaps the consequence in restlessness and worry.

The same uncontrollable urge may dominate the person's thought-life. He may be the prey of *obsessive* doubts about eternity, the fate of mankind, or — more prosaically — whether he did or did not sign the pledge on that quiz paper, did or did not turn off the hot water heater, did or did not lock his car. (An interesting case has been furnished the reader on page 23.) The compulsive individual may persistently have to fight the desire to touch a lighted match to the hay in the barn or to Santa Claus's beard; or he may be convinced against his judgment that he has committed the unpardonable sin.

The Psychopathic Personality. For this kind of deviate person, the reader is referred to the discussion on pages 623 f.

All these personality patterns are called forms of *psychoneuroses*. In contradistinction, the clinician speaks of the graver forms of deviation as *psychoses* (in popular language, "insanities"). The distinction is mainly one of social adjustment. While psychoneurotic persons may cause great inconvenience to others, those properly termed psychotic are so completely unable to adjust to the conditions of life among their fellow men that they must be specially cared for and hospitalized. Only a few of the many varieties of psychotic patterns can be mentioned here.

(II) The Psychotic

The Manic-Depressive Personality. The manic-depressive psychosis is characterized essentially by morbid exaggeration of the ups and downs in thinking, in overt activity, and in emotion. In the manic or excited phase, the patient is exalted and on the heights, or irritable and quarrelsome, or erotically a nuisance. He may display a flight of ideas in rapid and unconnected speech. He may also become quite active overtly — for example, breaking up the furniture, somersaulting, howling.

When the depressed phase is on him, the picture is reversed. He may fall into a dull stupor, and as he sits in a corner by himself, contracted almost into a ball, he furnishes the spectacle of one overwhelmed by profoundly unpleasant emotions. His speech comes slowly and almost inaudibly. He may now be beset by hypochondriacal convictions of serious diseases within his frame, or by tormenting self-accusations.

One interpretation of this disorder is psychogenic. It seems that the patient, unable to resolve certain serious personal difficulties, adopts either — or alternately both — of two tactics. By becoming excessively active he forgets his problems, in a way; for by his very busyness he gives himself no time for thinking of them — a morbidly extreme and complicated manner of whistling in the dark. On the other hand, he may be "licked"; the problems that beset him will not be denied, and overwhelmed, he withdraws into a contemplation of his own moral depravity. After all, this type of psychotic personality only exhibits in extreme form the characteristics of the so-called "cyclothymic" (or circular) person, who is given to emotional ups and downs, and who may be encountered every day on the street.

The Schizoid Personality. Of all the disorders of behavior, this is probably the most common. It develops in individuals on college campuses, as elsewhere, for the late 'teens and twenties is the age-period of highest incidence. In the full psychotic form, "schizophrenia," it is not characterized simply and easily, for it has many variations. Its old name, "dementia praecox," signified an apparent *premature intellectual deterioration,* and to this might have been added an *emotional* deterioration as well. Its present name is more accurate (schizo = split; phreno = mind) as implying *disorganization* of the person's habits. Further, as is becoming increasingly recognized, there is a *desocialization* at the very heart of the picture. Private fantasies dominate the person so completely that he becomes inaccessible to us, his actions and his language (see pages 560 ff.) unpredictable and undecipherable [14, 5]. In the simplest form of this mental disorder, a patient who as a child had perhaps the usual amount of promise begins in his middle 'teens or later to slow down. He grows listless, inattentive, lazy, is easily tired, is the victim of insomnia and often of fleeting delusions and hallucinations. "Silly" is an adjective excellently describing much of his behavior. His verbal expression grows incoherent. He may give evidence of a split between his intellectual functions and his emotional reactions: he cries when he should be glad, or simpers in a silly fashion upon losing his home and property. The change takes also the common form of a dulling and deadening: he merely smiles where formerly he laughed aloud, or he becomes utterly callous and apathetic.

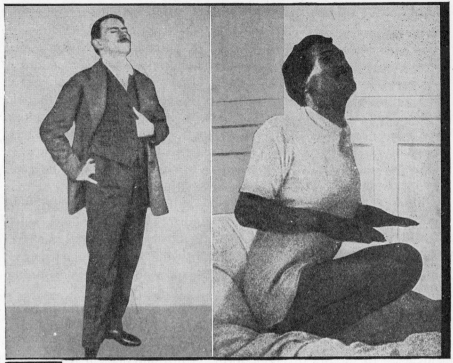

199 Two Varieties of Schizophrenia

Left: Paranoid variety. The attitude of tilted head, closed eyes, hand posturings, and all, are expressive of a delusion of grandeur.

Right: Catatonic variety. The patient had accepted the clinician's suggestion
of this posturing and maintained it for a half-hour.

(*From E. Bleuler,* TEXTBOOK OF PSYCHIATRY [*trans. Brill*], *Macmillan,* 1924; by
permission of the publishers.)

A condition often complicating the picture of the schizophrenic patient
is the development of *paranoid* trends. Mild delusions appear: he financed
Henry Ford; he invented "eenie, meenie, minie, moe"; or he is the new
Messiah and will (actually) preach for you by the hour. Or, in a more
serious form, he is hounded and persecuted by enemies, by telephones,
by mirrors, by voices, by cosmic rays (Figure 199).

A more dramatic though infrequent complication of the picture is
brought about by *catatonic* seizures. In his motor performances the
patient may show a negativistic contrariness in which he does nothing
he is asked to do (but may do the opposite); further, he may become
absolutely mute and take no notice of anything or anybody. In some
cases a "waxy flexibility" appears: for minutes or even hours or as long
as there is anyone to witness, he will maintain peculiar postures which

he himself has assumed or in which he has been placed by the clinician. On the other hand, his motor activity may take the form of an excitement expressed in mild and silly grimacing and attitudinizing, or may assume dangerous proportions in breaking windows, arson, murder, suicide — although these are infrequent occurrences.

When a disease is so diversified in nature, theories of its causes are likely to be many. However, a definite trend of the day is to emphasize certain psychological factors as central. A case is often traced back to a persistent habit of meeting frustration by complete withdrawal from social contacts. By this dangerous method of countering the thwartings of his motives, the individual becomes more and more shut in, less and less in touch with the actualities of life. Hence mental hygiene today places major emphasis on counteracting such specious methods of solving personal problems.

Involutional Melancholia. After the middle of life has passed, when a woman is entering her fifties or a man is a little older, it seems that one of life's critical periods is reached. With some persons a characteristic depression now sets in. It may take the form of a free-floating fear (as Freud picturesquely named it); that is, one which is subject to arousal by this, that, or the other incident, in the shape of a causeless anxiety and even self-accusations. This manifestation may have to do with the fact that old age (technically) is arriving and one's womanhood or manhood (for procreative purposes) is a thing now gone. And recognition of this fact furnishes a severe test of ego-regard and of emotional balance.

It is no wonder, then, that the general character of a person's behavior may now change in such a degree as to astonish his family and those who know him best. In a few cases he (or she) may affect gay costumes as if again in the twenties, and may show an interest in frivolous matters. Often other symptoms appear, such as paranoidal accusations against friends or against oneself. But usually these symptoms do not last long. As the patient, through long habit and through thoughtfully assimilating the present difficulty, comes to look at life more serenely, the melancholic moods and the regressions to earlier kinds of actions grow infrequent and disappear. Thus the patient often again makes a satisfactory adjustment to the world in which he lives.

The Paranoid Personality. We have spoken of paranoid trends in the schizoid. We must realize that this characteristic is not by itself diagnostic of that disorder, for it is to be found in other disorders as well; and certainly it may be the central or principle characteristic of otherwise normal personalities. When the delusion has become systematized and dominates the individual's life, there has been established a psychosis which is called "paranoia." Far more commonly observed, however, are the temporary, unconnected, more or less incidental false beliefs which still rate as paranoid by reason of being irrationally held in spite of good and sensible evidence against them.

The delusions of the paranoid personality take various concrete directions. One is toward the courts. The litigious individual is forever taking others before the law; and every experienced judge has learned to recognize this, in many a litigant, as a personal trait that deserves more attention than the legal issue brought before the bar. Again paranoia may turn in the direction of grandiose delusions. An ex-serviceman claimed that he had a half-million dollars coming to him for his eleven months' enlistment period. Another confided to the present writer that he had discovered the Secret Mathematical Formula which was unlocking all the gates to all the areas of knowledge. But there is a potentially more serious direction which many delusions tend eventually to take: they lead into delusions of persecution. The persecutors need not be any particular persons: they may be the Masons, or lawyers, or even non-personal agencies formulated out of the latest discoveries of science. Many a patient has been convinced that X-rays, or telephones, or logarithms — and soon, no doubt, atomic energy and atom bombs — are secretly pursuing him and plotting against him. Often, however, an irrational and unreasoning fixed conviction weaves itself about one's neighbors, who steal one's silverware and linens, or about one's in-laws, who are guilty of treachery and illicit affairs. Incalculable harm is sometimes the consequence of the paranoid's accusations, unless and until he is recognized as pathological.

The preceding forms of psychotic behavior are among those that are largely psychogenic in causation, that is, are *functional* disorders. Several kinds, however, have definite *organic* bases in structural changes of the body. Since they have psychological effects of some interest we must notice two groups of them.

The Paretic Patient. When syphilis germs happen to direct their attacks upon the cerebrum, the destruction they wreak on highly important interconnecting tissues plays havoc with the man's behavior. Paresis is typically a disorder that affects men, often apparently sound and prosperous ones in middle life. It can be described briefly as *progressive deterioration in all phases.* At the zenith of his mental and physical powers, a man may gradually become a votary of every form of vice, and if not understood and put under care he will waste his family's wealth and astonish both his social and his business acquaintances with his conduct. Not least striking are the very extreme delusions often shown: his wealth is in the quadrillions, he has children all over the world, or he fashioned the moon with his own hands. At first, besides the eccentricities just mentioned, the clinician will note definite sensory and motor disturbances: inability to enunciate such words as "hippopotamus" or "Methodist Episcopal," to write a legible hand, to sew on buttons, and the like. As the patient grows worse he becomes fat instead of fit, stupid instead of active, and along with other muscles those of the face lose their tone and grow flabby and expressionless. After he is bed-ridden his dementia becomes profound, his emaciation exaggerated, he lapses into coma, and he is little more than a bulk of living flesh before death occurs.

Various treatments for this degenerative disease have been developed which are especially effective if the disease is diagnosed in its early stages, but it would take us too far afield to discuss these special clinical techniques here.

Alcoholic Personalities. Surely one of the most formidable agencies for precipitating psychotic disorders is alcohol. Every hospital and every clinician recognizes its potency. The effects of alcohol differ greatly from organism to organism; and where the effects of long-continued doses of the toxic substances are so severe as to warrant the appellation of psychosis, the patterns vary. The delirium and the visual hallucinations of *delirium tremens* are a matter of common knowledge. In another alcoholic form, *acute hallucinosis*, the hallucinations are auditory in character; and they furnish a medium through which the patients hear accusing voices. These in turn are an expression of his own anxiety feelings; and they frequently lead him to report his imagined enemies to the police. In *Korsakoff's* psychosis, a profound impairment of the intellectual operations appears in the shape of a loss of ability to recall anything newly and recently experienced. It is as if the impact of experience leaves no abiding impressions; consequently the patient shows confusion and some disorientation in time and space.

There are still other ways in which the personality organization may be impaired through alcoholic poisoning. Enough has been said, however, to suggest its weighty contribution to psychotic disorders.

REFERENCES

1. Allport, F. H. *Social Psychology*. Boston: Houghton Mifflin Company, 1924.
2. Allport, G. W., and H. S. Odbert. "Trait-names: a psycho-lexical study," *Psychol. Monogr.*, 1936, *47*, No. 211.
3. Allport, G. W. *Personality*. New York: Henry Holt and Company, 1937.

4. Cameron, N. The functional psychoses, in J. McV. Hunt, ed., *Personality and the Behavior Disorders*. New York: Ronald Press, 1944.

5. Cameron, N. *The Psychology of Behavior Disorders*. Boston: Houghton Mifflin Company, 1947.

6. Cattell, R. B. "The principal trait-clusters for describing personality," *Psychol. Bull.*, 1945, *42*, 129–161.

7. Freeman, W. "Constitutional factors in mental disorders," *Med. Ann. Dist. Columb.*, 1936, *5*, 287–297, 336–344.

8. Guilford, J. P., and R. B. Guilford. "An analysis of the factors in a typical test of introversion-extroversion," *J. Abnorm. Soc. Psychol.*, 1934, *28*, 377–399.

9. Harrington, W. "Recommendation quality and placement success," *Psychol. Monogr.*, 1943, No. 252.

10. Hartshorne, H., and M. A. May. *Studies in Deceit*. New York: The Macmillan Company, 1928.

11. Humm, D. G., and G. W. Wadsworth. "The Humm-Wadsworth temperament scale," *Person. J.*, 1934, *12*, 314–323. Los Angeles: Doncaster G. Humm Personnel Service, 1940.

12. Kretschmer, E. *Physique and Character* (trans.). New York: Harcourt, Brace and Company, 1925.

13. Malamud, W. "The Psychoneuroses," in J. McV. Hunt, ed., *Personality and the Behavior Disorders*. New York: Ronald Press, 1944.

14. Masserman, J. *Principles of Dynamic Psychiatry*. Philadelphia: W. B. Saunders Company, 1946.

15. Murray, H. A., *et al. Explorations in Personality*. New York: Oxford University Press, 1938.

16. Naccarati, S. "The morphologic aspect of intelligence," *Arch. Psychol., N.Y.*, 1921, No. 45.

17. Page, J. D. *Abnormal Psychology*. New York: McGraw-Hill Book Company, 1947.

18. Paterson, D. G. *Physique and Intellect*. New York: Appleton-Century-Crofts, 1930.

19. Rosanoff, A. J. "A theory of personality based mainly on psychiatric experience," *Psychol. Bull.*, 1920, *17*, 281–299.

20. Sheldon, W. H., and S. S. Stevens. *The Varieties of Temperament*. New York: Harper and Brothers, 1942.

21. Wertheimer, F. I., and F. E. Hesketh. "The significance of the physical constitution in mental disease," *Medical Monogr.*, v. 10. Williams and Wilkins, 1926.

22. Wolfle, D. "Factor analysis in the study of personality," *J. Abnorm. Soc. Psychol.*, 1942, *37*, 393–397.

21

SOCIAL DETERMINANTS OF PERSONALITY DEVELOPMENT

FAMILY DETERMINANTS

IN SEVERAL PLACES throughout this book points have been presented which bear upon the story of how the individual personality becomes organized. In Chapters 7 and 8, emphasis was upon the inside story, the more intimate and individual processes whereby the motivations of the newborn eventually become more and more highly integrated. In Chapter 17 some attention was directed to the social side of the story. In the present chapter we want to go into this more fully. What are some of the molding influences that bear upon the individual from without, that help to shape the ways in which his personality is organized?

The Importance of Infancy

"The child is father to the man." "As the twig is bent, so the tree's inclined." Many such proverbs epitomize the popular observation that the early years of the individual's life are of tremendous weight in determining his personality and his manner of behavior toward other people. In Chapter 4 we saw that in respect of general and basic characterists we must recognize the heavy contribution of the intrinsic biological maturation; but in later chapters (especially Chapter 17) we have also had to recognize the directive influences of environmental — especially social — factors. And it is a cardinal principle in contemporary studies that the intimate family relationships of the infant and child are of great influence in shaping his later adult attitudes toward people and toward personal situations. There is unanimity among psychologists on this general point: their interpretations of it, however, are widely varied. We shall best appreciate this variation if we note briefly two opposed extreme views on a particular question. The mother, of course, is in nearly all cases the first and most present source of social contacts. *What are the consequences, for personality-shaping, of two contrasted types of mother-attitude toward the infant and child?*

Some Results of Excessive Mothering [1]

A summer camp counselor once exclaimed, "If the doting mothers would only forget to write, we might be able to make men of their kids." Every clinical adviser knows the kind of patient who is unable to stand on his own feet, to make decisions for himself, to assume responsibilities. In many such cases, now, it has been demonstrated that this pattern of behavior can be traced to his "mom" (as some contemporary writers call her [30]), to a mother who had failed to wean him emotionally as he grew up, who had refused to untie the apron strings that bound him to her. She had continued to give him "smother love."

There is, for example, the case of a young man who held an advanced university degree yet who, when talking about his various difficulties and disorders, brought his "mom" into the conversation again and again. Eventually the full story was brought to light.

> Ever since his childhood his mother, or more properly his mom, has dominated him. After college, when he left home to take a well-paying job in another city, she carried on her domination by long-distance telephone. She repeatedly accused him of shirking his responsibility as a son in spite of the fact that he was contributing more toward her support than either of his two brothers. As a result he finally gave up his job to take another that paid less and promised less of a future so that he could live at home. Now she continually reminds him, "Harry, you are head of the house now. If you go away you will be throwing up your responsibility."
>
> In spite of his twenty-six years, he has never had a date with a girl — he "knows" that his mom would not approve. Even mild flirtations in the office in which he works upset him. At the time he enjoys them, but when he gets to thinking about them he wonders "what mom would say?"
>
> The psychiatrist treating him suggested that he assert himself and move away from his mother, reminding him that he could still see that she lived comfortably and free from want. She was healthy; it was not a case of a sick woman requiring care. He agreed and berated his mother for her dominance, but when he arrived for his next appointment he admitted that

---

[1] Here and in the following section the term "mothering" refers to a general kind of behavior toward an infant on the part of any older person or adult, whether or not such a person is the individual's actual physical mother.

he had been unable to make the break. His mother had gone into one of her emotional tirades and had even threatened to take the matter to court.

This mom's boy realizes that his life is being ruined, yet, at the moment, he is unable to do anything about it. He lacks the decision of a mature person. He wants freedom, he wants life, yet he is completely submerged and confused." [1]

If a picture of the person who has been maternally overprotected when an infant were to be drawn in its essential pattern it would be that of a tyrannical, selfish man or woman who expects constant attention, affection, and waiting-on; who reacts to any frustration or delay with impatience, outbursts, even assaults; who is completely at a loss when alone and thrown on his own resources; who in conversation may perhaps be gifted and charming through knowing how to pull out all the stops for getting his own ends. It is the picture of an egocentric psychopath. True, a person's full development in such a pattern is often tempered by his experiences with realities; still the basis of selfish and undisciplined yet helpless behavior toward others — the behavior of mom's child — is met with monotonous frequency in clinics.[2]

Some authorities claim that this individual attitude toward an all-protecting mom can be discerned on a large group scale in authoritative political regimes. A Nazi version of "Silent Night, Holy Night" contained a line that ran "Alles schlaft, einsam wacht Deutschland's Führer." [3] His burden of care for eighty-five million Germans, so the worshipful Nazi held, was eighty-five million times as heavy as that of any one citizen. Can the psychology of a people be traced back to the nursery? (Cf. pages 487 f.)

Some Results of Insufficient Mothering

But if oversolicitous mothering has disastrous effects on the personality, some effects of insufficient mothering are likewise unhappy. Developmental tests were once given to the infants of eleven institutions in the city of Vienna; and among other items, record was kept as to whether each one was cared for entirely by the institution nurses in their routine way or was given at least partial care by his or her own mother. It was found that those handled by nurses ranged in their D.Q. (develop-

[1] From E. A. Strecker, *Their Mothers' Sons* (Philadelphia: Lippincott, 1946). By permission of author and publisher.

[2] We have not taken trouble and space to treat these phenomena in any analytic explanatory manner. The reader will find it an interesting exercise to trace out discernible principles previously enunciated in Chapters 7, 8, 15, and 17, especially (a) the dynamisms in psychogenesis and (b) conditioning.

[3] All are sleeping; only Germany's Führer is watchful.

mental quotient, analogous to intelligence quotient) from .91 to 1.02, while those handled by their mothers ranged from 1.06 to 1.16 [4]. Even though we should want more data about the two groups of infants before we would consider this finding as important evidence, still the results are suggestive. They are mentioned here because they point to a principle well accepted in pediatrics: lack of adequate mothering with its demonstrations of affection may actually be physically harmful to the infant. In Bellevue and some other hospitals it has become a rule that every baby shall be picked up, carried around, cooed and sung to, patted and stroked and rocked a bit; and in some cases a system of employment of "Pharaoh's daughters" is part of the regime. In short, bacteriological considerations are being supplemented by psychological. And from the hospitals the infants are sent as early as possible to homes. Cases of "marasmus," that disease of wasting away through no ascertainable cause other than lack of individual, personal, affectionate attention [26], tell the story dramatically (Figure 200). This phenomenon may puzzle the reader who thinks mostly in terms of physical proc-

200   **A Case of Extreme Atrophy from Lack of Mothering**

A. Condition on May 18, after weeks of institutionalized impersonal but hygienic care. Weight 9½ pounds. *B.* Condition on September 8, after personal affectionate care in a home. Weight 18½ pounds. (*From H. D. Chapin, "A plan of dealing with atrophic infants and children,"* ARCH. PEDIAT., *1908, 25, 491–496. By permission of the publishers, E. B. Treat and Co., Inc.*)

esses. However, mothering activities occasion important alterations in the infant's bodily position, and a really great variety of stimulations through his optic, auditory, cutaneous, kinesthetic, and static sensory avenues, not to mention gastric and muscular exercise and other involvements. Moreover, similar phenomena are reported for lower animals, too, such as the dog and the ape.

The effects of mothering are not limited to the physical well-being of the baby. We know too little about the emotional responses of infancy to make a clear analysis, but any observer notes the sighing, guzzling sounds by which very young infants at the breast express their enjoyment of nursing — a clearly affective element. And he notes later the social character of the smile reflex as it becomes established. Certainly the whole gamut of affectionate stimulations contributes toward establishing a feeling of security, emotional responsiveness toward others, and general alertness. Clinical reports show that children deprived of these contacts and attentions by the Spartan training so often given to habituate them to artificial schedules instead of their own natural rhythms, tend to show such behavior traits as tantrums, enuresis, speech-defects, sensitiveness, attention-craving, negativism, and other symptoms of personal insecurity, of inability to give or receive affection, of lack of normal responsiveness in general [2, 4].

We have the confirmatory results of a non-clinical survey of the ten-year-old and sixteen-year-old children of a midwestern city [9]. These children were rated by each other on various items that bore on their personal character reputations — for responsibility, honesty, loyalty, friendliness, moral courage. They were also scored on a family-relations questionnaire which included such items as: degrees of parental participation in their work and play, sharing of confidences with their parents, sharing in the making of family decisions, degree of parental approval. Between the two sets of scores a correlation coefficient of .51 was obtained.

Interesting confirmatory evidence comes also from experimentation with lower animals. In one series, for example, white rats that had suffered feeding-frustration in their infancy showed the effects months afterward when adults, by displaying hoarding behavior to a much greater degree than did the control animals. Going hungry when infants made them food-hoarders for life, even after long periods of plenty [18]. It requires no stretch of the imagination to see analogies in some human personality-patterns.

A Reconciliation

We have had presented here two opposed extreme viewpoints on the parent-child relationship. Obviously the degree to which the one or the other is to be applied will depend on the individual case — and on common sense. We may get some guidance from considering that the cases which were furnished to show the need for building up security feelings were chosen largely from infancy, while those which showed the need for developing independence were taken largely from childhood. This consideration suggests the following precept: First establish physical health, emotional responsiveness, and feelings of security in the individual; then, on that foundation, gradually help him to become self-reliant and responsible toward others.

Other Determinants in Infancy

In the preceding section we have taken notice, in its two extreme degrees, of one of the intra-family relationships that mean much in determining the personality-pattern shaping itself in the child. There are many others. What is the effect on the child of having many, few, or no siblings? Of being the eldest or the youngest child? [1]. Is his or her relationship to the parent of the opposite sex likely to be any different than that to the parent of the same sex? [12] What is the effect if the family lives in cramped quarters and the child must share his room? What if the family is broken by divorce or separation or by the death of one parent? Does the nature of the father's occupation make a difference? What if there is high incidence of mental disease in the immediate family? Or high incidence of delinquent and criminal behavior? [14] How much will the child's nature be shaped by the patterns of his parent's behavior — casual, actively rejectant, or actively acceptant (an extension of the question of mothering behavior)? [5]

These are some of the questions we could ask about personality-determining factors within the family. When we enlarge our purview to include the neighborhood, the proximity of playground or dance hall, the opportunities for schooling, the prevalence of street gangs, the population density of the area, and other numerous conditions that form the extra-family environment of the child, we find a staggering complexity. However, when Frances turns out to be an effective leader of her Scout troop, while Freddie becomes a persistent truant, it is well to bear in mind that putting one's finger on the true predisposing cause or causes in either case is anything but a simple process of tracing back from consequents to antecedents.

Control as a Goal of Development

All through our survey of psychology such terms as "integrated" and "organized" have frequently recurred. Let us now recognize more explicitly a particular feature of the conception to which such terms refer. Not only are the different functions of a man hitched together, interwoven, associated; they are arranged into *hierarchies of control*. What may have been prepotent or dominant activities at a primitive level of development have in most cases become subject to inhibition or release by other activities; and the lifetime process of learning has been to a large extent the arranging and rearranging of these dominances. The operating of controls is seen in what is generally intended by the word *character*. Though ethical writers have delineated character for centuries, psychology is not ready to present a natural science of character. We can, however, approach the matter in a negative way, by considering two kinds of personality in which the control factor is weak.

First, there is a general type of person known to the clinical psychologists as a *psychopath*. He has been described in various ways. "He is weak in inhibiting his impulses." "He has uncontrollable impulses to satisfy his present cravings regardless." "He shows immaturity." "He seems unable to grasp what other people really expect of him." "He cannot use foresight to appreciate the consequences of his actions." "He frequently is afoul of social customs and laws." "He is excessively self-centered." "What he wants he wants." "Has a talent for compensating and rationalizing." "May have a front of much charm; but that is just window dressing." "Can strike the postures and mannerisms of a friendly fellow, but —." "He seems very calloused." "A lie is to him an ever present help in time of trouble." We can reduce these characterizations to a simple form: The psychopath reveals lack of control, and in two senses: (1) He lacks control of his more primitive and immediate motives by his more rational, elaborated, and remote motives. (2) He lacks control of his own individual wants by consideration of society's demands. He is not civilized.[1]

The second kind of personality whose control is weak is the alcoholized person, who presents somewhat the same picture as the psychopath. Highly satisfied with himself, he grows indifferent to the usual expectations others hold of him. His inhibitions grow weak (cf. page 663), as he cuts loose in quarreling, weeping, ogling, or boisterous laughter. He is not himself. He is dis-integrated; that is, his actions are not as usual under the control of his own more evolved sentiments, nor are they controlled by his usual recognition of what other people think.

---

[1] The technical meaning of the term *psychopath* is as given here. In common speech the word is sometimes used to describe all individuals who show marked behavioral disorders of any kind.

Upon examination, the two controls just mentioned are reducible to one. From evidence cited in other places in the present book, we know that the development of an individual's motives is certainly influenced by the attitudes and customs of his personal environment. And in nearly all discussions of such matters it is a central thread that just as "morals" are after all "mores" (tribal folkways of coercive sort), so most of the "higher" considerations that commonly direct a man's "lower" impulses are quite readily recognized as being the rules of the social group in which he lives.

The whole question of control is an area of psychology which, for all its great practical and theoretical importance, has not had the benefit of much scientific exploration. There are, to be sure, a few points of attack. Much has been discovered about "right of way" between reflexes, various forms of "inhibition," and like notions on a simple plane. A few studies have been made of how the organism tends to recover its internal equilibrium after it has been emotionally upset [11]. And the part played by the cerebral cortex in restraining the reflexes of sub-cortical levels especially involved in emotional behavior has been pointed out in a clinical way (see pages 324, 335 f.). But these scattered points remain scattered. We should, however, take some brief notice of the conceptions of a most influential recent authority.

Freud's Three "Components" of the Personality

The psychoanalytic notion of personality structure posits three chief aspects. The *id* is used collectively to include the manifold drives, passions, and motives of the human organism. It is the "great reservoir of libido[1]," the hinterland whence appear such biological urges as sex and aggressiveness. We see it clearly in the newborn who wants what he wants when he wants it. It may be styled "unmoral," or — we might say — "premoral." Only the controls of sensory pleasures and pains operate here — the so-called "pleasure principle." This is human nature in the raw. The *ego* is a name by which Freud and his followers personify in a collective way those controls that begin to operate when the child comes into contact with hard realities — the so-called "reality principle." His perceptual recognition that he can do this but cannot without pain and penalty do that, leads to that control of his behavior which we commonly call prudence or foresight. The prudent person is realistic. Finally, there emerges a kind of personal control which Freud has called the *super-ego*. In consequence of the pressures exerted by the individual's social group, he acquires many moralities and other inhibi-

---

[1] This term was briefly discussed on page 143.

tions. He develops what we call in common parlance a "conscience." This is the high product of the civilizing process. Not everyone achieves this form of control. It is glaringly weak or absent in the criminal or anti-social person, in the psychopathic or the alcoholized.

We do not need to personify the id, the ego, and the super-ego, as Freud and his followers seem often to do, in order to find the threefold notion useful. In everyday life, though we speak of "the conscience" and of its "still, small voice," we never really think of it as an independent agency operating from some inner secret seat. So likewise the three terms from Freudian literature need not be taken too literally; they can serve as useful shorthand terms for describing this or that character or degree of personality organization and control.

CULTURAL DETERMINANTS OF PERSONALITY [1]

The Principle Stated

We must admit the possibility that at least a fraction of the stability to be found in the organization of each individual is attributable to a stable environment in which he has been living. This carries us back to a previous question: What are the known effects of environmental controls on personality manifestations? If one's personality is, as we have defined it, a matter of his being both socially stimulating and socially

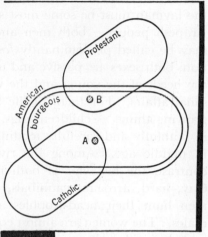

201 Membership in Groups as Determining Personalities

Individuals *A* and *B*, by virtue of their membership in the groups *American* and *bourgeois*, would be similar in their attitudes and behavior; but by virtue of their membership in the *Catholic* and the *Protestant* groups, respectively, they would be different in their attitudes and behavior in many situations. (*From J. F. Brown*, PSYCHOLOGY AND THE SOCIAL ORDER, *McGraw-Hill, 1936.*)

reactive, it is reasonable to suppose that his social surroundings have had much to do with its building-up.

One way of schematizing this importance to the individual of his membership in social groups is that used in Figure 201, wherein the make-up of the individual is shown to be determined in some degree by

[1] The material of this section supplements and is supplemented by the materials we have dealt with in Chapter 17, especially in the sections on the Socialization of the Individual and on Cooperation and Competition. There the point of view was more that of society; here it is more that of the individual.

his membership in certain social groups. A person's pattern of traits is chiefly determined by the groups in which he has membership.

Differential Effects of Divergent Primitive Cultures

The point just mentioned is being much emphasized by anthropologists today. Their view is clearly (if perhaps extremely) represented in a recent study on the primitive peoples on the island of New Guinea [24]. In the course of a two years' expedition to that island exhaustive observations made of three primitive tribes brought to light what to the layman must be some most striking facts. The mountain-dwelling Arapesh people — both men and women — reveal a personality that may be called predominantly *feminine*. Despite differences in occupation, both sexes are passive and unaggressive, cooperative, responsive to the needs of the young and the weak, and preoccupied with their personal affairs. For them, if life is an adventure it is an adventure in growing things — children, pigs, yams, coconuts. They are interested in faithfully and carefully tending their charges until happy retirement in middle age. Among the river-dwelling Mundugumor, in perfect contrast, the behavior of both men and women is actively *masculine*. Gay, hard, arrogant cannibals, they care little for human life. The men hunt their head-trophies among women, children, and weakly males. The women are almost equally careless of the young, the elderly, and the sickly. In contrast to both the other tribes, as well as to our own culture, the lake-dwelling Tchambuli present both the masculine and the feminine patterns of temperament but reversed as between the sexes. Every man is an artist in some line; he is concerned much with his role in society, showing little responsibility and much emotional and economic dependence upon women. The women are the fishers and managers, looking after the men and boys with solicitude. In courtship, too, women play the active role.

The malleability of human temperament and whole personality, revealed so strikingly for masculinity-femininity, has been the subject-matter of other anthropological studies of primitive tribes in which other sides of human nature have been taken as the starting point [7]. There is, for example, a marked contrast between the kind of American Indian who has grown up in the culture of the Kwakiutl and he who has grown up in the culture of the Zuñi. This point we have brought out in an earlier chapter (pages 497 f.).

Differential Effects of Different Civilized Culture-Levels

We have just seen how the encouraging-discouraging elements of an individual's surrounding culture can profoundly determine the temperamental pattern of his personality. It can determine its general breadth and richness, also. A wide range of traits is likely to be developed in a social organization where variety of experiences is provided — making contacts with many persons, handling many materials and instruments, encountering problems and difficulties. This was found, for example, by comparison of four different communities of English and Scotch-Irish ancestry in the Blue Ridge Mountain section.

In C. Hollow, (Colvin Hollow), cut off almost completely from the currents of American life, the inhabitants live in scattered, mud-plastered log huts. They have neither cattle nor chickens, and tend only small cabbage and corn patches. Their food is strictly of the hog-and-hominy sort. No general road leads to the outside world nor is there any system of communication between cabins. No church nor local government nor other common meeting-place affords contacts. R. Hollow, (typified by Briarsville), the other extreme of the four places studied, is a more substantial compact community. The cabins are solidly built and much better furnished. The cultivated patches are almost farms, and there is a fair amount of cash in circulation among the people. Food is more varied. A public road and daily mail service connect with the outside world. A seven-months' school term, ability to read newspapers and to order from mail order catalogs, furnish indirect avenues of contact with the world. The men and women are more friendly to each other, as well as to strangers. Even some social stratification is setting in. The contrast between the children of different hollows was evident at once, as is suggested in Figure 202.

Children of these four communities when examined by several intelligence tests showed a consistent increase in score from C. Hollow to R. Hollow. But what interests us more at present are the differences in their general modes of behavior, especially social and emotional. To take the two extreme cases, again, the children of R. Hollow as compared with those of C. Hollow showed a greater variety of interests and quicker apprehension of novel ideas. They adjusted themselves more readily to strangers, were more critical of other children, were more interested in matters of social prestige, and displayed more definite attitudes on matters of morals and propriety. Their worries were different: the C. children worried only about food and clothing, storms and cold, while the R. children worried about their school grades, and about personal matters such as the attitudes of others toward themselves. In a word, those children who had a *greater variety of social conditions and contacts developed more varied personality-traits and more flexibility or adaptability.*

202   **Culture-Level and Child Personality**

The two groups of children have a common racial ancestry, but are being reared in different levels of culture. Note not only clothing and building but also apparent attitude toward cameraman. *A.* A Colvin Hollow group, of extremely low living standards and general culture. *B.* A group from Briarsville, where the living and cultural standards are higher. (*From M. Sherman and T. R. Henry,* HOLLOW FOLK, *Crowell, 1933. Photos by courtesy of Dr. Sherman.*)

Is Mental Normality Relative to the Culture?

In the last section of the preceding chapter we reviewed a few of the well-recognized patterns of personality which are called "abnormal." At this point we should note that this classification of "abnormal" is one which *we* in *our* culture are applying to these different patterns. But are they all considered abnormal among all peoples, in all places, and at all times? Ruth Benedict is one of the several anthropologists who have pointed out the contrary [8]. We cannot hope to improve on some of her phrasings:

> The tribes we have described have all of them their non-participating "abnormal" individuals. The individual in Dobu who was thoroughly disoriented was the man who was naturally friendly and found activity an end in itself. He was a pleasant fellow who did not seek to overthrow his fellows or to punish them. He worked for anyone who asked him, and he was tireless in carrying out their commands. He was not filled by a terror of the dark like his fellows, and he did not, as they did, utterly inhibit simple public responses of friendliness toward women closely related, like a wife or sister. He often patted them playfully in public. In any other Dobuan this was scandalous behavior, but in him it was regarded as merely silly. The village treated him in a kindly enough fashion, not taking advantage of him or making a sport of ridiculing him, but he was definitely regarded as one who was outside the game. . . .

> Most ethnologists have had similar experiences in recognizing that the persons who are put outside the pale of society with contempt are not those who would be placed there by another culture. . . .

> In the Middle Ages when Catholicism made the ecstatic experience the mark of sainthood, the trance experience was greatly valued, and those to whom the response was congenial, instead of being overwhelmed by a catastrophe as in our century, were given confidence in the pursuit of their careers. It was a validation of ambitions, not a stigma of insanity. . . .

> Among primitive peoples, trance and catalepsy have been honored in the extreme. Some of the Indian tribes of California accorded prestige principally to those who passed through certain trance experiences. . . .

> The Puritan divines of New England . . . were the last persons whom contemporary opinion in the colonies regarded as psychopathic. Few prestige groups in any culture have been allowed such complete intellectual and emotional dictatorship as they were. They were the voice of God. Yet to a modern observer it is they, not the confused and tormented women they put to death as witches, who were the psychoneurotics of Puritan New England. A sense of guilt as extreme as they portrayed and demanded both in their own conversion experiences and in those of their converts is found in a slightly saner civilization only in institutions for mental diseases.[1]

[1] From R. Benedict, *Patterns of Culture* (Boston: Houghton Mifflin Company, 1934). By permission of author and publishers.

We can make a new application of Wesley's remark, "There, but for the grace of God, go I!"

Finally this viewpoint can be brought to bear upon our own culture of the present decade and the sort of personality it tends to produce. When regarded from the anthropologist's vantage position, the rugged individualism exalted in American life is seen to have, after all, much the nature of a megalomania, in which competitive self-aggrandizement leads to the accumulation of properties in order to keep up with and outdo the Joneses in conspicuous waste. It is a megalomania exceeded only by that of the Kwakiutl Indians of whom we learned in Chapter 17. And according to some psychoanalysts [17], this culture shapes up the kind of personality that combines fear with hostility; hence to unusual degree a person so constituted needs reassurance to relieve his fearful insecurity. Such is the neurotic personality created by our times.

METHODS OF EXPLORING PERSONALITY

The Questionnaire Inventory

Ever since Woodworth's pioneer attempt in World War I [32], a favorite procedure in attempting to get at an individual's personality structure, especially with reference to his nervous stability, has been to have him answer a list of statements about himself as "true" or "false." Today one of the best accepted lists is that of the Minnesota Multiphasic Personality Inventory (MMPI). Here are a few items that are similar to, but not identical with, items in that inventory.

> I hardly ever have dizzy spells.
> At home they find fault with me a great deal.
> I hate to have to make up my mind in a hurry.
> When ascending a stairway I usually count the steps.
> I believe in life beyond the grave.
> I like to play practical jokes on people.
> I just don't have patience with a slow person.
> Lots of times I can't help feeling something is going to happen.
> Overly friendly people don't fool me much.
> I like horse operas better than soap operas.
> Most people join church just for selfish advantage.
> When things go wrong I just feel like giving up.
> I like fixing electric light connections.

Such statements may strike the reader as too narrow in their reference and as too subject to qualifications in many cases. But the whole set consists of over five hundred statements, so that these accidental faults of individual items tend to be absorbed by the very number of the items. In any case, the proof of the pudding is in the eating. Has the inventory method proved useful? Many forms and revisions of the method have shown high *reliability* (self-consistency, cf. pages 105 f.). And in the MMPI the *validity* also has frequently been satisfactory, as in sorting out cases that need guidance on a college campus [15], or in screening out enlisted men in the Army Air Force [28]. In such applications the results checked well with clinical diagnoses based on other methods of examination.

Another fault the reader is likely to find with such a list of personal statements is that it would seem easy for an examinee to give a deceptively favorable picture of himself by falsifying on many items. This is all too likely to be the rule rather than the exception when self-ratings are factors in obtaining a job or a promotion; but the danger is small when the self-ratings are for the information of a clinician or counselor whose aid is being sought by the examinee. In anticipation of this danger, however, the MMPI includes a number of statements that, if answered in certain ways, will reveal that the subject has chosen in every case the response that he thinks places him in the most acceptable light socially. Furthermore, just as in the case of other questioning devices, a personality inventory can be cast into the form of *forced-choices* where the subject is faced repeatedly with what he takes to be equally-acceptable or equally-unacceptable answers, but where only one answer has actually been found by the examiners to be indicative. Since in each item the examinee has no choice between what he supposes the examiner will score as a better or a worse answer, he is likely to be more objective and factual in his choosing. For example, employees in a cotton mill were offered an opportunity to decide what work they would like best. They were given pairs of words like the following, and instructed: "You MUST choose one word from each pair; just take the one that is MORE like you."

(1) temperate in everything	(1) thick-fingered
(2) give no unasked-for advice	(2) submissive
(1) stand up for your rights	(1) up and down in moods
(2) conscientious	(2) a daredevil

The Rating Scale

The questionnaire inventory is concerned with what a man says he does. However, we often want to know what others say he does. By rating scales the general character sketch, such as that mentioned on page 601, is refined in two ways. The particular dimensions or *traits* are *specified* by the inquirer; and the rater is asked to indicate, in respect to each, *how much* of it is revealed by the subject.

Rating scales have been employed in several practical fields: in commercial and industrial firms, for selecting and promoting employees; in teachers' and other employment bureaus, for fitting square pegs to square holes; on college campuses, for assisting the individual to understand and meet his emotional and social problems; and in the armed services, to assess the qualifications of officers.

One thing is at once apparent. Even the best rating scales depend definitely upon the cooperation obtained from the raters. For there is the well-known "halo effect," whereby the rater's general impression of his man influences his marking of a particular trait. And equally dangerous is the all-too-human tendency to let one's personal liking or disliking dictate one's judgments, sometimes quite intentionally. Here the

TABLE

XLVI   Forced Choice Rating of Army Officer Traits

A. Hot-tempered

B. Fails to demonstrate originality

C. Reserved

D. Impresses people favorably

A. Boastful

B. Inspires pride in the organization

C. Lacks tact

D. Thoughtful of others

The rater is to black in those spaces that indicate his judgment as to which of the four traits in each box are most and least descriptive of the candidate in question. The marking by one rater of one candidate is shown.

From an Efficiency Report, Department of the Army.
By permission of Major General Edward F. Witsell.

forced-choice technique is again a safeguard — doubly so in a scale developed for use with Army personnel, wherein the rater indicates which one of four traits (two favorable, two unfavorable) is *most* like the subject and which is *least* like him. Two sample items, and their blanks for machine scoring (cf. page 174) are shown in Table XLVI.

The Thematic Apperception Technique

Neither of the methods of personality study so far described allows the examiner a very intimate view of the examinee's underlying drives, needs, motives. To get at this aspect of his make-up, certain *projective* techniques have been devised. As we have seen earlier (pages 187 f.) any person tends to read himself into other people, and so (often unawares) to reveal his emotional trends, his attitudes, his persistent personal problems.

One of the most useful projective methods is Murray's Thematic Apperception Technique [25], in which a number of pictures (see Figure 203) are presented to the subject, one at a time, with such instruction as the following. "I shall show you a picture, and I want you to make up a plot or story for which it might be used as an illustration. What is the relationship of the individuals in the picture? What has happened? What are their thoughts and feelings? What will be the outcome?"

This provides opportunity for a person to project or read into the situation and the persons of the picture his own personal situation-

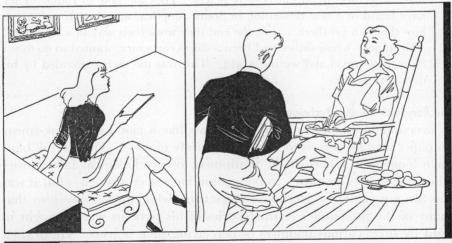

203   **Pictures Similar to Thematic Apperception Technique**

The use of pictures of this general type, but not identical with either of these. is described in the text.

problems and his own emotional and thought reactions. It is known that many a literary creative artist tends to embody in his fictional characters, wittingly or unwittingly, his private likes and dislikes, ambitions, disappointments, rebellions, fantasies, and the like [23]. And any clinician recognizes the manifold ways in which any normal person gives away his secret feeling-attitudes by the way he speaks of others. So through the thematic apperception technique the discerning and practiced examiner, after getting his subject's full unhurried stories for all pictures in the series, can often divine some unifying themes running through them all. One of the original subjects at Murray's Harvard clinic will serve as an example.

In his stories three of the scenes were laid on board ship, two in the Orient. About a picture which illustrates a middle-aged man talking to a younger man, the subject said: "The older man is educated and has traveled a lot. He convinces the other to travel; to take a job that will take him to different places." In a picture which illustrates a young man sitting in a chair brooding rather disconsolately, this subject said: "This is a business man who runs quite a business in town. He is weighing the possibility of a European trip. He has been arguing with his wife on the subject. She got angry because he would not go, and finally took up her hat and left. He is thinking it over. He changes his opinion, goes out and buys tickets." In another picture illustrating two laborers engaged in conversation, the same subject said: "These two fellows are a pair of adventurers. They always manage to meet in out-of-the-way places. They are now in India. They have heard of a new revolution in South America, and they are planning how they can get there. . . . In the end they work their way in a freighter." This subject, whose father had been a ship's carpenter, wanted to go to sea himself, to travel and see the world. This was the theme revealed by his dominant fantasy.[1]

The Rorschach Ink-Blot Technique

Everyone knows how an irregular mass like a cloud or an ink-smear on paper may be perceived in a great variety of ways. Printed ink blots have long been a part of the equipment of psychological laboratories where the factors operating in perception have been studied. But it was the Swiss psychiatrist Hermann Rorschach who came to see also that many of the profounder characteristics of his patients were brought to light by their various manners of perceiving such objects. He devised a set of ten blots, some in black and gray, some with colors added; and on the basis of acute analyses of how his different patients reacted to

[1] From *Explorations in Personality* by H. A. Murray, copyright, 1938, by Oxford University Press, New York, Inc. By permission of the publishers.

them, he eventually worked out elaborate methods of tabulating and scoring. Comparing these analyses with the case histories and the independent psychiatric diagnoses of his patients, he tentatively set forth a system which, in the years following his untimely death, has increasingly gained favor with clinical examiners. It certainly deserves to be presented in a general way to the inquiring student of psychology, even though, being a clinical tool, it should not be publicly exhibited in detail [27].

Figure 204 shows an ink-blot of a type similar to many in the Rorschach standardized set. Suppose it is displayed to an examinee with the question, "What might this be? What do you see on this card?" Of course, there are countless different ways of "seeing" it. One might see at first a fixed column or gargoyle with two faces,

204 Ink Blot Test of Rorschach Type

Similar to those of the Rorschach series, but not identical with them. Discussion in text.

or a descending angel with high spread wings, or even the antenna of a crayfish (at the top) or perhaps a two-headed ape. These and other answers can then be analyzed from different standpoints.

1. Does the examinee regard the figure as a *whole* (*W*) or does he see *details* (*D*) first? If details, are they normal ones or unusual or minute ones (*Dd*), or ones that are seen as representing some piece of a thing (*Do*), or are they white spaces (*S*)?

2. Is his *way of regarding* it determined more by its form or visual design (*F*), or by kinesthetic or movement influences (*M*), or by the color when color is present (*C*)?

3. As to *content*, does he note animals (*A*), human beings (*H*), inanimate objects (*Obj.*), or a landscape (*ldscp.*)?

Both the initial way the subject regards it and any succession of changes are matters for the examiner to record. Recent work with the Rorschach has increased the number of factors taken into account in making an interpretation of a protocol: texture, shading, vista, reaction time, originality or banality of productions, and many others.

From Table XLVII we can get some notion of how some of the results are set down at one preliminary stage. It shows Rorschach's abbreviated recordings of four subjects as they reacted to four out of the series of ten plates. We note that this is clearly not an assembly of data to be counted and calculated: the differences from person to person in responses to a given card are essentially qualitative differences. Indeed it is not the scores so much as the inter-relationships of scores, their ordering into a consistent perspective, their falling into a picture, that become revealing. To be able to give them such value the examiner must be versed in Rorschach's observations, and those of his more recent exponents, and by all means must have had many cases of his own to observe, both with and without supervision. The training demanded is not simple, for the richness and complexity of the psychological meanings to be attributed to this and that detail of record — or better, to the totality of records — for a given examinee defy simple statement.

TABLE XLVII

Beginnings of Some Rorschach Records of Responses to Four of the Cards

Plate I	W F+ A	Dd F— Ad orig.	W F+ A	D M+ H
Plate III	W M+ H	Do F+ Hd	W M+ H	W M+ H
Plate VI	W F Obj. orig.	Do F+ Ad	W F+ A	W F+ Obj. orig.
Plate IX	S F— A orig.	D C— map orig.	D F— A	S F+ Obj.

The clinician actually tabulates the responses of his subject in far more elaborate form than that shown in the table. He inspects his array carefully. He is *not* to add up results as scores or to introduce other quantitative procedures. Rather he is to inspect his whole array of data much as he would a picture; and from the inspection he is to get the true portrait of his subject as a unified personality — his emotional temperament, his expressive movements, interests, talents, occupational tendencies, and even his philosophy of life [6, 19]. And the same response element may have different meanings in different personality patterns.

To the experimentalist and to the statistician long rigorously trained in the precise manipulation of accurate mechanical instruments and of detailed mathematical formulae, both Murray's and Rorschach's procedures at first might seem the loosest and most dangerously unscientific kind of guesswork.

Here let us note that a profound difference of attitude has formerly been observable between American psychological work on the one hand and German-Swiss psychological work on the other. From the viewpoint of the latter, the fruitful way to investigate personality is to make an intensive examination of a very few individual subjects so as to determine the general pattern or style of behavior for each [3, 31]. We dare not hastily decry this claim. We have seen in our study of Perceiving that the adequate recognition and appreciation of a given thing, person, or situation, is often achieved through insight. Perception is a configural performance. Similarly, it is claimed, a true understanding of another person is not obtained by mechanically adding up his scores on a number of tests. You must "get" him as you would a picture or a tune — as a unique unity. This is sound enough. One important reminder, however, is in order. Consider the clinical practitioner in psychology and in medicine: he, too, tentatively sizes up and ultimately understands each of his patients in just this way, but it must be remembered that he has not become a skillful practitioner by merely exercising hunches through the years. Judgment ripens out of abundant specific experiences.

The Psychoanalytic Method

The most celebrated method of exploring the personality is that first developed by Freud, a physician of Vienna. It is not, however, simply and primarily a method for determining the general pattern or structure of personality; it is rather a method for probing for something in particular. It is not adaptable to the problems demanding the kinds of personal assaying that we have been reviewing in this section: it was originally devised for diagnosing the cause of neurotic illness. In his interviews with psychoneurotics Freud found it effective to let the perturbed patient *talk it out*, as fully and freely as possible, by encouraging him to let himself go and say anything and everything that came to mind. If successful this method leads to an *emotional catharsis*, a release from guilt and anxiety. Yet psychoanalysis is far from being as simple a procedure as this sounds.

Free association, constantly encouraged in the patient, is expected to lead him eventually to recall some incident or desire, often of his earlier years, that has been crucial in producing his illness. The incident is one which is so unacceptable and painful that he simply cannot bear to think about it; it has been *repressed* from his conscious experience. In his sessions of free talking-out the patient will at times experience a block or *resistance* to the recalling. And that is interpreted by the analyst as a manifestation of repression, or *censorship*. One way of partially circumventing this censorship the analyst finds in examination of the patient's *dreams*. For it is when dreaming that one's guard is lowered; and telltale fragments of the content of the dream may prove revealing if freely interpreted. Quietly following up such leads, the analyst may assist the patient to work back around the point of blocked recall (the resistance) and eventually to bring to light the repressed incidents or desires. The repression may be revealed in other ways than mere blocking of recall: it may force the patient's ideas and words into distorted or *symbolic* or *just-reversed* forms — anything in fact to prevent their being recognized. All the skill of the analyst may be required to work through these disguises [12, 13, 16].

Many hour-long sessions of analysis are held in the hope that, once the repressed memories are brought to light again, they may be seen to be harmless after all, or at least to be something which the patient can be helped to deal with in a direct and positive way. If either of these ends can be achieved, his neurotic illness is expected to disappear.[1]

Psychoanalytic doctrine has in it much that strikes certain critical psychologists as fantastic, far-fetched. But as a central doctrine it has achieved so strong a place with many psychiatrists, psychologists, and anthropologists, that the manifest need now is for translation of the concepts into more scientifically acceptable biological-psychological terms. In this place we cannot follow the matter further. However, in order to give the reader some of the feel of psychoanalysis, we present here one of Freud's cases, though without much mention of procedure.

A Case for Psychoanalysis

In this simple case the reader should be able to break the story down into principles and concepts with which he is not unfamiliar. He will find especially relevant material in Chapters 7, 8, 9, 14, and 17. The case, while a simple one as Freud's cases go, yet presents a few of the cardinal points in psychoanalytic theory. Note the heavy emphasis upon motives; upon emotional reactions to frustrating circumstances; upon the difficulty one has in really understanding himself; upon the further manifestation of this difficulty in resisting deep probings, though all unaware of such resistance; upon the active nature of forgetting.

> A young officer, home on short leave of absence, asked me to treat his
> mother-in-law, who was living in the happiest surroundings and yet was
> embittering her own and her family's lives by a nonsensical idea. I found
> her a well-preserved lady, fifty-three years of age, of a friendly, simple dis-
> position, who gave without hesitation the following account of herself. She

---

[1] This is certainly a highly condensed account! The reader who is interested will find the italicized terms useful as suggesting some of the key notions with which he would want to become familiar and with which he would start in order to organize his grasp of the subject.

is most happily married, and lives in the country with her husband who manages a large factory. She cannot say enough of her husband's kindness and consideration; theirs had been a love-marriage thirty years ago, since when they had never had a cloud, a quarrel, or a moment's jealousy. Her two children have both married well, but her husband's sense of duty keeps him still at work. A year before, an incredible and, to her, incomprehensible thing happened. She received an anonymous letter telling her that her excellent husband was carrying on an intrigue with a young girl, and believed it on the spot — since then her happiness has been destroyed. The details were more or less as follows: she had a housemaid with whom she discussed confidential matters, perhaps rather too freely. This young woman cherished a positively venomous hatred for another girl who had succeeded better in life than herself, although of no better origin. Instead of going into service, the other young woman had had a commercial training, been taken into the factory and, owing to vacancies caused by the absence of staff on service in the field, had been promoted to a good position. She lived in the factory, knew all the gentlemen, and was even addressed as "Miss." The other one who had been left behind in life was only too ready to accuse her former schoolmate of all possible evil. One day our patient and her housemaid were discussing an elderly gentleman who had visited the house and of whom it was said that he did not live with his wife but kept a mistress. Why, she did not know, but she suddenly said: "I cannot imagine anything more awful than to hear that my husband had a mistress." The next day she received by post an anonymous letter in disguised handwriting which informed her of the very thing she had just imagined. She concluded — probably correctly — that the letter was the handiwork of her malicious housemaid, for the woman who was named as the mistress of her husband was the very girl who was the object of this housemaid's hatred. Although she at once saw through the plot and had seen enough of such cowardly accusations in her own surroundings to place little credence in them, our patient was nevertheless prostrated by this letter. She became terribly excited and at once sent for her husband to overwhelm him with reproaches. The husband laughingly denied the accusation and did the best thing he could. He sent for the family physician (who also attended the factory), and he did his best to calm the unhappy lady. The next thing they did was also most reasonable. The housemaid was dismissed, but not the supposed mistress. From that time on the patient claims to have repeatedly brought herself to a calm view of the matter, so that she no longer believes the contents of the letter; but it has never gone very deep nor lasted very long. It was enough to hear the young woman's name mentioned, or to meet her in the street, for a new attack of suspicion, agony, and reproaches to break out.

First, I shall ask you to notice this incomprehensible detail; that the anonymous letter on which her delusion is founded was positively provoked by the patient herself, by her saying to the scheming housemaid the day before that nothing could be more awful than to hear that her husband had an intrigue with a young woman. She first put the idea of sending the letter into the servant's mind by this. So the delusion acquires a certain independence of the letter; it existed beforehand as a fear — or, as a wish? — in her mind. Besides this, the further small indications revealed in the bare two hours of analysis are noteworthy. The patient responded very coldly, it is true, to the request to tell me her further thoughts, ideas, and recollections, after she had finished her story. She declared that nothing came to her mind, she had told me everything; and after two hours the attempt had to be given up, because she announced that she felt quite well already and was certain that the morbid idea would not return. Her saying this was naturally due to resistance and to the fear of further analysis. In these two hours she had let fall some remarks, nevertheless, which made a certain interpretation not only possible but inevitable, and this interpretation threw a sharp light on the origin of the delusion of jealousy. There actually existed in her an infatuation for a young man, for the very son-in-law who had urged her to seek assistance. Of this infatuation she herself knew nothing or only perhaps very little. . . . Such an infatuation, such a monstrous, impossible thing, could not come into her conscious mind; it persisted, nevertheless, and unconsciously exerted a heavy pressure. Something had to happen, some sort of relief had to be found; and the simplest alleviation lay in that mechanism of displacement which so regularly plays its part in the formation of delusional jealousy. If not merely she, old woman that she was, were in love with a young man, but if only her old husband too were in love with a young mistress, then her torturing conscience would be absolved from the infidelity. The phantasy of her husband's infidelity was thus a cooling balm on her burning wound. Of her own love she never became conscious; but its reflection in the delusion, which brought such advantages, thus became compulsive, delusional and conscious.[1]

This case is free of the more bizarre concepts of psychoanalysis. The almost fantastic nature of such concepts, however, can be better understood if we bear in mind two things. First, they have grown up in the course of a clinical practice which has boldly attempted to bring to the surface and to understand the emotional undercurrents of human beings. These undercurrents had gone undetected through the centuries, and began to be recognized only when abnormals were viewed as "people" and given study. In the second place, the urgencies of clinical practice have not encouraged the application of controls by experimental and statistical checks. Here, however, the present-day growing interest in experimental psychodynamics is a promising discipline.

[1] From S. Freud, *A General Introduction to Psychoanalysis* (trans. by J. Reviere; Garden City, N.Y.: Garden City Publishing Company, 1935), pp. 221–222, 224–225. By permission of the Liveright Publishing Corporation.

REFERENCES

1. Adler, A. *Problems of Neurosis.* London: Kegan Paul, Trench, Trübner, 1929.
2. Aldrich, C. A. "The role of gratification in early development," *J. Pediat.*, 1939, *15*, 578–582. With M. Aldrich. *Babies are Human Beings.* New York: The Macmillan Company, 1939.
3. Ansbacher, H. L. "German military psychology," *Psychol. Bull.*, 1941, *38*, 370–392. "Murray's and Simoneit's methods of personality study," *J. Abn. Soc. Psychol.*, 1941, *36*, 589–592.
4. Bakwin, R. M., and H. Bakwin. *Psychologic Care during Infancy and Childhood.* New York: Appleton-Century-Crofts, 1942.
5. Baldwin, A. L., J. Kalhorn, and F. H. Breese. "Patterns of parent behavior," *Psychol. Monogr.*, 1945, *58*, No. 268.
6. Beck, S. J. *Rorschach's Test.* 2 vols. New York: Grune and Stratton, 1944, 1945.
7. Benedict, R. *Patterns of Culture.* Boston: Houghton Mifflin Company, 1934.
8. Benedict, R. "Anthropology and the abnormal," *J. Gen. Psychol.*, 1934, *10*, 59–82.
9. Brown, A. W., J. Morrison, and G. B. Couch. "Influence of affectional family relationships on character development," *J. Abn. Soc. Psychol.*, 1947, *42*, 422–428.
10. Ellis, A., and H. S. Conrad. "The validity of personality inventories in military practice," *Psychol. Bull.*, 1948, *45*, 385–426.
11. Freeman, G. L., and J. H. Pathman. "The relation of overt muscular discharge to physiological recovery from experimentally induced displacement," *J. Exper. Psychol.*, 1942, *30*, 161–174.
12. Freud, S. *The Basic Writings of Sigmund Freud.* New York: Modern Library, 1938.
13. Freud, S. *A General Introduction to Psychoanalysis.* Garden City, N.Y.: Garden City Publishing Company, 1943.
14. Glueck, S., and E. T. Glueck. *One Thousand Juvenile Delinquents.* Cambridge, Mass.: Harvard University Press, 1934.
15. Hampton, P. J. "The Minnesota Multiphasic Personality Inventory as a psychometric tool for diagnosing personality disorders among college students," *J. Soc. Psychol.*, 1947, *26*, 99–108.
16. Healy, W., A. F. Bronner, and A. M. Bowers. *The Structure and Meaning of Psychoanalysis.* New York: Alfred A. Knopf, 1930.
17. Horney, K. *The Neurotic Personality of our Time.* New York: W. W. Norton and Company, 1937. *New Ways in Psychoanalysis.* Norton, 1939.
18. Hunt, J. McV., H. Schlosberg, R. L. Solomon, E. Stellar. "Studies of the effects of infantile experience on adult behavior in rats: I," *J. Comp. and Physiol. Psychol.*, 1947, *40*, 291–304.

19. Klopfer, B., and D. M. Kelley. *The Rorschach Technique.* Yonkers, N.Y.: World Book Company, 1942.

20. Kluckhohn, C., and H. A. Murray. *Personality.* New York: Alfred A. Knopf, 1948.

21. Levy, D. M. *Maternal Overprotection.* New York: Columbia University Press, 1943.

22. Masserman, J. H. *Principles of Dynamic Psychiatry.* Philadelphia: W. B. Saunders Company, 1946.

23. McCurdy, H. G., "Literature and Personality: an analysis of the novels of D. H. Lawrence," *Char. & Pers.*, 1940, *8*, 181–203, 311–322.

24. Mead, M. *Sex and Temperament in Three Primitive Societies.* New York: William Morrow and Company, 1935.

25. Murray, H. A., *et al. Explorations in Personality.* New York: Oxford University Press, 1938.

26. Ribble, M. A. *The Rights of Infants.* New York: Columbia University Press, 1943.

27. Rorschach, H. *Psychodiagnostics* (trans. by Lemkau and Kronenberg). Berne: Hans Huber (Grune and Stratton), 1942.

28. Schmidt, H. O. "Test profiles as a diagnostic aid: the Minnesota Multiphasic Inventory," *J. Appl. Psychol.*, 1945, *29*, 115–131.

29. Sherman, M., and T. R. Henry. *Hollow Folk.* New York: Thomas V. Crowell Company, 1933.

30. Strecker, E. A. *Their Mothers' Sons.* Philadelphia: J. B. Lippincott Company, 1946.

31. Vernon, P. E. "The American and the German methods of approach to the study of temperament and personality," *Brit. J. Psychol.*, 1933, *24*, 156–177.

32. Woodworth, R. S. *Personal Data Sheet.* Chicago: Stoelting, 1919.

22

CONDITIONS OF EFFICIENCY

EFFICIENCY is a word of first importance in contemporary American life, not only as it is applied to machinery and tools, accounting systems and sales devices, but as it is applied to the human factor as well. In our survey of some of the principles of motivation we have already observed that many psychological processes make for or against a man's fitness for his work and for activities in general. These we need not rehearse. It has also been assumed, in the discussion, that man's fitness depends as well upon distinctly physiological as upon distinctly psychological conditions; and that these physiological conditions in turn depend upon his regimen of living or upon environmental influences that operate upon him not as specific stimuli but as general physical-chemical conditioners.

FATIGUE

The Nature of Fatigue

In everyday life there is no more common set of phenomena than the many different forms of what goes by the name of "fatigue." There are numerous kinds of "being tired": a person may be tired after a long run or after hours of heavy-lifting work; he may be tired from a long automobile or train trip during which he did little but sit on some well-cushioned seats; he may report being tired after a long afternoon of reading in his easy chair; or he may tire of the sound of his neighbor's radio; and a neurasthenic is tired all the time. Clearly the word "tiredness," and even the more technical one, fatigue, is variously used; and upon examination it becomes painfully apparent that a disentangling,

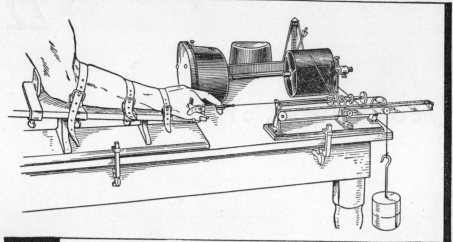

205 **Mosso's Ergograph**

The middle finger in a stirrup pulls against a free-hanging weight, the other fingers and the arm being confined to permit isolation of the muscle to be fatigued. As the finger alternately draws and releases the sliding carriage to which the weight is slung by a pulley, a pointer attached to the carriage records its excursions on the revolving smoked drum of a kymograph driven by clockwork. Contractions are made at regular intervals to the sound beat of a metronome. The smoked paper when removed from the kymograph shows graphically the work done by the isolated muscle throughout the task. (See Figure 206.)

standardizing, and relabeling of the various meanings are very much to be desired [2, 21]. Even in its narrower technical usage, the term "fatigue" — *the reduction of capacity to do work in consequence of long-continued work of the same kind* — is still somewhat ambiguous, since different structures may be affected at different times.

As is true in most fields of inquiry, the first scientific method of attack on the nature of fatigue was highly analytical and addressed to as small and elementary a case of it as was obtainable: the fatiguing of a small and isolable muscle-group. The ergograph (of which one model appears in Figure 205) was devised to isolate the muscles that bent the middle finger and to record graphically the results of their work, without the participation of other muscle-groups and the shiftings of burden from one to another part of the body which happen so commonly in the course of any ordinary work.

Staying for the present at this very analytical level, we should note some established phenomena of fatigue-onset. Figure 206 shows some ergograph tracings made in the University of North Carolina laboratory. On the left is a record of repeated pulls in a 2-kilogram weight. Here the onset of fatigue is shown as a progressive decrement in work on the part of the muscle to a point at which it loses ability to contract. But the rest of the graphic record is evidence that total inability to move a given weight does not signify total loss of power to move any weight at all.

Fatigue as More General Impairment

So far we have used the term "fatigue" as referring to purely quantitative changes in work done. This is much too narrow an application, for qualitative changes occur also. As Bartlett found in his Cambridge study of British airplane pilots, after prolonged work of highly skilled nature it is the coordination of movements and their nice timing that begin to suffer. As the skilled operator begins to show impairment, he may still perform the correct movements rather than wrong ones, but he will perform them at the wrong times, or he will perform the several component activities in a disconnected way. On the perceptual side, his whole stimulus field (such as that shown in Figure 207) tends to fall apart. Some signals improperly assume prominence over others, and some he no longer notices at all [1]. He loses alertness [23]. All in all, it is a picture of disintegration. The fatigued automobile driver or drill press operator may be doing much muscular work; but his movements are jerky, not made in smooth sequences, and he is all too likely to overlook sounds and sights that may be danger signals. The deterioration in a man's skilled performance is manifested primarily not as a decrease in his total activity but as an increase in the errors he commits.

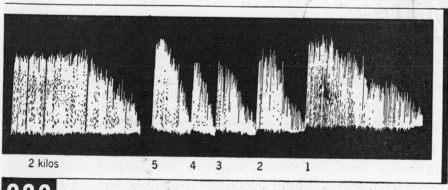

206 **Kymograph Tracings Made on a Mosso Ergograph**

The tracing on the left is a record of repeated pulls against a 2-kilogram weight. The composite tracing on the right is a record of repeated pulls against a load decreased in amount at intervals. When the muscle appeared "fatigued" for a given weight, reduction of the load led to apparent renewal of contracting power: shown for reduction of 5-kilogram weight to 4 kilograms, then to 3, to 2, to 1.

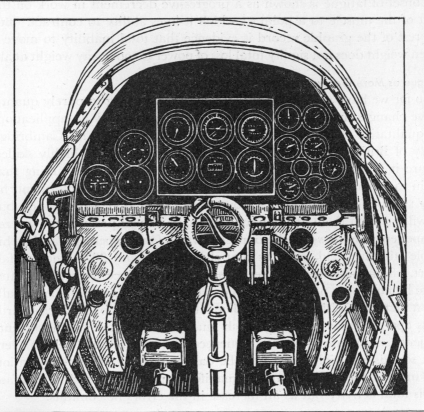

207   **The Cambridge Cockpit**

The situation presented to the pilot examinee, who was being tested in the psychological laboratory of Cambridge University, England. (It resembles the Link Trainer much used in America in teaching how to fly by instruments only.) Note the number of dials on dashboard which have to be watched and responded to appropriately. (*From D. R. Davis*, PILOT ERROR: SOME LABORATORY EXPERIMENTS, *Appl. Psychol. Res. Unit, Med. Res. Council, Great Britain, 1948. By permission of the controller of H. M. Stationery Office.*)

Properly to understand "fatigue," then, we must take cognizance of much more than the changes involving one isolated muscle-group. Indeed some scientific contemporaries broaden the term to apply to a condition of the whole person [2]. And in military terminology, similar breadth of meaning is implied by such expressions as "battle fatigue," "flying fatigue," "operational fatigue."

Rest Pauses

Some results of an early Italian investigation employing the ergo-graphic technique set an interesting practical and theoretical problem. It was found that if a subject were put to work pulling a weight of 6 kilograms, (*a*) when only 2 seconds were allowed for rest after each contraction he would be completely unable to move the finger after about 1 minute, and would need a 2-hour rest to return to his full former efficiency. (*b*) When he was compelled to work at the same rate for only ½ minute, he would need but half an hour for return to full efficiency. Finally, (*c*) when he was allowed a 10-second rest after each contraction, he could continue this sort of work indefinitely with no evidences whatever of fatigue. Now, if these findings be applicable to a day's work of approximately 8 hours, the three methods would result in the following respective total outputs (allowing 2 seconds for each contraction): (*a*) 120 contractions; (*b*) 240; (*c*) 2400. The data are recapitulated in Table XLVIII. This is eloquent and logical testimony, drawn from a laboratory source, as to the central importance of introducing rest pauses in work.

TABLE XLVIII   Effect on Output of Length and Frequency of Pauses

Length of Pause Following Each Contraction	Total Length of "Spells" of Work	No. Contractions Made Per "Spell"	Time Required For Recupera-tion	Theoretical Output (No. Contractions) In 8-Hr. Day
2 sec.	1 min.	30	2 hrs.	120
2 sec.	½ min.	15	½ hr.	240
10 sec.	continuous		0	2400

Observations in actual industrial and business situations have pointed in the same direction. In an English shoe factory heavy cutting presses required two girls as operators. If the usual plan was followed whereby the two girls worked continuously throughout the working day, the weekly output of the plant was 42 gross in a 46-hour week. But if three girls were put to each press and worked 40 minutes and rested 20, in rotation, the weekly output was increased to 49 gross in a 30-hour week. Significant, too, was the testimony of all the operatives that their health had improved and a day's work no longer left them tired out.

Illustrations of the same principle could be multiplied easily, and from a wide range of human work-activities. Let us consider some of the points involved. From several studies the generalization seems war-

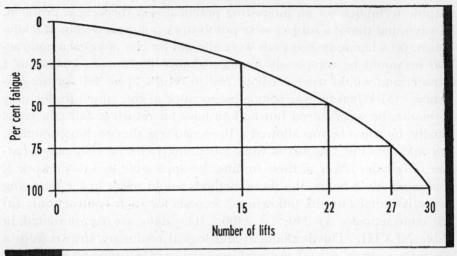

208 Rate of Fatigue During Continuous Work

The data from the ergograph experiment mentioned in the text, with interpolations. If 30 lifts of the weight produce a complete fatigue, and 15 lifts produce a degree of fatigue that requires one-fourth as long for recuperation, the rate of fatiguing is seen to be positively accelerated. (*From A. T. Poffenberger,* PRINCIPLES OF APPLIED PSYCHOLOGY, *Appleton-Century-Crofts, 1942, p. 113. By permission.*)

ranted that, in the course of uninterrupted activity, *loss of effectiveness occurs at a rate with a positive acceleration;* that is, the longer one keeps at the work, the more rapidly do the fatigue effects appear.

Here we may well refer back to the Mosso data. In case (*a*) the muscles moving the finger were exhausted after pulling up the weight 30 times; and it took 2 hours for complete recuperation. In case (*b*) the working was stopped after the weight had been lifted half as many times (15); and complete recuperation took only a fourth as long (½ hour). From these two cases, Poffenberger has drawn a hypothetical curve of recovery, shown in Figure 208.

A practical problem is to discover just when a pause should be introduced. A safe generalization would be: Find that length of working time after which *a drop in production first begins to appear,* and insert the pause there.

This is complicated somewhat by a distinctly psychological factor. In several types of industry the anticipation of the pause makes for improved output just before it is due to occur. In one case where individuals were occupied in adding digits morning and afternoon, on certain days a mid-morning and a mid-afternoon pause were introduced. The workers' output on these days was greater than their output on the days when no pauses were allowed, not only in the periods following the pauses but also in the periods preceding the pauses. Thus, not only the physiological rest during the pause but also the *anticipation* of it promoted increased efficiency.

This matter of pauses is one of prime importance to the student, to the houseworker, and to the businessman. There can be no doubt whatever that a mid-morning and mid-afternoon pause means much to a person's fitness for work. In an English study, a 12-minute rest pause was introduced in the middle of a 2-hour stretch of work which consisted of doing arithmetic problems without pencil and paper [4]. The gains in achievement with different methods of filling the rest pause were:

Walking	2%
Tea	3%
Music	4%
Sitting, talking, smoking	8%
Complete relaxation in easy chair	9%

To this could be added another effective method — the restoring benefits to be obtained by a very brief mid-day nap. If conditions make a nap impossible, nearly anyone can learn to induce a complete relaxation of muscles that approaches the conditions of sleep [9]. For many people a brief loss of consciousness (and the relaxation of muscles) makes the individual as effective on what would otherwise have been a dull afternoon as he is normally on an alert morning.

A more recent research shows that the advantage of rest pauses holds for clerical occupations as truly as for the more muscular. In this study, 16 comptometer operators were given regular 12-minute rest pauses in mid-morning and mid-afternoon, with a resulting increase of output by 29 per cent and a reduction of time lost in voluntary rest pauses by 60 per cent. We should note also that there was increased group morale [15].

Mental Blocks as Fatigue Symptoms

When a person is kept at a repetitive task, such as adding pairs of numbers or calling out the names of color patches exposed on a sheet of paper, the experimenter usually notices that often the smooth performance is momentarily interrupted at times in the course of the task [3]. The subject is for the instant blocked in his response. But it is only for a moment; and he resumes the task at once, sometimes unaware of the interruption. The same is true also, but in lesser degree, of work that is not so repetitive in character. Furthermore, these blocks appear less frequently after much practice in the task and more frequently after long continuation in the task at the same sitting, and errors seem to occur more frequently just before and less frequently just after a block. Such facts argue for some relationship between the course of fatigue and the occurrence of the blocks. Can it be that they serve as an *automatic protective device?*

Much the same supposition may be presumed to explain one of the well-recognized symptoms of fatigue, namely, fluctuations of attention. After long-continued application to an intellectual task, one commonly experiences an inability to keep intruding irrelevant ideas out of one's mind. Is this similarly an automatic protective device?

Amount of Energy Consumed Depends upon the Nature of the Task

Here, as everywhere else, when it comes to applying scientifically derived principles to particular concrete cases, the sensible reader will recognize that much judgment must be used. For one thing, the term "work" embraces many kinds and degrees. The reader should note, from Table XLIX that the measured consumption of energy varies enormously from one occupation to another. This table lists the energy expenditures of a man of average weight during an hour each at different tasks. Note, for instance, that sitting in a chair uses up some 50 per

TABLE XLIX	Energy Expenditure at Various Common Tasks (For a man weighing 70 kilograms)

Task	Calories Per Hour
Sleeping	65
Awake lying still	77
Sitting at rest	100
Dressing or undressing	118
Singing	122
Typewriting rapidly	140
Ironing, dishwashing	144
Walking slowly (2.6 miles per hour)	200
Carpentry, metal working, industrial painting	240
Walking moderately fast (3.75 miles per hour)	300
Walking downstairs	364
Sawing wood	480
Swimming	500
Running (5.3 miles per hour)	570
Walking upstairs	1,100

From H. C. Sherman, CHEMISTRY OF FOOD AND NUTRITION *(6th ed.), copyright, 1941, by The Macmillan Company, and used with their permission.*

cent more energy than sleeping, typing or ironing about 50 per cent more and walking about 100 per cent more than sitting and that walking upstairs consumes $5\frac{1}{2}$ times as much energy as slow walking.

Automobile driving is certainly a common task. Since it entails many consequences besides mere decrease of output, it deserves special attention. In one experiment six experienced drivers were engaged as subjects. On each of the 128 experimental days they drove standardized courses of about 300 miles, and on the 28 interspersed control days they spent the time in recreation (playing checkers, watching boxing matches, attending movies). Tests were administered to the operators at the beginning and at the end of every experimental and control day, as follows: (1) Vascular skin reaction: length of time for a faint white streak left by a blunt instrument to begin to fade (time had been found in other studies to decrease after muscular exertion). (2) Postural steadiness: amount of body sway when eyes are kept closed. (3) Hand-eye coordination: (a) number of side-contacts made by stylus inserted into a series of diminishing holes, and (b) number of contacts during repeated insertions in the same hole. (4) Visual focusing: total time one can maintain the letters "li" in clear focus. (5) Color naming: time taken and errors made in naming 1200 patches of 10 different colors. (6) Adding: time taken to add correctly 21 columns of 15 digits each.

TABLE L

Effect of Sustained Automobile Driving on Performance Test Scores

Shown as percentage changes between morning and evening test scores, averaged separately for experimental and for control days

Tests	Percentage of Change		Diff.*
	Driving Days	Control Days	P.E._diff.
Vascular skin reaction	− 12.38	− 1.21	12.93
Postural steadiness	+ 8.32	+ 0.20	3.83
Hand-eye coordination: A	− 2.92	+ 0.39	3.64
Hand-eye coordination: B	+ 23.58	− 9.78	7.76
Visual efficiency	− 2.62	− 0.80	6.62
Color naming: time	+ 3.93	− 1.65	8.92
Color naming: errors	+ 46.79	− 16.28	12.45
Adding	+ 8.46	− 3.59	8.31

* In this form of the "critical ratio" (pages 121 f.) a value of 4 is usually considered as indicating that the difference is completely reliable.

From A. H. Ryan and M. Warner, "The effect of automobile driving on the reactions of the driver," AMER. J. PSYCHOL., 1936, 48, 409 ff. By permission of the editor.

The findings, furnished in Table L, show the mean percentage gain or loss between scores made on the morning and on the evening tests, as averaged separately for the experimental days and for the control days. On every test except that for hand-eye coordination there was a greater loss in score between morning and evening on those days when the driving was done than on those of no driving (and on six tests the difference is statistically significant). It was therefore demonstrated that a day's work behind the wheel entailed definite losses of effectiveness in certain sensory, motor, and association processes that are similar to processes involved in automobile driving.

Some Subjective Aspects of Fatigue

So far we have confined our discussions to fatigue in its objective meaning — decreased ability to work in consequence of work. We must now repair our omission of the subjective aspect by analyzing the state of "feeling tired."

One broad statement can be made at once. *A person's experience of feeling tired is not a valid indicator of his ability to work*. Indeed, in certain stages of tiredness he may actually do far better work, whether it be heavy labor or thinking. It seems that the toxins when produced in certain amounts affect the neural centers, and probably the endocrine and other systems, in a way to increase one's general excitement; and this condition of heightened energy leads one to throw greater power into the work and to continue it longer. Surely the reader can cite from his own experience instances of surprising things accomplished when he has felt "done." This phenomenon is of a piece with the accelerated tempo at which one lives and works during the first stage following an energy-depletion, such as loss of sleep — a compensatory phenomenon. One should bear in mind, however, the fact that this heightened level of work in the first stage of fatigue often turns out to be a temporary extravagance in the expenditure of energy, the organism living recklessly, as it were, on its capital.

Conversely, it not infrequently happens that an experience of freshness and avidity is misleading and is based upon a condition of actually decreased productivity. This state is not unlike a certain stage in alcoholic poisoning, when a man's emotional expansiveness ill consorts with his heightened clumsiness and ineptitude.

The subjective state of an individual — the way he feels — is a function not only of his general physiological state (muscular, neural, endocrinal, and so on) but also of his preceding thinking processes. Anticipation of the end of a job, as we have already noted, is an important factor. On the other hand, the monotony of an endless, inexorable, and unremitting

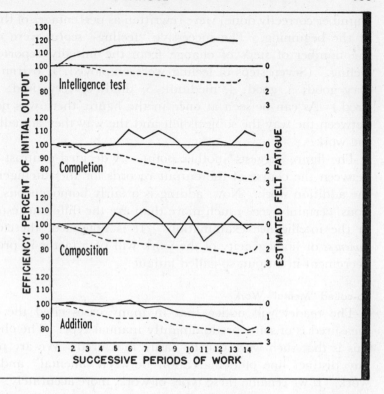

209 Relation Between Objective Output and Subjective Feelings in Mental Work

Solid lines: outputs. Broken lines: feelings. The successive output scores were calculated as percentages of the initial score made. The successive feeling scores were calculated as number of steps of change from the initial feeling reported. (*From A. T. Poffenberger*, PRINCIPLES OF APPLIED PSYCHOLOGY, *Appleton-Century-Crofts, 1942. By permission of author and publishers.*)

repetition of the same little set of motions hour after hour becomes for some people a restraint and frustration that has serious consequences not only for the job output but for the nervous and mental health of the workman. Much concern over the effects of monotony is to be found throughout the critical literature written by industrial experts as well as by literary observers. We need not expand the theme.

The discrepancy so often found between the worker's objective output and his reports of how he feels is well shown by the results graphed in Figure 209. The experimental subjects worked at four different mental tasks: answering intelligence test questions, completing sentences with written words, judging English compositions, and doing continuous adding (to an announced number, adding first 16, then 17, then 18, and so on, until a new number is announced). The successive scores of output (number correctly done) were rewritten as percentages of the score made at the beginning. The successive "feeling" scores were calculated as the number of steps of change from the initially reported degree of feeling. (Seven steps of feeling were employed. 1, extremely good; 2, very good; 3, good; 4, medium; 5, tired; 6, very tired; 7, extremely tired.) As can be seen at once in the figure, there was no parallelism between the way the subjects felt and the way they actually turned out the work.

The figure suggests another point. A decided contrast is noticeable between the course of the output records for the intelligence tests and the addition work. Now, adding is a fairly homogeneous set of operations, certainly very much more than are the different tests to be found in the intelligence examinations. It is suggested, therefore, that the *sameness* or homogeneity of the work will be a factor in production of a decrement in output, so-called fatigue.

So-called "Mental" Work

The reader will notice that in many cases cited the work that is measured is of some predominantly manual type. The chief reason for this is that such work can be easily measured. We are not to assume any distinct line of demarcation between "mental" and "muscular" work. If we rename these types of work, more accurately, "verbal" and "manual," the distinction is clearly shown to be a fine-drawn one, for many occupations involve both kinds of activity. And in point of fact, the very same principles of work and fatigue apply to many jobs of the verbal type just as they do to heavier manual or muscular labor.[1]

It would seem that if any distinction is to be drawn between different kinds of work, it should be between the more repetitive and the more creative tasks. This is a distinction that any student can find in his own activities. And to hazard a general statement, we may say that, the psychotechnical principles that have been derived to date are primarily applicable to the repetitive activities of shop and of office. Their applicability to such activities as writing a theme for an English class, solving a problem in calculus, or making a qualitative analysis of a chemical compound is extremely limited. For instance, if a rest pause is introduced as per a schedule, it is as likely as not to fall just when the thinker is immersed in his problem, has succeeded in reawakening his relevant sources of knowledge, and is hot on the trail of his quarry. There would seem to be abundant reason why creative workers so often observe

[1] For a thorough critical analysis of work and fatigue in the more ideational activities, Thorndike should be consulted [22].

living hours that scandalize those who work at more routine tasks between punchings of the clock. They may apply themselves feverishly all day and most of the night and repeat the procedure on the next day; then when a task is finished, an answer obtained, or a thesis worked out, they may lapse into hours and days of seeming idleness.

To what extent, then, the reader should apply to his own case the principles of psychotechnics — that is, the practical application of psychology — cannot be decided with a simple formula. He should realize that the most important thing practically is not this or that particular plan, but his own attitude of inquiry and criticism addressed to his own working program.

Is "Mental" Work Fatiguing?

(I) The power a person has to continue work, if only the incidental feelings be neglected, was exhibited in a study at the University of Southern California in which each subject set herself the task of memorizing and then multiplying 4-place numbers by 4-place numbers without use of paper and pencil, for a continuous 12-hour period on 4 successive days. (If the reader will try to memorize and multiply a 3-place number by a 2-place one — a vastly easier task! — without benefit of pencil, he will appreciate better the implications of this experiment.) After months of preliminary practice, each subject proceeded as follows: (a) she drew from a stack a slip of paper bearing two 4-place numbers; (b) she recorded the precise time on a corner of the slip; (c) she memorized the numbers; (d) she turned the slip over and proceeded with the mental multiplication, recording only the answer when she eventually had it in its entirety; (e) she noted down the precise time when she had completed writing the answer. (The complete process between the two time-recordings was found on analysis to consist of exactly 100 operations.) Then she proceeded to the next example. And so on through the 12-hour period. The obtained data are strikingly shown in Figure 210. It seems demonstrated that the *purely intellectual* operations in a task of this sort are practically unfatiguable. The decrements which would certainly have appeared, and in gross amounts, if one were to do anything like these same operations as routine tasks in a clerical commercial job, would then be a function of the many non-intellectual complications entering in. These subjects jotted down brief notes on their feelings of tiredness, boredom, or physical or nervous discomfort, but there was no clear parallelism between these feelings and the appearance of errors. Under the conditions of high motivation the subjects were able to continue their intellectual operations quite regardless of discomfort.

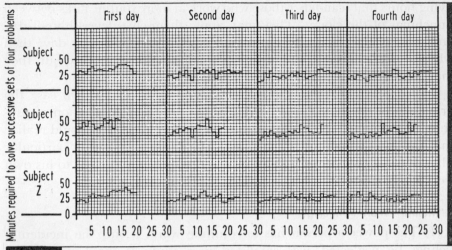

210   **Curves for Continuous Intense Mental Work**

For convenience the whole course of the work is divided into sets of four successive problems. The height of each short horizontal crossbar represents the time in minutes (corrected for errors) taken to solve one set of four problems. For example, subject *X* on her first day took 24, 31, and 29 minutes each on her first three sets of four problems, and in the course of that 12-hour day she solved 20 sets of four problems. (*From Z. L. Huxtable, M. H. White, and M. A. McCarter*, Psychol. Monogr., *1946, 59, No. 275.*)

(II) Even when long-maintained work of the eyes is involved in sedentary activity, there need be no decrement in a person's efficiency. In a recent experiment, 20 high school and 20 college students read a book for 6 hours. Eye-movements were recorded on each subject throughout that period of time, by means of the technique illustrated in Figure 163 on page 472. The measures included: number of blinks, fixations, regressions, and lines read. No statistically significant change in eye-performance was shown by any of these objective measures in any of the students throughout the 6-hour period of work. Nor was there any loss in comprehension of the material.

Subjective symptoms did appear in feelings of tiredness, of eyestrain, of wishing to stop. And a clue appeared in the finding that a work decrement had indeed been observed in a preliminary work-out when the student-subjects had been less highly motivated with rewards and competition [5].

Overwork versus Overworry

It is a fact of immense practical and personal importance that in most instances what has been described as nervous breakdown is a result not of excessive work but of excessive worry. In the first place, such breakdowns occur much less frequently among workmen who do heavy labor than among white-collar workers and professional and business men on higher economic levels. It is true that the laborer's health may be undermined by over-long hours; but the ill-health takes the form of general weakness and greater susceptibility to systemic infectional diseases. The source of nervous breakdown must accordingly be sought outside the working muscles and neural connections. In a very few cases it is diagnosed simply as resulting from infections at tonsils or teeth or other foci; and in other cases the endocrine system has been seriously unbalanced. But the most important inducing condition is that of prolonged worry and emotional stress, sometimes incidental to the work itself, sometimes set up by extraneous problems in a person's private life. Worry is worse than work.

The principle underlying the theme of the preceding paragraphs may be more widely applied. The deleterious effect of an agency may not be directed primarily at an individual's working apparatus, in the strict sense, but at his emotional apparatus. This we shall see demonstrated again.

OTHER PHYSIOLOGICAL CONDITIONS

Sleep as a Natural Phenomenon

Of all the conditions making for human efficiency, sleep is probably the most important. It is the one most necessary to normal metabolic activity — and the one most neglected by college students. Experimental animals deprived of any sleep whatever die within a very few days,

211 **Fluctuations in the Depth of Sleep During the Night**

Schematic representation. Height of curve above base line represents the auditory sensitivity of the sleeper, that is, the degree of intensity of a sound necessary to awaken him. This sound is emitted by a loudspeaker, and its intensity is measured by the voltage of the sound-producing current. When the curve touches the base line, the subject is awake or nearly so. In general, the sleep becomes shallower and in shorter periods. But there is much irregularity in both respects. (*From N. Kleitman*, SLEEP AND WAKEFULNESS, *University of Chicago Press, 1939. By permission of the publishers.*)

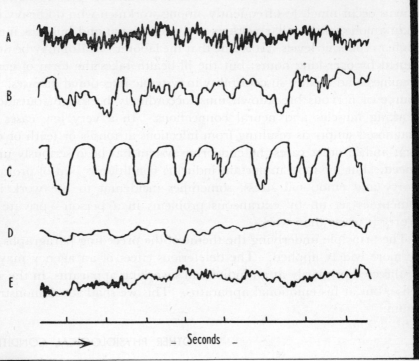

Seconds —

212 **Change in the Brain Waves of a Person Going to Sleep**

A. Alpha rhythm of wakefulness.   *B.* Alpha and delta waves of light sleep
C. Delta rhythm of deep sleep early in the night.   *D.* "Null" rhythm which
later replaces the delta rhythm.   *E.* Alpha rhythm on awakening.   (*From N.
Kleitman,* SLEEP AND WAKEFULNESS, *University of Chicago Press, 1939. By permission of the publishers.*)

no matter how well they may be fed, watered, and housed. Since the
physiologists are not agreed as to what constitutes the essential nature of
sleep, it would be foolish to be wise on that question. And instead of
asking, How explain sleep?, we might more fittingly ask, How explain
waking? We shall therefore content ourselves with the view that it is a
period of cessation of nearly all overt muscular activities and of nearly
all sensory functions. It differs in depth just as waking life differs in
vividness and intensity, to form the other half of a continuous scale.

The depth of one's sleep is lighter in the later hours of the night than
in the earlier. However, there is much fluctuation throughout the night;
the sleeper actually wakes occasionally, though the next morning he is
usually unable to recall having done so. Figure 211 is a schematic

representation of both the foregoing statements. Changes in the sleeper's electroencephalogram (Figure 212; and cf. also pages 336 ff.) offer a promising line of evidence.

The sleeper does not lie like a log throughout the night. On the contrary, a typical sleeper shifts his position frequently. This we know from repeated photographs taken of him [10] and also from continuous kymograph records of displacements of his bed communicated from large tambours placed under it. He will make movements twenty to sixty times in the course of the night. It seems that the muscles, the skin, and the internal organs develop conditions analogous to fatigue when kept in any one long-continued position; and each shift of posture provides a change, a specialized rest.

Effects of Sleep Deprivation

What are the psychological effects of the loss of a considerable amount of sleep? Experiments have taken the form of abstention from sleep for sixty or more hours, with tests administered before, during, and after. The results of such researches at first seem puzzling. After one night of sleep loss, the subject may feel much as usual, except for a slight malaise and drag, especially noticeable when he sits down. In his emotional attitudes and particularly in his performances on tests he is likely to be at his normal level, or even sometimes to be above it. Here it seems that the impediments put upon the organism are not so great as not to be compensated by extra effort automatically put forth — on a biological level below the subject's awareness of it.

With considerably greater sleep loss, lasting for 60 hours, say, the story is different although likewise somewhat confusing. On a wide variety of psychological tests (color naming, canceling, computing, aiming, steadiness, etc.) no impairment has usually been found even in subjects deprived of sleep for sixty hours. No one who has worked with men in this condition can fail to be impressed with their ability to perform well on such tasks.

A significant thing is to be noted, however. The sleepless subjects do fall down when it comes to tasks demanding persistent and *sustained attention*. They may be able, say, to name a hundred color patches with normal speed and accuracy, but they cannot do so with a thousand, as they can when fresh. They may be as skillful in parking an automobile as anyone else, but on a long driving trip they would tend to lapse into sleep. In the same connection, another obvious thing is to be considered. Whatever their objective achievement scores, all subjects show or report vivid and impressive *illness symptoms* of other sorts: buzzing in the head, burning eyes, headache, "musty feeling in the head," feeling of being dazed, of being "almost dead," and the like; and their general deportment becomes irritable and nervous, or else silly. They feel almost "tight," and laugh at anything. How can the test results showing only slight impairment in specific short tasks be reconciled with failure in sustained tasks and with these general bodily symptoms of disorganization? One key to the problem may be found in the phenomenon of *compensation*. The dull weight imposed upon a man's activities by his sleepiness operates, as any other impediment is likely to do, to arouse in him extra effort to overcome it. And because of its costliness, the extra effort cannot be maintained. This principle is supported by some evidence on the physiological side. It has been found that the energy consumed (as measured by metabolic rate) during an arithmetic task was something like three times as great with subjects who had lost only two hours of sleep as with those who had lost none: the excess muscular effort put forth in keeping oriented to the task was costly.

Another characteristic of the sleep-deprived person is his *sluggishness in shifting his set* from task to task or even item to item. It is difficult to redirect his activity. Once started on a given line he can hardly be drawn from it. This behavior may at first seem to contradict the point made above; but there it was stated that it is the excess effort that is short-lived, rather than a general orientation. Now, this sluggishness in turning from one task to another has been strikingly found in other experimentally induced conditions of impairment: deprivation of oxygen, alcoholic poisoning, excessive fatigue. And it is a noticeable feature in life outside the laboratory: the alcoholized person is not easily diverted; the tired, goggle-eyed child does not want to move or go to bed; the student working on into the night finds himself more and more reluctant to quit and seek his rest, though he may well know he is slowing down.

Exactly how much sleep makes for highest efficiency it is impossible to say, for individuals differ in the depth of their sleeping. We know that the value of sleep is a function of its depth multiplied by its length. This is shown by the fact that after long hours of vigil a person ordinarily can catch up with a much shorter sleep if it is undisturbed and profound than if it is broken.

Finally, sleeping has many elements of the *habitual*. A person can learn to sleep only at certain times — or at any time by merely lying down and closing his eyes; he can learn to sleep only in certain places on certain kinds of beds — or in any place. Tomes have been written on how to fall asleep, and the methods recommended — counting sheep, stroking one arm, taking a hot bath — are innumerable. The writer would recommend two peripheral devices especially: eliminate sensory stimuli as far as possible, and relax all possible muscles — open the hands, drop the jaw, and "look over" the body to see if there is tenseness in a muscle group anywhere [9].

When one thinks of sleep, one often thinks of *dreaming*. Concerning dreams some points have been made on preceding pages (195 f., 462, 637 f.); but whatever connection dreams have with one's efficiency of work — our immediate interest in this chapter — is probably remote.

Alcohol

Safe generalizations on the subject of alcohol and its effect on human efficiency are not easily made, and for two reasons in particular. Susceptibility varies from individual to individual in a way that is baffling. The effect of different amounts on any one individual is likewise surprisingly different from time to time. Because of their failure adequately to control certain factors, most of the experimental studies have helped very little in clearing up the great popular confusion on the general subject. A principal error is that of *suggestion:* a subject, if he knows when he is and when he is not taking the dose, will expect himself to perform differently in the two cases, and this expectation serves to induce or influence the very behavior supposed to be in question. In such a welter of conflicting opinions and discordant findings we shall do well to limit ourselves to the evidence from three of the best-accepted pieces of research.

One experiment was concerned primarily with the simpler motor phenomena. Some of the findings appear in Table LI. A glance at them will reveal a fact that is at variance with one strong popular opinion: alcohol proves to be a *depressant*, at least of the functions measured, reducing either the strength or the quickness of an action.

Another study was devoted to more complicated processes such as are tapped with some well-known psychological tests. Six men were given a battery of tests at half-hour intervals before and at similar intervals after a noon drinking of genuine beer of three different strengths, and similarly on other days when the beer contained no alcohol. The subjects were unaware of the differences in the beers. (One man was a total abstainer, one a regular drinker, and the others occasional drinkers.) The results of drinking the beer with alcoholic content are briefly summarized in Table LII. Again the depressing effect of alcohol is shown, and this time on distinctly psychological performances.

These results are reinforced by those of another study in which the effects of alcohol were as shown in Table LIII.

TABLE

LI Influence of Alcohol on Efficiency: I

	Per Cent
Latent time of the knee jerk increased	10
Thickening of the thigh muscle decreased	46
Protective eyelid reflex, latent time increased	7
Extent of eyelid movement decreased	19
Eye reactions, latent time increased	5
Speed of eye movements decreased	11
Sensitivity to electric stimulation decreased	14
Speed of finger movements (tapping) decreased	9

From R. Dodge and F. G. Benedict, PSYCHOLOGICAL EFFECTS OF ALCOHOL *(Carnegie Instn. Publ., 1915).*

TABLE

LII Influence of Alcohol: II

Hand steadiness..........decreased	Naming opposites ....slower
Hand-eye coordinations.......poorer	Adding ....slower
Tapping ....slower	Learning substitutes ....slower
Color-naming ....slower	Memory, paired associates ....slower

From H. L. Hollingworth, J. ABNORM. SOC. PSYCHOL., *1923–24, 18, 204–237, 311–333.*

TABLE

LIII Influence of Alcohol: III

Pulse rate..............increased	Visual acuity..............less keen
Skin temperature ....increased	Finger movement ....slower
Patellar reflex ....decreased	Eye-hand coordination ....poorer
Eyelid reflex ....slower	Typewriting, errors ....increased
Eye reaction time ....slower	Typewriting, speed ....slower
Word reaction time ....slower	Using code ....slower

From W. R. Miles, ALCOHOL AND HUMAN EFFICIENCY *(Carnegie Instn. Publ., 1924, No. 333).*

From everyday observations of people we would be warranted in asking for an interpretation of such results as these. Do not light doses of alcohol excite rather than depress, increase rather than diminish? Does not many a man testify sincerely to the supporting effect of a small drink? The fact is that popular experience and the laboratory data are not really in conflict. The *depressing effects at first concern the very highest inhibitory functions*, and as these dampers are removed the emotional functions are released. The result is increased experience of well-being, good fellowship, freedom from timidity before a crowd, increased confidence in one's own powers — a condition that on further poisoning passes into an emotional exaggeration in sentimental weeping or absurd anger, gesticulations, and much loud talk. *In vino veritas* has only this much truth in it. When a person is in this alcoholized condition it is only in some false senses that we can speak of his increased efficiency. There is an apparent increase from the point of view of the man's feelings, and an increase in any other way only in the negative sense of the removal of inhibitions [13].

Miles, a leading authority on the subject, has this to say:

> Although beverage alcohol appears to give subjective stimulant action to a person, its real effect is a depressant action on most of the functions of body and mind. The alcohol effect which interferes with driving ability is fourfold: (1) A poorer grade of attention to external signals and environment; (2) Slower responses of eyes, hands and feet; (3) Less dependable, that is, more variable, muscular responses; (4) Increased self-assurance which prompts to the assumption of right-of-way and willingness to take a chance. Although alcohol is directly mentioned in only 7 to 10 per cent of fatal highway traffic accidents, it is the belief of informed traffic officials that one-third of such accidents are at least partly chargeable to use of alcohol by the driver.[1]

And for airplane operation Sir Frederic Bartlett at the Cambridge University laboratory found that the disorganizing effects of alcohol are equally definite.

> On nearly every occasion on which subjects carried out a test in the Cambridge Cockpit [laboratory facsimile of air pilot's cockpit, shown in Figure 207] after taking alcohol, the performance was most adversely affected. All but one of the ten pilots who were given 100 c.c. (about four tots) of a good brand of Scotch whiskey before a test obtained scores which placed them in the worst quarter of a large group of subjects.[2]

[1] From W. R. Miles, "Alcohol and motor vehicle drivers," *Proc. 13th Ann. Meetg. Hyway Res. Bd.*, 1933.

[2] From D. R. Davis *et al.*, *Pilot Error: Some Laboratory Experiments* (London: H. M. Stationery Office, 1948).

Caffeine

Caffeine is the active principle in coffee, tea, and certain proprietary drinks, which are taken the world over to increase one's fitness. The best evidence bearing on the effect of caffeine is the following well-controlled experiment. For a 40-day period subjects were given capsules, on some days containing caffeine in different amounts and on others a milk sugar of similar appearance. The contents of each day's capsule were unknown both to the subjects and to the assistants serving as their examiners. The subjects were given several times daily a battery of tests. A comparison of scores made by all subjects after different-sized doses on the caffeine days and on those of the caffeineless days led to some fairly definite conclusions. These are summarized in Table LIV. The effect upon simpler motor performances (Tests 1, 2, 9) tended to be one of stimulation. On the more definitely psychological functions (3, 4, 5, 6, 7, 8) the effect was stimulating, with a few exceptions for certain sizes of dose. In general, then, *caffeine makes for heightened efficiency,* at least in the period immediately following the dose. An interesting and important incidental fact is that in no case was there a secondary reaction of let-down.

It remains to be said that caffeine is clearly *habit-forming;* that is, he who uses it frequently comes to depend upon it, as witness the numbers of people who experience headaches, dizziness, and other discomforts when denied their usual caffeine-bearing beverage.

TABLE

LIV   Effects of Caffeine on Efficiency

Test	Small Doses	Medium Doses	Large Doses
1. Tapping	+	+	+
2. Complicated tapping	+	0	—
3. Typewriting			
(a) Speed	+	0	—
(b) Errors	—	—	—
4. Color naming	+	+	+
5. Naming opposites	+	+	+
6. Adding	+	+	+
7. Discrimination reaction time	—	0	+
8. Cancellation	—	?	+
9. Steadiness	?	—	—
+ = increase	o = no effect		— = decrease

From H. L. Hollingworth, "The influence of caffeine on mental and motor efficiency" ARCH. PSYCHOL., *1912, No. 22.*

Tobacco

The question of the effect of tobacco upon a man's work is today a football being booted about by rival interests in a game that knows few rules. While they were under the ban of certain reforming organizations, cigarettes — otherwise known then as "coffin nails" — were in many states not sold to minors under legal penalty; and even yet they are not used by women as freely as by men in certain sections of the country, a faint taint of iniquity still adhering to them. Since World War I, however, an unparalleled orgy of advertising has been devoted to them, and nonsensical and even false claims have been pressed in untempered and fulsome language. Where does the truth lie? We may surmise offhand that it lies in neither extreme position.

As for scientific evidence, there is little available. To be sure, a host of investigators here and there have followed such procedures as comparing the scholarship or the athletic records of smokers and non-smokers, but where does the tobacco come in? Is it cause, effect, symptom, or accident?

One experiment seems to have been conducted with an adequate appreciation of the checks and controls that need to be employed. In all studies of the effects of drugs a disturbing factor of very great importance has been the subject's knowledge of when he is and when he is not being administered the drug, and the resulting operation of suggestion. This factor has been particularly difficult to eliminate in the case of tobacco smoking. In the experiment referred to, however, the following check was devised. The subjects were blindfolded and were allowed to suppose that tobacco would be smoked on each occasion. On the tobacco days a full pipeful of tobacco was placed in their mouths, while on the tobaccoless days they were given pipes of exactly the same shape, empty of tobacco, but with an electric heating-coil that warmed the air drawn into the mouth from the pipe. While puffing on the latter they smelled tobacco smoke produced in the room from other sources. This control was apparently effective. In fact, in one case a confirmed smoker went through the motions of blowing smoke rings when he had the warm-air pipe in his mouth.

A battery of tests was run before the "smoking," just after a 25-minute "smoke," and at two approximately half-hour intervals later. The data obtained are summarized in Table LV. As the reader can see, no single conclusion as to the effect of tobacco smoking upon the more strictly psychological functions can be drawn from this study. (A) Different psychological functions were differently affected. (B) They were affected sometimes in opposite ways depending upon whether the

TABLE

LV

Effects of Tobacco Smoking on Efficiency

Function Tested		Non-Smokers			Habitual Smokers		
		test 1	2	3	test 1	2	3
Pulse	(increased)	+	+	+	+	+	+
Tremor of hand	(increased)	−	−	−	−	−	−
Tapping		0	0	0	0	0	0
Muscular fatigue	(decreased)*	+	+	+	+	0	0
Cancelling of A's, speed		0	0	0	0	0	0
Cancelling of A's, accuracy		0	0	0	0	+	+
Reading reaction-time		+	+?	+	+	+?	+
Learning reaction-time		+	+	+	+	+	+
Adding, speed		−	−	−	+	+	+
Adding, accuracy		−?	−	−?	0	0	0
Memory span		−	−	−	−	−	−
Rote learning		−	0	0	−	0	0

+ = gain in efficiency on tobacco, as compared with no-tobacco days.
0 = no decided change.
− = loss in efficiency.

From C. L. Hull, "The influence of tobacco smoking on mental and motor efficiency" PSYCHOL. MONOGR., 1924, 33, No. 150.

subjects were habituated to smoking. (C) Where definite increases or decreases are indicated, the original figures have but low reliability. We are left to conclude either that the technique of experimentation is not adequately perfected to reveal the true effects of smoking, or (more probably) that tobacco smoking has little if any definite and consistent effect upon psychological functions.

It may be in order to add that besides whatever physiological and psychological effect the tobacco has as a drug, some of the motivation to smoking possibly lies in the pleasure derived from cigarettes, cigars, pipes, and even chewing-tobacco as something to be handled and mouthed.

CONDITIONS OF THE PHYSICAL ENVIRONMENT

Noise

Even though city-wide anti-noise campaigns do not figure so prominently in newspaper headlines as they did a decade ago, noises remain a matter of considerable concern. First of all they are generally accounted a nuisance, an addition to the emotional trials and tribulations of human life. A second count against them is the part they play in decreasing one's working efficiency. What are the facts?

An experimental program in Bartlett's Cambridge University laboratory was admirably conducted and broad in scope; and as the outcome represents well the findings of others before and since, it will serve our purpose here. A protracted series of different kinds of work were assigned to successive sets of subjects. They included: eye mazes, in which one was to follow out complicated lines; card sorting; picking out and replacing pegs in a moving bed; building a new piece of apparatus out of a supply of wheels, washers, axles, and the like; "number setting" in which two sets of levers had to be manipulated in complicated ways to produce certain combinations of letters and numbers on a dial; making up words beginning with a given letter and spelled with other letters to be taken from a few supplied. All in all, the tasks furnished a variety of work, from simpler sensory-muscular coordinations to thoughtful and creative activities. In the noises used, variety again was kept in mind. Through headphones the subjects heard loud clicks delivered at different tempos; piercing whistles; filing sounds on a piece of tin; a wooden rattle; a claxon horn; a very loud and continuous noise like that of a machine shop; the same delivered in discontinuous bursts; and finally loud phonograph renditions of humorous dialogues, or barely audible renditions of the same. Finally, the lengths of the work-spells varied up to eight hours [18].

What did these many different tests of work under various conditions of noise bring out? It was discovered that differences in the likelihood of a noise's interfering with a piece of work depended upon (a) the nature of the noise (for example, somewhat interrupted, intense, indistinct), and (b) the character of the task on which the subject was employed (for example, not routine, complex, inherently difficult). But such differences were often statistically unreliable. We can cast the more striking findings into the form of statements that have considerable reliability and generality as representing the series of experiments as a whole.

(1) Noises do frequently excite conscious experiences of dislike, unpleasantness, irritation. There is no doubting these subjective reports: noises frequently are a nuisance. Especially is this true at the beginning of a task.

(2) But what as to their effect upon a person's working efficiency? Often there is initially some not-very-great adverse effect, when measured quite objectively in terms of speed and accuracy.

(3) This initial adverse effect wears off rather speedily, and the worker's performance tends to resume its normal course.

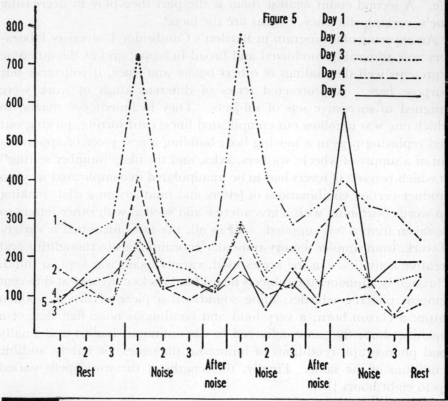

213 Muscle Action Potentials Under Noise

Average magnitudes of the action potentials of four persons before, during, and after periods of noise, separately plotted for five successive days. The 1st day shows intense muscular tension at the beginning of each noise but a rapid reduction as it continues; the 2nd day shows the same to a minor degree; and on the 3rd, 4th, and 5th days there is almost complete negative adaptation. (*From F. C. Davis*, INDIANA UNIV. PUBL., SCI. SERIES, *No. 3, 1935. With the permission of the author.*)

(4) This return to normal efficiency occurs in spite of the subjectively reported feelings, mentioned in (1).

(5) This return is due to at least two factors. One is *compensation*. The worker puts forth some extra effort to combat the effect of the noise. He grits his teeth and applies himself all the harder. This is a special case of a more general biological principle we have noted previously.

(6) A second factor bearing upon the return to normal efficiency is *negative adaptation*. The worker rapidly gets used to the noises so that they become less and less effective (cf. sensory adaptation, page 233).

It is possible to note this phenomenon even in the records taken of the minute action potentials in the forearm muscles of the workers. This is shown in Figure 213.

It should be added that these laboratory results accord well with business and industrial field observations; and the experimentalist's interpretations are useful in understanding many practical conditions and results.

Ventilation

Oxygen, as every school child knows, is essential to life; the more active the organism, the more oxygen it requires. This is a commonplace. Yet certain details and qualifying facts need to be considered. Ventilation is more than a matter of oxygen supply. The air in which one works and breathes has a certain *temperature*, a certain *humidity*, and a certain amount of *circulation;* and variations in each of these characteristics should be considered.

All three were rather thoroughly investigated in a research project sponsored by the New York State Commission on Ventilation. The subjects of the investigation worked in an airtight room in which the air could be experimentally controlled as to oxygen content, temperature, humidity, and circulation. For work of the heavy muscular type the men lifted heavy dumbbells. At a temperature of 86° F. and a humidity of 80 per cent they accomplished 28 per cent less total work than at 68° F. and 50 per cent humidity. Or again, taking their output in 68° F. fresh air as 100 per cent, their outputs under other conditions were: in 68° F. stagnant air, 91 per cent; in 75° F. fresh air, 85 per cent; and in 75° F. stagnant air, 77 per cent. This is definite testimony to the importance of oxygen content, of temperature, and of humidity, if the work to be done is of a muscular type. An important finding was that any change which will remove the excess heat from the skin — as by stirring and circulating the air with fans — will generally reduce unfavorable symptoms.

When work of the thinking type is in question, the results of the Commission's investigation are much more surprising. When subjects were given some well-known psychological tests of thinking efficiency, no reliable differences appeared in their accomplishments under considerable variations of the atmosphere. Some typical data are selected from the report and presented in Table LVI. The report concludes that, with the forms of work listed and the lengths of period used, when a person "is urged to do his best he does as much, and does it as well, and improves as rapidly, in a hot, humid, stale, and stagnant air condition . . . as under an optimal condition."

TABLE

LVI   Psychological Test Scores under Different
           Atmospheric Conditions

Tests	68° F., 50% Humidity Fresh Air	86° F., 80% Humidity, Same Air Recirculated
Naming colors	49	49
Naming opposites	53	55
Cancelling	101	102
Adding	74	76
Multiplying	57	57

What can such results mean? For the industrial manager they indicate the importance of conditioning the air of his factory. For the student and other brain workers they indicate that so far as his subjective experiences of comfort and discomfort go, the *atmosphere and weather is an important item in his motivation but not in his capacity.* His diminished inclination to work in hot weather is not to be taken for inability to work.

In the aeronautical age in which we now live, the oxygen requirements for efficient performance of duties have acquired special interest as part of the problem of altitude, for with increasing altitude there goes reduction of atmospheric pressure and, in the same degree, reduction of the oxygen component. From his work in the Andes mountains, McFarland reported that climbing to 16,000 feet resulted in measurable deteriorations in both simple and complex functions; and climbing to 20,000 and 25,000 feet was clearly incapacitating. Again, it was demonstrated that during a rapid ascent by plane a pilot would become increasingly inaccurate both in his movement coordinations and in seeing and hearing. Some pilots grew hilarious and laughed uncontrollably, while others became very angry and destructive. There was commonly a growing carelessness and indifference about taking precautions, frequently a loss of capacity for sane judgment and self-criticism and for realizing one's incapacities — serious matters indeed for airplane pilots, as military and civilian authorities know. In slower ascent by train, impairments of efficiency also occurred. These appeared in tests such as the making of choice reactions to lights of different colors, in hitting dots on a moving tape, in speed of apprehending four-letter words, in writing from code, in naming colors, and in remembering words (Figure 214). It is interesting that one form of the deterioration was a tendency for the subject to perseverate, to keep on doing whatever he was doing: an inability to shift his set from task to task.

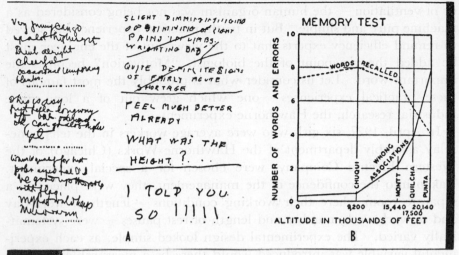

214 **Some Psychological Effects of Decreasing Oxygen Supply**

A. Effects on handwriting. *B.* Effects on memory. (*From R. A. McFarland,* "*The internal enironment and behavior. I,*" AMER. J. PSYCHIAT., *1941, 97, 858–877. By permission of the author.*)

Similar psychological impairments from lack of oxygen are found in men caught in mine cave-ins. One victim jotted down notes as he awaited the hoped-for aid. An excerpt from the notes betrays his increasing disorganization of thought and of motility:

"2 P. M. Good-bye, we are all dying, your Clement. I fear we are all dying, good-bye, all my darlings all, no help coming good-bye, we are dying, good-bye, we are dying; good-bye, good-bye, we are dying no help comes . . . No . . . or scarcely any, we are done, we are done, godo my darlings." And all the while this victim dimly realized that by walking some twenty feet he could reach safety: he simply could not initiate the necessary action.[1]

The effects on the central nervous system of a low supply of oxygen have been likened in general to the impairing effects of excess alcohol.

MOTIVATION REMAINS A CARDINAL FACTOR

It is high time that we recognized more explicitly another side to the whole question of human efficiency. The reader may have wondered whether, in some of the foregoing discussions — as of "mental" fatigue

[1] From J. Barcroft, *The Brain and its Environment* (New Haven: Yale University Press, 1938), p. 96.

or of ventilation — the human organism was not being considered as a machine pure and simple. But in truth, practical experience has served to remind efficiency experts that to the viewpoint of the engineer must be added the viewpoint of the biologist. "Motivation" becomes the important word. Let us consider what is probably the most famous of these practical experiences — one which grew out of a long-range industrial research, the Hawthorne experiment.

In April, 1927, six girls who were average workers in the telephone-relay assembly department of the Hawthorne Works (Chicago) of the Western Electric Company, were chosen for a special experiment. Taken into the confidence of the management, they were placed in a separate room where their working conditions — length of work-day and of work-week, number and length of rest pauses — were systematically varied. The experimental design looked simple: as each experimental variable was introduced would there be a measurable increase-decrease of output?

Table LVII presents us with interesting results. As we read down the third and fourth columns to note the changes systematically introduced and the consequent changes in total weekly production, we see that with almost any change the girls' production went up, even when the change was a return to an earlier experimental condition. Clearly the steadily increased output was not to be attributed to rest pauses, nor to changed length of work-day or work-week. The experimenting management had to look in another direction for the explanation.

Let us bear in mind that the six girls chosen had been told the objectives of the experiment, and that their cooperation had been solicited. Their relation to their work, to their overseer, and to each other became different from the relationships prevailing on the shop floor. Supervision was much less strict. New ideas were suggested to them for criticism before being instituted. Each girl was given more individual attention. She was allowed to work at her own comfortable pace. Free conversation was permitted. Considering these things, the management eventually realized that the increased output resulted from a new attitude toward a job on the worker's part, an attitude in which the worker's self was respected and given attention. The ego-involvement was of crucial value. More broadly, it was the enhancement of the workman's motivation that was most responsible.

In the present chapter we have canvassed a few of the many external conditions that bear upon the effectiveness of a person's work with hand or brain. The conclusions drawn from scientific studies are not meant

TABLE LVII

Changes in Working Conditions and Their Effects upon Output of a Chosen Group

Experimental period	Duration of period, in weeks	Experimental conditions of work	Relative output per week
I	2	In shop: preliminary	taken as 100%
II	5	In test room: regular shop conditions	101
III	8	Improved rate of pay	105
IV	5	Two 5-minute rests	109
V	4	Two 10-minute rests	112
VI	4	Six 5-minute rests	113
VII	11	15-minute A.M. rest with lunch; 10-minute P.M. rest	116
VIII	7	Same; stopped at 4:30	123
IX	4	Same; stopped at 4:00	125
X	12	Same; stopped at 5:00	124
XI	9	Same; Saturday morning off	123
XII	12	Regular conditions, as in II	122
XIII	31	Rests, as in VII	131

Adapted from F. J. Roethlisberger and W. J. Dickson, MAN-AGEMENT AND THE WORKER (Cambridge, Mass.: Harvard University Press, 1939). By permission of the publisher.

to serve as practical prescriptions. They are not rules of thumb. They are laid before the reader for his serious consideration and for his thoughtful adaptation to the concrete practicalities of everyday life.

REFERENCES

1. Bartlett, F. C. "Fatigue following highly skilled work," *Proc. Roy. Soc.*, 1943, *B 131*, 247–257.

2. Bartley, S. H., and E. Chute. *Fatigue and Impairment in Man.* New York: McGraw-Hill Book Company, 1947.

3. Bills, A. G. *The Psychology of Efficiency.* New York: Harper and Brothers, 1943.

4. Burtt, H. E. *Psychology and Industrial Efficiency.* New York: Appleton-Century-Crofts, 1929.

5. Carmichael, L., and W. F. Dearborn. *Reading and Visual Fatigue.* Boston: Houghton Mifflin Company, 1947.

6. Davis, D. R., *et al. Pilot Error: Some Laboratory Experiments.* London: H. M. Stationery Office, 1948.

7. Davis, R. C. "The muscular tension reflex and two of its modifying conditions," *Ind. Univ. Publ., Sci. Ser.*, 1935, No. 3.

8. Ghiselli, E. E., and C. W. Brown. *Personnel and Industrial Psychology.* New York: McGraw-Hill Book Company, 1948.

9. Jacobson, E. *You Must Relax.* New York: McGraw-Hill Book Company, 1934.

10. Johnson, H. M., T. H. Swan, and G. E. Weigand. "In what positions do healthy people sleep?" *J. Amer. Med. Ass.,* 1930, *94,* 2058–2062.

11. Kleitman, N. *Sleep and Wakefulness.* Chicago: University of Chicago Press, 1939.

12. Loveday, J., and S. H. Munroe. "An experiment with rest pauses," *Grt. Britain: Indust. Health Res. Bd.,* Rep. no. 10.

13. Marshall, H. "Alcohol: a critical review of the literature," *Psychol. Bull.,* 1941, *38,* 193–217.

14. McFarland, R. A. "Psycho-physiological studies at high altitude in the Andes," *J. Comp. Psychol.,* 1937, *23,* 191–225. "The psycho-physiological effects of reduced oxygen pressure," *Res. Publ. Ass. Nerv. Ment. Dis.,* 1939, *19,* 112–143.

15. McGehee, W., and E. B. Owen. "Authorized and unauthorized rest pauses in clerical work," *J. Appl. Psychol.,* 24, 605–614. 1940.

16. Moore, H. *Psychology for Business and Industry.* Second edition. New York: McGraw-Hill Book Company, 1942.

17. Poffenberger, A. T. *Principles of Applied Psychology.* New York: Appleton-Century-Crofts, 1942.

18. Pollock, K. G., and F. C. Bartlett. "Psychological experiments on the effects of noise," *Grt. Brit.: Indust. Health Res. Bd.,* Rep. no. 65, 1932.

19. Robinson, E. S., and F. R. Robinson. "Effects of loss of sleep," *J. Exper. Psychol.,* 1922, *5,* 93–100.

20. Roethlisberger, F. J., and W. J. Dickson. *Management and the Worker.* Cambridge, Mass.: Harvard University Press, 1939.

21. Ryan, T. A. *Work and Effort.* New York: Ronald Press, 1947.

22. Thorndike, E. L. *Educational Psychology.* Vol. III, pt. I. New York: Teachers College, Columbia University, 1914.

23. Travis, R. C., and J. L. Kennedy. "Prediction and automatic control of alertness. I, II," *Amer. Psychologist,* 1947, *2,* 331–332.

23

CONCLUDING ORIENTATION

THE PSYCHOLOGICAL VIEWPOINT RESTATED

THROUGHOUT THIS BOOK we have treated man as an object of scientific investigation, with a view to determining what cause-effect relationships obtain in his life. "Human nature" has been viewed not only as "human" but as "nature," as a natural object involved in natural events. In concluding this survey, let it be said again that this is not claimed to be the only legitimate and proper way of regarding man. Human beings are to be valued; and the items and incidents of their surroundings that contribute to their living are to be regarded as weals and woes. Just as the accurate knowledge of details of chemical properties and processes does not in any way invalidate nor displace personal interests in foods as things good-to-eat, and as the precise formulation of physiological laws and principles does not conflict with a desire for health, so likewise an increasingly exact science of the laws of human behavior does not challenge any values to be placed upon human personalities and their behavior. Rather, as in the other two cases mentioned, science should materially further such interests by providing the bases for practical techniques — techniques to be employed in the service of securing those things valued by man.

The natural science method is non-moral; and to psychology as such "goods" and "bads" are irrelevant. But for ethics of the future there is being built a solid foundation in the fundamentals of psychological science. As we obtain increasingly adequate data and laws as to why this juvenile delinquent or that adult habitual criminal, this public benefactor or that private distributor of blessings, conducts himself as he does, then we shall be equipped in increasingly adequate ways to set into operation just those forces that contribute to the making of approved types of character and conduct and not those forces that work toward an opposite result.

The same interpretation applies to all the other valuational aspects of life. The determination of the details of stimuli that arouse esthetic types of response, for example, in no way invalidates nor challenges artistic endeavor and artistic appreciation. It should, in fact, support and further them. To adapt a phrase from Santayana: the true philosophy looks to science for its view of the facts and to the happiness of men on earth for its ideal.

As the nineteenth century and first half of the twentieth century were notable for the unprecedented advance in man's control of his non-personal environment through the technological application of the physical and biological sciences, it may be fairly anticipated that the second half of the twentieth century will become remarkable for the development of psychotechnology. The "pure" science of psychology though still in its swaddling clothes, is today being rapidly expanded in many directions, and — what is more important — is being built upon more solid and certain foundations. And as the fundamental principles and formulae of this science become determined with increasing degrees of accuracy, technological applications are sure to follow. Already trends of practical usefulness are becoming evident, as a steadily growing host of investigators are engaged in working out the applications of the laws of human behavior to the fields of medicine, education, industry, commerce, law, and national defense. That "man may become master of his fate" is a phrase invested now with new and fruitful meaning.